THE UNIVERSITY OF WISCONSIN

A History, 1848-1925

Volume II

Charles R Van Hise.

The University of
WISCONSIN

1848   *A HISTORY*   1925

Merle Curti &
Vernon Carstensen

Two Volumes · II

Madison · 1949

UNIVERSITY OF WISCONSIN PRESS

Acknowledgments

O UR indebtedness to the many people who helped in the preparation of these volumes was expressed in the preface to Volume I. Volume II has increased our indebtedness to some and added others to the list of those whose help has been invaluable. It is impossible to give appropriate acknowledgment to all, but these few at least must be named: Dean George Clarke Sellery, who read and criticized all of Volume II; Fulmer Mood, who read page proofs of both volumes; June Stalker, who prepared the index; John N. Stalker, Jr. and Kendall A. Birr, who helped in innumerable ways; and Neil G. Cafferty, University controller, and Harlan H. Schiffer, who compiled the statement of University receipts which appears as an appendix to this volume.

The illustrations for both volumes have come from so many sources that it is impossible to name individually all to whom thanks are due. We must content ourselves by expressing gratitude to the following offices and to their staffs: the University Library for the use of the Meuer Photoart collection, *The Wisconsin Alumnus* and the Wisconsin Alumni Association, the Manuscript and Map Section of the Library of the State Historical Society of Wisconsin, the University of Wisconsin News Service, the University Photographic Laboratory, the library of the College of Agriculture, the Office of Buildings and Grounds of the University, and the fraternities Phi Delta Theta and Kappa Kappa Gamma. We wish also to acknowledge a debt to

Floyd A. LaFayette of the museum of the Historical Society for assistance in identifying the scenes of the University.

Contents

Contents

Illustrations

THE UNIVERSITY IN THE NEW CENTURY

Part Five

1.

President Charles R. Van Hise

I N THE first twelve years of the twentieth century the victories of the Progressives under "Fighting Bob" La Follette and his followers brought Wisconsin into the national limelight. Reformers took inspiration from legislation designed to strengthen political democracy by breaking the bosses and the machine. Labor legislation promoted social justice. The Wisconsin Idea involving the cooperation of experts in framing and administering legislation for the regulation of corporate wealth won glowing praise in liberal circles throughout the country. In the words of one crusader, Wisconsin was "an experiment station in politics, in social and industrial legislation, in the democratization of science and higher education. It is a laboratory in which popular government is being tested in its reaction on people, on the distribution of wealth, on social well-being."[1] More commanding voices spoke in the same vein. In 1912 Theodore Roosevelt, impressed by the way in which Wisconsin had achieved substantial improvements without resorting to sweeping experiments, declared that "all through the Union we need to learn the Wisconsin lesson of scientific popular self-help, and of patient care in radical legislation."[2]

The chapters on Van Hise have benefited from the research and suggestions of Maurice M. Vance, whose doctoral dissertation, begun before this history was written, will be a full-length biography of President Van Hise.

[1] Frederic C. Howe, *Wisconsin, An Experiment in Democracy* (New York, 1912), vii.

[2] Quoted in the introduction to Charles McCarthy, *The Wisconsin Idea* (New York, 1912), x.

3

Confronted by a new situation, the University, not without doubts on the part of some of its faculty members and vigorous criticism by conservatives throughout the state, adapted itself to the innovations and even played a role of importance in many of them. Members of the staff helped to draft reform legislation and served on the regulatory commissions. The doctrine of "service to the state" was implemented in the large-scale extension work and in sponsoring research of obvious economic benefit to Wisconsin. These activities were given wide publicity which helped the University to acquire the reputation for being at the forefront of higher education. The success with which the University served the new forces in the state likewise explains its influence on other institutions both in America and abroad.

At this period the state of Wisconsin was being enriched by the contributions of its foreign population. Of the two million residents of the state in 1900, a quarter were foreign-born and another forty-six per cent had at least one foreign-born parent. Almost a hundred thousand persons over ten years of age were unable to speak English. The Germans made up the largest foreign segment and the Scandinavians, among whom the Norwegians were most numerous, were the second largest group. Primarily hard-working and efficient farmers, both groups represented a tradition of orderliness, of respect for the expert, and of devotion to progress through orderly procedures. German industrialists and Norwegian political leaders carried these traits into their fields of influence. Various smaller groups also contributed from their European heritage to Wisconsin's cultural growth. As the bearers of these foreign cultures gained familiarity with their new home, they became more articulate. Because this articulateness sprang from the common experiences of the immigrants and their children in the new world and from their absorption of the often new idea of free expression, it was tempered by the American scene and by American traditions. In short, Wisconsin was becoming Americanized, and the foreign overtones, though present, were increasingly subordinated to the fundamentals of American life.

Wisconsin in 1900 was still predominantly agricultural. Fifty-seven per cent of the population was classified by the census of 1900 as "rural"—that is, as living on farms, in unincorporated communities, or in villages with a population of less than twenty-five hundred. The majority of the state's population was thus more or less directly dependent upon agriculture, and the agricultural interests inevitably affected the state's attitude toward the University and its activities. For example, the shift from grain- to dairy-farming had been encouraged by the University, and it proved profitable. The utilitarian aspect of the University program was partly, though by no means wholly, a response to the demands of the state.

Apart from the development of dairying, the most striking phenomenon in Wisconsin agriculture was the growth of farming in the northern part of the state, an area previously devoted largely to lumbering. Beginning shortly after 1890, the legislature and the College of Agriculture had tried to attract farmers into the cutover area, which proved to be largely untillable. The northern counties in the first decade of the twentieth century increased in agricultural population at a strikingly greater rate than did the rich farming sections in southern Wisconsin. But the farming of cutover regions was difficult, and the conditions favored the revival of the Grange and the growth of new agricultural protest organizations such as the Society of Equity and, indeed, the Progressive movement itself.

The steady growth of agriculture was more than matched in these years by the industrial development of the state. Though more persons were dependent upon agriculture than upon industry, the value of the state's industrial products by 1890 had exceeded the value of its agricultural produce. For a brief time (1899–1905) after the depletion of the Michigan forests, Wisconsin produced more lumber than any other state. Even after the decline of the Wisconsin timber supply, lumbering and the manufacture of wood products continued to be a leading industry. The stage was set, belatedly, for the movement to conserve the forests and other natural resources.

The growth of industries meant that the population of Wisconsin, like that of many other states, was shifting from the country to the towns. Although most of the people in 1900 lived in rural areas, the cities were growing more rapidly than the villages and farms. This urban growth was most marked during the 1890's, when Green Bay and Superior more than doubled in population and Racine, Milwaukee, and Sheboygan all gained about 40 per cent. In a less spectacular manner this trend continued through the first decade of the new century, when the increase of town dwellers was almost 24 per cent and that of the rural population only 5.7 per cent. By 1900 Wisconsin's 9,721 manufacturing establishments employed an average of over 180,000 wage earners. These developments explain the advance of the labor movement in the industrial towns and the progress of the Socialist Party in Milwaukee.[3]

The University was inevitably affected by the social changes in the state. The student body grew so rapidly that serious consideration was given to the suggestion that the state shift a large part of the instruction of the first two years to the private colleges, the normal schools, and to a six-year program in the larger high schools in order that the University might concentrate on training upperclassmen, graduate students, and professional students.[4] In view of the growing enrollment at the University and the increasing wealth of the state, larger appropriations were in order, and campaigns for more state support had to be made. The changing character of the state's economy indicated the need of a readjustment in the work of the University. Indeed, on one occasion, the brewers asked the administration to incorporate a training school for brewers. Above all, the relation of the University to the various cultural and political developments in Wisconsin presented special problems.

Wisconsin, like the rest of the country, was being increasingly secularized. Though organized religion remained a potent interest, the religious organizations and the Christian colleges had at last come to accept the University. At the same time there was a fairly wide feeling that something must be done to protect the religious life of students in Madison, a feeling the Univer-

[3] This account is based on the Eleventh (1890), Twelfth (1900), and Thirteenth (1910) Census Reports, Washington, 1895, 1902, and 1913 respectively.
[4] Charles R. Van Hise, *Recent Progress of the University and its Future,* commencement address (Madison, 1908); Van Hise to Arthur J. Puls, June 8, 1909, Presidents' Papers. All letters to and from Van Hise are in the Presidents' Papers unless otherwise indicated.

sity could not ignore. The University also recognized its obligation to take the lead in harmonizing relations with the private colleges.

Among certain denominations there was still a marked indifference toward formal education of any kind. This, together with the foreign make-up of a large part of the population, explains the fact that in 1900, some 74,800 persons over ten years old were unable to read or write. But this illiterate bloc, less than five per cent of the people, was reduced by 1910 to nearly half that figure. By and large the high literacy of the population provided fertile ground for a vigorous new extension movement.

In Frank H. Hutchins, brilliant and imaginative secretary of the Free Library Commission, the University had a worthy ally. The Free Library Commission, established in 1895, had begun to extend library services not only by setting up permanent centers but by adopting and improving on New York's scheme of sending out boxes of books to rural communities. In 1901, again on the initiative of Hutchins, the unique Legislative Reference Library was launched. This agency, headed by the energetic and resourceful Charles McCarthy, former football star and holder of a University doctorate in history, provided legislators with information and aided them in drafting bills. This greatly decreased the power of professional lobbyists and opened the way for University experts to give advice and provide assistance in the drafting of bills for various types of political and economic reform.[5]

The increase of newspapers, reflecting the growth of urbanism and the conflict of interests in the state, posed problems for the University. With the foreign-language press, which in 1900 included nearly a hundred German and twenty Norwegian and Slavic papers, Wisconsin readers had seven hundred and fifty journals at their disposal. Most of these were, to be sure, local enterprises with limited news and editorial features. But the movement for large-scale journalism was under way, the *Milwaukee Sentinel* and the *Milwaukee Journal* taking the lead. These influential journals were at best equivocal in their support of pro-

[5] See McCarthy, *The Wisconsin Idea*, 196–197, 214 ff., and Edward A. Fitzpatrick, *McCarthy of Wisconsin* (New York, 1944), chapter 4, *passim*.

gressive developments. But the La Follette movement was promoted by the Milwaukee *Free Press,* thanks to Isaac Stephenson,
a wealthy lumberman who for a time lent his purse to this venture in "independent" journalism. Socialism found an organ
in the *Milwaukee Leader.* The *Wisconsin State Journal* in Madison was sometimes on the side of liberalism, especially as time
went on and after Van Hise lent money to its editor. Thus, in
spite of the fact that a large number of newspapers opposed the
Progressives, the Wisconsin public was not without agencies able
and willing to speak as the people's champion. The University
could not be indifferent to the press nor to its influence in shaping popular attitudes toward its program. It became necessary
for the University to cultivate press relations.

Movements in arts and letters which displayed so much vigor
in some parts of the country affected Wisconsin only slightly.
In architecture, for example, the state showed little interest in
her one architectural genius. Frank Lloyd Wright was building
his experimental structures, not in Milwaukee and Madison,
but in Buffalo and Chicago. Nor did Wisconsin contribute
much to the literary awakening of the period. Hamlin Garland's
interests were rapidly shifting away from Wisconsin. John
Muir, the gifted naturalist, and Ella Wheeler Wilcox, sentimental and popular versifier, no longer maintained any connections with the state in which they had grown up. All these writers were to do justice to it in their autobiographies, but these
were not yet written. Almost no one appreciated the literary
potentialities of the rich Paul Bunyan folklore in the lumber
camps; writing was still in the genteel tradition. If Wisconsin
could claim a literary center at all, it was in Milwaukee. There
George Peck, owner of *The Sun* and author of *Peck's Bad Boy,*
and General Charles King, who continued to turn out his popular Civil War and army stories, provided a literary nucleus. And
in Milwaukee young writers like Edna Ferber and Zona Gale
were acquiring writing experience on various newspapers.[6]

Although the older German poets in Milwaukee had largely

---

[6] The Wisconsin backgrounds of these writers are portrayed in Hamlin Garland,
A Son of the Middle Border and *A Daughter of the Middle Border;* Ella
Wheeler Wilcox, *The Worlds and I;* John Muir, *The Story of My Boyhood and
Youth;* Edna Ferber, *A Peculiar Treasure;* and in August Derleth's biography
of Zona Gale, *Still Small Voice.*

had their say in the vernacular press, Wisconsin's leading city was still the seat of a considerable German-American culture. With this the German department of the University made profitable contact. The drama flourished in Milwaukee's well-known German theater. The city was also the home of vigorous musical activity, centering in the Sunday afternoon concerts in Turner Hall on the west side of the city. Heinrich Vianden, Wisconsin's first landscape painter, died in 1899, but the influence of his pupils, especially of Carl Marr, was felt when the Society of Milwaukee Artists was organized three years later. Yet in view of the accentuated Americanization of the rising generation, German-American culture was of the past, not of the future.

In brief, if the University were to reflect the interests of the state, it was hardly likely to nourish creative movements in literature, architecture, or in any other one of the arts. It would, rather, mirror the utilitarian interests of those in Wisconsin who were frankly dedicated to a larger measure of political democracy and a wider sharing of the material benefits of civilization. Wisconsin was one of the chief spearheads in the political revolt against the alliance of corporate wealth with political machines. Wisconsin did not initiate this revolt, nor should its contributions, important as they are, be isolated from those of the neighboring states and the urban East. Nevertheless it did produce a notable revolt, a constructive program, and a great leader.

For almost two decades before his election to the governorship, La Follette had challenged the privileged politicians and their allies among the lumber and railway barons. But even in 1900, when on his third attempt he won the governorship, he was faced with a largely hostile legislature. La Follette, who enjoyed politics and public service, who was masterly in his command of facts and figures and powerful on the platform, which he had begun to conquer as a student orator, inspired loyalty among the plain people. "Fighting Bob" was bent on breaking the power of the machine and of wealth in the interest of political democracy and the well-being of the little fellow. With dynamic enthusiasm he had set a goal of "freeing" the commonwealth. He had no intention, despite poverty and illness, of calling quits when it proved impossible during his first term (1901–1903) to push through his long-cherished plan for direct primary nominations by which the citizens themselves might name candidates for office and thus break the strangle hold of the machine. The election campaign of 1902 kindled feverish heat, and La Follette won the day. On May 18, 1904, at the last Republican convention preceding the first direct primary in Wisconsin, La Follette, with the assistance of University football men, prevented the meeting from being taken over by delegates who he was convinced were unauthorized. With the establishment of the direct primary law, one of the first in the country, the ground was laid for breaking the machine and for inaugurating a people's program.[7]

La Follette had also determined to introduce into Wisconsin the new system of ad valorem taxation which had originated in Indiana. In the words of Professor John R. Commons, "this system based the taxation of railways and other public utility corporations, not on the older ideas of corporeal property located in the state, but on the newer idea of the state's share in the total value of the 'intangible property' of the corporation as a unit throughout the United States, evidenced partly by the sale-value of its securities on the New York stockmarket."[8] In carrying out this program, La Follette enjoyed for the time the support not only of small businessmen and farmers but also of the lumbermen, eager to shift a larger portion of taxation to the railroads. As a result of the ad valorem tax law of 1903, railway taxes in the next five years added up to four million dollars more than they would have under the old system. Not until 1905 with the setting up of the Wisconsin Railroad Commission did La Follette succeed in establishing control of intrastate railway rates and services to end discrimination.

It was natural for La Follette, an alumnus of the University and a disciple of Bascom's doctrine of the responsibility of education in the struggle for right, to look to the University for

---

[7] See *La Follette's Autobiography* (Madison, 1913), 323–326. See also Albert O. Barton, *La Follette's Winning of Wisconsin* (Madison, 1922), and Benjamin Parke De Witt, *The Progressive Movement* (New York, 1915), 54–88. For a criticism of La Follette see Emanuel L. Philipp, *Political Reform in Wisconsin* (*Milwaukee*, 1910).

[8] John R. Commons, *Myself* (New York, 1934), 97.

support. In so far as the University responded to this expectation it won the enthusiastic acclaim of Wisconsin Progressives and of liberals throughout the country. But in so doing, it also encountered criticism and opposition from the Wisconsin Stalwarts, La Follette's Republican opponents. The controversy raised fundamental issues involving the University administration and faculty, the regents, the governors, the legislature, and the agricultural and business communities of the state.

IT WAS in the midst of the fight for ad valorem taxation that La Follette played his part in the selection of President Van Hise. In fact, it has been often said that La Follette put Van Hise into the presidency.[9] Professor Edward Kremers, writing in later years, asserted that one regent told him that he had been appointed to the Board by La Follette in order to strengthen Van Hise's candidacy.[10] It is true that a majority of the regents appointed by La Follette's predecessors did not look with favor on Van Hise. It is also true that in the Board which finally offered him the presidency two holdover regents from the earlier regime were still in the opposition while the majority of the La Follette appointees cast their votes for Van Hise. Furthermore, Van Hise, a classmate and personal friend of La Follette, not only kept in close touch with him during the interval between his first election to the governorship and the final decision of the regents, but also made clear his gratification at La Follette's political success.[11]

Whatever the role of La Follette in the choice of Van Hise,

[9] Interview, Merle Curti with Edward A. Birge, November 26, 1944. President Birge recalled that sometime after the resignation of President Adams, Colonel William Vilas remarked in the presence of Birge and Breese Stevens that Governor La Follette seemed to be wanting to interfere in the appointment of the new president, and that he had better be put in his place. Others have made similar declarations. See, for examples of the statement, the *Milwaukee Journal*, November 30, 1908, p. 2, and Howe, *Wisconsin, An Experiment in Democracy*, 30.

[10] See Edward Kremers, Sketch of Van Hise, Kremers Papers, State Historical Society of Wisconsin. Kremers' statement that La Follette boasted in an address at an educational meeting in Indianapolis that he had put Van Hise into the presidency has not been verified.

[11] This is clear from Van Hise's letters to his wife throughout the summer of 1902, Van Hise Papers, State Historical Society of Wisconsin.

the appointment was made only after other candidates had refused the position. The regents took over a year and a half to make their decision and showed in that interval not only internal differences but a good deal of independence. The committee on selection made overtures to President Benjamin Ide Wheeler of the University of California but he declined to accept.[12] Ex-President Adams, on whom the Board leaned heavily, also considered Nicholas Murray Butler but Columbia acted first. Other non-Wisconsin men were also talked of,[13] despite the advice of the presidents of Harvard, Yale, and Johns Hopkins to appoint someone from within the University.[14] In this category Birge, the acting president, was the chief rival of Van Hise, notwithstanding Adams' private assurance that no man from the faculty would be taken. In April, 1903, when the committee on selection at length reported its inability to agree, an informal ballot indicated that of the nine regents four favored Birge.[15]

The evidence at hand does not explain the opposition to Van Hise. It was not because he was a scientist rather than a humanist, for there had been scientists among the presidents, and Birge, the chief contestant, was a zoologist. To some, Van Hise seemed crude, awkward, and devoid of appreciation of the humane and aesthetic values, at least in comparison with Adams. Possibly a few shared the querulous opinion of Professor Kremers that in faculty meetings Van Hise had wearied his colleagues by laboring points already made. Perhaps his ill-concealed eagerness for the position acted unfavorably on others. It is likely that some resented the influence of a faculty group, the Frances Street cabal—including Turner, Slaughter,

[12] Charles Forster Smith, *Charles Kendall Adams: A Life Sketch* (Madison, 1924), 95–96.

[13] Professor George E. Vincent of the University of Chicago was supported by the "Yale" party, while Henry Pritchett, subsequently director of the Carnegie Foundation for the Advancement of Teaching, enjoyed considerable favor. Frederick Jackson Turner to Van Hise, February 15, 1902, and Regent James Kerwin to Turner, June 6, 1902, Records of the History Department, University of Wisconsin. See also, Van Hise to his wife, July 9, 1902, Van Hise Papers.

[14] President Ira Remsen of Johns Hopkins University specifically recommended Van Hise. Puls to Van Hise, June 22, 1909.

[15] Records of the Board of Regents, F:30–31, April 21, 1903. Birge, in an interview on November 26, 1944, stated that the regents who voted for him did so as a means of defeating the effort to have a La Follette man appointed.

Van Hise, and Slichter—which was particularly energetic in promoting Van Hise. Indeed, Professor Freeman spoke of Turner as the Warwick in the case, and with some reason, for it is clear that he worked effectively in breaking down opposition both within the staff and in the Board of Regents.[16] Finally, if La Follette's support was as vigorous as there is reason to believe, his critics among the regents may well have resented his activity and feared that the appointment to the presidency of his old friend and classmate would throw the University into politics on the governor's side. In spite of all these considerations the regents by a very narrow margin finally voted to offer the presidency to Van Hise.[17] His acceptance was immediate and, unlike that of his predecessors, not hedged by qualifications.[18]

The student body celebrated the election of Van Hise with cheers, an immense bonfire on the lower campus, and a pilgrimage to his home. Unlike Wisconsin's previous presidents, Van Hise was one of the University's own sons. The *Alumni Magazine* declared: "A new regime begins and with it an experiment but little tried in the West—the administration of a university by an alumnus of the institution."[19] Van Hise was not only an alumnus: he had taken all his advanced training at the University and had been, in fact, the first on whom the doctorate was conferred. A native son of farming parents, he had entered the University in the autumn of 1874, the first year of Bascom's tenure. He had transferred from the general science curriculum to the course in mining and metallurgy and from Professor

[16] This is supported both by the letters of Van Hise to his wife and by Turner's correspondence. Among the latter, of special significance are letters to Van Hise dated February 15 and to Dana Carleton Munro, April 16 and June 12, 1902. Records of the History Department. See also the letter of Regent James Kerwin to Turner, June 6, 1902, in which Kerwin reports that some support has shifted to Pritchett and asks Turner to make a comparison of the qualifications of Pritchett and Van Hise. Records of the History Department.

[17] Records of the Board of Regents, F:30–32, April 21, 1903. One regent abstained from voting in the final ballot; one vote was given to Turner, and one to the Reverend James Bashford, four to Birge, and five to Van Hise. However, before his death in 1908 Vilas, who was in the opposition, said he was convinced that Van Hise was making a better president than any other possible candidate could have done. Puls to Van Hise, June 22, 1909.

[18] Van Hise to the secretary of the Board of Regents, April 23, 1903, Papers of the Board of Regents, April 21, 1903.

[19] *Wisconsin Alumni Magazine* (Madison), 5:11 (October, 1903).

Irving had learned the methods of the exact scientist. Even as a student, he was, according to Chamberlin, among the first to use the microscope in determining the nature of the crystals of complex rocks. He quickly became the outstanding American authority on this technique. As Irving's assistant and presently as his junior colleague, Van Hise supplemented his mastery of laboratory techniques with field work for the United States Geological Survey. In investigating the crystalline rocks of the Wisconsin valley and the iron-bearing formations in the Lake Superior area he indulged his love of the forces of nature and rubbed elbows with practical mining engineers. Here he learned the bearing of geological study on economic pursuits. Here he confirmed his faith in the existence of an ordered universe, governed by ascertainable laws; and he nourished his passionate desire to find the truth.

In 1888, after Irving's sudden death, Van Hise succeeded his chief as director of the Lake Superior Division of the Geological Survey. In this capacity he continued the detailed examination of the mineral-bearing areas of the region and wrote, with the collaboration of various associates, seven monographs which were published by the Survey over the next two decades. These volumes discussed in detail the geological structure of the iron- and copper-bearing districts and were of great practical value to mining men of the region. In addition they correlated the field observations with geological principles in such a way as to place them among pioneer works in geological theory. For example, Van Hise's discussion of the deposition of ores pointed, in a practical way, to the location of deposits. At the same time, his study of underground waters minimized volcanism as a causal factor in mineral deposition and, as Chamberlin pointed out, robbed the doctrine of a molten earth of practically all field evidence and gave a reinterpretation to the early chapters of earth history.

Van Hise's study of the changes undergone by components of the earth's crust led to the publication, in 1904, of his most important geological work, *A Treatise on Metamorphism*. In his own words, it was "an attempt to reduce the phenomena of metamorphism to order under the principles of physics and chemistry, or, more simply, under the laws of energy. It is but a part of the larger task of reducing to order under the same laws the entire subject of physical geology."[20] In this volume Van Hise discussed the forces which contribute to earth changes, presented scores of reactions which were known to take place within the earth's crust, and explained, in terms of the volume and heat changes in the various reactions, why some minerals occur more frequently than others. To the extent that any one man's work may be given credit, *Metamorphism* may be said to mark the rise of geology from the stage of classification to that of the formulation of principles which define geological relationships and determine geological changes. The importance of the work was recognized at once, and when, in 1910, Van Hise went to Stockholm as president of the International Geological Congress, he was hailed by his European colleagues, not as the president of "America's leading state university," but as the author of *Metamorphism*.

It was inevitable that Van Hise's geological activities should be relegated to a lesser place after his appointment to the presidency. Furthermore, as his work brought him in contact with new problems, his working interest shifted from geology to conservation, to the regulation of business, to the war, and finally to the problem of establishing a successful League of Nations. However, he did manage, particularly in the nonlegislative years, to devote considerable time to his various geological activities. In 1903 it was his intention to use his spare time in scientific work. Chamberlin, who knew from personal experience how administrative duties could curtail a scientist's work, congratulated Van Hise on his election in terms not unmixed with regret. In reply, Van Hise expressed his determination not to give up his research. "I have acquired a habit of many years standing," he wrote, "of turning to my investigative work every moment which was not required for teaching or executive work. Upon this habit I have a certain amount of reliance."[21] From the beginning he resolved not to let his new job swamp him, and to do nothing himself which he could get someone else to do.[22] His ability on leaving his office to dismiss for the time even

[20] *A Treatise on Metamorphism*, monograph of the United States Geological Survey, No. 47 (1904), 32.
[21] Van Hise to Thomas C. Chamberlin, April 25, 1903.
[22] Van Hise to Lucy C. Thompson, April 29, 1903.

the most vexatious issues served him in quite as good stead as did his efficient habits, and for several years he was able to accept special Geological Survey assignments, to do some field work, and to publish occasional articles. He was consulted frequently by other geologists both at home and abroad, and when, in 1907, the directorship of the Survey became vacant, he could have had the position.[23] He collected material for a book on the influence of minerals in world history and delivered lectures on various phases of this subject. Nevertheless, because of his presidential duties and his newer interests he devoted less and less time to geology, and when, in 1915, he was asked to prepare an article for a new scientific publication he refused, saying that he was "geologically bankrupt."[24]

Professor Charles K. Leith, now emeritus professor of geology at the University of Wisconsin, and in geological work successively Van Hise's secretary, assistant, collaborator, and successor, has the highest regard for Van Hise as a scientist. Van Hise's driving energy, his grasp of detail, his ability to perceive relationships and to make valid generalizations on a mass of data made a lasting impression on the younger man. As a collaborator, Leith recalls that Van Hise was generous to a fault, often giving his associates credit for ideas that had originated with him. He was always ready to consider the ideas of others and, when the evidence showed he had been wrong, quick to abandon a thesis he had vigorously defended.[25] Nor was Leith by any means alone in his appreciation of Van Hise's work. In electing Van Hise to the presidency of the Geological Society of America (1907), the International Geological Congress (1910), the National Academy of Sciences (1915), and the American Association for the Advancement of Science (1916) his fellow scientists made clear their esteem for the man and his work.

Established geologist though he was at forty-six when he took over his new office, Van Hise was as yet unknown in the fields of general education and in what Albert Shaw called economic statesmanship. Yet the foundations for what he accomplished were already laid. Van Hise's developing social and political ideas were, of course, intimately related to his temperament and his background. His boundless energy, his drive, his optimism, and his way of looking at things in terms of their potentialities were certainly his emotional endowment. So too, probably, was his unshadowed faith in the future. Unlike Henry Adams, he had no scruples in accepting unreservedly the doctrine of progress; his acceptance seemed to be inherent. His directness, sincerity, and penchant for fusing the practical and the idealistic, no less than his enjoyment of power, were also part of his personal endowment. Deep-rooted in his personality was his ability to hold no grudges. "It apparently never entered his mind," Professor Leith has written, "that differences of opinion, even when they amounted to petty criticism, were to be taken personally. As he often expressed it, it was 'all a part of the game' and any man who allowed personal considerations to influence his judgment or to affect his temper failed in playing the game."[26]

At the same time his exuberance, drive, optimism, practicality, and readiness to "live and let live" also reflected the outlook of the pioneer society in which he had been reared. Like so many Americans he attached importance to results, wanting, himself, to get things done and to have others get them done. His correspondence is full of such admonitions as "We must vigorously push the matter" or "I shall expect you to push the matter vigorously." It was often by sheer force of personality rather than by logic that he carried his point; when confronted by opposition his voice became shrill, his goatee bristled upward, and his vehemence often subdued less vigorous and less militant spirits.[27] Devoted as he was to the practical things of life, he naturally looked with favor on the applied sciences and on what were called the practical aspects of education. In defending research, as he so often did, he never tired of citing examples of the far-reaching implications of disinterested or un-

[26] Leith, "Memorial of Charles Richard Van Hise," 104–105.
[27] Interviews, Curti and Carstensen with Dr. Joseph Evans and Dean Sellery.

specialized investigations. Nor were these the only ways in which his outlook on life reflected a pioneer environment. As became a son of polyglot Wisconsin, he sympathized with peoples of various stocks and assumed that just as mixed populations within the state had got along with one another, so might those on the world stage. As a means to this end he welcomed the Cosmopolitan Club movement in the universities[28] and favored the international program of Woodrow Wilson.

But a heritage in no sense peculiar to the frontier also influenced Van Hise. The new president shared the traditional American faith in the ability of the people to work out their problems and to advance their interests once they saw them clearly. He came to be a zealous champion of popular education in the widest sense of the term. Education, he felt, much as Thomas Jefferson and Horace Mann had insisted, was the means by which talent was to be discovered and used for the benefit of mankind. Education, moreover, was the most effective long-time guarantee of honesty in public life and of responsibility in government officials. Above all, education was the means by which ever increasing knowledge was to be popularly assimilated for human well-being. Van Hise was challenged by the fact that man knew so much more than he made use of.

Immediately related as Van Hise's outlook on life was to his temperament and background and to main currents in American life, it also owed much to the men with whom he had come in contact and by whom he had been influenced. Among these, as Van Hise himself recognized, was John Bascom. As a student he had been impressed by the New Englander's emphasis on the moral and social responsibility of the scholar to the public interest and on the role of education in promoting the social and spiritual as well as the material well-being of the people. Others reinforced the influence of Bascom. From the writings of Lester Frank Ward, Van Hise learned the importance of conserving human talent and the social significance of the advancement and the dissemination of knowledge under government

---

[28] Louis Lochner, "Cosmopolitan Clubs in American University Life," *Review of Reviews*, 37:316–321 (March, 1908).

auspices for the extension of democracy and the acceleration of social progress. To La Follette and Turner, Van Hise owed an incalculable debt. They aroused his interest in politics as a weapon and made him see some part of the economic basis of politics; they also sharpened his concern for social justice.

It is impossible to say, of course, just how Van Hise's thought would have developed in the presidency had he not come under the influence of these realistic and progressive minds. Yet the general movement against special privilege was strong enough to provide fertile soil for the growth of the seeds planted in his mind by Bascom and nourished by Turner and La Follette. Thrown into the arena of political and economic upheaval from which the University could not possibly be isolated, he learned quickly. He enriched in new and striking ways the concept of the University as an integral arm of the state. He believed in the pre-eminent role of the expert in any complex society. Indeed, the emphasis he put on the regulatory commission of experts somewhat tempered his faith in the masses. Van Hise faced many problems squarely as they arose. To say this is not to deny a certain intellectual naïveté which displayed itself from time to time. Nor is it to claim that his desire to get things done with the least possible antagonism of powerful conservative interests did not sometimes lead him into inconsistencies in both thought and action. At the same time Van Hise unquestionably moved from the level of the scientist and administrator to that of publicist and statesman. The publicist he became fairly readily. It was more difficult to become the statesman.

Of the two principal social issues on which Van Hise's reputation as a publicist and economic statesman rests, his drive for the conservation of natural resources was most intimately related to his scientific interest. As early as the 1870's, leaders in the American Association for the Advancement of Science took up the long-overlooked pleas of John Quincy Adams and George Perkins Marsh that natural resources be used with more regard for future needs. The Geological Survey also sounded warnings. In 1893 at the World's Fair in Chicago the conservation issue was put before the public for the first time. Van Hise's interest in the problem owed something to his association with the Geological Survey; it may have been stimulated by the movement at the World's Fair, for at this time he was a nonresident professor at the University of Chicago. The first lectures on conservation at Wisconsin were given by Professor Bernhard E. Fernow in 1896. Whatever the importance of these factors, Van Hise himself in his field work in northern Wisconsin had seen the devastating effects of forest depletion on water sites and on the environment in general.

Van Hise served on the state conservation commission and took part in the White House conference which President Roosevelt called in 1908. But his chief service to the cause was the book which he published in 1910, *The Conservation of Natural Resources*. "It is my hope," wrote Van Hise in the preface, "that this book may serve a useful purpose in forwarding the great movement for conservation which, as it seems to me from the point of the not distant future of the human race, is more important than all other movements before the people." Based on University lectures, the book made no claims for the originality of the data, carefully selected and documented from public records, but it might well have claimed originality for its synthesis. The essence of Van Hise's teaching was that the state should assure development of natural resources without waste; this implied that franchises should be granted on terms attractive to capital, and the state should take responsibility for preventing waste and unfair monopoly in the development of natural resources. Thus, in developing water power Van Hise favored elastic legislation administered by a nonpartisan expert commission in such a way as to protect the resources and at the same time encourage capital.

The difficulty of drawing and maintaining a line between these two objectives was exemplified in an episode which involved Van Hise and his associates in a controversy of some significance. A group of promoters interested in constructing a power dam on the Wisconsin River acquired the necessary franchises from the state and spent considerable money in lining up businessmen in support of the project. Two regents of the University, Magnus Swenson and G. D. Jones, were involved in the enterprise. It was discovered that the plans ran counter to the conception of public interest entertained by the Wisconsin Conservation Commission, of which Van Hise was a member. It was also discovered that a report on riparian law prepared by Professor Eugene A. Gilmore of the law school threatened the undertaking. The University experts were attacked before a legislative committee for interfering with the plans of honest businessmen. The University in its corporate capacity was not involved in the issue; but sections of the public press and leading figures in the power schemes, failing to distinguish between the institution itself and the services and views of a few of its experts on state commissions, attacked the University.[29] When Van Hise became convinced that the project not only possessed a proper franchise from the state but also presented no conceivable danger to the future water supply, he used his influence to persuade the Army Engineer Corps to add its approval.[30] Despite the fact that the zeal of Van Hise and his colleagues for the protection of water sites did not block this particular enterprise, some of the increasing criticisms of the University from conservatives derived from Gilmore's brief and the initial concern of the conservation commission.[31]

In the years that followed the University was bitterly attacked by the Stalwart opponents of La Follette progressivism on the ground that it was a hotbed of radicalism and that it was taking part in political controversies. During these attacks Van Hise's integrity as a conservationist was questioned by some newspapers. The Milwaukee *Free Press,* apparently being without full possession of the facts, clamored indignantly that Van Hise, while an employee of the University and of the Geological Survey, had betrayed the ethics of his profession and of the conservation movement by obtaining title to large Canadian tracts rich in silver and cobalt and then selling these tracts to a syndicate for development.[32]

In 1910 Van Hise had reprimanded a professor for indiscretion;[33] what he had done was not ethically wrong, Van Hise had said, but the man should have realized that his action might serve as an opening for criticism of the University. In this in-

[29] G. D. Jones to Professor Eugene Allen Gilmore, March 4, 1909; Jones to Birge, July 10, 1909; Van Hise to Jones, July 19, 1909, all in the Presidents' Papers.   [30] Van Hise to Brigadier General Alexander Mackenzie, July 8, 1909.
[31] *Milwaukee Journal,* July 17, 1909, p. 6.
[32] Milwaukee *Free Press,* June 27, 1911, pp. 1–2.   [33] See pp. 63 ff.

stance Van Hise himself perhaps failed to distinguish with sufficient perspicacity between the rectitude of his actions and their implications. Though criticism is often facilitated by "indiscretions," it is seldom stopped by the lack of them. The evidence indicates no ethical betrayal. While Van Hise was dealing with organizations of the type sometimes violently opposed to conservation, it should be remembered that the mineral wealth of his tracts could never have been developed without capital, and that his program as a conservationist consistently included the encouragement of development of resources as well as the prevention of waste. Nor should he be criticized on professional grounds. Van Hise could undoubtedly have become wealthy had he marketed to the full his talents as a geologist. He did not, however, engage in activities prohibited by his connections with the Geological Survey, nor did he receive pay for any work as consulting geologist while he was president of the University.[34]

It was almost as inevitable that Van Hise should become involved in the public controversy over the politics of conservation as it was that his own devotion to the cause should be questioned by his critics. In the Ballinger–Pinchot controversy he did not hesitate to support Pinchot in articles in the *World's Work* and *Collier's*. After a public speech in St. Louis in which Roosevelt and Pinchot were praised for their contributions to conservation, the press interpreted Van Hise's remark as a criticism of Taft. He was quick to assure Taft of his appreciation of the good work he had done and tactfully to invite his continued support of the movement.[35]

In championing the cause of conservation Van Hise had emphasized the efficient use of natural resources and the importance of the principle of public control. Thus, despite the fact that many questioned his competence as a writer on complex economic subjects, it was natural for Van Hise to ponder the growing concentration of corporate wealth and to consider methods of dealing with it. Early in November, 1911, in an address at Harvard, Van Hise first publicly announced an analysis

[34] Leith to Curti, July 3, December 23, 1947. Van Hise's personal property at his death was cited at $155,577 and his real property at $16,700. *Daily Cardinal*, December 16, 1918.

[35] Van Hise to William Howard Taft, January 12, 1910.

Charles R. Van Hise in 1905

The University in 1880

and a prescription, which he developed in his *Concentration and Control: A Solution of the Trust Problem in the United States.* He sent advance proof sheets to Roosevelt who, though "worked to death," read it at once.[36] Roosevelt paid public tribute to the book at the Progressive National Convention which nominated him for the presidency in 1912. Van Hise may well have influenced Roosevelt in clarifying a position toward which he had been moving.[37]

Concentration and Control, which was read and discussed almost as much as *The Conservation of Natural Resources,* analyzed the data relevant to the increasing concentration of capital and brought to the fore many aspects of the problem. Making use of case histories accumulated in government investigations, Van Hise produced a book at once scholarly and readable. He generously recognized the help of colleagues at the University. He wrote the book, he declared, "to present an outline picture of the situation regarding concentration of industry in the United States, and to suggest a way to gain its economic advantages and at the same time to guard the interests of the public."[38] Assuming large-scale aggregations of capital and industrial organization to be necessary for the efficient use of natural resources, Van Hise rejected as both unrealistic and undesirable any proposal to dissolve the trusts. Thus he found himself in good standing with the Chamber of Commerce when it fought legislation for the dissolution of huge combinations which the older antitrust laws had failed to touch. As a result of an address given before the United States Chamber of Commerce he was appointed to the legislative committee of that organization to present the case of big business to the congressional committees. At these hearings he appeared along with the powerful representatives of leading corporations.[39]

The proposal stated in *Concentration and Control* went farther than mere opposition to the movement for dissolving trusts. It involved in effect an extension of the Wisconsin Idea:

[36] Theodore Roosevelt to Van Hise, June 4, 1912.

[37] Van Hise to John T. Dow, September 17, 1912.

[38] Charles R. Van Hise, *Concentration and Control: A Solution of the Trust Problem in the United States* (New York, 1912), v.

[39] Van Hise to James G. Wray, December 23, 1914.

trusts were to be controlled by a commission of experts in the interests of the public. "If this book," he wrote, "has the good fate to assist in the rule of enlightment, reason, fair play, mutual consideration, and toleration, and thus advance the solution of this problem, the author will have been repaid many fold for his labor in its preparation."[40] In the achievements of the Federal Trade Commission his program was in some measure implemented.

In view of the growing strength of organized labor both in Wisconsin and in the country at large, Van Hise was compelled to concern himself with the relative claims of management and the working class. Van Hise was neither for nor against labor, although his actions generally supported management. In the spring of 1912 a threatened strike of the Brotherhood of Locomotive Engineers against eastern railroads promised to tie up a considerable part of the nation's transportation system. The contestants agreed to accept informal, nonstatutory arbitration and Chief Justice Edward White asked Van Hise to sit on the arbitration board. As chairman he had an important part in the final report. The full claims of the engineers were not met: the board cut the requested increase, allowing an advance of only seven per cent of existing wages. In a dissenting report the labor representative on the board, P. H. Morrissey, challenged the statistics on which the recommendations were based.[41] The *Locomotive Engineers' Monthly Journal,* however, held that the settlement as a whole should meet with the general approval of the brotherhood and especially approved that part of the report which for the first time worked out a standardized wage arrangement for a large number of railroads.[42] The representative of the brotherhood on the board and the *Journal* of the brotherhood both strongly opposed the recommendation for the compulsory arbitration of

[40] Van Hise, *Concentration and Control,* v.

[41] *Report of the Board of Arbitration in the matter of the controversy between the Eastern Railroads and the Brotherhood of Locomotive Engineers* (Washington, 1912).

[42] W. S. Stone, "Award of the Arbitrators," in the *Locomotive Engineers' Monthly Journal,* 46:1161 (December, 1912). The *Journal* devoted surprisingly little editorial comment to the award.

disputes in the future. Although this recommendation was not new, it had "never before been so conspicuously and effectively presented in connection with an important labor arbitration."[43] Van Hise and the majority of his colleagues maintained that railway workers were engaged in a public service comparable to that of teachers, soldiers, and sailors and that therefore strikes paralyzing transportation must be prevented. The report argued that if railroad labor accepted a qualified right of free concerted action, its interests should be protected through an interstate wage commission. The public press and specialists in railway economics applauded this recommendation, but the brotherhood angrily maintained that it "must retain some control over the supply of our kind of labor." Van Hise's proposal would "leave us standing as individuals subject to the dictates of some commission as to how we should be treated and paid for service rendered."[44] This represented a shift of attitude on the part of organized labor which, at an earlier stage when it had little power, had looked favorably on the idea of compulsory arbitration. Now, holding the balance of power, it had little to expect from compulsory arbitration. To Van Hise, however, the recommendation was eminently sound: it extended the role of the nonpartisan, fact-finding expert and evoked the principle of control in the public interest. It was consistent for him, a few years later, to oppose the Adamson Act which railway labor had wrung from Congress without resort to arbitration provided for by the Newlands Act of 1913.

In one instance Van Hise's interpretation of the public interest led him to take a position in a local labor dispute. A building trades union in Madison asked the Dane County circuit court for an injunction to stop work on the remodeling of the engineering building on the ground that, contrary to a state statute, the working day was longer than the stipulated eight hours. The president described the extent to which the University's work would be hampered if the injunction were

[43] William J. Cunningham, in the *Quarterly Journal of Economics*, 27:293 (February, 1913).

[44] "Our Future Needs," in the *Locomotive Engineers' Monthly Journal*, 47:82 (January, 1913).

granted, Judging the interest of the University to be of public nature, the court refused the request for the injunction.[45]

Van Hise was a liberal, not a radical. He emphasized the role of the expert in government, rather than that of the electorate. The people's function, as he saw it, was to lay down, through chosen representatives, broad lines of policy. He himself not only preached but practiced the doctrine that the scholar is under obligation to serve the state. Neither Van Hise nor other progressives of the time expressed any great enthusiasm for the idea that public responsibility might well extend to the enrichment of the spiritual and aesthetic lives of the people. His conception of service was that of the progressives of his day; it emphasized efficiency and honesty in government and the advancement of the material welfare of the people. In the conflict between those favoring an extension of the powers of the state in the public interest and those opposing such extension, Van Hise, in greater degree than many educational leaders of his time, stood among the critics of laissez faire. If his progressivism was limited by his acceptance of the competitive and profit-making motives in the economy, we must remember that in this he was in accord with most of his fellow progressives. It is indeed true that, perhaps as a result of his tussles with conservative politicians who attacked the University as a hotbed of radicalism, perhaps in consequence of the shift in state politics in 1914 toward the Stalwarts, his liberalism was less militant in the later years of his administration. Charles McCarthy was only one progressive who felt that Van Hise was doing much too little in the way of carving out new frontiers for the advancement of the ideal of University service to the people. Furthermore, Van Hise could and did take in sail, even in a matter like academic freedom, when he feared that a forthright stand threatened financial support for the University or might bring too sharp criticism from the cautious.[46] It was of course easy for his critics to forget that the University had to be financed.

Van Hise's admirable qualities were quite naturally tempered with some limitations that influenced his career as a

---

[45] Copy, court record of Van Hise's testimony, September, 1910. Presidents' Papers, filed under Jones and Schubring, Attorneys.   [46] See pp. 65 ff., 71 ff.

president. His contacts with men of affairs and with other educational leaders increased his skill in personal relations, but to the end his forthrightness occasionally led him into ineptitude. His letters were often direct and brief to the point of bluntness; a two-page inquiry or request often received a sentence in reply. In expressing his ideas he betrayed the fact that words were not the tools with which he worked most easily. Although the president trained himself to keep his voice on a lower pitch, thus overcoming one of his most obvious faults in public address, he never became a polished speaker.

Professor Pyre, who was not unappreciative of Van Hise's great contributions as president, maintained that his principal lack was in the sphere of aesthetic values. According to Pyre, he failed to appreciate men of discriminating taste and cultivation as much as he did the experts and administrators who came to play an ever greater part in University affairs. He never grasped, Pyre felt, the fact that the cultivation of aesthetic values might be as much a public service as that of utilitarian ones. Though he realized that the University was failing to make adequate provision for the fine arts, he did not push this part of his program with the success that he pushed his more cherished interests.[47] There is an element of truth in this picture. Yet Van Hise was not without fine sensibilities. The intimate advisers on whom he leaned most heavily—Evans, Slaughter, Slichter, Turner, Birge, and Sellery—were all men of cultivation. It must be conceded that it was more difficult to persuade regents and legislators of the importance of the arts than it was to present the claims of laboratories and extension services. Thus Van Hise pushed for what he felt he could get and waited for an opportunity to advance the aesthetic arts. Although in general he had a good sense for what was possible, he may have been wrong here. Van Hise had limitations and made mistakes. He was not always adequate in promoting his own sincerely held objectives, and in some respects these objectives were themselves circumscribed.

But his limitations were overshadowed by his remarkable gifts and by his no less remarkable success in building boldly

---

[47] James F. A. Pyre, *Wisconsin* (New York, 1920), 330.

and well with the materials at hand, on the foundations already laid. For giving publicity to, fighting for, and implementing the idea of the service-university, Wisconsin is deeply indebted to him. For what he did to promote the increase of knowledge, to disseminate it and to facilitate its useful application, the country itself is indebted to him. It is not easy to exaggerate the enthusiasm which Van Hise kindled among students, the faculty, and the people at large. His warmth and imagination, his devotion to the University and the state, his capacity to learn, and his remarkable statesmanship, all added up to greatness. His belief in Wisconsin, his capacity to make others share his belief, and his record in creating and leading an organization which justified that belief, were unparalleled in the annals of American higher education.

VAN HISE possessed many talents which insured his administrative success. Many who worked under him have testified to his integrity and his complete dependability. He was willing to make decisions and stand by them. He never double-crossed or "let down" a subordinate. True, the new president found it difficult if not impossible to realize his determination to do nothing himself that could be delegated to others. In the first few days of his incumbency he was overwhelmed by protests from alumni indignant because the room hitherto used exclusively by the Philomathia literary society had been converted into a lecture room, and to these protests he gave careful consideration. His attention was called to the fact that at a mass meeting held in the gymnasium the side doors were not open, and he gave instructions to avoid the repetition of so petty an inconvenience. Complaints were brought directly to him regarding the improper cleaning of the gymnasium and he took steps to see that it was kept in suitable condition. It was necessary to discipline a janitor given to drunkenness and disorderly conduct. Students reported to him the inadequate lighting in the handball courts and he took appropriate action. In fact there was no end to the nuisances that piled up. When a professor complained about the noisy, indecently clad bathers who were using the piers near his home and demanded that these be closed to outsiders, Van Hise declined to take so drastic a course but ordered all bathers to be clad decently, that is, in "suits which extend from the shoulders to the knees." A plethora of inquiries continued to come to him which he did not ignore. In 1912, for example, he was asked to answer such questions as these: If a balloon went up into the air and stayed still for a period of time and then came down straight to earth, would it land in China? . . . Which is the greatest man, emperor or king? . . . Does a snake bite or sting? . . . What sort of a foundation is best for a house? . . . What is the matter with my daughter when she does not eat any breakfast, and is otherwise very well? . . . How build an icebox? He was also frequently asked advice on mining ventures, apparently by complete strangers, and sometimes his counsel was sought regarding investments.[48]

Little wonder that, in the middle of his administrative term, he wrote to his intimate friend, Frederick Jackson Turner: "I remember the happy days when I used to escape from Madison for six weeks or two months at this period of the year, but now I am 'on the wheel of things.' How many times I shall be obliged to allow the wheel to go round before I escape is one of the questions which I cannot yet answer, but I sincerely hope the number may be small."[49]

Yet Van Hise did not permit himself to be swamped by details. Heretofore the president had given a large part of his time to the College of Letters and Science. As one of his first administrative actions, the new president increased the responsibility and work of its dean, Edward Birge, thus not only lessening his own burden but placing the deanship on the same level as that enjoyed by the principal administrators of the other and less central colleges.[50] His sense of logic and efficiency, so apparent in his geological treatises, led him early in his presidential career to bring about a reorganization which discontinued the semiautonomous Schools of Pharmacy, Commerce, Education, History, and the School of Economics and Political Science. These were integrated with the College of Letters and Science,

[48] This paragraph is based on letters in the Presidents' Papers.
[49] Van Hise to Turner, March 11, 1907.
[50] Van Hise to Birge, and Van Hise to the Board of Regents, June 10, 1903.

in which they had always been active elements. In making the proposal to the faculty Van Hise had said that the directors, recognizing the anomaly of such schools, recommended the change. Notwithstanding his explanation and despite the fact that the faculty had approved the program,[51] some felt that the president had forced the reorganization. At least one director later said that the president had been highhanded.[52] Van Hise subsequently maintained that the change preserved the unity and harmony of the College of Letters and Science and removed virtually all friction and jealousy between the heads of the various schools without in any way interfering with or weakening the courses.[53] The reorganization certainly simplified the administrative tasks of the president. The inclusion of quasi-professional cores of study within the College of Letters and Science, proved, in many ways, a happy solution. By checking the development of independent "schools" of commerce and education, it insured a pre-eminence to the College of Letters and Science which similar colleges did not always enjoy in other institutions. Van Hise approved of this. Moreover, he believed that students took hold of their work more effectively if they could see, early in their undergraduate training, how it pointed toward a career. The combination of liberal education with preprofessional work also squared with his belief that a clear-cut line between the cultural and vocational aspects of education was misleading.

Yet the reorganization, important though it was from an administrative point of view, was insufficient to make all the wheels run smoothly. As an administrator Van Hise had to meet the test of making readjustments fast enough to keep pace with a rapidly growing institution. This was the core of the report of the joint legislative committee on the affairs of the University which was appointed in 1906. As the committee insisted, the methods of administering a small institution would not altogether apply in a large, fast-growing university: "To the failure to make methods of administration keep pace with growth

[51] Van Hise to the faculty of the College of Letters and Science, November 13, 1903.
[52] See Kremers' biographical sketch of Van Hise. Kremers Papers.
[53] Reports to the Regents, E:21–22, October 10, 1904.

is due most of the defects discovered."[54] Thus reinforced in his original determination not to do things which others could do, Van Hise urged the appointment of an able vice-president. In 1907, when invited to become director of the Smithsonian Institution, the president was promised, as an inducement to remain at Madison, the assistance of a competent vice-president. Van Hise sanguinely hoped that with this help he might even be able to devote his mornings to his own research.[55] But no vice-president was appointed. A partial substitute was conceded three years later in the creation of the office of business manager. The bylaws of the regents provided that the business manager should "be the executive head of those officers and employees that are not attached to the instructional force" and that he should have "authority based on the rules and regulations of the Board of Regents to supervise business affairs of the University both at Madison and at other University centers throughout the State." In outlining the qualifications of the prospective incumbent, Van Hise emphasized a knowledge of accounting, an ability to perform duties without encroaching on the field of others, the energy and force to get things done, a respect for subordinates, and an understanding of the University in general.[56] Hermon C. Bumpus, director of the American Museum of Natural History, was called to the new position. After he left to become president of Tufts, the position was not immediately filled. However, Halsten J. Thorkelson, Bumpus' assistant, took over the work the day Bumpus left and was subsequently made business manager. Van Hise often said that the business manager relieved him of a great many responsibilities. Nevertheless, Van Hise continued to the very end to discharge a great many of the ever-increasing duties of the presidency.

Van Hise's ideas on the internal organization of the University, and especially on the relations between the president, deans, faculty, regents, and the public, were exemplified not only in his day-by-day and year-by-year practice but in state-

[54] *Report of the Joint Legislative Committee on the Affairs of the University,* 1906, pp. 14–15.

[55] Van Hise to James B. Angell, January 14, 1907; Van Hise to Chamberlin, January 25, 1907.

[56] Van Hise to Frank E. Doty, October 20, 1910. These qualifications, it may be noted, corresponded to Van Hise's ideas of the qualifications of a good president.

ments to the faculty, in papers presented to the National Association of State Universities, and in letters of counsel requested by officials of other universities. He was thoroughly
committed to the Wisconsin tradition of keeping both the college of liberal arts and the colleges of the applied sciences on
the same campus. This pattern, he believed, promoted both
economy and proper breadth of training for all groups and
at the same time lessened the competition from partially duplicating institutions. He was also happy in the fact that the University was located in a town of moderate size, thus avoiding the
domination of the institution by a great city. It was fortunate,
he believed, that the seat of the University was at the same time
the capital of the state. This, he pointed out to a committee
engaged in the organization of the new University of Saskatche-
wan, militated against the sort of misunderstanding that so easily
arose when university and capital were separated by a considerable distance.[57]

Gratified though he was by the fact that instruction and research in the practical arts centered on the University campus,
Van Hise saw no comparable advantages in bringing the University, the normal schools, and the school of mining under a
centralized board of higher education. When a legislative committee considered it he mustered evidence against the proposal
from the experience of institutions in other states. If a single
board should replace existing agencies, Van Hise insisted, it
would have a full-time job on its hands and could function only
on a professional basis. But that meant that if the compensation were small, only inferior men would seek the office; if
large, the unfit. A nonpaid board, he contended, in which membership carried honor and prestige, had succeeded in attracting
such outstanding men as Vilas, men who would never have accepted a position on a professional board. Moreover, in those
states which had a single board, there was evidence of much
trading: the board member coming from a district with an educational institution would often support the proposal of a member eager to help out some other school or college. Van Hise
feared that such a board would tend to elevate the normal

[57] Van Hise to Walter C. Murray, October 24, 1908.

schools to the same level of importance as the University.[58] He also feared that a central board might usurp faculty powers, arouse resentment, and drive away able scholars and teachers.[59] Closer harmony between the several institutions he believed might be obtained through a conference board; in any case he admitted that the movement for the centralized board was likely to gain strength as long as overlapping and undue competition between existing boards prevailed.

With a single exception all the regents saw eye to eye with Van Hise on this issue.[60] The president's opposition was an important factor in the rejection of the proposal, when it was first advanced and on subsequent occasions.[61] There was beyond doubt some merit in Van Hise's arguments against the consolidated board. Nevertheless, the continuation of the existing agencies resulted in overlapping, waste, and competition at a time when planning was becoming increasingly necessary to meet adequately the needs of the state in higher education.

⟡

AN ABILITY to work with the Board of Regents harmoniously and effectively was the first requisite of a successful president. For a state which was still largely agricultural the farming interest throughout the period was definitely underrepresented on the Board, despite occasional requests from agricultural organizations for a proportionate representation.[62] Delbert Utter, J. W. Martin, Enos L. Jones, and James L. Jones at various times represented the farming population, as did former Governor Hoard, the influential publisher of *Hoard's Dairyman,* and Benjamin Faast, who, like Hoard, was quite as much a businessman as an agriculturalist. Representatives of the professions, as

---

[58] National Association of State Universities, *Transactions and Proceedings,* 9:62–104 (1911).   [59] Papers of the Board of Regents, December 1, 1909.
[60] Records of the Board of Regents, I:316–317, June 16, 1915.
[61] *Daily Cardinal,* April 8, 1911. After 1915 he seemed to favor a single board, but this was not achieved. See Chapter 8.
[62] This point was made by Professor Andrew W. Hopkins in presenting to the governor the resolutions of the Wisconsin Livestock Breeders Association. Hopkins to Francis E. McGovern, February 6, 1914, McGovern Papers, State Historical Society of Wisconsin; resolution of the farmers' institute of March, 1913, in Papers of the Board of Regents, April 16, 1913.

well as of agriculture figured inconspicuously on the Board. Dr.
Gilbert Seaman was a politician as well as a physician; and the
only educators to sit on the Board during the period were
Professor Frederick W. A. Notz of Northwestern College at
Watertown, Frances G. Perkins, truant officer, and Elizabeth
Waters of the Fond du Lac high school. The women of the
state were represented for the first time by Mrs. Edmund
Ray Stevens who, irritated that she had been appointed without her knowledge, resolved to be completely inactive. Mrs.
Florence Buckstaff, on the other hand, was an active member of
the Board. An alumna, formerly a teacher, and a leading figure
in the women's club movement, she made her influence felt.[63]
There were political leaders and lawyers on the Board but, with
some exceptions, these were closely associated with banking and
business. James F. Trottman and Frederick C. Thwaits were
among them. Indeed, a study of the Board shows that business
was the predominant personal interest of the regents. Lucien
Hanks and Adolphus P. Nelson were bankers; Magnus Swenson,
Alexander J. Horlick, Walter J. Kohler, John E. Morgan, and
Pliny Norcross, industrialists and promoters; Gustav Keller,
watchmaker and jeweler; Theodore Hammond, publisher; E. M.
McMahon was in insurance; and Thomas E. Brittingham, in
the lumber business. G. D. Jones, lawyer, was active in paper
mills, utilities—including water-power development, chemicals,
real estate, and banking; he typified the newer businessman with
versatile interests. Few members of the Board were more influential than Jones, who served from 1909 to 1922. Labor, as such,
was entirely unrepresented during the period.

In political views the regents largely represented the dominant Republican party. The Stalwart faction on the whole pre-
dominated until the Progressive sweep in the elections of 1910.
But the triumph of Governor Philipp in 1914 swung the pen-
dulum once more in the conservative direction. In making appointments to the Board, the several governors were influenced
by a number of considerations. For example, those who wrote to

[63] Early in 1909 Assemblyman Fred W. Kubasta introduced a bill into the legislature designed to give women increased representation on the Board and Assemblyman George P. Hambrecht favored its consideration and passage. *Daily Cardinal*,
April 15, 1909.

Governor Francis E. McGovern in support of candidates made seven references to political availability, seven to high moral character, and three each to business ability, education, experience in the field of education, administrative experience, and friendliness and loyalty to the University. Unlike the situation in the early days of the institution, the office of regent was now sufficiently honored to be seldom refused and, indeed, to be frequently sought.

The charge was frequently made, by Stalwarts as well as Progressives, that both the appointments of the regents and their actions reflected political considerations. Thus the *Milwaukee Journal* declared, when Hoard resigned from the Board in 1911, that his retirement marked the removal of the last survivor of the Davidson regime, which had stood out against the freedom of teaching and research, and which had sought, for conservative reasons, to hamper the University.[64] One of his colleagues on the Board lent support to this view in declaring that there had been no politics until the advent of Hoard. "Then, for the first time, as you will recollect," he wrote to Van Hise, "we had secret meetings at the home of one of the regents," after which certain Board members would act together on the basis of these prearranged decisions.[65] In his letter of resignation Hoard wrote, "Failing health and an unwillingness to longer remain as a member of a body that has lately been reconstructed upon the basis and for the main purpose of political partisanship for the La Follette faction in politics are my chief reasons for resigning."[66] This, he declared elsewhere, was in contrast with the excellent nonpartisan appointments of Governor Davidson. Although Thwaits and Lamoureux had done good work on the Board, he continued, McGovern did not reappoint them because they had not been subservient: "They were not partisans of La Follette nor always backers of the ideas and ambitions of President Van Hise, who was and is La Follette's chief factotum in the University."[67] To this McGovern replied that Hoard was more of a factionalist than any of his

[64] *Milwaukee Journal,* March 31, 1911, p. 1.
[65] William J. McElroy to Van Hise, April 1, 1911.
[66] *Jefferson County Union,* April 7, 1911, p. 2.
[67] Milwaukee *Free Press,* April 2, 1911, pp. 1, 4.

own new appointees—Elizabeth Waters, Theodore Hammond, Thomas E. Brittingham, and Dr. Gilbert Seaman, none of whose appointments were political.[68] Hoard nevertheless continued to charge McGovern with appointing regents the president could manage and with getting rid of those he could not.[69] A few years later the president of the Board, Regent Trottman, also resigned the presidency in protest against what he declared to be partisan opposition to the economy program of Governor Philipp[70] on the part of the holdover McGovern-named regents. These charges and countercharges lend support to the argument that political considerations did in some degree enter into appointments to the Board and that its members were not entirely free from partisanship.

Van Hise's relations with the Board were complicated by the fact that he was called on to work with a governing body which, at different times, represented Stalwart and Progressive majorities. In view of his own convictions on the Progressive side, he was confronted by difficult and delicate problems. He had to cooperate with a Board weighted by Stalwarts in order to push his financial and educational program; he had to consider the frequent allegations that this Board would seize any occasion to oust him from his office. And when the Progressives enjoyed a majority, he had to face the charge that he was unfairly using his position to strengthen that group.

Several considerations explain the success of Van Hise in steering his course between dangerous shoals. In the first place the Wisconsin system of having regents appointed by the governor rather than elected met with his full approval; he let it be known that, in his opinion, this resulted in securing superior men, since many of the most able and desirable simply would not enter a political campaign for the position.[71] Van Hise fre-

---

[68] *Milwaukee Journal*, March 31, 1911. W. D. Hoard noted that McGovern did not say that these regents were not Progressives. *Jefferson County Union*, April 7, 1911, p.2.

[69] Milwaukee *Free Press*, November 24, 1941. Hoard wrote to Dean Harry L. Russell, "I am no longer persona grata with the Board of Regents, as you know, owing to my disgust over their subservience to the La Follette game and his tool, Van Hise." Papers of the Dean of the College of Agriculture, Hoard File, July 21, 1913.

[70] See pp. 93–95.   [71] Van Hise to Doane Robinson, December 11, 1906.

quently declared that the regents were genuinely devoted to the interests of the University as they understood them and frequently expressed appreciation of the self-sacrifice they made for the institution. Whatever he thought, in public he defended the regents against charges of political bias.[72] The president of the Alumni Association said that when he asked Van Hise whether the regents always voted right in the end, he answered that they did.[73]

Other attitudes and practices still further explain Van Hise's generally successful relations with the regents. For example, he presented matters of policy to the Board "in a free form, so that they may not feel hampered by the necessity of refusing to adopt the recommendation of the president if they cannot agree to the change. Both from the point of view of the results to be obtained and from the point of view of good feeling between the regents and the president, I feel certain that this policy is the best one."[74] Moreover, in approving the establishment of the faculty-regent conference committee,[75] the president shifted from his own shoulders to those of the regents and faculty some part of the friction which generally fell on the president in his capacity of liaison officer to the Board.

Nor must the president's skill in educating the Board be overlooked. Recognizing that the regents possessed final legal authority in educational as in financial matters, he nevertheless tried to make clear to them the wisdom of leaving educational issues to the faculty. Even when he had not favored a given faculty decision he presented it to the Board as cogently as possible; and on at least one occasion, fearing that he could not do justice to the point of view of the faculty on athletic policy, he asked Professor Turner to present the arguments to the regents.[76] It was

[72] For example, see Van Hise's statement in the Milwaukee *Free Press*, April 1, 1911, pp. 1, 3; and Van Hise to George F. Merrill, June 20, 1909.

[73] Lynn S. Pease to McGovern, February 7, 1911, in the McGovern Papers.

[74] Van Hise to Joseph Jastrow, May 8, 1909. M. E. McCaffrey, secretary of the Board, has stated that this was a consistent Van Hise policy.

[75] In 1909 a conference committee was appointed by the regents and by the faculty for the purposes of "general discussion with reference to University matters." This committee was systematized in 1912. Records of the Board of Regents, H:328, April 25, 1912.

[76] George C. Sellery to Merle Curti, June 28, 1947.

especially in the financial sphere, however, that Van Hise was at his best in bringing the regents to see the needs of the University. Thus in his report of 1905 he dealt almost exclusively with the financial condition of the institution, outlining needs and carefully justifying expenditures already made in the light of the long-range program. His next report dealt largely with the problem of promotions and recruitment of new faculty members. In 1907 Van Hise met, with an able and comprehensive summary, the request of the governing board for a statement on the administration of the courses in the various departments. These and other reports to the regents were bolstered by the evidence gathered from students and faculty and from officials of other universities. He made his points not only with facts and figures but with analogies familiar to the businessmen on the Board. He phrased his requests in such a way that the regents would have to negate their own expressions of educational policy if they refused what he asked. Always he made it clear that his requests were not mere patchwork but part of a large, long-range program for increasing the facilities of the University in proportion to the growing population of the state, the demands of the students, and the multiplying services of the institution to the commonwealth.

In spite of Van Hise's faculty for meeting the regents at least halfway and for working with them on points of difference as harmoniously as possible, it was inevitable that conflicts should arise. One involved the position of the College of Agriculture. Van Hise, notwithstanding his penchant for achieving practical results and for buttressing the University in the eyes of the state by the constant demonstration of its usefulness, shared the feeling of a group in the College of Letters and Science that the regents failed to appreciate both the importance of pure research in the humanities and social studies and the basic importance to the applied fields of the general work of the College of Letters and Science. Regent Hoard, in writing to the president in October, 1908, asked why in so many of his recent addresses he seemed obsessed by the idea that the College of Letters and Science was suffering, or was in danger of suffering, in both student and public appreciation. If anything, Hoard maintained, it could claim "an undue share of money and attention. . . . Should you not as the mouthpiece of the University in its most influential sense, say more for the upbuilding of the minor colleges, when, by the very drift of events, the College of Letters and Science will take the lion's share anyway?"[77]

In replying Van Hise made his position clear. Recently, he pointed out, the regents had questioned the policy of having research professors in the College of Letters and Science. Yet both in the College of Agriculture and in the College of Engineering provision had been made for research professors. Since only two professors in Letters and Science had been granted a mere half year for investigative work, it seemed obvious that the regents were discriminating against research in that college. He concluded by indicating that, as a result of his discussion with the regent conference committee on the state of the University, he had been assured that there was no intent so to discriminate and that his mind was greatly relieved.[78]

If Van Hise was thus reassured, Hoard was not, for before long he was expressing annoyance at reports of "ill concealed sneers of certain professors in the faculty of the College of Letters and Science toward the College of Agriculture."[79] Van Hise replied by emphasizing points of agreement. Had he not again and again in public addresses upheld the work of the College of Agriculture on the ground that it directly promoted the conservation of the human race? Moreover, the strongest men on the faculty of Letters and Science fully appreciated the great work of the College of Agriculture, were proud of it, and were trying to make their own college as efficient. If there was some talk about Wisconsin's having become a "cow university," this was to be regarded as the sort of joke men make when the joke does not express their real conviction.[80]

The differences between the two men on this point were too fundamental to be thus easily resolved. Hoard subsequently expressed the view, which he declared other regents shared, that a considerable portion of the so-called research led nowhere. In support of his view, he cited an article by President David Starr

---

[77] Hoard to Van Hise, October 12, 1908.   [78] Van Hise to Hoard, October 14, 1908.
[79] Hoard to Van Hise, April 16, 1909.   [80] Van Hise to Hoard, April 19, 1909.

Jordan of Stanford.[81] Van Hise declared in his reply that "in order to get large results in research it will be inevitable that a considerable amount of relatively fruitless work will be done." "The situation," he continued, "in reference to research is something like that of a mine. The man who deals with mines takes a dozen prospects which look good with the expectation that probably a half or two-thirds of them will not fulfill their promise. However, if but one fulfills its promise this will more than compensate for the expenditure of the dozen."[82]

But the president's efforts to educate Hoard to his own way of thinking left the great practical dairyman unconvinced. Hoard's devotion to applied science and suspicion of pure research in the humanities and social studies were on subsequent occasions brusquely expressed. He took Van Hise to task for supporting Dean Birge in the ardent defenses he made of members of the faculty of letters and science whenever any of them were subjected to criticism. Specifically, Hoard agreed with the alumnus who criticized Professor Cunliffe for making an assignment on Chaucer's use of Italian derivatives in *Troilus and Criseyde* and resented Dean Birge's defense of Cunliffe. "The entire Board of Regents are becoming somewhat weary of this attitude on the part of Dean Birge," Hoard complained, "and a much wiser and sagacious policy would be to admit the possibility that things are not always going right."[83] Such complaints lent support to the growing feeling in the College of Letters and Science that the regents were unduly interfering in the purely educational affairs of the University.[84] Van Hise did not conceal in his private correspondence his opinion of Hoard when, after his retirement from the Board, he criticized the University in the press for policies for which as a regent he had borne responsibility.[85]

Hoard was not the only regent with whom Van Hise crossed swords. Although the tone of his correspondence with G. D. Jones was on the whole friendly and although the president

[81] Hoard to Van Hise, January 30, 1911.
[82] Van Hise to Hoard, February 4, 1911.
[83] Hoard to Van Hise, January 13 and February 1, 1910. The correspondence does not indicate what position Van Hise took in regard to this complaint.
[84] See pp. 57 ff.   [85] Van Hise to former Regent McElroy, May 15, 1911.

was convinced that this leading industrialist was devoted to the University, in the fall and winter of 1910 their relations became badly strained. In the conflict arising between his own interest in the Wisconsin Valley Improvement Company and the Conservation Commission, Jones had expressed regret that his colleague, Neal Brown, had openly attacked the University for endangering the plans of Wisconsin's businessmen. Jones had properly distinguished between the University itself and the position of some of its officers as members of state commissions. But he subsequently felt that the Forestry Commission, of which Van Hise was also a member, pursued policies inimical to business enterprise.[86] It is certain that Jones thoroughly disliked the support Van Hise gave to the Progressives. In his eyes this was a "revolutionary policy" and equivalent to political interference on the part of the experts on the University staff participating in the regulation of business enterprise. He particularly disliked the growing tendency of the muckrakers to hail the University as an institution whose precocious sophomores pretended to tell businessmen how to run their affairs.[87] Jones took Van Hise to task for making the faculty suspicious of the regents, for indicating unwillingness to come to an understanding with the governing agency of the University, and for opposing Regent Charles P. Cary's proposal for taking from the University the inspection of high schools. "I have come to seriously doubt your fairness and openness," he said.[88]

The president was thoroughly irritated. He agreed with Jones in holding that the president certainly should not stir up the faculty against the regents but quickly denied that he had ever done any such thing.[89] Replying to the reflections on his fairness and openness, Van Hise minced no words: "It is therefore useless for me to discuss the points mentioned in your letter. It is only on the basis of your acceptance of my fairness and openness that I am willing to consider with you the various questions you raise."[90] Although apparently this affair was patched up, Jones continued to feel that Van Hise was on the

[86] Jones to Van Hise, March 6, 1911.
[87] *Ibid.*, November 9, 1909.
[89] Van Hise to Jones, November 8, 1909.
[88] *Ibid.*, November 5 and 9, 1909.
[90] *Ibid.*, November 13, 1909.

side of those criticizing the regents for permitting their own conservatism and their business affiliations to influence them in their alleged interference with educational policy. Van Hise could and did yield to the regents against his own preference often enough. For example, in the appointment of an acting dean of the law school in 1912 Van Hise wanted Gilmore and told him he would serve. Jones was definitely opposed to Professor Gilmore either by reason of the brief he had drawn on riparian law in Wisconsin or for other reasons. Although he favored Gilmore, Van Hise, in a Board meeting, did acquiesce in Jones's desire that Professor Smith be named. He had, however, in the pressure of preparing his work for the railroad arbitration committee, neglected to notify the law school and, in consequence, Gilmore proceeded on the basis of the original arrangement. The president, while expressing the embarrassment he would feel if Smith were made acting dean, indicated his willingness to leave the decision to the regent committee on the law school. Gilmore was permitted to act as dean; but Jones must have added this to his list of reasons for feeling dissatisfied with the president.[91]

[91] Jones to Van Hise, October 3, 1912; Van Hise to Jones, October 2 and 4, 1912.

2.

Van Hise: Academic Leadership

T HE internal administration of a university, Van Hise thought, should, like that at Wisconsin, be democratic. As he saw it, the faculty should initiate educational policies and the regents should approve their recommendations. "I am so strongly of the opinion that this is the only wise government of a university," he wrote to an inquirer, "that I would sooner forego my own opinions than have them introduced when they are not acceptable to the faculty. ... The reason for this," he continued, "is that the progress of the university is largely a function of the harmony of the different administrative factors. Upon the whole, an institution will make the most rapid advance by having favorable action of the faculty upon the suggestions of the president than it will if the president takes matters in his own hands and disregards the faculty." In other words, Van Hise thought of the president as the leader rather than the director of the faculty.[1] The faculty, he believed, was the true focus of the University. In practice this meant that although the president took the initiative in matters of appointment and removal, he did not make recommendations to the regents on these points without the approval of the chairman of the department and the dean of the college.

In the interest of efficiency Van Hise approved the practice of delegating many issues to the faculty committees; in the inter-

[1] Charles R. Van Hise to Eugene A. Smith, April 15, 1908, Presidents' Papers. All letters to and from Van Hise are in the Presidents' Papers unless otherwise indicated.

43

est of democracy, of having committee recommendations on important issues threshed over by the faculty as a whole.[2] At the same time Van Hise confessed that there was no doubt whatever that "the faculty and committee method of government is exceedingly expensive in time, energy, and efficiency as compared with the directorial method." He encouraged Turner to work out a more efficient method of administration but said he did not think that any method which curtailed the powers of the faculty would be acceptable to them. Citing illustrations of faculty resentment at recent proposals for handling certain purely administrative details involving athletics and an improved course for teachers, the president remarked: "The fact of the matter is that the faculty is unwilling to follow the method which any good administrative officer must, if successful. If the faculty do handle the matters themselves, they complain about the time and energy required for the work. Upon the other hand, if they delegate a piece of work to a chairman or a committee, they are not content, as any administrative officer must be, to give that committee a free hand, asking only that satisfactory results be secured—they want to reserve the power constantly to modify and regulate."[3]

Van Hise was doubtless sincere in his belief that his relations with the faculty were democratic. Though the faculty unanimously urged him to stay when a call came to another position,[4] there was some feeling on the faculty that the administration might be more democratic. In a cogent essay in J. McKeen Cattell's volume, *University Control,* Joseph Jastrow, without explicit reference to Wisconsin, condemned many practices with which he was familiar. But it is worth noting that of the thirteen Wisconsin professors who responded to Cattell's invitation to comment on his plan for a more democratic system of ad-

[2] Memorandum labeled "Kansas" and filed under K in the Presidents' Papers.
[3] Van Hise to Turner, July 31, 1907. In the meeting of the faculty on October 7, 1907, Van Hise pointed out the wasteful effects of committee work and suggested that the legislative and executive functions of committees be separated, the executive ones being delegated to chairmen. He added, however, that he proposed no general faculty legislation, suggesting merely that each committee consider the problem and work out its own solution. Minutes of the Meetings of the Faculty, 6:83, October 7, 1907.
[4] Van Hise to Thomas C. Chamberlin, January 25, 1907; Van Hise to I. A. Holmes, January 16, 1907.

ministration, only four spoke in its favor—a smaller percentage than those of a similar mind in Michigan, Cornell, and half a dozen other universities.[5] This suggests that, if the thirteen professors were a fair sample, the faculty was largely satisfied with Wisconsin procedure. We shall see that, as a result of the regents' interference, faculty discontent in the second half of the Van Hise administration led to a reorganization of the relations between faculty and regents. This was not, however, because of any general feeling that the president failed to represent the faculty adequately before the Board. Indeed, an instance in which Van Hise did fall down badly in interpreting the faculty to the regents seems to have been the exception rather than the rule. In the spring of 1907 he made certain statements to the executive committee regarding the faculty's position on athletics. To test the truth of these statements a circular letter was sent to the full professors asking for a free expression of opinion on intercollegiate athletics. The replies, according to Professor Scott, left in the minds of the regent committee "an impression almost diametrically opposed to that which the President's statement had left."[6]

In his personal relations with individual members of the faculty Van Hise thought of himself as the friendly leader and counselor rather than as master. When a professor sought his permission to arrange his work so that he might accept an invitation to lecture on the west coast, Van Hise told him to decide for himself whether he thought his work would suffer and to be guided by his own judgment.[7] He was, of course, accessible to members of the staff by appointment; in addition, busy as he was, he set aside an hour each morning when anyone might see him briefly without previous arrangement. When controversies arose between members of the faculty, like that between the director of physical education and the commandant or that between Ely and Commons concerning credit for the industrial history project, the president arbitrated the differences. And

---

[5] J. McKeen Cattell, *University Control* (New York, 1913), 23.

[6] William A. Scott to Richard T. Ely, May 9, 1907, in the Ely Papers, State Historical Society of Wisconsin. Scott indicated that except for one or two members of the Board, the regents did not oppose the president despite this misrepresentation and other actions.

[7] Van Hise to Joseph Jastrow, September 23, 1903.

although he regarded himself as the representative of the faculty with the regents, on at least one occasion he arranged for a department chairman whose request for a salary increase he did not see fit to support, to present his own case before the Board.[8] In the later years of his administration, when liberals often criticized particular professors for an overly conservative position on such issues as the cooperative movement, Van Hise defended them, insisting they might be too cautious, but that they were honest searchers for truth and that their caution might be the result of a deliberate effort not to push too far ahead of public opinion. In his individual dealings with faculty members Van Hise fairly well realized his conception of a friendly leader. Although Professor Pyre felt that the president's program was sometimes carried through "by bringing into play the full pressure of administrative prestige supported by dark allusions to Demos,"[9] the formal records of Van Hise's relations with the faculty seem neither to bear this out nor to evidence lust for power.[10]

He considered it wise policy for distinguished scholars to offer an introductory course, not only on the ground that this enabled underclassmen to come in contact with eminent men but that it also stimulated specialists to think in terms of the whole field. According to his own testimony, Van Hise tried to inspire the staff to reach higher levels in both instruction and research, not to regiment or force them into activities against their will. Thus on one occasion he remarked that there was no necessity for any standardized method of teaching; he hoped, however, that the various departments might exchange information on their methods of instruction, so that new ideas could be widely tried.

Suggestions like this, as well as his warnings to the faculty against the duplication of effort in overlapping courses,[11] and

[8] Papers of the Board of Regents, June 20, 1905. The regents upheld the president.   [9] James F. A. Pyre, *Wisconsin* (New York, 1920), 351.

[10] It must, of course, be kept in mind that records often fail to reveal important undertones. Thus, much would have depended upon the president's manner in emphasizing in faculty meetings—as he did so frequently after the Visitors, the regents, and even a legislative committee had taken a firm stand—the matter of maintaining a high level of instruction in the first two years.

[11] Minutes of the Faculty, 7:3, October 3, 1910. A committee, appointed to look into the matter, made constructive proposals. Minutes of the Faculty, 7:10, December 5, 1910.

his calling of their attention to such experiments as the tutorial and honor systems in other institutions, were no doubt well enough received; his constant emphasis on the importance of research was not always so fortunate. A man must be a scholar, he declared again and again, if he were to be an effective member of a university faculty. Only research men, he maintained, could attract graduate students; and even on the undergraduate level investigation enriched instruction. "The most effective plan for accomplishing these things," he admonished, "is for each member of the staff to resolve that he will become a recognized scholar in his field and begin at once some piece of productive work."[12] That this reiterated emphasis on research should irritate certain members of the faculty was only natural. Some felt that the president failed to take into account the fact that original investigation in such fields as Latin was more difficult than in the natural sciences, and that, furthermore, excellent teachers might better maintain their excellence by enriching their minds with wide reading and reflection than by investigation frequently unimportant if not actually trivial.

Van Hise's reports to the regents were marked by continued and vigorous efforts to persuade the Board to find means for increasing the salary scale of the faculty. This, the president insisted, must be done in simple justice to the faculty, called on to meet the constantly rising costs of living and the mounting competition from other institutions. In these efforts Van Hise met with less success than he wished, but his record was impressive. In comparing the salary scales of 1904 and 1907 he indicated an increase of 13.4 per cent for professors, 8.8 per cent for associate professors, 4.6 per cent for assistant professors, and 13.6 per cent for instructors—an average increase of 10.9 per cent. Progress was also recorded subsequently; yet the president was far from satisfied with his achievements.[13] Although he was opposed to jumping a professor's salary much above the top rate and believed that merit increases should be made regardless of outside invitations, Van Hise, like other administrators, again

[12] Van Hise's address to the faculty, October 2, 1916, in Papers of the Board of Regents, October 11, 1916.
[13] Papers of the Board of Regents, October 15, 1907. Van Hise was, in fact, less successful in winning salary increases than either Chamberlin or Adams.

and again tried to meet academic competition by individual salary increases.[14]

Pertinent to the economic well-being of the faculty was the whole question of retirement pensions. Several private universities had a pension plan, but among the state universities California was the only one to have any provision for it. When the Carnegie Foundation was established to arrange for a pension system for college teachers, Van Hise quickly moved to take advantage of it for Wisconsin. As the representative of the National Association of State Universities at the first annual meeting of the board of trustees of the foundation, he argued in favor of including the state universities.[15] On the score that the states should themselves assume responsibility for professors' pensions there was some hesitancy about including state universities. Van Hise, however, won over President Eliot of Harvard, one of the most influential of the trustees,[16] and the foundation decided to open its doors to the publicly supported institutions. At the same time Van Hise was trying to persuade the regents that in justice to the teaching staff, and in order to meet competition from other institutions, the University must either set up its own retirement system or accept the Carnegie arrangement.[17] The latter course proved more acceptable. The legislature, in response to a request from the Board, adopted a resolution authorizing and directing the president to make the arrangements.[18] In recognition of the important role of Van Hise in broadening the base of the pension system, the foundation made him a trustee when the first vacancy occurred.

In making appointments and in recommending promotions, the president worked within a framework originally prescribed

[14] For Van Hise's fullest statement see National Association of State Universities, *Transactions and Proceedings,* 1910, pp. 284–285.

[15] Carnegie Foundation for the Advancement of Teaching, *Second Annual·Report* (New York, 1907), 62.

[16] Charles W. Eliot to Van Hise, February 4, 1908. For Van Hise's discussions in the meetings of the Association of American Universities, see *Journal of Proceedings and Addresses,* 8th Annual Conference (Chicago, 1906), 65 ff.

[17] Records of the Board of Regents, F:371, 376, January 16, 1906; Reports to the Regents, E:69, 84, January 16, April 17, 1906; Records of the Board of Regents, F:508–509, December 18, 1906.

[18] *Laws of Wisconsin,* 1909, p. 808; Carnegie Foundation for the Advancement of Teaching, *Fourth Annual Report* (New York, 1909), 38.

by academic practice. During the first decade of the twentieth century, several papers appeared in the educational journals contending that the powers of presidents in American universities were autocratic in matters of appointment and promotion and that such powers ought to be turned over to the faculty. In 1910 Van Hise presented his ideas on the subject to the Association of American Universities. His analysis of prevailing practice in twenty-two universities indicated that the great majority of presidents, in making recommendations for appointments, acted with the advice of the departments concerned. For universities where there was no clear understanding of appointment procedure, Van Hise recommended clarification. He felt that in the interest of harmony and unity it was necessary and desirable for the faculty to exercise some authority in administrative matters; but he opposed the idea that it should have complete charge of appointments on the ground that this could be accomplished only at the cost of time taken from teaching and research. In general, Van Hise believed that the president should exercise his appointive power only on the advice of a responsible academic body;[19] and it was his custom to be guided by departments and deans. This practice was occasionally suspended. At one time, convinced that the English department was lagging, he urged the regents to go above the top salary in order to attract Bliss Perry, then editor of the *Atlantic Monthly*. At another time he appointed a new chairman of the English department. Van Hise no doubt justified these acts on the score that one of the major contributions of any president was the improvement of the faculty by careful use of his appointive power.

Deeply concerned at Van Hise's emphasis on research, and fearful lest this militate against good teaching—especially on the freshman-sophomore level, the regents recommended that in the election and promotion of staff "due regard should be given to the teaching ability of the candidate"; they again expressed their conviction that "the ability to pursue original investigation and research work, when not combined with teaching

[19] Charles R. Van Hise, "The Appointment and Tenure of University Professors," Association of American Universities, *Journal of Proceedings and Addresses*, 12th Annual Conference (Chicago, 1910), 50–61.

ability, should not constitute sufficient qualification for membership in the faculty of the University, unless such research investigation is specifically provided for by Federal or State appropriation or by specific action of the Board of Regents."[20] But, as almost anyone knew, teaching ability was hard to measure, while a capacity for turning out research monographs was patent. Many probably felt that in making or approving new appointments or promotions Van Hise overemphasized the research record and slighted gifts for teaching. It is not clear whether the quality of appointments was in any sense affected either by the directive of the regents or by their resolution later in the year that the qualifications of women scholars should be taken into account in recommending new faculty members.[21]

✺

In the same paper in which Van Hise discussed the appointive power he clarified his ideas regarding tenure. Devoted as he was to efficiency, and convinced that an institution existed not for the faculty but for the students and the public, he was certain that there could be no possible excuse for retaining an inefficient professor; efficiency implied competency in teaching or in research or in both. "The responsibility of the governing board and the executive educational officers to the students and to the people is vastly greater than any obligation to the professor." The ultimate authority for removing an incompetent professor must rest with the governing body acting with the advice of the officers who make recommendations for new appointments.[22]

In actual practice the president followed no single procedure in implementing his somewhat nebulous ideas about the removal of faculty members for inefficiency or for misbehavior. If an administrative officer was directly implicated it was, of course, incumbent on him to take a positive stand. Thus the regents themselves requested Van Hise to recommend whether or not Assistant Professor George Knapp of the College of

[20] Records of the Board of Regents, G:200, June 16, 1908.
[21] *Ibid.*, G:234–235, December 16, 1908.
[22] Association of American Universities, *Journal of Proceedings and Addresses,* 12th Annual Conference, 50 ff.

Agriculture, who had become involved in a conflict with Dean William A. Henry, should be retained or dismissed. The president thereupon interviewed Professor Knapp, who declared that there was general dissension in the school, that Dean Henry was the cause of it, and that he was unfit to remain in his position. Van Hise then interviewed other members of the agricultural faculty, first separately, and then in the presence of Professor Knapp. All of them denied the existence of any dissension and upheld Dean Henry. Van Hise took the position that if Knapp had voiced his criticisms only to faculty members and to the president he would have been within the bounds of propriety, since it was the duty of the faculty to consider the welfare of the University, however mistaken their judgments might prove. But the president felt that Knapp exceeded his rights when he condemned Dean Henry in many Madison quarters, including legislative circles, as well as at Minnesota and at the Washington meeting of the Association of Agricultural Colleges at which he was representing the College of Agriculture. The president, having made this report, asked the regents for instructions. The Board recommended the removal of Knapp.[23] Van Hise's handling of the problem was judicious: he tried to be sure of the facts, to balance the interests of the individual with those of the University, and to leave the final decision to the regents.

Issues of tenure which did not directly involve an administrative official Van Hise was content to leave largely in the hands of the interested department and the appropriate dean. For example, when criticism developed both within and without the University regarding the business activities of Professor Van Velzer, Dean Birge handled the case. According to the records Professor Van Velzer was given the choice of withdrawing either from his business or from the University; he resigned from the University.[24] Apparently the president did not question the fairness of Birge's decision.

A more difficult situation arose in the School of Music. One of its faculty was charged with taking undue liberties with young

[23] Reports to the Regents, E:74–75, January 16, 1906; Records of the Board of Regents, F:400–401, April 17, 1906.
[24] Reports to the Regents, E:72–73, January 16, 1906; Papers of the Board of Regents, January 16, 1906.

women students, with crudeness of language, and with conduct generally unbecoming to a professor. The president approved the appointment of a committee to investigate the charges. The committee found that the reports had been exaggerated, and that the professor had been in no sense guilty of impropriety toward the young women; but, it said, he "has been at least obtuse and offensive in his relations with students, where he should be sensitive." The committee recommended that the regents direct the president to omit the man's name from the faculty list for the coming year.[25] Van Hise seems to have stayed in the background. Whether he was justified in playing quite so negative a role in a more important situation, involving Director Louis Coerne of the School of Music, is less clear. The official records fail to indicate precisely the case against Coerne. The faculty of the school had been sharply divided before Coerne came. He did not resolve these cleavages; and apparently he alienated some of his associates by his egocentrism. The procedure followed in the dismissal of Coerne is not known exactly. One of his principal critics in the school recalls that Dean Birge told both him and Coerne that the only way out of the situation was for them both to go.[26] Professor Coerne was not alone in feeling that he had been done an injustice in being asked to resign. The regents received petitions urging his reinstatement from students, from the First Congregational Church, and from the Madison Singing Society. Professors Hohlfeld, Slichter, and Smith, all prominent members of the faculty, informed the regents that the recent action regarding the two members of the School of Music staff had "aroused great concern among their colleagues" and that, if the action stood, the University would undoubtedly suffer in academic circles from the accusation that tenure was uncertain and that it failed to meet standards set at leading institutions.[27] Nothing resulted

[25] Papers of the Board of Regents, February 8, 1913.
[26] Arthur Locke to Merle Curti, May 24, 1947.
[27] For Professor Louis Coerne's defense of himself see his statement "To the Dean of the College of Letters and Science, to the President of the University, to the President and to the Board of Regents," April 10, 1914, Presidents' Papers. Coerne to Van Hise, December 14, 1914, Papers of the Board of Regents. Papers of the Board of Regents, April 15, 1914.

from this protest. It is an open question whether Van Hise was justified in this case in keeping his hands off, as he apparently did.

There is no doubt that Van Hise genuinely and sincerely believed in academic freedom as he conceived it. In his mind an institution in which this freedom did not prevail lacked the essential soul of a university. He spoke out for academic freedom when it seemed to be threatened. In his commencement address of 1910 he made one of his few general public statements on the subject. His speech followed closely on a series of incidents involving the principle of academic freedom and preceded the final decision of the regents to accept formally from the class of 1910 the plaque inscribed with the famous "sifting and winnowing" statements of academic freedom adopted by the regents at the time of the Ely trial. Van Hise pointed to the traditional freedom of university scientists to proclaim scientific truth as they made discoveries. Are investigators, he asked, to be forbidden to teach, proclaim, and advocate the truth in political matters? Van Hise did not perceive the difference between the degrees of certainty attached to conclusions derived from research in the natural sciences and from research in political thought, but in view of the prevailing tendency among social scientists to regard their findings and interpretations as objective, he was merely following current professional opinion. He was not disturbed when one of his correspondents, in referring to the commencement address, expressed the fear that the participation of the University in state activities might mean that politics would envelop the institution.[28]

An even more important public statement on academic freedom was contained in his commencement address of 1912. At that time Professor Max Otto of the philosophy department was being attacked by orthodox religious groups for his antitheistic position in a course entitled "Man and Nature." Some of Otto's friends believed that the whole issue should be fought in the open, and at the suggestion of one of them a Chicago reporter had visited Madison and written a front-page story which gave the affair the color of an attack on academic freedom. In

[28] Lynn S. Pease to Van Hise, July 6, 1910.

his commencement address Van Hise pointed out, first, that the duty of a university is to advance knowledge not only in the sciences but in the field of human relations, that this means a constant re-examination of old statements of truth in the light of new knowledge, for "nowhere is there fixity or completeness in regard to human relations any more than with regard to physical or chemical relations. This freedom of thought, this inquiry after truth for its own sake, this adjustment of the knowledge of the past in the light of the newest facts and highest reason,—this is the essential spirit of a university, *which under no circumstances should it yield*. Without this spirit an institution is not a university; with this spirit, it is a university, whether it be large or small." Van Hise recognized that the spirit of disinterested search for truth would inevitably make a university the center of conflict. Today, as in the past, he declared, "the spirit of the university is in irreconcilable conflict with those who hold that the present state of affairs is the best possible, who believe that existing conventions, morals, and political and religious faiths are fixed." Nor was there any way to escape from this situation but to destroy the university as an institution. Continuing, Van Hise said that freedom did not imply arrogance and dogmatism and propaganda on the part of professors. Conflicting opinions should be fairly presented, and personal opinions should be expressed with humility and "the realization that ultimate truth has nowhere been reached, that the advance of tomorrow may modify the statement of today." The recognition of the university spirit, he concluded, meant that the people must retain largeness of vision. "They must be willing to give freedom for its own sake, without regard to the belief of the teaching staff. They must have faith to believe that it is best that truth shall prevail, faith to believe that truth will prevail if there be full liberty of teaching and learning."[29] These were noble words, courageous words.

[29] Charles R. Van Hise, *The Spirit of a University,* commencement address (Madison, 1912). Van Hise repeated and amplified these ideas in an address to the Wisconsin expedition of the City Club of Philadelphia, May 23, 1913. "Since it is the function of the university to inspire, adjust, and advance civilization, it becomes the very food of disturbance. There is between the university and the reactionary an irrepressible conflict." This was especially true in the field of human relations.

The First Dean of the Graduate School and the
First Dean of the College of Letters and Science
George C. Comstock and Edward A. Birge

The University in 1890

On other occasions Van Hise was less forthright. In his paper on "The Appointment and Tenure of University Professors," he maintained that in cases involving academic freedom the authority must rest with the appointive power and, since such cases were exceptional, it was best to make no rules regarding procedure. If the governing power exercised its prerogatives in an arbitrary manner the public would hold it responsible. The University would suffer since able men would refuse to accept appointment and would leave at the first opportunity. "The punishment of the offending University by public condemnation is the most effective protection for the professor against arbitrary or unjustifiable removal."[30] Van Hise somewhat naïvely assumed that an informed public, duly concerned for academic freedom, actually existed, and that, moreover, it was so well informed and so deeply devoted to freedom of investigation and teaching that it could withstand propaganda, the influence of pressure groups, and waves of hysteria. It is also clear that his conception eliminated the idea of academic freedom as an absolute and abstract value and emphasized its pragmatic nature.

In 1916 Professor Ely sent the president a report quoting from the *Bulletin* of the American Association of University Professors in which it was laid down that before dismissal or demotion every university professor should have the charges against him stated specifically in writing and that he should be entitled to a fair trial on those charges before a special or permanent judicial committee chosen by the faculty senate or council, or by the faculty at large. At such a trial the accused should have the right to present evidence, and if the charge were one of professional incompetency, it should be preceded by a formal report upon his work made by teachers in his own or related departments and, if he so desired, by a committee of fellow specialists from other institutions, appointed by a competent authority. Van Hise, in replying to Ely, expressed his complete disagreement with this point of view. In the first place, he considered that the publicity connected with such a trial might do the accused a great disservice. But, he went on, his objection

[30] Van Hise, "The Appointment and Tenure of University Professors," 50–61.

was even more fundamental. The report in the *Bulletin,* he said, was "written wholly from the point of view of the professors. The rights of the students and the public ... are wholly ignored. These in my opinion are paramount to the individual. The thing to do in case a man is not adapted to his place is, without making any public display, find a place to which he is adapted. ... The Association of American [University] Professors is, I believe, the only trade union that has ever made a proposal that a man employed must have a trial if his service is not continued for life."[31] Thus Van Hise, the administrator, rejected the procedure designed to protect academic freedom which the leading scholars in the newly launched association of university professors had proposed.

But this was not the only instance of qualifications of academic freedom made by Van Hise. In September, 1914, he officially requested the faculty to "refrain from using the university platform, either in classroom or otherwise, for discussing any of the questions relating to the war," and to refrain "so far as practicable from active participation" in such discussions outside the classroom.[32] Regent James Trottman, a Republican lawyer in Milwaukee, at once called Van Hise's attention to the implications of his statement for academic freedom: "In making a statement of that kind to the faculty there must necessarily be implied some direct or hidden suggestion to the effect that members of the faculty not complying with your suggestion will receive some form of punishment." "I believe," he continued, "that a request that members of the faculty refrain from using the University platform or the classroom, for discussion of questions pertaining to the War, is reasonable. ... Since you have gone further and have sought to control the action of members of the faculty without the classroom, in reference to the great questions involved in the present War, you have, as I view it, taken the first step in breaking down faculty independence by exercise of coercion, however mild that coercion may be. The way may now be open, since the precedent is established, to con-

---

[31] Ely to Van Hise, May 17, 1916; Van Hise to Ely, May 18, 1916.
[32] "Summary of part of Address by President Charles R. Van Hise to the University Faculty, September 28, 1914," Presidents' Papers, filed under War.

trol the opinion and actions of the several members of the faculty."[33] In replying to Trottman, the president declared it had been his idea, in making the suggestion, "to keep the university entirely free from any entanglement over questions in which race feeling is aroused." "That the statement," he continued, "could possibly be interpreted as interfering with academic freedom never occurred to me."[34] Van Hise no doubt meant well in asking the faculty not to stir up more bitterness of feeling—President Wilson had urged circumspection in maintaining neutrality of thought and word. It must be remembered that Milwaukee was a German center. Professor Max Otto, who was opposed to the entrance of the United States into the war, had little trouble in convincing himself that the president was asking the faculty "to protect the University *and its freedom*" from what might happen if classrooms were turned over to expositions of personal feelings about the war.[35] At the same time it cannot be denied that Van Hise failed to see the implications of his statement and that a regent found it necessary to champion academic freedom.

In view of the fact that Van Hise's statements on academic freedom were noble on the one hand and somewhat limited and expedient on the other, it seems advisable to test his position by examining his actions. Statements in both newspapers and magazines in the summer of 1909 to the effect that the regents were interfering with academic freedom brought about a crisis in University affairs. The opening gun was fired by Richard Lloyd Jones, an alumnus associated with *Collier's*, in an article in the July 17, 1909, issue of that then widely read, muckraking magazine. The article declared that some of the more powerful and active regents had been interfering in purely academic affairs; that, for instance, they had tried to curtail the economics department and to alter its character; and that, moreover, many friends of the University believed that these regents would, if they dared, depose Van Hise. Behind this, the *Collier's* piece declared, was the resentment on the part of these regents

[33] James F. Trottman to Van Hise, September 30, 1914.
[34] Van Hise to Trottman, October 3, 1914.
[35] Max Otto to Merle Curti, July 12, 1947.

toward the role of the University in promoting independence in state politics and in its growing determination to control public utilities and conserve the resources of the commonwealth.[36]

Van Hise was perturbed. He informed the regents that neither the University Press Bureau, for which Professor Bleyer was responsible, nor the department of economics had furnished Jones with any of the information appearing in his article.[37] Moreover, Jones had written the article before leaving New York for Madison for the unveiling of the Lincoln statue with the understanding that he would wire the editor, Hapgood, whether or not to publish the piece. As a result of his visit to Madison, Jones decided that it would be inadvisable to have the article appear, but he put off notifying Hapgood until it was too late. The president further informed the Board that he had tried to prevent the publication of material such as that appearing in *Collier's*. He had persuaded Lincoln Steffens not to publish a piece along the lines of the *Collier's* article, and he had succeeded in having an article in the *Chicago Record Herald* revised.[38] Despite the energetic efforts of the president to check such criticisms of the regents, the *Milwaukee Journal* declared that the business-minded Board, or at least certain members of it, had supported those who criticized the University for the role of certain professors in checking private exploitation of natural resources, that they had opposed having the University advise and assist the legislature in this effort, and that they were opposed to research on current problems affecting corporate wealth.[39] The decision of Professor Turner in November, 1909, to accept an invitation to Harvard, allegedly on the ground of dissatisfaction with the regents' methods of interference in academic matters, lent further support to the now widespread story that academic freedom no longer flourished at Wisconsin.

[36] *Collier's*, July 17, 1909, p. 9.
[37] Van Hise to the regents, November 3, 9, 1909, Papers of the Board of Regents.
[38] Papers of the Board of Regents, December 1, 1909. Earlier in the year, on January 28, 1909, Van Hise had written to Lincoln Steffens, "In reference to the magazine article, I would not think of suggesting that you attempt to modify it, considering all the circumstances." This is the only reference to Steffens on the point that Van Hise made to the regents in the Van Hise letters of this period. The Van Hise letters to Steffens are in the possession of Granville Hicks, of Grafton, N.Y. [39] *Milwaukee Journal*, July 19, 1909, p. 1.

Although Van Hise himself professed to disclaim any foundation for the statements in the press, and, as we have seen, tried to check their repetition, he frankly told the regents, at their meeting of December 1, 1909, that many professors did believe that the regents had threatened academic freedom and that the faculty was in a state of unrest. After naming the details he went on to say: "They base their belief upon the statements directly made to them in some cases, but more frequently I think upon hearsay reports as to what individual regents have said at various times and places in reference to teaching revolutionary doctrines in the university." The president suggested as the first remedy for the situation that the regents provide those faculty members chosen as a conference committee an opportunity to outline the bases of faculty unrest.[40] No one could say that the president was trying to throttle the malcontents or that he was blocking an investigation of the whole situation.

The proposed meeting, no less exciting than it was important, took place on the afternoon and evening of December 10, 1909. The regents were represented by Enos Jones, Swenson, Cary, Trottman, Buckstaff, and Thwaits, the faculty by Harper, Hohlfeld, and Reinsch in addition to the several deans and President Van Hise. In his final report, Regent Thwaits wrote that "it was agreed by all that there was a great deal of dissatisfaction, uneasiness, and apprehension in the minds of the members of the faculty; that this feeling was due to various actions of the regents which had led the faculty to distrust the motives and the purposes of the regents. This feeling culminated with the announcement of Professor Turner's resignation. It was the understanding of all that Professor Turner's resignation was due to his treatment by the regents and to his distrust of the policy of the regents and his dissatisfaction with the general situation in the university as brought about by the regents."[41] Regent Thwaits went on to specify the reasons for the feeling which many professors shared with Turner. The

[40] Papers of the Board of Regents, December 1, 1909. Dr. Edward Evans, one of the regents, applauded Van Hise's course, Evans to Van Hise, December 22, 1909.

[41] Report by Regent Frederick C. Thwaits, Papers of the Board of Regents, January 19, 1910.

faculty had come to be uncertain of their tenure because of a "number" of resignations brought about by the regents.[42] Such uncertainty not only made it hard to keep able men but created an atmosphere not prejudicial to good work. The regents, on the one hand, had made promotions and adjustments of salaries without the recommendations of the appropriate departments or the president; and, on the other hand, they had failed to make certain promotions recommended by the departments and the president. The department of philosophy had been crippled by the refusal of the Board to make increased appropriations for its work. The regents had consulted directly with members of the faculty concerning their own work or that of other departments; and "this had caused a feeling of fear, apprehension, and uneasiness as to the motives and purposes of the regents." Thus the regents had shown a disposition to take the initiative in strictly educational matters. They had misplaced their emphasis on the importance of having professors give elementary courses and had shown an undue concern over the weekly teaching hours of the staff. One regent even attended and in a somewhat critical way took part in a doctoral examination. The indictment also showed that the faculty thought the Board was departing from the established policy of the University in belittling research and in discriminating against original investigation in all fields except those of the applied sciences. All these things in their cumulative effect indicated to the faculty a tendency on the part of the regents to interfere with academic freedom.[43]

Thanks to the detailed notes taken by Professor Reinsch it is possible to reconstruct in part the discussion on which these generalizations rested. Since the resignation of Professor Turner had crystallized the growing discontent of the faculty it may be useful to summarize the discussion regarding his decision. Two years before, when he had been invited to Stanford, the regents in order to keep him had consented to an arrangement by which he was freed every other semester for research. Some

---

[42] According to the *Milwaukee Journal*, of November 30, 1908, Samuel Sparling, member of the political science department and of the Civil Service Commission, was one of these. Sparling was an assistant professor on a three-year appointment.

[43] Thwaits's report, Papers of the Board of Regents, January 19, 1910.

of the regents felt that the complaint of the students that they were thus deprived of the opportunity of taking Professor Turner's classes was justified. At a meeting at the president's house which Turner attended, it appears that one or more of the regents had taken him to task or at least indicated dissatisfaction. In any case, Professor Harper declared at the December 10 meeting that the remarks made on the earlier occasion "must have been to such a man almost equivalent to a request to resign." Regent Cary quickly retorted that Turner had in effect told the regents that they ought to know their place. During this discussion President Van Hise, whose sympathies must have been with Turner, apparently kept silent. But Dean Birge interjected the significant comment that "the trouble came because the arrangement which had been freely made was pulled up again and again." "A man should," he pointed out, "be able to depend on such arrangements."[44]

The most crucial part of the discussion involved freedom of teaching. Regent Swenson, powerful in public utilities and in various business enterprises, asked for comments on the accusation that the regents had interfered with teaching in the University. Professor Harper, in reply, spoke of the remark of a regent at the meeting at the president's house to the effect that the University should not deal with anything affecting property rights. Regent Trottman thereupon asked whether the regents should permit a professor to teach socialism. Harper replied that he believed in "complete and absolute" academic freedom. At this point Van Hise suggested that there were different usages of the word socialism: "It has no definite signification and is applied very differently according to the opinions of the speaker." Regent Swenson remarked that when he went about the state, people often "jumped" on him for "keeping a nest of socialists." The regents present thereupon agreed that while individual members of the Board may have commented on socialism, the subject had never been an official issue nor even discussed. Professor Reinsch stated the point of view of the faculty in declaring that University teaching did not, as

[44] Paul Reinsch minutes of the joint committee, Papers of the Board of Regents, January 19, 1910.

the regents seemed to suppose, impress dogmatic principles
upon students—that a university could not teach "socialism"
or any other system of thought. But, he insisted, "you cannot
close any field of inquiry without impairing the students' faith
in the honesty of teaching."

In summarizing the discussions Professor Reinsch stated the
faculty's case: If the regents adhered to the spirit rather than
the exact letter of the law; if they chose administrators to whose
guidance they were willing to relegate such matters as the hours
of teaching and time for research as well as appointments and
promotions; if, when students made complaints, they remembered that visiting a classroom was no substitute for the considered judgment which colleagues might make of a professor's
ability—then the situation would greatly improve. There was
no dissent to Reinsch's summary of the point of view apparently held by the regents at the end of the discussion: "The
regents have no intention of interfering with the customary
methods of educational administration by the faculty; . . . they
will continue to allow to the faculty the initiative in formulating educational policies; . . . they desire appointments to
be made through the regular channels as developed in the
custom of the University."[45] On their part, the professors present at the meeting agreed to communicate to a special faculty
meeting their conviction that the acts of the regents which
caused complaint were "not caused by improper motives or
animus and that it was the intention of the regents to conform
to the provisions of their bylaws." The regents, on the other
hand, specified that it must be clearly understood that the acts
complained of were made "within the legal and technical rights
of the regents" and that furthermore they had a right to change
their bylaws.[46] The way was still open for trouble. Yet the victory was clearly with the faculty. Although the president took
little part in the discussions his moral influence was on the side
of the faculty. The real test for Van Hise lay ahead in a series
of episodes, all occurring in the early months of the following
year, 1910, and all important in the cause of academic freedom.

[45] *Ibid.*
[46] Thwaits's report, Papers of the Board of Regents, January 19, 1910.

In the latter part of January, 1910, Emma Goldman visited Madison. No member of the faculty and no student had had anything to do with her coming, but she received the impression during her stay in Madison that, thanks to such men as Ross, Jastrow, Commons, and others, the University was far more enlightened than most institutions.[47] When the president of the Socialist Club noticed the announcement of her lectures tacked up on poles and trees, he arranged for a round-table discussion with the members of the club at the student Y.M.C.A. No public notices of the meeting were given, and no more than twenty members were present. Miss Goldman discussed differences between Russian and American university students, emphasizing the Russian conception of education as a means of social uplift rather than as an avenue to an individual career. "Our talks on this occasion," Emma Goldman wrote many years later, "were followed by spirited discussions and proved to us that our audiences had become very much aware of their relation to the masses and of their debt to the workers who produced all wealth."[48] When the trustees of the Y.W.C.A. refused the use of the room for further discussions, the "advertising," according to Emma Goldman, swelled the audiences of her downtown public meetings.

During the visit of the famous anarchist to Madison, Professor Ross, in the middle of a lecture to his elementary sociology class in which he was discussing the development of government from the coercive to the beneficent state, remarked that he understood that a Madison lady had torn down the posters announcing Emma Goldman's lectures on anarchism. Making it clear that he himself took no stock in anarchism, he stated his belief in the right of free speech, and he announced that Miss Goldman was speaking that evening in the Knights of Pythias Lodge.[49] He did not attend the lecture, but the next day Miss Goldman called on him at his office and he conducted her about the campus, pointing out its beauties.

Harmless as all this was, it occasioned sensational charges in

[47] Emma Goldman, *Living My Life* (New York, 1931), 1:462.
[48] *Ibid.; Daily Cardinal*, January 26 and 27, 1910.
[49] Statement of Edward A. Ross, Papers of the Board of Regents, March 2, 1910.

the press. The *Madison Democrat* sounded the alarm against "the spirit of anarchy and revolution" rampant at the University. In view of the recent mood of the faculty and of the widespread feeling that academic freedom was none too safe at the University, the attack in the press proved to be a genuine test of the recent declaration of the regents. Professor Ross reiterated publicly his opposition to anarchy. "I am not interested in it myself nor in fostering an interest in it among the student body. Miss Goldman was not here under the auspices of the University, but as long as she chooses to remain here, I believe she should be allowed free speech." [50] In response to many telephone inquiries the *Cardinal* published a letter from a senior setting forth clearly the fact that Miss Goldman had not been entertained in rooms furnished out of University funds, that not a single "socialistic preceptor of the faculty" had attended the meeting, and that not a person present believed in the doctrines of Emma Goldman; they had attended as students of political philosophy prompted solely by a desire to learn and to know. [51] In view of the situation, what would the governing authorities do? Would they ignore the matter? Would they make a positive statement in behalf of academic freedom? Would they seize the occasion to discipline Professor Ross, long regarded in conservative circles as an archradical?

The first officer of the University to take a public position was Regent Trottman. While emphasizing his opposition to a doctrinal teaching of any kind, he made it clear that he was not opposed to the study of anarchism or socialism or any other subject, and that he saw no reason why students and professors should not listen to Emma Goldman's exposition of her doctrines if they cared to do so. [52] Quite unsolicited, the Board of Visitors appointed a committee to investigate the Emma Goldman incident and to discover whether or not socialist teaching existed at the University. Its report, published before being presented to the regents, set forth clearly the main facts in the Goldman episode. It took Professor Ross to task for failing, as a public officer of the University, to exercise the special care

[50] *Daily Cardinal*, January 29, 1910.
[51] *Ibid.*, January 28 and 29, 1910.   [52] *Ibid.*, January 29, 1910.

necessary to prevent public censure from descending on the University when it should fall on the individual alone. The committee also reported that it had examined students, curricula, and books and had found no evidence of socialistic teaching. On the contrary, it remarked, "The investigation disclosed striking instances of foreigners who have come to the university as students believing in anarchism and violence, who have been led to discard such beliefs through the instruction given in the university."[53] Individual regents found the publication of the report highly discourteous to the Board. Although the committee of the Visitors explained that in allowing previous publication of its report it had intended neither discourtesy nor any forestalling of action on the part of the Board, the regents regarded the investigation as quite outside the proper sphere of the Visitors.[54]

The role of President Van Hise in the episode is fairly clear. Three days after the publication of Regent Trottman's statement upholding the right of professors and students to attend the meeting of an anarchist, the president publicly set forth the facts in an effort to correct misstatements and to demonstrate that "a great injustice is done the University by the implication that the university authorities sympathize with or give encouragement to the doctrines advocated by Miss Goldman." His references to Professor Ross were all that could be expected: he indicated the unfairness of attaching to his announcement of the Goldman lectures any sympathy for the cause since in that very class he had condemned anarchism and indicated his approval of the extension of governmental functions in the interest of social welfare.[55] But in his private interview with Ross the president said that he felt that Ross had made a serious mistake in judgment in mentioning Miss Goldman's lectures to his classes; any such announcement was bound to be interpreted as sympathy and would arouse public passion. Ross replied with the assurance: "I agree entirely with you that for the reasons you state my announcement of Miss Goldman's lecture was an impropriety. You can rest assured

[53] Papers of the Board of Regents, March 2, 1910.
[54] *Ibid.*, March 2, April 20, 1910.   [55] *Daily Cardinal*, February 1, 1910.

that sort of mistake I shall not commit again."[56] The president was obviously bent on preventing unjustified criticism of the University.

Yet in another episode involving Professor Ross the president valiantly upheld him although convinced that certain regents were eager to dismiss him, not, to be sure, for indiscretion but simply because of their dislike of his ideas. In fact, Van Hise told Ross that ever since the publication of his *Sin and Society* in 1907 some of the regents had been gunning for him, only waiting for a suitable pretext.[57] On January 31, four days after Miss Goldman left Madison, Parker Sercombe lectured in University Hall, at the invitation of Professor Ross, on "Education in a Democracy." When Regent Swenson inquired about the lecture, Van Hise learned that Ross had invited Sercombe without the knowledge of the committee on lectures. But Professor Michael V. O'Shea, whom Ross had consulted on receiving Sercombe's offer to come to Madison for a lecture, saw no objection, approved the outline of the lecture, and announced it in his courses. Subsequently O'Shea testified that Sercombe, in emphasizing the idea that schools are too bookish and that instruction in a practical workshop or garden should accompany textbook teaching, was in accord with the best contemporary thought in education. Ross said, when he was criticized, that he did not know he was transgressing "channels" by not having the matter routed through the lecture committee; he had assumed that a professor might have an outsider talk to his class without securing special permission. Confronted by the charge that Sercombe's character was questionable, Van Hise learned from inquiries in Chicago that his personal worth and integrity were widely vouched for. Nevertheless, in reporting to the regents, the president called Ross's action an "indiscretion." The regents, at the meeting of March 2, unanimously adopted a resolution of censure and disapproval. At the meeting of April 20, the minutes were amended to read that the resolution of disapproval had had "the approval of the President."[58]

Van Hise may well have given his approval with his tongue

[56] Ross to Van Hise, February 4, 1910, Papers of the Board of Regents.
[57] Edward A. Ross, *Seventy Years of It* (New York, 1936), 290.
[58] Records of the Board of Regents, G:451, 519, March 2, April 20, 1910.

in his cheek in order to prevent action more drastic than mere censure. He had cabled Ross, who was now in China, "to expect the worst" and Ross was fully prepared for his dismissal. Meantime the president had gathered protests from various liberals throughout the state against the possible ousting of Ross. He informed the regents that the faculty conference committee wanted a session with the Board before it took drastic action. Certainly Van Hise made a very strong case for Ross before the regents. He cited the excellence of his textbooks and the praise his periodical articles had received and he pointed out that in his *Social Control, Foundations of Sociology,* and *Social Psychology* Ross had taken a stand for law and order, for adherence to government, and for high moral and ethical standards. Despite Ross's "indiscretions," the president argued, he was far too valuable a man for the University to lose. Moreover, to ask for the resignation of a man of such stature for so slight a reason would be unwise. "The effects . . . would not be overcome for years." The president also emphasized the fact that Ross was highly regarded by students as an inspiring force and that he had been willing to give elementary courses—a particularly precious point in the eyes of the regents.[59] Although the evidence at hand does not document Ross's belief that Van Hise thus converted into a minority that majority of the regents who were bent on ousting him, it is not unlikely that in making the strong case for Ross at the same time that he conceded "indiscretions" Van Hise won a major victory for academic freedom.

The victory was the more impressive because the University was under widespread attack on the score that the alleged "welcome" of such radicals as Emma Goldman was tantamount to support of anarchistic doctrine. Some papers, however, blamed this attack on the water-power monopolists and on the Stalwart conservatives who were, they maintained, seeking ammunition for an attack that might kill "the ideals of public ownership taught at the University."[60] Regent G. D. Jones for

[59] Van Hise's report to the regents, Papers of the Board of Regents, March 2, 1910.

[60] *Manitowoc Daily Tribune,* February 28, 1910; *La Crosse Tribune,* February 4, 1910; *Milwaukee Journal,* July 19, 1909.

his part called such allegations defamatory of Wisconsin's honest businessmen and made clear his disapproval of the University's muckraker friends who were continually picturing the University as the foe of the "interests."

The fight was not over. At the time of the Ross affair and in the spring that followed, Wisconsin was the scene of bitter antagonism between the Stalwart faction of the Republican Party and the La Follette Progressive Republicans. The crucial autumn elections were in the offing. Most of the regents had been appointed by Governor Davidson, who, since his break with La Follette in 1906, had led the Stalwarts.[61] Some of the regents, especially the two immediately concerned with water-power development, had objected to the brief Professor Gilmore had prepared at the request of the state Conservation Commission, on which both Birge and Van Hise sat. The critical attitude of the regents toward Ross provided further evidence that at least some of the University's governing authorities were alarmed at what they considered dangerous radicalism in the institution. Hoard, for example, asked Van Hise what position Dean Birge would take regarding the "anarchistic" professors in the College of Letters and Science. There can be little doubt that the regents also knew that a considerable part of the student body—especially in the senior class—was ardently pro-La Follette. Nor were the regents unaware of the fact that many of the seniors and many other students looked with disfavor on the Board for its alleged interference with faculty control of educational policy and for its threatening attitude toward academic freedom.

Shortly after the Goldman–Sercombe affairs Lincoln Steffens appeared on the campus, eager to find out just what the situation was. Almost a year earlier the *American Magazine* had published his article on the University which, although highly complimentary, had suggested that possibly academic freedom was not secure. He had been informed, he wrote at that time, that while there was no socialist on the faculty, several men were more radical than they dared to indicate in their teach-

[61] Theodore Herfurth, to whose monograph the authors are much indebted, estimates that ten of the regents were Stalwarts; five, liberals. Theodore Herfurth, *Sifting and Winnowing, A Chapter in the History of Academic Freedom at the University of Wisconsin* (Madison, 1949).

ing.[62] It was probably on his return to the campus in the early part of 1910 that he remarked to Fred MacKenzie, class of 1906 and editor of *La Follette's Weekly*, that the noble sentiment regarding academic freedom adopted by the regents at the time of the Ely trial had never been given adequate publicity and deserved to be more widely known. This gave Mac-Kenzie an idea. For many years it had been customary for the graduating class to present the University with a memorial, usually a stone engraved with the class number and placed somewhere on the campus. MacKenzie suggested to James Thompson, editor of the *Cardinal*, that the seniors might appropriately give the University, instead of the usual meaningless stone, a plaque bearing the "sifting and winnowing" sentiments of the regents of 1894. He cautioned Thompson not to mention the fact that Steffens had said the resolution ought to be more widely known, for fear the regents, hating Steffens as a radical, might reject the plaque. The memorial committee of the class readily accepted the proposal. There must have been some suggestion of the possibility that the regents might not accept the plaque, for it was subsequently recalled that there were discussions as to what might be done if the gift should be refused.[63]

Before the annual meeting of the Board, class officers approached members of the executive committee with the request that the plaque, which was to be presented with exercises as usual on class day, be displayed on Bascom Hall or some other specified prominent place. The regents thus approached indicated that only the full Board could take action on the proposal. By this time Regent G. D. Jones had become convinced that the class had been duped by clever radicals into rebuking the regents for having presumably jeopardized academic freedom. He even suspected the hand of Steffens and other La Follette sympathizers. The regents, both the Progressives and the Stalwarts, fell in with Jones's suspicion and rejected the request of the class. We do not know whether Van Hise acquiesced without objection. We do know that in his commencement address he pointed out the dangers to state universities

<hr>

[62] Lincoln Steffens, "Sending a State to College," *American Magazine*, 67:349–364 (February, 1909).   [63] Herfurth, *Sifting and Winnowing*.

resulting from political control, from the demand for returns measurable in dollars and cents, and from restriction of freedom of teaching.[64] Speaking a few days after commencement in Fond du Lac, his home town, Class President Francis R. Duffy, declared that the memorial committee had not been influenced by any outside interest in making the selection but had chosen the plaque "in order that their class might leave a memorial that was really worth while." Duffy lent support to Regent Jones's suspicion by adding that the action of the Board was certain to occasion widespread discussion and that among those who would write articles would be Lincoln Steffens.

In the autumn, the La Follette-dominated platform committee strongly favored academic freedom by writing the words of the plaque into their platform, thus by implication condemning the regents for their action. Meantime the plaque had been gathering dust in a cellar. There the matter stood until April 25, 1912, when, after having four times postponed further action, the Board, now more heavily weighted with Progressives, voted simply to accept the tablet.[65] The *Cardinal* noted that this action was largely the result of two years' effort on the part of Duffy.[66] But the end had not come yet, for the regents in accepting the plaque had not accepted the proposal that it be riveted to the façade of Bascom Hall.

In preparation for the fifth reunion of the class of 1910 it was decided that to insure a good attendance the long-drawn-out quarrel with the regents should be settled by requesting them to permit the plaque to be properly dedicated at Bascom Hall. Considerable publicity, including a letter to the *New Republic,* revived the animus of Regent Jones, who determined to prevent the plaque from being hung unless the class officers and the reunion committee explicitly retracted all the statements and implications that the regents in 1910 had jeopardized academic freedom or behaved in any way other than conducive to the best interests of the University. Jones was influential enough, even in a Board in which the Progressives now en-

[64] *Wisconsin State Journal,* June 22, 1910, pp. 1, 8.
[65] Records of the Board of Regents, H:227, 239, 283, 298, 330, October 11, December 13, 1911, and January 17, March 13, April 25, 1912.
[66] *Daily Cardinal,* April 27, 1912.

joyed a majority, to prevent the proposal of the class officers from being accepted. Van Hise acted as the compromiser, persuading the class officers to accept a very general statement admitting that there had been many misunderstandings and some misstatements of fact, and clearing the 1910 Board of any implied violation of academic freedom. The statement was, perhaps purposely, vague;[67] in any case, neither Regent Jones nor the class emerged the complete victor. But at last the plaque was hung. The president made a strong statement on academic freedom. In the course of the dedicatory address he paid the highest tribute to the words inscribed on the plaque, words which Regent Jones finally decided were themselves harmless and inoffensive although somewhat dogmatic.[68] The resolution, Van Hise went on, "marks one of the great landmarks in the history of the University. And from that day to this, no responsible party or no responsible authority has ever succeeded in restricting freedom of research and teaching within these walls."[69] Van Hise's remarks were reiterated in other language by Joseph E. Davies, whose letter declared that the principle of academic freedom had been settled for all time, "cemented into the very foundations of the University," and that "never again will the question be raised."

Such, unfortunately, was not to be the case. To understand the continuing struggle, carried on in other areas, it must be borne in mind that the Progressives were defeated in 1914 and that Van Hise was confronted by the problem of winning the support of a conservative party and of a governor frankly admitting his hostility to the University. The effort to win over the conservatives made Van Hise more cautious if not less liberal—no doubt the part of wisdom. Professor Ross was only one among those who felt that with the conservatives' victory the president shifted ground, no longer encouraging members of the faculty to serve on state commissions and in other respects militantly to champion the Wisconsin Idea.[70] Somewhat later

---

[67] Records of the Board of Regents, I:312–313, June 15, 1915. See especially the letters of Van Hise to Blair, May 17, 1915, and to G. D. Jones, June 9, 1915, in the Presidents' Papers, filed under Memorial.

[68] Jones to the regents, May 25, 1915, Presidents' Papers, filed under Memorial.

[69] *Wisconsin State Journal*, June 16, 1915, p. 6.   [70] Ross, *Seventy Years of It*, 104.

Van Hise himself confessed his "repugnance to the use of the phrase 'The Wisconsin Idea.' "[71] Charles McCarthy wrote to Ely early in 1916 that "the University is so hopelessly reactionary, and the professors as a whole have shown such a timid spirit" that it seemed useless to make any suggestions.[72] In writing to Van Hise in behalf of the cooperatives C. A. Lyman of Rhinelander spoke of the work of the College of Agriculture as "colorless." There should be one man at least, he went on, "who believes in the cooperative movement, and in the uplift of the masses. If there are such men in the college now, they should be given a freer hand."[73] It was against this background that the cry was again raised that academic freedom was in danger. In the eyes of Van Hise there was little or no foundation for all these fears and criticisms. He insisted that Governor Philipp (1915–1921) and the conservative Republicans quickly learned the value of the services of University experts and made full use of them. And he could point with justifiable pride to his refusal to submit to the pressure of the religious groups who attacked Professor Max Otto for denying the truth of theism.[74]

But there was another side to the picture. No one, apparently, challenged the statement attributed to Governor Philipp in the autumn of 1915. According to the *Milwaukee Journal* the governor declared that, since in the natural order of things some men are born to be captains of industry, it was not "wise to permit the teaching of half-baked theories of government that never have been demonstrated to be a success, that intimidate capital, and that close the factory doors."[75] On August 8, 1915, the *Milwaukee Leader* declared that courses on socialism had been dropped and that socialist speakers had been discriminated against when they attempted to reach the students. An intellec-

---

[71] It is possible that he was here objecting to the term "Wisconsin Idea" since he felt that it had been too loosely used if not abused. Van Hise to Felix Frankfurter, November 3, 1917.

[72] Charles McCarthy to Ely, March 8, 1916, Presidents' Papers, filed under McC.

[73] C. A. Lyman to Van Hise, April 21, 1916.

[74] John W. Morgan to Van Hise, August 24, 1915; "Summary memorandum by C. R. Van Hise of Position taken at conference with pastors, 2 p.m., Wednesday, January 26, 1916," Presidents' Papers, filed under Otto. For a discussion of the Otto case see the account of philosophical teaching in the College of Letters and Science, p. 333.   [75] *Milwaukee Journal,* November 5, 1915, p. 20.

tual leader of the Socialist Party, Harry W. Laidler, came to Madison expecting to make a speech under University auspices but, according to his account, found at the last minute that "higher-ups" had canceled his lecture. These events and rumors of events lay back of the resolutions of the North Wisconsin Teachers' Association which, after noting the widespread feeling that academic freedom was being threatened at the University, deplored any effort to abolish courses or to make them conform to outside opinion.[76]

Early in 1917 a crisis arose which had important bearing on the question of freedom of discussion. The Wisconsin Forum, a students' organization, had been formed to promote the discussion of controversial points of view in economics, religion, and the arts which were either ignored or treated gingerly by University lecturers. "The practical result of this unavoidable circumstance," declared the officers of the Forum, "is that these tendencies of thought have no adequate and fair representation on the campus or before the students; thus contrary to the spirit and the ideals of the University, and undoubtedly contrary to the intentions of those who administer its affairs, there is brought about an abridgment of the opportunity for that freedom of discussion which alone guarantees the freedom of thought."[77] The Forum invited as its first speaker Max Eastman, the well-known editor of the socialist journal, *The Masses*. Dean Goodnight gave permission for the affair and arrangements were made for a room in the Biology Building. Late in the afternoon of the day preceding the scheduled lecture, Dean Goodnight told the Forum that President Van Hise had notified him that Eastman would not be allowed to speak in a University building. Both the dean and the president informed the Forum that the decision in no way abbreviated the right of free speech on the campus but merely followed

[76] North Wisconsin Teachers' Association to Van Hise, October 18, 1915. A study of the catalogues for the years between 1913 and 1916 indicates that courses on socialism in the economics department were apparently given in certain years, and that in 1915–16, a course on modern socialism was consolidated with one on labor history. It is not clear whether these changes affected the content of instruction or whether they were made for reasons of departmental convenience.

[77] Wisconsin Forum to the Board of Regents, March 12, 1917, Presidents' Papers, filed under Forum.

the rule forbidding the dissemination of propaganda from a University platform. The authorities further declared that the use of University buildings had been withheld in the past not only from socialists but from suffragists and Christian Scientists. Van Hise maintained that if student organizations were permitted to arrange public lectures in University buildings the institution could be used as a "platform on which to spread propaganda not only in regard to desirable things but also in regard to all sorts of wild notions by propagandists." Was there any university in the world, the president asked subsequently, in which a self-constituted group of students could use the institution as a platform upon which to propagate the doctrine of any speaker chosen by the group?[78]

The officials of the Forum took issue with the president. "The difference between the propaganda which he approves by giving it recognition and that of which he disapproves is a difference of point of view only, and not one of distinctive merit. The whole method and point of view of the administration of this question is a direct contradiction to the policy for which Wisconsin has become justly famous, and of which the University has been the staunchest advocate and the most effective promulgator."[79] In support of its contention the Forum denied the allegation that Eastman was coming to spread propaganda and pointed out the inconsistency of the administration in permitting in a University building the scheduled lecture of the great prohibitionist propagandist, William Jennings Bryan. The Forum further appealed to the regents to set aside a building for student-sponsored speeches with the understanding that the University would not be responsible for utterances in it. Although the Visitors lent support to the Forum's proposal the regents sided with the president and the request for the use of a University building was denied.[80]

[78] *Daily Cardinal,* January 16, 17, 1917; Van Hise to William Brockhausen, March 8, 1915, and to Clark Getts, May 4, 1917, Presidents' Papers, filed under Forum.

[79] *Daily Cardinal,* January 19, 1917.

[80] *Ibid.,* January 19, March 14, 1917; Scott Goodnight to Van Hise, March 9, 1917, and Van Hise to Clark Getts, May 4, 1917, both in the Presidents' Papers, filed under Forum.

A flood of criticism, implicit and explicit, descended on Van Hise. Professor Oscar J. Campbell of the English department introduced Eastman at the Woman's Building, where the speaker declared that he had given exactly the same exposition of socialism the night before under the auspices of the University of Illinois. To a *Cardinal* reporter Eastman remarked that in reality there was less freedom of speech at Wisconsin than elsewhere.[81] The issue of the *Cardinal* which carried Van Hise's justification of his course also published statements from Dean Goodnight and from Professors Westermann, Feise, and Guyer expressing approval of the Forum's objectives. Outside the University, liberals and radicals were indignant. Mayor Daniel Hoan of Milwaukee declared that Van Hise's action was a disgrace to the state and the Socialist Party considered it an insult. Labor unions deprecated the president's surrender to "the black and evil forces that are striving to suppress free discussion and keep the public mind in ignorance of the predatory character of the dominant class in the existing social order."[82] Richard Lloyd Jones, editor of the *State Journal,* compared Van Hise's course with the Russian suppressions of publications bearing the words *truth, freedom, hope,* or *democracy.*[83] The New York Wisconsin Alumni Association protested against the blow it believed had been dealt academic freedom. These and other criticisms indicated that Van Hise had forfeited some part of his claim to liberal leadership. If his position had not in the technical sense violated freedom of learning, it had restricted free discussion in student circles.

One of the administrator's most difficult problems is to keep his progressive and conservative supporters in harness together. In order not to lose the support of a group entirely it may at times be necessary to yield something to it. Van Hise's attitude toward the Forum may have been influenced by some such expediency. But he preferred in his spoken and written justification to rest his case on a distinction between objective knowl-

[81] *Daily Cardinal,* January 17, 1917.
[82] *Milwaukee Leader,* January 19, 1917, p. 1; Federated Trades Council of Milwaukee to Van Hise, January 18, 1917, Presidents' Papers, filed under Weber.
[83] *Wisconsin State Journal,* January 17, 1917, p. 10.

edge and propaganda—a nebulous distinction. At the University
during the first World War, the dilemma in administration became even more acute.

✐

In his inaugural address Van Hise had taken a bold and constructive stand for a policy which he considered of great importance to student life. The University had made provision for
housing some of the male students, but at the time Science Hall
burned the immediate pressure for space had resulted in the
abandonment of the dormitory system. Van Hise proposed the
establishment of dormitories which would be not merely much-
needed residence halls, but units for such activities as debating
and athletics. In his mind this arrangement was a necessary
part of education, for by living together students learned how
to handle themselves in human relations. "If the University
of Wisconsin," the president declared, "is to do for the sons
of the state what Oxford and Cambridge are accomplishing for
the sons of England, if it is to do even what the eastern universities are accomplishing for their students, not only in producing scholars and investigators, but in making men, it must
once more have halls of residence, and to these must be added
a commons and a union."[84] In a commodious and beautiful
union, fitted with reading and recreation rooms, he continued,
the students not only would find stimulus and fellowship, they
would find less engaging "the coarse attractions of the town."
Above all, in view of the rapid increase in numbers and the
disparity of means among the students, the plan would
strengthen the democratic tradition. In his annual reports Van
Hise returned to this program again and again, urging for it
both private gifts and state support.[85] Student opinion bore
out the president.[86] By keeping the ideal alive he not only won
their applause but laid the foundation for the partial realiza-

[84] Van Hise's inaugural address, in *The Jubilee of the University of Wisconsin*
(Madison, 1905), 113.
[85] Report of the president, *Regents' Biennial Report*, 1907–08, pp. 22–23; 1909–10,
p. 13.
[86] *Daily Cardinal*, November 10, 1903; October 24, 1905; October 4, 1911; November 13, 1912.

tion of the program in subsequent years. In his own time the dream was not realized. The only accomplishment in this direction was the extension of the inadequate residence and recreational facilities provided for women in Chadbourne Hall by the construction of Lathrop and Barnard.

Van Hise's awkwardness and lack of social perception did not make it easy for him to win the confidence and admiration of undergraduates. Because of an inept effort at humor, he had made a bad beginning: in commenting to the student body on the coming Jubilee he had thrown out the suggestion that it might be well to revive some of the biblical customs of jubilee year—debts and even examinations might be canceled! Unfortunately Van Hise left town the next day. There was no one who could state definitely that his comment should not be taken seriously, and more and more students easily persuaded themselves that the omission of examinations was a definite University plan. When Van Hise came back, completely amazed that his joke had misfired, he was compelled to set the students straight. For the rest of the semester "it's a joke" was a campus byword; no student antic was complete without a solemn assurance to the faculty that it was "just a joke."[87]

His early difficulties no doubt taught the president the importance of cultivating skill in his relations with the student body. He quickly sensed the widespread opinion of the students that the faculty was unfair in its attitude toward athletics and social affairs and realized that as a leader of the faculty he was included in their indictment. He enjoyed telling convocations that the ideal relation between faculty and students should be that of "comrades working together for a common purpose—older and younger comrades, it is true, each with their own privileges but still comrades."[88] The best government of the faculty, he told the students, was by leadership, not by authority. If the faculty assumed this attitude, he pointed out, it had the right to expect cooperation on the part of students for the general good.

Convinced that faculty-student relations could be improved

---

[87] *Ibid.*, April 25, May 13, 1904. We are indebted to Halsten J. Thorkelson for supplementing the record of this episode.   [88] *Daily Cardinal*, October 2, 1908.

if the students understood what the faculty was thinking, Van Hise asked each of the men's organizations to choose a delegate to a student conference committee. At the meetings of this group, the president solicited student opinion, explained the faculty's position, and asked the delegates to carry back to their organizations the upshot of the discussions. Gradually student hostility toward the faculty decreased. The president was convinced that the next step was to shift responsibility from the faculty to the students in troublesome matters of student discipline. Making it clear that he approved of sport and fun, he pointed out to the students that he could not approve of hazing when it degenerated into brutality. He therefore urged the conference committee to take responsibility for regulating the freshman-sophomore rush. This it did. It was apparent that the new system worked much better than the old effort of the faculty to prohibit the whole business. In 1907, however, Van Hise declared that, in view of the great numbers participating in the rush and in consideration of the unhappy events occurring in connection with it, the whole custom must be abolished, preferably by the students themselves.[89]

Gradually the student conference committee developed into a representative legislative body for the men students; the women, thanks to the initiative of Dean Annie Emery, already had a self-government association. The president attended the meetings of the committee less and less frequently, thus encouraging student self-discipline and responsibility. These meetings, he believed, provided the best possible training for young men destined to enter into a larger society in which public opinion was the ultimate authority.[90] In explaining the course of self-government during his administration, Van Hise concluded that the experiment had proved his contention that the greater body of students was right-minded and that it was

[89] *Ibid.*, September 25, 1912. Actually, hazing continued to be reported.
[90] The student conference committee led to the creation of the student court which enjoyed jurisdiction in all cases save those involving academic dishonesty. The faculty was ready to delegate the detection and penalizing of cheating to the court, but a referendum indicated that the students were unwilling to have that body assume such a responsibility. In 1913 the regents, feeling that the student court was dilatory, expelled a student for the writing of "The Blackbird," an objectionable publication. Van Hise had no sympathy for anything approaching the lascivious, but he indicated that on the very day that the regents took their

feasible to develop through student responsibility an adequate machinery for dealing with the troublesome few.[91]

The fact that student self-government did not cover athletic activities, the students' major interest, lent support to the charge that the Van Hise administration was after all essentially paternalistic.[92] The truth was that the president was confronted by a serious conflict between student and faculty opinion regarding the status of athletics. When influential members of the faculty, including Turner, demanded that intercollegiate athletics be entirely abolished as the only adequate means of eliminating professionalism and restoring the priority of academic interests in student life, Van Hise played a mediating role. He himself was convinced that the general physical development of every student through intramural sports was preferable to competitive intercollegiate athletics.[93] But much as he wanted to see intercollegiate athletics subordinated, Van Hise did not consider the complete abolition of the system feasible. He knew the zeal of students and alumni for the great games and he recognized the strength of that which was by now an institution. With the support of Dean Birge, the president finally persuaded the faculty that intercollegiate athletics were worthy of perpetuation provided that they could be subordinated to other aspects of University life and provided their abuses could be eliminated. Although the president exerted all his influence to maintain the standards established by the Intercollegiate Conference[94] and to encourage intramural sports and other types of student interest, he did not urge that responsibility for the control of athletics be returned to the

hasty action, the court was scheduled to take testimony. The regents also amended the charter of the student court, taking away full jurisdiction in discipline cases. Although the evidence is not clear, it appears that Van Hise was instrumental in persuading the regents to withdraw the amendment of the charter in the interest of the further development of self-government. *Daily Cardinal,* March 7, April 15, 1913.

[91] "Self-Government at the University of Wisconsin," in National Association of State Universities, *Transactions and Proceedings,* 10:256–263 (1912).

[92] See chapter sixteen for a discussion of athletic policy.

[93] Later, when George W. Ehler had been brought to Wisconsin to develop this type of program, Van Hise gave him unqualified support despite considerable pressure from alumni to dismiss him. Van Hise to John H. Finley, June 14, 1916.

[94] The president was ready, for example, to favor the suspension of Michigan from intercollegiate athletics for two years rather than to have the standards of the conference relaxed. Van Hise to Albion W. Small, March 28, 1907.

students. Devoted as he said he was to the principle of student self-government, Van Hise was nevertheless unwilling to have the faculty entrust the determination of athletic policy to a student body which in his opinion could be trusted neither to administer the existing system efficiently and honestly nor to modify the system in the interest of the wholesome well-being of the students themselves.

In the matter of the religious life of the students the president defended the constitutional provision prohibiting sectarian instruction in the University. When some seven hundred students petitioned the regents to permit the department of Hebrew and Hellenistic Greek to introduce a nondoctrinal Bible course,[95] it was referred to a committee of which Van Hise was a member. The committee did not favor the proposal. But this was certainly not because Van Hise was unappreciative of the importance of religion in the lives of undergraduates. True, he himself seems to have taken a consistently naturalistic view of the universe and, while contributing to the support of the Unitarian Church, seldom attended its services. But he urged the several denominations to take up religious work among the students affiliated with their churches and encouraged the establishment of suitable devotional quarters. Although he favored a union religious center instead of separate denominational houses, the movement for separate houses had already won too much favor.[96] When a proposal was made to set up an interdenominational theological seminary in Madison in order that students preparing for the ministry might have the advantage of University instruction and the use of University libraries, Van Hise expressed approval.[97] He knew, to be sure, that it was highly unlikely that the several denominations would cooperate in such an enterprise.[98]

In Van Hise the students found an able champion when adverse criticism descended upon them. He minimized the opinion that the student body had become aristocratic in temper, and he championed "the less conspicuous nine-tenths," par-

[95] Papers of the Board of Regents, June 17, 1913.
[96] *Daily Cardinal*, January 26, 1916.
[97] Van Hise to Bishop William E. McDowell, October 25, 1915; to Richard C. Hughes, November 29, 1915. [98] Van Hise expressed this view to George C. Sellery.

ticularly the students who were supporting themselves finan-
cially, as "the real university."⁹⁹ Such sentiments naturally
pleased the students, and Van Hise's work to promote student
self-government, a student loan fund, a housing system, and
such enterprises as the Cosmopolitan Club, in addition to his
achievements in winning greater support and reputation for
the University, gradually won him their thoroughgoing esteem.
Accordingly, when in 1907 Van Hise was considering leaving
the University to become secretary of the Smithsonian Institution, the students expressed alarm and subsequently rejoiced in
his decision to remain.¹⁰⁰

✐

PRESIDENT Van Hise's relation to undergraduate interests cannot be dismissed without considering the repercussions of an
address which he delivered in 1907 at the Boston meeting of
the Association of Collegiate Alumni. Stating his belief that
coeducation had given satisfactory results for both sexes and
that its adoption in the western universities had led to the
higher education of tens of thousands of women who otherwise
would have been deprived of college training, the president
nevertheless declared that certain problems had arisen and
that certain modifications of the system were in order. There
was a natural but unfortunate tendency, he pointed out, on the
part of both men and women to refrain from taking courses
in which the great majority of the students were of the opposite
sex. Thus some women hesitated to take certain political science
courses that were popular with the men, while men avoided
literary courses in which they would be outnumbered by the
women. That this tendency was due to the nature of the courses
Van Hise denied, citing the popularity of literature and languages in men's colleges and the interest shown in many wom-
en's colleges in science, economics, and political studies. Although the professional schools of law, engineering, medicine,
home economics, and nursing had always been essentially one-
sex institutions, it was undesirable to permit any one department in a liberal arts college to become associated primarily

⁹⁹ *Daily Cardinal*, September 27, 1907. ¹⁰⁰ *Ibid.*, January 10, 16, 1907.

with one sex, since every department had something of importance to contribute to each. To whatever extent the presence of the other sex curtailed the opportunity of either to study in any academic field, to that extent a remedy was needed. Various presidents of coeducational institutions had expressed concern about the problem, he added.[101]

Was not the answer, Van Hise asked, to provide in those large courses in which many sections existed some special divisions primarily for the men and others primarily for the women? "If the actual opportunities for women will be enlarged by offering courses in political economy for them, perhaps adapted to their special interests when they would not otherwise pursue this subject because of the number of men, why should this not be done? If the opportunities of the men will be enlarged by offering courses in literature for them, when otherwise they would not take such [a] course because of the large number of women, what valid objection can be urged to the proposal?"[102] In conclusion, Van Hise reiterated his belief in coeducation and declared that in arranging for segregation in those subjects attractive to both men and women, coeducation in the colleges of liberal arts might be strengthened and preserved.

Segregation of a sort existed at Wisconsin as it did at Kansas, Washington, and Chicago. Classes in physiology and hygiene were taught separately. The history department had occasionally transferred the handful of men or women in a quiz section predominantly made up of the other sex in order better to meet specific interests in the assignment of special readings. Professor Ely, eager to attract more women into economics courses, asked permission to establish separate sections and to emphasize, in those designed for women, their peculiar interests. Professor McGilvary likewise requested a separate course in ethics for men.[103] Thus in raising the issue in his address Van Hise, in the first instance, merely described what he considered to be a tendency not only at Wisconsin but at other

---

[101] Charles R. Van Hise, "Educational Tendencies in State Universities," *Educational Review*, 34:504–520 (December, 1907).   [102] *Ibid.*
[103] Papers of the Board of Regents, April 21, 1908; Alfred L. P. Dennis to Van Hise and D. C. Munro to Van Hise, April 14, 1908.

state universities and, in the second place, made a proposal which he thought would solve one of the problems of coeducation more efficiently and also strengthen its cause in the liberal arts colleges.

At a meeting of the regents held in December, 1907, the president, after presenting the case for organizing separate classes for men and women in political economy and ethics, recommended that the requests be granted. Considerable discussion followed. Mrs. Florence Buckstaff, a member of the Board, moved a resolution to the effect that the regents were not in favor of the segregation of the sexes in college classes at the present time; the resolution was referred to the committee on letters and science with the understanding that no further steps were to be taken until it had made a report.[104] A faculty committee proceeded at the request of the regents to prepare a statement of the distribution of the sexes in the several departments. This indicated that there had been an increasing tendency for women to concentrate in language and literature and in education, and for men to emphasize the social studies, mathematics, and the natural sciences. The committee attributed the situation to "the natural taste" of women for the humanities and of men for science and public affairs; to the fact that most students preparing to teach were women, and that they preferred the humanities; and to a tendency to concentrate in a certain field of study and to neglect courses not directly related to it. These factors, in the committee's opinion, were augmented by the tendency of students of either sex to dodge courses taken almost exclusively by the other.[105]

The storm which presently began to rage was precipitated by the publication of a pamphlet by Mrs. John M. Olin, wife of a leading Madison attorney and well known as a militant alumna. The pamphlet attacked the president's proposal and insisted that this segregation would jeopardize the full equality and opportunity of coeducation.[106] Van Hise called the pamphlet "inflammatory and misleading," and Dean Birge at-

---

[104] Records of the Board of Regents, G:63, December 17, 1907.
[105] Papers of the Board of Regents, June 16, 1908.
[106] Helen R. Olin, *Shall Wisconsin University Remain a Co-Educational Institution,* n.p., n.d., [Madison, 1908].

tempted to rebuke Mrs. Olin. Mrs. Olin then undertook a campaign which included the presentation to the regents of a petition signed by two hundred and seventy-five graduates, vigorously protesting against segregation. Senator and Mrs. La Follette, in guarded language, wrote to the regents that they would "regret to see the University of Wisconsin take any step that might, directly or indirectly, be construed as a recognition of the principle of segregation."[107] No doubt instigated by Mrs. Olin, former President Bascom prepared a piece, printed in the *Cardinal*, in which he declared that the whole battle for coeducation had been fought and won years ago, that its success had been amply proved, that in its present form it adequately covered the ground in the most simple and direct way, and that, above all, it was not a thing of compromises or halfway measures.[108] The *Milwaukee Daily News* repudiated the suggestion that the scope of the inquiry into coeducation had been misapprehended and declared that it would be better to oust President Van Hise and all his followers than to jeopardize coeducation.[109]

The president, genuinely shocked and pained at the charge that he was betraying coeducation, again reiterated his complete devotion to it. So far as he knew, he continued, there was not a single member of the faculty opposed to the present system of education, which gave men and women alike the fullest opportunity to obtain higher training.[110] Van Hise was flooded with letters. Most of the women correspondents were clearly disturbed although, with the exception of Mrs. Olin, they expressed due respect for the illustrious president. Van Hise, in replying to Mrs. Olin, did not conceal his resentment at what he regarded as her unfairness or his bewilderment and

[107] Papers of the Board of Regents, April 21, 1908.
[108] *Daily Cardinal*, April 13, 1908. [109] *Milwaukee Daily News*, April 17, 1908, p. 6.
[110] *Daily Cardinal*, April 4, 1908. Only ten days later, however, Professor O'Shea, head of the department of education, entered the lists as an advocate not only of segregation but of separate institutions for girls during the adolescent period. A disciple of G. Stanley Hall, O'Shea was convinced that the "inherent physical and psychological differences" of women, particularly of girls during adolescence, made it inadvisable to subject them to the same type of education provided for boys. The fact that O'Shea was a widely recognized authority and also editor of the *Wisconsin Journal of Education* gave his opinion special weight with the public.

sense of helplessness in a situation where logic seemed ineffectual. A few men confessed to Van Hise their own dislike of coeducation and applauded his stand. But by far the greater number expressed their amused understanding, indicating that they too on occasion had suffered from unpredictable feminine wrath. Many saw in the Olin diatribe merely a humorous tidbit in the teapot tempest the president had unwittingly called forth.[111]

At its meeting on June 16, 1908, the Board of Regents adopted, as a sop to the women, a resolution declaring that "men and women shall be equally entitled to membership in all classes in the University." Van Hise, who had never dreamed that his proposal, advanced to meet a practical situation in an efficient way, would occasion such an explosion, accepted the decision in good part. The regents further resolved: "There shall be no discrimination on account of sex in granting scholarships or fellowships in any of the colleges or departments of the University."[112] Although this had not been a major point in the controversy there was some evidence, the *Cardinal* felt, for believing that such discrimination existed.[113] There the matter might properly have rested.

At the next session of the legislature, however, Assemblyman George P. Hambrecht of Grand Rapids introduced a bill providing that "all schools and colleges of the university shall in their respective departments and class exercises, be open without distinction to students of both sexes."[114] At the hearing Van Hise made it clear that he was not advocating segregation. In response to an inquiry Hambrecht admitted that, so far as he could see, there was nothing in his antisegregation bill to prohibit the arranging of classes primarily for men or for women, the only consideration being that the faculty must admit men and women to any class if application be made or desire shown on the part of either men or women to enter it.[115] The *Cardinal*, citing Dean Birge as its authority, declared that the bill, if passed, could have no possible effect on the Univer-

---

[111] See Presidents' Papers, 1907–08, Coeducation File.
[112] Records of the Board of Regents, G:198, June 16, 1908.
[113] *Daily Cardinal*, March 5, 1909.   [114] *Laws of Wisconsin*, 1909, p. 387.
[115] George Hambrecht to Van Hise, June 7, 1909.

sity curriculum, which already admitted men and women to all classes. The editor whimsically added that nowadays when anyone mentioned segregation "we have a vision of a little yellow dog alone in a frost. Once Prexy was said to have [said] a kind word to it and it has followed him around ever since like Wags, the dog that adopted a man; but, as a matter of fact, Prexy disowns it in accord with the rest of us."[116] But the bill passed. In spite of the temporarily unfortunate consequences of Van Hise's ill-considered efforts to introduce a greater measure of "educational efficiency" through segregation, and several other awkward blunders, his general relations with the student body showed marked administrative talent.

[116] *Daily Cardinal,* March 6, 1909.

3.

Van Hise: The Larger Public

V AN HISE's concept of the University's proper place in the life of the state was one of his great contributions. As he saw it, the University had three main tasks: the first was to contribute to the undergraduate's preparation for his life work and intelligent citizenship; the second was to advance knowledge; and the third was to take knowledge to the people and to aid in its application to the economic, social, and political problems. But it was the invigoration of extension and the crusade for research that brought the University into the main currents of the life of the state. When Van Hise took office few accepted the idea that opportunities for research might be as great in a state-supported institution as in a private one. But in his inaugural address Van Hise boldly declared, "I am not willing to admit that a state university under a democracy shall be of lower grade than a state university under a monarchy," and "if the University of Wisconsin is to do for the state what it has a right to expect, it must develop, expand, strengthen creative work at whatever cost."[1] If this was to be done, the state must support research and creative scholarship in every field; there could be no limitations on the lines of the University's endeavor unless the state were to be the irreparable loser. Nor could research, he continued, be confined to subjects deemed practical, for "the practical man of all practical men is he who,

[1] Charles R. Van Hise's inaugural address, in *The Jubilee of the University of Wisconsin* (Madison, 1905), 125.

87

with his face toward the truth, follows wherever it may lead, with no thought but to get a deeper insight into the order of the universe in which he lives." "It cannot be predicted," he declared, "at what distant nook of knowledge, apparently remote from any practical service, a brilliantly useful stream may spring. It is certain that every fundamental discovery yet made by the delving student has been of service to man before a decade has passed."[2] With such convictions Van Hise was obligated to "sell" Wisconsin the idea that it must support research in every field—no easy task. Opposition to the idea was widespread and persistent.

A further responsibility of the University, preached by Bascom and forwarded by Chamberlin and Adams, was to assume leadership in the application of knowledge for the direct improvement of the life of the people in every sphere. To this function Van Hise gave drama and publicity. Its fulfillment would involve two main lines of activity. The first would be the contribution of the expert, not only in the improvement of agriculture, in the building of railways and bridges, and in sanitation, but in helping to solve complicated economic and social problems. In his inaugural address Van Hise called attention to the services of the German scholar to his government. The German professor was a man of affairs, serving as a non-partisan expert in all sorts of ways. In America, too, scholars had begun to serve on tax commissions and to aid in the evaluation of railroad investments. By 1908 forty-one members of the University faculty were serving the state on one or more commissions: Van Hise himself and Dean Birge were each on five state commissions, and many were on two or more. Although such service was not unknown in other states, Wisconsin led the way and carried the movement further than any other commonwealth.

The second aspect of the idea Van Hise so often expressed in the phrase "service to the State" involved the invigoration and development of the extension movement. "I shall never be content until the beneficent influence of the University reaches every family in the state," he declared. "This is my

[2] *Ibid.*, 123.

ideal of a state university."[3] He gave his full support to the revived University Extension. "The aggressive business man does not wait for the consumer to go to the wholesale establishment to purchase his articles. He gets his products out to the retail stores by advertisement, by travelling agents, and in other ways. Also, more and more, the manufacturer is beginning to establish retail stores in various parts of the country to sell his goods. Are we going to be less aggressive in education than we are in business?"[4] This analogy with business was not only a reflection of the way in which the dominant mores affected the University administrators; it was also no doubt calculated to appeal to an influential segment of the public. Two-week short courses for farmers and for housewives, the dispensing of debate materials to every nook and cranny in the state not only to help schoolboys but to familiarize adults with the issues of the day, the support of traveling professors who held classes in many communities—these were the means by which the University was making the campus include the whole state. Thus the president could justifiably claim that a large part of the work of the University was not for the students on the Madison campus but for the two and a half million people in the state. The use of the University expert on the state commissions, the extension movement, the work that had been done and was being done to improve agricultural production, the achievements of the engineering college in operating classes for artisans and in advancing sanitary construction and electrical engineering, the practical applications of research in the social sciences—all of these and other enterprises the University sponsored.

Such, then, was Van Hise's conception of the relation of the University to the state. To insure its acceptance and development it was necessary to publicize the program. Van Hise lost no opportunity. The jubilee celebration, held in June, 1904, was the first tangible effort to dramatize the University to the people. On that occasion Van Hise himself, as we have seen,

[3] Van Hise's address to the Wisconsin Press Association, February, 1905, in the Presidents' Papers.
[4] *Regents' Biennial Report*, 1907–08, pp. 18–21. For a discussion of University Extension during the Van Hise administration and of the contributions of Dean Louis E. Reber and others to it, see chapter seventeen.

expounded his conception of what the University must do for the people. He was ably supported by former President Chamberlin and by Governor La Follette. "The state welcomes the ever increasing tendency to make the university minister in a direct and practical way to the material interests of the state," La Follette declared. "Upon every citizen rests the obligation to serve the state in civil life as the soldier serves the country in war. To this high duty the children of the university are specially called."[5] It was, indeed, as the *Cardinal* had hoped it might be, a soul-stirring jubilee.

But this was only the beginning. In his reports to the regents, in his testimony at legislative hearings, in his correspondence with political leaders and others, and in his public addresses, Van Hise reiterated the program again and again, apparently never tiring of what he said, and never at a loss in meeting objections. With confidence and equanimity even in the face of obstacles, he continued his crusade. In the process he created an ally. When he assumed office, Van Hise found that the comments on the University in the state newspapers were largely confined to athletics and social affairs. The president decided to change this. He asked Professor Bleyer of the English department to revive the weekly bulletins to be sent out to the newspapers of the state. These told, in an attractive way, the story of discoveries, inventions, and innovations at the University. The press made generous use of the bulletins, and the people became familiar with what the University was doing to make knowledge useful. The president was convinced, however sharp the criticism leveled at the University, however regrettable reverses were, that in the long run, if the people only understood the University, they would never let it down.[6]

It not only was necessary to educate the people to larger conceptions of the University's role and importance in their lives; it was imperative to expand the financial support of the institution, both to provide for the ever growing body of

[5] Ellen Torelle, comp., *The Political Philosophy of Robert M. La Follette* (Madison, 1920), 293, 294. The quotation is from La Follette's address at the inauguration of Van Hise, June 7, 1904.

[6] National Association of State Universities, *Transactions and Proceedings*, 1905, 3:148–149.

students and for the maintenance and improvement of teaching, and to make possible the research and extension activities which in Van Hise's mind were no less important than the instruction of undergraduates. He encouraged students to help obtain favorable legislation for the University and took care to express appreciation for their efforts.[7] He took an active part in encouraging the more effective organizing of the alumni, including the improvement of the *Alumni Magazine* and the establishment of an employment bureau. This, he pointed out, would strengthen the ties between the University and its former students. The alumni, he repeated again and again, could benefit their alma mater not only by making gifts for pressing needs not provided for by the legislature but by telling the people of its achievements and by securing proper legislation and preventing unfortunate legislation.[8] He appeared at legislative hearings armed with facts and figures and with arguments for new appropriations, now pointing out that it was impossible to separate the cost of instruction in Madison from the total cost of operating the University to the limit of its service to the people, and again indicating why the requests represented the minimum on which the University could efficiently function.

It is, of course, impossible to indicate the exact contributions of the president, regents, governor, and friends of a university in and out of the legislature in securing financial support for an institution. When Van Hise became president, the income of the rapidly growing University was substantially stationary as a result of the recent abolition of the fractional mill tax and the substitution of a biennial appropriation. It was, as the new president saw it, impossible to maintain the University under such circumstances. "This being the situation," he wrote subsequently, "I took up the matter of having the mill tax restored."[9] His files during the session of the 1905 legislature, which restored the mill tax, indicate that Van Hise was hard

---

[7] *Daily Cardinal,* September 29, 1905.

[8] Van Hise to Lynn S. Pease, summer and fall, 1908; Van Hise to Frederick Whitton, March 7, 1911; Van Hise to Mrs. C. R. Carpenter, May 23, 1912, all in the Presidents' Papers, where all letters to and from Van Hise are deposited unless otherwise indicated. [9] Van Hise to H. M. Dunlap, March 29, 1907.

at work organizing support for the mill-tax bill. He wrote to alumni, legislators, newspapers, and others—to someone, in fact, in almost every county. In reporting his activities to the regents the president remarked that he had devoted the major portion of his time to working for the mill-tax support for the University.[10] It was with some pride that he wrote, two years later, "By everyone connected with the university, faculty and regents alike, this mill-tax law is regarded as our greatest bulwark in planning for the future."[11]

Van Hise's technique for persuading public officials of the University's needs improved with time. His correspondence in the autumn of 1906 with Governor Davidson, who apparently did not like him, reveals considerable skill in "buttering up" the chief executive. Quite unexpectedly the Committee on Claims reported damaging amendments to a bill in the legislative session of 1907 which provided for appropriations for student buildings and medical education. "Every minute of my time and all my energy as well as that of many friends of the university was required to get this work of the committee on claims reversed."[12] We can be sure that Van Hise on this occasion was forceful and yet propitiatory, vigorous with his general arguments, heavy but persuasive with his facts and figures. Nor was the president the man to give an inch, even when the regents favored retreat. Writing to the Board in the spring of 1909, he expressed his strong disapproval of the suggestion that in view of legislative opposition the amount asked for be reduced. The president pointed out that this would be a bad precedent, that the bills were honest bills, and that the regents, once having approved the requests, should not, by reneging, make it appear that Van Hise had testified not on the authority of the Board but merely on his own authority.[13]

The Van Hise campaign for funds involved further techniques. According to Regent Hoard, the president in asking for increased appropriations from the legislature played up the remarkable contributions of the College of Agriculture and the

[10] Papers of the Board of Regents, June 1, 1905.
[11] Van Hise to Dunlap, March 29, 1907.
[12] Van Hise to W. N. Fitzgerald, June 15, 1907.
[13] Van Hise to the Board of Regents, April 24, 1909.

College of Engineering to the prosperity of the state. In these colleges, he knew, were "mainly to be found visible signs of progress upon which he can lay hold for testimony that shall reconcile the mind of the state to the burdens of taxation for the University as a whole. There is the fountain that nourishes the whole."[14] Sometimes, in a pinch, Van Hise called on an outstanding political leader for special aid in putting through an appropriation bill. For example, he regarded Joseph E. Davies as an important adviser on handling the Democrats in the legislature. On more than one occasion Davies was asked to make them "see the situation in its true light."[15] When, in 1913, Davies gave special assistance in the fight to retain the mill tax, the president was especially warm in his thanks.[16]

The most critical test of Van Hise's talents for winning financial support came, indeed, at the very time he was calling on Davies to stand by. In 1914 the tide had begun to turn against the Progressive administration of Governor McGovern. The high cost of government, the Stalwarts declared, was the result of extravagance; and they gave notice that the dominant issue in the autumn campaign was to be economy and retrenchment. Thus confronted by curtailment in case the Progressives went out, Van Hise and some of the regents conferred on April 14, 1914, with Governor McGovern. It was agreed that no construction of new University buildings was to be undertaken for the present and the governor was to submit a written statement to that effect, which he did, with an expression of appreciation and with the warning that even more drastic economy might be necessary. President Trottman of the Board of Regents subsequently stated that this understanding was not a mere temporary arrangement made for campaign purposes but a genuine effort to secure some measure of relief from taxes. The understanding implied, he felt, an obligation on the part of the regents to do nothing in the way of new construction until the 1915 legislature had had an opportunity to consider the wisdom

[14] *Hoard's Dairyman*, 41:888 (August 26, 1910). Hoard went on to say that it was inconsistent for Van Hise in his commencement address to emphasize the idea that the college of liberal arts is the glory and basis for progress.

[15] Joseph E. Davies to Van Hise, February 6, 1915; Van Hise to Davies, March 11, 1915.　　　　　　　　　　　　　　[16] *Ibid.*, June 5, July 3, 1913.

of the appropriations that had been made for building purposes.[17]

The Stalwarts swept McGovern and the Progressives out of office in the November elections. The new governor, Emanuel L. Philipp, was not only pledged to economy: he was generally believed to be unfriendly toward the University and to dislike Van Hise.[18] Besides, the president was certainly aware of the opinion that in its intention to cut the University's appropriations the new conservative regime was trying not to serve the taxpayer, but to punish the institution. It is impossible to determine whether these considerations played any important part in the decision of the regents' constructional development committee, three days after the election, to let the bids for the physics building. Trottman, in voting against this action, held that it would be construed as a violation of the agreement made the preceding April. It would, in other words, be interpreted as meaning that the University had tried to influence the campaign in McGovern's favor by suspending building operations and then, with his defeat, hurrying the completion of the specifications and contracts in order to have them approved by McGovern rather than awaiting the inauguration of Philipp. When it became clear that the building program was to go ahead, Trottman resigned the presidency of the Board. He seized the occasion to declare that in his opinion the present government of the University was neither efficient nor economical.[19]

In answering Trottman, the regents flatly denied his interpretation of their motives in resuming building operations. They insisted that their actions in letting the contracts in no way violated the agreement with McGovern to defer payment of $800,000 of the University's appropriations. Haste was needed in order to get the building ready for occupancy. McGovern had approved the action. Further, the situation had been put before Governor-elect Philipp with the view of promoting cooperation between him and the regents; he had seen the desir-

[17] James F. Trottman to Governor Francis E. McGovern, December 14, 1914, in Papers of the Board of Regents, March 3, 1915.

[18] G. D. Jones to Van Hise, March 27, 1916.

[19] Trottman to the regents, February 26, 1915, in Papers of the Board of Regents.

ability of distributing appropriations for buildings in such a way that in no single year too heavy a burden would fall upon the state.[20] President Van Hise likewise announced that the action had in no way broken faith with Governor McGovern.[21]

This incident was analogous to Van Hise's early experience with the new economy regime of Governor Philipp. During the long legislative session of 1915, Van Hise was often in difficulty; great cuts in the University appropriation were imminent; the governor was highly critical of some of the activities of the University; and the final appropriation was much less than Van Hise wanted. Yet in the end, Governor Philipp became less critical.[22]

The success of the president in the sustained drive for funds was not the only item on the credit side of his relations with the state. He determined to improve the relations between the University and the private colleges. At a conference in the autumn of 1904 the respective presidents agreed that the private colleges would emphasize their undergraduate programs, leaving graduate and professional training to the University. Another conference worked out programs of study for the advanced students of the smaller colleges which would fit them for more specialized work at Madison.[23] In addition the University established a graduate scholarship for each state college, to be awarded by its faculty to a member of the senior class. Lawrence and Ripon adopted the same entrance requirements as those of the University, enabling their students to be admitted to the University in full standing at the end of the sophomore year. Ripon invited the University to send inspectors, thus anticipating the action of the North Central Association in its efforts to standardize collegiate work; the arrangement worked satisfactorily. The cordial relations with Ripon were cemented when Van Hise used his influence

[20] Papers of the Board of Regents, March 3, 1915.
[21] *Daily Cardinal,* March 2, 1915.
[22] Papers of the Board of Regents, August 19, 1915. On March 27, 1916, G. D. Jones wrote to Van Hise: "I think we both agree that Governor Philipp entered his administration with some prejudice. I think he concluded it practically free from prejudice . . . I know he had an entirely changed opinion of yourself and that he sincerely wishes to cooperate with you."
[23] Reports to the Regents, E:25, October 10, 1904; Van Hise to R. C. Hughes, president of Ripon, March 9, 11, 1908; Hughes to Van Hise, March 12, 1908.

with the General Education Board, one of the Rockefeller agencies, to secure funds in the school's behalf.

But the president's relations with the normal schools and other state institutions were less happy than those with the private colleges. He frequently clashed with Superintendent of Public Instruction Cary, an ex-officio member of the Board of Regents. Van Hise wished to retain for the University the inspection of high schools and control over entrance requirements; Cary wished to have the state superintendent of public instruction take over this function.[24] To make matters worse, Cary on more than one occasion attacked Van Hise in the public press. In turn Van Hise declared openly that Cary wilfully misrepresented the facts or displayed "such amazing ignorance as to belittle his intelligence."[25] The contest with Cary did not, however, prevent the state teachers' association from electing Van Hise as president in 1915. Although the heads of the normal schools did not apparently follow Cary's example in publicly denouncing Van Hise, the president's opposition to a bill permitting these institutions to grant degrees must have dampened the cordiality of their relations. But Van Hise felt he was on firm ground since none of the normal schools at the time offered even the first two years of the bachelor's program.[26] Yet it was natural for the other state educational institutions, which under his system would be confined within carefully prescribed limits, to interpret his stand as an effort to maintain the power which a monopoly of educational functions gave to the University.

[24] Report of the Committee on Entrance Requirements and Inspection of the Changes Proposed by Superintendent Charles P. Cary. Presidents' Papers. Cary maintained that University inspection duplicated the necessary work of the state's Department of Public Instruction; that the University dominated the high schools; and that the University could suffer no possible loss in relinquishing inspection. The committee took Van Hise's view in maintaining that the University could not dominate the high schools as long as a state department set the course of study; that the schools entered freely into the association with the University and could voluntarily break off relations at any time; and that the University and high schools alike profited from the closer relationship which inspection involved.

[25] *Daily Cardinal*, April 11, 1912.

[26] Van Hise to R. C. Hughes, April 19, 1907. Van Hise sought and obtained the support of Ripon in the stand he took against the proposal.

In the earlier phase of the Van Hise administration, before his program was fully developed, the University was spared unusual criticism. It is true that the *Wisconsin State Journal*, as early as the autumn of 1903, had decried the effort of Governor La Follette "to build up a political machine" in the law school.[27] The reorganization of the student Republican Club occasioned a flurry, but the *Cardinal* probably expressed a common feeling in declaring that it was altogether desirable for those benefiting from superior training to take a more than perfunctory interest in politics.[28] Yet the editor, in the autumn of 1904, protested the introduction of politics into the affairs of the institution as antagonistic to its best interests: "We can commend a legislature that aids the university. We can condemn any faction that buys university support with patronage. We will countenance none of that in the future."[29] These comments, unimportant in themselves, reveal a belief that the University was already too closely tied to the La Follette regime to suit conservative tastes.

No doubt this feeling provided impetus for the legislative investigation of 1905. The immediate occasion, however, was what the *State Journal* called a "financial crisis" in the University. In November, 1905, the La Follette administration boasted that its economies made it unnecessary to levy a state tax; but within a month the University confessed, at a special session of the legislature, to what the *State Journal* insisted was a deficit of $450,000. The newspaper implied that the University, in requesting continuation of the policy of borrowing from the state to tide it over until tax appropriations became due, was as guilty as the La Follette administration in concealing the actual state of financial affairs.[30] The request of the University to have monies transferred from the general fund to the University evoked criticism and led to the appointment of a special committee empowered to inquire into the management and needs of the University. President Van Hise at once publicly announced his satisfaction. He declared that not only were the

---

[27] *Daily Cardinal*, November 5, 1903.
[28] *Ibid.*, January 8, 1904.　　　　　　　　　　　[29] *Ibid.*, November 9, 1904.
[30] *Wisconsin State Journal*, December 7, 1905, p. 4. See pp. 168 ff. for an account of the legislative investigation.

authorities of the University pleased but that they hoped that the policy inaugurated at this extraordinary session of the legislature would become permanent, so that the legislature in the future might rely on the reports of its own committee concerning the needs of the University rather than to have to depend on statements of University authorities which in some eyes were regarded as biased.[31] Dean Henry feared that the investigation might have disastrous results for the financial support of the College of Agriculture—one of the points at issue. But Van Hise maintained that the committee's report would be fair to the University.[32]

When the special investigating committee reported, the president was not disappointed. The state, the report declared, was justly proud of its University, which stood for "the highest ideals in scholarship and in economical and practical effort.... The success that has attended its labors in bringing the most practical sciences into the services of the people, is most gratifying as it is profitable to the state. The man who does brain work and the man who does hand work, the theorist and the practical man, each and everyone is today profiting by the investigations, experiments, and the practical problems that have been undertaken and given a practical interpretation by the university."[33]

The report was not a complete bill of health. It made certain recommendations designed to correct the failure of the administration to keep pace with the growth of the institution. These recommendations favored closer oversight and a more minute division of responsibility. At the same time the committee deplored the fact that in a few cases heads of departments had shifted as much as half of their regularly assigned work to their assistants. Several faculty members, on account of inadequate remuneration, had given considerable time to work outside the University. In general the understanding between the University and the agencies for which these professors worked was

[31] *Daily Cardinal*, December 13, 1905.
[32] Van Hise to William Arnon Henry, July 6, 1906.
[33] *Report of the Joint Legislative Committee on the Affairs of the University* (Madison, 1906), 14–15.

satisfactorily clear. Only in one or two cases was there any evidence that such faculty members had neglected their University work in the pursuit of their outside activities. At the worst, some professors appeared to have neglected their students outside class. The committee therefore recommended that research work be encouraged "only so far as that can be done without detriment to the instruction to which students are entitled." The committee further recommended that teaching be so arranged that all students in all classes enjoy the opportunity of contact with full professors. "We do not disparage the work of the specialists who write books, or through research, enlarge our knowledge of man or nature. . . . What we do contend is, that the best efforts of the best teachers should be expended in actually teaching. Unless some provision is made for giving to the lower classes enlarged opportunities for instruction by the strongest teachers employed, before long the state will be obliged to provide outside of the university instruction covering the first, and possibly the second year, of most of the courses as now outlined." [34] The report, in brief, revealed moderate doubts concerning Van Hise's emphasis on research, but it did not impugn the financial management of the University, nor did it stigmatize the institution for undue promotion of the La Follette conception of public service.

Nevertheless the questions raised about research and teaching were not buried. The *Wisconsin Alumni Magazine,* declaring that many teachers neglected their classes for research, called these men "self-deceiving dreamers who solace themselves with the idea that they are doing for the world a service by their books, while their class work goes unheeded." [35] Except in the College of Agriculture, whatever President Van Hise maintained, research was less important than instruction, which ought to be the criterion of promotion. The editor of the magazine spoke for many alumni and other citizens in belittling the graduate school as a "foreign element" in the University, recruited largely from out-of-state students lacking "the Wisconsin spirit," and opposed, because of its great size, to the best

[34] *Ibid.,* 9–11.   [35] *Wisconsin Alumni Magazine,* 7:301–302 (April, 1906).

interests of the University.[36] No wonder that Van Hise began
to turn his attention to the alumni and to cultivate a more cordial attitude toward his administration.

As appropriations increased biennium after biennium, the
critics of the Wisconsin Idea declared that the University was
costing the state far too much and that other educational institutions, especially the common schools, were suffering.[37] The
leading exponent of this idea was, of course, Superintendent
of Public Instruction Cary. He declared that the gross cost of
educating students was far too high in comparison with the
cost in neighboring universities. Van Hise, on his part, demonstrated with facts and figures that Cary's analysis failed to allo-
cate the appropriate sums to extension and other educational
services. The move in 1908 to audit the University's books was,
according to a leading regent, designed less to help the University than to provide data for attacks on the institution.[38]

It was natural, in view of the increasing means of many whose
sons attended the University and of the natural growth of a
more elaborate social life, for some to feel that the institution
had become "aristocratic." In spite of the president's effort to
give publicity to constructive achievements, this feeling was encouraged by the tendency of the press to feature news stories,
sensational and exaggerated, regarding the fuss and feathers of
student life. The *Cardinal* pointed out that such unfair criticism injured an institution dependent for its support on a
legislative assembly.[39] Farmers bringing daughters to Madison
for study were shocked at what seemed to their plain eyes the
lavish appointments in the women's dormitories and in Lathrop Hall.[40] Most were doubtless unconvinced by the contention
that Wisconsin was now old and rich enough to afford the
amenities of life and to promote "culture." In responding to
the criticism of a normal-school officer, Dean Birge denied that

[36] *Ibid.*, 7:389 (June–July, 1906).
[37] *Milwaukee Sentinel*, April 3, 1915, p. 6.
[38] J. F. Trottman to G. D. Jones, June 8, 1909, Presidents' Papers filed under T.
[39] *Daily Cardinal*, November 2, 1905; October 4, 30, November 24, 1906; March
14, 1907.
[40] See Charles Belmont Davis, " 'Court' Circles at Wisconsin," *Collier's*, July
23, 1910, pp. 14–16; Honoré Willsie, "Propagating Culture by Luxury," *Collier's*, January 20, 1912, p. 18.

the University was "aristocratic": "I would not call aristocratic
the innovation of a short course of farming; a branch of
schools in shops in Milwaukee; of classes among workingmen;
of correspondence courses, where the student has the advantage
of personal supervision; of exhibits, like the tuberculosis exhibit, which we have here."[41]

All this was light artillery fire compared with the mounting
indictment of the University for its alleged partisanship of the
La Follette Progressives and for its growing influence in the
state. Professor Gilmore's report on water power, threatening
as it seemed to the plans of private utility interests; the roles of
Van Hise, Birge, and a score of professors in the various commissions of the state; and the enthusiasm the muckrakers expressed for the University's leadership as a public service institution—all these pointed, in the minds of the Stalwarts, to dangerous partisanship. There were murmurings during Governor
Davidson's administration; but with the defeat of the Stalwarts
in 1910, the feeling rapidly mounted. The University became a
focus of major attacks.

Early in January, 1911, state officials grew concerned over the
bill Professor Commons was drafting to set up a commission to
take charge of all commissions, an agency, moreover, on which
the president was to be one of the four members; they therefore
declared that the University was trying to control the state.[42]
Hoard, former governor and regent, having resigned because he
was tired of the way in which the Board, now Progressive, had
"played politics," joined the hue and cry; Van Hise, he was
reported as saying, headed a group of men seeking to dominate
the state.[43] Another vehement critic was the state superintendent
of public instruction, Regent Cary. In a much-publicized statement he proclaimed that unless the University was checked in its
scramble for power, the people would have "a university state instead of a state university."[44] Attorney General Bancroft was
quoted as saying that Cary's statement was much too weak: "We

[41] *Daily Cardinal*, November 14, 1908.
[42] *Milwaukee Sentinel*, January 29, 1911, section 1, p. 15.
[43] Milwaukee *Free Press*, July 15, 1911, p. 6. Reprint from the *Jefferson County
Union*.
[44] *The Survey*, 27:1569 (January 13, 1912).

have hell in our legislative halls and hell in our university."[45]
Leading editors and businessmen denounced the "so-called so-
ciologists" in "control" of the University, declared that the
institution was a "hotbed" of socialism, excoriated "Professor"
McCarthy's "bill factory," proposed the abolition of all state commissions and agencies, fumed over the high taxes—which were
laid at the door of the University, and insisted that the people
must teach the University that it was the creature of the state.[46]
Others assailed the University by praising the private colleges
for their freedom from graft and politics; raised the old complaint that professors, and the president himself, took outside
pay while they neglected their inside work; and, ignoring Babcock's notable precedent, denounced faculty members for "com-
mercializing" their research to fatten their own pockets.[47] The
Wisconsin Retail Lumber Dealers' Association objected when
members of the faculty recommended that farmers compare
prices of mail-order houses with those of local merchants.[48]
When Governor Philipp gave friendly consideration to the University, one of his northern Wisconsin followers let loose his
fury: "Whenever the Tax-eating Idol—the 'head push' of the 'U'
appears, the 'U' graduate members of the Legislature are either
ready to 'kow-tow' to him, or hold the bag? That is FIERCE.
It accounts for the erratic, damfool laws our statute-books have
groaned over.... When the educational 'High-Muck-a-Mucks'
are controlled and curbed, the tax-payers of Wis. will enjoy
freedom again. 'Extravagance' appears to be the watch-word of
the school system in Wis. Our 'U', upon which we based so
much pride, is a tyrant nearly past control: ready to stultify and
besmirch clean politics, rob the tax-payer, bamboozle the lawmakers, defy the Governor and raise particular HELL generally, if things don't come their way. You find their ideas

---

[45] *Milwaukee Sentinel*, February 19, 1912, p. 1.

[46] Milwaukee *Free Press*, August 7, 1912, p. 1; Milwaukee *Evening Wisconsin*,
March 9 (p. 6), and June 15 (p. 5), 1914; *Milwaukee Sentinel*, April 10, 1913, p.
1; *Milwaukee Daily News*, August 17, 1915, p. 3.

[47] *Milwaukee Sentinel*, June 29, 1911, p. 8; Milwaukee *Free Press*, July 2 (p. 2),
July 6 (pp. 1, 5, 6), and July 7 (p. 1), 1911; February 19 (p. 1), February 23 (p. 3),
1912; June 21, 1914, section 2, p. 18; *Oshkosh Daily Northwestern*, March 30,
1912, p. 6.

[48] Milwaukee *Evening Wisconsin*, February 19, 1914, p. 1.

spreading like a cancerous growth into our Normal, High and Common schools: and every 'Professor' connected with these institutions, who has fed at the public crib a long time, thinks the public 'pap' must be given HIM for the good of the State. The County Boards of Education are but a step toward the complete and eventual elimination of local school officers—any way to strike another blow at the right to GOVERN ourselves."[49]

President Van Hise deftly devoted himself to the defense of the institution. Never faltering in his supreme confidence that the people would give the University what it wanted if the University gave the people what they wanted, he met the attacks both directly and indirectly. He spared no effort to enlighten the public regarding the contributions of the University to the common welfare, writing for the *Wisconsin Alumni Magazine,* making statements to the press, and reassuring inquirers agitated over the sweeping indictment of the institution.[50] In reply to the father of two University students, the president was bluntness itself: "In response to your letter . . . I have to say that the misrepresentations regarding the university are largely due to the inaccurate, misleading, and frequently false statements made by the state superintendent which he has widely disseminated thru letters sent at public expense to all parts of the state."[51] An effort was made to cultivate the business community: Ely wrote three articles which appeared in the *Wisconsin State Journal* early in 1915 demonstrating that the University was a great commercial asset. The department of economics sponsored a conference to which leading businessmen were invited and at which problems of the business community were sympathetically presented by members of the faculty.

And Van Hise rallied friends to refute allegations against the University and to emphasize its great contributions.[52] The University, declared the *State Journal,* was bound to rise above Gov-

[49] George B. Carley to Assemblyman John Gamper, April 5, 1915, Philipp Papers, State Historical Society of Wisconsin.
[50] *Wisconsin Alumni Magazine* (Madison), 13:226–230 (February, 1912); University Press Bulletin, quoted in the Milwaukee *Free Press,* February 21, 1912.
[51] Van Hise to Thomas Edwards, March 5, 1913.
[52] *Milwaukee Journal,* March 29, 1915, p. 1; *La Crosse Tribune,* February 23, 1915, p. 1.

ernor Philipp's attempt to control it by subordinating it to his kind of politics.[53] *La Follette's Weekly* insisted that back of the whole campaign was the water-power interest, sorely troubled by Professor Gilmore's brief for the public.[54] The *Milwaukee Leader* declared that the real object of the attack was to put the University in the hands of the big business crowd whose efforts to loot the state had met with resistance within the institution. "The talk of economy from the defenders of the gang that are looting the state of more each year than the university has cost since its foundation, is cheap demagoguery."[55]

Public officials eventually spoke out against the crusade. Ex-Governor McGovern defended both Van Hise and the University. Chief Justice John B. Winslow of the supreme court of Wisconsin defended the institution by pointing out that legislation affecting it could not be entirely judged upon the basis of dollars and cents and reminding the public that the good the University had done far outweighed any errors or inefficiency.[56] Finally, Governor Philipp himself, having modified his suspicions and unfriendly attitude, reported in the autumn of 1915 that he had ousted professors either from their positions on state commissions or from academic posts, and that in consequence the University was now divorced from politics and that all was well.[57] The *State Journal* remarked that he had either hidden his real reasons for the campaign against the University or he had been ignorant of the truth and had found that the institution was of great aid in the administration of state business.[58]

Although Governor McGovern declared that the investigation which the Board of Public Affairs instigated in the spring of 1914 was in no sense to be a criticism of President Van Hise or of the regents, the members of the Board of Public Affairs indicated that it was not unrelated to the mounting criticism of the Van Hise regime.[59] As was becoming to an administrator

[53] *Wisconsin State Journal,* April 2, 1915, p. 14.
[54] *La Follette's Weekly,* July 2, 1910, pp. 3–4.
[55] *Milwaukee Leader,* April 2 (p. 8) and April 3 (p. 8), 1915.
[56] *Milwaukee Journal,* June 7, 1915, p. 3.   [57] *Ibid.,* November 18, 1915, p. 2.
[58] *Wisconsin State Journal,* November 4, 1915, p. 4.
[59] *Daily Cardinal,* March 21, 1914.

given to emphasizing fact finding and prone to cooperate with critics in order to bring them to appreciate his own position, Van Hise urged the faculty to aid William H. Allen, director of the survey. The recommendations of the investigators might, he pointed out, be useful to the University. When he saw the drift of the proceedings and the nature of the recommendations, he announced to the faculty that Allen and his associates had not accepted as many of the criticisms of the University as they might have been expected to, and that, furthermore, the University had not accepted as many of the survey's criticisms as Allen thought he had reason to make.[60] Van Hise turned over to a faculty committee, in which Dean Birge and Professor George C. Sellery played leading parts, the task of demolishing Allen's work.

At the first general meeting of the faculty in the fall semester of 1914, Van Hise summarily declared that "the survey is quickly disposed of, since while Dr. W. H. Allen, its chief conductor, was an undoubted annoyance, neither the benefits nor the evil effects of his work have been important." It was indeed a misfortune, he continued, "that the principal director of the survey did not conduct his work in an enlightened manner; for had he so done, the results would have been of great assistance to the university. As it turned out, we must depend upon ourselves for improvement."[61] The faculty thereupon proceeded to assess its own work and to make recommendations for increasing its effectiveness.

It will be recalled that Van Hise and Turner had been concerned with the problems posed by the increasing demands which the faculty committee system put on the teaching staff and that the president had expressed, as early as 1907, the hope that the faculty might be willing, in the interest of conserving its time for teaching and investigation, to separate policy-forming from policy-executing functions. The crisis of 1910 over the respective roles of the regents and the faculty in determining educational policy had again raised, without settling, the problem of faculty organization for effective policy-forming and ad-

[60] Minutes of the Meetings of the Faculty, 7:215, November 30, 1914.
[61] *Ibid.*, 7:273, October 4, 1915.

ministrative functions. Finally, in response to the challenge the Allen investigation offered for faculty reconsideration of the efficient use of its time, there was appointed in May, 1915, a committee on organization of the faculty, consisting of William A. Scott as general chairman and Gilmore, Leith, and Paxson.

The report of the committee, which was submitted to the University faculty on February 8, 1916, reviewed the regents' allocation of certain educational policies to the faculty and outlined two classes of faculty function, policy-determining and administrative. Assuming that the faculty should give its principal attention to the former in the interest of conserving time for teaching and research, the report recommended the "elimination or reduction to the minimum of time spent on matters essentially routine or administrative in character" and "the fixing of responsibility for, and expediting the execution of, measures enacted by the University Faculty." To accomplish this, the committee recommended that such jurisdiction as the faculty had over administrative matters be exercised through small committees, the actions of which in all ordinary cases became faculty action automatically upon report, and that the secretary of the faculty henceforth be regarded as its chief administrative officer. A new standing committee, the University committee, was to be created to keep the faculty informed of all actions affecting the educational interests and policies of the University and to bring before it educational questions which it should properly consider by reason of the jurisdiction and powers the regents had conferred on it. In addition to the elected University committee, an administrative committee, composed of the president, the deans, and the secretary of the faculty, was to prepare a calendar for each faculty meeting and to supervise the execution of the routine matters which the faculty committed to its secretary. The duties of the secretary of the faculty, of the administrative committee, and of the nominating committee were clearly indicated, and other faculty committees were classified according to whether they existed chiefly for the determination of policy or for administrative functions.

The report, which the faculty adopted, was a landmark. It

went a long way toward solving the problem of maintaining democratic faculty control over educational policy and of relieving the teaching staff from routine matters.[62]

While the faculty concerned itself with internal reorganization, Van Hise and his lieutenants anxiously and skillfully combated any unfavorable influence the Allen report might have on opinion in the state. Taking satisfaction in the criticisms of the report in various newspapers, Van Hise declared that the persistent dissemination of the Allen material throughout the state by means of a publication called *Everybody's Business* had made little impression.[63] The president took equal or even greater satisfaction in the circumstance that notwithstanding the report the University had enjoyed the good will and support of the state administration and of a great majority of the legislature. Despite the stormy outlook at the beginning of the legislative session, the institution had come through "the squall without receiving more than a few scratches, and none of these were more than skin deep."[64] Van Hise must have felt that his confidence in an enlightened public has been vindicated.

THE University had achieved a country-wide and even an international reputation as a leading state university even before Van Hise became president, and he augmented it. When the distinguished Mosely Educational Commission came from Great Britain in 1903 to study American institutions of higher learning, it ranked Wisconsin as second among the state universities, giving the first place to Michigan. But the commission paid especial tribute to the library resources, regarding the collection in the field of American history as "perhaps the best on the continent"; it commended the research work associated

[62] Report of the committee on organization of the faculty, special order for University faculty meeting, Tuesday, February 8, 1916, Records of the Secretary of the Faculty.

[63] According to the *Wisconsin State Journal* of June 18, 1915, the Wisconsin Efficiency Bureau, the agency circulating the publications attacking the University, was financed by members of the Milwaukee Merchants and Manufacturers Association. See pp. 278 ff.

[64] Minutes of the Faculty, 7:278, October 4, 1915.

with Ely, Turner, and others; and it was duly impressed by the program of the agricultural college in experimentation and dissemination.[65] The Jubilee, which, as we have seen, did much to make the people of the state realize for the first time, as Van Hise put it, "the magnitude of the University," also resulted in the wider appreciation of the institution by leading scholars, American and foreign. In 1905 Oxford granted junior and senior students advanced standing—Harvard was the only other American institution enjoying these privileges.[66] A leading English educator reported, after a study of American institutions, that the English could learn more from the University of Wisconsin than from any other educational agency. From the princely state of Mysore in India an educational commission reported that of the American universities visited, Wis-

[65] *Reports of the Mosely Educational Commission* (London, 1904), 121, 254, 287. "Hon. William Henry Jones, member of parliament, who is visiting this country with the Mosely delegation which has for its purpose the study of higher educational methods in America, is much impressed with the growth of democracy in education here, and finds the state universities much superior to the old, privately endowed colleges of the east.

"In a recent statement Mr. Jones said it would be difficult to name the first five great American universities, as we have so many institutions of unquestionably high standing and large purpose, but that, if he were to do so seriously he probably would have to name them, following the sun—Harvard, Cornell, the University of Michigan, the University of Wisconsin, and the University of California.

" 'To name the first ten,' he said, 'would be still more difficult, as that would put a larger number of great institutions into competition, but that, if he were to do so, it would be almost impossible for him to add any five to the first list mentioned that did not include the state universities of Illinois, Nebraska, Minnesota, and, possibly, Kansas and Tennessee.

"He states that, if there is any one college that would have preference with him it probably would be the University of Wisconsin.

" 'This university,' he says, 'is strong in numbers. It is democracy, where merit alone counts; its standing in scholarship is of the highest; its degrees are recognized by every university in the world; and its spirit and purpose are as broad and inclusive as the universe. Unlike the older colleges of the east, it is not circumscribed and hampered by a conservative, classic curriculum, nor is it intimidated by its benefactors, as are some of the colleges founded by the predatory rich.

" 'It is the wholesome product of a commonwealth of three millions of people; sane, democratic, industrial and progressive; with ideals, and unafraid of ideas. It responds to every need of humanity; it knits together the professions and labor; it makes the fine arts and the anvil one. There are many of these state universities that have much or all of this; but to this must be added the natural endowment of the University of Wisconsin—its location is sublime.' " From the *Milwaukee Sentinel*, November 29, 1903, p. 1.

[66] *Wisconsin Alumni Magazine*, 6:295 (June, 1905).

consin had the most to offer toward the plans for Mysore's university. A larger number of out-of-state students came each year; Superintendent Cary complained in 1912 that the number was larger than the entire enrollment at Iowa or Indiana. But Van Hise pointed out that the presence of these students was a broadening influence, necessary if the University was to be a national rather than a provincial institution.[67] The press bulletins went not only to the journals of the state but to eastern and western metropolitan papers and to the bureaus furnishing news service. In 1909 Albert Shaw, editor of the *Review of Reviews,* included Wisconsin in the account of four American universities he was asked to prepare for the *London Times.* The popular magazines, including *Collier's, American Magazine,* the *Survey,* the *Review of Reviews,* and the *Outlook,* all gave publicity to the University. The University also came off very well in such books as Edwin E. Slosson's *Great American Universities* and John Corbin's *What University for the Boy?* When President Eliot of Harvard conferred the honorary degree on Van Hise in 1908, he called Wisconsin the leading state university. Its national character was also reflected in the neverending stream of distinguished men and women who visited Madison to lecture; among these were James Bryce, Jane Addams, William Jennings Bryan, William Howard Taft, Justice Louis Brandeis, and Theodore Roosevelt.

Other universities sent delegations to Madison to study the extension division, the role of the University experts in the state commissions, the organization and support of research, and other aspects of the institution which were distinguished or unique. In 1904 forty delegates from Georgia, including the chancellor of the university, members of the board of trustees, the governor, the editors of leading newspapers, and members of the legislature, visited Madison to study and to take home for application those features which made the University of Wisconsin "a model northern state university."[68] The General Education Board, one of the Rockefeller philanthropies, in thanking Van Hise for hospitality to the governor of Arkansas

[67] Report of the president, December 1, 1904, *Regents' Biennial Report,* 1903–04, pp. 11–12. [68] *Ibid.*

and his party, wrote that "the visit will be of great benefit to education in Arkansas. . . . The University of Wisconsin is at the top and we are all looking to you for counsel."[69] After visiting Madison a group of Cincinnatians made tentative arrangements for a working connection with Ohio State University, stating that both the governor and the faculty were pleased at the prospect of such cooperation as they had observed in Wisconsin.[70] Leading Philadelphians also visited the University to see how it did things and to make use at Pennsylvania of what they had learned. The delegation, impressed by the contributions of the University to the enlightenment of the people and to the promotion of better government, studied the Wisconsin Idea in all its ramifications, especially in the extension division.[71] Kansas sent a delegation, headed by the governor and the chancellor, and including William Allen White; prominent Texans launched a movement to have their state university revamped along Wisconsin lines. No wonder that Lincoln Steffens could write Van Hise in 1908: "When you stop work to look beyond your own state you must find no little personal satisfaction in the thought that you are leading not only your neighbors but the whole round world."[72]

The national and international reputation of the University was, of course, the result of many factors, but among these Van Hise's personality, his leadership, and his flair for publicity bulked large. The part he played in the Association of American Universities was creditable; and no one in the National Association of State Universities rivaled him in influence. His relations with the new foundations were cordial and his energetic support of their program won enthusiastic praise. His relations with President Eliot reflected his talent for making a good impression on the right people. His influence was widely recognized. "I want to tell you again what I have told you before," wrote President James of the University of Illinois, "that I have gotten more ideas from you than from any other

---

[69] Wallace Buttrick to Van Hise, October 15, 1908.

[70] James W. Faulkner to Van Hise, December 15, 1912.

[71] Morris Cooke to Van Hise, February 27, 1912; Gregory Mason, "Educating a Democracy," in *The Outlook*, 105:742–744 (December 6, 1913).

[72] Lincoln Steffens to Van Hise, December 25, 1908.

man."[73] President Angell of Michigan often sought his advice, as did the presidents of many other colleges and universities. David Starr Jordan considered him "easily the peer of any college president in the United States," and a delegate to the American Association for the Advancement of Science meeting in 1909 wrote that it was no exaggeration to say that he "ranks with the very ablest of University Presidents."[74] Lincoln Steffens told Madisonians on a visit in 1913 that Van Hise was "in a class by himself among college presidents. He has the broadest conception of what a university should teach, how it should teach it, what it should represent and stand for, what it should work for, and what its relations to the people and the problems of the present should be, of any college president in the United States, bar none."[75]

Van Hise would have been the first to associate the leadership of the University and its wide recognition with the policies in which it had been a pioneer. These policies he did not originate; but he crystallized them, implemented them, and gave them publicity. In his report to the regents in 1911, he made a special point of the fact that while within the state the University staff was criticized for all those things it did which were not directly concerned with teaching, such as research, extension, and public service, outside the state the University was praised for these very things. And he quoted from a recent article in the *Outlook* Theodore Roosevelt's statement that "in no other state in the union has any university done the same work for the community that has been done in Wisconsin by the University of Wisconsin."[76]

THE faculty, in describing what it had done during the initial year of America's participation in the first World War, declared that the state had not been educationally prepared

[73] Edmund J. James to Van Hise, March 1, 1907.

[74] Orlando Clark to Arthur J. Puls, June 25, 1909; Dr. J. C. Bloodgood to Puls, June 30, 1909; Puls to Van Hise, July 6, 1909.

[75] *Daily Cardinal*, November 14, 1913.

[76] Papers of the Board of Regents, December 13, 1911.

for undertaking the issues of the struggle.[77] There were several reasons for this. At least ten per cent of the people had been born in Germany and another seventeen per cent were of German parentage. The Progressives, under the leadership of Senator La Follette, believed in general that domestic reform was paramount and regarded the war as an Old World struggle in which the United States should take no part. Wisconsin shared the isolationism of the Middle West. In addition, if the faculty was correct in its assumption that the people were not educationally prepared for the war, Van Hise's admonition to the staff early in the autumn of 1914 to refrain from discussing the war from the University platform and to keep out of wartime activities may have contributed to the lack of understanding. In any case, in the early stages of the war, there seems to have been little discussion at the University, either in the *Cardinal*, in general lectures, or in the extension program.

Once the national movement for military preparedness got fully under way, voices within the University spoke vigorously in its behalf. In the spring of 1916, for example, the *Cardinal* favored a sham battle between the cadet corps of Wisconsin and Illinois as a means of arousing patriotism and stimulating preparedness.[78] The University commandant, Lieutenant Wrightson, gave a series of lectures on the training of volunteer officers, and various professors, including Ely, Scott, Fish, and Dennis, spoke out for preparedness. Dennis worked for the establishment of a national council of defense which would include the secretaries of war, navy, and state, military personnel, and civilian experts, and Van Hise assisted in presenting the idea to the administration.[79] Another member of the history department, Professor Eugene H. Byrne, stirred the University to join belatedly with other institutions in sending ambulance drivers to the European fronts for relief work. The fact that there was less enthusiasm or, as the *Cardinal* said,

[77] University Faculty Documents, No. 90, Records of the Secretary of the Faculty, April 24, 1918.

[78] *Daily Cardinal*, April 21, 1916.

[79] Council for Defense file, in the Presidents' Papers, especially A. L. P. Dennis to Newton D. Baker, April 20, 1916, and the telegrams, Van Hise to Dennis, and Dennis to Van Hise, April 19, 1916.

"military hysteria" on the campus than in many eastern universities may well have resulted from the fact that Wisconsin had long had military drill whereas the private institutions on the seaboard had not.[80] Yet practically the entire student body turned out for Madison's loyalty parade a few days before the declaration of war. According to the *Cardinal,* student opinion, as soon as war was an actuality, overwhelmingly favored the bill for compulsory military service. The student organ and the officials of the University urged everyone to do some constructive service for the war effort during the summer; aside from the men who joined the services, 1,650 took part in the food-production program or in industrial enterprises. All this President Van Hise ardently supported. Like other educators, however, he took the position that high school boys of intellectual ability should come to the University to prepare themselves for efficient national service until they were drafted. The faculty, he insisted, should try to help students realize that their greatest patriotic contribution might well be to continue their studies until the government designated other duties.[81]

In the period between the outbreak of the war in Europe and the American decision to enter on the side of the Allies, President Van Hise, unlike his old classmate and friend, Senator La Follette, had been moving in the direction of an internationalism in which the United States was to play a leading role. He refused Henry Ford's invitation to take part in the Peace Ship crusade to end the war, suggesting instead that an interested member of the faculty be asked.[82] But he became a charter member of the League to Enforce Peace, served on one of its important committees, helped organize branches in Wisconsin, and wrote to former President Taft that it was the one organization he had joined and with the purpose of which he was in full sympathy.[83] It was thus natural for Van Hise to champion Wilson's program for a League of Nations.

Meantime, once the country had declared war, the University

[80] *Daily Cardinal,* December 19, 1916, and March 17, 1917.
[81] Van Hise's statement to the faculty, in Papers of the Board of Regents, December 5, 1917.
[82] Van Hise to Henry Ford, November 25, 1915.
[83] Van Hise to William Howard Taft, January 26, 1916.

was confronted by a series of difficult problems—the making of
a new budget which would take into acount the probability
of a shrinking enrollment, the granting of leaves to students
and faculty as they went into war service, and the consideration
of the whole matter of academic freedom. A few days after war
was declared Van Hise asked German citizens on the faculty
to give him "a parole not to take part directly or indirectly in
any way whatsoever in any matter which relates to the war."[84]
Professor Hohlfeld gave Dean Birge the written resignation of
Professor Ernst Feise, a German national, to be used if and
when it seemed wise, and Van Hise approved Birge's acceptance
of the resignation when Feise made a "scurrilous" remark
about a colleague's liberty button.[85] But there was no general
onslaught against the large and thriving German department.
Complaints were publicly made that it was larger than all the
other modern language departments combined. "My contention is," wrote Richard Lloyd Jones, editor of the *Wisconsin
State Journal*, "that the University has always been Germanized
up to the time you made the cut from twenty-seven to fifteen"
members of the department. But Jones was still most unhappy
that the cut in budget had been a mere four thousand dollars
and that in numbers the department still overshadowed the
French department. No doubt the strength of the German element in the state helped to explain the fact that the University
did not follow the example of many other institutions in virtually suspending German studies. Yet it would be unfair to
assume that Van Hise's devotion to the freedom of learning and
teaching was not also a factor. One faculty member of German
origin, known to be opposed to the war on pacifist grounds, has
testified that the administration put no pressure on him whatever and that any pressure he did encounter came from members of the faculty who told him he could have a great future if

[84] Van Hise to Guy Potter Benton, April 9, 1917.
[85] Papers of the Board of Regents, December 5, 1917. The dismissal of Feise
was an index to the near-hysteria which pervaded the University. Feise's "scurrilous remark" was that his colleague, earlier pro-German in his outlook, ought
to wear another liberty button on the seat of his pants so that, when he turned
his back on a class to write something on the blackboard, evidence of his patriotism
would still be apparent. While the remark was in bad taste, perhaps, it was
hardly scurrilous, although many so regarded it.

he would go about the state telling the German-speaking population that it was a wonderful war to which they should rally
with all their might.

The question of academic freedom during the war must not
be dismissed without some mention of the famous "round
robin" which the overwhelming majority of the faculty adopted
early in 1918. This was a protest against the utterances and
actions of Senator La Follette "which have given aid and comfort to Germany and her allies in the present war." The signers deplored "his failure loyally to support the government in
the prosecution of the war."[86] Van Hise strongly believed that
La Follette's war policies were dangerous to the country.[87] Yet
he made it clear to members of the faculty who felt they could
not in conscience sign the statement that they should feel under
no compulsion to do so.[88]

In the autumn of 1917, some months before the great majority of the faculty expressed its disapproval of Senator La
Follette's war position, Van Hise was called on to defend the
University for lack of patriotism. A prominent alumnus complained that while he was in the East he had found himself
unpleasantly on the defensive; he questioned whether the University had done all it might to make it clear that it had no
sympathy with La Follette and Louis Lochner, a well-known
graduate, journalist, and internationalist. Van Hise replied that
it was obviously unfair to judge the University by the attitudes
of two men and called attention to the war services of professors and students.[89] His correspondent thereupon professed to
be unconvinced, contending that such enumerations "do not
carry great weight with industrial organizations who have

[86] Papers of the Board of Regents, January 16, 1918.
[87] Van Hise to President John S. Lord of the Wisconsin Alumni Association,
December 27, 1917, copies in the Presidents' Papers and in Papers of the Board
of Regents, January 16, 1918; University of Wisconsin Press Bulletin, January 23,
1918.
[88] Van Hise to William Ellery Leonard, January 21, 1918, and Van Hise to
Max Otto, January 18, 1918; Max Otto to Merle Curti, July 12, 1947. According
to Professor Otto, Dean Birge was said to have felt that the time might come
when it would be in the interest of the University to have had some members
on the staff who had refused to sign and who had not been made to suffer.
[89] Charles F. Burgess to Van Hise, October 5, 1917; Van Hise to Burgess, October 6, 1917.

turned over their entire staffs and resources to public welfare."[90] Thoroughly irked, Van Hise replied, "If the facts are
gone into, I shall put the patriotism and self-sacrifice of the university organization against that of any industrial concern,
which in no case, so far as I know, has made any arrangement
with the government which has not yielded very handsome
profits."[91]

More serious was the publicly made charge of Assistant Secretary of Agriculture Carl Vrooman in the second of two addresses made in Madison in the autumn of 1917. As the representative of President Wilson, Vrooman had reviewed the University cadets and had spoken to them on the subject of patriotism. He subsequently declared that "they were less responsive
than any audience I have talked before . . . in three-fourths of
the states." He went on to say that this was the first loyalty
meeting held at the University and asked, "Has the University
the right kind of patriotic leadership? Is it guided by a milk
and water patriotism, a kind of platonic patriotism? If this
University is not most outspoken, if it does not express a militant patriotism at this time, it expresses no patriotism at all.
. . . What they [the students on parade] need is patriotic inspiration, patriotic leadership, patriotic education. . . . Is this
state university giving them this kind of education at this time
when it is so needed?"[92] As President Van Hise was quick to
point out in a protest to President Wilson, Vrooman was entirely incorrect in stating that the meeting had been the first
of its kind; there had been a whole series of loyalty get-togethers
addressed by such men as Secretary McAdoo, Sherwood Eddy,
Major Stanley Washburn, General Vignal of the French Em-
bassy; and, moreover, twice weekly, members of the University
staff had lectured on war issues. "The nature of the address of
Mr. Vrooman," continued Van Hise in his letter to Wilson, "is
called to your attention for the reason that the regents, the
faculty and the students deeply resent the serious reflection
made upon the patriotism of this institution by a high public

[90] Burgess to Van Hise, October 10, 1917.   [91] Van Hise to Burgess, October 13.
[92] Quotation from Vrooman's address included in Van Hise's letter to President
Wilson, November 27, 1917.

official." He called attention to the number of professors and students in war service. "This University," he concluded, "has aggressively taken the initiative in many lines of effort to assist in the prosecution of the war and has given prompt and complete response to all suggestions and demands from the outside."[93] While the *Milwaukee Journal* felt that Van Hise had missed the point in failing to answer whether the leadership of the University was truly inspirational in creating a fighting, patriotic spirit,[94] the *Capital Times* remarked that if froth and gush were patriotism, then the University was unpatriotic, but if action counted, then the University was above criticism.[95] Indignant at Vrooman's insult, the *Cardinal* reported that the students were preparing a mass meeting to counteract the mistaken statements of men of national prominence, the ill-chosen criticism of the University in the state press, and the activity of a small minority of obstructionists and pussyfoot patriots among the student body.[96]

But this was nothing in comparison with the sensational fury resulting from the indictment of the University by Princeton's Professor Robert McNutt McElroy. As a representative of the National Security League, he had, on April 6, 1918, addressed a large audience in the Stock Pavilion. After he returned to the East, the *New York Tribune* published an interview in which McElroy reported his story in detail. From the outset, he declared, the audience, made up of students and of the cadet corps wearing the United States Army uniform, took strangely little interest in his effort to tell them about America's aims and ideals in the war. "They sat with folded arms, staring wearily up at the ceiling. From time to time they'd turn and look at each other and smile superciliously, sort of pityingly. There was a good deal of fidgeting and shuffling of feet. Several times, generally at the most strongly patriotic portions of my talk, sounds which bore every sign of being subdued hisses would be heard. . . . When I began to quote some of President Wil-

[93] Van Hise to President Wilson, November 27, 1917.
[94] *Milwaukee Journal,* December 5, 1917, p. 12.
[95] *Capital Times,* December 14, 1917, p. 8.
[96] *Daily Cardinal,* December 4, 1917.

son's messages, the rattle of snapping rifle triggers throughout the audience . . . sounded very much like an attempt to break up the speech. . . . Finally I couldn't stand it any longer . . . . So I leaned forward and I deliberately insulted them. 'Do you know what I think of you from your conduct tonight?' I said. 'I think you're a bunch of damned traitors!'" According to his story, McElroy was astounded to see that there was no reaction whatever except the snickering of a few men in the back of the room. "I've often wondered what it would be like to speak before a Prussian audience. I think I know now."[97]

Great indeed was the indignation in almost every quarter when news of this interview reached Madison. The faculty adopted a resolution asking for "a reparation, full, explicit, and emphatic." The faculty, on the one hand, and Chief Justice John Bradley Winslow, Dean Birge, and President Van Hise, on the other, brought forward the facts in the case. The weary, drenched cadets, who had marched two and a half miles to the Stock Pavilion, had become restless and inattentive in the uncomfortably cold pavilion. In fact, a large proportion of the students present had had to be put under medical care and two citizens who had taken part in the proceedings died from exposure. Members of the faculty seated near the speaker testified that his one derogatory remark was so softly spoken that no one more than a few feet away could possibly have heard it; this explained why there had been no response when McElroy remarked that he believed "there are a lot of damn traitors in this audience." The few that did hear the remark had disregarded it as evidence of petulance on the part of a speaker who had failed to hold his audience. President Menken of the National Security League, who visited Madison to investigate the affair, made an infuriatingly equivocal statement and in the end refused to repudiate McElroy.[98]

The faculty, President Van Hise, the regents, and leading

[97] *New York Tribune,* April 17, 1918, p. 16.
[98] C. R. Van Hise, E. A. Birge, and J. B. Winslow, *Report upon the Statements of Professor Robert McNutt McElroy and the Executive Committee of the National Security League relating to the University of Wisconsin* (Madison, 1918). This report consists chiefly of statements and the correspondence between the University and Security League officials.

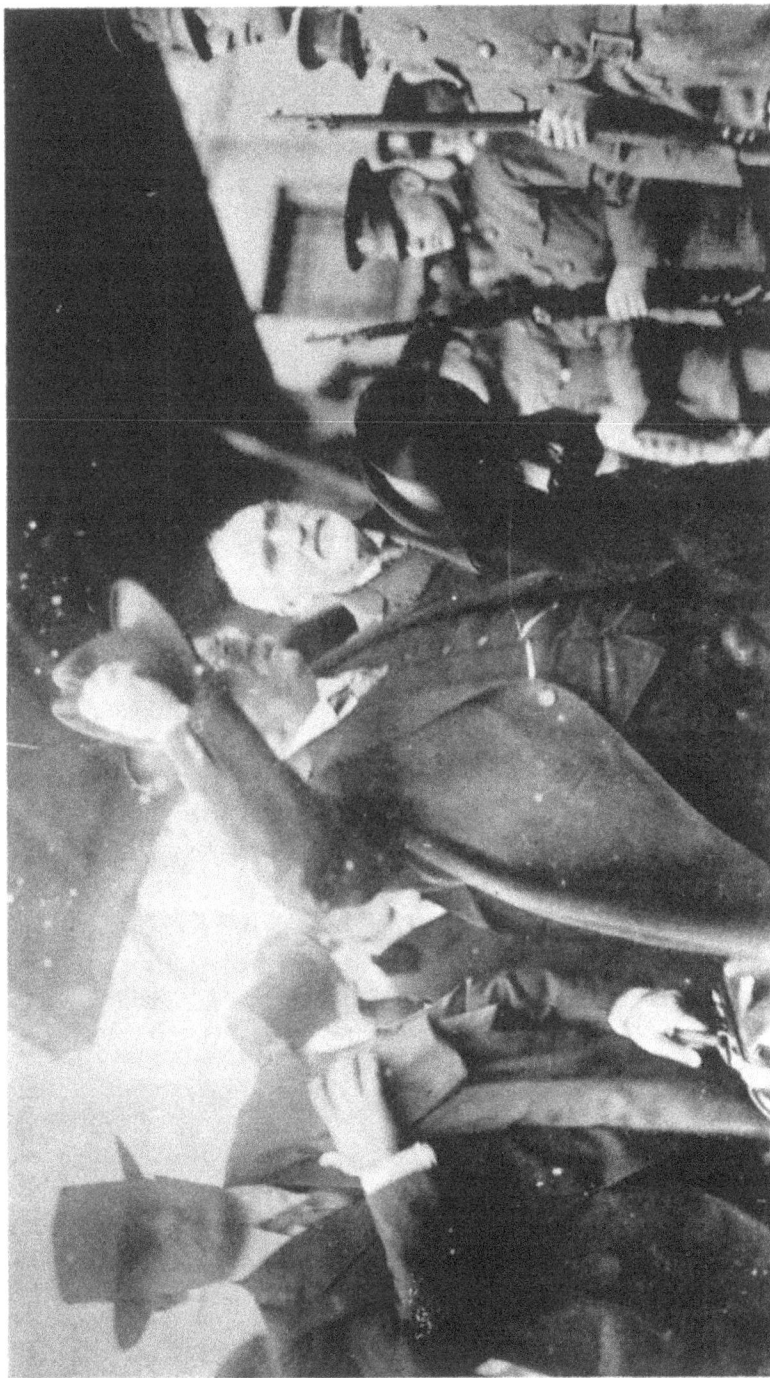

Van Hise and Theodore Roosevelt, May 28, 1918

The Loyalty Parade Preceding the McElroy Address in the Stock Pavilion, April 6, 1918

citizens regarded McElroy's interview as an insult to the whole University. The *Wisconsin State Journal* branded his remarks as untrue, caddish, and slanderous fulminations. Professor Fish and Professor Paxson, history colleagues of Professor McElroy, made it plain that they believed he had grossly misstated the facts. A throng of students, mostly cadets, burned McElroy and the Kaiser in effigy while they shouted and snake-danced in a patriotic rally. President Van Hise wrote to President Hibben of Princeton protesting the unjust charges made against the University of Wisconsin, and Chief Justice Winslow declared that McElroy had done more harm than he could repay in a lifetime of devotion.[99]

The circumstances of the meeting itself and a whole array of positive achievements left no doubt as to the essential loyalty of the student body and the patriotism of the University. The regents revoked the honorary degree given in 1910 to Count von Bernstorff, German ambassador at the time the United States entered the war. The overwhelming majority of the faculty criticized Senator La Follette for his lack of sympathy with the struggle. The University oversubscribed the liberty loans, sent more faculty officers into the armed forces than any other educational institution, and boasted of being near the top in the number of students serving in the armed forces. President Van Hise's idea of the expert in public service was thoroughly realized: the chemistry department sent ten of its staff and many of its advanced students to work on gases and explosives; the geologists contributed to the increase of the country's stocks of manganese, iron, and nickel; the physicists and engineers did useful work in submarine and aviation research; the medical school trained personnel for special war services; the language departments provided translators and prepared teaching materials for the army; and the historians made their contributions to the propaganda crusade. At the same time the College of Agriculture helped increase wheat production and the home economics department did its bit in

[99] *Daily Cardinal*, April 16, 20, 27, and May 2, 1918; University Faculty Documents No. 90, April 24, 1918; *Wisconsin Alumni Magazine* 19:213–214 (July, 1918).

suggesting ways and means for providing bread and meat substitutes. The extension service helped train Red Cross workers
and spared no effort in enlightening the people regarding the
issues at stake.[100] The University was conducting, the faculty
declared in the spring of 1918, a "systematic campaign of education on the issues and measures of the war, a campaign that
has helped in the establishment throughout the state of a fighting patriotism as vigorous as any section or element in the
country can show."[101]

In all these activities President Van Hise himself took a
leading part. Within the University he worked on the war committee which guided the innumerable readjustments. These
included, in the late summer and autumn of 1918, the establishment of the Student Army Training Corps. On the national stage the president took the leadership in the drive to
conserve food, mineral, and other resources for war use. This
involved cooperation with the shipping board, the priority
board, the war industries board, and the food and fuel administrations. Van Hise also prepared written material on conservation and the war effort which was widely circulated for instructional purposes in schools, colleges, and other agencies.
On the international stage the president likewise labored in
promoting cooperation among the Allies and in helping lay
foundations for a just and lasting peace to be built and maintained by an effective world organization. To this end he
visited England and France in the latter part of the war and outlined his conceptions of peace planning in a notable paper,
"The Foundations of a New World Order," first delivered as an
address before the Wisconsin state convention of the League to
Enforce Peace on November 8, 1918, just a few days before the
armistice. It was an intelligent and ardent defense of the emerging League of Nations, definite and clear-cut in its rejection of
American isolation and, in its several proposals for international machinery, firm and vivid in its vision.[102] It must have
been at about this time that the president also prepared a

[100] *Ibid.,* January 10, 1918.
[101] University Faculty Documents, No. 90, April 24, 1918.
[102] Charles R. Van Hise, *The Foundations of a New World Order,* (New York,
n.d.).

Christmas greeting for Wisconsin men in combat—a message in which, on behalf of the University, he expressed pride in the service of the two thousand undergraduates and all the other Wisconsin men: "Through the years to come we shall proudly recall that it was from our doors you went out to battle; your gallantry will inspire the men and women who come after you, and will give a new radiance to the spirit of Wisconsin."[103]

Within a week of the armistice Van Hise was dead. He had suffered for years from a chronic nasal infection, and during the fall of 1918 his breathing had become uncomfortably obstructed. An operation was prescribed. It was not expected to be serious, let alone dangerous; Van Hise did not consider the matter serious enough even to mention it to many of his friends, and he took with him to the hospital the proofs of his latest book to check over during the day or two he expected to remain. However, infection set in, and death followed within forty-eight hours.

In the war as in peace Van Hise had exemplified his own definition of patriotism: "He who thinks not of himself primarily, but of his race, and of its future, is the new patriot." The *Cardinal* recalled that he was a self-made man, that he had worked his way through the University in his student days, and that he had become one of America's greatest educators. It spoke of his modesty, of his simplicity and straightforwardness, of his courteous sympathy. He felt, the student writer said, that he could never do too much for anyone. The regents, in their resolutions, pointed out that for forty-five years he had maintained an unbroken connection with the University—every faculty member and nearly every living alumnus had come into intimate personal contact with him. "To know him was to love him, to serve with him a privilege, and to serve under him a benediction," the regents said. William Ellery Leonard wrote:

> A son of earth, he probed and proved his stock,
> Walking with giant footsteps, wise and free;
> He searched out wisdom in her cloven rock,
> He entered in the springs of ice and sea;
> He conned the crystals and her ores of fire

[103] Papers of the Board of Regents, December 4, 1918.

For laws of change, dynamic as the sun;
Then, fraught with surge and scope of her desire,
Foretold the output of her living on.

A son of man, he built with faithful hands
New roads from hills of thought to humble hearts,
Highways to shop and farm and inland beach;
And now, when drifts the war-smoke from all lands,
Touched to still larger issues, he departs—
Even as his lips are moving to new speech.

Perhaps Van Hise had accomplished all that was his to accomplish. That he would have had to continue the fight for research and extension is clear from the letter of a prominent regent written within the year before his death. That the new temper of the country was hostile to his kind of progressive idealism was soon evident. His greatness had been less in the invention of new ideas and policies than in his work for their implementation. Perhaps, despite Leonard's noble words about the new language he had begun to speak, Van Hise would have been able to provide no new platform. Perhaps he could no longer have fought with anything like the old success. But he had fought well; he had temporized with circumspection; he had clearly shown academic statesmanship and greatness of spirit and action. He had made his mistakes, but the mistakes only served to emphasize his achievements.

4.

President Edward A. Birge

AT THE regents' meeting on December 4, 1918, Dean Edward A. Birge was named acting president and a committee was appointed to make recommendations for a successor to President Van Hise.[1] Twelve days later the regents voted to make Birge president in spite of the attempt of a group of the faculty to have him continued as acting president.[2] Birge accepted the office on condition that the regents promptly begin searching for "a man to whom the office may be committed with full expectation that he may hold it for a long term."[3] This condition the regents accepted and a committee was appointed to hunt for a new president.[4] A desultory search apparently was conducted during the next year, but in December the regents adopted a resolution asking Birge to withdraw his conditions of acceptance and agree to an indefinite term of office. This he did on the same day, acknowledging that "the progress of events . . . has shown that my term as president ought not to be ended as soon as seemed to me wise at the opening of the year."[5]

Dean Birge had many admirers on the Board. In 1917 G. D. Jones had written Van Hise asking that Birge's plan to retire be forestalled. "He is certainly one of the great men

[1] *Daily Cardinal*, December 5, 1918. [2] *Ibid.*, December 17, 1918.
[3] Birge to the regents, December 17, 1918, Papers of the Board of Regents; *The Wisconsin Alumnus*, 44:11 (November, 1942). The letter as printed is misdated.
[4] Records of the Board of Regents, J:250, January 15, 1919.
[5] *Ibid.*, J:401–402, December 3, 1919.

whose names have been associated with our university."[6] Theodore Hammond of Milwaukee and Charles Vilas, president of the Board, were also among his supporters. These three men had constituted the special committee to select a president in 1918. In the uncertainty and confusion which followed the end of the war, Birge no doubt represented a kind of stability. There was another consideration which may have weighed with the Board: Birge could occupy the post until the regents, in their own time, selected the man they wanted.[7] The election of Dean Birge to the presidency was regarded by some people as an assurance that the University would be brought back to its prewar position. Others expected it to become more conservative. Gilbert E. Vandercook, a Milwaukee editor, wrote to President Birge saying that he had in the past "not always been friendly to some phases of university work, policies and politics, and in a newspaper capacity sometimes I have been obliged to assume a harsh attitude. . . . With your selection, coupled with your long experience and fitness, I am confident that our great institution could be in no better hands."[8] G. D. Jones, who had been a persistent and forthright critic of Van Hise, wrote to Birge in 1920, "I most sincerely congratulate the University on the wholesome situation in 'governmental' matters. I am sure my views of your especial fitness as our president have been amply verified and I most sincerely believe it is the wish of every friend of our University that you may long continue to serve as our president."[9]

The man who was selected to follow Van Hise and to guide the University through the most critical years since its found-

[6] G. D. Jones to Charles R. Van Hise, January 3, 1917, Presidents' Papers.

[7] When Chamberlin resigned in 1892, Dean Birge had been mentioned for the presidency. When President Adams was absent, Dean Birge had served as acting president, and he had held this position from the time of Adams' resignation until the selection of Van Hise in the spring of 1903. Van Hise had refused to accept a salary of more than $7,000 a year unless faculty salaries were raised. The president of the Board confided to Birge that this had caused the Board considerable embarrassment. When Birge was made president, he was given a salary of $10,000 a year. *The Wisconsin Alumnus*, 44:15 (November, 1942).

[8] Gilbert E. Vandercook to Birge, December 10, 1919, Presidents' Papers, filed under Drought. All letters to and from Birge are in the Presidents' Papers unless otherwise indicated.

[9] G. D. Jones to Birge, October 13, 1920. Jones repeated these sentiments three years later. Jones to Birge, December 26, 1923.

ing was rich in administrative experience. Born in New York State in 1851, he had attended Williams College and had there been instructed by two men who were to serve as presidents of the University of Wisconsin, Chadbourne and Bascom. In 1875 he had come to Wisconsin to teach in the preparatory department and later, while on leave, had continued his education at Harvard and in Germany. On his return he had taught biology and had helped to inaugurate the premedical courses in the College of Letters and Science. He rose to the deanship of the college in 1891 and held this position until 1918. In spite of his administrative duties he continued to teach for a number of years. A leader in the field of his specialty, limnology, he possessed wide and active intellectual interests besides. One of his colleagues recalled that while he was a member of the library board Dean Birge read all the new books that came to the library. In addition to his teaching, administrative work, and scientific investigation, he found time to serve on various state commissions, on the Madison school board, and on the library board, as well as to teach Sunday school.

In 1899 Charles Kendall Adams gave his opinion of Birge to a member of the governing board of the University of Iowa: "My own relations with Dean Birge have been so intimate during the past seven years that I find it difficult to speak with entire impartiality. Our offices have been adjoining, our relations have been of the most intimate, cordial, and unreserved nature during the whole of that period, and I should feel that it was giving away my right hand to say anything that would create any probability of his going elsewhere. . . . He began as an instructor and at the time of my coming here he was appointed Dean of the College of Letters and Science. In that position, he has acted as the chief executive officer of the college over which he has presided, and has had far more to do with the relations of students to the University than any one else. He has administered these duties with almost faultless energy and wisdom. He is a remarkable teacher, and for his integrity and fairness has the entire confidence of all the members of the Faculty and of the student body. His mind is remarkably quick and alert; his scholarship is of the best; and, what is very unusual in a man with such qualities, his judgment in relation to University matters is almost invariably discreet and sound. He is a strong, forceful, cogent public speaker. Without any oratorical gifts, and without any rhetorical show, he has a persuasive way of analyzing a subject and presenting the gist of it in a manner that is always strong and generally convincing. As a debater he has remarkable skill. He is known and is popular with the teachers of the state and is everywhere heartily welcomed as a speaker and lecturer. . . . That he is highly esteemed outside of the University may be inferred from the fact that he is Director of the Geological and Natural History Survey of the state; Secretary of the Fish Commission of the state; is President of the Wisconsin State Library Association; is President of the Madison Public Library Board; and is a member of the School Board. of the city. . . . I ought perhaps to add that he is an officer in the Congregational church in this city, and may always be relied upon as taking a foremost part in every good work that may be undertaken by a Congregationalist of a very liberal type.

"As contrasted with these rare and high qualifications, there is hardly anything to be said on the other side. He would not by a stranger be thought to be particularly impressive as a personality. He is rather small in stature, but the keenness of his eye will seldom fail to impress itself upon any one who scrutinates him carefully. By some his nature is thought to be cold and unsympathetic. Perhaps that would be the judgment even of some of his friends, but it is, I think, rather to be regarded as an indication that he keeps his emotions in rather remarkable reserve. From these characteristics you will naturally infer that by his colleagues and friends he is not so much beloved as admired and respected. This perhaps would describe his relations to students as well as to his colleagues and the public at large." [10]

Twenty years later Pyre wrote of Birge: "Familiarity with every detail of the university, breadth of knowledge and intellectual sympathy, unusual powers of analysis, precision and balance of judgment, and keenness in debate, made him a master of compromise and a mediator peculiarly invaluable in a period

[10] Charles Kendall Adams to W. I. Babb, Mt. Pleasant, Iowa, February 10, 1899, Presidents' Papers.

of transition. To him, more than to any other individual, is due the preservation of the central college and the continuity of its influence in the university."[11] The testimony of former students—both by their professional success and by their words—as well as that of his colleagues and a host of others bespeaks the exceptional capacity and achievement of Birge as a teacher, scholar, and dean.[12]

But the dean was not without limitations. One of the regents observed to Van Hise that, as dean, Birge was too willing to accept what was given him for the college and try to get along on that.[13] Himself a man of Spartan tastes, he had once told a colleague that all a scholar needed was a table, a chair, and a couch. The funds that were entrusted to him for administration he dispensed with a frugality reminiscent of Regent Napoleon Bonaparte Van Slyke. Professor Edward Kremers, in one of a number of unenraptured sketches of his colleagues which he prepared after his retirement, complained that Birge had devoted himself to the details of the dean's office without reserve. He even made corrections in the statements prepared for the catalogue. "Surely," wrote Kremers, "if the capacity to unload administrative routine is regarded as a characteristic of either a good dean or president Birge ought never to have been either."[14]

Birge came to the presidency of the University at a crucial time in the history of the institution. The enlarged student enrollment following the close of the war brought new problems and forced the University into new directions; the increases also placed a great strain on the physical plant, which had not been materially expanded since 1913. The growing needs of the University had to be dealt with in the political turmoil which emerged in Wisconsin after the war. During the war, it will be recalled, the University faculty had split with La Follette and his supporters. The followers of La Follette, and Wisconsin

[11] James F. A. Pyre, *Wisconsin* (New York, 1920), 265.

[12] See *Edward A. Birge, Teacher and Scientist,* addresses delivered at a dinner, September 5, 1940 (Madison, 1940).

[13] Florence Buckstaff to Van Hise, March 4, 1917, Presidents' Papers.

[14] Edward Kremers, Sketch of E. A. Birge, Kremers Papers, State Historical Society of Wisconsin.

liberals in general, had charged again and again that the University had turned its back on liberalism, that it had become the agency of the conservatives. Then the La Follette forces came into power in the state government in 1920 and remained there for the rest of the Birge administration.

The attempts of the University to win financial support commensurate with its larger activities and greater enrollment are told elsewhere,[15] but it should be noted at this point that the most successful attempts to win increased appropriations from the legislature occurred at the special session in 1920 when Governor Philipp undertook what amounted to the major responsibility for getting an enlarged appropriation for University salaries and for obtaining the authorization and funds for the construction of a hospital. The regular session of the legislature in 1921 added little to the general appropriation and provided a small amount of money for additional buildings; the legislature of 1923 became entangled in a fierce struggle over the kind of taxes which should be levied to support the University and adjourned without having adopted an appropriation bill for the operation of the University. This left the University to continue with the same funds for operation that had been granted under the law of 1921. The legislature in 1925 made a handsome contribution to the support of the University but made it in the full realization that by the next year the University would be under new leadership.

In part the failure to obtain adequate funds was a product of forces and developments completely beyond the power of the president to control; in part it reflected the disinclination of President Birge to push as vigorously as his predecessor for liberal support of the University. Birge had accepted the office reluctantly and at first for only one year, impelled more by a sense of duty than by any personal desire for the office. To Franklin Carter he wrote that his fate had in a sense been decided in 1891 when he accepted the deanship of the College of Letters and Science. "Everything else has come along in the natural course of events and in a way from which there was no escape. I need not say however that this last change to the presidency

[15] See pp. 202 ff.

was one which I should have been glad to escape. No one at my age desires to undertake the duties of a new and arduous position. Least of all would I have wished to come to the presidency as a result of the death of Dr. Van Hise and the consequent great loss both to the university and to the state. Yet as matters stood after his death it was obviously right, both for the university and for myself that I should undertake the position."[16] To the president of the University of California he wrote the next year: "I believe that the next ten years will witness more changes in university life than perhaps any earlier decade. For myself I can neither expect nor wish to take an active part in university life for so long a time as even a decade."[17] It had been his duty to accept the position, to help keep the University going, but he had wanted to undertake no major changes. In his reminiscent piece written in 1942 he gave reasons for not sponsoring or encouraging a reorganization of the University. Such a task, he felt, "should be undertaken by a man in middle life, who is in close and sympathetic touch with the men of his own age. The wisdom or the folly, with which such large measures are carried through, comes far more from the right *feeling* of the leader than from his intellectual processes. His arguments are still less important. But my age was approaching the three score and ten which has always been the natural limit of life; and I did not intend either to push my old-fashioned ideas upon the University or to accept the ideas of those whose lack of administrative experience made them unsafe counsellors."[18] Furthermore, since his administration would be relatively short, he did not want to saddle his successor with a reorganization partly carried through. His relation with the faculty was influenced by the same reasoning. The faculty pay scale could be adjusted by his successor.[19] Major appointments were postponed for the

[16] Birge to Franklin Carter, August 4, 1919.

[17] Birge to President David P. Barrows, University of California, March 16, 1920.

[18] *The Wisconsin Alumnus*, 44:16 (November, 1942).

[19] Birge's reason for inaction, namely, that he could not see the reforms carried through, brought the following protest from the ever-critical Kremers: "I certainly regret that you should be influenced by such a reason. So far as I am concerned I do not recall that I have ever been influenced by such an argument. If I know a thing to be right, I want to begin it right and am more than willing to leave it to my successors to see it through." Kremers to Birge, May 25, 1921.

same reason. Dean Louis Reber of the extension division wanted to retire in 1923, but Birge urged him to stay on until a new president was selected.[20]

Birge, whose period as acting president from 1900 to 1903 had consisted largely of carrying on the institution as Adams had left it, now devoted the seven years of his administration to carrying on what Van Hise had left. His notion of the office of the president differed somewhat from that of his predecessors. Chamberlin, Adams, and Van Hise had all revealed in their actions that they conceived it as a position of vigorous leadership. Birge however held a somewhat more modest conception. He wrote to President Frank L. McVey of the University of Kentucky: "My conception of the office for many years has been that it is similar to the office of Prime Minister of England, that of a leader among equals. This at least was my conception before I had the place, but whether I shall be able to realize that ideal even partially is quite a different question." Birge was convinced however that the faculty had not the ability to consider the University budget. "I agree with you fully that no large body of men, like the faculty, each of whose members has a personal interest in the framing of the budget, is competent to make a budget or even discuss it intelligently."[21]

And though he sympathized with Van Hise's conception of the function of a university, his own view was more moderate. In a baccalaureate address in 1902 he emphasized that information and skills were only a part of what students should learn at a university. "The main purpose of the higher education is to produce a certain temper of mind, a certain way of looking at things."[22] Again and again in his reports as dean he had pointed out the necessity for the college to strive toward producing that "certain temper of mind," whatever other professional or technical training it offered. In an article in the *Atlantic Monthly* in 1909 he had developed a similar thesis.[23] As president he con-

[20] Even the editor of the University Press Bulletin could not resign because Birge did not want to select a successor for him. Interview, Irvin G. Wyllie with Grant Hyde, August 9, 1947.

[21] Birge to President Frank L. McVey, University of Kentucky, October 12, 1920.

[22] Edward A. Birge, *University Ideals*, baccalaureate address (Madison, 1902).

[23] Edward A. Birge, "A Change of Educational Emphasis," *Atlantic Monthly*, 103:189–200 (February, 1909).

tinued to urge these views. In a statement on the University after the war, prepared for the *Badger,* he recognized that the war had driven the students into vocational training, but he hoped that this limitation of purpose would not continue. "A university which limits its teaching to vocational instruction ceases to be a university, and students who look only to preparation for the immediate duties of the future are not university students." The chief task of the University, he said, was "to serve the immediate needs of the state and not to lose touch or to let its students lose touch of those wider aspects of learning on which the intellectual life of the state depends and on which in the end rest its prosperity and happiness." [24]

Not hostile to professional and technical training, he nevertheless stood firmly against giving it pre-eminence in the University. Nor was he willing to urge a college education as a means of earning a better living. In an address before the National Education Association in 1919 he took issue with those who feared that the college and its "impractical" learning would lose its constituency because the "cash rewards of brain workers are so far inferior to those of craftsmen. . . . The inadequate reward of learning has been for centuries and for millennia the theme of poet and scholar. It is no new thing, or one brought to light by this war. It has rather been well known since the Trojan War. The world has had time to become adjusted to this fact. No man here, therefore, who went to college, I venture to say, did so in the expectation of getting rich. We knew this fifty years ago as well as the youth of today can know it—that college offers no road to wealth. Yet we chose this higher education, as our spiritual ancestors had done for many generations, undeterred by the certainty of small financial gains. The reason for our choice is plain. Look at the plumber, or any other wealthy craftsman. . . . If we may trust the official attitude of the organization to which they belong they have little or no love for their work. They regard it as the price which they pay in order to find enjoyment elsewhere and they constantly struggle to make this price as small as possible. We, on the other hand, chose the higher education in order that we might find happiness and

[24] *The Badger, 1920* (Madison, 1919), 51.

pleasure in our daily work, not outside of it. The result has justified our hopes; and as long as human nature remains as it has been during all time there will be many who believe that life is more than meat, who will look for happiness in life's activities and will be more than willing to pay the cash price of such happiness."[25]

He was in basic sympathy with the program initiated by Chamberlin and carried forward so energetically by Van Hise in making the University the servant of the state. A year before he retired from office and on the eve of Senator La Follette's campaign for the presidency, Birge prepared a statement on the senator which revealed his attitude toward the Wisconsin Idea. "Let me say a word about that public relation in which I knew him best—his relation to the University of Wisconsin. Our University in the early and formative years of Dr. Van Hise's presidency was in a unique and very fortunate position. Governor La Follette and President Van Hise were not only close personal friends but were in complete harmony regarding the fundamentals of public policy and especially regarding the relation of the University and State. Thus Governor La Follette not only put the 'Wisconsin Idea' into operation by means of administrative organizations like the Railway Commission, but he also enlarged its scope by bringing the University and its faculty into active cooperation with public life. Such an enlargement of the ideals alike of public service and of university life was greatly needed twenty years ago and it would be effected only through the initiative of a Governor who was persuaded of its wisdom and who acted in cooperation with a university president equally in sympathy with the policy.

"The results were obvious in the exceptionally rapid growth of the University in size and in influence, both in the state and in the nation. Less easy to see but all the more important was the change in its inner life which came with the enlarged conception of service and with the sense of a greater public responsibility. Thus Senator La Follette, always devoted to his alma mater, not only gave distinguished aid to its development

[25] Edward A. Birge, "Effect of the War on Higher Education," in National Education Association, *Addresses and Proceedings of the 57th Annual Meeting...* *Milwaukee, Wisconsin, June 28–July 5, 1919,* vol. 57, pp. 217–219.

but also at a critical period in its history and in that of state education, he was able to exert a powerful and determining influence in adapting it to a new era of the commonwealth. I cannot expect that those whose lives are outside of university work will see today the importance of this service as I do. But in the perspective of history it will rank among the first of Senator La Follette's permanent contributions to the life of his commonwealth."[26]

In his attitude toward the press and the uses of publicity President Birge differed appreciably from Van Hise. After Van Hise's death, articles discussing aspects of the University virtually disappeared from the pages of general magazines of national circulation. Birge often seemed indifferent to the uses of a friendly relation with the newspapers and suspicious that news reports would provoke hostile editorials. He checked many of the items sent out by the University Press Bulletin and occasionally made corrections with acid vehemence.[27] Some newspapers objected to his uncooperative attitude. Early in Birge's administration, the *Capital Times* added another to its growing list of complaints about the University: "We believe that the whole method of publicity pursued at the university is wrong. Nothing can ever be gained for the university by seeking to cover up and distort the real facts. The university will gain in the long run by being absolutely frank and open with both the newspapers and the people of the state. This is a people's university and the people are entitled to the fullest knowledge concerning what happens at the university. If the university authorities expect to receive fair treatment from the newspapers the university authorities must be equally fair in giving the newspapers the real facts."[28]

Unlike Van Hise, who was often ready with an opinion when solicited, Birge refused to give opinions for publication on matters outside his special field. When the editor of the *Literary Digest* solicited his opinion on the policy of the United States toward the Permanent Court of International Justice, he refused to give a statement because he was a zoologist and university administrator and in neither capacity had "such knowl-

[26] Birge's statement, dated March 28, 1924, Presidents' Papers.
[27] See Birge to Grant Hyde, June 9, 1922.   [28] *Capital Times*, March 23, 1921.

edge of international politics or international relations as to make it right for me to push my opinions upon the public."[29] On the other hand, when questioned on prohibition, as he often was, he held frankly to the position that although he favored prohibition he did not think the nation was ready for it. To a federal prohibition director in Milwaukee he wrote, "I looked forward to troubles of the kind which we have been meeting in the enforcement of the law." He thought that the number of students who drank had not increased with prohibition, but that those who had formerly been satisfied with a glass of beer could now get only bootleg whisky and sometimes drank to excess. The situation was no worse than it had been; it merely got more attention.[30] When the editor of the *Independent* asked for a statement on prohibition, he refused it; he did not think the prohibition law was being more openly violated than the license laws which had preceded it. Moreover, he took the editor to task for having urged that prohibition be enforced on the basis that "drinking is a sin." Perhaps it was a crime, but it was not a sin. "All of the religious public derive their ideas of sin from the Bible, and drinking *per se* is not so treated either in the precepts of the Bible or in the example of our Lord. . . . If, therefore, I should comment on the issue, I should have to dissent sharply from your editorial because it seems to me to make a demand of a kind which would make it impossible to succeed in enforcing prohibition."[31] In the main he steadfastly refused to give opinions on public problems outside his field.

Birge was drawn somewhat unwillingly into a nationally reported exchange with William Jennings Bryan. Bryan spoke in Madison early in May, 1921, on "Brother or Brute." At the close of the address Birge thanked Bryan and told him that he had found the address "especially interesting since I had not heard such a sermon on Darwin for nearly fifty years." Birge also recorded the next day that he was not sorry that the students had heard the address which was "of the kind so often listened to by their fathers and grandfathers. . . . The address was, as

[29] Birge to William Seaver Woods, February 26, 1923, Presidents' Papers, filed under *Literary Digest.*

[30] Birge to James A. Stone, Milwaukee, September 22, 1921.

[31] Birge to Harold De Wolf Fuller, editor of the *Independent*, October 30, 1923.

you all know, vigorous, eloquent, clear, and beneath it lay a moral purpose none the less high because, as I believe, it was fundamentally mistaken in its methods and conclusions." He added, however, that he regretted that the speech "contained as little of the religious gains of the past half century as it did of its scientific advances. I must say plainly that when one attempts to induce young people to unite their religious faiths to discredited scientific doctrines, he commits a very grievous error and endangers the religious life of those he is trying to help. The leaders of religion in general have learned this lesson, and I can only regret that Colonel Bryan has not done so."[32] In a speech at Monroe, Wisconsin, on September 2, 1921, Bryan attacked Birge. Reports of Bryan's talk were published fifteen days later in the *Capital Times* of Madison and several Chicago papers and were quickly relayed through the country. Newspaper reporters called on Birge and asked for a statement, which Birge was unwilling to make at that time—he wanted to wait until Bryan had completed his charges. Having concluded what he thought was the formal part of the press interview, Birge told the reporters that he had no intention or desire of entering into a newspaper controversy with Bryan. In response to a question he made a statement which one reporter translated to say that Bryan was crazy. The story "leaked" to the *Milwaukee News* and several Chicago papers and was also quickly spread across the country.[33]

Although newspaper comment continued for some months, kept alive largely by the *Capital Times,* and although Birge received communications from widely scattered places throughout the country, both condemning and favoring his position or his alleged position, little interest in the affair was manifested in Wisconsin.[34] Birge himself felt that it had been disposed of

[32] Statement prepared by Birge, May 6, 1921, Presidents' Papers, filed under Bryan.

[33] *Capital Times,* September 17, 1921, p. 1; Aaron Martin Brayton, editor, *Wisconsin State Journal,* to Birge, September 22, 1921. Interview, Irvin G. Wyllie with Grant Hyde, August 9, 1947.

[34] On February 7, 1922, the *Capital Times* printed a long rejoinder written by Bryan. This was followed by a letter printed in the papers (*Capital Times* and *Wisconsin State Journal,* February 17, 1922) and a pamphlet written ostensibly by Birge to his pastor setting forth his religious convictions. Another letter from Bryan and a response by Birge (*Capital Times,* March 7, 27, 1922) completed

in a story which came to him from a professor who, unobserved in a drug store, overheard a salesman telling a group that "all the citizens of the state knew that 'Birge had slept in his pew in the First Congregational Church every Sunday for the past forty years. . . . Birge an atheist! Oh, Hell!' "[35]

Charles Kendall Adams had said that Birge was thought by some people to be cold and unsympathetic. Many could testify that he had a sharp tongue and a sharper pen, that his wit was often mordant, sometimes brutal. When the business manager of the *Octopus,* the student humor magazine, wrote to him apologizing for an advertisement which had appeared in the *Cardinal,* Birge accepted the apology but remarked that "it had never occurred to me that it was notably below the standards of the *Octopus* as regards either taste or wit"; he suggested changing the name of the *Octopus* to the *Tea Hounds' Review* since its chief aim seemed to be "to give the university 'tea hound' a place in which he may publicly show off his uncontrollable amorous propensities, after the manner common to his kind."[36] He reserved his most pungent comments for the makers and circulators of questionnaires. To a young instructor at the University of Michigan who was collecting information on "the modern American university as a social organization" Birge wrote saying that while he never found any pleasure in questionnaires, "I am bound to say that yours seems to be a peculiarly obnoxious one." Birge interpreted a question on socialism as a trap for the unwary. He himself refused to be trapped, but he charged the author with being naïve and remarked, "Indeed,

the exchange in the month before the important question of control of outside speakers came before the regents for final decision.

[35] *The Wisconsin Alumnus,* 44:13 (November, 1942).

[36] Birge to Willard J. Rendall, March 7, 1921. To the editor of the *Cardinal* he once wrote, "I have long recognized the fact that it is useless to make a reference to the Bible in an address. I had not known before that David Copperfield was also included in the list of books which are outside of the reading list of the average student." Birge to the editor of the *Daily Cardinal,* November 19, 1907, Papers of the Dean of the College of Letters and Science. To a member of the faculty who complained about the penetrating and distracting quality of a classroom bell, Birge responded, "You must remember that it is intended to stop a professor, and that this task is not always easy to accomplish." Birge to A. R. Hohlfeld, December 17, 1906, Papers of the Dean of the College of Letters and Science.

one can hardly help wondering how a person with so great naïveté has reached the position of instructor in the University of Michigan."[37] To another information seeker, he wrote, "I wonder how much you can get out of a questionnaire of this sort? I must own that it looks to me something like the survival of the Laputan idea of extracting sunshine from cucumbers. I am obliged to confess that I am not that kind of cucumber. However, let me say on the other side that while I am receiving questionnaires in practically every mail, yours is in a new form and I think you may be congratulated on adding a new terror to human life—at least so far as human life is shared by college presidents."[38] Frederick B. Robinson, secretary-treasurer of the Association of Urban Universities, wrote to President Van Hise, reporting that the University's dues had not been paid. Birge replied that the University of Wisconsin was not a member and was not in a position to contribute much to the discussion of problems of urban universities. "It is, of course, regrettable that institutions should thus fall into classes, but the absence of close connection between your work and ours may perhaps be indicated by the fact that you address your letter to President Van Hise, not knowing that his death occurred more than a year and a half ago." Birge's victims almost never responded, but in this case Robinson answered. He pointed out that the adult education program of urban universities was closely connected with Wisconsin's well-known extension work and that there were many other points of mutual interest. "I am writing these things to you," he concluded, "not in order to persuade you to have your institution represented in our Association, but rather to convince you that I am well aware of what is being done in your University of Wisconsin and am also desirous of encouraging a man in your position to regard an institution like the University of Wisconsin as a great public university, rather than a private rural college in a small town."[39] The pungency was not all on Birge's side.

Even with friends his tone was sometimes sharp, his humor

---

[37] Birge to Robert Angell, University of Michigan, April 30, 1923.

[38] Birge to L. C. Marshall, University of Chicago, April 30, 1925.

[39] Birge to Frederick B. Robinson, May 24, 1920, Robinson to Birge, June 4, 1920, Presidents' Papers, filed under Association of Urban Universities.

wry. When Florence Bascom, daughter of John Bascom, wrote just after the 1920 elections, "Were you among those who stoned the prophet?" Birge responded: "Nobody stones a prophet. He always stones somebody else's prophet. I have no doubt I have done it, though I did not know it at the time. You must tell me whose prophet has been stoned and the kind of stones they were before I can lay claim to any of them." "I am sure you know the prophet to whom I alluded," returned Miss Bascom, "the *only* prophet now in public life, and, pardon me, the more shame to you if he is not your prophet. The prophet is Wilson and the stone is a Harding vote." Birge had the last word. "As to the prophet: To tell the truth I had supposed that La Follette was the prophet that you had in mind rather than Wilson. I am quite ready, however, to accept Wilson as a prophet; all the more because he has made such a mess of things as an administrator. That ordinarily goes with the prophetic temperament. Anyway, I voted for Cox, and you must decide whether that is throwing a stone or a bouquet at the prophet."[40]

During Birge's administration and partly upon his urging buildings began to be named for past presidents. Birge had been instrumental in fixing the name of Paul Chadbourne upon Ladies Hall. He had proposed Chadbourne's name not only because the dormitory was built during his administration but because it amused him that the name of the president who most bitterly opposed coeducation would be permanently fixed to the oldest women's residence hall on the campus.[41] Florence Bascom later wrote indignantly and sadly that at meetings of the "ridiculously young" alumni of the University at Philadelphia she had "been forced to recognize the fact that the name of John Bascom is quite unknown among them." She remarked

[40] Florence Bascom to Birge, November 25, 1920; Birge to Bascom, December 13, 1920; Bascom to Birge, December 18, 1920; Birge to Bascom, December 27, 1920.

[41] To Rudolph Frederick Schuchardt, president of the University of Wisconsin Club of Chicago, Birge explained: "I suppose that I have more responsibility for the selection of that name than any other one person must assume. My reasons were two. First, President Chadbourne secured the appropriation for the building. . . . My second reason is a private one rather than public. I thought it was only fair that Dr. Chadbourne's contumacy regarding coeducation should be punished by attaching his name to a building which turned out [to be] one of the main supports of coeducation." Birge to Schuchardt, March 11, 1922.

that it was "the irony of fate that the name of Chadbourne, whose stay was so brief and whose influence was relatively so ephemeral, should be known to every alumnus of the University." She asked whether some building was to be named for her father.[42] During the next year it was planned to name the central building for John Bascom, and on June 22, 1920, the building was formally dedicated Bascom Hall.

Out of sympathy although certainly not out of touch with the educational changes which began sweeping the country after the first World War, and unwilling to sponsor major changes in either the organization or direction of the University during his term in office, Birge was nevertheless completely devoted to the University he had served so long in so many capacities. And while from time to time he was disturbed by the presence of large numbers of students and felt that the University was crowded beyond its capacity, he never lost his basic sympathy with the rights of students; as dean he had always responded to honest appeals for advice, whether from prospective students, from students in difficulty, or from parents seeking guidance. His formula for success was honest hard work and as dean and president he urged this course upon the students. He never minimized the difficulties which might be in a student's way. In his relations with student malefactors he was always firm, impersonal, and usually inflexible. Though he was no doubt often touched by sympathy for parents or for students in disgrace, his sympathy never noticeably influenced his judgment. These traits he retained as president. Although he lacked the warmth of Adams, he was no less anxious than Adams had been that students should enjoy the stimulating intellectual atmosphere of the University.

In Birge, both as dean and president, the students had a defender. In matters concerning the personal conduct of students, he agreed to a large extent with Bascom in desiring as few controls as possible; to the numerous complaints that came to him as president, many charging excess of drinking among the students, his characteristic response was to minimize the charges.

---

[42] Florence Bascom to Birge, September 4, 1918.

When Regent Florence Buckstaff complained that the general tone of student behavior was low and that boys were learning to drink at the fraternity houses, Birge replied: "The situation regarding drinking among the students is unquestionably a very bad one. There is a great deal less miscellaneous drinking of the light type which used to go on—beer, etc.—but there is decidedly more drinking of whisky." He was not sure that there was more drunkenness; what there was, was more conspicuous. But the problem was not restricted to the University of Wisconsin; all other universities faced it. Drinking, which had once been the vice of the poor, was now the vice of the well-to-do. Nevertheless he was sure the University must not appoint, as Mrs. Buckstaff proposed, a University agent to spy out things of this sort.[43] When Mrs. Buckstaff again complained, this time that members of the Haresfoot Club had been drinking at Oshkosh, Birge calmly replied that such reports were made "with regard to substantially every party that is given at the University. . . . We regret such a situation as much as any one can, but the inference that all of these boys are drunkards is wholly unjust." He agreed that prohibition had increased the difficulties of the University in the matter of student drinking but suspected that the condition would continue so long as whisky could be easily obtained. "Incidentally, I am told that it is especially easy to procure whisky in Oshkosh, though I have no personal knowledge of the facts."[44]

If not an uncritical champion of the students, Birge firmly refused to take a parochial view of their behavior. Sometimes he lectured those who complained about student conduct. The manager of a local teachers' agency wrote demanding that a student accused of stealing evergreens from the grounds of a Madison resident be permanently expelled. "It seems to me that any action short of permanent expulsion would be insufficient. University funds ought not to be wasted in the attempt to educate such criminals." Birge replied that students had paid for the damage. He observed that people were often anxious for the

[43] Florence Buckstaff to Birge, September 12, 1921; Birge to Buckstaff, September 14, 1921.
[44] Birge to Florence Buckstaff, April 20, 1922.

expulsion of "students guilty of misconduct, so long as the case is an abstract one; as soon, however, as it develops that the son or daughter of a neighbor is the person concerned the anxiety for expulsion is immediately converted into an equally great anxiety to 'give the student another chance.' "[45]

FEW problems of the Birge administration attracted more attention and, in some quarters, more unfavorable notice, than that of the control of visiting lecturers invited by student organizations to speak before the student body. The regents had delegated authority to the president to approve or disapprove all applications from student groups for meeting places in University buildings. Van Hise had not formulated a wholly satisfactory policy in this matter and his judgments had in several cases caused both indignation and consternation. President Birge had similar experiences.

The postwar period, it will be recalled, was one of intense and often irrational feeling. During the war men had been sent to jail for words said or written—Eugene Debs and Victor Berger among them. Immediately after the war had come the notorious "red hunts" conducted by the Department of Justice, the deportations of "undesirable aliens," the revival of the Ku Klux Klan, and many other nativist activities. Yet while the nation drifted toward "normalcy" with Harding and Coolidge, the progressive wing of the Republican Party triumphed in Wisconsin. In the state the trend seemed to be to the left rather than to the right. But the support Governor Philipp had given the University, coupled with the opposition of prominent members of the University faculty to Senator La Follette's stand on the war, led to the charge that the University was becoming an agency of conservatives. We need not here be concerned with whether this was true or not. The charge was frequently made, and Birge's policy on outside speakers was often interpreted in these terms. The moves to displace Professor Kahlenberg and to remove Professor Bruns had been construed in some quarters as evidence

[45] W. E. Chase to Birge, January 16, 1922; Birge to Chase, January 19, 1922.

of nativist inclinations in the University.[46] Various rumors, some of them growing out of the war, supported this belief. Thus in 1919 a correspondent informed President Birge that Professor Robert Herrick of the University of Chicago had declared publicly that the daughters of Victor Berger had been "ostracized" at the University. President Birge, contending that the girls had not been ostracized, admitted they were unpopular because they believed thoroughly in their father and shared his opinions. "Since Mr. Berger's opinions were sufficient to secure him a conviction in court and exclusion from Congress, they were not likely to be very popular among the young women at the university."[47]

Evidence of a public touchiness was apparent. At the January meeting of the Board of Regents, the Wisconsin State Association Opposed to Women Suffrage protested the use of University buildings by the suffragists, contending that the University "has no right to permit the use of the University for the promotion of any disputed issue."[48] The regents proposed that the complaint be answered by pointing out that the policy on use of buildings by students was to grant requests "as far as physical conditions permit providing the purposes in view are not inconsistent with objects sought in the creation of the University."[49] Late in the month, the *National Equity News,* published in Madison, denounced John R. Commons for his part in a public discussion of unemployment and urged that farmer members of the legislatures in the various states see to it that no more appropriations be given the universities until the farmer was given a square deal.[50] Within the next months the University was criticized by left wing members of the legislature then in session for being intolerant and reactionary,[51] and a bill was

[46] John S. Roeseler to Governor E. L. Philipp, February 3, 1919, Presidents' Papers, filed under Kahlenberg; Frederick Bruns to Birge, March 5, 1920, Presidents' Papers, filed under Hohlfeld; Birge to Hohlfeld, March 15, 1920. See pp. 324 ff.

[47] Ruth Marshall to Birge, November 16, 1919; Birge to Marshall, November 26, 1919.

[48] Papers of the Board of Regents, January 15, 1919; Records of the Board of Regents, J:245, January 12, 1919.

[49] Papers of the Board of Regents, March 5, 1919.

[50] *National Equity News* (Madison), January 30, 1919, p. 4.

[51] *Daily Cardinal*, February 3, April 2, 1919.

introduced to give labor and agriculture representation on the Board of Regents. President Birge was opposed to such legislation. He refused "to accept the idea that America is definitely and permanently composed of classes or interests, and that these classes and interests ought to be represented as such on our educational governing boards."[52] The bill was not passed, but the next year before elections the *Wisconsin State Journal* warned that the representatives of the Non-Partisan League and the Socialists were preparing an attack on the University in the next legislature because, it was charged, the University and the Philipp administration had limited free speech and free thought and destroyed the policy of democracy which had existed when La Follette was governor.[53]

The University was belabored also from the right. A lumber merchant of Rhinelander protested to the regents about Professor E. A. Ross's "decided 'Pro-Red' opinions." While not urging that Ross be dismissed without further investigation, he proposed that if it were proved that Ross was "sympathetically inclined toward sovietism" he should be dismissed.[54] A Milwaukee attorney complained when he heard that syndicalist William Z. Foster was to speak at the University. While not opposed to Foster's appearance, the writer felt the students should know what his doctrine would lead to, "stripped of all disguises," so that an honest judgment could be made on him and his work.[55] President Birge in this case reported that Foster had not been offensive in his speech. He explained that the organization which brought him, the Social Science Club, wanted to have speakers who represented all shades of opinion, and that it was making a sincere effort to bring all sides of social questions to the attention of the student public.

"I think you will see," he concluded, "that under such conditions any attempt on the part of the University to refuse to allow such an organization to bring speakers here would be very unwise, unless we felt sure that the speech would be one of a revolutionary character. A censorship of speeches in this coun-

---

[52] Birge to State Senator Roy P. Wilcox, April 14, 1919.

[53] *Wisconsin State Journal,* July 30, 1920.

[54] Webster A. Brown to the Board of Regents, April 12, 1920, in Papers of the Board of Regents, May 26, 1920.   [55] George E. Morton to Birge, January 7, 1921.

try is ordinarily unwise, and a very clear necessity for such censorship must be shown before a public institution should attempt to exercise it."[56] Birge here outlined a policy which, had it been followed scrupulously, might have avoided a great deal of unfavorable publicity later. His correspondent was satisfied with the answer although he reported that he had "heard a great deal of complaint in the last few years that the University of Wisconsin was a hotbed for 'parlor socialism.' " He felt that with proper precautions this reputation could be minimized.[57]

The local newspapers, particularly the *Capital Times,* were alert for evidence of repression of "liberalism" at the University. In June, 1921, the *Capital Times* reported that a professor of English had resigned to accept another position, and implied that it was because he could not hope for advancement at Wisconsin. "There is a cabal in the faculty that is opposed to the promotion or advancement of members of the faculty who have any liberal or advanced ideas. For the good of the university, this inside ring eventually ought to be smashed." The professor, who had introduced Max Eastman in 1916, flatly contradicted the *Times's* interpretation.[58]

In 1921 events rapidly moved to a crisis. In June the *Delineator* presented the first of a series of three articles by Vice-President Calvin Coolidge entitled "Enemies of the Republic." In these articles Coolidge discussed radicalism in the colleges and universities and asserted that the University of Wisconsin Socialist Club was "said to be the largest" in the country.[59] The charge was of course noticed by Wisconsin papers.

Whether for this or other reasons, President Birge became uneasy and the Board of Regents reluctant to have the buildings of the University used for certain speakers that the Social Science Club wanted to bring to Madison. In October, 1921, the regents refused the request of the Federated Press League of Madison for use of the gymnasium for an address by Lincoln Steffens.[60] Others, no more inflammatory, were denied the use of University rooms to make public addresses sponsored by the

[56] Birge to Morton, January 12, 1921.   [57] Morton to Birge, January 13, 1921.
[58] *Capital Times,* June 1, 4, 1921.
[59] Calvin Coolidge, "Enemies of the Republic," *The Delineator,* 98:4, 5 (June, 1921).   [60] Records of the Board of Regents, K:123, October 12, 1921.

Social Science Club. No ban was more widely advertised than that imposed upon Scott Nearing. Nearing had not yet attained the fame which was to be his after the president of Brown University broke up a Nearing meeting by turning out the lights, but he did have the distinction of being called a "dangerous radical."

The initial decision to refuse the student group the use of the gymnasium for Nearing had been made by a faculty committee of which Professor Jastrow was chairman, but the decision had been approved by President Birge, who received both the credit and the blame. For once the two newspapers in Madison were in agreement. In a front-page story the *Capital Times* spoke of the "arrogant spirit" of the institution and announced: "The university rostrum is still closed to liberals of the country seeking a hearing at the university."[61] Naturally the speech was given full coverage.[62] The student paper protested the president's decision in an editorial entitled "Shall We Know the Truth?"[63] President Birge promptly wrote to the *Cardinal* charging that the editorial contained only "a modicum of that most desirable product." He explained that University platforms were "affected with a public interest." Public lectures, given in University buildings, he wrote, were regarded as a part of the "educational opportunities" of the University. Under the regents' rules, the president had to pass on the men who appeared on the University platforms. "So long as this is the situation, the president must use his best judgment in every case presented to him, and he ought to use it and does use it with the widest sympathy toward every student organization."[64]

The *Wisconsin State Journal* devoted all of its editorial space to a discussion of the case. The *Journal* felt that the University had managed to give Nearing more advertising than he could otherwise have gotten. It questioned the wisdom of the University policy, asserting that the students could listen to such men without being corrupted. It warned, "Offer bibs and sugar teats to a football-nurtured student body and you are sure to provoke

[61] *Capital Times,* October 31, 1921.
[62] *Ibid.,* November 1, 1921.
[63] *Daily Cardinal,* November 1, 1921.
[64] Birge to the editor, *Daily Cardinal,* November 1, 1921.

an intellectual riot."[65] A Milwaukee engineer, while dissociating himself from the ideas Nearing represented, protested what he thought was an abridgment of free speech. A teacher in the New York School of Social Work took a similar position.[66] Julius Kiesner, Socialist member of the Wisconsin Assembly, was incensed that a person in as "high and noble standing as Scott Nearing" should be denied the right to speak.[67] On the other hand, a Rhinelander businessman wrote to Birge and Jastrow expressing his "deepest appreciation for the splendid attitude you have taken in this matter."[68] To both the Socialist and the businessman Birge wrote that whatever he did he was blamed, and to the former he declared, "I shall have to do the best I can under such conditions, and . . . the people of the state will have to appreciate the situation and to bear with me."[69]

The president's best was widely questioned. Several days before the regular December meeting of the regents the *Capital Times* reported that members of the Board had received petitions from the Social Science Club asking that the "ban" on speakers be lifted. The mayor of Madison and the editor of the *Capital Times* were among those who had signed the petition.[70] Several days later the *Wisconsin State Journal* ran a long article, including front-page pictures of prominent members of the Social Science Club, discussing the "contest" between the club and the Board of Regents. Theodore Kronshage, newly appointed member of the Board, it was reported, would lead the fight for the removal of censorship. The opinions of Governor Blaine, President Birge, and a number of others were given. Michael Olbrich, a prominent Madison attorney closely associated with the Blaine administration, offered Justice Holmes's statement from *Abrams vs. United States*: "The best test of truth is the power [of the thought] to get itself accepted in the competition of the market." In an editorial which appeared the same day, the *State Journal*

[65] *Wisconsin State Journal*, November 3, 1921, p. 3.
[66] Arthur J. Sweet to Birge, November 2, 1921; John A. Fitch to Birge, November 18, 1921.
[67] Julius Kiesner to Birge, November 7, 1921.
[68] J. W. Jones to Joseph Jastrow and Birge, November 4, 1921.
[69] Birge to Kiesner, November 15, 1921; Birge to Jones, November 15, 1921.
[70] *Capital Times*, December 1, 1921.

again discussed the Scott Nearing case and sympathized with the Social Science Club.[71]

At the regents' meeting, President Birge presented two papers on the problem of outside speakers; the first was largely a report and the second a discussion of the request of the Social Science Club. He talked of having permitted William Z. Foster to speak and of refusing to permit Scott Nearing to use a University platform. He had been condemned for both decisions. Because of this he wanted his position clearly understood. The student organizations had not been forbidden to have speakers that they wanted to hear: those who had been banned had wanted to address the general student body. They were speakers who proposed to discuss social and political matters and often they were representatives of propaganda organizations. When the University authorities did give permission for the use of its platform, many people assumed that this gave a "sort of quasi-endorsement to the views thus presented to students." Birge would not acknowledge the validity of this assumption, but he felt that from it stemmed the principal difficulties. He drew a distinction between the speakers who appeared before a general University assemblage and those in regular lecture rooms where all views were presented and discussed. The general lectures, he said, were "devoted rather to advocacy than to discussion and intended primarily to influence those who have made no study of the subject." He asserted that "the fundamental principle of those who present these social speakers to me is that every one has an equal and complete right to the university platform for the purpose of urging his views upon the students at large and that no distinction should be made between speakers whether bigot, conservative, liberal, radical, revolutionist, or crank, and whether in the scientific, social, or religious fields." This position he felt differed widely from that long held by the University, which did not approve of "instruction that is partisan in politics or sectarian in religion." He felt that his discretionary power under the regents' rules should be used not to limit freedom of University teaching but to extend it to the widest limits

[71] *Wisconsin State Journal*, December 4, 1921, pp. 1, 3.

consistent with maintenance of that freedom. If that power was exercised, criticism from both sides was bound to follow and "since actions will necessarily concern 'marginal cases' in my own judgment it may well be that both criticisms will be right." Such decisions, he said, "will represent my best judgment, and . . . I should welcome any rule or statement of principles by the regents which may direct my decision and so relieve me of the duty of exercising that judgment." [72]

Birge made a longer, somewhat similar statement in connection with the request from a representative of the Social Science Club for a definite statement of policy from the regents by which a speaker would be approved or refused, and for the establishment of an open forum committee on which the students would be represented. [73] Birge doubted that the propaganda which Calvin Coolidge deplored had much ill effect—after all students for a thousand years had had "such ideas presented to them and much ferment has thereby been caused." He thought that the students would go to hear propagandists whatever the University did. Nor did he think that the question of free speech was involved: "Any agitator can find a place to speak without let or hindrance." The real question was which persons ought to be permitted to speak before University students from a University platform. This was a question of administration rather than of constitutional principle. He reiterated his belief that a speaker who appeared on the University platforms was considered to have been approved by the University; and he said that there were many propagandists who wanted to speak to students. On the other hand, parents had entrusted their children to the University to be educated. "The question which I have constantly asked myself as any concrete case arises is 'What would the wise parent of a boy or girl who is here want me to do in this case?' " If the open forum was permitted, he said, "every propagandist of every sort of doctrine—religious, scientific, or social—is to be given full and free opportunity by the regents to use the facilities of the university to teach his doctrines and to secure proselytes from among the

[72] Birge to the regents, n.d., Presidents' Papers, filed under Social Science Club.
[73] Records of the Board of Regents, K:134–135, December 7, 1921.

youth committed to us by their parents." This he did not think parents would condone. At the same time he recognized that not all could be satisfied. Students must come in contact with the movements of thought in the world. "I believe that while people may and do differ with regard to the wisdom of our decision in a given case, they have confidence in our general policy and the motives which determine it. But I do not believe that they wish this matter of lecturers determined by propagandist societies outside of the university or by students affiliated with such societies or sympathetic with their work. The responsibility of deciding on lecturers belongs in large measure to me." On the other hand he felt that parents did not expect their children to be "kept in a sort of intellectual cotton wool. They are to be trained to face the problems of the day as they will meet them in after life." Yet he felt that the University could enjoy a large freedom within the rules proscribing instruction "sectarian in religion or partisan in politics." He concluded with the question, "Is it at all clear that the operation of the 'open forum,' converting the university lectures into a 'free for all' among contending propagandists and proselyters, would seem to the people of the state so much a 'forward movement' to be hailed with delight, as an intolerable nuisance to be abated?"[74]

Against this view the student petitioners had but little chance of winning approval for establishment of an open forum. After discussion by the Board, it was recommended that the representative of the Social Science Club bring the matter before other student groups to work out a plan acceptable to all students. The plan could then be presented to the regents.[75]

This decision apparently satisfied no one. The *Capital Times* announced that the student petition had been smothered by the regents and denounced the action in an editorial.[76] The *State Journal,* although more temperate, was also unsatisfied.[77] At the January regents' meeting, the student representatives were again present, this time with a proposal of a constitution, already

[74] Birge to the regents, in Papers of the Board of Regents, December 7, 1921.
[75] Records of the Board of Regents, K:135, December 7, 1921.
[76] *Capital Times,* December 8, 1921, pp. 1, 12; December 10, 1921, p. 1.
[77] *Wisconsin State Journal,* December 11, 1921, pp. 1, 3.

approved by the Student Senate, for a student forum board. It provided for a forum board consisting of six students and a member of the faculty who would be appointed by the Student Senate. This board would pass on all speakers brought to the University by student organizations. The decisions of the forum board would in turn be controlled by a set of guiding principles, one of which was that the speaker should be known "to present material of educational value as opposed to an emotional or similar appeal."[78] The regents also received at this meeting a petition from the University of Wisconsin Club of Duluth which opposed giving "propagandists" the right to use University buildings.[79] The regents followed President Birge's reasoning in disposing of the student request. They adopted a resolution declaring that the regents had the "ultimate control of university buildings and a measure of responsibility for the speakers who speak from a university platform. The regents cannot, consistently with their duty, divest themselves of this control and responsibility."[80] They then turned the student request over to the regent committee on student life and interests.[81]

Birge in the meantime had begun to doubt whether the Social Science Club wanted both sides of a question represented. In response to the proposal from Regent Florence Buckstaff, member of the regent committee on student life and interests, that the plan of the Student Senate be given a trial, Birge declared that the club had always been a "definitely propagandist organization for socialistic doctrines. . . . They are now trying to get their organization into a position where it will be recognized by the Regents as substantially the official purveyor of extracurricular instruction in matters relating to economics and society." This he thought was unwise. He felt a solution to the problem might be found either by continuing the present situation, under which he would exercise the final control, by establishing a student-faculty committee with faculty outnumbering the student representatives, or by permitting a stu-

[78] Papers of the Board of Regents, January 18, 1922; Records of the Board of Regents, K:148, January 18, 1922.
[79] Papers of the Board of Regents, January 18, 1922.
[80] Records of the Board of Regents, K:150, January 18, 1922.   [81] *Ibid.*, p. 151.

President Birge

The University in 1923

dent committee to pass on speakers. Although asserting that he had no strong feeling as to which policy should be adopted, he felt that if a student committee was to be named, care must be taken to have the committee representative.[82]

When the regents met on March 1, they received a communication from the Student Senate with a new plan for an open forum and an acknowledgment that final authority rested with the regents.[83] Action on the communication and on the report of the committee on student life and interests was postponed to the next meeting.[84] But if the regents felt that postponement of a decision would lessen interest in the question, they were to be disappointed. Several related and unrelated incidents served to give the next meeting of the regents exceptional prominence. Early in February, Thomas A. Edison had circulated a questionnaire on money and banking to leading authorities for the purpose, he said, of collecting authoritative opinions on problems of finance. Professor William A. Scott was among the experts to whom he had appealed. At the end of February, Scott, thinking, as he later told President Birge, that Edison was collecting this information to "supply material for Henry Ford's propaganda of monetary heresy," wrote Edison a very frank note saying that nothing short of a "treatise on the subject of Money and Banking" would answer his questions. He went on to say that he could not understand how a man who had seriously studied the subject could ask such questions. "They betray to me an utter lack of comprehension of even the ABC of the subject. . . . I doubt very much whether at your age and in what seems to be your present state of mind it would be worth anyone's while to attempt to teach you those elements." Edison reported the matter to President Birge, the members of the Board of Regents, and the Board of Visitors. Scott immediately apologized and Edison accepted his apology and pronounced the end of the incident.[85] Less than a week later the *Capital Times* obtained

[82] Birge to Florence Buckstaff, February 24, 1922.
[83] Papers of the Board of Regents, March 1, 1922.
[84] Records of the Board of Regents, K: 167-168, March 1, 1922.
[85] William A. Scott to Thomas A. Edison, February 27, 1922; Scott to Birge, March 8, 1922; Edison to Birge, March 3, 1922; Edison to Scott, March 16, 1922.

copies of the letters and published them. A storm broke.[86] It was predicted that the regents at their next meeting would accept Scott's request for a year's leave of absence.

Then in April, William Jennings Bryan returned to his attack on Birge for religious unorthodoxy. His letter was given full space in one of the Madison papers.[87] The Social Science Club, far from subdued, had come to the president with a list of speakers to ask informally which of them he would approve. He would not approve Mrs. Kate Richards O'Hare, Socialist candidate for the vice-presidency in 1920, if application were made, and he would not approve Upton Sinclair unless a speaker were found to present the other side of the question.[88] Accordingly the Social Science Club did not ask permission for Mrs. O'Hare. Instead, arrangements were made to have her give her address in the capitol.[89] State officials, rather than President Birge, were attacked in this instance.[90] One other incident focused attention on the regents' meeting. Two University students had married secretly. Dean Goodnight discovered it and asked them to withdraw from the University because they had violated University rules. The students, both of legal age, carried the matter to the Board of Regents.[91]

Five days before the regents met, Upton Sinclair had arrived in Madison to visit his son, then a student at the University, and to give a public address under the auspices of the Social Science Club.[92] It was already reported that Birge had refused to give him permission to speak in a University building.[93] Sinclair announced that he intended to discuss the matter with the presi-

[86] *Capital Times,* March 22, 1922.
[87] *Ibid.,* April 7, 1922.
[88] Birge to Benjamin Faast, March 29, 1922.
[89] *Capital Times,* March 28, 31, 1922.
[90] The accompanying uproar amused President Birge. "When I look at the row in Clark University over Scott Nearing and consider the difficulties which the officials at the Capitol are finding in the matter of Mrs. O'Hare, I must own that I feel that I guessed right in keeping the University out of those situations. I cannot suppose however, that Mr. Sygman [president of the Social Science Club] will agree with me." Birge to Faast, March 29, 1922.
[91] *Capital Times,* April 28, 1922.
[92] *Ibid.* Upton Sinclair later stated that it was Birge's unwillingness to allow him the use of a University platform which induced him to stop off at Madison. Upton Sinclair, *The Goose-Step: A Study of American Education* (Pasadena, 1922), 223.　　　　　　[93] *Capital Times,* April 28, 1922.

dent.[94] At the meeting, Birge suggested that Sinclair write a letter and he would answer. This Sinclair did, giving his reasons for wanting to speak from a University platform. He invited Birge or any member of the faculty or the students to question him.[95] Birge however had made up his mind. He felt the matter of deciding the question of public speakers was in the hands of the regents, and he would not change his first decision.[96] Sinclair then gave copies of the letters and an interview to the *Capital Times*. The superintendent of public schools offered the use of the high school for the address Sinclair proposed to deliver.[97] But it was not just a hall that Sinclair and his friends wanted. It was a room in a University building. The *Capital Times* came up with an editorial attack on Regent Horlick;[98] the *State Journal* published the notice that the Madison council of the Federated Press League, which had entertained Sinclair at a dinner, was petitioning the regents to permit Sinclair to make his speech in a University building.[99] Sinclair himself announced his decision to carry his request in person to the regents.

It was in the midst of this turmoil that the regents came together on May 2 to dispose of the vexatious problem of control of outside lecturers. University authorities had meanwhile sought advice from other institutions[100] and much advice had been offered gratuitously. The Gun and Blade Club, an organization of two hundred disabled veterans of the World War,

[94] *Ibid.* Sinclair's account of the interview appears in *The Goose-Step*, 223–226.
[95] Sinclair to Birge, April 28, 1922, Presidents' Papers, filed under Social Science Club.
[96] Birge to Sinclair, April 29, 1922, Presidents' Papers, filed under Social Science Club.
[97] *Capital Times, Wisconsin State Journal,* April 29, 1922.
[98] *Capital Times,* May 1, 1922.   [99] *Wisconsin State Journal,* April 30, 1922.
[100] Dean Sellery canvassed his former colleagues, William L. Westermann at Cornell, Dana Carleton Munro at Princeton, Frederick Jackson Turner at Harvard, and Thomas Sewall Adams at Yale. He explained the difficulties which the University was experiencing and asked each whether something comparable to the proposed open forum existed at his university and what type of control the university exercised. (Sellery to Westermann, and others, April 19, 1922.) All answered, but none described a situation which Wisconsin could very well imitate. Adams wrote: "I should lean always in the direction of the open forum; and would refuse the use of University rooms and halls only if it were reasonably certain that the people of Wisconsin, through their represenatives, objected to the 'open forum' in this sense." Adams to Sellery, April 27, 1922, Papers of the Dean of the College of Letters and Science. Earlier Sellery had consulted with

presented a resolution condemning the Social Science Club "without reserve, as a group of un-American radicals and extremists, who are continuously inciting unrest among the Student Body" and requesting that the regents abolish the organization and "go on record as strongly opposing the uncensored right of irresponsible groups or clubs to bring any and all speakers to the University." In transmitting the resolution the president of the club came suspiciously close to threatening violence by saying that a repetition of the Kate Richards O'Hare incident "would precipitate a crisis which the heads of Service Organizations here could not prevent, and cause a probable riot in which some would be sure to be hurt."[101]

The Madison newspapers seemed more interested in Upton Sinclair than in the settlement of the general problem. The *Wisconsin State Journal* announced in a banner headline that the Sinclair case was taken up by the regents.[102] In the *Capital Times* of May 2 love interest competed with Upton Sinclair. The newspaper gave one headline to the reinstatement of the married students, another to Upton Sinclair. In an editorial the *Capital Times* denounced the regents for violating the law by conducting closed meetings.[103] The *Cardinal* exhibited a discreet interest in the regents' decision, although the opening games of the baseball schedule and a campaign to get freshmen to wear green caps occupied more space.[104]

Upton Sinclair formally presented three communications to the regents: a request for an opportunity to explain to the Board his reasons for wanting to use a University hall to address the students; a protest against the regents' "violation of the law by discussing the question of academic control of speakers secretly, when the public wishes to know what is going on"; and, last, a

deans of the colleges of liberal arts of the state universities of the South and Middle West and found in almost all cases approval of outside speakers rested with the dean and the president. "It was the general opinion in conversation with these men that their institutions could not tolerate a situation in which the president would not be able to exclude an objectionable speaker. One of the men remarked that it would be preposterous to think that the admission of speakers to a university platform could be transferred by the regents and their chief official, the president of the university, to any student organization or committee." Sellery to Birge, April 24, 1922.

[101] Papers of the Board of Regents, May 2, 1922.

[102] *Wisconsin State Journal*, May 2, 1922.

[103] *Capital Times*, May 2, 1922.   [104] *Daily Cardinal*, May 2, 1922.

statement that if the use of the gymnasium were granted, "I shall not make use of the occasion to refer to any controversy concerning this matter."[105] Sinclair was given ten minutes to present his case to the regents. He took thirty-five. Then, on motion of Theodore Kronshage, the regents voted informally to express approval of the request. The motion was carried by a vote of 7 to 4.[106] This was notice to Birge to give Sinclair and the Social Science Club permission to use the gymnasium. The Madison papers announced the "victory" in headlines.[107]

There was, however, one unexpected result. Professor Ross had agreed to introduce Sinclair. But Sinclair in an interview declared: "It is a class struggle and President Birge is on the side of special privilege." Whereupon Professor Ross indignantly refused to introduce the speaker. He resented, he declared in a public statement, the attack on Birge, "I have been here sixteen years and I have never experienced from Dr. Birge as dean or president, the least pressure to say or not to say, do or not do, anything my conscience prompted." Nor, so far as he knew, had anyone else.[108]

More significant was the action of the regents on the matter of the open forum constitution. Birge had opposed granting to a student group the authority to approve outside speakers. His desire was respected. Regent Elizabeth Waters reported for the committee on student life and interests, recommending that the students' request for approval of an open forum constitution be refused. Instead the committee proposed the following addition to the bylaws: "The action of the Board of Regents in 1894, 'whatever may be the limitations which trammel inquiry elsewhere, we believe that the Great State of Wisconsin should ever encourage that continual and fearless sifting and winnowing by which alone the truth can be found,' shall be applicable to teaching in the classroom and to the use of university halls for public addresses, under the control of the President of the University with appeal to the Regents." This proposal was adopted by the Board.[109] Its action largely escaped the notice of the press, but

[105] Upton Sinclair to the Board of Regents, Papers of the Board of Regents, May 2, 1922. [106] Papers of the Board of Regents, May 2, 1922.
[107] *Capital Times,* and *Wisconsin State Journal,* May 3, 1922.
[108] *Capital Times,* May 3, 1922.
[109] Records of the Board of Regents, K:180–181, May 2, 1922.

it was significant in affording the president another and perhaps better touchstone than the one he had hitherto employed in making his judgments. Upton Sinclair in his own account of the incident made no mention of this decision of the regents, although he gave space to various details of the meeting.[110]

But the decision seemed to have broken the tension. Thereafter, criticisms of the University became fewer, and President Birge even managed to add a jovial touch in some of his rejoinders to complaints.[111] Only once thereafter did the president appeal to the regents for a decision on an outside speaker. In the spring of 1923 the Social Science Club asked for permission to use the gymnasium for an address by Eugene Debs. Birge wrote to all members of the Board asking their opinions. Regent Kohler replied that if it were a matter of personal preference he would oppose it, but that if the room were denied there would be "an engineered storm of public protest by a few."[112] Only one regent opposed. Unfortunately, somebody managed to turn out the lights in the gymnasium after the audience gathered to hear Debs, so the meeting did not escape wide notice. In fact, some irresponsible people even attempted to hold President Birge personally accountable. Although the president continued to receive objections about outside speakers, no excitement comparable to that engendered during 1921 and 1922 developed during the remainder of his term. It had been demonstrated that the great statement of 1894 was a shield as well as a weapon.

⌒

PRESIDENT Birge reached his seventieth year in 1921 and began his forty-sixth year of service in the University, but there was no open discussion of his retirement.[113] As he approached

---

[110] Sinclair, *The Goose-Step*, 227–228.

[111] In 1923 George Banta wrote objecting to something said by an assistant in economics. Birge pointed out that even if the person had made the remark as charged, it was in a personal conversation. "The university professor," he wrote, "has the same right to make a fool of himself in conversation that belongs to every free-born American citizen." Birge to Banta, March 8, 1923.

[112] Kohler to Birge, March 29, 1923; Birge to S. H. Goodnight, April 2, 1923, both in the Presidents' Papers, filed under Debs.

[113] *The Wisconsin Alumnus*, 44:17 (November, 1942).

his fiftieth year in service, the decision could no longer be postponed. The conservative forces in the state politics had given way to the La Follette Progressives in 1920, and in the ensuing years, as had been the case during Birge's earlier period of service as acting president, the complexion of the Board changed. By 1924 appointees of Governor Blaine were beginning to predominate; a year later, they did. In 1924, the Board again created a committee to search for a new president. The elder Senator La Follette interested himself in helping to find an incumbent. It was an open secret that he sought to have Professor Robert Morss Lovett named to the position.[114] But apparently neither the Board of Regents nor Lovett was much interested.[115] Lincoln Steffens intimated to La Follette his willingness to be considered for the position, but nothing came of it.[116]

The nominating committee at length proposed Dean Roscoe Pound of the Harvard Law School, and the selection was approved unanimously by the regents. A committee went east to talk with Pound, and Birge wrote cordially to him expressing his satisfaction with the choice. Pound, however, declined the offer, because, he explained to Birge, "There are great things to be done in legal scholarship, and on full consideration my life's task seemed to be there. Likewise, Mrs. Pound shrank from assuming the duties necessarily devolving upon the wife of the President of a great University."[117] Having failed to attract Dean Pound, the nominating committee delayed briefly in the East. One of the members, generally supposed to be Regent Zona Gale, proposed Glenn Frank, then the editor of the *Century Magazine*. The proposal attracted attention; Frank

[114] Based on memoranda and letters in the Olbrich Papers, State Historical Society of Wisconsin.

[115] Milton Mayer ascribed Lovett's lack of interest to a message from John R. Commons: "A Christian like you wouldn't last a week." Milton Mayer, "Portrait of a Dangerous Man," *Harper's* (July, 1946), 63.

[116] *The Letters of Lincoln Steffens* (2 vols., New York, 1938), 2:696–697.

[117] Birge to Roscoe Pound, January 23, 1925; Pound to Birge, February 9, 1925. There were numerous other explanations for Pound's refusal. As is often the case in such matters, candor is not expected, and the real reason and the stated reason are often mixed in the conveying. Thus one regent wrote Birge to say that one of the reasons that Dean Pound refused the offer was his dislike "for some of Wisconsin's politics." Alexander Horlick to Birge, February 19, 1925. The *Wisconsin State Journal* reported that he refused because of the poor financial condition

himself showed interest. At a special meeting on May 29, the regents formally approved the appointment of Glenn Frank as president. At the regular meeting in June the Board ratified an agreement made with the new president, who was to enter office September 1, 1925. At the same meeting the Board accepted President Birge's resignation and elected him president emeritus.[118]

For the first time in twenty-five years the presidency of the University was entrusted to a man unfamiliar with the institution; for the second time in history the regents selected a man for president whose experience lay largely outside of university life. On the first occasion, perhaps unknown by the Board of 1925, the president's uneasy tenure of office had been terminated awkwardly by the regents.

of the University and because he feared that politics would hamper his work if he accepted. The *Wisconsin State Journal*, February 4, 1925. Walter J. Kohler sent Birge a clipping from the New York *World* quoting Felix Frankfurter as saying that "if Roscoe Pound should leave his job here to become President, even of Harvard, it would be one of the most crying wastes in our history. It would be a piece of unwisdom reaching the height of a calamity . . . . If the law is to continue to be made for men and not men for law the job must have the utmost abilities of men like Dean Pound." Kohler to Birge, February 12, 1925.

[118] Records of the Board of Regents, L:78,79, June 22, 1925.

5.

Getting and Spending: 1903–1914

D URING the first decades of the twentieth century the University moved rapidly from its position as a medium-sized business venture into that of a large-scale agency. In the fiscal year 1900–1901 the total receipts of the University from all sources amounted to $502,341.01. Twenty-five years later the total receipts of the University amounted to $6,951,340.77. This rate of increase did not continue over the next ten years. During the fiscal year of 1936 total receipts amounted to $7,717,814.25. Five years later they exceeded ten million.

As late as 1910 the contribution of the state amounted to more than three-quarters of the whole amount, but ten years later it had decreased to a little more than half of it. In part this showed the reluctance of the state to continue increasing its contribution; in part it indicated the increased contribution from the federal government and from private gifts, but in large measure it reflected the widening business activity of the University, which involved management of dormitories, dining rooms, the Memorial Union, the hospital, athletic contests, sale of farm products, and numerous other enterprises. On the whole these receipts shown each year in the official report merely represented collections by the University for bedding, feeding, and entertaining students; the disbursements canceled out the receipts. Although these activities were necessary in the academic community, they represented essentially noneducational

159

functions. The law required an annual report showing all receipts and expenditures. The careless reader of these reports often derived a wholly distorted impression of the prosperity of the University. But this bookkeeping should not obscure the large part the state's contribution had played and must play in maintaining educational activities of the University.

Like all other growing organizations the University had to accommodate itself to its enlarged business activities by adding new officers with new duties. In 1906, partly as a result of legislative criticism, the University accounting system was reorganized and the office of University auditor established. Up to then general supervision of the University accounts had been in the hands of the secretary of the Board of Regents, and auditing had been done by a committee of the Board. The new system, with an auditor to make a daily check on receipts and disbursements, went into operation on July 1, 1906.[1] Five years later the regents created the office of business manager.[2] In this office was lodged responsibility for supervising all business affairs of the University. Certain members of the Board, in making the business manager responsible to the regents, had hoped to divest the president of some of his power. Their attempt was not wholly successful. The creation of this office was probably inescapable in view of the large sums of money handled by the University and the wide variety of business activities in which it engaged. Similar offices were created in other institutions. The development was not looked upon with favor by all university presidents or by others who saw in the rise of business managers a genuine threat to the faculty and to presidential control of educational policies. In 1922 President David Kinley of the University of Illinois wrote to President Birge: "I am strongly, indeed bitterly, opposed to having our educational policy formulated, modified or determined by the business

[1] *Regents' Biennial Report*, 1905–06, pp. 19–20.

[2] *Ibid.*, 1911–12, p. 6. In 1911 Hermon Carey Bumpus, formerly director of the American Museum of Natural History, was appointed business manager. Three years later, when Bumpus resigned to accept the presidency of Tufts College, Halsten J. Thorkelson was appointed. Thorkelson had graduated from the University in 1898 and after several years in business had returned as a member of the engineering faculty. When he resigned in the early 1920's to accept an appointment with the General Education Board, another member of the faculty, Professor James David Phillips, was made business manager.

agents of the Universities. From what I have seen of the reports of the meetings of these business agents, they have been, whether conscious of the fact or not, undertaking to do that very thing in a large way and in important matters."[3] Supervision of the accounts whether by business managers or budget directors appeared to encourage the supervisor to venture into the creation and control of academic policy.

Behind the tall columns of figures of the annual report of the business manager there lay the University's biennial appeal to the legislature for funds. In the academic community, particularly in the more sequestered portions of it, the biennial joust with the legislature was often misunderstood. The function of the sound and fury was to vote money for the University, but beyond that the political and personal needs of the legislators had to be satisfied. In the tradition of American politics, requests for appropriations are often accompanied by oration. The oratory, whether in the legislative chamber or in the newspapers, very often becomes intemperate, inflammatory, even abusive, depending on the political necessities to be served. Politicians have a biennial if not perennial capacity for shocked surprise and pained indignation upon learning publicly what the professors are doing or what they are not doing.[4] The legislature during this period, however, always gave funds to the University, but its support was less generous after the first World War.

In 1895, it will be recalled, the University, having been granted a tax of 17/40 of a mill for each dollar of assessed valuation of property in the state, enjoyed perhaps the largest millage tax of any university in the Middle West. In 1899 the mill tax was repealed and in its place a fixed money appropriation was made. University authorities sought to recover the mill

[3] David Kinley to Edward A. Birge, January 27, 1922, Presidents' Papers.
[4] Fitzpatrick tells of a hearing when University officials were being grilled by a legislator on the subject of how much time the professors worked. Upon learning that some taught only seven hours of classes a week, he was preparing to object but was cut short by McCarthy, watchdog of University interests: "Mr. Chairman, you're all wrong in your kind of question. If you are asking the value of a bore [sic] pig or a stud horse, you wouldn't ask him how many hours he works, you'd ask what his product is. That's what you ought to ask about University Professors." Edward A. Fitzpatrick, *McCarthy of Wisconsin* (New York, 1944), 238.

tax but failed in 1901 and again in 1903. It became Van Hise's first great objective to win back and increase the mill tax for University support and, in addition, to reduce if possible the number of specific appropriations made by the legislature. This practice of specified appropriation had reduced the discretionary power of the Board.

In getting money from the legislature Van Hise enjoyed a large measure of success, but it must be observed that the proportion of state taxes given to the University decreased. One investigator has reported that "in 1910 the citizen of Wisconsin contributed to the support of his University five cents out of every dollar of tax money which he paid out for all purposes. In 1920 he paid two and seven tenths cents."[5] This decrease was partly the result of less generous support of the University by the state and partly the result of the many new and increasingly expensive activities which the state had launched. The new state boards and commissions, the state-supported highway construction program, and even the slowly increasing state aids for public schools, all demanded increasing amounts of money. Indeed, less than thirty-five years after the state highway-building program was launched, more money was being devoted annually for highway construction and maintenance than had been given to the University for buildings and land during ninety-odd years of its existence. Although there was a decrease in the percentage of the total tax collections of the state that went to the University, it must be recognized that many new and valuable governmental functions had been added and the total amount of money collected by the state increased with almost terrifying rapidity—so rapidly in fact that before 1915 several prominent groups had argued that the tax burden had become intolerable. And in a sense the complaint was justified. The new expensive agencies of the state, attributes of an urban industrial society rather than an agricultural one, were being largely maintained by a tax system based chiefly upon land and physical property. And Wisconsin's wealth was less in her soil than in her industry and commerce.

[5] Richard Rees Price, *The Financial Support of State Universities* (Cambridge, 1924), 126.

The struggle of the University officials for greater amounts of money and the reaction of the legislature to these demands constitute the central part of the story of University finances. The interest of the legislature in what the University did increased with the amounts of money it appropriated. This interest was reflected in periodic investigations of one aspect or another of University activity, in the movement to reduce the power of the regents and president by specifying exactly how money was to be spent, in the attempt on the part of the legislature to control the expenditure of University income not derived from the state, in the determination by law of tuition fees for out-of-state students, and in various attempts of the legislature to influence educational policy, to investigate and advise on matters of student conduct and even of professorial behavior. Often, even though the legislature failed to pass a certain law, the consideration of it caused the regents or the faculty to make changes to meet the criticism implicit in the proposed legislation. Thus the legislature not only provided money and determined larger matters of policy, but it influenced, directly and indirectly, such matters as University entrance requirements, the prerequisites for a degree, and the courses of study.

It is, of course, impracticable to attempt a discussion of all legislation bearing on the University. The number of bills relating to some aspect of the University increased each session; in 1915 forty-two bills were introduced relating to the institution; in 1923 eighty-two such bills and resolutions were introduced. Most of them did not pass but, because they had influence, some attention must be given to these measures.

Long before the legislature of 1905 came into session, Van Hise gave notice of his intention to press for larger and more secure support from the state. In his report to the Board, he pointed out that rising costs of living required an increase in faculty salaries, and that the great increase in the number of students required additional appointments to the faculty and an extensive building program. He complained that in terms of income the University of Wisconsin, in comparison with neighboring institutions, was losing ground. The states of California, Michigan, Illinois, Iowa, Nebraska, Colorado, and North Dakota were all relatively more generous in the support of their institutions of higher education than was Wisconsin. Under the present system of support, the regents could not plan ahead, could only do what each successive legislature provided for. Van Hise asked for support of a program under which the income of the University would not only be assured but would expand with the prosperity of the state. This meant, of course, a mill tax.[6]

Governor La Follette reiterated Van Hise's requests. He pleaded for additional funds and pointed out the valuable contributions made by the University to the economy of the state. There were other contributions, La Follette said: "The true and constantly growing spirit of democracy fostered by the state university is by no means one of its least valuable returns to the commonwealth. This spirit is essential to and insures permanency of popular government in its best form."[7]

Identical bills providing support for the University on a mill-tax basis and appropriating other funds to the University were introduced in the Assembly and the Senate on February 14, 1905.[8] The one in the Assembly, presented by Herman L. Ekern, was permitted to die; the Senate bill, presented by William H. Hatton, was the one on which action was taken.

Even before the bills were introduced, Van Hise and other University officials were busily engaged in winning popular support. Copies of the *Jubilee* volume, containing Van Hise's inaugural address and many other speeches, had been widely distributed along with the biennial report of the Board. A circular letter, prepared by Van Hise, outlining the needs of the University, had been sent to political leaders, University alumni, and prominent citizens. Van Hise and others wrote numerous letters asking for support of the bill. They received a sympathetic hearing and many promises of help. Emil Baensch, president of the Wisconsin Press Association, wrote: "You know the views I have held for many years, that the institution should be put on a firm basis, that its representatives and friends ought not to be biennially and eternally forced in[to] the disagree-

[6] *Regents' Biennial Report,* 1903–04; pp. 42–44.
[7] *Senate Journal,* 1905, pp. 102–103.
[8] *Assembly Journal,* 1905, p. 359; *Senate Journal,* 1905, p. 329.

able ranks of lobbyists."[9] Malcolm C. Douglas, managing editor of the *Milwaukee Sentinel,* wanted to promote the best interests of the University and promised that the columns of the newspaper would always be open to Van Hise to make public the work of the University.[10] So carefully did Van Hise select people to assist, and so persuasive were his letters, that in the large collection of letters and answers in his legislative file of that year, only one letter registered a clear-cut refusal to help.[11]

Most of the work on the appropriation bill was done in the Senate. The Hatton Bill, which had provided a levy of 2/5 of a mill for the support of the University, and other appropriation measures were referred first to the Committee on Education. Van Hise's correspondence files show that, in addition to his extensive campaign to win popular support for the bill, he had collected pertinent information as to the way in which other universities were supported. For the committee hearings he tabulated the data from other states on the use of mill taxes for university support. For the Committee on Education he prepared a long statement again showing the needs of the University and advantages of the steady but elastic support offered by a mill tax. He lamented that the tax of 17/40 of a mill which had existed until 1899 had been repealed. He appealed to the state pride of the members of the committee by pointing out that through the generous and stable support of the University given in the 1890's under a mill tax, the prevalent distrust of state universities had been allayed, and that the University had been able to attract good men to the faculty. The system of biennial appropriations was undermining the confidence which had been created.[12]

In April the committee was ready to report with a bill which

[9] Emil Baensch to Charles R. Van Hise, March 25, 1905, Presidents' Papers, filed under Legislative. All letters to and from Van Hise in this chapter are in the Presidents' Papers filed under Legislative, unless otherwise indicated.

[10] Malcolm C. Douglas to Van Hise, March 25, 1905.

[11] This man had been "grieved by the expensive mode of living of the average student there [at the University], caused largely as I believe by the fraternities, which I deem an abomination, and so long as I view the situation as I do now, I am not disposed to render the assistance you desire." Clarence C. Coe to Van Hise, January 14, 1905.

[12] Syllabus for education committee, 1905, Presidents' Papers, filed under Legislative.

had reduced the millage tax from 2/5 to 2/7 of a mill; changed a provision granting specified sums for repair, construction, and support to a general provision granting $200,000 a year for building and improvements in the order of greatest need as determined by the regents; and included a section, not in the original bill, providing that no new school or college was to be established without the authorization of the legislature.[13] On the recommendation of the Committee on Education the bill was referred to the Committee on Claims.[14] For the Committee on Claims, Van Hise prepared another long statement setting forth the needs of the University, arguing the wisdom of a steady and growing support of the University to match its greater needs and increasing student body. He sought to win back a part of the support lost when the education committee reduced the sum from 2/5 to 2/7 of a mill by asking for 3/10 of a mill. In his pleas to the committee he said, as he had said before and would say again, that he held the view "that a University in a democracy may be as high grade as a University under a monarchy." To hold the opposite view "would be the most fundamental charge which was ever made against a democracy."[15] To the provision which had been added, directing that no new colleges be established without the consent of the legislature, Van Hise had no objection.[16]

The Committee on Claims, like the Committee on Education, was friendly. In May the bill was reported to the Senate for passage.[17] It came up for debate on May 26. Senator John M. Whitehead of Janesville proposed an amendment to substitute a specific money appropriation instead of the mill tax.[18] The amendment found little support. Senator Hatton argued that the University should have a steady and dependable income. Senator Julius E. Roehr echoed Van Hise in declaring that the

---

[13] Senate Bills, 459S, 1905; *Senate Journal*, 1905, p. 870. Hereafter the bills and joint resolutions will be cited by number only, the S signifying that the bill was introduced in the Senate and the A, in the Assembly. Printed copies of these bills are bound serially for each legislature and are preserved in the Document Room of the State Historical Society of Wisconsin.

[14] *Senate Journal*, 1905, p. 870.

[15] Syllabus for claims committee, 1905, Presidents' Papers, filed under Legislative.

[16] *Ibid.*

[17] *Senate Journal*, 1905, p. 1035.　　　[18] *Ibid.*, 1234–1235.

University should not be required to live from hand to mouth and upon the favor of the legislature. Senator Andrew L. Kreutzer thought that it would be a good thing for the University to show the legislature around the campus and explain to members the need for the money asked, but he would bow to the will of the Committee on Claims.[19] When the amendment came to a vote, it lost by a vote of 20 to 7.[20] The next day the bill passed the Senate by a unanimous vote.[21] In the Assembly the bill was read a first and second time and ordered to a third and final reading without going to committee. On June 2, it was passed by a vote of 77 to 2, with 21 assemblymen not voting.[22]

The bill, which thus became law upon the governor's signature, was brief. It provided for the levy and collection of a state tax of 2/7 of a mill for each dollar of assessed valuation of the taxable general property in the state. This money was appropriated to the University Fund income to be used for current and administrative expenditures and for additions and improvements in the facilities of the University. The regents were restricted only to the extent of being required to apportion funds to the various colleges as stipulated in the *Statutes* of 1898. Since property taxes would not be collected in time to provide for the first half of the fiscal year, the law provided that the regents might borrow money from state trust funds. The money was to be repaid with interest after taxes were collected. The law also provided $200,000 a year for three years for construction and equipment. Although release of these funds from the state treasury required the approval of the governor, and the general purpose of the fund was stipulated by the legislature, the regents were given wide latitude in determining how the funds were to be used. Lastly the law contained the provision that no new schools or colleges were to be established unless authorized by the legislature.[23] Because there

[19] *Wisconsin State Journal*, May 26, 1905.   [20] *Senate Journal*, 1905, p. 1235.
[21] *Ibid.*, 1252.   [22] *Assembly Journal*, 1905, pp. 1683, 1730, 1773.
[23] *Laws of Wisconsin*, 1905, pp. 491–493. The 2/7 mill tax of 1905 was, to be sure, smaller than the 17/40 of ten years before, but the tax rate alone does not tell the story. In 1901 the state assessment had been increased from $630,000,000 to $1,436,284,000. Nils P. Haugen, "Pioneer and Political Reminiscences," *The Wisconsin Magazine of History*, 12:180 (December, 1928).

was little money available in the state trust funds a supplemental law was passed authorizing the secretary of state, upon approval of the governor, to transfer from the general fund to the University Fund income such money as might be necessary to meet current expenses of the University. As soon as taxes were collected, the money was to be returned by a transfer.[24]

A number of other laws were adopted in the same session, mostly noncontroversial, providing funds for cranberry and tobacco experiments by the College of Agriculture, permitting the regents to establish branch experiment stations, providing funds for the state hygienic laboratory which had been established two years before, establishing a state forestry board on which the president of the University and the dean of the College of Agriculture were to be members, and making provision for the preparation of a history of Wisconsin soldiers in the Civil War in which the "head professor of American history in the state University" was to have a part.[25]

Van Hise was pleased with the results of the session. In an address before the representatives of the Association of State Universities in November, 1905, he spoke of the important steps which had been taken. He described the mill tax and declared: "The amount derived from this tax is placed almost without restriction in the hands of the Regents to be distributed between the various needs of the University as seems most desirable. The legislature held that this continuous body was the one that could wisely decide as to the distribution of the income among the various departments."[26]

Van Hise's elation was premature. The legislature came into special session late in 1905. Several things brought the University to its attention. A professor in the agricultural college had been dismissed and had publicly charged that there were ir-

[24] *Laws of Wisconsin*, 1905, pp. 804–805.

[25] *Ibid.*, 760–761, 620, 109, 809, 383, 456.

[26] The quotation was taken from a manuscript copy of the address. Dean Henry, it might be added, had opposed this legislation, fearing that the agricultural college would suffer. In a long and agitated letter to Van Hise he reviewed the history of the agricultural college, declaring that only the legislative safeguards placed on the funds, the alertness of several members of the regents, his own vigilant efforts, and the occasional intervention of the governor had kept the Board from diverting the agricultural funds to the other colleges. William A. Henry to Van Hise, February 22, 1905, Presidents' Papers.

regularities in the management of the college. Moreover, a wide discrepancy apparently existed between the amount of the University funds in the records of the secretary of state and in those of the regents, and charges were made that the University had been guilty of extravagance. The charges were based on a misunderstanding of University finances. From 1899 until the end of the fiscal year of 1904–1905, University appropriations had been made from the general fund and were available at the beginning of each period as needed. Under the reinstituted mill tax no funds could be claimed until taxes were collected. The fiscal year of the University began on July 1, 1905. Mill taxes were not collected until the first quarter of 1906. This left a period of over six months during which the University had to be financed but had no money. To cover this period, it will be recalled, the legislature had authorized the University to borrow from the state trust funds and from the general fund on condition that the borrowed money be returned as soon as funds collected under the mill tax became available. Another element in the financial misunderstanding may have been that political opponents of La Follette were willing to use any opportunity to embarrass or discredit the governor. The plain facts of the law and bookkeeping should have been simple enough for almost anyone to understand. La Follette himself had suggested that the mill-tax law be amended to provide more fully for the temporary transfer of funds from the general fund to the University Fund income.[27]

On December 7, Assemblyman P. A. Cleary introduced a joint resolution providing for an investigation of the University. "It is reported," ran Cleary's resolution, "and rumored that extravagance and waste in the financial affairs of the University of Wisconsin exist, and that, notwithstanding the liberal appropriations made by the legislature from year to year for the maintenance of that institution, there now exists a large deficiency."[28] Van Hise promptly prepared a statement for the legislature and for publication denying the charges and explaining the financial condition of the University.[29] He made it

[27] *Assembly Journal*, Special Session, 1905, p. 41.
[28] *Ibid.*, pp. 66–67.
[29] *Wisconsin State Journal*, December 8, 1905.

clear, however, that officials of the University would welcome an investigation of its finances. The *Wisconsin State Journal* reported that the legislative committee would also look into Professor Knapp's charges of irregularities in the agricultural college. Though asserting its impartiality, the *Journal* remarked that the excitement over University finances served to emphasize a point. The state administration, while claiming to reduce taxes, had been the most expensive in history. "The important facts are that the money has been spent, and that in the face of increasing burdens to the tax payers, the administration jugglers issued their no-state-tax announcement, and then a few weeks later it is shown that the tax payers must make good a deficit of nearly a half million in the University's income." [30] Two days later the *Journal* printed a story summarizing the opinion of the attorney general in support of the legality of the University's borrowing from the state. [31]

Meanwhile the Cleary resolution had been sent to the judiciary committee to consider the admissibility of the resolution at the special session. It was here amended so as to link the investigation directly to the mill-tax law passed in the regular session. [32] The substitute was adopted and sent to the Senate, where it was passed. [33] The Assembly and Senate Committees on Education had met jointly, considered "certain apparent discrepancies in the university accounts," and appointed a subcommittee to investigate. This committee reported that under the mill-tax law funds were not available during the first six months of the University year, and the funds adequate for University operations were not available in the state trust funds. Accordingly money had been obtained from the general fund. Under this arrangement $302,000 had been advanced to the University and it was estimated that this amount would be increased to $350,000 by February, 1906, when the whole sum would be repaid. On July 1, 1906, advances would again have to be made, but according to University estimates the whole advance should not exceed $250,000. In view of the expected large expenditures of the University, and the period

[30] *Ibid.*, December 9, 1905, pp. 1, 4.   [31] *Ibid.*, December 11, 1905.
[32] *Assembly Journal*, Special Session, 1905, p. 67.
[33] *Ibid.*, 115; *Senate Journal*, Special Session, 1905, p. 107.

of time which must elapse between the beginning of the fiscal year and the time of tax collections, the University would in the future have to anticipate its income and borrow to meet current expenses.[34]

This matter-of-fact report allayed some suspicion. Van Hise, meanwhile, publicly welcomed the appointment of a legislative committee. He declared that the regents had long urged the creation of a legislative committee on University problems. He hoped subsequent legislatures would appoint similar committees which would report to the governor before the meeting of each legislature. "By adopting this policy," Van Hise declared, "each legislature will have a complete and exhaustive statement as to the management, condition and needs of the university, as a result of an investigation made by one of its own committees, and therefore will not have to rely entirely upon the statements of the university authorities, which some may think biased. Such a report will relieve the university authorities from much of the embarrassment under which they have labored in the past when university legislation was pending."[35]

The resolution of the joint committee, as adopted, called for a full inquiry into the "conditions, affairs, management, expenses, and needs of the University with reference to any amendment which may be germane to chapter 468 of the law of 1905, or to any subject mentioned there, also into all transactions between the university and its agents, employees and other persons, it being the intention hereby to give such committee the fullest power and authority and not to limit in any wise the extent and manner of its inquiry." The committee was to be made up of two senators and three assemblymen and to report to the governor before November 1, 1906.[36] Ten thousand dollars was appropriated for the investigation.[37] The legislature also amended the mill-tax law, again permitting transfer

[34] Statement from the Committee on Education, James Huff Stout, chairman, *Assembly Journal*, Special Session 1905, pp. 135–137.

[35] *Daily Cardinal*, December 13, 1905.

[36] *Laws of Wisconsin*, Special Session, 1905, p. 41.

[37] *Ibid.*, 13. In approving the appropriation, Governor La Follette said there might be some question about the constitutionality of considering a measure not specifically provided for in the proclamation convening the special session,

of funds from the general fund to the University Fund income but providing that the University must pay interest at the rate of three and a half per cent for such funds.[38]

Thus the resolution to investigate the University, born of suspicion and perhaps hostility, was adopted. The inquiry now had the public support of the governor and University authorities. The suspicion had certainly been allayed. Van Hise had given notice that he would try to turn the investigation into a broad and intelligent effort to inform the legislature about all phases of the University.

The committee was in session for forty-five days between February 5 and October 25, 1906, and collected 2,055 typewritten pages of testimony. With its counsel, accountant, and clerks, it manifested a catholic interest in all the affairs of the University. One hundred and forty-four witnesses appeared before it to give information or opinions, or to make objections. Some witnesses came because they were called, some because they wanted to, and some appeared because they happened to be passing by while the committee was in session. The committee's interest ranged from fraternities (which it did not like), football, and out-of-state tuitions to the working hours of professors, the conduct of secretaries at the agricultural college, the personality of the farm superintendent, the relations of Dean Henry to his staff, the financial system of the Board, the procedures of the executive committee, the methods of acquiring land, the construction of buildings and the methods of inviting bids. The *Wisconsin State Journal* followed the hearing with the ill-concealed hope that some scandal would turn up. Late in February, Assemblyman Cleary appeared as a witness and acknowledged that the charges he had made against

but that he would not veto the bill. "To veto this bill for any reason, might operate to prejudice the university with the public. The work which that great institution is doing is worth millions of dollars annually to agriculture and to other material interests of the state. The confidence and support of the people of this commonwealth is vital to full accomplishment of its high mission. I am confident that the authorities at the university will welcome the most careful scrutiny of its management." He objected, too, that the amount of money for the inquiry seemed "extravagant" but was sure the committee could exercise "prudence and economy." With these reservations he had approved the bill. *Senate Journal*, Special Session, 1905, p. 115–116.

[38] *Laws of Wisconsin*, Special Session, 1905, pp. 30-31.

the University were based on hearsay.[39] Early in March the *State Journal's* interest revived when the dean of the College of Agriculture, the dean's secretary, the farm superintendent, and others were called to testify. There were hopes that the agricultural college linen would be washed in public, and the testimony, which at least revealed the irritability of the dean, was fully reported. The *Milwaukee Sentinel* also began to carry stories on this part of the investigation.[40] The *Madison Democrat*, on the other hand, made light of the investigation and studiously avoided the gossip. But it reported when the committee found the records and accounts of the college in good order[41] and informed its readers before the end of the month that the agricultural college had been vindicated by the investigation.[42]

By the time of the April meeting of the Board the inquiry had gone far enough for Van Hise to be confident that he could report on the principal conclusions which the committee would reach. Among those upon which Van Hise looked with disfavor were a recommendation that the business system of the University would be reorganized and the University required to submit a budget for the approval of the governor, secretary of state, and treasurer, and another recommendation which would urge that the president of the University be relieved of all financial responsibility. He felt that the adoption of the first would mean the virtual abolition of the Board of Regents. As to the second, he felt that the president should not be relieved of financial responsibility, since the most important expenditures were for educational purposes, and if the president were to direct educational policy he must not be separated from financial responsibility. He also reported that the censure of Dean Henry, if it were made, should carry with it recognition of Henry's great contribution to the state and nation.[43]

When the committee's report was published in October, it was milder and more helpful than Van Hise had anticipated.

[39] *Daily Cardinal*, February 24, 1906.
[40] *Wisconsin State Journal*, March 2, 10, 12, 15, 1906; *Milwaukee Sentinel*, March 3, 9, 10, 13, 14, 15, 17, 1906.
[41] *Madison Democrat*, February 23, March 3, 11, 1906.
[42] *Ibid.*, March 25, 1906.   [43] Reports to the Regents, E:81–83, April 17, 1906.

It found that the agricultural college had "suffered through a distrust that has become somewhat prevalent in the college" and that this was partly responsible for the loss of several good men. Dismissal of Knapp was not, the committee held, fully justified, but the resignation of the farm superintendent had "in great measure, reestablished confidence, and given promise of improved conditions in the future."[44] Dean Henry was not mentioned by name. The committee criticized the system of letting contracts, objected to the illegal practice, sometimes followed, of purchasing property from persons connected with the University, supported the principle of extension work but opposed engaging in it on the grounds of economy, urged that out-of-state students be required to pay higher fees, and urged the regents to become better acquainted with the work of the institution; and it disapproved of fraternities and college athletics but felt that these matters had best be left in the hands of the faculty.[45] The committee also recommended that an emergency appropriation of $250,000 be made to the University to enable it to meet expenses from the beginning of the next fiscal year until the time when tax money under the mill tax would be available. Moreover, it recommended adoption of a law providing that each year's budget be approved by the governor, the secretary of state, and the treasurer; requiring the University to remain within the limits of the budget; and requiring further that all funds be used for the purpose for which the appropriations were made.[46]

The last was the recommendation Van Hise least wanted, since it would impose restrictions on the regents' disposition of the funds allotted to them. In effect, if carried out, it would immediately cancel the advantages gained from the law of 1905 which gave wide latitude to the regents in the expenditure of funds. As it turned out, however, this recommendation, like the one calling for an appropriation of $250,000, was not enacted into law.

On the whole the report of the committee was fair and square.

[44] *Report of the Joint Legislative Committee on the Affairs of the University* (Madison, 1906), 6.
[45] *Ibid.*, 8–14.   [46] *Ibid.*, 10.

Before it was released the *State Journal* had prepared its readers for such a report. It had pointed out that the charges made by Professor Knapp after his dismissal and the reports that the University was bankrupt had combined to produce "a panicky effect on the minds of the legislators, most of whom know little of the university except by hearsay, and the resolution had easy sailing through both houses."[47] The *Journal* did not add that its own reports had contributed not a little to the "panicky effect." Nor was it content to accept complete vindication of the University. On October 25, it reported that reforms advocated by the committee, whose report had not yet been released, were already under way. The next day it published a report of the committee findings under the headline, "Legislative Report in Scorching Roasts of Frats, Regents, and Profs," a palpable exaggeration of the strictures of the committee.[48] The *Madison Democrat,* on the other hand, found the report "favorable" and declared that the University had been given "a clean bill of health."[49] The *Democrat* next day gave a front-page headline to the committee recommendation that the University be given another $250,000 and declared that this was the most important result of the investigation: "The investigation was born in sensationalism, rumor, jealousy and envy. It was fortunately placed in the hands of men of ability, common sense and fairness. Their report shows how exhaustively and with what earnestness they did their work. The great institution has been given a thorough trial—the result is the recommendation for a gift of $250,000, and for some changes of administrative character."[50] Commenting four days later, the *Democrat* thought "the investigation was not amiss. It will do good, but, just the same here's a cheer for the university! and throughout the great commonwealth will be heard a swelling chorus of reverberations."[51]

The committee, as the *Democrat* remarked, was fair and sensible; but the motivation of the investigation and the newspaper accounts distinguished it slightly from earlier legislative investi-

---

[47] *Wisconsin State Journal,* October 8, 1906.

[49] *Madison Democrat,* October 26, 1906.

[50] *Ibid.,* October 27, 1906.

[48] *Ibid.,* October 26, 1906.

[51] *Ibid.,* October 31, 1906.

gations of the University. The accusations were vaguely connected with attacks upon La Follette, whose good friend was president of the University. To be sure, there had been political bias in earlier investigations, but bias of a somewhat amorphous character; the president of the University, though sometimes attacked, had not been considered the creature of one political group. He had been merely a state official, fair game for any political attack.

When the next legislature met in 1907, President Van Hise not only was prepared to ask for additional funds for the University functions already established, but he presented a long argument for the establishment of a school of medicine. He rested his plea in part upon the fact that almost all state universities in the states adjacent to Wisconsin had medical schools, that in the very beginning the legislature had stipulated that a department of medicine must be a part of the University, and that this provision had not been wholly dropped by succeeding legislatures. Chiefly, however, he argued that Wisconsin students must now leave the state for medical training, that distinguished authorities in medical education and outstanding graduates of the University who were now practicing physicians urged that a medical school be established, and that excellent medical education, for at least the first two years, could be offered by the University. He submitted a plan prepared by Professor Charles R. Bardeen outlining the groups of studies needed for medical education. The University could easily provide the first two years of training and he therefore advocated incorporation of a two-year medical course.[52]

The legislative program of the University moved forward smoothly. Van Hise conducted a wide correspondence spreading information about the nature and purpose of the University, asking and seeking support in all quarters, while Professor Bardeen conducted an extensive correspondence with medical men and others to win support for a two-year medical school. There were two medical schools in Milwaukee and opposition to the establishment of a medical school at the University came from both of them. Early in March, Bardeen warned Van Hise

[52] Van Hise to the regents, *Regents' Biennial Report*, 1905–06, pp. 40–58.

that Dr. Washburn of the Wisconsin College of Physicians and Surgeons at Milwaukee was "bent by hook or crook, chiefly the latter, to force us to take over his school or remain unincorporated."[53] Later Washburn informed Bardeen that his school could not accept students from the University; still later he said he could see no reason why "friendly and cordial relations" should not exist between the University and the Wisconsin College of Physicians and Surgeons.[54] Meanwhile, Van Hise informed another inquirer that up to then nothing had been decided about what to do in the matter of training in clinical medicine, that he himself would approve having one or both Milwaukee institutions joined with the University of Wisconsin.[55] Such cordiality did not exist between the Milwaukee Medical College and the University. The material presented in a statement by the lobbyist of this institution to the Committee on Claims was subsequently published anonymously in a twenty-seven-page pamphlet entitled, *Some Facts and Figures Concerning the State University*. Mainly intended to defeat the plans for a medical school, the pamphlet was an inaccurate and inflammatory attack upon the University, particularly for its profligate ways. The institution, the pamphlet charged, was "becoming a deplorable example of the evils of money lust." The inaccuracies in the statistical data of the pamphlet were quickly revealed, its source identified by University authorities, and its influence largely negated.[56]

Authorization to establish a medical school was contained in the appropriation bill for the University. Supporting opinion was strong enough to check any effort in the Senate to remove the provision from the bill. In the Assembly an amendment was offered to strike out the clause authorizing the medical college, but it was promptly defeated by a vote of 58 to 13.[57] The bill passed both houses with substantial majorities. Be-

---

[53] Charles R. Bardeen to Van Hise, memorandum on a letter of Dr. Henry Vining Ogden to Bardeen, March 1, 1907, Presidents' Papers, filed under Legislative.

[54] Dr. Washburn to Bardeen, March 6, 16, 1907, Presidents' Papers, filed under Legislative.

[55] Van Hise to a Dr. Francis, March 18, 1907.

[56] Pamphlet and memorandum concerning a pamphlet, Presidents' Papers, filed under Legislative.   [57] *Assembly Journal,* 1907, p. 1147.

sides authorizing the medical school, the appropriation bill specifically provided that the secretary of state transfer not more than $250,000 each year from the general fund to the University Fund income. The building appropriation of $200,000 a year for three years was extended to cover a five-year period, and another appropriation of $100,000 a year for a period of four years was voted for the construction and equipment of men's dormitories and a women's building with a gymnasium. The legislature directed that the women's building should be constructed first.[58] In other appropriation bills the legislature contributed $20,000 a year for an extension department in the University, increased to $20,000 a year the funds available for farmers' institutes,[59] and passed a law giving the regents somewhat more power in acquiring land.[60]

At the instigation of Superintendent of Public Instruction Cary the legislature had considered, but it refused to adopt, resolutions modifying the entrance requirements of the University;[61] it had adopted a bill providing that no license could be granted for the sale of liquor "to be drunk on the premises within 3,200 feet of the main building of any state university";[62] and it had adopted a resolution condemning the plans of University students to hold a regatta on Lake Mendota on Memorial Day.[63] These acts indicated that the legislature was increasingly willing to consider matters of educational policy, student morals and conduct; that some of its members were prepared to inform the University authorities about the proper requirements for admission to the University and the prerequisites for graduation. In part, this was an outcome of voting larger appropriations; in part, it must be accounted a result of Van Hise's policy of encouraging the legislature to inform itself

[58] *Laws of Wisconsin*, 1907, pp. 73–74, 1069–1070.

[59] *Ibid.*, 352, 1045.

[60] *Ibid.*, 144–145, 932.

[61] Joint Resolutions, 56A, 1907; *Assembly Journal*, 1907, pp. 198, 399; *Senate Journal*, 1907, pp. 393, 516.

[62] *Laws of Wisconsin*, 1907, pp. 364, 1228. The bill originally stipulated that the distance be half a mile from the campus.

[63] The resolution denounced "such and all similar celebrations, fetes, and amusements, as a desecration ... of Memorial Day and a disregard and violation of its sacred and solemn character." *Laws of Wisconsin*, 1907, p. 1283.

about the University. If, as Van Hise insisted, the University existed to serve the state, then indeed the people's representatives had to concern themselves with the quality of the service and the effectiveness of legislation in widening or limiting it.

Van Hise asked the legislature of 1909 for increased funds. He wanted legislative approval for participation in the Carnegie plan for retirement allowances of University professors, and among the needs of the University he listed increased salaries and staff, additional buildings, research funds for the College of Letters and Science, new departments, a heating plant, additional land, and many other things, including an increased appropriation for residence halls. He asked that the mill-tax rate be increased from 2/7 to 3/8 of a mill. He concluded his request with the statement, almost a part of his catechism, "If the amounts asked for are granted, it is our confident belief that every dollar will be returned many fold to the state, even if the material point of view alone be considered."[64]

His proposals were not cordially received. The first enthusiasm for Van Hise apparently had worn off, and newspapers had begun to snipe at the University. Its increased cost and rapid growth and prosperity made it a conspicuous target for any politician. Its lengthening list of activities could not please everybody. Even before the 1909 legislature met, the *Jackson County Journal*, published by Merlin Hull, assemblyman-elect, carried an editorial entitled, "The Champion Wanter." Van Hise was accused of making excessive demands for funds.[65] A Boscobel lawyer, on the other hand, warned that there were "a bunch of dinky newspapers in this section of the state . . . who delight in making attacks upon the State University on account of its alleged extravagance."[66] Assemblyman Henry E. Roethe on March 3 delivered a hostile speech, accusing the University of extravagance, opposing funds for a medical building, and objecting to the continuous requests from the University for more money: "We all know how these things go, it's the same story

[64] Report of the president, *Regents' Biennial Report*, 1907–08, pp. 24–45.
[65] *Jackson County Journal*, Black River Falls, Wisconsin, December 30, 1908.
[66] Otto Kuenzli, Boscobel, to the registrar, March 31, 1909, Presidents' Papers, filed under Legislative.

over and over again, always more money needed, and I wish to compliment the University right here that its lobbyists are the slickest and the smoothest that ever came down the pike."[67]

The work being done at Madison, particularly by the extension department, won the enthusiastic and often uncritical approval of the reformers throughout the country. In February, 1909, Lincoln Steffens' article, "Sending a State to College," appeared in the *American Magazine*. Steffens was already known as a leading muckraker. The admiring articles he had written about La Follette and the Progressives identified him as a supporter of La Follette, and his enthusiasm for the University was construed as evidence that the University was carrying out the program of the Progressives. The very fact that Steffens approved what the University was doing was for many a sufficient reason to oppose the University program. His reference to the "Tory Regents," a mere qualification in his essay of headlong approval, did not escape the sensitive Board.

There was another element in the situation. The old titans on the Board were gone, the men who had been so potent in helping to steer the University through the roiled political waters of the 1890's, who had given respectability to academic freedom in 1894, who by virtue of their eminence maintained, if not a nonpartisan, at least a bipartisan aura about the University. General Lucius Fairchild had died in 1896, John Johnston in 1904, and Breese Stevens in 1903. William F. Vilas, one of the last and perhaps most powerful of them all, died in 1908. These men, and others like them, both Republicans and Democrats, had given great support to the University. Vilas, in his will, attested his belief in the University and in academic freedom by providing that eventually his whole estate be devoted to the University. His stipulations as to the salary to be paid to the William F. Vilas professors and the teaching duties to be demanded of them stood, and perhaps were intended to stand, as a biennial rebuke to the stinginess of the legislature. To a former regent, Van Hise confessed that he missed Vilas very much. "His death has indeed been a loss to us this year. In legislative matters he and [I] worked as one. Each one knew

[67] *Madison Democrat*, March 4, 1909.

exactly what the other did at all times, and the remarkable legislation which we secured four years ago and two years ago was very largely due to that fact."[68]

The character of the Board had changed. Men friendly to Van Hise had been replaced. State Superintendent Cary, regent ex officio, was becoming more and more shrill in his denunciations. Among the new appointees to the Board were G. D. Jones, a graduate of the University, wealthy, conservative, and outspoken; Magnus Swenson and Pliny Norcross, also conservative alumni; and William D. Hoard, former governor, early supporter of La Follette, an important influence in the agricultural college, who now in his last years was about to break with La Follette and denounce Van Hise for seeking to create a governing aristocracy. Swenson was the most irascible. G. D. Jones, whose initials suggested a nickname to the irreverent, stoutly opposed Van Hise on many issues. Against Van Hise's pleas that the regents stand firm in their defense of the full demands of the University, Jones objected that the regents should accept modifications "in the spirit of fairness."[69] Jones, then new on the Board and suspicious of Van Hise, wrote him in May objecting to the statements of the Socialists in the legislature and complaining that Van Hise allowed himself to be "unduly influenced" by them. "Thank God the State of Wisconsin is not socialistic. I am afraid it is true, however, that the University of Wisconsin allows itself to be influenced more by these theories than by any others in the state." Jones was angry at what he had heard about the "poltroonery and the disloyalty of the regents to the University. I am sure that without intending to do so you have encouraged this feeling. It is a most absurd and ridiculous charge, and I feel that you should see to it yourself that it is promptly and vigorously refuted. The Regents of the University are not only loyal to the University itself, but they have shown a loyalty to the president of the University that has not been reciprocated."[70] A week later Jones, his temper unimproved, wrote Van Hise to excoriate Professor Gilmore's theories about prop-

[68] Van Hise to Major C. Mead, May 24, 1909.
[69] G. D. Jones to Van Hise, March 31, 1909.   [70] *Ibid.*, May 3, 1909.

erty.[71] Hoard, too, wrote Van Hise about attacks against the regents which had been made in the legislature.[72]

Major C. Mead, a former regent, sought to console Van Hise by telling him what a great work he was doing for the University. "Your splendid efforts are thoroughly appreciated by the alumni everywhere and by the good people of the state, generally, and it is disgusting to me to know, as I do, that you have these guerillas on the board of regents."[73]

Some aspects of the difficulties of the years 1909 to 1911 have been treated in the chapters on Van Hise. They are noted here only in relation to the legislative program. In view of the attacks being made upon the Board and the evidences of distrust for Van Hise among some members of the Board, perhaps it was remarkable that the legislature turned out to be as liberal as it was. For all the uproar, charges against the University were not taken too seriously, and Van Hise and other University officials were effective in winning support and meeting objections. Van Hise as usual had appealed to alumni throughout the state for assistance in explaining the purposes of the University and assuring legislators of their support of appropriations.[74] On the whole, the legislative program went off well. Although not enthusiastic, Governor Davidson was cordial to the University.[75] The legislature refused to increase the mill-tax rate to 3/8 of a mill, it repealed the appropriation of $100,000 a year for building women's dormitories, and it refused a number of other requests, but it did provide a two-year grant of $100,000 a year for general purposes, $50,000 a year for two years for books, apparatus, furniture, and equipment, and it extended the $200,000 annual building appropriation for seven years after 1905. It also provided $125,000 for the next two years for extension but incorporated the extension budget into the University budget; and it made an additional appropriation for the agricultural college.[76] The legislature also considered limiting the mill-tax appropriation to only two years,

[71] *Ibid.,* May 11, 1909.　　　[72] William D. Hoard to Van Hise, May 3, 1909.
[73] Major C. Mead to Van Hise, May 16, 1909.
[74] Van Hise, circular letter to the alumni, October 14, 1908, March 11, 1909.
[75] *Senate Journal,* 1909, pp. 29–30, 290.
[76] *Laws of Wisconsin,* 1909, pp. 335–338.

an action which Van Hise gloomily predicted would of necessity drive the University into politics.[77]

Many other laws bearing on the University were passed. The legislature authorized the regents to apply to the Carnegie Foundation for the benefits of the retirement fund. It displayed remarkable solicitude for the women, first by providing that at least two members of the Board of Regents be women, and second, partly in answer to the ill-advised suggestion of Van Hise that some segregation of the sexes should be made in teaching certain classes, by decreeing that all schools and colleges of the University, "in their respective departments and class exercises," be open "without distinction to students of both sexes." It also attached the Library School more closely to the University, authorized the regents to establish two branch agricultural experiment stations and appropriated funds for that purpose, assigned nursery and orchard inspection duties to the agricultural college, directed the dean of the agricultural college to serve on a board to determine the proper location of county schools of agriculture and domestic science, and placed him on the state Board of Immigration. It approved the expenditure of a possible $50,000 of University funds for the construction of a forest products laboratory for cooperative work with the United States Forestry Service. It provided funds for paving Park Street "with asphaltum" from Lake Mendota to University Avenue and generously promised to give the old dome of the state capitol, which had survived the capitol fire of 1904, to the regents to be placed on the "main hall of the university building," if the regents or the legislature in the future so provided. The removal and reconstruction cost could be no more than $25,000. It also adopted one resolution requesting the regents to investigate the fraternities and sororities for the purpose of remedying the antidemocratic and cliquelike tendencies of these organizations, and another providing for a joint committee to investigate University supervision and inspection of high schools.[78]

---

[77] Van Hise to Thomas Lloyd Jones, May 11, 1909.
[78] *Laws of Wisconsin*, 1909, pp. 808, 723, 73, 509, 48, 650–651, 582–586, 342–343, 542–543, 831, 843, 345–346, 845, 844.

But in addition to the ones passed, the legislature had considered bills fixing the terms of admission to the University, changing the course of study of the normal schools, providing for a chair of "race culture" in the medical school to promote the "study of human degeneracy and deterioration";[79] numerous bills which would have increased the funds appropriated for extension work; a bill to abolish the medical school;[80] a bill to regulate the faculty in its handling of discipline cases;[81] and bills directing the establishment in the college of agriculture of a poultry department and chairs of plant pathology and entomology.[82]

Before the next legislature convened, although the carping criticism of the University and the differences between the Board on the one side and the president and faculty on the other had not entirely disappeared, the air had been cleared somewhat by the frank discussion which had taken place between a committee of the faculty and the Board. Fully as important was the fact that in the election of 1910 the Progressives had been triumphant. Francis E. McGovern, a graduate of the University, was elected governor. The legislature elected at the same time was to be known throughout the country for carrying through one of the most remarkable programs of reform legislation ever witnessed in an American state.

In his report Van Hise again called for an increase of the millage tax from 2/7 to 3/8 to provide for the growing needs of the University, an increase in salaries, and the establishment of new departments. He boldly outlined a building program which called for an outlay of between $805,000 and $930,000 for educational buildings, $1,000,000 for student dormitories and other student buildings, additional funds for the extension work, and funds for an addition to the historical library building, now crammed from attic to basement.[83] Again Van Hise assured the Board that every dollar would be "returned many fold to the state even if the material point of view alone be considered." The president of the regents, Wil-

---

[79] Assembly Bill 708A, *Assembly Journal,* 1909, pp. 281, 558.
[80] Assembly Bill 204A, *ibid.,* 170, 380.
[81] Assembly Bill 276A, *ibid.,* 186, 870.   [82] *Ibid.,* 185, 186, 899.
[83] Report of the president, *Regents' Biennial Report,* 1909–10, pp. 31–53.

liam D. Hoard, in transmitting the report to the governor repeated Van Hise's words, saying: "It is my belief that in the
future as in the past the investment of funds in the University
will be one which will be returned to the state manyfold."[84]

In his message to the legislature, McGovern was almost as
unreserved as Van Hise. Pointing to the work of the extension
division and other branches of the University, he recommended an adequate appropriation. "If those for whom it exists
still cherish the high educational ideal which it has fostered
and championed, that the boy or girl of humblest parentage
but with brilliant intellectual endowment should have an opportunity for education equal to that enjoyed by the children
of the most wealthy, it will not now fail of proper support. I
desire only to remind you that grants of revenue for the maintenance of the University should be regarded as investments."[85]

The legislature of 1911 did not grant all that was asked, but
it did increase the mill tax to 3/8 of a mill as Van Hise had
requested. It increased the $200,000-a-year grant for construc-
tion to $300,000 a year for the fiscal years beginning July 1,
1912 and July 1, 1913, providing however that $50,000 a year
of this increase should be used for purchase of books, apparatus,
furniture, and equipment. It did not provide a million dollars
for student buildings, although it granted a total of $150,000
for the next two years for a women's dormitory, gave generously
to the extension division and to the traveling schools of agriculture, and granted funds for the purchase of additional
property. This appropriation bill was the first passed by a legislature in which the regular appropriations to the University and
the other state institutions were submitted together.[86] Attempts
in the Senate to substitute a cash appropriation instead of the
millage tax and to require out-of-state students to pay a fee
equal to the cost of instruction were defeated.[87] The legislature
also provided funds for construction of an additional wing of
the library.[88]

Laws were also passed which governed the printing of University catalogues and other publications,[89] extended the term

[84] *Ibid.*, 2.
[86] *Laws of Wisconsin*, 1911, 831–836.
[88] *Laws of Wisconsin*, 1911, pp. 729–731.
[85] *Assembly Journal*, 1911, pp. 63–64.
[87] *Senate Journal*, 1911, p. 1116.
[89] *Ibid.*, 953, 955–956.

of the regents from three to six years,[90] authorized further agricultural demonstration stations, and modified the law under which the college maintained the stallion-registration service.[91] The legislature appropriated $10,000 for the purchase of two stump-pulling machines to be used by the College of Agriculture in land-clearing experiments and demonstration.[92]

Although the legislature passed no bills to hamper the University, and passed a great many helpful ones, its admiration was apparently tempered. It enacted a statute creating the state Board of Public Affairs, the precursor of the budget department; but it expressly stipulated that no member of the University faculty might be appointed to this board which, among its other functions, was intended to study the operation of the government and make recommendations for its greater efficiency. The legislature also considered but did not pass bills designed to abolish the farmers' institutes, require the University to purchase a flag and display it daily on University Hall, investigate University purchasing methods, require all male students entering the University to sign a written pledge promising to abstain from the use of intoxicants while at the University, prohibit the sale of liquor within one mile of the University, authorize the establishment of municipal universities to cooperate with the University, and establish an accident prevention museum.[93] It also considered a bill which would have fixed the admission requirements to the University,[94] and one which would have abolished the Board of Regents and established a central board of education.[95]

[90] *Ibid.*, 308.   [91] *Ibid.*, 61, 826–827.

[92] *Ibid.*, 565–567. The removal of stumps from cutover land in northern Wisconsin and Minnesota had been the subject of cooperative investigations for several seasons by the United States Bureau of Plant Industry and the Minnesota and Wisconsin Experiment Stations. This was, Dean Russell had reported, "the most serious drawback to the rapid settlement of this region." *Regents' Biennial Report*, 1909–10, p. 162. This law was introduced, appropriately enough, by Assemblyman A. J. Plowman. *Assembly Journal*, 1911, p. 212.

[93] Assembly Bill 710A, *Assembly Journal*, 1911, pp. 252, 581; Joint Resolution 345, *Senate Journal*, 1911, pp. 788, 816; Assembly Bill 45A, *Assembly Journal*, 1911, pp. 131, 1433, 1487; Joint Resolution 96A, *ibid.*, 432, 1173, 1273; Assembly Bill 188A, *ibid.*, 141, 641, 673–674, 741–744; Assembly Bill 747A, *ibid.*, 255, 1293; Assembly Bill 974A, *ibid.*, 499, 1446–1447, 1607.

[94] Assembly Bill 932A, *Assembly Journal*, 1911, pp. 283, 878.

[95] Assembly Bill 278A, *ibid.*, 159, 1412.

The legislature of 1913 was the last with which Van Hise enjoyed large success. The great well of energy within the University was perhaps subsiding. More important, the Progressives were divided. Senator La Follette had unsuccessfully sought the Republican nomination for the presidency in 1912. The Progressives were divided over the problem of whether to remain within the Republican Party, which La Follette did, support Roosevelt, which McGovern did, or bolt the party to support Wilson, which John J. Blaine of Boscobel did. The La Follette men apparently held nothing against Blaine for supporting Wilson, for La Follette himself campaigned in the summer of 1914 for Blaine, who ran for the Wisconsin governorship as an independent. But McGovern and his followers were not forgiven. McGovern, many La Follette men believed, had conspired with Roosevelt to deprive La Follette of the nomination in Chicago. When Roosevelt failed to get the nomination, McGovern had followed him into the Bull Moose campaign. McGovern retained the governorship in 1912 but Wisconsin returned its electoral votes for Wilson.

Van Hise appealed to the legislature for additional funds. He again asked for money for higher salaries, $878,000 beyond what had been appropriated for educational buildings, $607,000 for student buildings, and additional sums for miscellaneous purposes. He argued more specifically than ever before about the money value of the University to the state. Besides taking considerable pains to defend University expenditures on a purely material basis, he also protested the frequent misrepresentations of the cost of the University. These misrepresentations resulted from taking the total sum reported as spent and giving it as the cost of the University to the state. Van Hise properly denounced such "reckless" statements.[96] They took no account of the contribution made by the federal government, or of private gifts, or of income derived from donations, from the farm, or from other sources.

In his message to the legislature McGovern explained that the pre-eminence of the University was due "principally to its willingness to serve all the people of the state, especially those

[96] Report of the president, *Regents' Biennial Report,* 1911-12, pp. 31-45.

who have never been within its walls as resident students." He acknowledged that there had been criticisms of the institution but "the fear of university interference with the liberties of the people which in some quarters has taken the place of the primitive prejudice against higher education, is due entirely to a failure to recognize this function. The man who is working in the dark does not regard the bringing of light as an interference with his liberty unless he happens to be a safe blower.... Instead of interfering with freedom the University stands and through its extension division reaches out as the servant of all the people, holding aloft as its motto the inspiring greeting: 'And ye shall know the truth, and the truth shall make you free.' "[97]

In terms of money grants alone the University fared well with the 1913 legislature in the requests for funds both for operating expenses and for buildings. Over one million dollars was appropriated for land purchase, educational buildings, and student buildings. Some of these appropriations would not become available until the next legislature was in session, but the grants were impressive. For other University activities, too, the legislature was far from niggardly in its appropriations.[98]

This appropriation bill was noteworthy not only because it was the product of the last reasonably generous legislature for many years but because the legislature in 1913 returned to the practice of specifying the purpose for which appropriated monies should be spent. Moreover the legislature in its appropriation act chose to invade the prerogatives hitherto belonging to the regents. It appropriated funds which were derived from sources other than the state. This problem had been raised while La Follette was governor and had been put to rest. Now it was raised again, largely for the same reason, and for four years the legislature was to insist upon appropriating to the University all funds expended by the regents, whatever the source.

The appropriation bill of 1913, like the bill of two years before, was introduced by the Joint Committee on Finance and

---

[97] *Senate Journal,* 1913, pp. 45–46.
[98] *Laws of Wisconsin,* 1913, pp. 1123–1139.

provided funds for both the normal schools and the University. Unlike the earlier bills, it was long, detailed, and explicit, and for the University appropriation it added some thirty new subsections to the statutes. Seventeen of these new sections merely provided the amount of money to be used for each specified activity of the University during the coming two years. In appropriating $645,500 for construction of educational buildings, the legislature named the buildings which should be built and the amount of money which should be spent, although a clause was inserted giving the regents authority to reapportion up to ten per cent of the funds so obligated. Thereafter, a number of subsections were inserted to assure that all income of the University would be turned over to the state treasurer for deposit. The income was appropriated by the legislature to support the activity from which it was derived. The legislature, moreover, not content with what it had done, added another section which outlined the sources of funds to be used for the support and endowment of the University, stipulated that the income of all these funds should, "so far as appropriated by the legislature," be placed at the disposal of the Board of Regents, and further provided that the 3/8 mill tax be added to the University Fund income to be used "as specifically appropriated by the legislature." The legislature in this bill also fixed the rate of tuition for out-of-state students at one hundred dollars a year,[99] a provision which reflected the belief that out-of-state students were not contributing their full share to the support of the University. Attempts to increase the out-of-state tuition to $125 a year and to require the regents to collect from out-of-state students tuition fees equal to the per capita cost of instruction and operation of the University had been defeated.[100] Governor McGovern signed the appropriation bill but objected to passing appropriations for public institutions in an omnibus bill which, since the governor had to approve all or nothing, deprived him of his power.[101]

Other legislation adopted was of minor or passing impor-

[99] *Ibid.*, 1133.
[100] *Assembly Journal*, 1913, pp. 1503–1506; Assembly Bills, 1196A, Amendments 2A, 11A, 1913.   [101] *Assembly Journal*, 1913, pp. 1688–1692.

tance. A law was passed requiring the regents' meeting to be open to the press and public, although the regents' right to hold executive sessions was granted, provided the decisions of the session were made part of the record.[102] There were also laws relating to the establishment of a pharmaceutical experiment station, of county agricultural representatives, and of a soils laboratory and legislation on eradication of contagious diseases among animals, on the manufacture of hog cholera serum, on tuberculin tests of cattle, and on stallion enrollment.[103] Three laws were passed relating to the improvement of the Camp Randall Memorial Park.[104]

Many of the bills which were introduced but not passed indicated drifts of opinion. A central board of education was proposed.[105] A law was passed altering the composition of the Board of Visitors and extending its power, but it was vetoed by the governor.[106] Several bills were introduced directing that the University conduct research or offer instruction in phases of cooperative activity.[107] Bills were also introduced relating to the sale of liquor near the University.[108] Interest in student conduct was attested by a resolution calling for another investigation of the fraternities and sororities, a resolution under which the president of the Senate would have appointed a committee to confer with the Board of Regents of the University regarding "immoral conduct" in Madison, and another bill which would have prohibited dancing in state-owned buildings.[109]

[102] *Laws of Wisconsin,* 1913, p. 205.
[103] *Ibid.,* 446, 763–765, 842–844, 80–81, 408–409, 403, 163–170.
[104] *Ibid.,* 25, 32, 449.
[105] Assembly Bill 727A, *Assembly Journal,* 1913, pp. 144, 199. One, strongly opposed by Van Hise, made the Board of Regents elective. Assembly Bill 276A, *ibid.,* 154, 966.
[106] *Ibid.,* 1467–1469.
[107] Assembly Bills, S402A, 819A, 1913; Senate Bills, 387S, 1913.
[108] Assembly Bills, 411A and 558A, 1913.
[109] Assembly Bills, Joint Resolution 47A, 1913; Senate Bill 105S, *Senate Journal,* 1913, pp. 292–293.

6.

Getting and Spending: 1914–1925

T HE legislature of 1913 was the last moderately generous legislature for a long time. The building program, pushed each year by Van Hise with relentless
purpose, was first reduced in 1915 and then, because of the
war, virtually suspended. Van Hise died a week after the armistice, and Birge was president for the next seven years. When
construction of University buildings was resumed, somewhat
deliberately and under the pressure of a doubled enrollment
and higher costs, precedence was given to revenue-producing
buildings—dormitories, the Memorial Union, the hospital, field
house, and stadium. The major construction of educational
buildings had been all but completed before 1915.

The split which took place among the Progressives in 1912
had not been healed by the time the 1914 elections took place.
A representative of the conservative faction of the Republican
Party, Emanuel L. Philipp, a conservative businessman and an
outspoken opponent of La Follette, won the Republican nomination for the governorship. John J. Blaine of Boscobel ran
against him as an independent but, in spite of La Follette's
help in the campaign, was defeated in the election. McGovern,
who ran for the Senate in the same election, lost to his Democratic opponent. Before and during the campaign, Philipp had
pronounced various strictures upon the University; he had condemned radicalism, charged that the University was too expensive, insisted that the state of Wisconsin must not be re-

quired to provide expensive buildings largely for the use of out-of-state students whose tuition did not represent the full cost of their education, and urged that to assure the more efficient use of state funds a central board of education should be created to control the whole publicly supported educational system of the state. Philipp was charged with being hostile to the University, as indeed he was—at least to some of its activities. And the suggestion of a central board and the proposals of economy were denounced as attacks upon the University.

Van Hise to a large extent shared the fears about Philipp's intentions. In his report, however, he set forth the needs of the University, perhaps somewhat trimmed to suit the nature of the new administration, but stated in energetic and characteristically bold fashion. Again he spoke for increased salaries, but he did not urge any large appropriations for construction in addition to the funds which were granted in 1913 but were not yet available. Total requests for additional buildings for the biennium amounted to only $358,000, in which the largest amounts were for a student infirmary and a plant pathology building. Construction of a physics building, provided for from funds voted two years before, would relieve the congestion in Science Hall, he felt, and afford ample housing, temporarily at least, for the growing Medical School.[1]

In his report, without acknowledging directly the nature of some of the attacks upon the University, Van Hise discussed the causes of increased costs. He showed how much more work the University was doing, how the student body had increased, and he itemized the sources of support other than the state.[2] Van Hise's pleas for additional buildings encountered a snag in the report of the Allen Survey. This survey and some of its consequences are more fully treated elsewhere, but mention must be made here of one phase of the versatile Dr. Allen's work: his investigation to determine whether University buildings were being adequately and efficiently used. His line and block charts, showing clearly, if somewhat inaccurately, that classrooms and laboratories were not being used forty-four

[1] Report of the president, *Regents' Biennial Report,* 1913–14, pp. 23–34.
[2] *Ibid.,* 34–42.

hours a week (his standard for optimum usage) gave the legislators adequate reason to object to building appropriations.[3]

University officials encountered much difficulty in the legislature of 1915. The governor was intent upon getting a central board, and he got it. He wanted to reduce expenditures and he wanted to have out-of-state students pay more tuition. Here too he was successful. Two major appropriation bills were passed. The first, among other things, appropriated the sum of $1,296,269 for the year beginning July 1, 1915, and $1,372,449 for the following year. This sum was smaller by almost a hundred thousand dollars than the amounts contributed two years before. The bill limited to $10,000 the amount which could be used for salary increases. It also contained various miscellaneous appropriations.[4] A second appropriation bill renewed building appropriations made earlier, although it modified the amounts. Under this bill $129,400 was to be made available for construction in 1915–1916; $225,000 was to be available the following year, and the regents were authorized to devote $190,000 of it to the construction of either a medical or a physics building.[5] Additional appropriation bills were passed to provide for the University extension division, branch agricultural stations, and the hog-serum plant.[6] On the other hand, the legislature repealed the law of 1913 under which $350,000 was to be available for construction and furnishing of a men's dormitory.[7] A bill passed the Assembly which would have deprived the University of the benefits of the mill-tax support.[8] Another bill was passed amending the statutes to provide specifically that the Medical School be restricted to "courses of instruction customarily covered in the first two years of a medical curriculum."[9] This amendment, introduced by Senator J. Henry Bennett of Viroqua, was designed originally to restrict the course

[3] *Report upon the Survey of the University of Wisconsin: Findings of the State Board of Public Affairs and its Report to the Legislature* (Madison, [1915]), 723 ff. This publication will be cited hereafter as *Survey of the University*.

[4] *Laws of Wisconsin*, 1915, pp. 917–921.　　　　[5] *Ibid.*, 956–957.
[6] *Ibid.*, 732, 771–772, 893.　　　　　　　　　　　[7] *Ibid.*, 342.
[8] Assembly Bills, 238A, 1915; *Assembly Journal*, 1915, pp. 176, 1232–1233; *Senate Journal*, 1915, pp. 894, 1130. See chapter five, note thirteen.
[9] *Laws of Wisconsin*, 1915, p. 345.

to nonclinical subjects, but it was further modified to limit the entire course to two years. The amendment was a product of medical politics and had wide support among the doctors in Madison who feared the establishment of a University hospital. The legislature also passed a law directing the raising of out-of-state tuition to $124 a year.[10] The demand for an increase had been part of the platforms of both parties in 1914, but it was opposed by the president of the University, who feared that the higher fees would exclude many students from the University and result in provincialism.[11]

In addition to the legislation adopted, some of it showing hostility and much of it reflecting the desire of the legislature to invade the prerogatives of the Board of Regents, the legislature of 1915 appointed a joint committee to investigate purchases and sales of lands by the University.[12] The committee, consisting of Frank H. Hanson, chairman, Lewis G. Kellogg of the Senate, and Carl Hansen, Fred Hess, and H. J. Grell of the Assembly, began hearings on April 7 and completed them on May 23, 1915. Twenty-nine witnesses were called, including President Van Hise, a number of the regents, and various individuals knowledgeable about Madison real estate. In general, the committee confined itself to an investigation of land purchases, although attempts were made to embarrass Van Hise. Among the more amusing pieces of testimony was the attempt of the committee questioner to get Regent G. D. Jones to admit on the witness stand that Van Hise dominated the Board of Regents. This, of course, was an absurd and impertinent question to put to Jones.[13] After a thorough and in part hostile investigation, the committee brought in a report declaring that there had been disagreement among witnesses as to the necessity of many of the land purchases, that specific reasons for some purchases were absent, that the regents had not been unanimous in support of some purchases, that the purchases

[10] *Ibid.*, 741.

[11] Syllabus regarding Bill 47A, Presidents' Papers, filed under Legislative; *Assembly Journal*, 1915, pp. 33–35.

[12] *Laws of Wisconsin*, 1915, pp. 983–984.

[13] *Testimony and Report of the Special Legislative Committee to Investigate and Examine into the Purchases and Sales of Lands for and by the University of Wisconsin* (Madison, 1915), 158–162.

were not always carefully surveyed, that the land was often over-priced, and that the University already had enough land. "Your committee feels that the course of the Regents and the president, who appears to have dominated the Regents and who takes, in his testimony, the credit and the blame for all these purchases, has been unwise, unsystematic, wasteful and without regard to the welfare of the state."[14] Yet the report did not stop further appropriations for this purpose.

The legislature also entertained various hostile or restrictive measures. Bills were proposed to prohibit members of the faculty from holding appointive or elective municipal offices,[15] to abolish the regents and place their power with the superintendent of public instruction,[16] and to limit the functions of the student health service to examination, diagnosis, and first aid.[17] There were also bills to investigate nonresident tuition[18] and to prevent hazing[19] and a number discussed below relating to the inspection of high schools and the admission of high school graduates to the University.

Before the end of the session the Allen Survey had been generally discredited and the press had rallied to the support of the University. Moreover, Governor Philipp found that the University had many friends and his opinions about it seem to have changed. How much his attitudes changed between January and August it is difficult to say, but certainly it was moderated, partly because he frequently had to elaborate it, and partly because he learned more about the institution. But he had not yet come to trust Van Hise completely. As the session approached adjournment, several state newspapers assailed the legislature. The *Milwaukee Leader,* Victor Berger's Socialist paper, charged that academic freedom was already under ban[20] and quoted Harry Laidler's charge that the faculty had failed to defend it against the attacks of the Philipp forces.[21] The Milwaukee *Evening Wisconsin* circulated through the state Van

---

[14] *Assembly Journal,* 1915, p. 1449. [15] Assembly Bill 37A, *ibid.,* 82, 245.
[16] Assembly Bill 649A, *ibid.,* 404.
[17] Senate Bills, 222S, 1915; *Senate Journal,* 1915, pp. 176, 424; *Assembly Journal,* 1915, pp. 597, 1107, 1167.
[18] Joint Resolution 26S, *Senate Journal,* 915, pp. 200, 432.
[19] Senate Bill 9S, *Senate Journal,* 1915, pp. 60, 781.
[20] *Milwaukee Leader,* August 7, 1915. [21] *Ibid.*

Hise's warning to the Senate that a cut in the University appropriation would "turn the University into a college. This would destroy the very heart of the institution."[22] The next day the Milwaukee *Free Press* announced that the Philipp forces had won a victory in cutting University appropriations by a total of $458,000 for the biennium.[23] Governor Philipp, however, informed the legislature that the reduction in the appropriation was only $150,000 and that the amount could be replaced in case of an emergency.[24] Governor Philipp was probably closer to being right than his critics. Van Hise himself, when he addressed the faculty at the opening of the fall semester in 1915, declared that the University had only been scratched.

The legislature of 1917 was the last regular session which Van Hise dealt with. In general the tensions of 1915 had relaxed; the mutual suspicion which had characterized the relations of Van Hise and Governor Philipp had been largely dissolved. Governor Philipp, an undramatic man, had the ability to modify his views. He had gathered around him a group of young men, mostly graduates of the University, who were sympathetic to the institution. Among these were Lawrence C. Whittet, '98—speaker of the Assembly in 1915 and 1917 and associated with Philipp from 1915 to 1925, Michael J. Cleary, George Hambrecht, and others. Dr. Joseph Evans of the Medical School became a close friend and adviser of Philipp, as did Professor John G. D. Mack and Dean Charles Bardeen. Halsten J. Thorkelson, business manager of the University, was also trusted implicitly by the governor.[25] It is often asserted that Van Hise won Philipp over to the University; perhaps it would be nearer the truth to say that the governor had around him men sympathetic to the University and that he himself, through them, came to a better understanding of its problems.

How this affected the president in his recommendations to

---

[22] Milwaukee *Evening Wisconsin*, August 12, 1915.
[23] Milwaukee *Free Press*, August 13, 1915.
[24] *Senate Journal*, 1915, pp. 1327–1328.
[25] Lawrence C. Whittet is of the opinion that Thorkelson's work as business manager was of first importance in bringing Philipp to modify his views about the University. The governor never completely lost his doubts about Van Hise, but on Thorkelson's word he relied absolutely. Interview, Carstensen with Whittet, December 30, 1947.

the legislature of 1917 is not, of course, on record, but the recommendations, prepared before the end of the year, were less defensive than in 1915. Again Van Hise was demanding as of old. Nothing less than the world's greatest university should be the possession of Wisconsin. Again in his recommendations to the Board he pleaded for higher faculty salaries. He buttressed his argument with extensive quotations from the recognized publications on prices and business trends. He asked for specific appropriations for research for the College of Letters and Science and for the College of Engineering; he wanted a department of art; he wanted $105,000 for a new administration building, a music hall, auditorium, and many other small buildings and improvements. He asked for $50,000 for a student infirmary, $240,000 for a men's dormitory, $200,000 for a student union, $200,000 for a medical building, and $135,000 for reconstruction of University Hall, the dome of which had been destroyed by fire on October 10, 1916. For the purchase of additional land he asked another $120,620. Van Hise also proposed that the statutes be amended so that all disbursements of the University would not appear to be derived from the state. Since under the law the receipts of all University income funds were shown as funds appropriated by the state, many people assumed that the money had been raised by taxation. He complained that when the appropriation to the University for the year 1915–1916 was reported to be $2,765,330.30, many supposed that all of it came directly from the state treasury, although actually only $1,664,602.27 had been contributed by the state. Accordingly, he stated that "in order that misconceptions which honestly exist in this respect may be dissipated it is proposed that all the funds which the University receives from other sources than the state be set aside for the University by general acts as funds to be used by the University for the purposes appropriate to the source of the money. To do this is only fair and reasonable. By such action the University will be saved many embarrassments and misconceptions which have heretofore existed in regard to the amount of money derived from the state."[26] He asked, too, that the law governing nonresident

[26] Report of the president, *Regents' Biennial Report*, 1915–16, pp. 32–33.

tuition be modified so that minors whose parents had moved to Wisconsin and adult students who had become citizens could enjoy the benefits of the University, to which as citizens they were entitled, without having to pay nonresident tuition.[27]

How much Van Hise and the University supporters might have received had conditions not changed rapidly it is of course impossible to say. In his message to the legislature Governor Philipp had advised that new construction be postponed if possible because of the high cost of materials and the shortage of labor. Public construction, he urged, should be reserved to help out in the depression which was expected after the war.[28] But there was little doubt that the governor was now friendly. A large part of the program would probably have passed in one way or another, but war was declared while the legislature was in session. Immediately after the declaration of war, when it was urged that the University be closed, a proposal was made that the University give up all its requests for capital outlay, retaining only the operation and maintenance budget and requests for necessary repairs and improvements. Van Hise was not willing to give up everything. He wrote Governor Philipp that only one building of any consequence remained in the request—the administration building.[29] Even so, the University appropriation bills moved along so smoothly that the *Milwaukee Leader* remarked sourly that this showed the result of Van Hise's deserting the Progressives for Philipp's camp.[30]

Seven appropriation bills were passed: one provided the major appropriations; two provided special funds for the agricultural college, for land-clearing experiments and for agricultural education and demonstration;[31] two provided funds for a student infirmary, the one to pay rent for a temporary infirmary, the other to finance the construction of a new building;[32] one provided funds for University extension work;[33] and one supplemented the main appropriation bill, providing funds for improvements and construction.[34] The major appropriation bill

[27] *Ibid.,* 33–34.   [28] *Assembly Journal,* 1917, p. 28.
[29] Van Hise to Governor Philipp, April 14, 1917; Thorkelson to Senator Platt Whitman, chairman of the finance committee, April 13, 1917, both in the Presidents' Papers.   [30] *Milwaukee Leader,* May 10, 1917.
[31] *Laws of Wisconsin,* 1917, pp. 838–839, 1188–1189.   [32] *Ibid.,* 967, 1003.
[33] *Ibid.,* 818–819.   [34] *Ibid.,* 1129–1130.

contained substantially all that had been asked for and some things, such as an appropriation of $5,200 a year for the department of Semitic languages and Hellenistic Greek, which were not sought by the administration. The bill provided the sum of $1,572,556 for operations in 1917–1918, and for the next year, $1,584,556 for operations, and additional miscellaneous sums; these amounts were substantially larger than those voted two years before.[35] At the same time the legislature, while enlarging and making more representative the Board of Education, virtually destroyed it by providing that all funds in the appropriation bills which had been given to the Board of Education for the institutions designated were to be turned over directly to the institutions named.[36] It left the Board of Education, during the remainder of its existence, an agency which approved the budgets of the higher institutions and transmitted the budgetary requests to the governor.

It was also significant that, in accordance with Van Hise's request, the appropriation bills provided that the various monies received by the University become revolving funds to be used for purposes appropriate to the source of the money. The governor was also empowered in the general appropriation act to suspend "either in whole or in part, the activities and functions of any or all departments of the University."[37] The legislature also modified the law governing nonresident tuition as requested by Van Hise.[38] Other laws passed provided assistance for blind students,[39] authorized the regents to establish a "training school for public service,"[40] and made other miscellaneous changes.[41]

Few hostile gestures were made. A resolution calling upon Van Hise to explain both his refusal to permit Max Eastman to speak at the University and his permission for Bryan to do so was passed by the Assembly but defeated in the Senate.[42] A bill intended to permit the readmission of students who had left the University because of academic failure and to admit special

[35] *Ibid.*, 756–761.
[36] *Ibid.*, 787–791, 1195.
[37] *Ibid.*, 761.
[38] *Ibid.*, 612–613.
[39] *Ibid.*, 1000–1001.
[40] *Ibid.*, 678–679.
[41] *Ibid.*, 807–809, 1014–1024.
[42] Assembly Bills, Joint Resolution 13A, 1917; *Assembly Journal*, 1917, pp. 103, 107; *Senate Journal*, 1917, pp. 103–104.

adult students also passed the Assembly but was defeated in the Senate.[43] Another bill which would have reduced the size of the Board of Regents and placed representatives of labor upon it passed the Assembly only to be defeated in the Senate.[44]

The war into which the United States plunged in April, 1917, cut across the development of the University. In the fierce flames of patriotism, sometimes real, sometimes synthetic, which burned during the war, the clarity of purpose was lost. The war experiences in Wisconsin hung for years like somber shadows over the University and its faculty. There is no need here to blame or praise but rather to understand the changes which had been wrought and the antagonisms which developed over this great conflict. Wisconsin's population was largely of German origin—"hyphenated Americans" Theodore Roosevelt had called them. La Follette, re-elected to the Senate in 1916, had opposed the drift toward war. He was a conspicuous member of that "small group of willful men" denounced by President Wilson. After war was declared La Follette continued to be outspoken. He denounced profiteers, demanded a draft of property, and in a speech in St. Paul on September 20, 1917, was mistakenly quoted as saying that he "did not believe our grievances were sufficient to warrant entering the war."[45] That La Follette had said something else did not matter. The speech had been made before the Non-Partisan League and reports of it in various garbled forms appeared in the nation's press. A Senate committee was designated to investigate.[46]

Meanwhile charges were being made in Madison and elsewhere that the University was not doing its war duty. Carl Vrooman, Assistant Secretary of Agriculture, aired such charges. There were others. The *Capital Times,* launched early in December, 1917, denounced these attacks upon the University, saying they had no basis in fact. Only a few days later the editor of the *Capital Times* was refused membership in the Madison

[43] Assembly Bills, 630A, 1917; *Assembly Journal*, 1917, pp. 698, 995; *Senate Journal*, 1917, pp. 695, 820.

[44] Assembly Bill 344A, *Assembly Journal*, 1917, pp. 268, 981; *Senate Journal*, 1917, pp. 679, 878.

[45] From the *Wisconsin State Journal*, September 21, 1917. See Ellen Torelle, comp., *The Political Philosophy of Robert M. La Follette* (Madison, 1920), 349–350.

[46] *Ibid.; Capital Times*, December 20, 1917.

Association of Commerce on the grounds that in the last legislature he had voted against a resolution pledging loyalty to
President Wilson. On December 29 it was announced that Senator La Follette had been expelled from the Madison Club for
his stand on the war.[47]

The embarrassment of the McElroy incident was still to
come, but already many felt that the University must dissociate
itself from La Follette and the charge of Germanism. Van Hise
took the lead. The day before the senator was expelled from
the Madison Club, Van Hise had written to John S. Lord, president of the Alumni Association, asserting that the University
did not support Senator La Follette. For a record of the University's participation in the war, Lord was referred to the February issue of the *Alumni Magazine,* which would contain a full
statement. As for La Follette, Van Hise declared, "I strongly
believe the policies of Senator La Follette in relation to the war
are dangerous to the country."[48] Van Hise's letter was made
public shortly afterward. Early in January the Wisconsin Loyalty Legion was organized at Madison with Richard T. Ely as
president.[49] And on January 15 it was announced that a faculty
petition was being circulated condemning La Follette's stand
on the war.[50] The *State Journal* greeted the news of the faculty
action with delighted approval.[51] The Board of Regents
adopted a resolution officially approving the work of Van Hise
and the University faculty and, by implication at least, the attacks on La Follette.[52] The faculty petition, the famous "round
robin," bore the names of two hundred and ninety-nine members of the faculty, including those of Van Hise and the deans, a
full ninety-three per cent of the whole body. Men who had
stood with La Follette since 1900 signed.

It was within this tangled skein of political conflict and war-
born antagonism that the University had to operate in the
years immediately after the war. The legislature of 1917 was

[47] *Capital Times,* December 14, 19, 20, 29, 1917.
[48] *Ibid.,* January 7, 1918, p. 2. The letter was reprinted in full in the *Wisconsin State Journal,* January 16, 1918.
[49] *Capital Times,* January 11, 1918, p. 2.
[50] *Ibid.,* January 15, 1918, p. 8.
[51] *Wisconsin State Journal,* January 15, 1918, p. 10.
[52] *Ibid.,* January 16, 1918; *Capital Times,* January 16, 1918, p. 2.

twice called into special session, once to arrange for replacement of a senator, and the second time, in September, 1918, to provide funds and authority for the University and other state institutions to maintain the Student Army Training Corps. The legislature provided funds as requested.[53]

The reduction of both student body and faculty during the war had resulted in various savings. In April, 1918, Van Hise wrote a colleague that although fees from students had declined, the University had stayed well within the state appropriations, and that it was anticipated that in the next year the University would fail to spend approximately $80,000 of its appropriation.[54] Van Hise had gone off to visit Europe in August of 1918, leaving the preparation of his annual report to Birge, who was acting president. Only a short period passed between the time of his return and his death.[55] The regents then made Dean Birge president. Because of the uncertainty caused by the war and the larger uncertainty emerging from the cessation of hostilities in November, the president's report contained no program for the biennium except the statement that the needs of the University remained largely as they had been two years before. The statement of construction needs was presented in the report of the business manager.[56] In short, the University officials came to the legislature without much of a program. Their requests were based upon a faulty analysis of future needs. It was expected that student enrollment would not exceed the 1916–1917 average and that prices would decline at once.[57]

The University had relatively little trouble in getting the legislature to meet its modest requests in 1919. The major ap-

[53] *Laws of Wisconsin*, Second Special Session, 1918, pp. 3–5.
[54] Van Hise to President Marion LeRoy Burton, University of Minnesota, April 3, 1918, Presidents' Papers.
[55] The report of 1917–18 bore Van Hise's name, but he had not seen the material. Report of the president, *Regents' Biennial Report*, 1917–18, p. 13, fn.
[56] *Ibid.*, 331–333.
[57] In his report as president in 1920, Birge wrote of the plans for 1919–1920: "The financial measures to be presented to the Legislature of 1919 for the current biennium were discussed with the State Board of Education in the fall of 1918—in the days preceding and immediately following the Armistice. The following principles were agreed upon: (1) The number of regular two semester students in 1919–20 was not likely to exceed 5,000—the number present in 1916–17; (2) Prices were likely to fall rapidly as the army was broken up and

propriation bill provided substantially the same amount of money for operations as had the bill two years before, plus additional miscellaneous sums for construction purposes. The operations budget was to consist of $1,577,056 for the year 1919–1920 and $1,635,344 for the next year. Twenty-eight thousand dollars was voted for a soils building and $80,000 for a medical or physics building was again approved. The bill also authorized a full medical course.[58] Additional bills provided funds for agricultural experimental work in Door County and at Marshfield and for county agricultural representatives; another bill altered the regulation of University and other trust funds held by the state.[59] And the legislature passed a joint resolution honoring Van Hise in death as it never had in life.[60]

Other pieces of legislation were considered which indicated the current interests of the legislature. Bills were introduced in both houses proposing that the Board of Regents be constituted on a basis of professional and occupational representation.[61] Bills were also introduced exempting honorably discharged veterans from payment of tuition and incidental fees at the University and the normal schools[62] and appropriating funds for construction of freshman dormitories,[63] but they failed to pass. At this session the most conspicuous opposition to the University appropriation bill came not, as it often had, from the conservatives but from the Socialists. In March the *Capital Times* reported that Senator Louis A. Arnold, Senate leader of the small Socialist group, had attacked the University bills on the grounds that reactionary forces had appeared in the Uni-

the conditions of peace were restored; (3) All matters of building and similar permanent improvements were postponed until the full return of peace." Report of the president, *Regents' Biennial Report*, 1919–20, p. 16. Birge gave substantially the same explanation to Senator A. C. Anderson, February 20, 1920. Birge to Anderson, Presidents' Papers. Nothing is said about the reason for having agreed upon this set of guiding principles, although President Birge twenty-two years later explained in part the basis for his belief in the imminent fall of prices. Edward A. Birge, "The University of Wisconsin: Its History and its Presidents," *The Wisconsin Alumnus* (Madison), 44:13–16 (November, 1942).

[58] *Laws of Wisconsin*, 1919, pp. 124–131.

[59] *Ibid.*, 167, 344, 606–607, 756–759, 1109.

[60] *Ibid.*, 1384–1385.

[61] Senate Bills, 309S, 1919; Assembly Bills, 458A, 1919.

[62] Assembly Bills, 396A, 1919.   [63] Senate Bills, 465S, 1919.

versity during recent years.[64] The next month the Socialists voted against the appropriation bill because the faculty had circulated the "round robin."[65]

The legislature of 1919 had also adopted a soldiers' bonus law.[66] A bill providing for veterans' schooling had passed both houses during the regular session but was vetoed by the governor on the grounds that the benefits offered under the bill would be available only to those who could meet the entrance requirements of the institutions designated for veterans' education; it made no provision for increasing educational facilities and staffs.[67] The governor, however, conducted an investigation to determine how many veterans wanted an educational bonus and what kind they desired. When the data had been tabulated, he called a special session of the legislature to present the results and to ask the adoption of the appropriate legislation. He proposed that the law should express the gratitude of the state to all who served in the military. He thus included the nurses. All who had been in the service on November 1, 1918, should be offered the benefits. Veterans should be permitted to have the kind of education from which they would benefit.[68] The legislature adopted a bill incorporating the principal features of the governor's recommendation. It provided that the state would assist any honorably discharged veteran of the war to secure four years of education. Veterans who elected this opportunity were entitled to draw $30 a month. The state emergency board was authorized to apportion funds to the institutions in accordance with needs growing out of attendance of veterans, and a tax of not more than one-eighth of a mill, plus a surtax on incomes, was voted to supply funds.[69]

Even without the added enrollment encouraged by the adoption of this bill, University authorities discovered that they had misjudged the future. On the one hand, all prices had moved steadily upward; on the other, instead of the five thousand students that had been expected, seven thousand appeared in the fall of 1919 and the number was swelled another five hundred

[64] *Capital Times*, March 26, 1919. [65] *Ibid.*, April 11, 1919.
[66] *Laws of Wisconsin*, 1919, pp. 1163–1166. [67] Senate Bills, 348S, 1919.
[68] *Senate Journal*, Special Session, 1919, pp. 5–9.
[69] *Laws of Wisconsin*, Special Session, 1919, pp. 1658–1664.

before the end of the year. In short, the University quickly and unexpectedly found itself in grave difficulty. The number of students, increased by roughly fifty per cent, had to be accommodated in buildings which were barely adequate five years before with a student population of less than five thousand. The increased number of students required an increase in the University staff. And while the University was trying to obtain additional instructors, other universities also were bidding for the limited number of teachers, and the cost of living, instead of retreating, as the regents and the president had expected, increased.

Even before the legislature adjourned, there had been protests from the faculty, at first restrained and later almost shrill, on the difference between salaries and the cost of living. In May a faculty committee reported that living costs had risen forty per cent during the last five years and salaries for men in the lower ranks from four per cent to thirteen per cent.[70] The president was unmoved. To a department head who wrote him about an offer from another institution at a higher salary, Birge gave little sympathy. If any salary increases were to be allowed at all, they would go to the men on smaller salaries.[71] Yet some action had to be taken.

In June the regents authorized the executive committee to grant bonuses. A sum not to exceed $50,000 was to be apportioned to instructors and assistant professors receiving salaries of $2,500 or less.[72] But in the fall with the unexpected rush of students, the need for additional instructors, and the continued upward rise of living costs, President Birge at last became reluctantly convinced that something must be done. Accordingly he began a wide correspondence to gather data on salary increases at other institutions. At the October meeting of the Board, data presenting a comparison of salary rates between Wisconsin and Minnesota, showed that Wisconsin lagged far behind.[73] But still no definite steps were taken. A mass meeting of the faculty was called and a committee formed to educate the

[70] *Daily Cardinal,* May 12, 1919.
[71] Birge to Hugh Smith, June 5, 1919, Presidents' Papers.
[72] Records of the Board of Regents, J:337, June 24, 1919.
[73] Papers of the Board of Regents, October 8, 1919.

public and the administration on the need of salary adjustments.[74] The *Wisconsin Alumni Magazine* took up the question. In November it reported that the big problem at Wisconsin was to make faculty salaries meet the seventy per cent increase in the cost of living since 1914.[75] A month later it announced that the alumni council was pledged to support an early demand for salary increases, and still later the council appealed to all alumni to acquaint legislators with the problem.[76] The *Daily Cardinal* supported the faculty agitation for increased salaries and before the Christmas holidays invited students to carry word of the plight of the University to all parts of the state. It warned that the University was on the verge of losing "several of its strongest faculty members." [77]

In December, 1919, President Birge presented the details of the gloomy picture to the regents. He now pointed out that the budget as adopted by the legislature represented a reduction of $612,203 below the departmental requests of the University. The budget had been based on the expectation of a student body of five thousand, and already the enrollment approached seven thousand. "Study of the history of university attendance would indicate that this number is but little above the attendance that might have been expected if conditions for the past five years had been normal." He argued, by statistical and other means, that the enlarged enrollment need not be regarded as a short-time phenomenon; all indications pointed to its continuation. Additional funds must be obtained to support the institution. He proposed that the mill-tax rate be increased from $\frac{3}{8}$ of a mill to $\frac{1}{2}$ mill. This increase would give the University an additional income of $500,000 a year, but if living costs continued to go up, even this increase would not suffice for long. Salary schedules at Wisconsin, he asserted, had changed little since 1915; living costs had risen sixty per cent. Wisconsin, moreover, had lagged behind the other universities in the region in making salary adjustments. He presented a table showing that only Ohio State University had lower average salaries

[74] *Wisconsin State Journal,* October 23, 1919.
[75] *Wisconsin Alumni Magazine* (Madison), 21:2–3 (November, 1919).
[76] *Ibid.,* 21:35 (December, 1919); 21:63–65 (January, 1920).
[77] *Daily Cardinal,* November 7, December 4, 1919.

than Wisconsin. He asked for emergency increases of salaries and pointed out that large additional sums would be needed to meet increased operating expenses. Some money for the present year could be obtained from the Emergency Board from unappropriated balances in the income fund—balances which had been built up over the years to bridge the gap between the beginning of the fiscal year and the time for collection of taxes under the millage bill. If this were done, additional funds would have to be secured for the next year, probably by a special session of the legislature.[78]

Some of the regents appeared more disturbed by the situation than the president. Regent Florence Buckstaff wrote Birge urging that "we go the limit" and warned that faculty feeling was "somewhat similar to the feeling in the days when we lost Turner and Harper." She advocated raising salaries the next semester.[79] Birge responded cautiously but promised that he would shortly announce salary increases: "I believe that such an announcement as this will satisfy the faculty without their demanding that the details of next year's budget be made known at once."[80] At the regents' meeting later in the month the faculty presented data showing that to restore faculty salaries to their 1913–1914 buying power would require increases ranging from forty-one per cent for instructors to fifty-six per cent for professors and deans.[81] Early in February, Birge announced that official approval had been given for the use of the University Fund surplus to raise salaries in all ranks above that of assistant, but the increase would not go to any who had joined the faculty after the current budget was adopted, or to any faculty members who had announced that they were leaving during the semester or at the end of the current year. The increases would range from twenty to thirty per cent.[82]

This action meant, of course, that an attempt would be made to have the governor call a special session of the legislature. Dr.

[78] Birge and Thorkelson to the regents, December 3, 1919, Papers of the Board of Regents.
[79] Florence Buckstaff to Birge, January 22, 1920, Presidents' Papers.
[80] Birge to Florence Buckstaff, January 24, 1920, Presidents' Papers.
[81] Communication of the University committee to the regents, Papers of the Board of Regents, January 29, 1920.
[82] Minutes of the Meetings of the Faculty, 8:237–240, February 2, 1920.

Joseph S. Evans, professor of internal medicine and director of
the student health clinic, was sent, as the unofficial emissary of
the University, to see the governor at his home in Milwaukee.
Governor Philipp, who was thoroughly conversant with the
plight of the University and sympathetic to the requests, was
at first dubious about a special session. He had already called
one such session to deal with the problem of the soldiers' bonuses. When Evans asked him to call another special session to
vote an estimated million dollars for the University, Philipp
wanted to know how the money would be raised. Evans proposed an increase in the mill-tax rate, an increase advocated by
University authorities for a number of years. The governor said
that he could call a special session and present the proposal, but
that probably somebody would then move immediate adjournment on the grounds that the business could just as well be
taken up by the next regular session. After more reflection Governor Philipp told Dr. Evans that he had formulated a plan: he
would call the legislature together to consider legislation under
which the money remaining in the soldiers' bonus fund would
be returned to the general fund and then appropriated for the
construction of a Wisconsin memorial hospital. The legislature
would not then dare to adjourn and legislation for the relief
of the University could be presented. Thus, besides getting
funds to meet the rising costs of the University, there was a
likelihood that the University would obtain a hospital. The full
medical course, approved by the legislature in 1919, could then
be developed.[83]

In May, 1920, Governor Philipp called a special session of
the legislature. In his proclamation he asked that the legislature
increase tax support for the University, increase appropriations,
and provide for a hospital by authorizing the transfer of the unexpended balance in the soldiers' bonus fund to the general
fund.[84]

President Birge's attitude toward this maneuver was apparently one of reluctant acquiescence. A man of simple tastes himself, he acknowledged the need of somewhat higher salaries for
the lowest paid members of the staff, but he was far from con-

[83] Interview, Curti and Carstensen with Dr. Joseph Evans, October 12, 1945.
[84] *Senate Journal*, Special Session, 1920, p. 4.

vinced that Wisconsin needed to match the salaries paid in other institutions. He had responded slowly to the mounting pressure within the faculty. In his recollections he acknowledged that he had sought a fifty per cent increase in salaries, which he thought would be enough to "enable the teachers to live in reasonable comfort" during the year or two immediately before them. Of Governor Philipp's attitude he wrote: "I am sure that he would not have approved action which doubled salaries. I felt also that he might have agreed to a somewhat larger increase than that which I proposed, but I have no direct evidence on that point."[85]

While Birge held back, seemingly more fearful of the consequences of a future depression than of the immediate inflation, others were busy carrying the story of the University's plight to the state. Basil King, in the weeks before the session, prepared a series of eight articles for the *State Journal* on the financial problems facing the University. He reviewed the early history of the University and told, inaccurately, how the regents had once been compelled to sell lots to help meet expenses; he discussed the need for a full medical course and a hospital; he rehearsed a history of the land grant and compared it with the handling of the Cornell lands; and he concluded with an article showing that the situation in which the University found itself was not of its own creation—the budget had been made on the basis of an expected enrollment of five thousand, not seven thousand students.[86] King's last article appeared on the day the legislature convened.

Governor Philipp was ready with a full exposition of the needs of the University. The Medical School needed a hospital or the medical course would have to be restricted or abandoned. Other states, he pointed out, had full medical courses and Wisconsin should offer one. He observed pointedly that a state so generous in appropriating funds to aid animal industry could well contribute to the health of its people. On the need for a general appropriation to relieve the University he was equally forthright. Prices had by now almost completely doubled. Enrollment had increased beyond expectations. He proposed in-

[85] *The Wisconsin Alumnus,* 44:15 (November, 1942).
[86] *Wisconsin State Journal,* May 12–15, 1920.

creasing the mill tax from 3/8 to 5/8 of a mill, which would increase the income of the University about a million dollars, and asked for appropriations, as proposed by University officials, of $998,529 for operations, $43,610 for maintenance, $25,000 for purchase of books and apparatus, $18,900 for extension work, and $90,700 for an addition to the chemistry building.[87] In addition Governor Philipp proposed an appropriation of $1,500,000 for a hospital, nurses' home, and equipment,[88] urging that the funds therefor be provided by the transfer of the surplus from the soldiers' bonus fund to the general fund. The governor told the legislature bluntly that the money had to be furnished. He was not willing to accept the responsibility for reducing educational efficiency and thought the legislature was also unwilling to accept such responsibility.[89]

On the large matters before it the legislature showed no inclination to dissent from the governor. Item for item the appropriation bill provided the exact sums he had recommended.[90] Similarly, in providing for a hospital, the legislature followed the recommendations of the governor except in the request for $300,000 for construction of a nurses' home. This amount was reduced to $150,000.[91] In two particulars the legislature differed from the governor. He had wanted the hospital to be called the Wisconsin Soldiers' Memorial Hospital and University Clinic. This the Senate changed, preferring the name of State of Wisconsin General Hospital.[92] Secondly, the governor had recommended that the surplus from the Service Recognition Fund be transferred to the general fund and from there transferred to the University income fund for use in construction of the hospital.[93] Instead, the legislature, on political and constitutional grounds, provided that the surplus from the Service Recognition Fund be transferred directly to the University Fund in-

[87] *Senate Journal*, Special Session, 1920, pp. 13–21. These items, with the exception of the addition to the chemistry building, were exactly what was asked for by the University and argued for before the legislative committee, and they were received to the last odd dollar. See the statement to the legislature regarding operation, maintenance, and capital in Papers of the Board of Regents, May 26, 1920.

[88] *Senate Journal*, Special Session, 1920, pp. 13–21. [89] *Ibid.*, 21.
[90] *Laws of Wisconsin*, Special Session, 1920, pp. 3–4. [91] *Ibid.*, 36–38.
[92] *Senate Journal*, Special Session, 1920, pp. 36, 41. [93] *Ibid.*, 22, 46.

come and credited to the appropriations allowed for the hospital.[94]

The sharpest break, and the most serious which occurred between the governor and the legislature, developed over the increased millage rate asked to support the larger appropriation for the University. The University requested an increase from 3/8 to 5/8 of a mill. This the governor recommended to the legislature, and a bill to increase the tax was introduced in the Senate by Senator Ray J. Nye. It immediately became embroiled in the conflict over tax theory. The full opposition to property taxes and millage support of institutions had not yet developed as a part of the Progressive program, but it was beginning. At the regular session, in providing funds for the soldiers' bonus, the legislature of 1919 had decreed that the funds would be raised by the levy of a surtax on incomes. Senator Nye's bill providing an increase of 2/8 of a mill in the millage support of the University was promptly amended. Senator Severson proposed that the old millage rate be retained but that additional funds be procured from a surtax on individual and corporation incomes.[95] After considerable jockeying a bill containing these amendments was adopted by the close vote of 14 to 13 and finally passed by a vote of 23 to 5.[96] The bill was immediately passed by the Assembly.[97]

[94] *Laws of Wisconsin*, Special Session, 1920, p. 37. The struggle over this matter had both political and legal bases. As Dr. Evans recalled, after the hospital bill had been introduced, a group of the Progressive Republicans in the Senate told him that they would not pass a bill which returned to the general fund money raised for a specific purpose and then reappropriate it for a hospital. If they passed a bill at all, it would be one that simply provided for the use of any surplus in the soldiers' bonus fund for the construction of a hospital. Evans carried the decision of the Senate leaders to the governor. He was highly exercised but refused to make a decision immediately. Shortly thereafter Evans was told by an able lawyer that the administration bill which returned bonus funds to the general fund was probably unconstitutional. Evans invited him to talk to the governor. Apparently he did, because Evans was subsequently called to the governor and told that he might tell the gentlemen from the Senate that the governor would accept their bill. Interview, Curti and Carstensen with Dr. Evans, October 12, 1945.

[95] Senate Bill 2S, Substitute Amendment 1S, *Senate Journal*, Special Session, 1920, p. 24.

[96] The close vote was on the adoption of the amendment incorporating the surtax provision into the bill; the other vote was on final passage. *Ibid.*, 52.

[97] *Assembly Journal*, Special Session, 1920, pp. 72–75.

Governor Philipp vetoed the bill. He objected to establishing a new tax policy under which proceeds from income tax would be used for a specific instead of a general purpose. Although he had approved of such a tax for a soldiers' bonus he thought it a special case. Under the new policy, the large majority might impose upon the small minority in high income brackets. This would lead to extravagance and wastefulness in government. He did not object to income taxes for general purposes if fairly distributed, but he felt that income taxes should be left to the federal government, pointed out that few states had income taxes, that the Senate by its close vote had shown itself divided on the question, and that, because incomes fluctuated, it would be an unsatisfactory means of supporting schools. He concluded: "There is still another vital objection. Our educational institutions have been created and are maintained for the benefit of all the people. We believe them to be democratic, and we wish them to remain so. If the university and the normal schools must look to a small number of businessmen and manufacturers for their revenues, they will ultimately be dominated by that class of people, a situation that none of us should desire."[98]

The legislature made no attempt to pass the bill over Governor Philipp's veto. On June 4 it went home. In reviewing epochal legislation affecting the University, President Birge later declared that the nine-day special session in 1920 would stand high on the list and the results of the session should be definitely and permanently associated with the name of Governor Philipp.[99] Leadership in getting financial aid had been taken by the governor.

The president of the University chose to defend Philipp's opposition to the use of income surtaxes for the support of the University. The occasion was an alumni banquet in June, 1920. Many, of course, approved Birge's action,[100] but his opposition to surtax support also provoked outspoken criticism. The *Capital Times* declared that as an economist Birge was a "back

---

[98] *Senate Journal,* Special Session, 1920, pp. 61–64.

[99] *The Wisconsin Alumnus,* 44:15 (November, 1942).

[100] Regent Florence Buckstaff wrote to Birge congratulating him on having taken the "taxation bull by the horns so neatly and firmly at the Alumni dinner. . . . They are right in saying that the *have-nots* will vote away the money

number." Reporting that he had opposed the support of the University through surtaxes on incomes, and that he had insisted that all should have a share in contributing to the institution, the *Capital Times* asserted: "Within the past ten years the sentiment of this university has changed. It too easily defends the profiteer and has little to say for the poor." The paper warned that if the University were to be supported liberally both property taxes and surtaxes on incomes should be used.[101]

We need not here follow in detail the actions of the legislatures of 1921, 1923, and 1925. Birge himself summarized this period by saying that there was no significant change in the income from the state for operation of the University during the years from 1920 to 1925.[102] During the same period the legislature contributed about $1,500,000 for buildings.[103] His summary passes over or obscures the nature of the relationship which obtained between the University and the legislature. However, the fact remains that no material increase of money was obtained from the state for operations although the student body increased by over a thousand. Several points stand out. Perhaps because of the split with the La Follette forces during the war, perhaps for other reasons which shape political opinion and condition political behavior, the University no longer found its most valiant supporters among the Progressives, the Socialists, and other reformers. It was no longer in their eyes a champion of reform. Neither President Birge nor any of those around him could consolidate support for it. The University became the victim of a split in the Republican Party over the proper means of raising taxes.

In his report to the regents, intended for the governor and the legislature in 1921 (the last report to be printed in conformity

---

of the *haves* in irresponsible ways, unless they too have a stake." The injustice of such voting, she felt, "is a stronger argument than democratic control of education." With the support of prominent men she did not fear a factional quarrel. Birge responded that he agreed entirely that "the important aspect of the question is that which you indicate." He said further that those who disagreed with Severson's bill ought to have a constructive program, that Wisconsin politics had too long consisted of the Progressives proposing a policy and their opponents merely opposing. Buckstaff to Birge, June 24, 1920; Birge to Buckstaff, June 26, 1920, both in the Presidents' Papers.

[101] *Capital Times*, June 23, 1920, p. 1.
[102] *The Wisconsin Alumnus*, 44:16 (November, 1942).   [103] *Ibid.*

with the law, which still remains in the statutes, requiring the regents to report each biennium), Birge explained the errors in the budget making of two years before and reported that faculty salaries had been raised fifty per cent by virtue of the grant of the special session. This salary increase, he felt, should be retained. He again explained the need for a larger income. Carefully skirting direct reference to surtax on incomes, the president pointed out that an attempt to increase the University income had failed through "executive disapproval." He pointed out that the funds needed for operations would be only slightly larger than those granted by the special session. "In order to finance these costs, it asks an increase of the revenue from that raised by the 3/8 mill to the equivalent of that raised by 5/8 mill. This is the same request as was made from the special session and the sum involved is also substantially the same as that contemplated in the tax law passed by that session." [104]

The president did not say specifically that the University wanted a 5/8 mill tax; it wanted an increase which would yield the equivalent. He asked also for money for buildings. Only the physics-economics building had been authorized since 1913. Requests aggregating three million dollars, he said, had been made for buildings and equipment. To illustrate the need for a building program he pointed out that although the University should have a library, gymnasium, and medical building, none of these was covered by the three million request. From the 1921 legislature Birge sought enough money to prevent salary reductions. To Dr. Joseph Evans, who represented him in many dealings with the governor and legislature, Birge wrote urging that he use every effort to make the governor understand that the operations budget "ought to be maintained without reduction." He asked him to emphasize that Wisconsin salaries had been the lowest at any institution in the region until the increases of 1920, that even now they lagged behind Michigan, and that requests for operations were lower than those presented by any neighboring universities with the exception of Iowa, which did not include an agricultural college. [105]

[104] Report of the president, *Regents' Biennial Report*, 1919–20, p. 22.
[105] Birge to Evans, February 23, 1921, Presidents' Papers.

Bascom Hall Burning in 1916

Volunteers Leaving for Military Service, 1917

But the legislature was not sympathetic. From 1921 until the time of Birge's retirement it was under the partial or complete control of the La Follette branch of the Republican Party. John J. Blaine, who had run against Philipp as an independent in 1914, was elected governor in 1920. The Assembly and, later, the Senate were captured by the Progressive Republicans. Many of the Progressives had come to view the University with an uneasy suspicion.

The general University appropriation bill of 1921 carried some slight additions to what had been voted for operating expenditures by the special session of 1920. But instead of the grant of $3,000,000 for capital expenditures the bill merely reauthorized grants made in 1919 and provided something more than $300,000 for miscellaneous buildings.[106] Special appropriation bills were also passed providing funds for the Ashland Junction experiment station, for the Door County experiment station, and for land purchase at the Hancock experiment station.[107] It was resolved to appoint a legislative committee to investigate the necessity of constructing or acquiring a building for use of the extension division in Milwaukee.[108] Other laws established a teacher retirement system which would include the University,[109] dealt with the administration of the educational bonus law,[110] modified the fiscal control of the University funds slightly,[111] and regulated the use of the Wisconsin General Hospital;[112] one piece of legislation appropriated from the general fund to the Service Recognition Fund a sum large enough to meet the appropriations which had been made from that fund for the hospital.[113] Bills reorganizing the Board of Regents were again presented providing that the Board of Regents, along with

---

[106] *Laws of Wisconsin,* 1921, pp. 1032–1038.

[107] *Ibid.,* 488, 881, 901.

[108] Joint Resolution 56A, *Laws of Wisconsin,* 1921, p. 1182.

[109] *Ibid.,* 762–768.   [110] *Ibid.,* 230, 472–473, 894–896.

[111] *Ibid.,* 1045–1047.   [112] *Ibid.,* 800–801.

[113] *Ibid.,* 608. This law was interesting. After construction of the hospital had been authorized from the surplus of the Service Recognition Fund, it developed that the surplus might not be sufficient. Hence, instead of procuring a grant directly from the general fund for that purpose, Dr. Evans got the legislature to agree to deposit in the Service Recognition Fund a sum sufficient to meet the obligations of the fund in the construction of the hospital. Papers of the Board of Regents, October 12, 1921.

other educational boards, should be made up in part on the basis of occupation.[114] Another bill was presented raising non-resident tuition at the University to $500 a year.[115] These bills were not passed.

Amendments to the University appropriation bill, establishing a surtax on incomes for the support of the University, were proposed in both houses. They failed,[116] and so did a separate bill presented by Senator Severson providing for the levy and collection of a surtax on incomes for educational purposes.[117] Thus the University received neither an increased mill tax nor additional support from surtaxes. The legislature in 1921 made it clear that no additional permanent support could be expected in the form of an increased millage tax. It also reflected a salient part of the Progressives' new program, the use of income taxes for the support of educational institutions. Although defeated, this idea had not been destroyed. The dissatisfaction with the membership of the Board of Regents betrayed the belief, often repeated by the Progressive newspapers, that the Board of Regents had become the stronghold of conservative forces. The reorganization, in part defended on the grounds of representation of economic interests, was clearly aimed at altering the complexion of the Board.

Within two weeks after the legislature had adjourned, one of the regents, Florence Buckstaff, warned Birge that Governor Blaine was already talking about the necessity of cutting faculty salaries, but the president was unworried. He acknowledged that there was always the possibility that there would be a political combination between the Non-Partisan League element and the governor's party. "That is the possible danger and I am certainly not worrying greatly about it at present."[118]

[114] Senate Bill, 98S, 1921; *Senate Journal*, 1921, pp. 144, 962. The bill passed the Senate but was defeated in the Assembly by the close vote of 45 to 40. *Assembly Journal*, 1921, p. 1349; Assembly Bill 367A, *Assembly Journal* 1921, pp. 477, 1062.

[115] This was overwhelmingly defeated in the Assembly. Assembly Bill 462A, *Assembly Journal*, 1921, pp. 738, 967–968.

[116] Assembly Bill 367A, *Senate Journal*, 1921, p. 1152; *Assembly Journal*, 1921, pp. 1660–1661.

[117] Senate Bills, 50S, 1921; *Senate Journal*, 1921, pp. 117, 1147–1148. The bill was defeated in the Senate by the close vote of 17 to 15.

[118] Florence Buckstaff to Birge, July 28, 1921; Birge to Buckstaff, August 1, 1921, Presidents' Papers.

The legislative session of 1923 was one of the most fractious on record. In 1922 La Follette had run for re-election to the United States Senate. He had swept into office with him the whole state ticket and what appeared to be a clear majority of Progressive Republicans, but they were tied together more by the common bond of opposition than by policy. Blaine was re-elected governor. The legislative session was marked by sharp and sometimes unseemly conflicts. There were incidents such as that which followed a committee hearing on the normal school academic program, when a legislator and the secretary of the normal school regents got into a fist fight outside the committee room.

In his communication to the legislature Governor Blaine, while protesting loyalty to his party's pledge of support to the University, spoke harshly about the tendency of the educational system to overdevelop administrative machinery. It caused institutions to "veer away from a democratic system of education, and the more the machinery is developed, the farther we get away from democracy." Having stated this questionable principle, Blaine attacked the University, where, he said, such machinery had developed "to a position where it is charged as lacking a broad democratic viewpoint." In the last twenty years, he pointed out, the staff had increased five and three-tenths times, attendance only three and seven-tenths times. "This means that a part of the staff must have much idle time, or their time is devoted to matters purely private. This condition has led to the serious suggestion that the University is made for the staff rather than for the students and the state. In fact the increase in the staff should have kept step only with the increase in attendance." Though he could not bring himself to say that the research conducted was without value, he urged that the appropriation for the operation of the University "should not be based upon the increase in the number of the staff; in fact, such appropriation should be reduced to an amount that will furnish the necessary and proper staff, based upon the student attendance."[119]

The governor subsequently acknowledged that his attack was based upon misinformation furnished by the secretary of the

[119] *Senate Journal*, 1923, pp. 41–42.

218 *University of Wisconsin*

Board of Education. It is indicative, however, of the widened gap between University administration and the state government that the governor, after two years in office, should have been so poorly informed upon the internal affairs of the University. The scapegoat of the governor's embarrassment was the Board of Education, which was eliminated.[120]

Shortly after the legislature met, Senator Henry A. Huber introduced a joint resolution declaring that the "round robin" contained "libelous aspersions on the record and character of Robert M. La Follette, Wisconsin's most distinguished citizen," that the members of the faculty had been induced to sign the document under duress and intimidation "and now desire [that] the wrong done to Senator La Follette be rebuked," that the documents were "emanations of hate and malice inspired by war profiteers and public enemies," and that Senator La Follette was a "most distinguished alumnus of the University." The documents on file were "false and a disgrace to their authors." The people of Wisconsin in the recent election had overwhelmingly endorsed La Follette's public record, thus "repudiating his detractors." The resolution then directed that the "round robin" should be surrendered and burned. Later, on the advice of Senator La Follette, the resolution was changed so as to condemn the action of the faculty of the University "as unworthy of men employed in Wisconsin's greatest educational institution," but the document was not ordered burned.[121]

One other incident of the session suggests the temper of this hectic period. A month after the resolution of censure was passed, Eugene Debs came to Madison to deliver a lecture in the gymnasium under the auspices of the Social Science Club,

[120] Birge published a statement showing the errors in the governor's figures. The governor then corrected his figures and publicly accused the secretary of the Board of Education of having given him misinformation. *Wisconsin State Journal*, January 18, 1923.

[121] Joint Resolution, 19, *Laws of Wisconsin*, 1923, p. 1038. *Senate Journal*, 1923, pp. 86, 428; *Assembly Journal*, 1923, pp. 419, 420, 422. In the Senate the amended resolution, with the burning feature stricken out, passed by a vote of 17 to 12, in the Assembly by a vote of 81–11. It is impossible to know exactly what this resolution meant in the terms of the legislative attitude toward the University, but everybody knew, because the *Capital Times* republished all the names on the "round robin," that the president of the University was one of the prominent signers.

a student association made up largely of socialists. A large crowd, estimated at around twenty-five hundred and including many legislators, turned out to hear Debs on the evening of April 18. Someone turned off the lights after the audience had gathered. It was almost an hour before a missing fuse was replaced.[122] Meanwhile, a delegation of legislators had called on Birge to demand that the lights be turned on again;[123] and some people professed to believe that President Birge himself had been responsible for the act.

In the legislature attention was focused upon the Progressive program of reducing property taxes and substituting additional income taxes. In the session of 1920 the advocates of the surtax had been content to use income taxes plus property taxes to support higher education. In 1923 they wanted only income taxes. The taxation issue was concentrated largely in several bills intended to change the basis of support for state educational institutions from a property tax to an income tax. Sponsored by the governor, these bills were introduced in both houses.[124] The Senate refused a third reading of its bill by a vote of 12 to 10.[125] But there was no doubt about the willingness of the Assembly to pass the income-tax measure. Several attempts were made to get the measure through the Senate by attaching it to other legislation, but they all failed. Assemblyman John Gamper of Medford offered a resolution on June 26 urging the Senate to concur in "tax legislation that will relieve the burden now borne by farmers."[126] It also attacked the war profiteering and tax dodging which had brought the farmer to the "brink of ruin." The resolution held that the Assembly had passed a bill, advocated by the governor, which "provides for the financing of higher educational institutions by income taxes in lieu of taxes on property." Under this bill "every citizen shall pay taxes according to his means and ability to pay." Accordingly the Assembly called upon the Senate "to give the farmers of this state a square deal in the matter of taxation and expresses to the Senate its determination not to vote any appropriations

---

[122] *Capital Times*, April 19, 1923.   [123] *Ibid.*
[124] Assembly Bills, 250A, 314S, 1923; *Senate Journal*, 1923, pp. 646, 1183.
[125] *Ibid.*, 1183.   [126] *Assembly Journal*, 1923, p. 1681.

for higher educational institutions unless financed by income taxes."[127] The Assembly adopted the resolution immediately. Thus, in effect, the Assembly told the Senate that unless the income-tax measure was passed, the educational institutions of the state would receive no additional appropriations. Under the law the appropriations made two years before would continue unless changed.

The resolution was received in the Senate with oratory and disorder. Senator Ridgeway protested that the Assembly was attempting to coerce the Senate, that it was violating the principles of representative government.[128] The next day the Senate defeated the tax bill by a vote of 16 to 15, and the Assembly promptly responded by attaching an income-tax provision to the University appropriation bill and passing it by a vote of 56 to 8.[129] The bill, as passed by the Assembly, carried an appropriation of $8,419,571 for the biennium—over $1,000,000 more than first recommended by the governor.[130] The Senate received the University appropriation bill and other educational appropriation bills and promptly removed the income-tax provisions. The University bill was then adopted by a vote of 14 to 12.[131] The Assembly refused by a large vote to accept the amendment.[132] A conference committee was appointed to attempt to reconcile the differences between the two houses. Neither side would retreat, so the committee was discharged and the appropriation bill permitted to die.[133] In the Senate the vote stood 13 to 12 on the question of whether to accept the committee report.[134] Thus, on the issue of taxation policy the University appropriation bill was killed and the institution required to operate until the next meeting of the legislature on a basis of funds voted in 1921. How much the lack of aggressive University leadership was responsible for this outcome it is impossible to say. A supporter might have been found among the thirteen senators who defeated the Assembly measures; or the two who did not vote on the final count might have been prevailed upon to vote. In any event, the result was a crippling blow.

[127] *Ibid.*, 181–182.   [128] *Capital Times,* June 26, 1923.
[129] *Assembly Journal,* 1923, pp. 1660, 1779; *Capital Times,* June 27, 1923.
[130] *Capital Times,* April 24, 1923, p. 16; July 2, 1923.
[131] *Senate Journal,* 1923, pp. 1485–1487.   [132] *Assembly Journal,* 1923, p. 1866.
[133] *Senate Journal,* 1923, pp. 1493, 1494–1495.   [134] *Ibid.,* 1494.

Although the legislature failed to pass an appropriation bill in 1923, it took numerous other steps in legislating for the University. It abolished the state Board of Education.[135] It reorganized the Board of Regents by increasing the size of that body to include one regent from each congressional district plus four from the state at large, the state superintendent and the president of the University as ex-officio members, and provided that in addition to the two "mandatory women," two members of the Board should be farmers and two engaged in the "manual trades."[136] It directed that military drill be made optional[137] and it opened the way for the construction of dormitories by permitting the regents to use surpluses from revolving funds to build or acquire dormitories, commons, or other buildings or permanent improvements, and further authorized the regents to lease University lands to a nonprofit corporation or corporations for the purpose of building dormitories or commons, the cost of which would be liquidated over a period of years.[138] It also appropriated $150,000 for purchase of a site and construction of an extension building at Milwaukee[139] and passed various other laws assigning miscellaneous duties to the University.[140] A resolution was introduced calling for legislative investigations of the educational system.[141] Another was introduced in the Assembly condemning the undemocratic social functions held at the University,[142] while the Senate considered and passed a resolution directing that the capitol should no longer be used for dances.[143] Attacks were made upon the Door County experiment station, the farmers' institutes, and the land-clearing demonstrations.[144] The session was a critical, difficult one, unmatched by any since 1915. In 1923 there was sorely lacking the vigorous leadership of a Van Hise or the calm, conservative balance of a Governor Philipp.

In contrast with the session of 1923, the 1925 legislature was moderate and contemplative. Representatives of the University, including the president of the regents, Theodore Kronshage,

---

[135] *Laws of Wisconsin*, 1923, p. 357.

[136] *Ibid.*, 375–376.

[137] *Ibid.*, 417–418.

[138] *Ibid.*, 691–693.

[139] *Ibid.*, 828.

[140] *Ibid.*, 295, 618, 664, 705–707.

[141] *Senate Journal*, 1923, pp. 678, 1045.

[142] *Assembly Journal*, 1923, pp. 66, 345.

[143] *Senate Journal*, 1923, pp. 451, 833.

[144] Assembly Bills, 729A, 223A, and 222A, 1923.

and the president of the Alumni Association, George I. Haight, early began a systematic campaign to assure an increase in funds. Numerous reports and newspaper articles pointing out the imperative need of a larger appropriation were circulated.[145] The hot and tempestuous differences of 1923 had cooled. The appointment of Glenn Frank as president was announced while the legislature was in session. The Board of Regents was largely in the hands of Progressive appointees.

In his message to the legislature, Governor Blaine omitted reference to the University, although he complained that too much was being spent for education.[146] However the appropriation bill not only increased the funds for operations but provided approximately $1,000,000 for additional buildings. The bill was passed without encountering a last-ditch fight over tax policy and the 3/8 mill property tax was permitted to stand.[147] Authority was granted to construct a field house,[148] and other miscellaneous bills were passed. The legislature again modified fees for nonresidents.[149]

In 1925 the acts of the legislature seemed to suggest that the University was on the way toward re-establishing itself as it had been in the days of Adams and Van Hise. There was promise of a brighter day ahead—if support could again be consolidated.

Writing about the University in 1927, President Glenn Frank expressed the opinion that the great energy which had characterized the University in the first decade of the twentieth century had begun to subside even before the war. "But an unexpected break came in the cycle. An unusual factor was injected into the situation. The United States became involved in the World War. And from this fact two results of fundamental significance to the University followed. Certain circumstances of this war period over which neither State nor University as such had control made a further slowing down in the development of the University inevitable. And, in addition to this slowing down that was enforced by economic necessity, certain other circumstances, induced and aggravated by the emotional instability, recklessness of judgment, and extravagance of expression that

[145] *Daily Cardinal*, February 23, 1925.   [146] *Assembly Journal*, 1925, pp. 24–25.
[147] *Laws of Wisconsin*, 1925, pp. 431–439.
[148] *Ibid.*, 91–92.   [149] *Ibid.*, 412–413.

marked the war period everywhere, brought a breach between many people in Wisconsin and their University. I realize that I am here treading on delicate ground. I see no reason, however, for dodging a fact that is as obvious as a street corner lamp post. And, clearly, the healing power of a new understanding cannot be reached save by the road of complete candor. Dating from the war period, a good many people in Wisconsin became convinced that the essential spirit of the University was at variance with their spirit."[150]

THE University had been given no large sums of money before 1900. The first substantial contribution, except the one for the Washburn Observatory, was made by President Adams. He gave all his property, subject to the life interest of his widow, to the University. Van Hise in his inaugural address publicly called for gifts to the University.

There was some response during the next years, but gifts did not contribute substantially to the working funds of the University. The amount reached three per cent in 1918–1919 but dropped again to less than one per cent of the total receipts of the University. In 1921–1922 such contributions exceeded three per cent and in 1933–1934 reached four per cent of the total.[151] The receipts consisted of income from funds held in trust by the University and gifts, mostly in the form of scholarship or research funds, turned over to the University for specified purposes. Trust funds increased from $64,634.25 in 1906 to $627,435.81 by June 30, 1926.[152] By 1941 University trust funds amounted to $1,144,670.16.[153]

In 1925 the propriety of the University's accepting gifts from certain sources was questioned by the older Robert M. La Follette. In a series of editorials and articles which appeared in *La Follette's Magazine* the preceding year he had attacked one

[150] *The Wisconsin Blue Book*, 1927 (Madison, 1927), 363.

[151] *Report of the Business Manager*, 1925–26, p. 10; 1934–1935, p. 47.

[152] *Regents' Biennial Report*, 1905–06, p. 212; *Report of the Business Manager*, 1925–26, p. 61. The trust fund had been almost doubled the year before through receipt of a gift of $300,000 from the estate of J. Stephens Tripp.

[153] *Ibid.*, 1940–41, p. 61.

monopoly after another. In January, 1925, he called attention to the contributions American millionaires were making to educational institutions and the warning that had been issued by the United States Industrial Relations Commission in 1916 of the "increasing control over education by great wealth." He attacked the Rockefeller General Education Board and the Carnegie endowments. "Our universities, colleges and other education institutions," he wrote, "are cringing and fawning for the favors of predatory wealth. Big business must be cajoled and propitiated. Money however dirty or rotten is made a God. It may reek with the filth of the sweat-shop, it may represent the labor of little children warped and dwarfed in body and mind. It may be coined from the anguish of broken homes, the horror of the trenches or the hell of war—it cannot be too vile or debased in its source to devote to the cause of higher education." He called upon the governing bodies of private institutions to be on guard. "As to state institutions which are maintained by general tax levy upon all the people, we are just about due to have a general awakening upon this subject."[154] A month later he returned to the subject, warning that the issue must be met. "More particularly," he charged, "the University of Wisconsin, with its old traditions of academic freedom, must take the lead in restoring that fearless 'winnowing and sifting of truth' which is paralyzed by the subsidies, direct and indirect, of the Monopoly System."[155] Four months later La Follette was dead.

At the annual convention of the Wisconsin Federation of Labor in July, 1925, Assemblyman William Coleman of Milwaukee introduced a resolution censuring the Board of Regents for having accepted a gift of $12,500 from the Rockefeller Foundation. The gift, to be used for medical research, had been accepted only after heated discussion by the Board and a tie vote which was broken when President Birge cast the deciding vote. The Coleman resolution was reported under a banner headline in the Madison *Capital Times*. In support of the resolution Coleman declared, "We cannot hope for free discussion and the truth in educational institutions influenced or con-

[154] Signed editorial, *La Follette's Magazine*, 17:2–3 (January, 1925).
[155] *Ibid.*, 17:19–20 (February, 1925).

trolled by wealth." In the proffer from the General Education Board he saw a sinister plan to capture the state University.[156] An attempt was made by Regent Michael Olbrich the next day to set the record straight. In a statement to the *Capital Times* Olbrich pointed out that the regents had merely followed the will of the legislature and a long-established policy in accepting the gift.[157] But this had no effect in quieting the editor of the *Capital Times,* who answered with a long editorial arguing that the regents should return the Rockefeller money, that Wisconsin had long been proud of its University maintained by the people, that "tainted" money was not wanted. Rockefeller was attacked, the dangers of this precedent pointed out, and the Board, dominated by Progressive Republicans, was chided. It was proposed that if the regents did not give the money back, the legislature ought to make them do so. "The soul of the University is not for sale to interests that are in the business of buying colleges and universities" to "aid in the preservation of the present economic frontiers."[158]

The attack was not countered authoritatively. President Birge had resigned. Glenn Frank had been appointed president and was to enter office in the fall. No one speaking officially for the University announced that the grant offered by the General Education Board carried no condition except that the money be used for the purpose for which it was granted, that is, for medical research. The only answer came from the student paper, the *Cardinal.* The editor defended acceptance of the gift and denied the influence of Rockefeller on the institution supported by his money. He pointed out that Robert M. Lovett, who had been sought by Progressives for the presidency of the University, had served many years at the University of Chicago without being corrupted. If the state wanted to be exclusively responsible for the support of the University, it could be, but it had been reluctant to assume full support.[159] Furthermore no one revealed what was already known to members of the Board: besides the $12,500 gift which the regents had voted to accept, addi-

---

[156] *Capital Times,* July 22, 1925, p. 3. *Wisconsin State Journal,* July 22, 1925.
[157] *Capital Times,* July 23, 1925, p. 3.   [158] *Ibid.,* July 24, 1925, p. 24.
[159] Quoted in the *Capital Times,* July 28, 1925, p. 16.

tional gifts amounting to $740,000 were in prospect for the Medical School and for John R. Commons' research.

There was of course an area for honest disagreement over the question of whether a state-supported university should accept private funds of any kind for any purpose. If it should not, the assumption would be that the state should so support the university that private gifts would be unnecessary, and the possibility of control by special interests would be avoided. This view, entertained by many responsible people, rested on the assumption that power exercised by public officials is on the whole less apt to be perverted than power exercised by individuals responsible to no one but themselves. This position is probably correct although a close examination of the composition of agencies that exercise power ought to indicate that no wholly adequate machinery exists which will guarantee that power resting either upon wealth or upon political preferment will not be abused.

On August 1, four days before the next regents' meeting, the *Capital Times* reported that some members of the Board would attempt to rescind the motion accepting the Rockefeller gift.[160] Three days later the same paper carried a double-column, front-page article by Regent John Cashman declaring that the money must be returned. The University, he insisted, must not be under obligation to a monopoly. The state could and would support the University. He also attacked the Cecil Rhodes foundation which was "working through a secret society for the extension of the British Empire, sending American young men over to Oxford to get the spirit and ideals of the Empire Builder"; denounced the Carnegie pension system as "pensioning professors, making the men who teach our youth subservient to the wishes and politics of the Carnegie organization"; and attacked Rockefeller. There was also another editorial demanding that the regents reverse themselves.[161]

Fifteen members of the Board of Regents were present at the meeting of August 5. The policy of the Board in accepting gifts came up again in connection with approval of the Medical School budget which contained the Rockefeller grant. This item

[160] *Ibid.*, August 1, 1925.   [161] *Ibid.*, August 4, 1925, pp. 1, 16.

was excepted from approval, whereupon the discussion, unrecorded in the minutes of the Board, turned to the matter of accepting gifts. Regent Grady proposed a resolution: "That no gifts, donations, or subsidies shall in the future be accepted by or on behalf of the University of Wisconsin from any incorporated educational endowments or organizations of like character."[162] There followed a stormy four-hour session. The group opposed to acceptance of gifts argued against acceptance of Rockefeller funds because they had been improperly solicited, because of their source, and because of the possibility of Rockefeller domination. They also argued that the state should furnish adequate support for the University.

President Birge, Theodore Kronshage, who was president of the regents, and Regent Michael Olbrich pointed out again and again that the state had not supported the University fully, and that acceptance of these donations did not entail control of the institution. At one point Olbrich objected that the regents could not look into the source of all funds offered the University: "We are not a morals squad. Let's be consistent and keep our halo on straight if we are going to wear one."[163] But the opposition had the votes. An attempt to postpone decision on the Grady resolution failed by a vote of 8 to 7. The resolution

[162] Records of the Board of Regents, L:185, 190, August 5, 1925. Regent Grady later explained his opposition as follows: "First, a by-law existed in the University of Wisconsin ... which forbade any member of the faculty from soliciting funds from the Legislature, corporations, or individuals, without the consent of the Board of Regents. Second ... in 1925 ... the educational foundations required as a condition of advancing any fund an application showing that the institution was in financial need, which showing, I insisted, could not be made by the University of Wisconsin in view of the fact that the Legislature was by implication, under the Constitution, required to maintain it adequately, and that no member of the faculty had a right to violate this by-law, nor could the University itself justly and truthfully make a showing that either the state was unable or the Legislature unwilling to provide adequately for it. Third ... the resolution which I introduced ... might have been more clear had I recited the requirements of the Foundations as to the showing of financial need or unwillingness of the Legislature to provide adequately. However, the ground of my objection was repeatedly stated to be against the *soliciting of funds,* and while reference was invariably made through the press and otherwise that the advancement was a gift, I insisted then and now that the State of Wisconsin cannot justifiably make the showing then required by the Foundation. It was not a gift, much less a voluntary one. It was a yielding to the application made without authority and certainly was not justified under the financial situation of the University." Daniel H. Grady to Merle Curti, March 4, 1949.

[163] *Capital Times,* August 6, 1925, p. 9.

then passed by a vote of 9 to 6.[164] The *Capital Times* approved the outcome in a jubilant and belligerent editorial.[165]

Thus the decision was taken. No Rockefeller money would be accepted. Two weeks later the *Capital Times* announced that the General Education Board and the Rockefeller Foundation were about to give the University $740,000, $600,000 for the Medical School and $140,000 for research in economics under the direction of John R. Commons. Newspapers and magazines in and out of the state discussed the regents' decision, while various alumni and other organizations prepared resolutions for or against the regents' resolution. Certain newspapers jeered at the "tainted money" argument which some members of the Board advanced in defense of their stand. It could have been pointed out that the regents had accepted money more freshly tainted than the Rockefeller funds. The *Christian Science Monitor*, however, pronounced the regents' decision a wise one.[166] *The Outlook* thought the incident must be understood in terms of the contest in Wisconsin to succeed the late Senator La Follette but conceded that perhaps "behind the political gesture lies something finer, something independent and healthy."[167] But support of the regents' action in the public press was scant. The *Capital Times* remained steadfast in support of the regents, but it stood almost alone. The *New York Times*, according to the *Milwaukee Sentinel*, disapproved and the alumni in the East denounced the action.[168] Theodore Kronshage and Daniel Grady argued the question in the newspapers.[169] Zona Gale, who only a short time before had prevailed upon the regents to accept a gift from an outdoor advertising company, issued statements of her own, insisting that state educational institutions must not look to monopolies for support.[170]

A committee of nine alumni met in Madison to launch an in-

---

[164] Records of the Board of Regents, L:190, August 5, 1925. Regents Bachman, Cashman, Casperson, Gale, Grady, Hirschmann, Nace, Richardson, and Schmidtmann, for; Callahan, Faast, Gunderson, Kronshage, Olbrich, and Waters, against.

[165] *Capital Times*, August 6, 1925, p. 16.

[166] Quoted in the *Capital Times*, August 13, 1925, p. 16.

[167] *The Outlook*, 140:541 (August 19, 1925).

[168] *Milwaukee Sentinel*, August 17, 1925, p. 3.

[169] *Wisconsin State Journal*, August 22, 1925; *Capital Times*, August 29, 1925.

[170] *Wisconsin State Journal*, August 24, 1925, p. 4.

vestigation.[171] The committee invited regents, professors, and others to testify.[172] The professors declared that the policy of the regents would be detrimental, and Professor Leith asserted that without research funds the University would be nothing more than a "glorified high school." Stories were circulated that distinguished professors were preparing to leave the University.[173] These rumors were later given point when members of the staff left for other positions and admitted to the assiduous *Capital Times* that the policy of the Board was their principal reason for moving.[174]

The new president, Glenn Frank, arrived while the regents' decision was still being widely discussed and his skill in creating nicely balanced statements was immediately put to the acid test. To the faculty he said, "We must assure to the research of this institution as nearly complete freedom as is humanly possible in an organized society and, as I see it, freedom of research in this institution implies freedom from the influences and dictates of organized wealth and freedom from the influence and the dictates of organized politics."[175] A month later in welcoming the convention of the National Academy of Sciences he said: "Speaking for the plans and purposes of the administration and for the scientific staff, I can assure you that the University of Wisconsin will neither cut itself off from the vast co-operative efforts of American and European scholarship nor retrench on its own research program."[176]

Meanwhile the alumni committee formulated its report. The Board of Visitors took the matter under advisement. When the regents met again in December they received but did not act upon a resolution from the Visitors asking that the regents reconsider their action. They also received a resolution from the Duluth Wisconsin Club protesting the action taken in August.[177] The alumni committee had failed to agree. A minority supported the Board.[178] The majority condemned it.[179] The board

[171] *Ibid.*, October 2, 1925.   [172] *Ibid.*, October 3, 1925.
[173] *Ibid.*, October 16, 1925.   [174] *Capital Times*, April 12, 17, 1926.
[175] *Wisconsin State Journal*, October 8, 1925.
[176] *Capital Times*, November 9, 1925.
[177] Papers of the Board of Regents, December 2, 1925.
[178] *Capital Times*, October 26, 1925.   [179] *Ibid.*, December 28, 1925.

of the Alumni Association approved the report of the majority
and both reports were subsequently printed in the *Wisconsin
Alumni Magazine.*[180]

The majority of the regents were unmoved. Having made
their decision they were determined to stick by it. Despite newspaper criticism, protests, and petitions to reconsider their action,
they refused to alter their policy. They were publicly supported
by the Progressive Women's League of Milwaukee and the
Madison Federation of Teachers.[181] To use Olbrich's phrase,
the regents had decided to wear a halo. It remained to be seen
whether they could keep it on straight. The test, the *Capital
Times* announced, was coming—the Engineering Foundation
had appropriated funds to conduct a three-year research program in the College of Engineering. The *Capital Times* pointed
out that the regents would have to decide whether this organization was an incorporated educational foundation.[182]

At a meeting on June 19, 1926, the regents decided to accept
the funds offered by this foundation.[183] At this meeting they
also accepted other gifts amounting to over $100,000, including
$50,000 from the Wisconsin Manufacturers' Association, and
gifts from the Quaker Oats Company, the Milwaukee City Milk
Products, the Wisconsin Utilities Company, and the Commercial Solvents Company. The *Capital Times* remarked that the
policy of the regents now seemed to be to accept anything unless
it came from Rockefeller or Carnegie.[184] Some of the newspapers
were at a loss to understand the action of the Board, but among
the regents at least one member saw no conflict between the
earlier resolution and the action of the Board.[185] The next year
an attempt was made to carry a resolution through the legislature directing the regents to suspend their resolution of
August 5. It was defeated in the Senate.[186]

So the matter stood until the end of the 1920's. In 1928
Walter Kohler was elected governor. At the March, 1930, meet-

[180] *Milwaukee Journal,* February 21, 1926; *Wisconsin Alumni Magazine,* 27:
91–95 (February, 1926); 27:124–125 (March, 1926); 27:155–156 (April, 1926).
[181] *Capital Times,* October 8, 1925.   [182] *Ibid.,* May 20, 1926.
[183] Records of the Board of Regents, L:289, June 19, 1926; Papers of the Board
of Regents, June 19, 1926.   [184] *Capital Times,* June 19, 1926.
[185] *Milwaukee Journal,* June 20, 1926; *Wisconsin State Journal,* June 21, 1926.
[186] *Capital Times,* July 30, 1927.

ing, the membership of the Board having been altered since 1925, Regent Callahan moved to rescind the resolution of August 5, 1925. The motion carried by a vote of 10 to 3, one member voting present.[187] The *Capital Times* disapproved, but the other papers approved.[188]

But the struggle did not end. In the primary election of 1930 Philip F. La Follette won the nomination over Governor Kohler. The *Milwaukee Journal* reported that the decision of the regents to accept gifts from incorporated educational foundations would probably appear as a political issue in the legislature, that a resolution would be offered directing the regents to reject offers of outside aid. The governor-elect was reported to have said that he had not altered his views of 1925 supporting the majority of the regents in their decision.[189] In December, a month before the legislature met, a Milwaukee assemblyman announced that he would present a bill to carry out the wishes of the governor-elect.[190] No such bill was passed. However, a resolution was presented and adopted by both houses directing the regents not to accept money if it placed the University under obligation to any individual, corporation, or organization, or if the gift was designed to promote the sale of commodities or services. No gifts were to be accepted which came from agencies for research "in any public or governmental policy."[191] An amendment to the resolution barring acceptance of gifts from incorporated foundations was rejected.[192] The regents in the meantime adopted a general policy controlling the acceptance of gifts.

The effect of this action of the Board is of course impossible to measure. For several years after the resolution was adopted, the amount of money contributed to the University in gifts was smaller than it had been in the years immediately preceding its adoption. Whether this was the result of the resolution itself or of a number of other factors it is quite impossible to

[187] Records of the Board of Regents, M:195, March 5, 1930. Regents Backus, Butler, Callahan, Clausen, Drexler, Eimon, Faast, Gunderson, Sholts, and Waters, for; Richardson, Runge, and Schmidtmann, against; Berger voted present.
[188] Capital Times, March 5, 1930, March 6, 1930, p. 20; *Milwaukee Journal*, March 6, 1930.   [189] *Milwaukee Sentinel*, November 25, 1930, p. 13.
[190] Milwaukee *Wisconsin News*, December 2, 1930.
[191] Joint Resolution 34A, *Laws of Wisconsin*, 1931.
[192] *Capital Times*, March 25, 1931.

tell. However noble the objectives of the men who sought to keep the University completely safe from the possibility of corruption through acceptance of "tainted" money may have been, however sincerely these men believed that the state must support the University fully and generously, the fact remains that they were unable to win such support.

7.

The University and the State System

OR forty years after John Bascom left the University, the adjustment of the growing institution to the other new and changing educational activities of the state presented many problems. The adjustments, in general, had to be worked out in terms of the prevailing belief in and acceptance of the notion that the state system of public education must extend in unbroken steps, from the most lowly rural school, through the high schools, to the University. The point of adjustment came where the high school, the normal school, or the private school or college touched the University. The constant aim of the University was to maintain and to elevate the educational standards, as defined by University authorities, in the subordinate members of the educational structure. The adjustment of these different parts of the educational system to each other was complicated at times by the fact that the University authorities seemed in their demands to check the natural growth of the high school curriculum and to block a healthy development of the normal schools.

The discussion of the relationship of the University to the other parts of the emerging educational structure has been divided into three parts. Each is closely related to the other; but each is a story in itself. The first deals with the University and the high schools, the second with the colleges and the normal schools, and the third with the part played by the University in defeating a plan for centralized control of education.

✐

WE HAVE already considered the first steps taken in the process of bringing the academies and the emerging high schools to serve as preparatory departments of the University. The pattern of the relationship was, broadly speaking, determined by the time Chamberlin came to the presidency. In the succeeding years there were still many problems to be solved, but year by year the number of high schools accredited by the University increased. By 1895, 138 secondary schools—17 academies and private schools, 105 free Wisconsin high schools, 7 other Wisconsin high schools, and 9 high schools outside the state—had been inspected and approved.[1] By 1901 the number had increased to 217.[2] By 1910 it had increased to 315, and 205 of the 286 free high schools as well as 79 secondary schools in ten neighboring states were on the approved list.[3] The number continued to increase. When the University in 1931 at last decided to drop its inspection, the complete list of schools accredited by the University within the state of Wisconsin totaled 451.[4]

The simple statistical statement which each year showed additional schools qualified to serve as preparatory schools to the University suggests the operation of a system which was satisfactory on both sides and which proceeded without incident from formulation to execution. This was far from being the case. The early, somewhat stormy, stages of the accrediting program have already been discussed. It will be recalled that in the late 1870's and early 1880's there was a conflict between University authorities and high school officials revolving first around the University's continued operation of the preparatory department and then, when this problem no longer existed, around the requirements which the University imposed upon

[1] *Regents' Biennial Report,* 1895–96, p. 33.
[2] Faculty File Book (1889–1907), 1:195, June 10, 1901.
[3] *Regents' Biennial Report,* 1909–10, pp. 253–254.
[4] *Bulletin of the University of Wisconsin, List of Accredited Schools, July 1931* (Madison, 1931).

the high schools—requirements which, in the minds of many, diverted the high schools from more important functions.

Under the accrediting system as first established the faculty, on the petition of the high school, sent a representative to inspect it. Necessary expenses were to be paid by the high school. Although the cost was never large, many schools found it difficult to raise the funds. In many cases a happy solution was found by arranging to have the University professor-inspector deliver a lecture at the high school. The money taken in for the lecture was then used to pay the inspector's expenses. Many University professors willingly contributed to the advancement of the accrediting system in this way—none more extensively than Professor John C. Freeman.

During the 1890's the University officers worked diligently to win the good will of public school administrators and teachers and to attract high school students. Adams and others welcomed opportunities to address the meetings of the Wisconsin Teachers' Association, and Adams invited the members of the association to visit the University. "Our success," he told President Theron B. Pray, "as well as our prosperity at the University, depends upon the existence of harmonious relations between ourselves and the preparatory schools."[5] The faculty even undertook several times to entertain a large number of principals and superintendents at a dinner, the cost of which, prorated on a basis of salary, was borne by the members of the faculty. Principals and superintendents of schools from the upper Michigan peninsula were also invited.[6]

The Board of Regents, for its part, provided copies of the student newspapers to all high schools in the state "during the spring and winter terms," and on one occasion even ordered the distribution to all accredited schools of copies of the college song book prepared by the senior class.[7]

The University inspected schools and maintained an ac-

[5] Charles Kendall Adams to Professor Theron B. Pray, President, Wisconsin Teachers' Association, October 12, 1893, Presidents' Papers.

[6] Minutes of the Meetings of the Faculty, 4:152, May 13, 1897; 4:265, April 23, 1900.

[7] Records of the Board of Regents, D:251, January 16, 1894; E:101, April 19, 1898.

credited list under the authority given the regents to fix the educational qualifications for admittance to the University. Graduates of high schools which complied with University requirements in courses of study and preparation of teachers were admitted to the University without examination. But inspection by the University, its officers always insisted, was entirely voluntary. Compliance with University standards was optional with the high schools, but if a high school was not on the accredited list, its graduates had to take an entrance examination. On the other hand, the state superintendent of public instruction was, under the free high school law and subsequent legislation, directed to prepare and recommend courses of study, determine requirements for teacher certificates, supervise some of the high school work, and certify schools that were eligible to receive state funds. He had both the legal power and the responsibility to inspect high schools.

In the 1890's the University and the state superintendent cooperated effectively. In 1889 the legislature had appropriated funds to provide for a high school inspector for the state superintendent of public instruction. The same year the superintendent published a new course of study, to become effective in 1892, for four-year high schools. A year later, in 1890, the faculty created a standing committee to take charge of all matters pertaining to accrediting schools. The committee was further directed to require annual reports from the accredited schools. Schools failing to report were to be dropped from the list. The faculty also voted to prepare a syllabus on the character and extent of instruction desired in the preparatory studies.[8]

But the faculty had no intention of ignoring the state superintendent. Chamberlin hailed the new high school courses established by the state superintendent and asserted that the faculty thought they should be given formal University endorsement. "We have heretofore endeavored to secure satisfactory preparation on the part of the accredited schools by inspecting the quality of work done by the teachers, and by specifying the

[8] Minutes of the Faculty, 3:131, February 3, 1890; Faculty File Book, 1:11, April 28, 1890; *Circular Issued by the University of Wisconsin to Schools and Academies on the Character and Extent of Instruction Desired in Preparatory Studies* (Madison, 1891).

amount of ground to be covered. It is now proposed, in addition, to specify *the time* that must be devoted, thereby completing the three essential elements of a good preparation: excellent teaching, an adequate range of study, and sufficient time."[9] Some time later Chamberlin declared that: "Educational methods should be shaped with reference to the environment of those to be educated." He felt that there should be "an interaction between the observation and experiences of life and the studies of the school room." The city schools, he thought, were already shaped with reference to their environment, but not the rural schools. These were only attempting to imitate the city schools. Chamberlin proposed that Wisconsin schools be organized bilaterally "on rural and urban bases; the first to end in the agricultural college, the other in the other colleges." Nothing came of this proposal, but before the end of the year the University had given formal approval to the new standard high school courses recommended by the state superintendent and had adopted them as its standards of admission.[10]

The question whether the high schools should and could serve as University preparatory schools was occasionally debated during the 1890's. An editorial writer in the *Wisconsin Journal of Education* in 1890 discussed the reluctance of eastern writers to accept the notion that high schools would ever be capable of training young people for college. Although readily conceding that this must not be the sole function of the high school, the *Journal* writer felt that there need be no wide separation between courses offered to those going to college and to those not going. Such a separation had been accomplished in the new curricula published by the state superintendent. "Thus the educational ladder is with us made to reach from primary school to the University, as it ought to."[11] A year later the *Journal* defended the system of accredited schools by saying that pupils from these schools ranked highest in the University.[12] In other articles the *Journal* defended the higher standards in the high

[9] Thomas C. Chamberlin to the regents, in Reports to the Regents, C:87, April 15, 1890.
[10] *Ibid.*, C:134–135, September 16, 1890; *Regents' Biennial Report*, 1889–90, p. 46. [11] *Wisconsin Journal of Education*, 20:468 (November, 1890).
[12] *Ibid.*, 21:169 (August, 1891).

schools.[13] The next year the *Journal* pointed out: "It is a mistake to represent University men as demanding classical or any other kind of instruction in the high schools. . . . The University demands certain things of those who seek admission to its classes, and promises to accredit high schools which prove their readiness and competency to teach these things satisfactorily. The arrangement, however, is a purely voluntary one, and the University men are foremost to urge that the first duty of a high school is to meet the needs of the community which supports it."[14]

The *Journal* reported in 1894 that the Committee of Ten on Secondary School Studies, under the chairmanship of President Eliot of Harvard, had agreed that all subjects taught in the high school should be taught "in the same way and to the same extent to every pupil as long as he pursues it, no matter what the probable destination of the pupil may be, or at what point his education is to cease."[15] The faculty committee on accredited schools, however, fully supported by the faculty, was unwilling to support the higher standards proposed by the Committee of Ten for the nonclassical course of study. The committee felt that the University should "devote its effort to bringing the schools fully up to the courses of study now recommended by the State Superintendent, before proposing further changes in the course."[16] In 1893 the Board of Visitors reported that the graduates of accredited high schools attained higher comparative averages during their first term than any others.[17]

President Adams, who had taken office in 1892, urged enlargement of University inspection services. Since the inspection of schools could be made only on application of the school and since expenses had to be paid by the school, the University had no means of making sure that the schools, once accredited, maintained their standards. He felt that the committee on accredited schools should have funds to pay the inspector's ex-

[13] *Ibid.*, 21:194 (September, 1891); 22:49 (March, 1892).
[14] *Ibid.*, 23:169 (August, 1893). In a circular published in 1891 the University faculty had indicated the kind and amount of preparation desired in Greek, Latin, German, algebra, geometry, physics, botany, physiology, history, and English.   [15] *Ibid.*, 24:98 (May, 1894).
[16] Minutes of the Faculty, 4:32, June 11, 1894; Faculty File Book, 1:84, June 11, 1894.   [17] Report of the Visitors, in *Regents' Biennial Report*, 1893–94, p. 62.

penses.[18] The University shortly began to pay the traveling expenses for such faculty members as were sent out on inspection trips. In 1899 the faculty finally adopted a resolution for the abandonment of the faculty rule requiring formal application on the part of high schools for inspection except for those seeking accreditation for the first time.[19]

In 1900 Adams again renewed his recommendation for an inspector. This time he proposed that the inspector's job, which would be seasonal, be coupled with that of managing a teacher placement bureau. In urging the creation of such a position, he pointed out that the neighboring universities had established such bureaus.[20] The proposal won the full support of Superintendent of Public Instruction Lorenzo D. Harvey and was adopted by the Board at the April meeting. A salary of $1,500 a year was authorized.[21] Shortly thereafter, Albert W. Tressler was appointed to this joint position, after very careful consideration by Birge, the acting president.[22]

The official attitude of the University toward the high school curriculum was probably most adequately stated by Birge in 1901 in response to a request to help establish a unified entrance examination to American universities. Birge explained that the University was "very intimately connected with the school system of the state. The courses of study in the high schools are determined by the department of education, although the professors of the university have always been consulted in preparing these courses. Since the high schools are by no means wholly, or even primarily, preparatory schools for college, their courses of study are necessarily not wholly such as a University would recommend for a strictly preparatory school." Yet the University had to adapt itself to this situation. "Our flexibility in terms of admission is secured by freely accepting equivalents in our terms of admission, so that students who are prepared for any university of equal degree to our own are admitted to the freshman class." Although the University could do little to change

[18] *Regents' Biennial Report,* 1893–94, p. 42.
[19] Minutes of the Faculty, 4:242, November 13, 1899.
[20] Adams to the regents, in Reports to the Regents, D:575, February 1, 1900.
[21] Edward A. Birge to Adams, April 25, 1900, Presidents' Papers.
[22] Birge to Adams, May 31, June 14, 1900, Presidents' Papers; *Regents' Biennial Report,* 1899–1900, p. 7.

the high school courses in the state, Birge said that the University would be glad to accept students who are prepared "in any manner which the leading Universities of the country may accept as satisfactory."[23]

Yet it is doubtful whether the University's influence was as inconspicuous or as tentative as Birge implied. Indeed, the reports of the high school inspectors on the competence of teachers were sometimes thought to be a determining factor in the renewal of teachers' contracts. Professor Turner, for example, was told by a former student: "I think my re-election depends entirely on what the University authorities say on my work, and as it is subject to re-inspection I wish you would come yourself and tell me just what you think of it."[24] In many cases the reports of the University inspector furnished the occasion for a spirited community struggle over high school improvements.[25] Few serious objections were made to the accrediting system during the 1890's.

In 1902 the state constitution was amended to lengthen the term of the office of the state superintendent to four years, to place in the legislature the power to determine the qualifications, duties, and salary of the office, and to open the way to making it nonpolitical. In the first election held under the new amendment, Charles P. Cary was elected state superintendent. He held the office until 1921. Cary was born in Ohio in 1856 and had graduated from the Ohio Central Normal School in 1879. After holding teaching positions in Ohio, Kansas, and Nebraska, he came to Wisconsin in 1893 as instructor of pedagogy and principal of the training department of the Milwaukee State Normal School. In 1901 he had become superintendent of the Wisconsin School for the Deaf at Delavan and served there for a year until he resigned to run for the state superintendency.[26]

[23] Birge to Cromwell Childe, editor of the *Brooklyn Daily Eagle*, August 30, 1901, Presidents' Papers.

[24] Clara A. Glenn, Viroqua, to Frederick Jackson Turner, March 12, 1902, Records of the History Department.

[25] At Stoughton, for example, in the middle 1890's, an unfavorable inspector's report on the high school precipitated a sharp community conflict over the school. At least one member of the school board welcomed the criticisms by the University professor for the help they gave in his fight to elevate the high school standards. Stoughton file, Teacher Placement Office, University of Wisconsin.   [26] *The Wisconsin Blue Book,* 1915 (Madison, 1915), 485.

Jealous of his prerogatives, opinionated, outspoken, conservative, opposed to the Progressives, Cary quickly became an opponent of the University. He aired his charges against it in the *Wisconsin Journal of Education,* in the newspapers of the state, and at meetings of the Board of Regents, of which he was an ex-officio member. Whether his antagonism rested upon a sincere desire to improve the public school system of the state, as he saw it, or whether it rested upon other less idealistic impulses, need not here concern us. Cary began by attacking the University inspection of the high schools, but before he had concluded he had assailed the University for spending too much time and money on graduate work and research, for engaging extensively in politics, for providing poor and inadequate teaching, and for a host of other things. In 1911 he furnished a slogan for the anti-University forces by asking whether the people of Wisconsin wanted a "university state" or a "state university."[27] The slogan was seized with delight by some conservatives in the political campaign of 1914.

Early in Cary's administration Van Hise and other University authorities offered cooperation in dealing with the state educational system, but the results of a conference on the subject were inconclusive.[28] In 1906 the relation of the University and the high schools was debated before the state teachers' association. The *Wisconsin Journal of Education* printed editorials to the effect that the high school courses must not be shaped by college requirements since only fourteen per cent of the high school graduates went on to college or the University. It also declared that the two-year foreign language requirement was unfair to graduates of smaller schools. The University, it was suggested, should change its admission standards to accept graduates of those schools not offering a foreign language.[29]

Dean Birge answered the criticisms calmly. The University recognized the multiple responsibilities of the high schools, but the University also had its responsibilities. The engineering

[27] *Wisconsin Journal of Education,* 43:282 (December, 1911).
[28] Memorandum of a conference between the State Department of Public Instruction and the Department of Education of the University of Wisconsin, held at the invitation of President Van Hise at his residence on Saturday evening, November 4, 1905, in Papers of the Dean of the College of Letters and Science.
[29] *Wisconsin Journal of Education,* 38:39–40 (February, 1906).

college, for example, could not admit just any graduate of a four-year high school; high school students planning to go to the University should select proper courses. The University should be reasonable, and he thought it was.[30] Cary had not yet come out openly, although in his annual report he questioned the value of the North Central Association of Colleges and Secondary Schools.[31]

Late in 1906 the *Wisconsin Journal of Education* twitted the University critics when the Bloomington high school was accredited. The announcement, it was reported, "brought forth a demonstration by the pupils, who paraded the streets carrying appropriate banners. . . . That's the way they all feel and it makes the University Professor laugh. High-schools raise an awful rumpus because the college requirements for accrediting are so rigid and then those same schools fall over themselves to get into line. The University is not forcing the schools upon its accredited list."[32] But some harsh things were also said. Neal Brown of Wausau denounced University inspection at the state teachers' meeting in December and charged that the inspectors were often incompetent.[33]

At this point Cary definitely joined the critics of the University inspection. In an article in the *Wisconsin Journal of Education,* he charged that the state had a "double-headed system of inspection." This was unnecessary. It caused friction. Although the influence of the University on the high schools had been good in the past, Cary felt that it had caused some schools to ignore "local needs, local conditions, and local limitations" and produced "in the high schools nervous strain and in the public mind jealousy and contention."[34] The University, he said, should accept the course of study outlined by the state department of education. He charged that the University representatives had agreed to do this and then had repudiated the agreement. Inspection of the schools by the department of edu-

[30] *Ibid.,* 38:247–249 (September, 1906).
[31] *Biennial Report of the Department of Public Instruction,* 1904–06, p. 105.
[32] *Wisconsin Journal of Education,* 38:360 (December, 1906).
[33] *Milwaukee Daily News,* December 29, 1906; *Milwaukee Sentinel,* December 30, 1906.
[34] *Wisconsin Journal of Education,* 39:45 (February, 1907).

cation, he said, should be sufficient for the University. Cary also complained that the University placed too much emphasis on graduate work, that it could not excel in all fields, that it should not compete with Harvard and other large universities, and that it ought to devote more time to teaching undergraduates.[35]

Cary's attack was timed to coincide with a joint resolution introduced in the Assembly in February, 1907. The resolution, which was not passed, accused the University of dominating the high schools and forcing a University student to study a foreign language "even though it is not his pleasure or desire." It urged a change of University entrance requirements, proposed a University degree which would not require a foreign language, and declared that the state superintendent should inspect high schools "in the manner provided by the law without unauthorized interference."[36]

As a result of this attack a conference was soon arranged between Dean Birge and Cary and his assistants. Subsequently a faculty committee took up the matter. Cary of course wanted the University to give up all inspection. He repeated the charges he had already made. The committee properly declared that the University could not dominate the high school so long as the superintendent outlined the course of study, that accrediting was not forced upon any school, and that inspection had to be maintained if the faculty were to continue to determine the entrance requirements.[37] Cary would have nothing to do with a proposal that the state and University inspectors work together. In his annual report, although he withheld public criticism of the University, he again pointed out that the high schools had many functions besides preparing students for college.[38] A movement was even started to get Cary out of office by having Birge run against him for the office of superintendent

[35] *Ibid.*, 39:44–48.

[36] Joint Resolution 56A, *Assembly Journal*, 1907, pp. 198, 399, 604; *Senate Journal*, 1907, pp. 393, 516. The resolution was adopted by the Assembly but voted down in the Senate.

[37] Report of the Committee on Entrance Requirements and Inspection on the Changes Proposed by State Superintendent Cary, in the Presidents' Papers. The faculty adopted the committee report. Minutes of the Faculty, 6:72, May 6, 1907.

[38] *Biennial Report of the Department of Public Instruction,* 1906–08, pp. 33–34.

of public instruction. Birge would have nothing to do with this proposal.[39]

But the fight against University inspection was not over. In 1909 Assemblyman Simon F. Wehrwein introduced a bill which would have required the University to accept for admission graduates of all Wisconsin four-year high schools whose course of study was approved by the state superintendent. It would also have ended the University inspection system.[40] Cary supported the bill with vigor and long arguments; Van Hise opposed it with equal vigor. He charged that it would lower standards of the University and of the better high schools of the state. The *Wisconsin Journal of Education* favored it, saying that "it would do away with this duplicate inspection and give to school boards a greater freedom in the selection of their high school teachers."[41] But against the support of the *Journal*, Van Hise could show that the Association of Superintendents and Supervising Principals had adopted a resolution giving hearty approval to "inspection by both University and State Department." Legislation that would deprive the high schools of the benefits of inspection by either the state superintendent or the University "should be opposed."[42] Although the bill did not pass, a joint recess committee was appointed to investigate supervision and inspection of schools and the advisability of reorganizing the educational system of the state under one commission.[43]

In order to forestall legislative action, University officials again tried to find common ground on which to work with Cary. It was proposed that the dual system be abandoned and that a board, made up of the state superintendent, the president of the University, the president of one of the normal schools, and a superintendent or high school principal, should take over the administration of high school inspection.[44] But

[39] Junius Thomas Hooper, Ashland, Wisconsin, to Birge, and Birge to G. D. Jones, January 19, 1909, both in the Papers of the Dean of the College of Letters and Science.   [40] Assembly Bill 720A, *Assembly Journal*, 1909, p. 281.
[41] *Wisconsin Journal of Education*, 41:234 (September, 1909).
[42] Copy of resolution of November 5, 1909, sent to Van Hise by Professor Edward C. Elliott, Presidents' Papers.   [43] *Laws of Wisconsin*, 1909, p. 844.
[44] The proposal was put forth by Professor Michael Vincent O'Shea in the *Wisconsin Journal of Education*, 42:1–2 (January, 1910), but it had been made earlier by Birge and Van Hise. See Van Hise to Edward Webster LeRoy, vice-chairman of the Wisconsin Legislative Committee on Education, November 30, 1909, in the Presidents' Papers.

Cary would not agree. There was, he insisted, only one solution. The University must give up its inspection and accept graduates of all high schools approved by the state superintendent. He advertised his opinions in circulars to the high school teachers and in the *Wisconsin Journal of Education*.[45] In his formal report later that year he declared that "it is highly desirable that the high schools should not be hampered by college and University dictation, whether direct or indirect."[46] Moreover he questioned the legality of spending University funds to maintain the high school inspection service. On this question the regents appealed to the attorney general for an opinion. The attorney general held that the high school inspection by the University was clearly within the power of the regents since they had authority to determine educational qualifications of those admitted to the University. Although there was no specific provision in the law permitting expenditure of funds to pay for high school inspection, this was clearly warranted under the general grant of power to the regents permitting them to appropriate funds for "current or administration expenses."[47] While Cary from time to time thereafter complained that University inspection was illegal, he never challenged the opinion of the attorney general in the courts.

Cary at last carried the fight into the Board of Regents. In October, 1910, he presented to the regents a resolution abolishing the University system of inspecting high schools. It provided further that "any graduate of a free high school in this state who has successfully pursued and completed a four-year course, shall, on the recommendation of the principal of the school as to moral character and ability to carry on the work of the university, and the presentation by the student of properly certified standings that are sufficiently high to satisfy the officer or officers of the university, whose business it is to pass upon the standings, that the student has done satisfactory work in the high school, be admitted to the University without examination."[48]

[45] *Wisconsin Journal of Education*, 42:40–42 (February, 1910).
[46] *Biennial Report of the Department of Public Instruction*, 1908–10, pp. 6–7.
[47] Frank L. Gilbert, attorney general of Wisconsin, to Lucien S. Hanks, vice-president of the regents, April 26, 1910, Papers of the Board of Regents.
[48] Records of the Board of Regents, H:24–25, October 12, 1910.

It was eight months before the resolution came to a vote. Meanwhile, at the next meeting of the regents on December 7, Van Hise introduced a substitute for Cary's resolution placing the regents on record as fully approving the University inspection system. The regents refused to accept the substitute.[49] However, the faculty decided to alter entrance requirements. Late in December, it voted to accept up to four high school credits for work done in "approved courses" in agriculture, domestic science, manual arts, and commercial work.[50] The same month the recess committee of the legislature brought in a majority report favoring passage of Wehrwein's bill of 1909. Although supported by a majority of the committee, the bill failed to pass the Assembly at the session of 1911.[51] After the Assembly voted indefinite postponement of the Wehrwein bill, Cary insisted upon a vote on his resolution. The Board rejected it by a vote of 10 to 1. Cary was the only regent to support it.[52]

Although defeated Cary was not silenced. During the next years he conducted a campaign against the University in the educational press and elsewhere. His criticisms and his charges often were based on only a shadow of truth. He denounced the University for being both timid and intolerant of adverse criticism. He proclaimed that Wisconsin was a "university state," and that the "capitol is an annex to the University to be used for experimental and laboratory purposes." He accused the University of spending great quantities of money on expensive land and expensive administration. He claimed that most of the highly paid teachers were not teaching but conducting research and that there was no supervision of teaching at the University. In 1913, when he ran for re-election, one plank of the twelve-point platform on which he stood was "the freedom from domination by higher institutions of learning."[53]

Answers were of course made to Cary's charges. Regent Trott-

[49] *Ibid.*, H:35–36, December 7, 1910.
[50] Elliott to Samuel Plantz, December 5, 1912, Presidents' Papers. The faculty had voted for this move on December 22, 1910; the regents approved it on March 1, 1911. *University Catalogue,* 1911–12, p. 108.
[51] *Assembly Journal,* 1911, p. 878.
[52] Records of the Board of Regents, H:118, June 20, 1911.
[53] *Wisconsin Journal of Education,* 43:282 (December, 1911); 44:51–52 (January, 1912); 44:62–63 (March, 1912); 44:183–185 (September, 1912); 45:67 (March, 1913).

University Cadets, Machine Gun Drill, 1918

Girls' Mechanics Class, 1918

man denounced Cary as an enemy of the University. He said that if Cary had criticism to make "he should be present at the regular meetings of the board, and make his suggestions or criticisms."[54] Van Hise defended the University's public service: "It will be the aim of the University of Wisconsin in the future, as it has been in the past, since the days of John Bascom, not only to be a leader in the state, but so far as lies within its resources and capacity, a leader in the nation and in the world."[55]

Cary was re-elected in 1913. A year later at the June meeting, he again presented a resolution to the regents abolishing the University high school inspection system. The system, he declared, was unnecessary and it was "a virtual interference with the official duties imposed by law on the office of State Superintendent of Schools, and furthermore, an unnecessary expense to the State." Van Hise arranged to have the resolution referred to the faculty.[56]

The faculty committee reported that the accrediting system worked effectively in maintaining standards in the high schools, that it stimulated the high schools to better work, and that it afforded a valuable means of contact between the University and the high schools. The attacks, the committee found, followed two lines: the first contention was that the University dominated the high schools; the second was that the University invaded the authority of the state superintendent. The committee categorically denied both charges. In connection with the first it pointed out that the University only offered advice. It called attention to the fact that some fifty units of work could be offered in the high schools but that only fourteen were specifically required for University entrance. University entrance requirements were elastic enough, the committee declared, to afford high school students a wide choice of courses. The com-

[54] *Ibid.*, 44:315 (January, 1912).
[55] *Ibid.*, 44:32–34 (February, 1912). Van Hise's patience was quickly exhausted by Cary's misrepresentations. Once he commented that Cary's latest letter showed the same "lamentable deficiencies" as his previous letters. "By each of them he has put himself into the unpleasant dilemma either of wilful misrepresentation of the facts or of such amazing ignorance as to belittle his intelligence." *Wisconsin Journal of Education*, 44:119–120 (May, 1912).
[56] Records of the Board of Regents, I:169, June 17, 1914.

mittee felt that University inspection was competently done and that the school officers approved. Finally, students were now being admitted to the University from nonaccredited schools without examination but on probation for one year. Hence the complaint about University domination was invalid.[57]

On December 2 the report of the faculty committee was presented to the regents. Cary also submitted a statement on the legal aspects of the school inspection.[58] Cary based his somewhat involved legal arguments upon an old decision of the supreme court that the University was a part of the educational system of the state.[59] This being true, Cary argued, and the state having delegated to the state superintendent general responsibility for the educational system, high school inspection was a function of his office. The University in "exercising its function of providing higher education has not been given the right to legislate and impose conditions in matters affecting the scope and character of work in other parts of the public school system." Cary had other "numerous and weighty minor objections" to dual inspection: it was uneconomical; it confused the schools; it took professors away from the University and their students; some inspectors were incompetent, some too specialized; and it was now unnecessary. The first year of the University, Cary declared, was the thirteenth year of the public school system. That was the intention of the lawmakers. The University should receive all high school graduates who came properly recommended and certified. He urged the regents "to abolish the annoying, useless and expensive duality of inspection to which reference has in the above discussion repeatedly been made."[60]

At the January meeting of the regents, a second report from the faculty committee was presented. The committee insisted that sole legal authority and responsibility for the supervision of the schools did not reside in the state superintendent, that the relation of the state superintendent to the free high schools

[57] Papers of the Board of Regents, December 2, 1914; *University Catalogue,* 1914–15, p. 136.
[58] Records of the Board of Regents, I:227–228, December 2, 1914.
[59] *Wisconsin Reports,* 54:159.
[60] Papers of the Board of Regents, December 2, 1914; Records of the Board of Regents, I:227, December 2, 1914.

of the state was analogous to the relation of the University to the accredited schools. The committee further declared, in answer to questions which had been publicly raised by the Board of Visitors, that it was quite possible for the University accrediting agency to cooperate with the state department, that as a matter of fact, such cooperation had existed before the advent of the present superintendent, but Cary had refused to consider any cooperation. "The only conclusion your committee has been able to draw from the events of recent years is that the present state superintendent had one definite object in view, *and that is to exclude entirely the university from any official contact with the other parts of the school system except as he may determine.*" The committee complained that the "low standard established by the State Department of Education for the approval of schools as free high schools, together with the critical and depreciatory attitude displayed by the state superintendent during recent years toward university standards and university scholarship, have rendered it extremely difficult for the university to maintain those standards of equipment, instruction and teaching staff considered essential for the proper preparation, in accredited high schools, of pupils for the University. We believe that the university has given way too easily under the pressure of those who urge expediency rather than educational worth, as a basis for educational policy. . . . The State Superintendent, in effect, urges that the university entrance be adapted to the free high school level established by him."[61]

Cary denounced the statement of the faculty committee as "utterly pointless, illogical and inconsequential. . . . I should make no reply to this communication were it not for the fact that if these gentlemen take themselves seriously, they might say that I have no argument to offer." Cary argued that the faculty was wrong in its legal interpretations. It was not the state superintendent's fault that educational standards were low in Wisconsin. He scoffed at the proposal that the University and state superintendent "cooperate." He had the power, and he had no intention of sharing it. "I earnestly hope," he concluded,

[61] Report of the Faculty Committee, Papers of the Board of Regents, January 20, 1915.

"that the Board of Regents may realize the best and wisest, in fact the only thing to be done under the present circumstances, it seems to me, is to abolish outright university inspection for accrediting purposes and accept the graduates of all high schools of the State without any 'ifs' or 'ands' and 'maybe so's.' "[62]

But the regents were not impressed by Cary's bluster and legalism. They voted 8 to 2 to reject his resolution. In four years of agitation Cary had won one vote among the regents.[63] Later the same year Cary was again publicly rebuffed when the state teachers' association unanimously elected Van Hise president for the coming year.[64]

While Cary ostensibly suffered defeat, in a larger sense he did not. His first attack had brought the faculty to accept high school credits in manual arts, agriculture, domestic science, and commercial work. His continued attack had helped to abolish the entrance examinations for students from nonaccredited schools and to establish the system under which students from such schools were admitted to the University without examination, on probation for the first year. On the more conspicuous issue of the University's retaining its inspection service, Cary was defeated although here too he enjoyed a kind of victory. The uproar he had made between 1910 and 1915 fixed in many minds the point that University inspection was wrong and probably illegal. When Conrad Patzer wrote his history of public education in Wisconsin, he accepted Cary's view.[65]

Cary's successor in office never followed Cary's tactics. Finally, in 1931, the University itself abolished its inspection service and

[62] Papers of the Board of Regents, January 20, 1915.

[63] Records of the Board of Regents, I:251, January 20, 1915.

[64] Delos Oscar Kinsman wrote to Van Hise on October 27, 1915, asking him if he would serve. Van Hise responded, saying he would not be a candidate, and if there were a contest, he would not accept. "If however, there is a general feeling among the teachers of the state that they desire me to act as president for one year in recognition of the relation of the University to the teachers, I shall regard it as a responsibility which I would accept." Van Hise to Kinsman, October 28, 1915, Presidents' Papers.

After his election one of his admirers wrote: "I was extremely pleased to have you elected President of the State Teachers' Association. At this time when both the state department of Education and the Governor are knocking the University and you personally, your election will stand as a vindication and this will please loyal alumni." Frederick Godfrey Kraege to Van Hise, November 8, 1915, Presidents' Papers.

[65] Conrad E. Patzer, *Public Education in Wisconsin* (Madison, 1924), 92 ff.

won from the Wisconsin Association of Secondary School Principals a resolution of approval as "a forward step in secondary education."[66] Cary's battle was at last won. High school inspection was taken over entirely by the office of the state superintendent.

The University system of inspecting and accrediting high schools had lasted fifty-four years. Under this system four hundred and fifty-one Wisconsin high schools had been accepted as preparatory schools for the University. Each of these schools had been visited by a University professor-inspector, some almost every year, from the 1880's until 1931. Whatever critics of University inspection might say, the record of the inspectors was one of patient service. In the early days the inspector had often had to give a public lecture at the school to help pay his expenses. He had spent the day before or after the lecture visiting the high school classes, observing the teachers, examining the courses of study. Upon returning to Madison, he had written his formal report to the University accrediting committee and, to the superintendent of the school he had visited, a letter giving his observations, criticisms, and suggestions. If his report called for action, the committee had to meet, discuss the matter, and often present it to the faculty for final decision. For each school on the University's accredited list, there still exists a file containing the records of these visits, the reports, committee actions, protests, explanations, and entreaties—dusty and all but forgotten records of one phase of the mechanics of that process which educational historians call the articulation of the high schools to the University. This file is a monument to the patient, time-consuming, painstaking effort made by University officials to work out relations with the high schools.

A MUCH less prominent phase of the University-high school relations was the University's assumption of responsibility for training teachers for the public schools. The preparation of teachers had long been claimed as one of the functions of the

[66] Papers of the Board of Regents, December 2, 1931.

University, but this activity was more honored in the abstract than in the course of study and the appointments of the staff. The normal department, instituted during the Civil War, had been permitted to die shortly thereafter, and not until 1884 was a chair of pedagogy established and a professor appointed. In 1878 a law was passed under which the state superintendent countersigned the diploma of a teacher who had graduated from the University and completed sixteen months of successful teaching. The diploma was then equivalent to an unlimited state teaching certificate.[67]

A year later the legislature provided that principals of free high schools must have a college or University diploma and in 1880 modified the certification law to require that the state superintendent countersign the diploma of the graduate of any college or university located in Wisconsin if the course of study was "fully and fairly equivalent" to the University course.[68] This law remained in effect substantially unchanged until 1907, when a pedagogical requirement was made a requisite for a teaching certificate and a life certificate was granted after one year of successful teaching.

The University, however, while seeking advantages for its graduates in the high schools, was little interested in offering courses in teacher training. The first legislative grant for the support of a summer school was assigned to the superintendent of public instruction and the president of the University, and it will be recalled that for a number of years the summer school had only a tenuous relation to the University. The faculty apparently felt that a college or university training was all that was needed for a young person who might enter the teaching profession. Superintendents and principals were not exacting, as witness a letter received by President Chamberlin asking for a teacher of Latin and Greek. The qualifications were sketchy. "I want," he wrote, "a pleasant, wholesome girl full of energy: better of some experience. I want her at once."[69]

The University faculty could not ignore indefinitely the

[67] *Laws of Wisconsin,* 1878, p. 677.

[68] *Laws of Wisconsin,* 1879, pp. 496–498; *Laws of Wisconsin,* 1880, p. 243.

[69] Albert Hardy, superintendent of schools, La Crosse, to Chamberlin, September 2, 1891, Presidents' Papers.

mounting insistence that teachers be given special training. In 1896, the Board of Visitors urged that arrangements be made with the public school system of Madison to permit the schools to be used by University students for observation and practice teaching.[70] A year later President Adams urged the improvement of teacher training at the University: "I do not hesitate to say that in my judgment one of the weakest points in this University, up to the present time, has been its failure to give the requisite amount of theoretical and practical training in the art of imparting instruction." It was largely for this reason, he felt, that University graduates were not more fully represented among the teachers of the state.[71]

But University graduates were becoming numerous among the teachers of the state, and calls upon the University for teachers increased in number, in part no doubt because of University inspection of high schools. In 1899 a faculty committee was created to consider the advisability of establishing a University teacher placement agency. Late in January, 1900, the committee reported that such agencies were operating effectively at other universities; the Universities of Michigan and Illinois had created teacher placement bureaus. The committee proposed the creation of a University committee on appointments made up of representatives of each department of the College of Letters and Science, the College of Engineering, and the School of Pharmacy. This large committee would in turn select an executive committee from its members. The executive committee would direct the work. In addition it was recommended that the placement committee be given a secretary, who should also be secretary of the high school accrediting committee. The knowledge gained in one position would be useful in the other.[72] The regents approved the recommendation, and the teacher placement bureau was established.[73]

The same year the faculty directed a committee to investigate

[70] Report of the Visitors, in *Regents' Biennial Report*, 1895–96, p. 53.

[71] Records of the Board of Regents, D:534, January 19, 1897.

[72] Faculty File Book, 1:176, January 28, 1900; recommendation adopted January 29.

[73] In 1900 Birge, the acting president, pointed out that already more than two hundred and fifty University graduates were teaching in the high schools of the state, and that often more requests for teachers were received than the

and propose requirements for special diplomas for graduates who intended to become teachers.[74] The first step was to change the law of 1878 under which a University degree, in addition to successful teaching experience, entitled anyone to an unlimited teaching certificate. The committee, under the chairmanship of Professor John William Stearns, met with the president and the state superintendent to discuss the matter. It was agreed that an attempt should be made to change the certification law so as to entitle a graduate of the University to a teacher's certificate if his diploma were "accompanied with a certificate that the bearer has completed the course of pedagogical instruction prescribed by the University for all persons who intend to teach."[75]

The law was not changed until 1907.[76] Nevertheless the faculty proceeded to establish special requirements for graduates intending to teach. On March 28, 1900, Professor Stearns's committee on requirements recommended that special diplomas be granted only to those who had taken a course in psychology and pedagogy in the School of Education, had demonstrated scholarly preparation for teaching in at least one department of work represented in the high schools, and had completed a course for teachers. It was left to each department to "determine for itself the amount and kind of preparation requisite for this diploma." The University teacher's certificate was then to be granted on the recommendation of the executive committee of the committee on appointments.[77] All this the faculty approved.[78]

Thus the University faculty, urged on by the director of the School of Education but unsupported by law, established standards for the certification of University graduates desiring to teach. Presumably a student might refuse to conform, but if he did, the services of the placement service would not be available

University could fill. The appointment committee had been created "to centralize the giving of information to the high schools regarding possible candidates for positions and to the graduates of the University in securing positions for which they had been trained in the University." The committee acted only on requests from schools; it made no attempt to find vacancies. *Regents' Biennial Report,* 1899–1900, p. 17.

[74] Minutes of the Faculty, 4:251–258, January 29, March 5, 1900.
[75] Faculty File Book, 1:178, March 20, 1900.
[76] *Laws of Wisconsin,* 1907, p. 1190.
[77] Faculty File Book, 1:180, March 26, 1900.
[78] Minutes of the Faculty, 4:262, April 9, 1900.

when he came to look for a job. The regulation continued even after the school was reduced to a department early in Van Hise's administration.

The Board of Visitors in 1906 urged that provision be made for a demonstration school in connection with the work of the department of education.[79] Van Hise in his report to the regents, later in the year, declared that the department needed a model school. Arrangements, he thought, could be made with the Madison schools, but only temporarily. Other universities had already established their own model schools. Wisconsin must do so if its department of education was to have "standing and influence" comparable to Chicago, Illinois, and Columbia.[80] At the same time Dean Birge in his report declared: "It is the duty of the University as a leader in the educational affairs of the state to give serious attention to the problem of preparing teachers for the secondary schools."[81]

Apparently it was high time the University took action. In December of the same year it was charged at a meeting of the Wisconsin Superintendents' and Supervising Principals' Association that the University was responsible for the inadequate training of prospective high school teachers.[82] Van Hise answered the charge by saying that four fifths of a teacher's training should be directed toward giving the student knowledge and enthusiasm for knowledge. The best methods of teaching, he insisted, were presented not in the education department but by the professors in the academic department. But he admitted the pressing need for a model high school for practice teaching and other purposes.[83]

Such public complaints may have stimulated the University department of education to press for a more extensive teacher-training program. In 1905 members of the department unsuccessfully sought an agreement with the state superintendent to restrict the normal schools to the preparation of rural and elementary school teachers, reserving to the University the prepara-

[79] Report of the Visitors, March 28, 1906, *Regents' Biennial Report,* 1905–06, pp. 197–198.
[80] *Regents' Biennial Report,* 1905–06, p. 65.   [81] *Ibid.,* 80.
[82] *Milwaukee Sentinel,* December 27, 28, 29, 30, 1906.
[83] *Madison Democrat,* January 15, 1907.

tion of high school teachers.[84] But before the end of the academic year, 1906–1907, the faculty adopted a plan submitted by the education department for the establishment of a course for the training of teachers.[85]

Dean Birge, in his report to Van Hise in 1908, declared that the teacher-training course offered "educational problems of considerable difficulty." The rapid increase in the number of high schools and the expansion of their work had created a large demand for teachers, but pay was still low. The professional life of a teacher was short. One quarter of the teachers each year were beginners. Young men used teaching as a steppingstone to other professions; young women, said Birge, "naturally and rightly" looked upon teaching as an occupation to fill the period between graduation from the University and marriage.[86] Birge looked forward to a change whereby the teaching profession would become stabilized but believed it would not come soon. In the meantime, the University faced the difficult task of providing courses for those who proposed to enter teaching as a permanent profession and for those who would be in it only temporarily. Professional standards must not be placed so high as to exclude the latter.[87]

It was this temporary group which concerned Birge two years

[84] Memorandum of a conference between the State Department of Public Instruction and the Department of Education at the University of Wisconsin, held at the invitation of President Van Hise at his residence on Saturday evening, November 4, 1905. Papers of the Dean of the College of Letters and Science. An attempt was made by one member of the department of education of the University to have the state superintendent agree to a policy of restricting the University to preparation of the secondary school teachers and the normal schools to primary and rural teachers, but Cary would have none of it. Cary, however, indicated his willingness to accept University assistance in his campaign for the improvement of the rural schools.

[85] The term "course" in this connection means a program of study directed toward attaining a professional or technical training in some special field. Shortly after Van Hise became president, all schools in the College of Letters and Science had been reduced to the status of departments. Very soon, however, courses embracing the work formerly offered by the schools were established within the College of Letters and Science under the control of a committee and a director. Thus the commerce, pharmacy, music, chemistry, journalism, and teachers' training courses appeared. Some remained merely courses, charted as it were, within the broad areas of the College of Letters and Science; others emerged in time as schools. The course for the training of teachers established by faculty action in 1907 became the School of Education in 1919.

[86] *Regents' Biennial Report*, 1907–08, pp. 50–51.   [87] *Ibid.*, 62.

later when again he discussed the matter, pointing out that the average period of service for high school teachers was only three or four years. For the University to provide extensive professional training to people who would remain in the profession for only a few years was wasteful. When only a college degree had been required to teach, not much special training was lost if a person remained in the profession only a few years. But conditions had changed: "The student's work in college is becoming controlled and dominated by the brief period of teaching which may succeed it. It loses much of its value as a liberal course of study, and the short period which the student gives to the profession prevents him from realizing any considerable part of its proper value as a professional course."[88]

In establishing the course for teachers, the faculty had agreed: (1) that professional study should be placed in the later years of the course and much of it, if possible, should be gained in graduate work; (2) that under present conditions it was not practicable to require graduate training as a condition of teaching, so professional training must be provided within the undergraduate courses; (3) special care should be taken to develop the professional spirit in those expecting to teach.[89] Accordingly the faculty provided both an undergraduate and an advanced course for the training of teachers, the first to be offered in the senior year, and the second, consisting of twelve semester hours, to be taken during summer school or one semester of graduate work.[90]

Professor Edward Charles Elliott of the department of education was made chairman of the faculty committee on the training of teachers. For the committee Elliott made an arrangement with the Madison public schools whereby the Board of Education and the regents jointly employed some teachers who would serve as demonstration teachers for University classes, and some of the regular high school classes were opened for student observers.[91] Since the state department could offer no legal recognition of the advanced professional preparation, the regents,

---

[88] *Ibid.*, 1909–10, p. 64.
[89] Birge to Van Hise, *Regents' Biennial Report*, 1907–08, p. 53.
[90] *Ibid.* [91] *Ibid.*, 75–82.

at the request of the committee, approved a special professional certificate for those who took twelve semester hours of approved educational courses beyond the requirements of the undergraduate courses. Although the cooperation with the Madison schools was continued, the regents arranged in 1911 to take over the Wisconsin Academy, renamed it the Wisconsin High School, and used it as a practice school. Shortly thereafter, the legislature approved funds for construction of a University demonstration school, which was opened and occupied in September, 1914. The school was established on a six-year basis.

Meanwhile Elliott and his committee sought to increase the amount of special training for teachers. Elliott proposed that the unlimited teaching certificate be given only on a basis of five years' training beyond high school graduation, the additional year to be devoted entirely to professional courses. He also proposed a four-year college requirement for high school teaching on a limited certificate and five years for the unlimited certificate.[92]

Although the state board of examiners refused to support the demand, the faculty in 1914 increased the requirements for the University teacher's certificate from twelve semester hours to seventeen, to become effective after January 1, 1916.[93] Thus again the University authorities exceeded the strict requirements of the state department in their attempt to establish higher standards for teachers going from the University to the high schools of the state. But this time they had gone too far. Few prospective teachers were willing to take the work. Accordingly the faculty voted to reduce the amount of professional work for a teacher's certificate to fifteen hours. The advanced course for teachers, established in 1908, was also dropped by faculty vote in 1916. "As long as the legal standards for certification in the State are as low as they are," the director reported, "it is doubtful wisdom to set standards for certification by the University so high that only about half of those preparing to teach are willing to meet them."[94] In this development it can be

[92] Elliott to Birge, *Regents' Biennial Report,* 1909–10, p. 110.
[93] *Regents' Biennial Report,* 1915–16, p. 70.
[94] Vivian Allen Charles Henmon, director, School of Education, to George C. Sellery, *Regents' Biennial Report,* 1919–1920, p. 51.

seen that some University officials were working to make the University a source of trained high school and junior high school teachers. Control of the program gravitated into the hands of the members of the education department. The same department came to have a large influence in the placement bureau and on the inspection of the high schools. In short, the department came to stand largely as the University agent in its relations to the high schools.

THE relation of the University to the high schools represented one aspect of the University's functions within the state system of education. The relation of the University to the private colleges of the state and to the normal schools represented another. Shortly after assuming the presidency, Van Hise arranged a conference with representatives of the Beloit, Ripon, Lawrence, and Milton Colleges to discuss common problems and to work out arrangements under which they would confine themselves to collegiate work, leaving professional, graduate, and advanced training to the University.[95]

In 1904 an arrangement was made under which the students of Lawrence and Ripon Colleges could, at the end of two years, transfer to the University with junior standing. Students with degrees would be accepted as graduate students. Other arrangements were made for students going into the professional schools. Cooperation was carried a little further the next year. The faculty recommended, and the regents approved, a program by which the University exchanged lists of accredited schools with Lawrence and Ripon and accepted transfers from those schools in the College of Letters and Science without loss of credits.[96] In effect these two colleges had adopted the same entrance requirements as the University.

Through the years Van Hise maintained cordial relations with the presidents of the private colleges, making it clear that he wanted to be helpful where he could but that he wanted to discourage technical or professional work in the small colleges

[95] Van Hise to the regents, in Reports to the Regents, E:25, October 10, 1904.
[96] Records of the Board of Regents, F:238–239, February 28, 1905.

in competition with the University. In 1908 he urged that these colleges attempt to give no more than the first two years of engineering courses and that they then have their students come to the University. He assured President Richard Cecil Hughes of Ripon College that he had always maintained that small schools had a legitimate place in teaching the liberal arts.[97]

During these years the cordial relations between University officials and the private colleges was in marked contrast to those between University officials and the normal schools. There were seven normal schools when Van Hise became president; one at La Crosse and one at Eau Claire were established during his administration. Directed by a single board of regents, supported by the diverse local forces, the normal schools competed with the University for state support. Often they seemed to constitute a real threat to the University. This was particularly true during the period that Theodore Kronshage was prominent on the Board of Normal School Regents. University officials had long alternated between attempts to capture the normal schools and convert them into preparatory departments and attempts to destroy them or to keep them as trade schools. Bascom had wanted them to be preparatory departments of the University. In 1890 an arrangement had been made by which graduates of the normal schools were admitted to the University with the rank of junior. This had not been wholly satisfactory. Early in January, 1896, a joint committee representing the University and the normal schools submitted a report recommending a two-year University course leading to the degree of bachelor of philosophy in pedagogy for normal school graduates. Normal school graduates who wanted a regular University degree had to satisfy the established requirements. The committee also asked that the normal school regents so modify the normal school curriculum as to provide one year's work in a science, extend the mathematics course to include trigonometry, and extend the German course to include what would ordinarily constitute the first year of German at the University.[98] The report, approved by the regents, was welcomed by the students of the University.[99]

[97] Van Hise to Richard Cecil Hughes, March 9, 1908, Presidents' Papers.
[98] Records of the Board of Regents, D:426–427, January 21, 1896.
[99] *Daily Cardinal,* January 22, 1896.

Except for those who wanted to take the special degree, acceptance of the recommendations meant that normal school graduates who transferred to the University would usually receive
only about one year's credit.[100]

In 1907 the normal schools attempted to enlarge their activities. A bill was introduced in the legislature giving these institutions the authority to confer college degrees. Van Hise was
opposed to the passage of the bill and he enlisted the aid of the
presidents of Ripon, Lawrence, and Beloit Colleges against it.
To President Hughes of Ripon he wrote: "I have been somewhat hesitant what attitude to take in reference to this matter,
but have finally decided to oppose a bill which seems to me to be
contrary to the highest educational interests of the state. However, as I have been obliged to oppose so many bills, I am
desirous to have the support of the Presidents of the colleges of
the state in this matter, who are as deeply interested in the
measure as the University." Hughes and President Samuel
Plantz of Lawrence both agreed to come to Madison to oppose
the bill at the hearing.[101]

The normal school bill did not pass. Van Hise promptly set
about to bring the normal schools into the orbit of the University by marking out fields in which they could work. He wanted
them to train elementary teachers and to serve as junior colleges
for students who would transfer to the University. In February,
1908, he called a conference of the normal school presidents and
was shocked to find that they planned to extend the normal
school work from two to three or four years, in order to prepare
teachers for secondary schools. Van Hise opposed this. Instead
he urged that the normal schools confine themselves to a two-
year program. Students who wanted to prepare for teaching in
the secondary schools could transfer to the University. He assumed that the plan was acceptable to the normal school presidents and accordingly proposed it to the faculty of the College of
Letters and Science. It was approved and a committee was appointed to confer with the normal school presidents.

But the normal school presidents in the meantime had recom-

---

[100] Van Hise to the Alumni Association, June 21, 1905, Presidents' Papers.
[101] Van Hise to Hughes, April 19, 1907; Samuel Plantz to Van Hise, April 20,
22, 1907, in the Presidents' Papers.

mended to their board of regents that the four-year course be developed as soon as possible. Van Hise felt that the University was better adapted to train high school teachers than were the normal schools. He was convinced that the normal schools were not prepared to offer the last two years of college work. He urged the regents to make every effort to cooperate with the normal schools to bring about a division of labor. If the normal schools refused—that is, if they persisted in their plans to develop four-year high school teacher-training programs—the University should extend its own work so that it could provide a sufficient number of secondary school teachers independently of the normal schools. This sounded like a threat more in keeping with the methods of the captains of industry than with those of University administrators. To the Board of Regents, Van Hise declared: "This position is taken not because it is advantageous to the University, but because it is fundamentally right—because it is for the best educational interests of the State. In considering this matter we should not treat it from the point of view of whether there will be more or fewer students in the University, but from the point of view as how best to provide proper training for the required number of secondary teachers at the least expense." [102]

The regents created a committee, with Van Hise as a member, to meet with representatives of the normal schools in an attempt to work out a cooperative program along the lines Van Hise suggested. This committee opposed extension of the normal school program to three or four years because it was expensive and entailed needless duplication, but the normal school representatives did not agree. The committee reported to the Board that it considered the plan of the normal schools an impractical one, threatening to injure "the welfare of the State and of its system of education." The committee feared that the emphasis of the schools would suddenly be shifted to training high school teachers. Every effort must be made to cooperate with the normal schools by getting them to follow Van Hise's proposal, not "because it is advantageous to the University, but because

[102] Van Hise to the regents, June 16, 1908, Papers of the Board of Regents; Records of the Board of Regents, G:158, June 16, 1909.

. . . it is believed to be for the best educational interests of the State."[103]

In 1909 a bill was again presented to the legislature authorizing the normal schools to grant degrees. Van Hise again marshaled the private colleges against it.[104] But even before the bill was defeated, Van Hise had succeeded in carrying through a part of the program of coordinating the work of normal schools and the University. Representatives of the University and the normal schools met for a third time in March, 1909, to arrange a program under which graduates of the two-year normal school curriculum could transfer to the University with junior standing. It was decided that graduates of the normal school German and Latin courses would be granted sixty hours of credit toward a bachelor of arts degree upon transfer to the University, while graduates of the English course would be given sixty hours of credit toward the degree of bachelor of philosophy. This arrangement was approved by the University regents in April of the same year and by the normal school regents in June.[105]

In 1911 the legislature adopted a law which provided that the first two years' work of the normal schools could count toward a University degree, but that the normal schools were not to extend their course of study further without legislative consent. Relations between the normal schools and the University were not improved under this act. Shortly after the law went into effect one of the University regents wrote Van Hise from La Crosse reporting that the normal schools throughout the state had solicited students, promising they would get two full years' credit at the University for work done at the normal schools. Some high school graduates at La Crosse had enrolled with this understanding, only to learn later that the University would not give full credit. "The same is true of Milwaukee, I have been informed," Regent Edward Evans wrote to Van Hise, "and also, I believe, of some of the other Normal Schools." Evans warned Van Hise that this was causing a "very considerable adverse

[103] Papers of the Board of Regents, December 16, 1908.

[104] William Clifton Daland, Milton College, to Van Hise, March 18, 1909, Presidents' Papers.

[105] William Kittle, secretary of the normal school regents, to Van Hise, July 8, 1909; Van Hise to Kittle, July 9, 1909, both in the Presidents' Papers.

criticism ... of the University" and would work against it in the next legislature.[106]

President Fassett A. Cotton of the normal school at La Crosse also wrote Van Hise complaining that after agreement had been reached between the presidents of the normal schools and the University and announcement of courses had been published and distributed to the high school graduates, some high school graduates had written to University professors to verify the normal school promise and had been assured that the University would not accept these courses for credit. Under the circumstances Cotton felt that Van Hise must make a statement of University policy.[107]

Van Hise was unwilling to make a positive statement because he felt that, although the law did not specify exactly, the college work referred to could be accepted only in the College of Letters and Science, not in the technical schools. He thought the University must accept in the "technical" courses that part of the liberal arts work which is included in the first two years of those courses: "It is my broad understanding of the law that when the normal schools have established two years' college work we are to accept this work flat in liberal arts; and furthermore that we shall accept this work in the professional schools so far as it meets the requirement." Van Hise regretted it if any faculty members failed to understand this arrangement.[108] Although the University officials could properly defend themselves on the grounds of maintaining standards, to many normal school officials it appeared that the University was unwilling to follow the law.

Again in 1913 the legislature considered a bill to give the normal schools the right to extend their program to a full four years, and again the University and the private college forces prevailed in defeating it. Van Hise objected that under their 1911 grant of power the normal schools were attempting to establish technical courses for which they had no equipment. He urged that the normal schools be restricted to liberal arts

---

[106] Regent Edward Evans to Van Hise, September 11, 1912, Presidents' Papers.
[107] Fassett A. Cotton to Van Hise, September 18, 1912, Presidents' Papers.
[108] Van Hise to Cotton, September 21, 1912, Presidents' Papers.

courses.[109] At least one of the legislators supporting the law to make the normal schools degree-granting institutions was reported to have done so in the hope of freeing high schools from "domination" by the University.[110] When the bill was defeated, Van Hise and the presidents of the private colleges rejoiced.[111]

The effectiveness with which Van Hise and his supporters checked the expansion of the normal schools and the attitude of some University officials toward the work offered by the normal schools effectively blocked friendly cooperation. University officers were sometimes officious; normal school officers were quick to feel a slight and quick to resent it. Thus, in answering an inquiry about a chemistry course, Professor Kahlenberg wrote that "the University has not given credit for work done in the summer sessions of any Normal Schools. So that as the matter stands, it would not be possible to credit the work in organic chemistry as you proposed." President Cotton of the normal school at La Crosse took the question up with Van Hise, charging that the decision was Dean Birge's and that Birge was prejudiced against the normal schools. Van Hise referred the letter to Birge for comment. Birge said that the matter was to be taken up by the University normal school committee soon. He denied the charge that he was prejudiced and made the countercharge that ever since arrangements had been made to accept normal school credits at the University the normal schools had "in one way and another, been pressing for additional credit." Van Hise sent Birge's reply to President Cotton; Cotton was indignant. He asserted that the chemistry course in question would be offered in summer school as it had always been, and that if the University refused to accept the credit he would "bring legal proceeding at once to test the matter." He denied that the normal schools had been pressing for "addi-

[109] Van Hise to Senator William H. Hatton, January 2, 1913, Presidents' Papers.

[110] Samuel Plantz, president of Lawrence College, to Van Hise, April 16, 1913, Presidents' Papers.

[111] Edward D. Eaton, Beloit, to Van Hise, May 28, 1913, Presidents' Papers. He wrote: "It was a great satisfaction to us to have the Normal School bill indefinitely postponed last week. . . . We feel under great obligation to you for your leadership in the matter, and information you have furnished us from time to time. I do not support the movement to elevate the normal schools into colleges in the end, but the present check must be a salutary one."

tional credit." Van Hise replied that there was no purpose in arguing the matter further. He was unworried about Cotton's threat of legal action. "I have no idea that any court will require the faculty of the University to accept toward a degree any work which it does not regard as satisfactorily done for that degree."[112]

For all the published statements about carrying education to the people, the attitude of University officials toward the normal schools ignored the fact, clear to anyone who looked, that educational opportunity was often a matter of geography. Whether or not young people went to college and university often depended on their nearness to an institution. It was at least an open question whether the "highest educational interests" of the state were served by opposing the development of the teachers colleges into the regional colleges which appear to be evolving at the present, or whether these interests might not have been better served if, instead of fighting the advance of the normal schools, University officials had encouraged their growth, generously and wisely, and helped them toward educational respectability and usefulness.

[112] Louis Kahlenberg to Cotton, May 13, 1916; Cotton to Van Hise, May 16, 1916; Van Hise to Cotton, June 16, 1916, all in the Presidents' Papers.

8.

The Allen Survey and the Central Board

I T WAS natural that the various problems of relationships with
other educational institutions and the preoccupation of
President Van Hise with business and political "Efficiency"
should one day bring up the question of unified control of state-
supported education. The public-school system had evolved
largely under local control. It was mostly supported by local
taxes, with some funds from the state treasury. With the state
contributions there came supervision by the state superintendent. The University meanwhile, through its accrediting system,
sought to exercise a unifying influence on the high schools.
Some states already had placed their higher institutions under
a single governing board, in the hope of saving money, equaliz-
ing educational opportunity, and eliminating the unseemly and
competitive scramble for funds among educational interests at
each legislature.

Mild agitation for a central board for Wisconsin had arisen
in the 1890's and it began again in the legislature of 1909.
Neither the University regents nor the normal school regents
favored the move and nothing came of it.[1] Two years later the
legislature considered and postponed two bills, one intended to
create a commission on education to investigate and report on
the educational system of the state, the other intended to create a central board of education to supplant the two boards

[1] William Kittle, secretary of the normal school regents, to Charles R. Van Hise,
January 19, 1909; Van Hise to Kittle, January 21, 1909, Presidents' Papers.

of regents governing the University, the normal schools, and other institutions.[2] The question again came up in 1913, but again no legislation was passed.[3]

Provision was made, however, to study the problem. In 1911 the legislature had created the Board of Public Affairs, the precursor of the budget department. It was directed, in addition to its other duties, to standardize state accounting and recording practices. In 1913 the legislature had enlarged the functions of the board, enjoining it to investigate, among other things, the wisdom of creating a central board of educational control, and the "efficiency of the teaching and educational methods used in the high schools, the normal schools, the training schools for teachers, and the University." It was given forty thousand dollars a year for the next three years to conduct its work.[4]

Educational surveys were still in their infancy when the project was proposed,[5] but Wisconsin had already been subjected to several. In 1911 the Board of Public Affairs had engaged the New York Bureau of Municipal Research to survey the rural schools. This survey had been made under the direction of William Harvey Allen, then one of the directors of the bureau. The following year a survey of the normal schools was begun.[6] The law of 1913 in effect made mandatory the completion of the normal school survey and the undertaking of a survey of the University to evaluate the "efficiency of teaching and educational methods."

The survey was not without its ironical aspects. It was conducted by the State Board of Public Affairs, most of whose members were supporters of the University. Van Hise was himself an apostle of efficiency. His trip to Pennsylvania a year or so before had included a visit to the industrial plants which

---

[2] Assembly Bills 278A and 933A, *Assembly Journal*, 1911, pp. 159, 283, 1021, 1412.

[3] Assembly Bill 527A, *Assembly Journal*, 1913, pp. 199, 1665; Joint Resolution 16A, *ibid.*, 114, 1334.

[4] *Laws of Wisconsin*, 1913, pp. 1021–1026. Edward A. Fitzpatrick discusses the establishment and early work of the board in *McCarthy of Wisconsin* (New York, 1944), 140–156.

[5] See Walter Crosby Eells, *Surveys of American Higher Education*, Carnegie Foundation for the Advancement of Teaching (New York, 1937), 15 ff.

[6] Conrad E. Patzer, *Public Education in Wisconsin* (Madison, 1924), 308–309.

had responded to the magic of that great efficiency expert, Frederick W. Taylor. In a sense, the creation of Wisconsin's Board of Public Affairs and the rise of the educational and other surveys bore witness to the effectiveness of Taylor and his followers in influencing not only the patterns of American industry but governmental structure as well. "Scientific management" was a slogan of vast possibilities.

There was a further irony in the selection of William H. Allen as the principal director of the survey. Allen had directed the survey of the rural schools launched in 1911 and had a hand in the survey of the normal schools begun a year later and completed in 1914 under the direction of August N. Farmer, one of his associates. Whatever the real merit of the rural schools survey, it had been followed by remedial legislation. Charles McCarthy and other leading liberals gave Allen their support.[7] They had reason to believe that a survey of the University would be conducted sympathetically, perhaps in such a way as to uphold some practices which had aroused conservative opposition to the University.[8]

Certainly G. D. Jones, a prominent regent and conservative Republican, felt this to be the case. Writing to McGovern shortly after the Allen Survey got under way, he declared that he had "no confidence in the investigators, nor with the spirit in which they are undertaking the work. I believe that they are all very close to Dr. Charles McCarthy, who has been the heaviest advertiser of the University through more or less erratic and socialistic and wholly irresponsible magazine writers, and others of that ilk. I very much fear these men have come with the purpose of making an altogether partisan report, and that the effect of it will not be really helpful to the University." He had heard that the survey would look into the connection of the University with politics. To this he was

[7] At the meeting of the Progressives in Chicago in 1912 one of William Allen's wealthy patrons had inquired of McCarthy whether the money he had contributed to the bureau was well spent. Fitzpatrick, later biographer of McCarthy, reported to Allen that McCarthy had given assurance that the money had been well spent. Edward A. Fitzpatrick to William H. Allen, December 18, 1912, copy in the Presidents' Papers.

[8] See the Presidents' Papers, 1913–14, Allen file.

opposed. "If these investigators, every one of whom is unquestionably in most cordial sympathy with the new propaganda favored by Dr. McCarthy and others of our faculty, make any report whatever in this matter, it is certain to be biased." Jones clearly wanted no such whitewash. There were important problems of University policy which he thought should be settled. The "really basic thing, I believe, is are we headed wrong in our attitude towards post graduate work, and towards research work, and in our policy to bring in a large number of non-resident students." He wondered if the University was not becoming indifferent to its instructional responsibility.[9] Jones was perhaps right in ascribing to McCarthy and his friends responsibility for Allen's appointment, but he was wholly wrong in assuming that Allen was McCarthy's or the Progressives' man. Allen, clearly, was working largely for Allen. As it turned out, none were more surprised than the Progressives and liberals at what the Allen Survey hatched.

William Harvey Allen was still a young man when he launched the rural school survey in 1911. Born in LeRoy, Minnesota, in 1874, he had received his bachelor's degree from the University of Chicago. After study in Europe he returned to the University of Pennsylvania, where in 1900 he was granted the degree of doctor of philosophy. He had entered social work and was for a time general agent for the New York Association for Improving the Condition of the Poor. In 1907 he had become a director of the Bureau of Municipal Research of New York City. He had helped to create in connection therewith in 1911 a training school for public service of which he was also a director. In 1907 he had published a book entitled *Efficient Democracy,* one of a number of books that came from his pen. For a young man he had traveled far, aided by a capacity for vigorous self-advertisement. He had early perceived the opportunities in educational surveys.

But even before he launched the University of Wisconsin survey, Allen's work had come to be regarded with considerable suspicion in responsible quarters. In February, 1914, Abraham

---

[9] G. D. Jones to Francis E. McGovern, April 6, 1914, McGovern Papers, State Historical Society of Wisconsin.

Flexner submitted to the General Education Board a devastating report upon the educational activities of the New York Bureau of Municipal Research. Unfortunately the report was confidential.[10] Flexner had investigated fully the surveys already conducted by the bureau. Of the report on the survey of the Wisconsin rural schools Flexner stated: "The document unearths no novelties; the conditions described were already known: the remedies had previously been suggested. The document therefore contains nothing of original value. It is essentially journalistic in character, 'playing-up' certain startling data with the obvious purpose of arousing public sentiment. It is therefore not a piece of educational investigation, that impartially and thoroughly presents a picture of the situation, but an *ex parte* argument, cleverly constructed with a view to procuring a certain effect." The bulletins issued by the bureau, Flexner declared, were "for the most part, little more than newspaper squibs, shrill in tone, impatient, not free from personal and partisan insinuation, at times unfair, trivial and even vulgar."

After discussing instances of unfairness, contentiousness, and partisanship, Flexner concluded: "I have no hesitation in saying that the Bureau does not possess a staff competent to deal with educational problems. The director in charge was careful to explain to me that in purely educational matters he had 'never pretended to go beyond where a layman could go.' His assistants are men of diverse but limited training and experience, and assuredly no one of them a person of independent judgment. They are dominated by the Director, despite the educational inadequacy which he himself very properly concedes." He found the spirit of the bureau under Allen to be "militant, partisan, personal and its interest superficial, where it should be impartial, deliberate, impersonal and thorough. Finally, its publicity methods are not calculated to develop an enlightened attitude, because they distort the facts, suppress important sec-

[10] A copy of *The Educational Activities of the Bureau of Municipal Research of New York; A report to the General Education Board,* by Abraham Flexner, February 15, 1914, was found among the Presidents' Papers. It was labeled confidential on the cover, and Van Hise had written in his own hand, "absolutely confidential."

tions of the truth, and convey false impressions as to the character and attitude of modern educators." By the same token Flexner found the training school without merit. He concluded that the educational activities of the bureau were not "on the whole, worthy of serious considerations."[11]

Nor did Flexner stand alone in the opinions he expressed. After Allen had launched his survey at Wisconsin, accompanied, as these things always are, by endless questionnaires, he solicited the opinion of President Eliot of Harvard on the questionnaire. Eliot's comments on the questions were acid, his attitude hostile, and his conclusion contemptuous. "The whole questionnaire, and the Survey itself," he wrote, "seem not to recognize the fundamental principle that the supreme value of a university teacher lies not in the regular performance of routine duties, but in his power to lead and inspire his students, through the influence of his own mental and moral personality and example. The conception of the Survey seems to be borrowed from that of the industrial method called 'scientific management.' So far as I have been able to see, 'scientific management' has no application whatever in education, although capable of increasing efficiency in some industries in a disagreeable way."[12] To Van Hise, Eliot wrote enclosing a copy of his letter to Allen, adding: "I did not think it necessary for me to state to him the most obvious objection to the Survey, namely, that he is a totally incompetent person to conduct it—both as to knowledge and as to judgment."[13]

The decision to employ Allen was not reached until the spring of 1914. At a two-day meeting of the Board of Public Affairs on March 17 and 18, 1914, after considerable discussion, it was agreed that a special committee of three outside experts, Professor Herman Schneider, the dean of the engineering college at the University of Cincinnati, Eugene C. Branson of the University of North Carolina, and William H. Allen as chairman, should meet with the Board of Public Affairs at the next meeting to discuss the survey. Edward A. Fitzpatrick, who had

[11] *Ibid.,* 13, 19, 25–27.
[12] Charles W. Eliot to Allen, unsigned copy, June 2, 1914, Presidents' Papers.
[13] Eliot to Van Hise, June 2, 1914, Presidents' Papers.

worked with Allen on earlier Wisconsin surveys, was delegated to discuss the matter with Allen in New York.[14] At the next meeting, on April 1, the board invited Branson and Allen to make the University survey in conjunction with the New York Training School for Public Service on "the terms stated in Senator Sanborn's report."[15] Branson was to survey the agricultural college, Allen the rest. The *Madison Democrat* made a front-page announcement of the appointment under the headline, "Deep Inquiry Into State University By Affairs Board."[16]

The "terms stated by Senator Sanborn" which were to direct the survey consisted of twelve questions. These questions directed the survey to determine whether the University was undertaking things the state did not want done; whether it failed to do things the state wanted done; whether it was doing well what it did; whether it was economical; whether parts of the work were inadequately supported; whether parts of the work were out of proportion to the rest; whether state support of the University was in proportion to state support of other educational activities; whether the business management was adequate and efficient; whether the legislature was given adequate information about the University and the other educational activities; what the relation of the University was to the rest of the public education system; what the standards of living were among the students at the University; and what needs of the state had not yet been met and what opportunities for retrenchment and efficiency should be reported to the next legislature.[17] These questions were largely unanswerable except in terms of clearly established standards of judgment. They were

[14] Robert A. Campbell, secretary of the Board of Public Affairs, to Allen, March 20, 1914, copy in the Presidents' Papers.

[15] Acting secretary of the Board of Public Affairs to the New York Training School for Public Service on April 6, 1914, Presidents' Papers. Allen was to be employed at a rate of $10,000 a year and expenses, more than the president of the University received. The surveyors were authorized to employ men from outside the state and from the New York Training School for Public Service to assist in the work.

[16] *Madison Democrat*, April 2, 1914, p. 1.

[17] Copies of the questions are given in full in *Report upon the Survey of the University of Wisconsin: Findings of the State Board of Public Affairs and its Report to the Legislature* (Madison, [1915]), 145. This publication will be cited hereafter as *Survey of the University*.

formally transmitted to the faculty late in April.[18] Governor McGovern had already made it clear that the investigation of the University was in no way to be construed as critical of the work of President Van Hise or the Board of Regents. He had declared: "It is merely one of several that have been made of the various state institutions to determine some of the problems that are confronting them and to make their organization more perfect."[19]

Van Hise and other University officials promised full cooperation with the survey, which was promptly launched in all directions by the vigorous Dr. Allen and his numerous assistants who materialized almost out of nowhere with their questionnaires, their notebooks, and their information sheets. Letters were sent to faculty, editors, and educators asking for comments on the twelve basic questions which had been posed, and Allen reported that 305 faculty members, 30 editors, 147 school principals and superintendents, and over 50 others responded.[20] An "extensive general questionnaire" was sent to faculty members and 502 filled it out and returned it. Students were polled on their likes, dislikes, habits, and attitudes. Allen recruited large numbers of high school teachers, principals and superintendents, and normal school students to visit University classes and participate in the evaluation of the "efficiency" of University professors.[21] Some classes were visited more than once before evaluations were made![22] The use of the buildings was charted and Allen found it a great waste that some buildings were not used to capacity for the full day. He did not advise a night shift, in order to make maximum use of the "plant," but he did

[18] State Board of Public Affairs to the faculty and officers of the University of Wisconsin, April 20, 1914, Presidents' Papers.

[19] *Daily Cardinal*, March 27, 1914.   [20] *Survey of the University*, 148.

[21] No report was ever made showing the full number of people actively engaged in the survey work but Allen later declared, "There were nearly forty of us." *The Survey*, 35:604 (February 19, 1915).

[22] The evaluation of University teaching, Dean Edward A. Birge and Professor George C. Sellery pointed out, was in fact only an evaluation of pedagogical procedure, based upon a claim of 432 visits. Birge and Sellery were given the written observations of only 287 visits. A tabulation of these observations showed that 39 related to the work of one professor, 31 to another. Fifty were the record of "single visits to the classes of some 50 teachers." *Survey of the University*, 197.

propose a forty-eight-week school year. This indicates the approach of the survey which, before it was completed, had collected a mass of information purporting to answer the initial twelve questions. It is unnecessary to summarize the survey here. The methods used, data developed, personnel employed, and attitudes expressed followed almost exactly the lines indicated by Flexner in his report.

In the face of such developments the cooperation of the faculty soon turned to suspicion, then to resentment, and finally to wholehearted opposition to Allen, his staff, and his methods. Organization of the defense of the University against Allen was assigned to Dean Birge and Professor Sellery, the latter carrying the lion's share. Thirty-seven faculty members chosen by Sellery—President Van Hise was then giving his chief attention to the legislature—assumed the burden of answering the general report and the thirty-six specialized "installments" later published as "exhibits" of Dr. Allen's survey. In July, Birge had warned Van Hise that "sooner or later we shall have to make a definite fight on Allen and the earlier we can get information together regarding him and the more of it we can secure, the better off we shall be."[23] A month later Birge had warned Van Hise that Allen seemed to want a permanent position in the University.[24] Before time for registration of students that fall, Allen proposed an "improved" scheme for registering the students. Men supplied by the survey would do it.[25]

Meanwhile, there was beginning to be public criticism of Allen. In the *School Review*[26] Charles H. Judd of the University of Chicago publicly questioned Allen's qualifications for conducting a university survey. Allen naturally protested.[27] In November, Birge wrote to former Senator Hatton enclosing an installment of the survey dealing with a research bulletin which had been attacked. Declaring that the procedure of the survey

---

[23] Birge to Van Hise, July 14, 1914, Papers of the Dean of the College of Letters and Science.

[24] Birge to Van Hise, August 17, 1914, Presidents' Papers.

[25] Birge to Regent James F. Trottman, September 4, 1914, Papers of the Dean of the College of Letters and Science.

[26] *The School Review*, 22:485–488 (September, 1914).

[27] *Ibid.*, 22:555–559 (October, 1914).

in this case was fairly typical, Birge said the matter had been handled in a manner wholly unfair. The bulletin was not of itself of sufficient importance to warrant the time and energy which the survey had put upon it, but, if the survey wanted to comment on it, Birge declared, its "criticism ought to have been thoroughly well-founded, but . . . it is wholly wrong."[28]

Late in November, Van Hise discussed the survey before a meeting of the faculty and indicated that some of the suggestions might be of value. Not yet ready for a complete and open break, he stated that in his opinion "the survey had not accepted as many of the university criticisms as it might have been expected to, and also that it might be said that the university had not accepted as many of the Survey's criticisms as the Survey thinks it had reason to make."[29] This was probably as complete an understatement as Van Hise ever achieved.

The next month the results of the survey were submitted to the Board of Regents at a joint meeting of the Board and the investigating committee.[30] At that meeting Allen submitted his report, and the faculty committee consisting of Dean Birge and Professor Sellery submitted detailed comment upon the method and procedures of the survey and the qualifications of the surveyors. On behalf of the faculty Birge and Sellery formally requested that the Board of Public Affairs refuse to accept the Allen report and exhibits in whole or in part, insisting that the board "ought not to take any action or draw any conclusions from report or exhibits without a careful independent review of the evidence for and against the Allen recommendations." Secondly, the University asked that if the board accepted any part of the Allen report or exhibits it also accept "in the same manner and degree the comment or reply which the university may make to the part in question"; and that if any part of the Allen report were printed, the University be given time to prepare "an adequate reply, and that this reply also be printed, section by section, along with the Allen material."[31]

[28] Birge to William H. Hatton, November 7, 1914, Papers of the Dean of the College of Letters and Science.

[29] Minutes of the Meetings of the Faculty, 7:215, November 30, 1914.

[30] *Daily Cardinal*, December 15, 1914.   [31] *Survey of the University*, 207.

The Board of Public Affairs was faced with a difficult decision. It could not accept the Allen Survey as its own. It obviously could not suppress it. Allen realized that.[32] Accordingly the Board of Public Affairs decided in effect to repudiate Allen and write its own report and to publish Allen's report as an appendix with accompanying comment by Birge and Sellery. This was followed by thirty-six exhibits prepared by Allen and his associates, each of which was accompanied by comment by members of the University faculty. Branson's report on the College of Agriculture and Dean Russell's comments on it completed the huge volume consisting in all of nine hundred and fifty-three large pages of closely packed type. The board which had ordered the survey went out of existence on December 31, 1914, before the report could be printed.

The massive volume came out in the spring of 1915. Allen in the meantime was attacked in the public press. In the preceding July a story had appeared in the *New York Times* saying that the directors of the municipal research bureau had disagreed and that Allen, then on leave to conduct the Wisconsin survey, had been, or would be, dismissed. This was followed the next day by a more authoritative story denying Allen's dismissal although making it clear that the directors disapproved of Allen's methods and that he was no longer wanted by the bureau.[33] In February, 1915, the New York *Evening Post* carried a story stating that Allen, whose relations with the bureau had been severed by this time, claimed that the separation

---

[32] A master at engineering propaganda on his own behalf, Allen was untouched by the direct and often rough rejoinders of the faculty. Only a few days after the December meeting of the Board of Public Affairs he launched the Wisconsin Efficiency Bureau which distributed semi-weekly a leaflet, *Everybody's Business*, dealing with public affairs in Wisconsin. To a large extent, directly and indirectly, he used *Everybody's Business* to advertise his survey and to discredit in advance the University comments upon his methods and accuracy. He had the effrontery to urge every citizen to read it and, where the University and survey disagreed, to "consult available public documents to VERIFY STATEMENTS OF FACT." If the interested citizen could not do this the Efficiency Bureau had "analyzed the university's reply to survey findings." This had not been included in the printed report, but if enough people wanted it, Allen was prepared to print and distribute it for twenty cents a copy. *Everybody's Business*, January 13, 1915.

[33] *New York Times*, July 18, 1914, p. 14, col. 1; July 19, 1914, p. 8, col. 1.

occurred because he had objected to taking Rockefeller money with "a string to it." This was authoritatively denied. In fact it was reported that Allen had asked for some Rockefeller money and had been given it. Except for an unfavorable report furnished by Flexner he would perhaps have received more.[34]

Allen had returned to New York after completing his survey, but in April he returned to Wisconsin at the request of Governor Philipp to "explain" his report to the legislature.[35] He remained in Madison until August as a part of Philipp's official family. Even before he returned to Madison, *Everybody's Business,* a leaflet published by his Wisconsin Efficiency Bureau, was busily engaged in attacking the University on the one hand and urging a favorable acceptance of the Allen Survey on the other. Allen, or whoever prepared the copy, proved to be an unscrupulous although unskillful phrase lifter.[36]

Allen also cultivated some opponents of the Progressives. Thus when Hoard, who had long since broken with the Progressives and with Van Hise, wrote to the Efficiency Bureau asking about the editorials in the *Evening Post,* Allen calmly claimed that if his report on the University had been dishonest,

[34] New York *Evening Post,* February 4, 1915, p. 8, col. 2.
[35] Minutes of the Meeting of the Board of Public Affairs, April 1, 1915, State Historical Society of Wisconsin.
[36] On May 5, 1915, *Everybody's Business* contained the following statement: "The university could not wish for a fairer or better report than that of the board of public affairs." Findings were "fair and intelligent." New York *Evening Post,* April 7, 1914. Clearly it was Allen's intention to have people assume that these words were meant for him and his survey. They were written by Victor S. Yarros, special correspondent of the New York *Evening Post,* who sent in a series of articles in March and April dealing with the general University situation. The lines quoted by Allen appeared in his dispatch of April 4, printed April 7. The first quoted passage followed certain explanatory matter showing that Allen's survey was a failure and stating that the Board of Public Affairs had accordingly decided to prepare its own report. "In point of fact," Yarros continued, "the Board's report is a complete vindication of the University. Every count of the indictment circulated against it, every charge, is either dismissed as wholly baseless or else declared to be grossly exaggerated. *The University could not wish for a fairer or better report than that of the Board of Public Affairs* and the representative advisory body that assisted the board." The words of the quoted phrase appear in the following sentence: "The University, indeed, is not greatly troubled by the immediate effects of the Allen report; but it knows that, in spite of the *fair and intelligent* findings of the old board, and in spite of the virtually complete vindication of the University by the board, the bitter foes of the institution, or of some of the members of the faculty, will eagerly drink at the monumental Allen fountain and exploit it for every malicious purpose." (Italics ours.)

it would have been pronounced a scholarly document and printed long before. But Allen had insisted upon being honest and so he was being denounced. "It was not easy," he wrote to Hoard, "to write reports showing that regents were not given information without asking for it or when they ask for it. You will see that it is just a trifle disappointing to have regents who know the truth of this kind of report join the University or the administrative group in questioning the validity of the report."[37] Later Allen complained to Hoard that from October on he had been continually interfered with by the University and was compelled to "show my hand through conclusions"; that the faculty, abetted by the former governor, made every effort to keep the report from being printed; and that after the decision was made to print it, every effort was made to confuse and delay it.[38]

But the tide was turning against Allen even before the report appeared early in April. Victor S. Yarros' dispatches to the New York *Evening Post,* beginning on March 24, spoke of the "gratuitous and unintelligent overhauling, 'ripping,' and 'surveying' ... that the institution has been subjected to under the direction of Dr. W. H. Allen." The situation in the University faculty was such that one professor wrote to Van Hise denying that he had flattered Allen in order to get a favorable report.[39] In April *School and Society* quoted the *Evening Post* statement that the survey was a "childish and mischievous futility."[40]

Allen shortly became the target of numerous assaults. In April and again in May the *Nation* carried articles which dealt with the University situation in general. The second contained a brief comment on Allen and his methods. "This gentleman falls short of greatness only in the fact that there is such a disproportion between his competence and his plausibility and assurance."[41]

More devastating was an article which appeared anonymously in the *Dial* under the title "A Bull in the Educational China-

[37] Allen to William D. Hoard, March 11, 1915, Philipp Papers, State Historical Society of Wisconsin.
[38] Allen to Hoard, March 17, 1915, Philipp Papers.
[39] Michael V. O'Shea to Van Hise, March 25, 1915, Presidents' Papers.
[40] *School and Society,* 1:564–565 (April 17, 1915).
[41] Observer, "Demos and the Professor," *The Nation,* 100:596 (May 27, 1915).

Shop." The writer spoke of the "inquisitorial methods" of Allen, the "versatile fallacies" and the "comprehensive distortions" of the survey. "Misstatements, misquotation, garbled reports, direct untruthfulness, insinuations, unwarranted implications, ignorant interpretations, mechanical manipulations of statistics, are all charged against Dr. Allen; and with a ruthless frankness, scathing in its charitable reserve, are proved to the hilt." The writer thought that "so extreme a genius for blundering must be unusual." Of the report he asked, "And does any person in his senses really believe that the cause of higher education, or any worthy cause whatever, can be advanced by industrious anthills of such petty, carping, querulous, specious pellets of inconsequence?" The whole thing, he thought, was "a colossal piece of impudence."[42]

Current Opinion reviewed the press comment on the Allen Survey.[43] Hermon C. Bumpus, formerly University business manager and then president of Tufts College, wrote critically of the Allen Survey in *School Review*, declaring that "efficiency cannot be increased through investigations or advice of those who are ignorant of University purposes and out of sympathy with University methods."[44]

Allen attempted to defend himself. A letter to the *Dial* merely provoked further critical comment by two University professors, George C. Comstock and William Ellery Leonard.[45] Allen protested to the *Nation* in a long letter denying the charges made in its columns, but he got no sympathy.[46] In September, the *Educational Review* carried an article by John Loomis Sturtevant giving mild support to Allen, but Dean Birge and Professor Jastrow answered it promptly.[47]

In December, George H. Mead, professor of philosophy at the University of Chicago, in a long, thoughtful article in the

[42] "A Bull in the Educational China-Shop," *The Dial*, 58:445–448 (June 10, 1915).

[43] *Current Opinion*, 58:419–420 (June, 1915).

[44] *School Review*, 23:417–418 (June, 1915).

[45] *The Dial*, 59:14–15 (June 27, 1915); 59:51–53 (July 15, 1915); 59:93–96 (August 15, 1915).

[46] *The Nation*, 101:201–203, 224–227 (August 12, 19, 1915).

[47] *Educational Review*, 50:109–119 (September, 1915); 50:325–347, 418–423 (November, 1915); 51:87–89 (January, 1916).

Survey reviewed the relation of the University to the state and the Allen report. Allen's survey, Mead declared, was "an example of how not to survey a university." Again Allen was given space to answer, but he could not meet the objections Mead had raised.[48] Nowhere in the nonpartisan press was Allen's survey approved. At the end of the year Professor Ellwood P. Cubberley of Stanford pronounced it an "outrageous investigation."[49]

Meanwhile Allen was still intent upon winning acceptance in the capitol. For a while Governor Philipp kept him on as an assistant, and Allen, in letters to state politicians, tried to win support for his work. To Senator Otto Bosshard he complained that he must not be held responsible for the "miscarriage of intelligence in presenting the report." The old Board of Public Affairs had printed his material in eight-point type, had removed his underscorings and other typographical aids for the reader, and had permitted the University faculty to write anything it pleased but had not given him space to answer.[50] To an assemblyman he wrote protesting that reports of the cost of the survey were exaggerated—it had not cost sixty thousand dollars, as had been announced.[51]

Allen was not even successful with the state politicians. In May, Senator Henry M. Culbertson introduced a resolution ap-

[48] *The Survey*, 35:349–351, 354–361 (December 25, 1915); 35:602–607, 610 (February 19, 1916).

[49] National Education Association, *Proceedings*, 1915, p. 756, cited in Eells, *Surveys of American Higher Education*, 35. Ellwood P. Cubberley wrote to President David Starr Jordan that Allen was a brilliant man who "preferred to be a crook to an honest man," and said Allen was caught "cheating with the cards. . . . Since then he has been fired from the Bureau of Municipal Research for his crooked work." Cubberley to Jordan, April 22, 1915. Original in the Presidents' Papers.

[50] Allen to Otto Bosshard, June 23, 1915, Philipp Papers. Dean Sellery declared on this point that "no restrictions were placed on Allen in revising his installments or supplementing them." Interview, Curti and Carstensen with Dean Sellery, December 14, 1947.

[51] Allen to Harry J. Mortensen, June 10, 1915, Philipp Papers. The total cost of the survey was claimed by Allen to have been $13,200 plus the $2,000 for printing. The secretary of the Board of Public Affairs reported that it had cost $17,802.47 as of July 9, 1915, but that not all bills were in. Secretary W. W. Powell to Governor Emanuel L. Philipp, July 9, 1915, Philipp Papers. Dean Sellery later estimated the cost, including the time the University was required to spend on it, at over $100,000. Eells, *Surveys of American Higher Education*, 327.

pointing a committee to investigate the Wisconsin Efficiency
Bureau and its publication, *Everybody's Business.*[52] The committee submitted a scathing criticism of the educational surveys
in connection with its report,[53] which concluded that the efficiency bureau was "an organization which issues publications
designed to influence public opinion and legislation on important matters, without disclosing the names of its owners,
promoters, managers, or contributors. Sound public policy
demands the condemnation of such procedure.[54]

In July the *Milwaukee Journal* spoke of Allen as associate
governor, demanded to know his qualifications for the post, and
protested that he had first been employed to look for faults in
the University and now sat in judgment over the legislative
measures proposed for the University.[55]

In August, Allen left Wisconsin, having first prepared a memorandum showing that he had had graduate work in more universities than Van Hise, Birge, and Comstock combined.[56] To
Professor A. W. Rankin of Minnesota he wrote that he thought
the country would wake up to the fact that "the campaign of
detraction which the Wisconsin hierarchy has pursued is absolutely anti-educational, anti-inspirational and anti-moral as
anything could be. Even as it is, the faculty has appointed committees to see what constructive use can be made of the Survey.
The pity is that the faculty did not wake up until the hierarchy
had done the damage." He now pictured himself as a martyr.
"It is worth all the drubbing I have gotten to have had a small
hand in bringing about a complete revision of the state's
method of making a budget which if carried out will be by all
odds the best provision ever made in any state of getting the
facts before the public about budget estimates."[57]

So far as the survey itself was concerned, its influence was not
lasting. In his remarks to the faculty in the autumn Van Hise
declared: "The survey is quickly disposed of, since while Dr.
W. H. Allen, its chief conductor, was an undoubted annoyance,

[52] *Senate Journal,* 1915, pp. 647–649, 821–830.   [53] *Ibid.,* 821–830.
[54] *Ibid.,* 829.   [55] *Milwaukee Journal,* July 17, 1915.
[56] Allen to Pratt, August 16, 1915, Philipp Papers.
[57] Allen to Professor A. W. Rankin, University of Minnesota, August 16, 1915,
Philipp Papers.

neither the benefits nor the evil effects of his work have been important. It was feared that the misinformation and misrepresentation contained in the Allen reports might affect adversely the attitude of the legislature; but it turned out that this report had no appreciable effect upon that body. . . . It is a misfortune that the principal director of the survey did not conduct his work in an enlightened manner; for had he done so, the results might have been of great assistance to the University. As it turned out, we must depend upon ourselves for improvement."[58]

Several years later Birge gave his opinion on the futility of education surveys. Insiders failed because they were too much under the control of the traditions of the institution. Outsiders "are apt to give quite too little consideration to these same historical conditions. They criticize the institution as if it were detached from the conditions under which it has grown and which have made it what it is, and their criticisms are very likely to be impracticable for this very reason."[59]

But the survey, or at least the report of the Board of Public Affairs, was responsible for some action. Six University faculty committees were established to study and make recommendations for improvements. These included committees on research, on graduate work and field work, on improvement of instruction, foreign language requirements, utilization of the University plant, faculty records, and improvement of faculty organization. The important work of these committees is considered elsewhere.

AMONG the questions which the Board of Public Affairs had proposed to consider was that of bringing about centralized control of all higher education or of all public education within the state. This proposition had been considered many times by the legislature. Proposals aimed at creating a single board to control even the higher institutions had met with the solid opposition

[58] Minutes of the Faculty, 7:273, October 4, 1915.
[59] Birge to Judge Cuthbert W. Pound, Cornell University, February 21, 1919, Presidents' Papers.

of the normal school regents and the University regents. Van Hise was energetic and highly articulate in his opposition. Although not made directly a part of the Allen Survey, this subject might have been permissible under a number of the questions which guided the survey, or the Board of Public Affairs in its own report might have commented. However, neither the board nor Allen chose to deal with the problem. Perhaps as the situation had developed, with Allen in control of the survey, everybody felt that enough fighting issues had been created without injecting another.

Despite the failure of either Allen or the board to consider the question, Governor Philipp was determined to push for the creation of a central board. A conservative Milwaukee businessman, Philipp had captured the Republican nomination for governor in 1914. Campaigning on a program of economy, representing the anti-La Follette forces in the party, Philipp had to campaign against a Democratic opponent and John J. Blaine, who, with La Follette's backing, ran as an independent. Philipp won the election, although former Governor McGovern, running for the United States Senate, lost to his Democratic opponent by a scant thousand votes. With the Progressive bloc divided into at least two factions, with an "economy" governor in office, the political situation was confused. During the campaign Philipp had promised to reduce expenditures, and he had criticized the University faculty for teaching socialism. He insisted that sons and daughters of Wisconsin citizens should be permitted to attend and graduate from the University and return home as loyal and patriotic Americans. He had criticized the University for appealing to out-of-state students and thus educating noncitizens, and he had demanded greater efficiency in the handling of University business. Since he proclaimed such a program, and since he represented anti-La Follette, anti-Progressive forces within the Republican Party, many, including President Van Hise, assumed that Philipp was hostile to the University.

In his first message to the legislature, Philipp proposed the creation of a single board to manage the whole public school system. He felt that the several boards of regents considered problems only in the light of the institution or institutions under their control and that the common schools suffered from neglect. Under the system which had developed he felt Wisconsin was building the educational structure from the top down instead of from the bottom up. This system was wrong and needed to be corrected in the interest of the people. He proposed a central board of thirteen members, eleven to be appointed by the governor from various professional groups, of which the educators were most numerous. "I believe that the instructional side of our educational institutions should be represented by educators and the business side by businessmen. A board so constituted would be evenly balanced to meet all requirements of these institutions."[60]

Van Hise and his associates were suspicious of the motives of Governor Philipp. The governor proposed a basic reorganization of the control of the University, he said, as an economy measure and as a part of a campaign for a better educational system. But Philipp's campaign attacks on the "socialistic teaching" at the University were construed as attacks upon academic freedom; his plan for a central board was construed as an attempt to gain control of the University by reorganizing the board and thus appointing all the new members. When it finally became clear that Philipp was not motivated by enmity, that his program represented an honest and sincere attempt to bring about changes which he conceived to be of vital importance to the University, a great show was made of having "won Philipp over."

In the beginning, however, Van Hise assumed that the governor had ulterior motives in proposing a central board and he vigorously opposed the creation of one. Shortly after the governor had delivered his message, Van Hise spoke at length on the question of a central board before a meeting of the Association of Deans and Presidents of Wisconsin Colleges. He recognized that central boards had been necessary in states with several large institutions; but he insisted that, since Wisconsin had no such problem, such a board was not needed. He neatly arranged eight arguments in favor of central boards against eight slightly

[60] *Assembly Journal*, 1915, pp. 35-37.

more weighty arguments opposing such boards. Van Hise thus early and clearly went on record as opposed to a central board for Wisconsin.[61]

The course of Governor Philipp's campaign for the creation of a single board of education to promote and direct the orderly development and growth of the whole public educational program of the state, and the vigorous countercampaign, cannot here be traced in detail through the Wisconsin politics of 1915, but the outlines of the contest must be sketched.

First of all, Governor Philipp's interest, whatever was written to the contrary, was sympathetic and intelligent; he wanted what he considered a constructive program. By his own acknowledgment he was little influenced by the Allen Survey. He proposed to act on his own knowledge or on a basis of new investigations.[62]

In February, Bert L. Van Gorden introduced in the Assembly an administration bill providing for centralization of the control of Wisconsin public education under a single head. Governor Philipp himself conducted a wide inquiry of college and university administrators and professors, prominent citizens, and others, asking what should be the particular features in a bill of this kind.[63] He early won the support for the principle of a central board from a number of prominent citizens including

[61] Minutes of Eighth Annual Meeting of the Association of Deans and Presidents of Wisconsin Colleges, January 8, 1915, Papers of the Dean of the College of Letters and Science.

[62] Victor S. Yarros, New York *Evening Post,* April 7, 1915, p. 4, col. 3.

[63] Governor Philipp's papers include scores of letters from leading educators in the country, including the following: Nicholas Murray Butler, president of Columbia University; Balthasar Henry Meyer, Interstate Commerce Commission, Washington, D.C.; President George E. Vincent, University of Minnesota; President Frank L. McVey, University of North Dakota; Claude Halstead Van Tyne, professor of history, University of Michigan; President Samuel Plantz, Lawrence College, Appleton; President Silas Evans, Ripon College; President Wilbur I. O. Carrier, Carroll College; President Ellen C. Sabin, Milwaukee-Downer College; President Frank J. Goodnow, Johns Hopkins; William Fletcher Russell, Teachers College, Columbia; President Edward D. Eaton, Beloit College; Professor Charles H. Judd, University of Chicago; President William C. Daland, Milton College; and Clyde Furst, Secretary, Carnegie Foundation for the Advancement of Teaching. While these men by no means all supported Philipp's proposal—and in fact a large number opposed it or advised extreme caution—the evidence of extensive correspondence clearly reveals that Philipp sought the advice of leading educators. He also asked advice from most of the state governors. Philipp Papers.

G. D. Jones, then vice-president of the University regents; Frederick C. Thwaits of Milwaukee, a former regent; Neal Brown of Wausau; and William A. Titus, member of the Board of Visitors. Brown favored Governor Philipp with a fourteen-page discussion of what was needed in such a board.[64] Titus told Philipp that if he carried through a workable plan for a state board it would "long be remembered as one of the large constructive measures" of his administration, and he advised Philipp on how the opposition arguments being formulated by Van Hise could best be met.[65] Thwaits early gave his support to Philipp.[66] G. D. Jones wrote to Philipp, "I am and for some years have been in favor of a central state board of education that, in conjunction with the state superintendent, should have the supervision of all our public schools. Of course this would include everything from our common schools to our state university . . . my chief reason for reaching this conclusion is that one needs a wider vision and a larger knowledge of the real educational needs of the state than is afforded by membership on a board that is mostly concerned with financial and business matters relating to one department only of education."[67]

Governor Philipp's attitude toward the central board was perhaps most fully expressed in a letter he wrote to the aged ex-Senator Spooner, then in New York. An explanation was due Spooner not only because of the prominent political position he had held, but because forty years before he had shepherded through the legislature the bill under which the state first granted a regular appropriation to the University. Philipp said that only one bill before the legislature was an administration measure. This was the bill providing for a central board to "unify and correlate the State's publicly supported educational activities from rural school to University. To say that this bill is aimed at the University or is hostile to the University is to misrepresent its origin and purpose."

Van Hise, Philipp said, had already acknowledged the need

[64] Neal Brown to Emanuel L. Philipp, April 6, 1915, Philipp Papers.
[65] William A. Titus to Philipp, April 6, 1915, Philipp Papers.
[66] Frederick C. Thwaits to Emanuel L. Philipp, March 29, 1915, Philipp Papers.
[67] G. D. Jones to Philipp, April 3, 1915, Philipp Papers.

of at least central financial control, and while there was difference of opinion as to how far centralization should go, there was a respectable movement in that direction. Of the Van Gorden bill Philipp said that the administration had asked all people testifying at committee hearings to give constructive suggestions "inasmuch as none of the details of the bill were considered of consequence. Out of the constructive suggestions received here at home and from the best informed students throughout the country, a bill is now in the last stages of drafting." On this bill he invited Spooner's criticisms. Of his general attitude toward the University, Philipp declared that he had no responsibility for other bills affecting the University which had been introduced. On three phases of the University management he had spoken: "That in a time of universal need for retrenchment it is fair to ask the University to retrench; that to accepting out-of-state students there is a limit of profit to the State and the State's ability to pay; and that the State had the right to expect its boys and girls to return from the University without having been subjected to propagandizing which decreases their respect for American institutions."

Philipp complained that the legislature's attempt to get the University to economize was construed as hostility to the University, a point which he denied emphatically. He complained that Van Hise and the University authorities refused to try to answer the question of the cost of taking care of the out-of-state students. Philipp declared himself much concerned over this problem, asking Spooner to suggest "some practical way of testing out-of-state students who wish to come so that our University will receive only those who give promise of making actual contribution of character and force and scholarship." Philipp professed complete surprise that he should be charged with threatening academic freedom. "President Van Hise has publicly stated that he has never heard any such intimation from me or the Legislature. Not a syllable of any measure before the Legislature proposes even remotely an intervention with academic freedom. On the contrary, the bill now being re-drafted takes precautions which do not occur in existing law to prevent Regents from interfering with the instructional staff and would

compel the central board to deal with instructional matters di
rectly and exclusively through the instructional heads of institutions.

"In answer to the issue raised by persons who claim to be
friends of the University I have on one or two occasions said
that I believed there should be no teaching at the University
which would cause Wisconsin boys and girls to have disrespect
for American institutions. To this day I cannot see how anyone
can find a menace to academic freedom in this expression of
personal opinion."[68]

But no matter how sincere Governor Philipp was in his attempt to carry through a great educational reform, he never
managed to create this impression publicly. Some of the reasons
for this failure were beyond his control. His reorganization bill
was presented at a time when the agitation accompanying the
Allen Survey was at its height. Although the governor indicated
that his bill did not rest upon Allen's survey, he himself created
doubts by bringing Allen back to Wisconsin to "explain" the
survey to the legislature. He then kept Allen on his staff until
August. Thus at a time when Allen's work was being increasingly discredited, after the Board of Public Affairs had dis-
sociated itself from the Allen Survey, Philipp welcomed the man
into his administration. Moreover, a total of forty-two bills relating to the University were presented to the legislature.
Among them were bills to remove the president of the University from the Board of Regents, to limit the scope and usefulness
of the medical school, to forbid the appointment of University professors to government advisory posts, and to eliminate
the University foreign language requirements. Whatever
Philipp said to the contrary, these measures were associated by
his opponents with the central-board bill.

Van Hise had early gone on record as opposing a central
board for Wisconsin and his opposition was known to all his
brother administrators, many of whom were under the impression that the consolidation bill was an attack upon Van Hise.
Hence, when Philipp solicited their opinions, it is quite probable that their answers were as often made in terms aimed at

[68] Philipp to John C. Spooner, New York City, April 20, 1915, Philipp Papers.

assisting Van Hise as in terms of helping Philipp.[69] The assistance of alumni, individually and collectively, was enlisted. A group of New York alumni appealed directly to Philipp and to the legislature not to do harm to the University—construing the consolidation bill as harmful.[70] Van Hise discussed the matter freely with the president of the Alumni Association and asked his help.[71]

Prominent alumni gave their aid. Evan A. Evans of Baraboo was appealed to, and Zona Gale, already a well-known literary figure returned from New York to her native Portage, kept in touch with Van Hise throughout the campaign. She, with the aid of Van Hise and McCarthy, worked diligently to win the support of Senator George Staudenmayer of Portage.[72] To Zona Gale, Van Hise later confessed: "It has been a hard fight, or rather a series of hard fights. Without the cordial support of individual alumni we could not have won. As an organization, however, they did little. You already know what I think of the value of your services."[73] Besides the support Van Hise enlisted, assistance came from other quarters. Opponents of Governor Philipp opposed the bill on political grounds. The state superintendent of public instruction and the Board of Normal School Regents opposed the bill.[74]

Van Hise wanted, if possible, the complete defeat of the gover-

[69] It is difficult to make a judgment in this matter. Philipp polled opinion widely, but he had perforce to consult Van Hise's friends among university administrators. Van Hise was at the same time keeping them informed of the Wisconsin situation and of his desires and fears. How far this conditioned these men in their responses to Philipp it is impossible to say; perhaps it would have been impossible even for them to determine. There is no question, however, that many hoped for a Van Hise victory. In August, after the watered-down Van Gorden bill had been passed and the University appropriation bill adopted, President Edmund J. James of the University of Illinois wrote of his delight in hearing the outcome. "I felt like throwing up my hat and crying 'Hurrah for Wisconsin and for Van Hise!'" James to Van Hise, August 11, 1915, Presidents' Papers.

[70] The Alumni of the University of Wisconsin in New York City to Philipp, March 26, 1916, Philipp Papers; *Senate Journal*, 1915, pp. 395–396.

[71] Van Hise to Ernst von Briesen, president of the University of Wisconsin Alumni Association, March 17, 1915, Presidents' Papers.

[72] Zona Gale to Van Hise, March 18 and 22, 1915, Presidents' Papers.

[73] Van Hise to Gale, August 23, 1915, Presidents' Papers.

[74] William A. Titus, writing to Philipp on July 1, 1915, reported: "Of course Supt. Cary does not want this department of school work [rural] touched by any board as he feels it is his personal domain, but he seems to be against the

nor's bill but, if that were not possible, he had prepared numerous proposals intended to limit the power of the central board to bookkeeping and the collection of various educational statistics.[75] His political effectiveness in this contest is reflected in the steady disintegration of the Van Gorden bill introduced in the Assembly on February 17.[76] The bill was intended by Governor Philipp to abolish all boards of regents and to centralize and unify control of matters common to all educational activities.

But the governor's bill was amended and modified and transformed beyond all recognition, first in the Assembly and then in the Senate. In July the governor was warned by supporters of the bill that it could not pass as he wanted it.[77] They were right. A bill was passed, but it was just an empty reminder of what Philipp had sought. Its only resemblance to the original bill was that it still bore the original Assembly number and established something called a State Board of Education. The several boards of regents were left with virtually all their powers intact. The new board consisted of five members. The governor, the secretary of state, and the state superintendent were ex-officio members. The other two were appointed, one by the normal school regents, and the other by the University regents.[78] The board was given "exclusive charge and management of all financial affairs of the educational activities of the state." It could ex-

central board idea anyway, and is doing it all the injury he can. Then there is the pernicious Normal School lobby which is a fester on the educational system of Wisconsin, and beside which the lobby of the University is a nothing. This Normal Schools lobby is said to be ready to trade anything for votes against your State Board of Education bill." Philipp Papers.

[75] Writing to Zona Gale, Van Hise declared that he had decided the board should not be merely a budget board. Instead "it is my proposal to call it a board of estimates and apportionment." Van Hise to Gale, April 1, 1915, Presidents' Papers. Titus wrote to Governor Philipp on April 6, 1915, saying, "I have heard him state that any Board of Education that began to interest itself in the management of the University would become an 'intolerable nuisance.' " Philipp Papers.

[76] *Assembly Journal*, 1915, p. 190. While opposition to a central board to control all public education was partly bolstered by the fact that under the constitution the state superintendent was given power to supervise the schools, this difficulty was not insurmountable. The constitution provided that "the supervision of public instruction shall be vested in a state superintendent and such other officers as the legislature shall direct; and their qualifications, powers and compensation shall be prescribed by law." *Constitution of Wisconsin*, Article X, Sec. 1.

[77] Titus to Philipp, July 1, and Thwaits to Philipp, July 15, 1915, both in the Philipp Papers.   [78] *Laws of Wisconsin*, 1915, pp. 630–633.

amine and study the business methods and management of the
public schools and the expenditures of public funds for them. It
had authority to collect various statistical and other data. It was
given certain auditing powers and the educational budget for
the next legislature was to be passed through its hands.[79] The
bill was approved by the governor on August 3, 1915—a clear
victory for Van Hise and the anti-Philipp forces.

Yet Philipp apparently bore little ill will. Before the end of
the month Van Hise and Thorkelson, the business manager, at
a conference with Governor Philipp reached a mutually satisfactory agreement on points of interest. The governor authorized new appointments on a basis of the regents' budget, agreed
that the building program should go ahead, declared that "Dr.
Allen would not be appointed to any place on this board or indeed any position in the state," and promised that the University
would not be further harassed by the Board of Public Affairs for
the next two years.[80]

It was, all told, a victory for Van Hise. In his address to the
University faculty at the beginning of the new academic year
he stated that the education board "under the new law is a
board of estimates and apportionment; and in addition has
authority in financial affairs. Since, however, the State Board
consists of the Governor, the Secretary of State, the State Superintendent, each of whom has large state responsibility in the performance of his regular duties; and the other two members are
representatives of the University and the normal schools, it
appears probable that the government of the university will continue much as heretofore, the Regents doing the immediate
work of government; their actions, however, being subject to
review by the State Board."[81]

Van Hise had wanted a board with little power, and this is
what he thought he had. For a short time, however, it appeared

[79] *Ibid.*

[80] Van Hise, Memoranda of Interview, August 20, 1915. Presidents' Papers. To
Zona Gale, Van Hise wrote that Philipp declared he "has no intention of con-
tinuing Dr. Allen in his employ." Van Hise to Gale, August 23, 1915, Presidents'
Papers.

[81] "Outline of address by Charles Van Hise to Instructional Staff at the first
meeting of the University faculty for 1915–1916." October 4, 1915, Presidents'
Papers.

that the Board of Education might, almost inadvertently, assume considerable power. In the last days of the legislative session, a bill was passed, by a unanimous vote in each house, directing that all funds appropriated to the University and the normal schools be used "exclusively by the state board of education."[82]

Under this grant it appeared that the board, with Superintendent Cary now in a position of power as chairman, would try to use its supposed power over expenditures to impose various restrictions upon the University and the normal schools. Cary attempted to bedevil the University into abandoning small classes. In June, 1916, Cary, for the Board of Education, had the temerity to recommend that the University drop all vacancies unfilled at that time and effect a saving of over seventy-five thousand dollars.[83] Cary's proposal was firmly rejected.[84] The board also, much to the annoyance of Van Hise, Dean Birge, and members of the Board of Regents, attempted to control new appointments.[85] But no very extensive attempt was made by the board to attain control over educational matters during its first two years of operation. In 1917 it was enlarged to nine members. But the legislature took away some of its power, reappropriating all money given to the state board for operation and maintenance of the University, normal schools, and the other institutions to the respective governing boards of these institutions.[86] Reduced to impotency and in part captured by its enemies, the Board of Education retained a shadowy life until 1923, when it was abolished.[87] There were later attempts to revive the notion of a state board, but none met with success.

It is impossible to say what the result would have been had Van Hise supported instead of opposed Governor Philipp's plan to bring the whole public educational system under the direc-

---

[82] *Senate Journal,* 1915, pp. 1269, 1314; *Assembly Journal,* 1915, p. 1720; *Laws of Wisconsin,* 1915, p. 923.

[83] Charles P. Cary of the State Board of Education to the regents, May 29, 1916. Papers of the Board of Regents, June 20, 1916.

[84] *Ibid.*

[85] Birge to Van Hise, August 12, 1916, and Florence Buckstaff to Van Hise, December 10, 1916, both in the Presidents' Papers.

[86] *Laws of Wisconsin,* 1917, pp. 787–791, 1196.

[87] *Laws of Wisconsin,* 1923, p. 357.

tion of a representative board, if he had used his great talent and energy to shape rather than to obstruct the movement. Perhaps the other forces which helped to defeat Philipp's bill would have been sufficient without Van Hise's opposition, although from the record it does not seem that this would have been possible. That Van Hise opposed a central board was in part a matter of principle, but he had been known to shift his position for good reason. In his attitude toward University Extension, for example, he completely changed his opinion. More prominent in Van Hise's opposition was his distrust of Philipp. He felt, in view of the various attacks which had been made upon the University in the political campaign of 1914 and by the legislature, that Philipp meant to harm the University and that the central board was a means to this end. Van Hise and Governor Philipp in time came to understand and respect each other and Van Hise to realize that Philipp's motives had not been inspired by a desire to damage the University. Van Hise lived to regret his opposition to the central board,[88] but the opportunity to repair the damage did not come. Van Hise died in 1918.

[88] Dr. Joseph S. Evans, for years an intimate and close adviser of Van Hise and a friend of Governor Philipp, recalled that Van Hise later acknowledged that he had made a mistake in opposing the central board. Interview, Curti and Carstensen with Dr. Evans, October 12, 1945. Van Hise never made a public acknowledgment of his regret. However, when the central board was enlarged in 1917 but before it had been completely reduced, Van Hise wrote to Regent G. D. Jones saying that he was willing to serve on the board as the University representative. Jones wrote back saying, "It is one of the great pleasures of my life to know that you and I are in such accord in reference to our university. I know there have been times when you have questioned my stand on matters and that this Central Board of Education was one of them. I sincerely believed two years ago that the underlying thought of a Central Board of Education was sound. Under the old system there was no correlation. Misunderstandings were certain to arise. I know of no class of people who are more suspicious of one another than schoolmen. The University was unfairly assailed in private and somewhat in public by pinheaded educators from the normal schools, from the industrial schools, etc. There was an air of intrigue in which the state superintendent's department was a factor. I never believed the State Board of Education would mean a smaller expenditure of money, but I believed it would be a wiser use, and that it would improve the whole situation. I am firm in that belief now." Jones to Van Hise, March 3, 1917, Presidents' Papers.

9.

Letters and Science: Policies

THE rapid rise of applied education in the last two decades of the nineteenth century alarmed many scholars at Wisconsin as at other universities. To them it seemed as if the ever greater importance attached to the applied sciences and to the practical implications of the social studies jeopardized the integrity and influence of the liberal arts. President Van Hise did not share these fears and in his inaugural address he sought to prove that there was no basis for them. In so doing he outlined his conception of the role of the College of Letters and Science in the whole scheme of the University.

The rise of applied education, Van Hise argued, merely reflected the needs of a new constituency. If the so-called practical fields attracted a few students who might otherwise have followed the more traditional liberal arts program, "the tremendously increased momentum of the educational movement produced by the large numbers that flock to the universities probably has brought to the liberal arts more students than have been lost to them by the rise of applied knowledge."[1] In proof of his point he cited the increase in the number of undergraduates in the College of Letters and Science from 383 at the beginning of Chamberlin's administration to 1,122 at the end of the Adams regime—the period of the most pronounced advance

[1] Charles R. Van Hise's inaugural address, in *The Jubilee of the University of Wisconsin* (Madison, 1905), 106–107.

of applied knowledge. It had been fortunate, he admitted, that the College of Letters and Science had become so firmly established before the great development of agriculture and engineering. "So strong," he continued, "are the liberal arts and pure science, that I have no fear that the college of letters and science will lose its leading position at the university." In Van Hise's eyes the new union of the University Library and the Historical Society Library in the magnificent classical palace and the recent growth of graduate work, chiefly in the Letters and Science fields, augured well for the sustained influence of the humanities and of knowledge for its own sake.

In his inaugural address Van Hise maintained, as he did so often throughout his administration, that learning and research, without reference to immediate or apparent application, are valid and important in their own right. But even in this concession he envisioned the practical uses to which knowledge pursued with utter disinterest might lead. "No knowledge of substance or force or life is so remote or minute, although apparently indefinitely distant from present practice, but that tomorrow it may become an indispensable need. The practical man of all practical men is he who, with his face toward truth, follows wherever it may lead, with no thought but to get a deeper insight into the order of the universe in which he lives."[2] This, in fact, was the key to Van Hise's thinking: what was regarded as pure scholarship and disinterested investigation, however "apparently remote from any practical service," might suddenly prove to be a useful stream. Thus the College of Letters and Science had to remain central in the whole scheme of the University. It provided the basic general education on which all specialization and application inevitably rested. It was, in other words, the handmaiden of all the technical schools. What was done in the classrooms, libraries, and laboratories in connection with the program of the College of Letters and Science was bound in some way or other to prove useful in agriculture, industry, and government.

The Van Hise thesis, then, neither defended knowledge for the sake of knowledge nor assumed that practical education it-

[2] *Ibid.,* 123.

self was either sufficient or desirable. It represented rather a synthesis of the ivory-tower conception of learning and of the primacy of the practical. A fusion of the two approaches, he insisted, meant life and vigor. His point seemed to be borne out in the growing prosperity of the departments which could and did make fruitful connections with the business of living. As chemistry turned its attention to the problems of agriculture, biochemistry was born, full of promises to be realized with startling rapidity. As botanists concerned themselves with the needs of farmers, plant pathology developed and began to yield welcome gains. As zoologists set out to be serviceable to fruit growers and other agriculturalists, entomology ushered in triumphs over pests and blights. In much the same way, as economists faced the problems peculiar to a farming population, agricultural economics emerged. As the needs of industry grew, the course in commerce took shape. These are only a few of the ways in which the liaison between theory and practice seemed to bear out Van Hise's contention.

What was thus happening at Wisconsin was only the continuation of a long trend at the University. The inauguration of Van Hise did not interrupt a growing emphasis on an education functional to the increasingly specialized necessities of American life. The Van Hise era did represent leadership in a wider movement in the whole country, a movement which the older private universities shared in some degree with the state institutions. But if the Van Hise program represented continuity rather than innovation, it was nevertheless marked by a great expansion in the applications of knowledge and in the acquisition of techniques vocational in character. The first two and a half decades of the twentieth century witnessed a steady advance of specialization and professionalization, not only in the Colleges of Agriculture and Engineering and in the developing medical school, but in the College of Letters and Science itself. The multiplication on the undergraduate level of specialized programs in chemistry, journalism, the industrial arts, library training, musical skills, and professional education, all more or less within the framework of the College of Letters and Science, was the most pronounced trend during the administrations of

Van Hise and Birge. While this mounting emphasis on professional and vocational values was most apparent on the undergraduate level, the splendid development of graduate training and of research was, in a sense, an identical characteristic in the sphere of higher studies.

Thus any unity which the College of Letters and Science may have possessed originally was a thing of the past by the end of the Van Hise regime. But the values of a liberal education as such were not altogether forgotten. However, these values, in the minds of many, were in conflict with the new effort to make pure knowledge functional without undermining its theoretical basis. To some of the more conservative the effort to unite theory and practice, especially as it was exemplified in the effort to encompass so many diversities in one administrative unit, militated against the imperatives of a liberal general education and flouted the time-honored faith in knowledge for the sake of the enrichment of the individual and the community. Nor, for that matter, did those of this opinion believe that the nominal contact of the specialized, vocational programs with the liberal arts core, or what was left of it, greatly enlarged or enriched the minds of those pursuing well-defined practical purposes. To them it appeared that the University was failing to do full justice either to those who wanted a liberal education, such as that which still prevailed in the more conservative older private institutions, or to those who were bent on acquiring vocational training.

Nor were those primarily concerned with functional education always tolerant of the Van Hise synthesis. To some it appeared that those who gave the instruction basic to the subsequent applied programs divorced what they did, wilfully and completely, from any functional approach. Others, sensitive to the increasing demands of the technical and vocational programs, militantly insisted on an ever larger share of the time of the undergraduate in Letters and Science and demanded virtual autonomy, within the college, for the programs in music, journalism, commerce, chemistry, education, and applied arts. Nor was the competition confined to demands for time and space: it was inevitably fought on the level of appropriations, influence, and power.

Such, then, is the frame within which must be viewed and interpreted the great increase of students in letters and science, the administrative issues, the curriculum, departmental policies and programs, the quality of instruction, and creative scholarship. Before assessing the outcome of the effort to move forward the Van Hise synthesis and to implement it in terms of increasing exigencies, pressures, and problems, it may be well to consider the leadership provided by the two deans of the College of Letters and Science.

IN MANY respects this college enjoyed considerable administrative autonomy within the University, limited, to be sure, in important educational respects by the budget, which lay largely beyond the powers and scope of the dean. The dignity of the dean's office was enhanced by the fact that Edward A. Birge was virtually an assistant president or, at least, the president's substitute when Van Hise was absent from Madison.

The general educational philosophy of Van Hise was in large measure shared by Dean Birge, who presided over the College of Letters and Science until 1918. Birge, it is true, said far less than Van Hise about educational policy and philosophy in the large sense of the term. His position became explicit only when he was called on to oppose a proposition which he did not like, as for example when he set himself against the recommendation made in 1912 by the director of the commerce course for a one- or two-year program in commercial subjects for students not expecting to take a degree. "The State did not establish the University and does not maintain it in order to provide short cuts into vocations," he said. "The University exists, partly to furnish training in fundamental subjects of thought; partly also to offer professional training based on a knowledge of such fundamental subjects. It aims at breadth of fundamental knowledge. It requires of its professional students much that will be of no immediate service professionally; much that will be of no direct service at any time. It requires much which the University believes will find its ultimate justification in a larger conception of the world of thought—not that of trade—to which the profession belongs, and in a larger handling of professional problems."[3] Trained in an atmosphere in which the function of science was less emphasized than it was in the Middle West, Dean Birge was less ready than some to yield to vocational pressures. But even had he spoken more frequently in positive and explicit terms, he would have been unable greatly to alter the direction.

Dean Birge looked with disfavor on the tendency to lop off from the College of Letters and Science various fields which from time to time were allocated to other colleges and to duplicate, in other branches of the University, work already being done in his own college. True, he made no objection to surrendering the then somewhat questionable course in home economics to agriculture. In his mind it was even permissible to surrender bacteriology to the Medical School and to the College of Agriculture on the score that "for the present its general interest has become a special and applied science." But he was very decidedly against having a similar procedure applied to chemistry, botany, and zoology. The University, he insisted, should have all these sciences in one college, except in so far as aspects of any one were specifically applied to agriculture or to engineering.[4]

In spite of these infrequent statements on general policies affecting the relationship between pure and applied studies, neither the reports of Birge as dean of the college nor the faculty records give evidence of much concern with large educational issues. No one could question his competence in discussing such matters as the number and distribution of students, the need for space and equipment, and the maintenance of academic standards and discipline. But he said relatively little about research as a college policy and, with the exception of medical education, little of the relation between the College of Letters

[3] *Regents' Biennial Report*, 1911–12, p. 51.
[4] Edward A. Birge to Van Hise, March 18, 1914, Presidents' Papers.

and Science and other branches of the University. Perhaps he considered these matters to be more properly within the president's sphere.

In any case, Dean Birge's part in maintaining an equilibrium between theoretical and applied knowledge can best be illustrated by reference to his handling of specific issues that presented themselves to him. In view of the fact that he had been a close rival of Van Hise for the presidency, he might have carried a chip on his shoulder. On the contrary, he cooperated loyally with the president, defending his larger policies when occasion required. Yet in his relations with the president, Dean Birge stood on his dignity and did not shrink from speaking curtly when he was certain that the law was on his side. He did not hesitate to criticize the president for his effort to have admitted to the College of Letters and Science a student who wished to elect work in home economics: he quoted chapter and verse to prove that he, rather than the president, had interpreted the rules correctly. "It seems to me an unusual thing for the President of the University, in a letter addressed to two deans, to make the statement that one of them has refused to carry out the plainly stated rule of his college. It seems also especially unusual for the President to make such a statement in an official communication without giving the person most concerned any opportunity for explanation. This point, however, is a mere matter of official courtesy and I do not press it in any way."[5] In other words, Birge stood his ground firmly against pressure to let down the bars to a student desiring to elect work in a subject like home economics.

Such a man, when he regarded his position as just, was not to be overawed by influential parents asking for special consideration. One especially prominent father of an erring son suspended for giving aid in an examination to a fellow student used all his persuasive powers in pleas for clemency: the boy was a noble lad; his act had been one of generosity; he deserved another chance; he was going into business with his father, and would it not be wise to have, in a future business leader of the state, a

[5] Birge to Van Hise, October 8, 1915, Papers of the Dean of the College of Letters and Science.

friend, rather than an enemy, of the University? But none of these arguments was of any avail—certainly not the last. The father came to the campus to discuss the matter with members of the faculty, who informed him that whatever the dean said in such matters was the law; the faculty, if called on to express an opinion, would accept the judgment of the dean. Thus frustrated, the parent resorted to other measures, for it was not his custom to accept defeat. Senator La Follette, on request, telegraphed Dean Birge that the punishment seemed very severe, that he hoped no injustice would be done the young man, and that if he were like his father he ought to reflect credit on the University rather than leave it in disgrace.[6] The dean, in his own good time, referred the matter to the faculty. That body made concessions to the young man in permitting him to make up work in the summer session. But it took its cue from Birge in refusing to jeopardize the prestige of the administration or the faculty itself. Dean Birge thus maintained what he deemed the integrity of standards against pressure and appeals to consider the relations of the University with men of power and influence in the business community.

The correspondence in the archives of the college throws much light on Dean Birge's relations with individual members of the faculty and with departments as such. His determination to show no favoritism to his own department of zoology led him to lean over backward, with the result that it was strengthened by no major appointment until 1912. Nor could it be justly said that his influence was used in behalf of the natural sciences at the expense of other fields. Although frugal by nature, Dean Birge believed it expedient on the whole to meet outside offers rather than to compete in the market for replacements; competing, he felt, was likely to cost more in the end.[7] Yet he showed little disposition to favor individual increases when there was no necessity for so doing. Professor Joseph Jastrow made a strong case for an increase in salary to put him in line with other full professors. But Dean Birge insisted that he had em-

---

[6] P. C. to Birge, May 9, 11, 16, 24, June 1, 1906, Papers of the Dean of the College of Letters and Science.

[7] Birge to Van Hise, September 21, 1907, Papers of the Dean of the College of Letters and Science.

phasized popularization at the expense of investigation and that his contributions in instruction were not outstanding. When called on to arbitrate between two members of the faculty, Dean Birge made every effort to understand the conflict, to find an acceptable middle ground without jeopardizing law or precedent, and to make sure that no threads were left dangling as an invitation to future discord. Thus, in a conflict between Professors Ernst Voss and Alexander Hohlfeld in which Voss had, apparently, criticized Hohlfeld on grounds both of character and of his management of the German department, Birge insisted that the formula outlined by President Van Hise be strictly adhered to. Professor Voss was required to rewrite the letter in which he retracted his statements in order to make perfectly clear that he was not implying that the charges were true and that he was not withdrawing them merely to keep the peace. In thus insisting that Voss's retraction, like Hohlfeld's, be immediate, specific, and unconditional, Birge showed the stern sense of justice and efficiency in which he took pride.[8] Yet with all this puritan devotion to his values, Birge was capable of appreciating genius even when it was exasperating. He was able to sense the human and tragic factors affecting a scholar's academic life, as is shown by the letters he wrote about William Ellery Leonard.[9]

In his relations with the faculty body Birge was the competent parliamentarian, formal and correct, eager to have the wheels of the machine run smoothly. If they did not run smoothly, and if sustained administrative effort failed to make them do so, then, but usually only then, was he inclined to favor any departure from rule and precedent. He had no tolerance for what he regarded as "cheap political tricks" on the part of any faculty member and did not hesitate to express himself on this matter. We may be sure that his influence was exerted against the efforts made by a group of professors in 1905–1906 to induce Van Hise to accept the principle of cabinet government.

Although Dean Birge was primarily concerned with the administrative details of his office, he was not without watchdog

---

[8] Birge to Ernst Voss, July 18, 23, 1906, Papers of the Dean of the College of Letters and Science.   [9] Birge to Van Hise, June 12, 1914, Presidents' Papers.

virtues when the larger interests of the college were at stake. One member of the Board of Regents did, indeed, feel that he was too much inclined to take what was given to the college and to make the best of it.[10] Yet his reports often called attention to the need of additional staff and invariably demonstrated the pressing need for more space. Perhaps his own puritan simplicity and frugality kept him from attaching as much importance as some did to salary increases, for which, as dean, he did not press with any great vigor.

George Clarke Sellery, a distinguished teacher and an authority on the history of the Renaissance, began his long career as dean of the college when Birge took over the presidency in 1918. One regent opposed the appointment on the ground that he often showed "lack of sympathy or even cooperation" in dealing with plans submitted by others. This, it was felt, might prove harmful in dealing with students. Many students did indeed find Dean Sellery firm in the interpretation and enforcement of rules. He fought ably for the maintenance of academic standards in an era of lush student life and of an immense expansion of the undergraduate body. Partly, perhaps, to soften the criticism that the University was the seat of shocking moral turpitude, Dean Sellery supported Scott Goodnight, the dean of men, in his effort to ferret out delinquencies and to maintain, so far as possible, the conventional moral code among undergraduates. Although at first some members of the faculty regarded Dean Sellery as capricious when he was not "tough," he respected and defended the Wisconsin tradition of faculty participation in college government. He proved to be a witty and skillful presiding officer in faculty meetings, displaying an amazing knowledge of parliamentary law. Sellery was also an efficient administrator. Not least among his contributions was his demonstration that it was possible to administer the college and at the same time remain a distinguished scholar and a great teacher.

But Sellery was also an academic statesman. He had proved, it will be recalled, a tower of strength in presenting the point of view of the faculty and administration at the time of the Allen investigation, and in tearing to shreds the ensuing report he

[10] Florence Buckstaff to Van Hise, March 4, 1917, Presidents' Papers.

demonstrated his gifts in strategy and tactics. A wisely conservative leader in the counterrevolution within the University, he found a formula in the controversy over language requirements which for a generation preserved the integrity of these requirements for the bachelor of arts degree and yet conceded a practical procedure to the critics. No more than his predecessor did Dean Sellery relish any move to split off from the college any one of its several divisions, unless a department seemed peripheral from the point of view of Letters and Science standards or purpose. He had no intention of permitting anything to happen, if he could prevent it, which might lessen the importance and prestige of the college within the University. After the departments of manual arts and physical education were set up to give degrees, chiefly through the influence of Van Hise, Sellery managed to shepherd them into the School of Education, which at the time was still part of the College of Letters and Science. He did this, he said, "against the day when the pressure of the School Superintendents of the State would compel us to set up an independent School of Education." When at last, during Glenn Frank's administration, the "co-ordinate School of Education" was established, Dean Sellery saw to it that the sub-departments were taken along into the new school.

Yet Dean Sellery was not a mere traditionalist in his championing of the liberal arts tradition and in his battle to preserve the central place of the College of Letters and Science in the University. Skeptical of what he regarded as educational fads and impatient with anything savoring of educational jargon and superficiality, he was, to be sure, one of the leaders in the nation-wide group which valiantly defended the humanistic conception of higher education. Yet he was too much a realist to close his eyes to the imperatives of the natural sciences and to the vocational and technical aspects of college work. He shared Van Hise's belief in a functional equilibrium between the arts and pure sciences and their application. The college, he said in a message to the class of 1923, still fostered the purpose of the founders of the University—it equipped youth for life by making it familiar with the best that man has thought and done. The original purpose had been broadened to include more consciously the development of personality, tolerance, and sympathy. "In addition," he said, "recognizing that the world needs special training, along many applied lines, the College has instituted many special 'courses,' as chemistry, commerce, journalism, and music." "The peculiar virtue of these courses at Wisconsin," he continued, "is that they are not narrowly technical, but include an unusually large element of the older 'humanistic' studies. . . . Our newer 'courses' are meant to train not only for a living but for living."[11]

THE GROWTH of the College of Letters and Science, and its continuing central position in the University, may be attributed to its fusion of theory and practice and to its part in supplying basic preparation for the specialized vocational programs. It continued to provide a large share of the instruction of students of engineering and agriculture in their first two years. In addition, its own enrollment increased out of all proportion to that in any other college. In the academic year 1903–1904 its student body numbered 1,325. In 1913–1914 the college comprised 2,653 students of its own. In 1916 Dean Birge pointed out that in the decade just ending the college had added more than 1,500 to its annual enrollment. But the greatest peaks in growth came in the two years preceding the country's entrance into the first World War and, more strikingly, during the years after the armistice. As in other universities, the expansion after the war was unprecedented. By 1925 the enrollment of the college had passed six thousand.

The actual increase in numbers was accompanied by the phenomenal growth of certain departments and the decline of several others. Political economy, chemistry, and Spanish attracted an ever greater number of students, while mathematics and the classics fell off in percentage enrollments. The war dealt a blow to the flourishing German department, one of the largest

[11] *The Badger, 1923* (Madison, 1922), 44; George C. Sellery to V. C. Anderson, associate editor of the *Badger,* January 18, 1922, Papers of the Dean of the College of Letters and Science.

in the college. The department of commerce enjoyed the greatest expansion of all: its enrollment jumped from 562 in 1918–1919 to 1,379 in 1919–1920. Nearly all the important problems of the college throughout the period were intimately related to the steady and striking increase in enrollment and, in lesser degree, to the shifts in student preference for certain departments.

Of these problems none was so taxing and so unsatisfactorily met as the overcrowding. Whereas agriculture was able to spread out comfortably in its splendid new Agricultural Hall and affiliated buildings, in report after report Dean Birge patiently and specifically called attention to the utterly inadequate physical plant of the College of Letters and Science. Van Hise bore out all that he said. Nevertheless the little that was done to provide added physical facilities was much too little. As the result of pressure on the part of the administration, the north wing of University Hall was at last ready in 1906; the Biology Building was completed in 1912; the addition to the Chemistry Building helped somewhat in meeting the requirements of the rapidly growing chemistry department; and the construction of Sterling Hall, into which the departments of physics and political economy moved in 1916, relieved some of the overcrowding. Even with these added facilities, at least seventy-five per cent of the instruction of the College of Letters and Science was crowded into three buildings—North Hall, South Hall, and University Hall.[12] In his first presidential report Birge noted the fact that there had been no appropriation for any sizable building since 1913, despite the phenomenal growth in the student body of the University and, especially, of the College of Letters and Science.[13] This was in marked contrast with developments at many state universities.

The additional buildings that did become available benefited chiefly the natural sciences, which were more closely geared to the specialized and vocational courses than were the traditional arts. Indeed, if any single agency suffered more than did any other from prevailing overcrowded conditions in the college, it was the library, which was to the humanities and the social

[12] *Regents' Biennial Report*, 1915–16, pp. 47–48; 1917–18, pp. 67–68.
[13] *Ibid.*, 1919–20, pp. 22–23.

studies what the laboratories were to the natural sciences. The growing tendency in the humanities and the social sciences to rely less and less on textbooks and more and more on collateral library readings would have put considerable strain even on a library adequate for an increasing student body. But the library at Wisconsin was not adequate. As President Birge pointed out in 1920, the library had been erected two decades earlier when the student body was only one fifth of the size it had reached by the end of the first World War. The new wing, completed in 1913, had increased stack space without in any marked way affecting facilities for reading. It was obvious that a reading room seating two hundred and sixty students was pathetically inadequate for a student population of seventy-five hundred.[14] In spite of the crying need for a new library building, a need which became desperate in the postwar years, nothing was done.

Nor was the library keeping abreast with other state universities in the acquisition of books. The librarian, Walter M. Smith, reported in 1916 that although the increase in books had in many ways been gratifying, the library was still greatly inferior to those of most of the universities with which Wisconsin was fond of comparing itself. Several explanations for this were suggested. The University had failed to appreciate the fact that the cost of books, old and new, had shot upward. It had not taken into account that the development of new departments in fields of knowledge which the library had made a systematic effort to cover put an added strain on its management.[15] On the threshold of our entrance into World War I, the University Library numbered 240,000 books and 50,000 pamphlets. The holdings of the Wisconsin Academy and of the Historical Society brought the total to 438,000 books and 246,000 pamphlets. Although this compared favorably with the situation at neighboring institutions,[16] some of them had begun to multiply the appropriations for their libraries at a more impressive rate than Wisconsin was doing. Thus, while Wisconsin from 1876 to 1900 grew rapidly, Minnesota by 1927 had almost as many volumes as the University of Wisconsin and the State Historical Society together. From 1900 to 1927 the two state institutions in Indiana increased

---

[14] *Ibid.,* 23.   [15] *Ibid.,* 1915–16, p. 284.   [16] *Ibid.,* 280.

their holdings more than fivefold. Iowa State College at Ames and the State University of Iowa increased theirs by the same proportion. But the University of Wisconsin and the State Historical Society together increased their holdings in this period less than fourfold. By 1945 the University of Minnesota had more holdings than the two Madison libraries. Both Indiana and Iowa had nearly as many and, besides, had so accelerated their rate of growth as to overshadow greatly that of Wisconsin.[17]

Of less moment, but still symptomatic of the general situation, was the lack of adequate museum facilities. In his report for 1906–1908 Dean Birge remarked that Wisconsin had given almost no attention to the development of a museum for the University. Appropriations had been completely inadequate.[18] Four years later he declared that in this field the University was behind all other institutions of its rank. "A museum," he wrote, "does not increase the efficiency of classroom instruction or of research to a degree proportional to its cost, yet there is hardly an instrument of education which adds more than does this to that enlargement of ideas which is so important a part of liberal education."[19] Although it was repeatedly urged that something be done to improve the situation, little was accomplished. Sterling Hall at best provided inadequate facilities for a museum in the field of physics. Even the new Biology Building left much to be desired. Missouri, Michigan, and other state universities had built admirable art galleries, but at Wisconsin other demands took precedence.

In an economy and culture which put much stock in material equipment, prestige, and comfort, it is curious that the physical plant in which the College of Letters and Science conducted its work should have been so much neglected. Little was done to alleviate a situation which the administration demonstrated to be so trying. Higher education was obviously a value which more and more of the people of the state set store by. In other spheres expansion was taking place—in road building, in

[17] This is based on a memorandum entitled, Some Data Relating to the Library Situation at the University of Wisconsin, prepared by Louis Kaplan and submitted by Gilbert H. Doane, librarian.

[18] *Regents' Biennial Report*, 1907–08, p. 62.   [19] *Ibid.*, 1911–12, pp. 58, 59.

the construction of manufacturing plants, in the improvement of farm equipment. Whatever the explanation for the failure to provide for the more pressing physical needs, such a failure meant that in matters of physical equipment the University was not keeping up with other state institutions of higher learning.

ℐ

THE REORGANIZATION immediately preceding the inauguration of Van Hise, which restored to departmental status in the College of Letters and Science the special schools of political economy, history, education, pharmacy, and commerce, promised to unify the College of Letters and Science without weakening its various specialized programs. This precedent was maintained in large part on the organizational level throughout the first quarter of the century. The actual number of departments remained virtually constant from 1905 to 1925, but the courses in commerce and chemistry became increasingly specialized and vocationalized; a course in journalism was organized; the course in education evolved into a school in 1919, still within the frame of the College of Letters and Science; professional courses in manual arts, in physical education, and in social service were launched; and speech, organized as a department in 1919–1920, was offering, five years later, twenty-four separate courses.

The increasing number of courses within departments reflected, in part, the growing specialization in scholarship and the weight increasingly attached to graduate instruction. In 1904–1905, 597 courses were listed; in 1924–1925, 986. Meantime, anatomy, physiology, and related subjects had been transferred to the Medical School, while home economics had been shifted to the College of Agriculture. Had these shifts not been made, the number of courses listed at the end of the period would, obviously, have been even greater.

This was not all. In many departments the multiplication of courses indicated not only the growth of specialized knowledge in the field but a tendency to break the field into compartments more directly related to professional training or to applications

The Dean of the Graduate School and the
Dean of the College of Letters and Science
Charles Sumner Slichter and George Clarke Sellery

A Faculty Group, 1924

Front: Rostovtzeff, Kremers, Ely, Hall, O'Shea, Gilman, Commons, Frost; *middle:* Ogg, Kahlenberg, Laird, Snow, D. W. Mead, Root, Bradley, McCaffery (below Bradley), Withey, Skinner, Jastrow (below Skinner); *top:* W. J. Mead, Joel Stebbins, Pearse, Henmon, Showerman, Russell, Bunting, Fish

to agriculture, industry, and teaching. This was especially true in the natural sciences; but it was also evident in some of the social disciplines, particularly in political economy and sociology.

In discussing the curriculum we shall see that minor shifts and changes and the inauguration of the new course in humanities after the World War represented a reaction to the prevailing tendency to emphasize within the College of Letters and Science those fields more or less immediately functional. But, in spite of the manipulation of the curriculum, specialization pushed into the background the broad conception of a general education.

THE TRUISM that buildings do not make a university no doubt entered into many discussions—if, indeed, the reiterated pleas of the administration for new buildings were discussed beyond the campus. Yet crowded physical conditions inevitably affected the quality of instruction. Space for student conferences was at a premium: in some offices a dozen instructors struggled valiantly to maintain contact with students.

Worse for instruction, however, than the implications of inadequate plant facilities was the flat statement, repeated more than once, that the quality of instruction was deteriorating as the student body expanded. The criticism was most vociferously expressed by State Superintendent of Public Instruction Cary, an ex-officio member of the Board of Regents, but several other regents shared his conviction. The Board of Visitors was of the same opinion.[20] Legislators echoed the view. It is true that a few outstanding lecturers, notably Benjamin Snow in physics, Louis Kahlenberg in chemistry, and Carl Russell Fish in history, developed reputations as great teachers. But there prevailed the impression that many scholars were devoting themselves largely to advanced instruction and that when they offered introductory courses, they did so reluctantly and in a slipshod fashion. More and more responsibility, especially in the first two years, was

[20] See pp. 96 ff.

placed in the hands of quiz masters who themselves were mere apprentice teachers pursuing their work for advanced degrees. In deprecating the practice of turning over instruction, in both technical and nontechnical subjects, to inexperienced graduate and even undergraduate teachers, the Visitors in 1919 maintained that the institution was falling short of its obligations. "Teaching is an art and a difficult one and we reaffirm the opinions heretofore expressed that freshmen ought as far as possible to be taught by men of rank and experience, and that the teaching of new and inexperienced instructors should be supervised."[21] The Visitors were not alone. In his report for 1918–1920 Dean Sellery minced no words in declaring that the quality of teaching had declined. The increase in staff, he continued, had not kept pace with the increase in attendance. Many discussion sections numbered from thirty-five to forty students.[22]

Nor was the decline in the quality of instruction felt only in the overcrowded quiz sections. The senior-thesis system, inaugurated in 1892, was admittedly an admirable means of deepening student knowledge of some part of a chosen field and of providing the undergraduate with relevant techniques. But the ever growing size of the student body in the College of Letters and Science put a great strain on the administration of the senior-thesis system. In 1910 the faculty modified the existing arrangement by permitting departments to offer in place of the thesis a so-called thesis course in which written reports were accepted. For a time only the language departments took advantage of the privilege; but many felt that the older standards in the thesis requirements were inevitably being relaxed. The requirements for the thesis were further relaxed in 1921–1922; and in 1931–1932, the thesis was virtually abolished as a requirement for graduation.

Partly as a result of the survey of the University undertaken in 1914 at the direction of the State Board of Public Affairs, the University itself, as we have seen, instituted a self-inquiry. The large committee appointed for this purpose was subdivided into smaller special groups, one of which concerned itself with the

[21] Report of the Visitors, June 24, 1919, Papers of the Board of Regents.
[22] *Regents' Biennial Report,* 1919–20, p. 32.

problem of improving undergraduate instruction. The special committee, while recognizing that each department must have independence in determining the methods of instruction most suited to its requirements, recommended the adoption of a method by which the knowledge of the practice of one department would be brought to the attention of the others. The deans were to call upon approximately half of the departments each year for biennial reports on the methods of supervision and instruction. The college faculties were then to consider the reports at an annual meeting; after due discussion the reports were to form the basis for an annual report by the deans to the president. It was the expectation that as a consequence of this procedure each department would take advantage of improvements in methods of instruction developed in other departments.[23]

The subcommittee on the improvement of undergraduate instruction further recommended that special attention be given to the needs and the development of students of exceptional talent. The means of achieving this were left to the departments themselves. In order to raise the general level of scholarship the grade-point system, which required the maintenance of a minimum grade-average for graduation, was installed. But students, especially the happy-go-lucky ones, contented themselves with barely sliding by in their first two or three years on the assumption that, by turning on the steam, they might achieve the minimum grade-average in their last years. To check this tendency the faculty in 1919–1920 modified the grade-point system. Henceforth in each of the first three years a student must achieve a stated grade-point average to remain in college.[24] It is impossible to evaluate the effects of these changes on undergraduate scholarship since grading is obviously a highly relative matter. Yet it is warrantable to assume that the system did tend to stimulate somewhat greater exertion on the part of the average student throughout his college course.

Academic standards, it was claimed, also suffered by reason of the rapid increase in the number of students entering the

[23] *Ibid.*, 1915–16, pp. 6–8.
[24] *Ibid.*, 1919–20, p. 27.

college with advanced standing. It was clear that such students came from institutions which varied greatly in the type of training offered. In the class of 1906, thirteen per cent of the graduating members had entered from other institutions. In 1916 Dean Birge noted that fifty per cent of the class of 1915 had entered with advanced standing. The faculty decided in 1916 that henceforth advanced-standing students would in general be expected to earn forty-five credits, at least thirty in residence, and that only in very exceptional cases would as much as three years of credit be given for three years of work elsewhere.[25]

The new specialized programs—by 1915 there were fifteen of them—opened at least some of their offerings to all Letters and Science students equipped to take them. At the same time, as Dean Birge pointed out in his report for the 1909–1910 biennium, the technical characteristics of these specialized courses were being constantly more and more emphasized. This meant that the college in effect had become little more than a congeries of courses for special training in which were more or less lost the spirit and purposes of a liberal education. By 1910 only one fourth of the members of the senior class were following a course which was not at least partly professional or technical in nature. The dean did not complain. The other state universities and even some private institutions were being affected by the trend. Yet, as he properly insisted, it was necessary to remember that "liberal education also has a spirit and a temper of its own and that the cultivation of this spirit is the peculiar and highest function of a college of liberal arts and is its especial contribution to education and to the community."[26] We shall consider, in discussing the curriculum, the attempts to strengthen the humanistic core.

[25] *Ibid.*, 1915–16, pp. 41–42; *University Catalogue*, 1915–16, pp. 106–107.
[26] *Regents' Biennial Report*, 1909–10, pp. 61–62.

10.

Letters and Science: Studies

T HE old classical course which held more or less intact until 1866 had been, as we have already seen, gradually fragmented until some reorganization was imperative. As the College of Letters and Science grew and as new subjects and professional programs knocked at the door, special course after special course had been added, each with its own degree. The general science course was established in 1866, the modern classical in 1876, the English course in 1887, and the civic historical in 1893. Four years later a so-called philosophy course for normal school graduates was set up. In 1901 the School of Commerce entered the lists. The bachelor of arts degree during this whole period had been reserved for students completing the ancient classical course. Those who fulfilled the requirements of the other courses received the bachelor of science, the bachelor of letters, or the bachelor of philosophy degree. But it was obviously impossible to maintain the pre-eminence of the ancient classical course, which had come to include only a bare handful. Moreover, the existing arrangements did not possess the advantages of the free elective or of the required-course system. Everywhere changes were under way. In these Wisconsin neither led nor followed. But it is worth noting that the new system established in 1903 was based on the same objectives that governed the changes President Lowell introduced at Harvard some years later. In general the new Wisconsin program was designed to provide students with freedom of choice in selecting studies at the same time that it avoided the evils following over-specialization or too great scattering.

In the new dispensation all existing courses, except those in pharmacy, in music, and in teacher training, were more or less welded together into a general course leading to the bachelor of arts degree. Candidates for this degree were required to study English in the first two years, to choose two foreign languages, and to select two fields from the science, mathematics, and history cluster. In the junior and senior years the program was concentrated on the major subject. Of the one hundred and twenty "hours" required for the degree, about half were stipulated and about half were free electives, the requirements in all cases except for English being so arranged that, while a general direction of studies was marked out, the student enjoyed a fair range of choice within that sphere. That choice was still further broadened by the provision that students in the College of Letters and Science might elect one sixth of the work for the bachelor of arts degree, or twenty semester hours, from specified courses in other colleges in the University. This was a concession, of course, to technical and professional interests. But, as President Van Hise pointed out, the opportunity thus at hand was one of the greatest advantages that a university could offer that a college could not.[1]

Two years after the inauguration of the new plan Dean Birge reported it had been so successful that no one wished to return to the former state of affairs. The new program involved a revision of the traditional class-officer system: henceforth a freshman was assigned to a temporary adviser and, ultimately, to an adviser in his major field. Other changes, all minor, were introduced from time to time. Students in the premedical and commerce courses were enabled to qualify, by a proper selection of electives, for the bachelor of arts degree. In 1908 the idea of synoptical lectures, inaugurated in 1891, and considerably modified by the passage of time, was revived with the adoption of a plan by which any department might offer courses providing general information in a wide range of subjects for which some credit might be received.

[1] Reports to the Regents, E:22, October 10, 1904.

The College of Letters and Science successfully resisted efforts of outside groups to have established a nonsectarian but essentially religious course in ethics. It was less successful in dismissing criticism by the State Board of Public Affairs of the foreign language requirements for the bachelor's degree. Conceding the value of the foreign languages, the board saw no reason why everyone except those in agriculture and engineering should be required to take them for graduation.[2]

The successive faculty committees named to study the problem presented two plans, each in more than one form. The first recommended the maintenance of the courses and degrees in operation, with a reduction from two to one in the number of languages required for the bachelor of arts degree and a diminution from 32 to 24 in the number of foreign language credits required in high school and college together. The other proposal recommended the maintenance in principle of existing foreign language requirements for the bachelor of arts degree and the establishment of a new course, leading to the degree of bachelor of philosophy, in which a foreign language was required neither for admission nor for graduation. Professor Sellery, who was principally responsible for this proposal, defended it with cogent arguments and the faculty adopted it in 1916.[3]

In the years following World War I there was considerable discussion in the circles of higher education of the whole course of study. This included a debate over cultural and vocational objectives and the merits of the elective as against the once-integrated program embracing what were regarded as the essentials of the humane and genteel tradition. At the same time an articulate group of educational leaders urged the need of applying in the field of higher learning some part of the approach commonly known as progressive education. These writers maintained that the colleges were not meeting realistically and constructively the new intellectual challenges of the day. Institutions were, it was felt, failing to provide students with any

[2] *Report upon the Survey of the University of Wisconsin: Findings of the State Board of Public Affairs and its Report to the Legislature* (Madison, [1915]), 32.

[3] Report of the Committee on Foreign Language Requirements, January 17, 1916, Presidents' Papers; Report of the Dean of the College of Letters and Science, *Regents' Biennial Report*, 1915–16, p. 39.

genuine understanding of the world in which they lived or even with the techniques for obtaining such an understanding for themselves. In response to this ferment several arts colleges revamped their programs. The most striking instance of this was the introduction of the new integrated curriculum at Columbia College in which the unity of knowledge rather than its fragmentation was underscored.

At the same time there was a growing recognition of the interrelationships and mutual dependency of the many branches of knowledge organized into departments for instructional purposes. In research and graduate training the University had recognized the ever greater interpenetration of related subjects by providing, in the reorganization of 1916, for the establishment, "wherever feasible, of related departments . . . into divisions, each division to be commissioned with responsibility for the encouragement and supervision of graduate and research work in its field."[4] The divisions, it was hoped, might guard against excessive competition and overlapping courses. Important though this might in time come to be, the provision did not in any sense interfere with the traditional autonomy of the departments nor did it affect in any noticeable way the academic programs of undergraduates.

In the spring of 1921 the curriculum committee of the College of Letters and Science explained, in a report presented to the faculty, that it had been confronted by two alternatives: the complete redrafting of the requirements for the degree and the presentation of minor amendments to strengthen the program "at points where it has shown itself susceptible of improvement." It chose the latter alternative, since it believed that the existing program compared favorably with those at other institutions and because it felt that there was no substantial agreement in the faculty regarding changes of a basic nature considered likely to improve the course in any material way. The minor changes affected the general course leading to the bachelor of arts degree and brought about the creation of a new course in the humanities, likewise intended for candidates for that degree,

[4] *Regents' Biennial Report,* 1915–16, p. 9.

and the negotiation of new agreements with the Law School and the Medical School making it possible for students to follow a six-year program rewarded by the bachelor of arts and bachelor of law degrees and by the bachelor of arts and doctor of medicine degrees.[5]

The changes in the general bachelor of arts course involved an additional requirement for the study of English literature with the possibility of a reduction in the time spent on English composition for students obviously competent in writing. The proposals increased the flexibility in the choice of foreign languages without altering the total requirement and also aimed to secure more effective instruction in elementary courses in mathematics for students electing that field.

Of more interest was the new humanities course. This required the study of three out of four languages—Latin, Greek, French, and German; a choice between mathematics and philosophy; and work in literature, science, and the social studies. No electives in professional courses were permitted except those required for the teacher's certificate. The program aimed at a broad introduction to the principal fields of knowledge, at the development of special competence in a major field through course and thesis work, and at the laying of foundations for professional and vocational training rather than providing such training. Much was to depend, obviously, on the type of course offered. The proposal did not encompass the establishment of new integrated courses, as at Columbia. It merely required work in the major fields without undertaking to make that work essentially different in content and spirit from whatever had been available in established courses. Nevertheless the program did correct some of the tendencies toward one-sidedness and vocational emphasis. The number of students electing the new humanities program was small, and it did not exert any marked influence on the main currents of the college.

These innovations comprised, for the time, all that the faculty could agree upon. The curriculum in the college was re-

[5] Minutes of the Faculty of the College of Letters and Science, 3:119 ff., April 11, 1921.

examined in 1930. Meantime, early in the regime of President Glenn Frank, the new Experimental College introduced a
limited number of undergraduates to a program which did indeed break new ground.

✐

THE humanities offered the most critical test of the effort to
maintain an equilibrium between the concept of knowledge as
desirable for its own sake in enriching individual lives and the
concept of knowledge as a tool for resolving the problems of
living. Among the humanities Latin and Greek seemed particularly removed from the possibility of application to the practical
service of society. Yet the classicists tried not only to uphold the
standards of scholarship in their instruction and to advance
knowledge through research, but also to show the value of Greek
and Roman literature to twentieth-century Americans.

The logical union of the Greek and Latin departments took
place in 1917—a step designed to promote administrative economy and to suggest the essential unity of the languages and literatures of two great Mediterranean cultures. The retirement of
Alexander Kerr and Charles Forster Smith in the second decade
of the century left teaching and research in the hands of Grant
Showerman, Moses S. Slaughter, George C. Fiske, Arthur Laird,
and a group of younger men. Standards of scholarship were not
relaxed and prospective secondary-school teachers received competent training. Devoting himself to instruction both at the University and at the American Institute in Rome, Showerman
shared his wide knowledge and enthusiasm for ancient Rome
with a large number of students. In 1914 the Loeb Classical Library published his editions of Ovid's *Heroides* and *Amores*.
Eight years later his *Horace and His Influence* appeared in the
series entitled *Our Debt to Greece and Rome*. His early interest in the religions of the ancient Mediterranean world was expressed in his translation of Cumont's work and in articles in
the more scholarly encyclopedias. *Eternal Rome,* published in
1924, *Rome and the Romans,* in 1931, and *Monuments and Men
of Ancient Rome,* in 1935, all bore evidence of his humanism,

for Showerman did not represent the exhaustive monographic type of scholarship.

His colleague, Professor Slaughter, likewise leaned toward the interpretive and appreciative side of classical scholarship. Slaughter's publications, which included studies of the character of Augustus, the scientific thought and poetic imagination of Lucretius, and portraits of other Romans, were marked by his passionate zeal for all that was alive in the literature which, as President Birge said, he not only taught but lived. Among the younger members of the department the productive scholar best known was George C. Fiske, whose work on the poetics of Horace, the oratory of Cicero, the theory of imitation, and the religion of Augustus won favor in classical circles.

The interest in linguistics and comparative philology was concentrated in no single department. Laird, in addition to giving instruction in Greek, offered courses in Sanskrit. Until his departure in 1913 for the University of Texas, Professor Eduard Prokosch of the German Department represented the Slavic and Celtic fields, interests which were allowed to fade until the 1930's. The department of Hellenistic Greek and Semitic languages continued, after the retirement of Professor William H. Williams in 1915, to provide instruction in Hellenistic Greek, Hebrew, Assyrian, Arabic, and related languages. Few students, however, worked in this field, despite the competence of Frederick T. Kelly and Louis B. Wolfenson, the assistant professors. The University, influenced by this fact and by the consideration that Chicago provided rich opportunities for research and training in Semitics, discontinued the department in 1931.

With one or two exceptions the period from 1904 to 1925 saw few significant changes in the modern language field. Julius Olson continued to cover the Scandinavian languages and literatures and, as we have earlier noted, to promote interest in the field rather than to contribute to learning either in philology or in literary history and criticism. Professor Edward T. Owen's successor in the Romance language department, Hugh Smith, was a competent scholar in Old French and shortly after World War I published a sound study of the French epic.[6] Professor

[6] Based in part on a memorandum prepared by Casimir D. Zdanowicz.

William F. Giese, ably assisted by Barry Cerf, represented literary history and criticism. The French House, founded in 1918, augmented the department's strength in its major emphasis, instruction and teacher training.

Spanish grew in popularity at Wisconsin as it did elsewhere; its utilitarian value in promoting trade with Latin America was largely responsible. The department profited from the curse which fell over German during World War I. The first notable appointment in the field was of Joaquín Ortega, whose versatility embraced experience in archaeology, journalism, and creative writing. With the coming in 1924 of Antonio García Solalinde, a great philologist who inaugurated a significant research program in the medieval field, Spanish studies at last came into their own. The department rightly took pride in the distinction Solalinde brought to it.

No modern language department, however, approached the German department in popularity and reputation. The interest of well-to-do German-Americans and of other friends of the subject expressed itself in gifts for books and fellowships and, above all, in the establishment of the Carl Schurz memorial professorship. The first appointment was a happy one. In 1912 Eugen Kühnemann came from Breslau, conducted a seminary and gave lectures on German literature. After the first World War the Milwaukee Seminary, an excellent training school for teachers of German, was discontinued and gave the University its endowment for the maintenance of a special professorship and fellowships as well as for the continuance of a well-established professional journal, *Monatshefte für deutschen Unterricht*. But the generous support of Wisconsin German-Americans did not alone explain the reputation and excellence of the department. In Ernst Voss, Edwin Roedder, Charles M. Purin, Eduard Prokosch, John L. Kind, Friedrich Bruns, Bayard Q. Morgan, and others it possessed distinguished teachers and productive scholars; and in its chairman, Professor Alexander Hohlfeld, it had a great leader. From the very year 1901 that Hohlfeld came to the University until his retirement in 1937 his influence was paramount. Sensing the need for far more emphasis than German departments throughout the country put on developing teachers, Hohlfeld provided first-rate training for teachers. The department pioneered in the use of visual aids and, through extension, lent slides and other materials to the teachers of Wisconsin and to those of neighboring states. In 1914 the German House was opened. This was the first residence center in any modern language field in this country and its influence was far-reaching. Courses in both the philological and the literary fields multiplied, and the department easily ranked first in the Middle West and was generally recognized as one of the two or three greatest departments of German studies. The election of Hohlfeld to the presidency of the Modern Language Association in 1913 was a tribute both to his own scholarship and to the leadership he had provided.

Convinced that a department of German in an American university was mistaken in duplicating in every respect the Germanic studies in German institutions, Hohlfeld from the start conceived and carried forward a remarkable program in the study of Anglo-American-German literary relationships. The reception of German literature in British and, especially, in American periodicals and literary circles was the principal emphasis; but this was conceived broadly, on the assumption that what foreign critics liked and disliked provided a valuable supplement to the estimation of a literature by its own nationals. A similar project had, indeed, been started by Henry Dexter Learned at Pennsylvania; but Wisconsin developed it along new lines and in the end inspired similar projects at Berkeley under Lawrence Marsden Price, at Stanford under Bayard Q. Morgan, and at Princeton under H. S. Jantz. Between the years 1904 and 1937, twenty-four doctoral theses in the field of Anglo-German literary relations were accepted at Wisconsin.[7] The only major publication in the field prior to 1925 was Morgan's *Bibliography of German Literature in English Translation,* which appeared in 1922 (second edition, 1938).

The outbreak of the war in 1914 made its impact on the German department. Its numbers and strength showed no imme-

[7] A. R. Hohlfeld, The Wisconsin Project of Anglo-German Literary Relations, manuscript in the University Archives. The authors are greatly indebted to this manuscript for the account of the German department.

diate diminution, but its staff, being for the most part pro-German, was harassed and soon put on the defensive. This was exemplified, for instance, in the attitude which Professor Hohlfeld took toward a French grammar and reading book edited by Professor Giese. Hohlfeld analyzed the stories in the manual and concluded that "the satire on things German is far more extensive and far coarser than what is said of other nationalities," and that such material had no place in a French grammar. Professor Giese insisted that no harm had been intended, that the book was used in several universities without anyone's having assumed that it was offensive, and that the Germans were by no means the only national group to have been satirized.[8] Prominent Wisconsin German-Americans took up the issue, declaring that the Giese text reflected "maliciously" and "offensively" on German scholarship, family life, and character. Editorials appeared in *Germania* and Van Hise received numerous complaints.[9] Professor Giese seriously considered offering his resignation, but several members of the faculty took the matter in hand and arranged a compromise. Giese and Hohlfeld agreed upon a statement which Van Hise released to the press.

When the United States entered the war the situation became critical. Most of the staff had sympathized with Germany, but with one exception they now maintained discreet silence or openly supported the war. As we have seen in the discussion of academic freedom during the war, one member—he was a German national—resigned after making a remark which deprecated the shift from pro-Germanism to pro-Americanism on the part of a colleague. Student enrollments fell off in far greater proportions than in other departments. In 1916–1917 the department numbered twenty-five and the registration approximated fourteen hundred. By 1918 there were only eight giving instruction and only two hundred and seventy-five students.

The situation was made worse after the war by the failure of many high schools to reinstate abandoned German courses.

[8] Hugh A. Smith to Edward A. Birge, January 12, 19, 1915; Giese to Hohlfeld, November 24, December 2, 1914; Hohlfeld to Van Hise, January 15, 1915, all in the Presidents' Papers.

[9] Emil von Schleinitz, editor of *Germania*, to Van Hise, January 6, February 20, 1915, Presidents' Papers.

President Birge, aware that all "right-minded" men wanted to get German instruction back on its feet, believed this could be done only if the department appealed definitely and positively to native-born Americans by shifting its policy and augmenting the American contingent on the staff. It was natural that the department should have been recruited largely from scholars of German birth or German heritage.

The president believed that Bruns, whom many thought to have been particularly identified with German-American propaganda, should be dropped.[10] Apparently Goodnight was the only member of the department sharing this view. Morgan pointed out that relations must be resumed and reconstructed with the "half-leavened Germanic masses throughout the state." If no action were taken against Bruns, he continued, the University would be in a position to claim that it had met the German element halfway and might expect that group similarly to make concessions to a new policy.[11] At a faculty conference which the president called, varying points of view were expressed, the most striking being that of Professor Evander B. McGilvary. He believed Bruns should be dropped since a good deal of pressure was likely to be put on the University to limit the freedom of teaching in political and economic matters. The safest thing to do, consequently, was "to surrender the relatively unimportant support of positions not vital, so as to strengthen itself for the support of real academic freedom."[12] Other members of the faculty, however, strongly opposed Birge's opinion, and Hohlfeld submitted a great deal of evidence regarding Bruns's scholarship and popularity as a teacher. In the end Bruns was retained. But the department made certain concessions to the new situation. It inaugurated, for example, courses on the German classics in English. The leadership and traditions in the department, moreover, were sufficiently strong to guarantee a comeback. Within a short time the enrollments had greatly increased. Thanks to the bequest from the Milwaukee German teacher-training insti-

[10] Memorandum, apparently by Birge, bearing the date February 4, 1919, Presidents' Papers.

[11] Bayard Morgan to Birge, February 3, 1919; Birge to Morgan, February 6, 1919, both in the Presidents' Papers.

[12] Evander B. McGilvary to Birge, February 13, 1919, Presidents' Papers.

tute at the time of its own demise, the department strengthened its resources. Something of the old spirit was gone, but German studies at Wisconsin resumed much of their earlier importance.

In the first decade of the twentieth century rapid headway was made in the modernization, specialization, and professionalization of fields in the English department, one evidence of which was the development of the course in journalism. The first comprehensive curriculum in journalism had been introduced at the Wharton School in 1893, but the initiative passed to other institutions. While several universities, notably Missouri, offered courses in journalism, the idea "caught on" as the result of the announcement in 1903 of Joseph Pulitzer's intention to establish a university school of journalism. Pulitzer's ideas for such a school were outlined the following year in a much-discussed article in the *North American Review*. By 1906 Illinois, North Carolina, Oregon, New York University, and Wisconsin were all offering some work in journalism. But it was at Missouri that a special school first took shape. After a long preparation, which ran back to a course offered in 1884 and to the interest of President Richard Jesse and the Missouri Press Association, the School of Journalism was opened in 1908. Under the leadership of Dean Walter Williams it quickly won nation-wide prestige. The next striking development was the opening, in 1911, of the graduate school of journalism at Columbia, which received on the death of Pulitzer a bequest of two million dollars. Under the direction of Talcott Williams of the *Philadelphia Press* the school quickly established its reputation.

Meantime the ideas outlined by Pulitzer in 1903 had steadily influenced developments at Wisconsin. In 1905 Assistant Professor Willard G. Bleyer of the English department offered a course in journalism. Bleyer had taken an active part in undergraduate journalism and had been associated with several newspapers. It will also be recalled that he had persuaded President Van Hise to improve the relations of the University and the newspapers by establishing the University Press Bulletin. In 1906 Bleyer outlined in the catalogue a four-year course in journalism described as "courses preparatory to journalism." In 1908 his title was changed to assistant professor of journalism and the following year his work was integrated in "the course in journalism." Four years later the "course in journalism" was given a budget of its own and Bleyer was named chairman. In 1916 Bleyer was accorded the title of professor of journalism, a title then rare in American universities.[13] In 1919 he became director of the course in journalism and in 1927 director of the School of Journalism, which nevertheless remained within the College of Letters and Science.

In many respects Bleyer's leadership was vigorous and imaginative. He conceived of educational journalism not merely in terms of the techniques of writing—though at first this was quite naturally the main approach—but increasingly in terms of historical, social, and economic forces affecting the newspaper and magazine world. Thus from a fairly early point the course rested on the basic social sciences as well as on psychology, languages, and literature. Bleyer was well abreast of the times, too, in his conception of the possibilities of research in the field. In 1909 the University established the first graduate fellowship in journalism in the country and named as its incumbent Louis Lochner, a graduate of the course and a man sensitive to the international implications of news. Bleyer did not write the first textbook in journalism or the first history of journalism in the United States; but his writings, along with those of James Melvin Lee, a practical newspaperman who became director of the department of journalism at New York University in 1911, were important contributions to a growing body of professional literature. At the same time, Bleyer was at the forefront in organizing professionally the college teachers of journalism. The national newspaper conference met in Madison in 1912. At this time thirty American colleges and universities were offering courses in journalism. Thus it had become a fairly well recognized field of study in higher education.

Bleyer was able to work out some cooperation with the Madison newspapers and to maintain fairly close relations with the press of the state. But he did not succeed in giving the course

[13] Willard G. Bleyer to Birge, June 28, 1910, Papers of the Dean of the College of Letters and Science; Records of the Board of Regents, I:428, May 24, 1916.

a working laboratory, with a printing press or a daily news-paper.[14] The school did presently obtain use of printing equipment with which students could obtain practical training in typography. But this was less adequate than facilities in a great many other places. Wisconsin, contenting itself with the *Daily Cardinal,* did not, for example, emulate Missouri in establishing a general daily newspaper. The emphasis on general education and particularly on writing and the social sciences was, however, of greater usefulness in developing competent journalists than preoccupation with artisan training.

The growing specialization and modernization of the English department, of which the growth of journalistic studies was symptomatic, was further reflected in the organization in 1906 of the department of public speaking. The traditional formal training in oratory, elocution, and rhetoric had become increasingly old-fashioned, if not obsolete, as voice training and phonetics appeared and as dramatics overshadowed the waning interest in debating. The new leader of the department, Professor James M. O'Neill, who became chairman in 1914, developed a group of specialists which included Gertrude E. Johnson, Andrew T. Weaver, Robert W. West, Harry Houghton, Joseph Gaylord, and others. In calling Smiley Blanton in 1914 to develop speech pathology, the department broke new ground. Indeed, in emphasizing the scientific and psychological approach, in developing a course in teacher training, and in introducing graduate work, Wisconsin became the leading center in the newer conceptions of speech training. A master's degree was given in 1920 and two years later the University conferred its first degree of doctor of philosophy in the speech field. Its recipient, Sarah Stinchfield, prepared standardized speech tests which marked a new point in the rapidly developing application of psychology to the study of speech. The broadening scope of the department's interest was reflected in 1920 in the decision to drop the term "public" in the official title: as Professor O'Neill pointed out, the "public" emphasis was now only a small part of the department's offerings. The new department was called the department of speech. With the development of broadcasting in the

[14] *Regents' Biennial Report,* 1915–16, pp. 84–87.

early 1920's the department of speech was quick to see an area of usefulness in which to pioneer. All in all the University could rightly feel that it had sponsored a new educational movement in which its own department made a contribution of first importance.[15]

The specialization in the English department, which had begun in the 1890's with the appointment of Johns Hopkins-trained Professor Frank G. Hubbard and other younger men likewise schooled in the historical and philological approach, gained momentum at the very time that journalism and speech were setting up housekeeping on their own.[16] In 1906 the traditional requirement of Anglo-Saxon, normally taken in the freshman year, was abandoned. Students were introduced to the department in the revamped course in English composition which Professor Edwin C. Woolley launched in 1909 and directed until his death (1916). For some time it had been obvious that entering freshmen had demonstrated decreasing ability to write satisfactorily and to give evidence of an elementary familiarity with English literature. The new spirit of freshman English was reflected in Woolley's *Handbook of Composition,* destined to remain one of the most widely used textbooks in the country. Students were trained, by systematic conferences and by carefully controlled classroom exercises, to express their ideas and to describe their interests and experiences in clear, grammatical English and to recognize the qualities of good writing. The modernization of the department was also reflected in the survey course in English literature, in which tutorial groups were set up about 1912, and in the ever-increasing introduction of courses in the modern periods and in special authors—Elizabethan poetry, Wordsworth, Emerson, Carlyle and Ruskin, Arnold, Poe, Whitman, the chief American poets, and courses in literary criticism.

The objectives of the department also became more professional. By 1907 the courses were described in relation to their aims: "(1) To train students in the use of English as a means

[15] Based in part on a statement prepared by Andrew T. Weaver on the history of the speech department.

[16] Merritt Y. Hughes prepared a statement on the development of the English department, to which this discussion owes a great deal.

of expression or communication for the ordinary demands of social, commercial, and professional life; (2) to continue that training to suit the special needs of those who take up journalistic or professional work; (3) to develop literary appreciation and extend the knowledge of those who find in English and American literature the readiest means of obtaining the advantages of a liberal education; (4) to fit students for and assist them in scholarly investigation; (5) to prepare teachers of English for school or college work." The requirement for the teacher's certificate was outlined in 1907: forty to forty-six hours in English with the emphasis upon language and grammar. Specifications for the doctorate were also laid down. The department was guided, after John C. Freeman's regime virtually came to an end about 1907, by Professor John W. Cunliffe, an English Shakespearian who had taught at McGill and won a reputation for his study of the influence of Seneca on the Elizabethan tragedy and for his notable edition of Gascoigne's works, which he completed during his five-year sojourn in Madison. Cunliffe went to the Columbia School of Journalism in 1912, being succeeded by Karl Young.

Old and Middle English as well as Elizabethan studies were well represented in this period both in instruction and in scholarly production. Professor Hubbard's publications were not numerous, but they were meritorious. In 1923 William Ellery Leonard published his translation of *Beowulf;* three years earlier he had brought out *The Scansion of Middle English Alliterative Verse.* When Karl Young came from Harvard to Wisconsin in 1908 he had established his name by the publication of *The Origin and Development of the Story of Troilus and Criseyde.* He continued to bring out units of his monumental study of the medieval religious drama which was to be completed at Yale in 1933. Arthur C. L. Brown, who came as a young man and remained until 1906, when he migrated to Northwestern, published noteworthy studies of Arthurian romances. The Elizabethan field was represented, in addition to Cunliffe's work, by Professor R. E. Neil Dodge's edition of Spenser which, immediately on its appearance in 1908, was accepted as the best critical text of the poet. In his later years Professor Henry Lathrop worked on the Elizabethans, and also concerned himself with the translators of the classics into English.

But the interest of the department lay primarily in the more modern period. Thomas Dickinson was a pioneer in introducing courses on the drama and in making available texts of the modern classical English and continental dramatics. He also organized the Wisconsin Dramatic Society. Oscar J. Campbell's critical work on *The Comedies of Holberg* and his translation of that writer were the first fruits of a distinguished scholarly career begun at Wisconsin and continued at Michigan and Columbia. Leonard's study of Byron's reputation in America, Arthur Beatty's work on Wordsworth, a high-water mark in Wordsworthian interpretation, Frederick W. Roe's editions of nineteenth century English prose writers, James F. A. Pyre's study of Tennyson's style, and Lathrop's work on the modern novel, all bore witness to creative scholarship in the modern field. Special mention should be made of Professor William B. Cairns, who, as we have already noted, carried forward the early interest of Carpenter, Freeman, and Pyre in American literature. His *British Criticisms of American Writers, 1783–1815,* was continued, chronologically, in subsequent publications, and the Oxford University Press brought out, in 1912, his *History of American Literature,* a landmark among manuals in the field. During the first World War, Cairns delivered at Oxford a lecture on "Shakespeare in America" which broke new ground. Finally, the department possessed in William Ellery Leonard not only a distinguished scholar, as his translations of Empedocles and Lucretius demonstrated, but a gifted poet. His occasional verse and sonnets, *The Vaunt of Man and Other Poems,* published in 1912, and *Two Lives,* which appeared in 1925, put him in the front rank of contemporary American poets.

The interest of William Ellery Leonard in the Latin poets suggested the interrelationships of the literatures in the various languages, the recognition of which lay back of the so-called synthetic department of comparative literature. This department, in the charge of a committee, offered instruction beginning in 1908–1909. It did not give an undergraduate major, but it enabled students, both undergraduate and graduate, to enrich their knowledge and appreciation of literature by working with such men as Olson, Giese, Showerman, Dodge, and Kind.[17]

In one great and important area in the humanities Wisconsin was shamefully deficient. As we have noted, President Van Hise early called attention to the need of establishing instruction in the history and appreciation of the fine arts. Despite his repeated emphasis on the neglect of this field, little was done. In 1911–1912 Showerman, Sellery, Jastrow, and Dodge gave a general survey course, and Showerman continued to give instruction in the history of art. But this was all that was done, with the exception of the lectures which Thomas Wood Stevens of the Chicago Art Institute gave in 1912 and 1913. Not until 1925 did the University establish the department of art history and appreciation and call from Göttingen Professor Oskar F. L. Hagen, a leading authority in the field.

Although often associated with mathematics, philosophy at Wisconsin was closely related to the arts, to science, and to the social disciplines. Professor Frank C. Sharp, the senior member of the department, continued the interest he had developed in the nineties in ethics, and in using the case method to determine the origin and degree of universality of moral principles he made a unique contribution. Drawing on a wealth of material from law cases, he applied this method to an empirical formulation of the principles of business ethics. His findings formed the substance of a text in the field and a course which generations of Wisconsin commerce and law students valued. Professor Evander B. McGilvary, a technically skillful philosopher, taught the introductory course and offered contemporary philosophy. Sensitive to the newer currents in philosophy represented by the neorealists and the pragmatists, he was unready to go the whole way with any group. He tried, rather, to work out a reconciliation between the traditional idealists and the modernists. His many articles in the first quarter of the century covered a wide range of philosophical subjects, but after 1920 he concerned himself largely with the theory of time. According to Professor Ramsperger: "The concepts of time and of simultaneity, which are of great importance in Einstein's theory of relativity, are also of cru-

[17] *Ibid.*

cial significance in the philosophy known as perspective (or relativistic) realism of which Professor McGilvary is perhaps the ablest exponent."

Any discussion of philosophy at once suggests Max Otto. Inheriting from Boyd H. Bode the course on man and nature, Otto adopted a frankly naturalistic view of the universe. His instruction occasioned criticisms on the part of the Madison clergymen, especially John W. Morgan, of the Baptist center, and this criticism extended into the hinterland. Yet, as we have seen, Van Hise sustained Otto in his right to teach the truth as he saw it. In offering one of the first courses in the country in American philosophy, Otto anticipated a development which has come to be widely recognized in our own time.

But the significance of Max Otto lay chiefly in his conception of philosophy and in his outstanding success in exemplifying it. If an important function of philosophy, in a state university that prides itself upon service to the people, is to develop in students an intelligent philosophy of life and to arouse them to a critical examination of the beliefs and values which motivate their behavior, then Professor Otto, in the words of one of his younger colleagues, has performed that function as few men have. "Through his influence, Wisconsin's department of philosophy has come to be known as one in which philosophy is a method to deal with the problems of the students who study it, not merely to deal with the problems of the philosophers they study. Professor Otto's concern for human values has thus made him not merely an outstanding interpreter of humanism and instrumentalism—for example, in his books *Things and Ideals* and *The Human Enterprise* and in many articles—but also a teacher whose effectiveness reaches out to all places where Wisconsin students are to be found."[18] Otto's general position was shared by Horace Kallen who for a few brief years offered instruction in aesthetics. In approaching the field in a naturalistic and pragmatic rather than in the traditional way Kallen was opening new vistas. The Otto position was also strengthened by a group of young men, largely trained in the department.

[18] The authors are greatly indebted for this discussion to a memorandum prepared by Albert G. Ramsperger.

As in other institutions, psychology was attached to the philosophy department. Joseph Jastrow continued to cover in the courses he offered a wide range of subjects, but his interest was becoming less and less experimental and more and more educational in his concern for exposing charlatanism in what passed for psychology. The early promise of distinguished leadership in the field, which he certainly exemplified during the first years he was at Wisconsin, was hardly fulfilled. In one of his junior associates, Clark Leonard Hull, who took his doctor's degree at Wisconsin in 1918, Jastrow had an able experimentalist. His *Evolution of Concepts,* which came out in 1920, his studies on the influence of tobacco smoking on mental and motor efficiency, and his work in aptitude testing all appeared before he left the University for Yale in 1929. Psychological studies also profited from the instruction and research of Daniel Starch, who took his doctorate with Carl E. Seashore at Iowa in 1906. His *Experiments in Educational Psychology,* published in 1911, and his text in this field represented the newer, objective approach in which Edward L. Thorndike at Columbia was the principal leader; and his pioneer work on the psychology of advertising, appearing in 1914, indicated the subsequent direction of his major interest. Starch went to Harvard in 1920. Vivian Allen Charles Henmon, who was trained by J. McKeen Cattell and Thorndike at Columbia and who came to the department of education in 1910, likewise represented educational psychology. During the first World War, Henmon was one of the leaders in applying the principles of psychology to aviation. After a brief interlude at Yale, he became professor of psychology in 1927, developing the work in tests and measurements. In their emphasis on applications Starch and Henmon indicated the cleavage with the humanistic, genteel tradition, a tradition which philosophy and psychology at Wisconsin represented in less degree than was found in the country as a whole.

✐

OF ALL the social studies during this period, history was most closely related to the humanities. Although a leader in aligning historical research with geography, economics, and sociology,

Frederick Jackson Turner appreciated the uses of literature in historical study and was genuinely concerned with values and ideals. Others in the department, notably Dana C. Munro and George C. Sellery in the medieval and Renaissance fields, were also pioneers in America in emphasizing the humanities in investigation and teaching.

The general outlines of the courses which were offered at the turn of the century remained more or less intact. Introductory lecture courses with quiz sections continued to be offered in ancient, medieval, modern European, and American history. Additional period courses, in both the European and American fields, and new topical emphases were introduced from time to time. Thus, to cite a few examples, American social and economic history, constitutional development, and diplomatic history were offered along with the histories of the South, New England, the West, and a famous course in American biography. The department also continued the early emphasis Haskins and Turner had put on the training of secondary-school teachers. Professor Wayland Johnson Chase, a member of the departments of history and education, offered courses in the teaching of history and his researches increased our knowledge of education in the ancient and medieval world.

The reputation of the department as a research center was maintained and reflected both in the growing number of graduate students and in the continuing emphasis on research and publication. Among the historians of note trained in this period only a few can be mentioned—Charles H. Ambler, Lois Kimball Mathews, E. Merton Coulter, Homer C. Hockett, August Charles Krey, Bernadotte E. Schmitt, Lowell J. Ragatz, Thomas C. Van Cleve, and Paul Knaplund. In addition to eminent visiting authorities, such as J. Franklin Jameson, Max Farrand, Andrew Cunningham McLaughlin, Paul Vinogradoff, and Ettore Pais, the department boasted distinguished scholars of its own.

Allen's work in ancient history was carried on by Dana C. Munro until 1908 when William L. Westermann joined the department. Trained in Berlin, Westermann was meticulous in his scholarship and yet recognized the importance of the larger social and economic forces in the civilization of the ancient Mediterranean world. His experience at Wisconsin prepared him to make, in later years at Cornell and Columbia, effective use of the papyri and to extend considerably our knowledge of the institution of slavery in the ancient world. When he left for Cornell in 1920, the department, at his suggestion, decided to make a bid for the distinguished refugee scholar, Michael I. Rostovtzeff. President Birge was informed by a member of the English department who met him in England that, unlike so many Russians known to Americans, he was not Semitic and that his handling of English was competent.[19] President Birge in turn assured the regents that he was no Bolshevik! During the five years in the department before he was called to Yale in 1925, Rostovtzeff published a study of a large Egyptian estate of the third century B.C., *Iranians and Greeks in South Russia*, and he finished in 1927 his great work on *A History of the Ancient World*. The Byzantine interests of Rostovtzeff were continued after he left by a leading authority, Alexander A. Vasiliev, who taught ancient history from 1925 to 1938.

Dana C. Munro, who had studied in Germany, came to Wisconsin in 1902 as Haskins' successor. With his younger colleague, George C. Sellery, who was trained at Toronto and at Chicago, he brought out in 1904 the first edition of *Medieval Civilization*. Munro's notable work in the crusades made Wisconsin a center of medieval economic history studies. One of his students, Eugene Hugh Byrne, carried on the work in medieval economic history when Munro left for Princeton in 1915. Byrne's study of Genoese commerce in the Middle Ages at once took its place as an authoritative work. Medieval studies were strengthened in 1920 with the coming of a Haskins-trained student, Carl Stephenson, who stayed for a decade during which he pushed forward his outstanding investigation of the transition of the medieval English town into the medieval city.

Sellery was a brilliant teacher of the Renaissance field. In the modern European field Victor Coffin continued until the first World War to give instruction in the period of the French Revolution and the Napoleonic era. His publications chiefly comprised manuals and popular accounts. Alfred Lewis Pinneo Dennis, who joined the department in 1906 and remained until 1920,

---

[19] William B. Cairns to Birge, July 20, 1920; Birge to Florence Buckstaff, December 29, 1919, both in the Presidents' Papers.

was known by his excellent Columbia dissertation on *Eastern Problems at the Close of the Eighteenth Century*. Dennis was interested in English history, especially in England's foreign relations in the modern era. He published little during his Wisconsin residence but did some of the work subsequently to appear in the field of Anglo-American diplomacy and the Anglo-Japanese alliance.

In the field of American history the department was one of the strongest in the country. Ulrich Bonnell Phillips, whom Turner had brought to teach the history of the South, pushed forward his investigations and publications during his all too brief stay. Carl Russell Fish did not become the outstanding authority in New England history that Turner hoped he might. But his publications in the middle period and his manual on the history of American diplomacy were favorably received, while his colorful, dramatic personality and popular lectures brought large numbers of students to the department. Winfred Trexler Root, trained at Pennsylvania, carried forward the interest Turner had shown in the colonial period. Lois Kimball Mathews, the dean of women, gave instruction until administrative duties absorbed much of her time. Turner was succeeded in 1910 by Frederic Logan Paxson, who had taken his doctorate at Pennsylvania. Although not a student of Turner's, he continued to carry on the work in western American history for which Wisconsin had become famous. Paxson's contributions to this field included his *History of the American Frontier*, published in 1924, the first rounded account of the western movement; his *Last American Frontier*, which came out in 1910; and some interpretative essays. Paxson was a true pioneer in the scholarly investigation and teaching of recent United States history. His little volume, *The New Nation*, appearing in the Riverside series in 1915, was an admirable synthesis, and his subsequent text was the first of many in an ever more popular field. His writings on America's part in the first World War appeared after he left Wisconsin in 1932. Reuben Gold Thwaites occasionally gave instruction in the history of Wisconsin, and the State Historical Society remained a great source of strength to American studies.

Eager to be of service to the nation in its great struggle, members of the history department served in various capacities. Dennis, as we have noted, was a leader in the preparedness movement and subsequently received a commission in military intelligence. Westermann was an adviser on Turkish affairs, chief of the division of western Asia in the American Commission to Negotiate Peace, and a delegate on the Greek Territorial Commission at the Paris Peace Conference. Paxson received a major's commission in connection with his work for the economic mobilization section of the historical board of the war plans division of the general staff. Fish donned overalls to work in a local munitions plant. Several members of the department contributed to the Wisconsin War Book. Designed to arouse loyalty and zeal for the war, this was, actually, a propaganda enterprise. The venture was undoubtedly well intended and perhaps was necessary to national morale, but little can be said for the objectivity of its historical "studies."

Throughout the country political science was in general taught in departments of history. The University of Wisconsin, in setting up a separate department of political science in 1901, preceded Harvard by seven years in making such a separation. The department, as we have already noted, was ably led by Paul Reinsch, who was a pioneer in colonial studies. His *World Politics at the End of the Nineteenth Century* was published in 1900, his *Colonial Government* in 1902, *Colonial Administration* in 1905, and *Intellectual and Political Currents in the Far East* in 1911. All were marked no less by scholarship than by a humanitarian sympathy with the so-called "backward peoples." Stanley Hornbeck, who took his doctor's degree in the department in 1911 and who published his useful *Contemporary Politics in the Far East* a few years later, returned to the University from an academic assignment in Chinese government colleges and took over the work of Reinsch in 1914. However, when Hornbeck went into government work under Wilson, the interest of Wisconsin in the Far East was allowed to disappear except for occasional undergraduate instruction which Frederic A. Ogg offered. The political science department was interested not only in international relations with the Far East but in Latin America as well. Reinsch was a member of the United

States delegation to the third and fourth Pan-American conferences in 1908 and 1910 and also took part in the first Pan-American Scientific Congress at Santiago in 1909. Chester Lloyd Jones, whose Wisconsin training had been broadened by study at Pennsylvania, Berlin, and Madrid, served as professor of political science from 1910 to 1920, when he resigned to continue the diplomatic work on which he had embarked and with which he was identified until his return as director of the School of Commerce in 1929. His many publications on the Caribbean countries and his participation in practical enterprises associated with this area gave him a deserved reputation as an authority.

The general study of political administration had been begun at Pennsylvania by Edmund J. James, at Columbia by Frank J. Goodnow and others, and at Harvard by A. B. Hart; and in the first decades of the twentieth century John A. Fairlie was developing this area at Michigan and at Illinois. Wisconsin lagged behind other universities despite the fact that Reinsch published studies in legislative methods and that the association of Charles McCarthy with the department provided a note of realism. In 1924 John M. Gaus brought to the department wide experience in administrative commissions in Massachusetts, New York, Minnesota, and Washington. Versatile in his interests, he became one of the outstanding figures in the academic concern with administration and planning. Meantime Frederic A. Ogg, who came to Wisconsin in 1913 and whose special interest lay in the field of comparative government, gave the Wisconsin department an international reputation as his texts became ever more widely adopted.

Political economy, or economics, continued to enjoy the eminent role which Ely's leadership had given it in the nineties. Ely displayed less and less interest in the liberal type of economics that had characterized his early career, but with such men as Frank A. Fetter, Henry R. Seager, Emory R. Johnson, and Frank W. Taussig he remained one of the leaders in the inductive, factual approach which had been so novel in the latter part of the nineteenth century. Like political science, the department emphasized not only the cultural values of the discipline, but, above all, the functional relationship of the several branches of economics to state and national problems. It gave special attention to training for citizenship and for positions of expert service in industrial management, taxation, transportation, and labor relations. A group of service working fellowships enabled some of the advanced students to apprentice themselves to the state tax commission, the railroad commission, the industrial commission, the state insurance commission, and to other state agencies. These men received training in statistical and other types of investigation assigned by the commissions with which they were associated.

The department also achieved national leadership in labor history and industrial relations, a subject in which Carrol D. Wright had made beginnings in Massachusetts and in Washington. Thanks to the tie-up with the American Bureau of Industrial Research, Ely, Commons, and their associates prepared the *Documentary History of American Industrial Society*. This was a landmark in cooperative scholarship in the social sciences. The work itself was chiefly directed by Commons, who developed the thesis that in the United States organized labor found itself when it abandoned the search for social utopias and ideologies and concerned itself in a realistic way with job-consciousness and collective bargaining. Yet Commons did not ignore the study of the socialist movements. Thanks to the project, the University Library and the State Historical Society acquired a remarkable body of materials on labor history. These included the William English Walling collection of books, papers, and pamphlets dealing with European socialism and social problems, the Hermann Schlüter collection on German and American socialism, the Henry Demarest Lloyd papers, and a vast body of employers' papers, proceedings of trade unions, and related materials. No institution approached Wisconsin in this era as a center of research in the history of American labor and related movements. Among the younger scholars trained in this field Don Divance Lescohier, Helen Sumner, Elizabeth Brandeis, Philip Taft, and notably Selig Perlman were to become outstanding authorities.

The interest in the history of labor and socialism led to the misapprehension that the Wisconsin department was "radical." Professor Ely, whose social and economic thinking was becoming steadily more conservative, pointed out to Van Hise that there was no basis in fact for such an idea. "I doubt if there is any American university of equal rank in which so little attention has been given to Socialism as has been given in the University of Wisconsin. . . . I may say that I think on investigation it will be found that no one of the great universities is more conservative than the University of Wisconsin in its department of political economy, while other institutions have men far more radical than anyone here—men whom I would not think of recommending for a position."[20]

Ely was overstating the case—the situation no doubt seemed to him to call for it: this was the very time when conservative regents, editors, and other leading citizens were attacking the University as a hotbed of radicalism. Commons, despite his sympathy with the job-conscious pragmatism of Gompers, was in no sense an advocate of laissez faire or of traditional economics. He was already a pioneer in institutional economics, having begun the approach which was to result in the *Legal Foundations of Capitalism* (1924). His students, including Sumner, Perlman, Taft, Lescohier, Brandeis, and others, continued the work Commons had begun in labor history and legislation. Thomas Sewall Adams, a member of the department from 1901 to 1910, represented a liberal point of view as an expert on the Wisconsin State Tax Commission; after he left to head the department at Washington University, he returned to Madison to help draft and to defend the Wisconsin state income tax law of 1911. Balthasar H. Meyer, who had begun in the late nineties to publish his significant studies on government control of railroads, continued an association with the department, broken by leaves for public service. His *History of Transportation in the United States before 1860* was published after he had become associated with the Interstate Commerce Commission, but the foundations of it were laid in the Wisconsin period. Henry Charles Taylor, the virtual founder of agricultural economics, not only was a pioneer in cutting out a new field but in many respects was a

[20] Richard T. Ely to Van Hise, February 15, 1910, Presidents' Papers.

liberal in his approach to economics, as were his students and younger associates, Percy Wells Bidwell, John Ironside Falconer, Benjamin Horace Hibbard, and George Simon Wehrwein. Edward A. Ross, who developed sociology within the department, was a force in progressive thought.

Yet the department as a whole, as Ely claimed, was in no real sense radical. It apparently did not think of calling Edward W. Bemis or Thorstein Veblen when their positions at Chicago were no longer tenable. The principal Wisconsin authority on economic theory, William A. Scott, interpreted sympathetically the classical economists. Such younger men as William H. Kiekhofer and Fayette H. Elwell were to develop into economists not very far left of center. Above all, the commerce course, which enjoyed the status of a quasi-separate school in Letters and Science, directed by Professor Scott, gave an essentially conservative tone to the economics department with which it was so closely identified. Its program was eminently practical, designed to turn out realistic business leaders. It emphasized the importance of efficiency in accounting, auditing, advertising, and marketing; the potentialities of industrial development in the state; and the promotion of profitable investments and trade. Of especial point in connection with the statement of Ely regarding the conservatism of the department was his own growing interest in the economics of real estate, land investments, and public utilities. This expressed itself in 1920 in the establishment of the independent but associated Institute for Research in Land Economics and Public Utilities. In 1925 Ely, who had often threatened to take a highly paid position in a New York corporation, but who had stayed on for one reason or another, left for the more advantageous precincts of Northwestern.

The department of political economy, as it was called until it became the department of economics in 1917, included anthropology and sociology. Anthropological studies in American universities had been developed by Daniel G. Brinton at Pennsylvania and by Franz Boas and others at Columbia. Although something was done in this field by the first lecturer on sociology, Jerome Dowd, the real beginning at Wisconsin was made in 1907 when the English archaeologist and anthropologist,

Top: Moses Stephen Slaughter and John R. Commons
Bottom: Carl Russell Fish and Louis Kahlenberg

Top: Julius E. Olson and Edward Kremers
Bottom: William A. Scott and Benjamin W. Snow

Charles Henry Hawes, began a brief sojourn in Madison. Although Commons and Ross gave instruction in anthropology, this field of knowledge lagged behind developments in many American universities.

Sociology was forging rapidly ahead at Michigan where the brilliant and original Professor Charles Horton Cooley was striking out on new paths in showing the significance of the small, face-to-face group as a socializing agency. At Chicago, Albion Small was founding a notable school. At Columbia Franklin H. Giddings was training many of the future leaders. Ely had recognized the importance of sociology and even dabbled a bit in it himself; as we have seen, he took the lead in organizing a University settlement house in Milwaukee and in bringing Dowd and other lecturers to Madison. In 1906 Edward Alsworth Ross joined the department as the first full professor of sociology.[21] He had been trained at Berlin and at Johns Hopkins. His *Honest Dollars,* published in 1896, was a pamphlet which offended many conservatives. He had to leave Stanford, after more than one tiff, because of the unpopularity of his stand on immigration with the circles which controlled the university. His *Social Control* (1901) had been received as an important contribution to the professional literature and as coming out forthrightly for ethical values as against undisciplined, greedy individualism and social chaos. The year after Ross came to Madison his book *Sin and Society* created something of a sensation. It took its place with the more serious of the muckraking literature of exposure. Theodore Roosevelt praised it. Conservatives, including some of the regents at Wisconsin, denounced it. Indeed, as we have seen, Van Hise himself was the authority for the statement that a good part of the animus of the regents toward Ross at the time of the Goldman-Sercombe episodes had come from the fact that they had not forgiven him for indicting capitalistic greed in *Sin and Society.* Ross's publications were all but perennial; his *Social Psychology* published in 1908 and his *Principles of Sociology,* which came out in 1920, were useful texts. A great traveler and writer, Ross made many Ameri-

[21] This account is based on a sketch of the history of the sociology department prepared by Thomas C. McCormick.

cans aware of the new social stirrings in China, Mexico, and Russia, which he presented sympathetically.

Sociological studies took a different turn in 1912 when John Lewis Gillin, a Columbia-trained scholar and an authority on criminology and poor relief, came to the University from Iowa. Although at first he devoted only a small part of his time to residential instruction, his influence was widely felt. On the extension circuit he studied the health, recreational, and other community needs of the state, organized the Wisconsin Conference of Charities and Correction, and educated the public to the need of more and better trained social workers.[22] During the war Gillin directed the Home Service for the Central Division of the American Red Cross and, on returning to the University, brought with him one of his associates in the war work, Helen Clarke, a trained social worker. Miss Clarke offered instruction in case work and supervised students in practice field work. The University became one of the earliest members of the American Association of Schools of Social Work, which was organized in 1919. Not until 1946 did social work become independent of the department of sociology.

ℐ

At Wisconsin, as at most American institutions, the emphasis in mathematics had traditionally been in making provision for effective training in the basic branches.[23] The founding of a strong department at the University of Chicago stimulated mathematical research throughout the Middle West. At Wisconsin the new emphasis on research in pure mathematics was chiefly carried out by Edward Burr Van Vleck, who began in 1906 a thirty-three-year term of service. An early member of the American Mathematical Society, an active figure in its editorial activities, Van Vleck was honored with the presidency of the organization in 1913. He was also a member of the National Academy of Science and of the leading foreign mathe-

[22] Helen I. Clarke kindly prepared a brief history of the development of work in social service training at Wisconsin.

[23] The following discussion is based in part on a memorandum prepared by Rudolph E. Langer and Mark H. Ingraham.

matical associations. In the field of analysis Van Vleck was generally regarded as a distinguished figure.

But the primary emphasis was the deliberate union of pure and applied mathematics—in which Wisconsin led the country. This involved, among other things, close tie-ups with physics, the College of Engineering, and the Geological Survey. Charles Sumner Slichter began in 1898 to report on his investigations of movements of underground waters and continued to advance knowledge in this field in connection with his work with the United States Geological Survey and the Reclamation Service. The practical emphasis of Slichter's mathematical interests was reinforced in 1908 when Max Mason joined the department. His contributions to submarine developments in the first World War were of importance. With Mason's transfer to physics and, in 1925, to the University of Chicago, Herman W. March carried on the work in applied mathematics. Warren Weaver, during his brief sojourn at Wisconsin, ably represented this sphere and, subsequently, Ivan S. Sokolnikoff maintained it at a high level. Others in the department, including L. W. Dowling and Ernest Brown Skinner, were notable teachers. Until the first World War it was customary for American students to seek the doctorate in mathematics in Germany, and although a few students took this degree at Wisconsin it was not until the twenties that work on this level became an important function of the department. The staff, strengthened by the coming of Mark H. Ingraham and of Rudolph E. Langer, interested respectively in algebra and in analysis, took an influential part in national mathematical affairs.

Until Sterling Hall, with its admirable laboratories and museum, became available in 1917, the department of physics was housed in the lower floors of Science Hall.[24] From 1893 to 1925 Benjamin Warner Snow served as chairman. A striking and forceful lecturer, Snow was largely responsible for building up extensive lecture-demonstration equipment and for establishing carefully planned and executed experimental lectures which were unusually interesting to students. In fact, instruction in

[24] Leonard R. Ingersoll prepared a brief statement on main developments in the physics department, to which this discussion is indebted.

physics, in which the department took justifiable pride, was far less unpopular than in most institutions. On the undergraduate level a great variety of courses met the special and widespread needs of students in the University, but on the graduate level, in contrast with most other departments, courses were kept at a minimum and students were almost at once inducted into thorough and sustained research training. Among the physicists trained in the department many became leaders in the field, including Lee A. DuBridge, director of the Radiation [radar] Laboratory during the recent war and head of the California Institute of Technology; Donald W. Kerst, who originated the betatron; Jesse Talbot Littleton, head of the Corning Glass physical laboratory; David B. Parkinson, inventor of a gun director; Robert Serber, one of the leading theoreticians; and C. Guy Suits, director of the General Electric research laboratory.

Although the department put great emphasis on instruction, on both the more elementary and the more advanced levels, it established, in the first decade of the twentieth century, an enviable reputation as a research center—a reputation which has been sustained. This distinction owed much to the appointment, about the turn of the century, of three men strong in the spirit and techniques of research. Robert W. Wood, who went to Johns Hopkins in 1901, initiated investigations in light which aroused wide interest; Augustus Trowbridge did notable work in electrical and mathematical physics; and Charles E. Mendenhall, who succeeded Wood and who remained at Wisconsin until his death in 1935, won distinction in many fields. Mendenhall's researches included such varied subjects as gravity measurements, galvanometer design, melting-point determinations, and radiation. He originated the V-wedge black body which proved of great value in pyrometry. In his later years he began systematic investigations of photoelectric effects. Cautious in publishing, generous in his recognition of the work of his students, thorough, precise, persevering, and catholic in his grasp of many departments of a rapidly changing field of knowledge, Mendenhall was no less vigorous and outstanding in teaching and in administration than in investigation. And Mendenhall was surrounded by able investigators who worked harmoniously and fruitfully together. Leonard R. Ingersoll's studies in the polarization of light phenomena in the region of the short infrared spectrum were pioneer undertakings. Hugo B. Wahlin's work in the nature of gaseous ions, electron motion in gases, emissivity of metals and alloys, thermionic emission, and mass spectroscopy brought distinction to the department. John R. Roebuck's measurement of the Joule–Thomson effect for common gases, over wide pressure and temperature ranges, was the most extensive and precise work in this category.

While the Wisconsin physicists were much concerned with theory and profited from the sojourns of such outstanding theoreticians as Hendrik A. Lorentz, Peter Debye, Erwin Schrödinger, Arnold Sommerfeld, Gregor Wentzel, Paul Dirac, and Léon Brillouin, their work was in no sense divorced from application. During the first World War, Mendenhall, Mason, Roebuck, Earle M. Terry, Louis B. Slichter, and Earl Downing Hay developed a submarine detector which played a major part in the battle against the submarine. Ingeniously constructed to ignore sounds of the ship on which it operated at the same time that it sensitively picked up the sounds of the submarine, the detector was the legitimate object of pride. Earle M. Terry and Albert H. Taylor were pioneers in the development of radio from wireless telegraphy. Terry was mainly responsible early in 1919 for launching radio station WHA, credited with being the first in the country to offer scheduled broadcast service. Among outstanding developments in research in the past quarter of a century, the physics department took an important part in the investigation of nuclear structure and experimental spectroscopy.

The retirement of William W. Daniells in 1907 opened the way to reorganization and expansion in the chemistry department. The University had been offering many courses in chemistry in several departments and colleges, and chemical work in its practical applications was well established not only in engineering and agriculture but in the Hygienic Laboratory, the State Dairy and Food Commission, and the pharmacy course. The new course in chemistry, as Dean Birge pointed out in his report in 1908, aimed to bring together and to correlate the vari-

ous endeavors and to prepare men more adequately for professional careers in chemistry.[25] This departure was warranted,
not only by requirements of efficiency within the University,
but by the rapidly growing demands for competent chemists in
academic institutions, agricultural experiment stations, health
and sanitary departments of municipalities, industries engaged
in the preparation of foods and other products for consumption,
and the metallurgical and building industries. "In many of our
industries," in the words of the descriptive statement of the new
course, "it is already realized that it is necessary to have the service of a chemist continually in order to properly inspect the
raw materials bought, to control and improve the process of
manufacture so as to avoid waste of power and material, and
to test the grade of the finished article." The statement further
indicated the opportunities for women as well as for men in the
expanding field.[26] Six sequences, designed to train agricultural
chemists, industrial chemists, soil chemists, physiological chemists, food chemists, and general analytical chemists, were outlined. Work in the cognate sciences and in French and German
were required aspects of the program. The new course was
indeed something of an innovation in its recognition of both the
specialization in the field and the need for special training in
the several departments and in its coordination of the work
hitherto done in many branches of the institution.

The head of the new course was Professor Louis Kahlenberg,
who at the same time succeeded Daniells as chairman of the
department. After taking the bachelor of science degree at Wisconsin in 1892 he was awarded the doctorate, *summa cum laude*,
at Leipzig, thereafter taking up his residence in Madison. His
research and publications lay largely in the field of solutions,
electrolysis, and osmosis. But he became known to students and
to the public through his laboratory exercises in general chemistry, his *Outlines of Chemistry* (1909), and his *Qualitative
Chemical Analysis*, published in 1911 with James Henry Walton. Kahlenberg was a dramatic, even a sensational lecturer in
the elementary courses, and he inspired hundreds of students

[25] Report of the Dean of the College of Letters and Science, *Regents' Biennial
Report*, 1907–08, p. 50.   [26] *University Catalogue*, 1908–09, pp. 259–260.

with an interest in chemistry. Brilliant and something of an egotist, Kahlenberg set himself rigidly in opposition to the newer ionization theory, which he felt failed to account for many phenomena. Van Hise thought highly of him and threw many favors in his way. Dean Birge, while professing to value his merits, did not share the president's enthusiasm and was chiefly responsible for bringing Victor Lenher to strengthen the work in the inorganic field. The organic field was chiefly represented by Richard Fischer, trained at Michigan, Marburg, and Berlin. Coming to Wisconsin in 1894 as instructor in pharmacy, he was named state chemist in 1903, a position which he held until 1909. Thereafter he was consulting chemist for the Wisconsin Dairy and Food Commission and was closely associated with various committees and agencies on food standards. His researches lay chiefly in the field of dye intermediates, furfural derivatives, and food, especially alkaloid, chemistry.

During the first World War, Kahlenberg and Fischer carried on the work of the department while Lenher, James H. Walton, Joseph H. Mathews, and Paul W. Carleton accepted commissions in the Chemical Warfare Service, as did Arthur S. Loevenhart and Harold C. Bradley of the medical school. Some of his colleagues had felt that Kahlenberg refused or failed to teach courses competently, and many deemed him pro-German, including his fellow workers in the Chemical Warfare Service in Washington. Van Hise apparently cooled in his attitude toward Kahlenberg. The Wisconsin chemists in Washington put their heads together and schemed a revolution against Kahlenberg. Dr. Bradley, writing to Van Hise on November 18, 1918, the very day that Van Hise died, pointed out that with the war's end a scramble for good chemists was certain to take place; that many academic chemists would not be returning to their old posts; that Lenher, Mathews, Walton, and Carleton themselves might not come back to Madison. He spoke of the nonproductivity in some fields, the general atmosphere of dogmatism, and the "notoriously pro-German" or "obviously" indifferent members of the staff who stayed in Madison during the war. "We need an entirely new organization in the Wisconsin Department of Chemistry, with a leader at the head, and a producer in organic chemistry." "This branch of the field," continued Bradley, "has been one of the great factors in this war. Wisconsin has had nothing at all to contribute in this field—either in men or ideas." Moreover, organic chemistry, as Bradley pointed out, was basic to medicine. For all these reasons the time had come to act and to clear up the mess.[27] Carleton reinforced Bradley by calling Birge's attention to what he described as the "constant bickering and suspicious attitude within the department," the "grinding teaching" load of the staff, and the monopolizing of graduate students by the chairman.[28] The discontent was nursed along by Lenher, who felt the chairmanship should have been his. Mathews submitted to Birge a plan for departmental reorganization which the Washington delegation had approved. On his part Edward Kremers maintained a friendly neutrality toward Kahlenberg on the ground that it was undignified and even contemptible for the Washington group to capitalize on its war service and on the popular anti-German war hysteria to move against the chairman at this particular time.[29]

Thus spurred on, Edward A. Birge, the acting president, cautiously called a conference of the heads of the science departments, to whom he proposed the deposition of Kahlenberg and the elevation of Lenher. The conference supported his move against Kahlenberg but stood firmly against the elevation of Lenher. When it proved impossible to have a chairman from the outside, Birge appointed Mathews.[30]

But the affair was by no means over. Kahlenberg fought tooth and nail against his removal from the chairmanship and headship of the chemistry course. He traveled over the state urging the active interference of friends and alumni. The president and the regents denied that they were penalizing Kahlenberg and Fischer because they were of German descent. They further denied the allegations of Kahlenberg and his friends, particularly Arden R. Johnson and Dr. Albert John Ochsner of Chicago, that it was their intention to remove Kahlenberg from his

[27] Major Harold C. Bradley to Van Hise, November 18, 1918, Presidents' Papers.

[28] Paul W. Carleton to Birge, December 9, 1918, Presidents' Papers.

[29] Edward Kremers, Sketch of Louis Kahlenberg, Kremers Papers, State Historical Society of Wisconsin.

[30] *Ibid.;* Birge to Dr. Albert J. Ochsner, June 4, 1919, Presidents' Papers.

professorship or to interfere with his freedom to oppose the ionization theory.[31] Kahlenberg himself presented his case to the regents.

The most important issue in the whole controversy involved the permanency of the chairmanship. Kahlenberg and his supporters maintained that a chairman could not be demoted without a trial or similar procedure in which the accused faced his accusers. Birge effectively refuted this argument. "I understand it to be the wish of the faculty," he wrote, "that the chairmanship of a department should be regarded as a temporary executive office, which is held from year to year and is commonly held so long as a man is willing to hold it, or so long as he exercises its duties to the satisfaction of the other men in the department." "It is not," he continued, "a permanent position to which a man has definite claim as of right; indeed, one thing which of all others the faculty desire to avoid is the notion that the chairmanship is a permanent position for the man who may be holding it at a given time." If, Birge continued, Kahlenberg and Ochsner really thought the rights of a professor were involved, then the case should have been processed through the local chapters of the American Association of University Professors, which was both strong and sensitive to violations of faculty rights.[32] Doubtless the Kahlenberg case was in large part responsible for the adoption by the regents in 1920 of the by-law providing for the annual nomination of chairmen by members of a department and appointment by the dean.[33]

The situation became so badly mixed up that President Birge despaired of being able to straighten it out. Dean Sellery interviewed Ochsner in Chicago, making it clear that Kahlenberg was not being forced out of the University, and won over Kahlenberg himself to the arrangement by which another professor might be chosen as director and chairman, and instruction in the elementary courses, so dear to Kahlenberg, was divided between him and Walton. He was given ample opportunities for offering advanced courses and for research. New men who had

[31] Ochsner to Birge, January 17, 1919; Birge to Ochsner, January 25, 1919; A. R. Johnson to A. P. Nelson, February 27, 1919, all in the Presidents' Papers.
[32] Birge to Ochsner, May 29, 1919, Presidents' Papers.
[33] Records of the Board of Regents, J:441, March 5, 1920.

not been identified with the controversy—Farrington Daniels, Homer Adkins, and others—were brought in and by their instruction and distinguished research greatly strengthened the department. A new sequence of courses designed to prepare students to work in the economic aspects of chemistry was inaugurated but later abandoned. Yet expansion in old and new fields took place steadily.

Closely associated with chemistry was the School of Pharmacy, founded by Frederick B. Power and directed, since 1892, by Milwaukee-born and German-trained Edward Kremers. As we have already seen, the Wisconsin school was the first in the United States to grant a four-year bachelor of science degree in pharmacy and the first to give graduate degrees, on both the master's and doctor's levels. Inspired with an evangelical passion for improving standards in pharmaceutical education and for advancing knowledge through fundamental research, Kremers and his associates and students made significant contributions to plant chemistry. Kremers' students were called to the staffs and headships of other academic schools of pharmacy and to key positions in the industrial phases of pharmacology, and his importance in advancing knowledge in his field, in training research investigators, in bringing pharmaceutical education to higher levels, and in bringing cultural elements into a technical program can hardly be exaggerated. It is, moreover, noteworthy that Kremers did all this with only modest support from the administration. His querulousness probably had something to do with the modest support for, according to his administrative heads, he was impossible to satisfy.[34]

With his associate, William O. Richtmann, Kremers made the school one of the leading centers in the world for the study of the history of pharmacy. The materials Kremers and Richtmann collected illustrating the development of chemical and pharmaceutical symbols were virtually unrivaled. In our own time Professor George Urdang has made excellent use of these materials. Through the Institute of the History of Pharmacy, which Kremers inspired and Arthur Hoyt Uhl founded, Urdang has brought out a series of sound studies, the most important of

[34] Kremers to Birge, October 2, 1920, Presidents' Papers.

which is the Kremers and Urdang *History of Pharmacy* (1940), the first systematic survey of the development of pharmacy.[35]

Astronomy remained the smallest department among the physical sciences. The telescopes were not powerful compared to instruments at Yerkes, Lick, and Harvard observatories. George Cary Comstock, who had followed James Craig Watson from Ann Arbor to Madison in 1879 and who assisted Edward S. Holden, became director of the Washburn Observatory in 1889 —a post he held until 1922. In the field of the astronomy of precision he displayed remarkable talents and achieved results equal in importance to those of colleagues in far better equipped observatories. His studies of the law of refraction of light in the earth's atmosphere followed his early investigations of the aberration of light in which he achieved notable results through an ingenious instrument enabling him to observe two widely separated stars simultaneously. For three decades he studied the motions of double stars. His observations and investigations of the orbits of these stars established the generality of the law of gravitation. Out of these studies developed Comstock's demonstration that the faintness of many stars is the result of an intrinsic low luminosity rather than, as had been supposed, of their great distance. As a teacher and administrator Comstock was an important figure both in the University and in astronomical circles. The Wisconsin emphasis on the applications of science to practical problems was reflected in his course for engineers and in the text he wrote on *Field Astronomy for Engineers* (1902). He was one of the organizers of the American Astronomical Society and served as both secretary and president of the organization. The National Academy of Sciences honored him with election in 1899—he was one of ten astronomers at that time listed in its membership.[36]

[35] This discussion is based in part on George Urdang's "Edward Kremers (1865–1941), Reformer of American Pharmaceutical Education," *Transactions of the Wisconsin Academy of Sciences, Arts, and Letters,* 37:111–135 (1945); "Historical Research in Pharmacy," *American Journal of Pharmaceutical Education* (July, 1946); "Why the American Institute of the History of Pharmacy was organized at Madison, Wisconsin," *Badger Pharmacist* (March, 1941); and on notes on interviews between Maurice Vance and Arthur H. Uhl, and Vance and George Urdang.

[36] This is based on Joel Stebbins' sketch of George C. Comstock in the *Dictionary of American Biography,* XXI, Supplement I.

Roland D. Irving, Thomas C. Chamberlin, and Van Hise had established in geological studies the tradition of a close association with the Wisconsin Geological Survey and the United States Geological Survey.[37] In fact, for a long period geology was subordinated to mineralogy and mining. As we have already noted, Van Hise, from 1900 to 1908, was in charge of the Pre-Cambrian and metamorphic geology for the entire country. Charles K. Leith, Van Hise's pupil, who had begun his career with the United States Geological Survey, succeeded Van Hise as chairman of the department and as a member of the United States Geological Survey. The classic monographs of the Survey on the geology of the Lake Superior region, so useful in the exploration of iron and copper ores, composed only part of the outstanding publications of Irving, Van Hise, Leith, and their assistants and successors, including J. Morgan Clements and Warren J. Mead. Wisconsin was the mecca for advanced students of Pre-Cambrian geology from all over the world.

Interest in mineralogy and petrography played an important role in the geological department from the very outset. William H. Hobbs, Alexander N. Winchell, and Richard C. Emmons all extended mineralogical studies. The scope of instruction and investigation was enlarged to include stratigraphy, sedimentation, and paleontology. These developments took place with the coming of Eliot Blackwelder in 1905, William H. Twenhofel, who succeeded him in 1916, and Norman D. Newell and Robert R. Shrock, who came in subsequent years. Lawrence Martin, a member of the department between 1906 and 1919, furthered the work in glacial geology and geomorphology but, above all, stimulated geographical studies. His manuals, his book on the physical geography of Wisconsin, and his Alaskan-glacier work all belonged to his Wisconsin period: he was easily at the forefront of his field. Armin Lobeck, who came to Wisconsin in 1919 to stay until his call to Columbia in 1929, worked in geology, geomorphology, and geography. Vernor C. Finch, who took his doctorate at Wisconsin in 1916, became a leading figure in economic geography, and Ray Hughes Whitbeck, who came in 1909, developed his special interest in this field. As the geo-

---

[37] Based in part on a statement prepared by R. C. Emmons.

graphical work increased in importance the department was in 1920 renamed the department of geology and geography, and in 1928 the department of geography was set up.

The gradual extension of the geology department's interest in mineral resources in their human relations owed much to Van Hise's concern for the conservation of natural resources. His participation in the White House conference and his writings in the field have already been noted. Leith carried on this interest, introducing courses in the economics of geology with emphasis on international relations and effects on war and peace —a pioneer innovation. Leith's articles and books in this field and his participation in the Paris Peace Conference of 1918–1919 and in more recent government activities made him the recognized leader in the field of conservation.

Wisconsin, in brief, played a leading part in introducing four major themes into American geology—Pre-Cambrian geology, structural geology, sedimentation, and human relations to mineral resources. The scientific standing of the department was indicated by the election of Van Hise, Leith, Mead, and Louis Slichter to the National Academy of Sciences and by the fact that members of the department served as presidents of all the national mineralogical, geological, and geographical societies.

In the biological as in the physical sciences Wisconsin witnessed a development in research and instruction closely attuned to practical problems.[38] This was especially true of the work in anatomy, which Dr. William Snow Miller pushed forward after his arrival in 1892, and which Dr. Charles R. Bardeen subsequently forwarded as part of the premedical work which Birge had inaugurated in the eighties. Others also lent strength to anatomy, notably Ferdinand Schmitter. Bennet Mills Allen, who brought a fresh experimental approach to the study of vertebrate embryology, began, shortly after his arrival in 1903, to publish his commendable papers on the origin of sex cells in the different classes of vertebrates. George Wagner, who likewise came in 1903, developed the work in vertebrate zoology and ecology. William Stanley Marshall, who joined the depart-

---

[38] L. E. Noland kindly prepared a brief history of the zoology department which has proved helpful in the following account.

ment in the nineties fresh from his studies with Leuckart in Leipzig, published excellent histological and embryological studies of insects and trained the first doctors in zoology at Wisconsin. In 1905 Samuel Jackson Holmes was brought to the department as an assistant professor and, from 1906 until he left in 1912 for California, served as chairman. Holmes was not a forceful executive, and he indicated to President Van Hise that the zoology department must inevitably suffer as long as Birge retained the key position, especially since he bent over backward as dean to avoid any suggestion of favoritism to the department.[39] Holmes published outstanding research papers on crustaceans, animal behavior, and morphogenesis, and his book, *Evolution of Animal Intelligence,* published in 1911, was an admirable exposition of the newer functional point of view which was revolutionizing the psychology of animal behavior.

No less practical in its implications was the work of Birge and Chancey Juday on the physical and chemical behavior of inland lakes as habitats for animal and plant life. These investigations, centered at first in Lake Mendota, launched the new field of limnology, which was well established with the appearance in 1911 of the celebrated report on the dissolved gases of inland lakes. As commissioner of fisheries and forestry and as a member of the Wisconsin Conservation Commission, Birge saw the application of the research to practical problems.

A new epoch began in 1911 with the coming of Michael Frederic Guyer, whose training at Chicago and Naples had been followed by distinguished work at the University of Cincinnati. Guyer's effective leadership made itself felt at once. Instruction in comparative anatomy and vertebrate embryology which had been taken over by the anatomy department when it was organized was now transferred to the department of zoology. New impetus and strength were given to the work in microscopical technique, and cytology was introduced as a subject of instruction and research. Research was also initiated in heredity, especially to determine the possibility of inducing hereditary

---

[39] Samuel Jackson Holmes to Van Hise, February 22, 1911, Presidents' Papers; Report of the Alumni Committee on Zoology to the University of Wisconsin Alumni Association [apparently 1910–11], Presidents' Papers.

changes (eye defects in rabbits) by the use of antibodies affecting the germ cells of the unborn young through the body of the mother. Among Guyer's students Harold W. Beams, Harlan W. Mossman, C. L. Turner, Alan Boyden, Harold Wolfe, Joseph Baier, Frederic Mohs, and others won distinction for their researches. Guyer's *Animal Biology, Animal Micrology,* and *Being Well Born* attracted widespread attention. Guyer was one of the promulgators of the Basic Science Board of the state, which did much to raise the standards of medical practice.

Other new recruits likewise strengthened the department. Arthur Sperry Pearse developed a research program in ecology and parasitology which helped several men to become nationally known for the additions to knowledge which they made: Frederick Lee Hisaw, who took his doctorate in the department in 1924, won national recognition for the research program in endocrinology he developed before going to Harvard in 1935; Lowell Noland, whose Wisconsin years began shortly after the first World War, worked principally in the fields of protozoology and the physiology of snails. He also won distinction as a brilliant lecturer in the introductory course. The physiological aspects of zoology became the object of special investigation, thanks, in part, to Samuel Lepovsky, trained in biochemistry, who joined the staff in 1925.

The new Biology Building, opened in 1912, was no less an asset to botany than to zoology.[40] Robert A. Harper, the leader in the department since 1898, left for Columbia in 1911, but meantime the University had profited from his work in cytology, mycology, and plant pathology. His younger colleagues, Charles E. Allen, James B. Overton, William G. Marquette, and Rollin H. Denniston, were all investigators in their respective fields of morphology, vegetable histology, cytology, dendrology, and hybridization. Allen, who had taken his degree at Wisconsin in 1904, was known both for his textbooks and for his research in cytology and genetics which brought him countless honors, including, of course, membership in the National

[40] The careful and detailed account of the development of botanical studies at Wisconsin prepared by George S. Bryan has been used to advantage in this discussion.

Academy of Sciences. In the second and third decades of the century the department was strengthened by the addition to the staff, for a brief term, of Ivey Lewis, whose interest in marine biology was already well defined; of Ezra Kraus in applied botany, who was lured to Chicago in 1927; and of a group of outstanding plant pathologists—Edward Gilbert, Lewis Jones, and George W. Keitt. The far-reaching significance of work in this field seemed to justify the establishment of a separate department of plant pathology, but its members remained in close touch with their colleagues in botany. Others, including George Bryan and Gilbert Smith, likewise began highly useful careers in the department. While theory was in no sense neglected, botanical studies, like the other sciences at Wisconsin, were cast in a strong practical mold. This tendency did not extend, however, into the field of forestry where, despite auspicious beginnings, the administration decided that, in view of the well-established programs at Minnesota and Michigan, resources might better be concentrated in other departments. The Forest Products Laboratory, which in 1912 moved into a new building, was, however, closely associated in many ways with the botanists and was already the foremost institution of its kind in the country and one of the leading centers in the world.

As we have seen, Wisconsin was a pioneer in the development of bacteriological studies.[41] The early interest of Birge and Trelease was taken up and greatly extended by a group of men in the College of Agriculture. Until 1912 bacteriology was a department within the College of Letters and Science. In addition to the introductory work, the two emphases were in agricultural and medical bacteriology. William D. Frost and, from 1908 to 1914, Dr. M. P. Ravenel developed medical bacteriology, in association with the state hygienic laboratory, which Dr. Ravenel directed. The work of these men was ably continued by Paul F. Clark, who came to the Medical School in 1914. The early interest in agricultural bacteriology associated with Dean Henry and Harry L. Russell will be discussed in connection with the College of Agriculture. Here it may suffice to call attention to the significant research in the bacteriology of dairy

[41] The memorandum of E. B. Hastings has been drawn upon for this account.

products and the bacteriological diseases of plants and animals. Edwin B. Fred, joining the group in 1913, conducted basic studies in soil bacteriology with results of great practical importance. The research, the bacteriologists who were trained, and the application of the science to agriculture, the canning industry, and agronomy gave great distinction to the University.

*

THE development of musical interest in American institutions of higher learning had taken, in the latter part of the nineteenth century, two main forms. In some institutions no effort was made to provide the sort of technical skill in performance that the conservatories offered, if the training in the glee club and chorus, and perhaps in the college orchestra, be excepted. These institutions attempted to develop an academic tradition for the integration of musical appreciation into general education on the one hand and to set high standards in musicology on the other. Harvard was at the forefront in this general development. John Knowles Paine, professor of music from 1875 to 1903, was himself a distinguished composer and an authority in the theoretical aspects of musical study. Under his leadership the Harvard department set unusually high standards in choral music, in harmony and counterpoint, and in the study and appreciation of musical scores. This tradition was continued after the retirement of Paine.

The second development was the training of professional musicians through the development of technical skill in performance, with some attention to the history, appreciation, and theory of music. In other words, this approach resembled the conservatory type of musical education. Michigan was at the forefront in this development. As the interest in public school music increased and as specially trained teachers were needed, university schools of music turned their attention to providing adequate work in musical education. Wisconsin represented this tendency.

The connection of the School of Music with the College of Letters and Science had never been more than formal and administrative.[42] A series of crises within the school did provide occasion for strengthening the influence of the dean in its affairs. These crises arose in part from the decision, in 1907, so to improve the standards for admission and certification that the school might properly be deemed of university grade. This involved putting the staff on a regular salary basis, thus making the members no longer dependent on individual student fees. The reorganization, based on the pattern provided by the School of Music at the University of Illinois, also limited the teaching load to forty hours a week and eliminated all elementary instruction. The entrance requirements were made equal to those stipulated for the College of Letters and Science. In part the crises also resulted from the fact that two of the directors on whom fell the burden of implementing the reorganization were inexperienced in administration and unable to solve problems of personnel.[43]

During the year 1915–1916 the program, which had gradually been expanded on both the theoretical and practical levels, was again reorganized. It was extended to four years, about half of the credits being assigned to the School of Music and the remainder to academic courses in Letters and Science. The degree of bachelor of music was thenceforth conferred on those completing the course. It continued to be possible, for a time, however, for students to acquire a teacher's certificate for three years of work in place of the traditional two. The regular four-year and three-year collegiate programs were still supplemented by a course open to persons not members of the University as well as to students who did not desire to enter the collegiate course leading to graduation. Much of the technical and practical instruction continued to be individual, but group work in chorus, orchestra, counterpoint and harmony, as well as in the history and appreciation of music, won much wider acceptance. Even before the coming of Peter W. Dykema in 1913 the school had emphasized training for the teaching of music in the public schools. Dykema, who remained until 1924, when he went to

[42] L. A. Coon submitted a helpful chronology of the principal developments in the School of Music.

[43] Papers of the Board of Regents, October 21, 1908, and June 19, 1909.

Teachers College, Columbia, developed this work. Edgar B. Gordon and others likewise promoted community music, working effectively in the extension division.

With a few exceptions courses in the school were open to qualified students in any college of the University. But the offerings in the history and appreciation of music, so popular and praiseworthy at Harvard, Michigan, and other institutions, did not appeal to any sizable section of the undergraduate body. This was unfortunate for, as Van Hise so often pointed out, the University was weak in the aesthetic sphere.

The staff included musicians of national reputation. Rossetter G. Cole, director from 1907 to 1909, had been trained in Germany and was in the midpoint of a long, productive career as a composer when he came to Madison. His subsequent work at Columbia and in Chicago, his writings on choral and church music, and his editing of periodicals put musical America in debt to him. His successor, Louis Coerne, possessed the first doctorate Harvard gave in music (1905) and was known both by his *Zenobia,* the first American opera to be performed in Europe (1905–1906), and by his *Evolution of Modern Orchestration* (1908). Arthur Locke and Leland Hall, on the threshold of distinguished careers which won them recognition after their migration to Smith, did much to stimulate interest in music in Madison. The directors of the men's glee club raised the standards in this field and contributed materially to the growing reputation of the club in the Middle West. Despite able men, the school did not rank with that of Michigan, Harvard, or Columbia. But it did reflect, in its emphasis on public school music, the Wisconsin concept of practical service to the state. And the period definitely saw it transformed from an old-fashioned and limited affair into a relatively competent University school.

THE professional library movement involved, of course, the idea of special training schools. The first such school was begun in 1887 when Melvil Dewey established at Columbia the School of Library Economics, presently to be moved to Albany and to become the New York State Library School.[44] In the Middle West, Illinois took the lead, adopting in 1897 the Armour Institute Library School. This had been organized three years earlier with a one-year course which had almost immediately been extended to the second year. The Wisconsin school, established in 1906, was the eighth such school to be founded. It was an outgrowth of the Wisconsin Summer School of Library Science which the Free Library Commission had established in 1895. But this was by no means the only evidence of the brilliant leadership of Frank A. Hutchins of the Free Library Commission. He had attracted the attention of librarians all over the country by the development of the rural traveling library idea and by the establishment of the Legislative Reference Library. The work thus begun was carried forward by Henry Legler, who became secretary of the commission in 1904. Legler laid the foundations for the new library school before leaving for a magnificent career as head of the Chicago public library system. In 1905 the legislature provided an appropriation to the commission to establish a "school of library science." The course hitherto given by the commission during the summers was lengthened to a year and the name Wisconsin Summer School of Library Science was changed to the Wisconsin Library School.

Four years later, in 1909, the legislature authorized the regents to cooperate with the school and to aid it with University funds. This step was taken in 1911. The school, while continuing to be administered by the Free Library Commission, thus definitely became part of the University.[45]

From the start the Library School took the sound view that general education was the best foundation for a successful career in public libraries—the field chosen for emphasis. But it did not seem feasible to insist on the ideal plan of a four-year college course as the indispensable preparation for a one- or two-year technical training program. The school, both before and after its integration into the University, admitted candidates to its one-year course by examination. It also introduced a four-year

---

[44] Mary Wright Plummer, "The Columbia College School of Library Economy from a Student's Standpoint," *Library Journal*, 12:363–364 (September-October, 1887).   [45] *Regents' Biennial Report*, 1915–16, p. 258.

program which included the necessary minimum technical training and which led to the bachelor of science degree in the College of Letters and Science. Under this arrangement a student spent his first two years in the regular freshman and sophomore work of the College of Letters and Science and substituted, in his last two years, twenty hours of technical courses in the Library School. In 1914 the plan was modified to develop a more professional attitude among candidates. This involved the completion of general education, including the major in the English department, during the first three years and, usually, an additional summer session, and the allocation of virtually the whole program in the senior year to the school. But the total credits for Library School courses remained at twenty, and the work of the senior year included the preparation of a thesis in the Letters and Science major department, English; the bibliographical part of the thesis was acceptable in fulfillment of the school's requirement in this type of training. Thus the combined course required the equivalent of at least 130 credits.

The school resembled other library schools in emphasizing field and apprentice work. A minimum of actual library experience was required for registration, and during February and March classes were suspended while students worked in the public libraries of the state. This not only provided needed practical experience but exemplified the Wisconsin Idea of bringing to the public agencies of the state the new specialized techniques and points of view being developed at the University. The school also pioneered in the development of courses for the training of legislative reference librarians and was quick to follow the new national trend of placing specially trained personnel in high school libraries. Under Director Matthew S. Dudgeon and his successor, Director Clarence B. Lester, and Preceptor Mary Hazeltine, the school proved invaluable in preparing trained librarians not only for Wisconsin but for other states as well.

DESPITE the intention of the founders to provide for the adequate training of teachers for the state, this lagged behind other developments in the University until the twentieth century. At Wisconsin, as elsewhere, the field of education was given grudging recognition. This did not, however, prevent the department of education, established in 1884, from developing, in the first two decades of the twentieth century, the same specialization and professionalization that characterized departments or schools of education in other universities. Indeed, it is hardly too much to say that no field was proliferated and professionalized to the extent that education was. At the turn of the century the history of education, educational theory—which was often little more than a somewhat sophisticated discussion of practice, and teacher training through observation and practice constituted the principal work of both the normal schools and the rising departments of education in universities. But thanks to the work of William James, G. Stanley Hall, J. M. Cattell, and Edward L. Thorndike, educational psychology made rapid strides in the next decade; educational administration, tests and measurements, and the social aspects of education all entered the scene. In 1905, G. H. Locke urged the investigation of school systems by outside agencies, and in 1911 the first school survey at Montclair was carried through. Thorndike's *Theory of Mental and Social Measurements,* published in 1904, introduced statistical techniques that were rapidly to be refined and extended by Henry H. Goddard, Lewis M. Terman, Fred Kuhlmann, Robert M. Yerkes, Olga Bridgman, and others. In 1916 Dewey's *Democracy and Education,* which brought together the results of theories and experiments in social education, marked an important point in educational development.

Wisconsin reflected and contributed to many of these developments. The approach of the department was fully abreast of the new tendencies in emphasizing the study of education not only in relation to its history and its functions in contemporary society but in terms of its relationships to the auxiliary fields of psychology and philosophy. The study of educational administration was put on a sound basis with the coming in 1905 of Edward Charles Elliott. Elliott's recently accepted dissertation at Teachers College, Columbia, on *Some Fiscal Aspects of Public Education in American Cities* was one of the first two studies to apply to school administration the new statistical procedures. Elliott was also one of three educators who conducted the survey of the Boise schools in 1912, one of the first three such surveys. Meantime he had published his important books on state and city school systems and on supervision and was pursuing scientifically inspired investigations of the costs of educational systems. When Elliott left Wisconsin in 1916 to become chancellor of the University of Montana he was one of the leading authorities on educational administration and was on the threshold of an even more important career in research and administration—he was to become president of Purdue in 1922.

But Elliott was not alone in representing the new scientific study of education. Daniel Starch, who took his doctorate in 1906 with Seashore at Iowa, came to Wisconsin in 1908 and before his departure in 1920 for Harvard had published *Experiments in Educational Psychology, Educational Measurements, Educational Psychology,* and his path-finding book on *Advertising.* The department also profited from the brief stay of Walter F. Dearborn, who published while he was in Madison his pioneer study, *Psychology of Reading,* and who began his work in the group testing of intelligence. V. A. C. Henmon, trained, as Elliott and Dearborn were, at Columbia, came to Wisconsin in 1910, succeeded Elliott as director for the teachers' training course in 1916, and did important original work in tests and measurements. The staff was too much burdened with instruction to carry on as extensive and intensive original work as the faculties of some professional schools of education were doing, but it nevertheless attracted attention to its researches in the field of administration and in the testing and measurement of progress in school studies.[46]

In 1908 the department implemented recent state legislation by setting up a new special course in the training of teachers. This led to the University teacher's certificate, which enabled its holder to receive from the state superintendent a license to teach for one year in any public school of Wisconsin. Such a teacher might, after two years' successful service, receive an unlimited state certificate. The new course, which assumed as a

[46] *Ibid.,* 74–78.

prerequisite a sound general education, was open only to students who had completed two years of college work. It comprised, in addition to a major and a minor field of concentration in given academic subjects, professional training by means of courses in psychology and education and specialized departmental courses in the teaching of the major subject. In addition the training included observation in the Madison schools. This was supplemented by practice teaching when the Wisconsin High School was established in 1911. The professional requirements in the course were augmented in 1916. In addition to the undergraduate course, an advanced course, based on one semester of resident graduate work or on graduate work through two summer sessions, opened the way to higher degrees.

The rapid development of the new course made inevitable the movement for transforming the department into the School of Education. In June, 1919, the Board of Regents authorized the establishment of a School of Education within the College of Letters and Science. The faculty consisted not only of the department of education and teachers in the Wisconsin High School, but also of instructors in charge of departmental teachers' courses and other courses required for the University teacher's certificate. The school emphasized both the professional preparation of teachers of general high-school subjects and the training of teachers in the industrial and applied arts, agriculture, home economics, physical education, and supervised recreation. All these specialities had been developing rapidly in the high schools of Wisconsin as they had been throughout the country. The need for training in these new fields had long been felt and, indeed, was partly met in the preceding decade. The school also included the Bureau of Educational Research, an agency for coordinating and facilitating research with particular reference to the public schools in the state. The bureau provided research facilities and issued bulletins and reports of investigations. The organization of the School of Education also gave new impetus to graduate work on the master's and doctor's levels.

The solution thus worked out meant that the School of Education did not enjoy the complete autonomy of the colleges of engineering, law, agriculture, and medicine. But the assumption that education, as an art and a science, rested on competence in the subjects to be taught made the association with the College of Letters and Science both logical and advisable. While the school was in no sense without influence in the University, it did not enjoy as much power over general educational matters as did the independent schools in some universities. However, the policy of having special methods courses in given subject-matter fields closely geared to the departments meant less friction between the academic group and the professional educational staff than existed in many institutions. The school was somewhat further restricted, in relation to comparable schools in many states, by the well-entrenched teachers colleges, of which there were considerably more than in most states comparable in population. The relations between the school and the department of public instruction have been discussed elsewhere; it may be recalled that this state agency was both militant and influential in the educational affairs of the state.

FROM the very start, and throughout the period, the defined purposes of graduate study emphasized the acquisition of "a larger and more thorough acquaintance with the scholarship and research of the world" than could be obtained in undergraduate courses. "It seeks to awaken in the minds of capable men and women an appreciation of high scholarship, research, and the advancement of learning," not only that they might extend the boundaries of knowledge, but also that they might more effectively aid in the promulgation of knowledge. The work of the Graduate School, in other words, while opening avenues to the pursuit of "pure research" at the same time was "in large part planned with reference to the needs of those who desired to fit themselves for the higher positions in the work of education."[47] Thus the development of graduate work during

[47] *University Catalogue,* 1905–06, p. 383.

the first two and a half decades of the twentieth century was an important aspect of the proliferation of general education.

It will be recalled that prior to 1895 graduate work was conducted by the several departments without any special arrangement for cooperation. Graduate instruction had grown out of advanced undergraduate instruction. It had begun with one or two Letters and Science departments and involved senior courses ("for graduates and undergraduates") and a seminary. It was carried on by regular Letters and Science professors and involved no budgetary changes. In 1895 the committee on graduate study was organized. At a meeting in January, 1904, it recommended organization of a graduate school, to be administered by a standing faculty committee. The regents at once approved the recommendation which the faculty meantime had accepted.[48]

Professor Comstock, director of the Washburn Observatory, assumed the chairmanship of the administrative committee of the school at an annual salary of $250. In his effort to create a real rather than a nominal graduate school, Comstock was handicapped by the growing opposition in influential circles to graduate instruction and research. In 1905 the legislature declared that no additional schools were to be established without its consent, and this action was no doubt related to the disapproval of the way in which the Graduate School had been established. Comstock also encountered the growing opposition to expenditures for research and to the large number of out-of-state students, many of whom came to Wisconsin for graduate study. Not deterred by these obstacles, Comstock pointed out in a memorandum presented to President Van Hise in 1906 that the school already had more students than the colleges of law and agriculture and that it should, therefore, have its dean.[49]

The regents, however, contented themselves with giving Comstock the title of director. This he held until 1914, when he was made dean. Meantime, in 1910, he had succeeded in obtaining

[48] Minutes of the Graduate Committee, 1:105–106, January 9, 1904, Graduate Office, University of Wisconsin; Records of the Board of Regents, F:127, January 19, 1904.

[49] Comstock to Van Hise, March 27, 1906, Comstock Papers, Department of Astronomy.

the status of a separate faculty for those giving graduate instruction. The graduate committee was abolished and replaced by a small committee advisory to the director and a large deliberative body identical with the graduate faculty.[50] The newly created but still dubious graduate school was, as Dean Sellery has picturesquely described it, a sort of bootleg affair. In his report for the 1913–1914 biennium, Comstock was happily able to announce that by regent action the graduate faculty now exercised powers comparable to those of college faculties with reference to undergraduate studies.[51] The Graduate School, however, still had no budget of its own. Professorial salaries were still paid by the respective colleges. The decision not to create a separate budget and a regularly established separate school rested on several considerations: general opposition to what seemed to some the introduction of a caste system and the fear that a separate budget for graduate work might attract the fire of critics of advanced studies. Furthermore, the absence of such a budget protected the University from the charge that the law of 1905, forbidding the establishment of any new college without the consent of the legislature, had been violated.

Comstock's contributions to the development of the Graduate School were in no sense confined to his persistent struggle to win status and power for it. He bent every effort to improve standards without closing his eyes to needs and realities and without sacrificing the valuable tradition of flexibility which departmental jurisdiction in many aspects of graduate instruction implied. Thus shortly after its organization the Graduate School, recognizing that it was impossible for many teachers and clergymen desiring a higher degree to devote full time to study, provided for the candidacy for the master of arts degree partly in absentia. In the years preceding the first World War the University was urged in various quarters to increase its facilities for graduate credit in absentia and to permit a larger use of such work for the higher degrees. The American Association of Universities recommended that the resident work for the master's degree be not less than five summer sessions or its equiva-

---

[50] *Regents' Biennial Report*, 1909–10, p. 197.   [51] *Ibid.*, 1913–14, p. 252.

lent in semesters. The graduate faculty, after discussing these opposing and conflicting tendencies, and after reviewing its own experience over a decade, decided to continue its policy of granting the master's degree for work equally divided between residence work and work done in absentia. Less than ten per cent of the master's degrees granted over a decade represented this category; and in view of this and of experience, the school decided to maintain its own standards and its own policy of flexibility.[52]

In the interest of maintaining high standards the background equipment of students entering the Graduate School from colleges with lower prerequisites for the first degree was frequently the subject of discussion. Such students were required to make up undergraduate deficiencies; but in the administration of this some concession was made to those whose graduate work proved to be eminently successful. In 1910 the preliminary examination, or an equivalent test, was set up for all candidates for the doctorate. This was to be held normally about a year prior to the final examination for the degree. "It is the purpose of this test to insure the candidates breadth of attainment and ripeness for the intensive work that should especially characterize the last year of candidacy for the doctorate."[53] At about the same time courses leading to the doctorate were reclassified. In 1914–1915 the requirements for the doctorate were revised. This involved a group organization of related departments, greater coordination in the various parts of the program for the degree of doctor of philosophy, and the distribution of responsibility for a candidate among several professors, including professors in the minor field or fields.

From time to time the Graduate School gave consideration to the policy of requiring publication of the thesis as a prerequisite for the doctorate. The general emphasis on flexibility within a frame of standards characterized Wisconsin practice. In 1908 the Graduate School formalized procedures by permitting a candidate whose thesis had been accepted either to deposit the required number of printed copies at the University Library or to file a copy of the thesis with an abstract certified as suitable

[52] *Ibid.,* 1915–16, pp. 236–237.   [53] *Ibid.,* 1909–10, p. 197.

for publication and to deposit fifty dollars which would be refunded upon publication of the thesis within two years. Otherwise the deposit would be forfeited and used for the publication of the abstract by the University.[54] In 1910 provision was made by which a candidate might, in place of depositing one hundred copies of his dissertation, deposit six copies if it had been printed in scholarly periodicals, or in the University series, or in bound volumes bearing the imprint of an approved publisher. In 1915 the University undertook to publish a series of thesis abstracts, the cost of which was to be paid from deposits hitherto required to secure publication. Candidates were further given one year in which to file one hundred printed copies. If they failed their deposits were forfeited.[55]

The steady increase in the number of graduate students, both in the regular sessions and in summer school, resulted from several factors. The growing reputation of the University as a research center; the opportunities provided in an ever larger number of scholarships and fellowships; the availability of more and more teaching assistantships as the undergraduate student enrollment multiplied; the bonuses offered by high schools; and the positions open to holders of higher degrees in industry and in the growing institutions of higher learning—all these considerations helped explain the growth of enrollment in the regular terms from 148 in 1905 to 377 in 1912 and to 507 in 1920. In 1925 over 900 students were pursuing graduate studies during the regular sessions. In 1905 thirty-four master's degrees and ten doctor's degrees were conferred; in 1910, 110 master's degrees and 18 doctor's degrees; in 1920, 164 master's degrees and 34 doctorates. Five years later, in 1925, 80 received the doctorate and over 300 the master's degree. As the period ended, in 1925, the University had conferred altogether 748 doctorates since Van Hise received the first one in 1892 and over 3,200 master's degrees. It was, in a sense, mass production. Yet the University took pride, justifiably, in the standard of graduate work which had been built up and maintained.

The great majority of the higher degrees continued to be

[54] Minutes of the Graduate Committee, 2:65–66, March 27, 1908.

[55] *Ibid.*, 2:266, April 26, 1915; Records of the Board of Regents, I:348–349, October 13, 1915.

awarded for work based on the offerings of departments in the College of Letters and Science, but an increasing number took their graduate work in engineering and agriculture. Even the degrees within the frame of Letters and Science represented in considerable measure vocational degrees, for they were worked for and treasured with professional ends clearly in mind.

Perhaps the greatest weakness of the Graduate School lay in the fact that it had no budget of its own and virtually no research funds under its control. In the biennium of 1914–1916 the College of Letters and Science received for the first time a stipulated sum for research ($10,000 and $15,000). This, of course, was allocated in support of work which directly affected graduate investigation. The annual grants were increased so that by the end of the period they had reached something like $25,000. A step of great importance was taken when the legislature began to make annual grants of between $50,000 and $60,000 for research, to be allocated by the dean in conjunction with the research committee appointed by the president. In 1930 Professor Kimball Young, in an elaborate report, demonstrated that the bulk of the money went to projects in the natural sciences. However deficient these research sums were, and however unsatisfactory their distribution was to scholars concerned with the social sciences and the humanities, a new era opened when regular sums for research in subjects with no obviously immediate and practical applications were forthcoming.

Dean Comstock retired in 1920 and was succeeded by Charles Sumner Slichter, a distinguished mathematician and a capable administrator. Dean Slichter's administration, which continued until 1934, represented a steady development without any radically new departures.

Such, then, was the story of graduate study at Wisconsin. Scholars trained in the Graduate School were well scattered over the country by the opening of the first World War; many were in educational or government posts in the Orient and in Latin America. To the larger world the University was known principally by the products of its Graduate School. Wisconsin citizens might and perhaps did raise their eyebrows from time to time—

many certainly would have had they known the titles of some of the dissertations and the monographs turned out by the faculty of the Graduate School. Fortunately President Van Hise did not have to justify in concrete terms his contention that research even in the less obviously practical fields was full of benefits— or potential benefits—for the people of the state. The opposition to the emphasis on research gradually melted away: by the end of the first quarter of the twentieth century it had all but disappeared. During the same period other state universities had likewise forged ahead in the training of research scholars and men and women equipped to offer instruction in the smaller colleges. But Wisconsin was well abreast of the movement.

In the effort to maintain an equilibrium between knowledge and culture in terms of personal enrichment and an indefinable social utility on the one hand and, on the other, education and research applicable immediately to practical problems, the College of Letters and Science neither succeeded nor failed. It did not succeed because general education steadily retreated before the pressures and demands of professionalization and specialization. In view of the prevailing philosophy of those who governed the University and of those who provided the constituency of the college, anything like an equilibrium satisfactory to the exponents of the cultural values as such was impossible. But neither was the Wisconsin effort to achieve a synthesis of theoretical and practical knowledge a failure. The college never became a short-cut vocational school. Even the most clearly defined preprofessional courses did demand some part of liberal education. Even the researches that were most sensitively geared to *ad hoc* problems rested on a broad and deep foundation in the theoretical aspects of the relevant divisions of knowledge. It could also be said in all fairness that the boundaries of knowledge were extended, often in significant ways, as a result of the fact that theory and practice walked hand in hand. What was really indicated, at the end of the Van Hise–Birge period, was a redefinition of objectives, procedures, and programs as well as topics for research, a redefinition in terms of a new chapter in intellectual history and the new threshold on which the state, the nation, and the world stood.

11.

The College of Agriculture

THE 1880's at Wisconsin were stormy years for agricultural education and research. It will be recalled that the move in 1884–85 for a separate agricultural school, divorced from the University and practical and popular rather than theoretical and academic, almost carried the day. This plan not only had the support of leading agriculturalists but was even abetted by William Arnon Henry, professor of agriculture. Those in the University who were favorably inclined toward the idea of practical training, either at Madison or elsewhere, had little idea of how to achieve it, for vocational education was only in its beginnings. Much energy was also frittered away in the conflict between those favoring a self-supporting model farm and those wanting one which would be equipped to attack concrete problems by empirical investigations and by inductive researches in the basic sciences.

If the eighties were years of storm and confusion, they were also years of far-reaching, constructive decisions.[1] The argument that agricultural education had more to gain in the long run from an intimate association with the University carried the day, and in 1885 a final blow was struck at the agitation for a separate school. Its champions did, however, win some of the main points for which they had contended. Wisconsin set herself earnestly

[1] For a detailed discussion of the problems and decisions of the eighties, see Volume I, pp. 459 ff.

A Faculty Group, College of Agriculture

Seated: Ocock, Woll, Henry, Babcock, Farrington, Alexander. *Standing:* Russell, Humphrey, Hart, Whitson, Otis

An Early Class in Cheesemaking, about 1895

to the task of taking to the farmers of the state the best prevailing agricultural practices. In the year that the move to set up a separate agricultural school failed, provision was made for farmers' institutes. Such meetings at which college staffs offered popular instruction in agriculture had been launched about 1870 in both Kansas and Massachusetts, and the movement had spread to other states. Closely knit to the agricultural group at the University and successful from the very start, the institutes offered a down-to-earth way of serving farmers through popularizing new knowledge and superior practices.[2]

In 1886 it was decided, again in deference to the champions of practical training, to offer a short course at the University each winter. Here Wisconsin was truly pioneering, for this was the first course of its kind in the country. The short course was to be open to any young man who had attended the common schools and was intended to be as practical as possible. With the best intentions in the world, however, it was hard for Henry and his colleagues, all trained in the academic mold, to implement the idea of a practical education in which barely literate boys might learn the principles of scientific farming on the activity level where they could operate effectively. John Dewey's philosophy of learning by doing had not yet been formulated. There was, to be sure, some tradition for such action in the all-but-forgotten Fellenberg and Pestalozzian movements of the second quarter of the century; but at best, vocational education was all but unknown. The failure of the short course to attract immediate interest was, however, only partly the result of the fact that no one knew what actual teaching methods could and should be adopted. The dearth of students in the first years also reflected the indifference of farmers and, equally important, their fear that any contact with academic walls might wean boys away from the farm. Nevertheless the staff was at least honestly committed to find ways and means for building a program truly functional in character. The decision to inaugurate the short course did not affect the established but largely ignored four-year program based on the sciences and cultural disciplines. De-

[2] For a discussion of the farmers' institutes, see the chapters on extension.

signed to provide a general education as well as special training in the theory and technique of agriculture, this course represented continuity with the largely barren past.

These were by no means the only far-reaching decisions made in the eighties. In establishing the Experiment Station in 1883 the regents and the legislature seemed to favor the program of basic investigations rather than that of a mere demonstration farm. The outlook for empirical investigations and for field and laboratory experimentation of a fundamental sort brightened with the regularization of state appropriations for the station and with the passage in 1887 of the Hatch Act, which brought federal funds for research. Thus several timely decisions more or less solved the troublesome conflicts and at last gave the interested parties a sense of direction if not an actual blueprint to work by. The final decision provided for a College of Agriculture within the University. Two years later, in 1889, the department of agriculture became the College of Agriculture.

ℐ

No SINGLE factor explains the outstanding success of the new college in the first fifteen years of its life. It owed something to the push President Chamberlin gave to research in the agricultural sciences. It owed a good deal to the farm spokesmen on the Board of Regents. Much of the success could be laid at the door of Hiram Smith and of William Dempster Hoard. Hoard, founder of the Wisconsin Dairymen's Association, editor of the leading farm magazine, and sponsor of the farmers' institutes, ardently championed scientific farming, gave the college invaluable support, posed problems of research, and effected an indispensable liaison between the college and the farmers in the state. The achievements of the college likewise owed much to a remarkable staff and to the teamwork it maintained. But no one can doubt the prime debt of the college to William A. Henry, first director of the Experiment Station and first dean.

Henry's background and personality were major assets. Born and reared on a farm, he had put himself through the first year of college at Ohio Wesleyan. At Cornell University, he earned his tuition and keep, his struggle with poverty reducing him for a time to sleeping on the floor of the botany laboratory where he worked as an assistant. In 1880 he completed the agricultural course, and that year Wisconsin called him to a professorship. Despite his college education and his thirty years he appeared to the farmers with whom he at once made contact as a mere rustic stripling. His shrewdness in exploiting his farm background and struggle with poverty was unexcelled. He never missed an opportunity of making friends with farmers he encountered in train coaches, and of course he wore his boots, overalls, and work jacket at the run-down University farm where anyone could see him introducing efficient management. Moreover he was to be seen in the same garb as he talked to endless gatherings of stockbreeders, dairymen, and horticulturalists. He did not bother to dress up even when he appeared before the appropriation committees in the legislature. On all these occasions he spoke bluntly in the vernacular, his vigorous talk punctuated with dramatic, quotable phrases, the more intriguing because of their cutting overtones. Yet all this was no mere opportunism and make-believe, for Henry was a man of fearless honesty and integrity. No one doubted his sincerity in identifying himself as he did with the farmers; his interest was theirs and theirs was his. Added to this ability was a boundless, contagious enthusiasm for whatever he thought might better the lot of the farmers, be it the introduction of sheep farming, the cultivation of sugar beets, or the opening up of the cutover areas of northern Wisconsin to settlers.

No less important than his background and personality in explaining his successful leadership was his grassroot practicality. An ardent champion of cooperation among agriculturalists, he spared no effort in showing the feasibility of this approach. But above all he carried to every corner of the state the gospel that scientific farming is economically sound. We shall see that the success of extension work and of the short course owed much to his unqualified belief in popularizing the findings of research and to his own skill in demonstration teaching. From the very start he realized that farmers had to be convinced that the agricultural department was an eminently serviceable agency. At the outset of his Wisconsin career he cajoled the legislature into granting the first appropriation for any sort of research in the University—the modest sum of $4,000 for investigating the ensilage of fodders and the manufacture of sugar from sorghum cane. His success in both projects was impressive. As a result of his experiments farmers saw the value of silage in feeding livestock and constructed more silos than were to be found in any other state. The farmers' confidence in Henry was deepened by a series of investigations all clearly fruitful. These included experiments in livestock feeding which showed that better hogs resulted from combining nitrogenous feed with corn; in superior methods for measuring butterfat in milk and for curing cheese; formulae for fighting blights and for combating pests and tuberculosis in herds; proof that mutton sheep could be profitably raised through the use of rape as a forage plant. Each practical success at the Experiment Station added to Henry's influence, which became almost legendary. Thus, for example, one farmer, in asking for an unusual type of aid, wrote, "I see you can do almost anything."[3] No mark of confidence, however, was more telling than his early election to the presidency of the Wisconsin Dairymen's Association.

The demonstrated value of the Experiment Station, important though it was in explaining Henry's success as a lobbyist, did not tell the whole story. In seeking appropriations he never failed to point out that they were in no way designed to promote his personal advantage or that of his associates. His reputation for integrity and for having no interest other than that of the farmers themselves reinforced the utilitarian arguments he could muster with greater effectiveness as the years brought one success after another.

The financial support of the college and the station, which seldom satisfied Dean Henry, was nevertheless impressive. There was rarely any occasion to complain about the allocation of University funds, for the College of Agriculture had its full share.

[3] E. S. Helderman to William A. Henry, undated, cited in Wilbur H. Glover's manuscript, The History of the College of Agriculture, on which this entire chapter is largely based.

Only on one occasion did Henry put up a fight within the University itself. In 1894 he successfully opposed a plan to reduce the share of the college from one third to one fourth of the regular mill-tax income.[4] Naturally he used his skill as a lobbyist in behalf of the college and the station, but he was also ready to lend a hand for augmenting general University appropriations when this could be done without jeopardizing the interests of the college. Henry was chiefly responsible for the special legislative appropriations which resulted in a far more generous budget than that of any other department of the University. In addition to barns, greenhouses, the residence of the dean, and a heating plant, Henry's administration saw the construction of eight buildings. Among these was the stately Agricultural Hall, unrivaled anywhere at the time of its completion in 1903. The Hill Farm, purchased in 1896 and later enlarged, was an object of pride. Dean Henry also obtained a ten-week annual vacation for the staff, but he himself refused to take advantage of it. We have already noted his success in winning, in 1881, the first legislative appropriation for research in the entire University. Appropriations for other projects followed. The means for research provided by the Hatch Act (1887) not only put the station on its feet but brought results which were invaluable when further approaches were made to the legislature. The second Morrill Act (1890) was another boon. Dean Henry's final legislative triumph, however, was his part in the passage of the Adams Act (1906) which brought, ultimately, an annual grant of $15,000 for research. It would have been easy, in view of the relatively generous support which the college and station enjoyed, to expand the program, for there was a legitimate demand for agronomy, poultry husbandry, and a veterinary department. But Dean Henry wisely resisted such pressures, insisting that it was better to do a few main jobs well than to attempt more than could be adequately supported with the available funds.

In his relations with his colleagues, Dean Henry was hardly less successful than he was with farm folk and agricultural

---

[4] Records of the Board of Regents, D:290, July 30, 1894.

leaders. He possessed an almost uncanny gift for making the right appointments. Stephen M. Babcock, Franklin H. King, and Emmett S. Goff, three of his early choices, were investigators of recognized merit. Fritz W. Woll, John A. Craig, William L. Carlyle, John W. Decker, Edward H. Farrington, and Ransom A. Moore, together with their colleagues, contributed to the growth of a remarkable teamwork. It is true that toward the end of Henry's administration there was resentment of a certain unreasonableness, a dictatorial bent, and an unreadiness to delegate authority; but his behavior was properly attributed to nervous exhaustion and overwork. More serious, however, was the charge, lodged by George N. Knapp, assistant professor of farm engineering, that he imposed needless red tape on staff members when supplies were to be ordered, divided the faculty into factions, and especially that he mishandled college finances. It will be recalled that Dean Henry asked for Knapp's resignation and that the University upheld this action. A legislative committee investigated the whole controversy, but its report revealed little to confirm any really serious criticism. The editor of the *Wisconsin State Journal* no doubt expressed a consensus in concluding that "Dean Henry's fame is secure. He will continue to be honored by the state for which he has done so much."[5]

THE idea of an experiment station was not new when Wisconsin established its station in 1883. In England the famous Rothamsted station had been active since 1843, while in Germany the even more noted station established in 1852 by the great agricultural chemist, Justus Liebig, boasted a notable record of success in both empirical and inductive investigations. Maryland's legislature established an agricultural college and provided for experimentation on the college farm as early as 1856. But the real beginnings in America date rather from the establishment in 1862 of the federal Department of Agriculture

[5] *Wisconsin State Journal,* March 19, 21, 1906; see also Volume II, pp. 173 ff.

which encompassed field research from the very start. Ten years later, the Commissioner of Agriculture called a convention of representatives of the recently launched land-grant colleges. This meeting recommended the establishment of experiment stations in the colleges. Connecticut and California proceeded at once to establish such stations. North Carolina, New York, and New Jersey followed in the next few years. Thus the decision in 1883 to set up an experiment station at the University of Wisconsin was merely part of a movement already well under way. Although Professor William Willard Daniells had tried his hand at a few investigations, agricultural research at the University really dates from the founding of the Experiment Station.

Managed at first by a committee made up of Professors Trelease, Armsby, and Henry, the Experiment Station was modestly housed in South Hall. In 1888 Henry was made director, a position he kept until his retirement in 1907. With solid financial support, augmented, as we have seen, by both state and federal funds, with steadily improving equipment in the laboratories, greenhouses, and barns, with a staff both imaginative and practical, and with the intimate associations with the farmers of the state who set problems and cooperated in scientific attacks on them, the Experiment Station continued to move from success to success.

Yet the task of convincing the farmers of the necessity of a scientific approach in agriculture was often difficult. Indeed, the close contact with farmers and their leaders, so fruitful in many respects, was sometimes disadvantageous. Experimentation occasionally suffered by reason of deference to the conventions of farming. In its early stages the Experiment Station was embarrassed by the expectation and even the demand that the University Farm show an operating profit. The understandable desire of Dean Henry and many of his colleagues to succeed by practical standards sometimes led to short cuts disastrous to carefully controlled, long-range, inductive investigations. When Babcock initiated what were to become extremely significant nutrition experiments, William Carlyle, in charge of the carefully selected station herd, was unwilling to have his beautiful heifers fed single-ration diets. Confirmed in his fears when one of the two cows selected died, he insisted on withdrawing the other and nursing it back to health.[6] In another experiment designed to test the popular belief that salt is an essential in milk production, the sick cows were restored to health by dosages of salt so that, while it was clear that salt was necessary to the well-being of cows, it was not clear that deprivation meant death.[7] Frank Kleinheinz, the station shepherd, likewise saw no reason why he should jeopardize his flock of prize-winning sheep and the outstanding success of his practical manual on sheep management by acceding to the demands of the biochemists.[8] It is not hard to understand how the desire of expert stockbreeders to develop perfect demonstration herds resulted in refusals to cooperate in theoretical investigations which threatened to ruin results developed only by great effort. Many on the station staff shared the impatience of Carlyle and Kleinheinz with the slow, obscure, and painful methods of experimental science.

In consequence of the importance usually attached to empirical methods, problems were frequently attacked with inadequate equipment and controls or undertaken altogether too lightly. Remedies were often hastily tried without regard either to thoroughness or to full understanding. This was true, for example, of Henry's efforts, begun in 1881 and resumed a decade later, to find a remedy for corn smut by treating the seed with copper sulphate, carbolic acid, and sulphur, with negative results. In other experiments, notably in the efforts to churn sweet and sour cream, the desire for quick, usable results no doubt led to a neglect of important elements in the controls. And sometimes, at the most critical juncture, the pressure against sacrificing a prize-winning herd to the imperatives of the inductive method was hard to resist. Henry brought himself only by a supreme effort and at the cost of great anguish to

[6] Paul de Kruif, *Hunger Fighters* (New York, 1928), 280–284; Stephen M. Babcock to de Kruif, October 10, 1927, cited in Wilbur H. Glover's manuscript, The History of the College of Agriculture.

[7] *Twenty-Second Annual Report of the Agricultural Experiment Station of the University of Wisconsin*, 1905, pp. 129–137.

[8] A. S. Alexander, History of the Wisconsin Experiment Station, manuscript, 91–92, Papers of the Dean of the College of Agriculture.

order the slaughtering of the station's prize herd which the new tubercular test indicated was infected: only pathological examinations could prove or disprove the tests.[9]

As the work of the station developed it was guided by a compromise between empirical tests, designed to tell how to solve specific problems, and experimental research, intended to explain why the problems arose. This was true, for example, in Henry's own feeding experiments. These proceeded along two lines. On the one hand he was guided by the "official" method of chemical analysis, which, although it probably seemed empirical enough to Henry, was at best tolerated if not actually distrusted by the empirical school; on the other, he resorted to long-term feeding tests, trying out, for example, feeding corn meal as against whole corn over a ten-year period, in order to check the findings of chemical analysis. The work of Henry and Babcock in dairy procedures was, again, both empirical and experimental.

The shifting of the proper balance between fundamental experimentation and empirical observation can be understood, as Wilbur H. Glover has pointed out in his history of the College of Agriculture, only in terms of the relations of the staff to the farmers of the state. When Henry succeeded in having the station set up in 1883 the confidence of the farmers in scientific investigation was by no means unlimited. In part, but only in part, this was the result of tradition and folkways, of the anti-intellectualism not uncommon in the American temper. But suspicion of laboratory research conducted along inductive lines was not entirely the result of shortsighted prejudices. Unaccompanied by empirical tests, laboratory investigations sometimes had misleading or unfortunate results. For example, devotion to the chemical analysis alone of feeds, without biological observations of their effects, delayed the discovery of vitamins. To cite an impressive example of the importance of supplementing laboratory work by empirical observations, Professor R. H. Chittenden of Yale was justly criticized for permitting the publication by commercial firms of laboratory results indicating the

[9] *Ibid.*

harmlessness of borax as a milk preservative without having determined its effect on the digestion of humans. If the station was to maintain effective relations with farmers, if it was to attack problems of immediate importance, and if it was to enjoy their cooperation in investigation and in popularizing results, it was necessary to accede in part to their misgivings and reservations.

Whatever the advantages and disadvantages of the Wisconsin compromise between empirical and theoretical investigations, between the immediate, ad hoc approaches and the long-range, controlled investigations, the work of the station was impressive. In many respects, including the inauguration of agricultural physics, it broke new ground. Franklin H. King's early efforts to apply the principles of physics to agriculture contributed both to the establishing of courses for the study of soils and to a new type of engineering. King, who had been a pupil of Thomas C. Chamberlin at the Whitewater State Normal School, had shown his originality when, as an assistant on the geological survey, he had begun a study of the economics of birdlife, a project he pushed forward at Cornell by examining the stomachs of 2,000 birds to find out what insects made up their diets.[10] Coming to the college in 1888 as the first American professor of agricultural physics, King inaugurated investigations which led to the construction of round silos, a greatly improved means of providing barn ventilation, and soil studies which made available solutions to problems posed by the long dry spells which had continued into the early 1890's.

As the trail-blazing step in the study of the moisture content in soils, a practical method was required for their mechanical analysis. King showed how by measuring the flow of air through a sample of soil it was possible to determine the effective surface of a unit volume of soil both for holding soil moisture and for the exposure of plant food to solvent action. The investigations included the ingenious weighing of large chunks of earth and the checking of ground water by systems of wells in a variety of soils. Applications of the resulting general principles of soil

[10] "Economic Relations of Wisconsin Birds," Geology of Wisconsin: Survey, 1873–1879, (3 vols., Madison, 1883), 1:476–610.

physics were studied in relation to the influence of subsoiling on soil moisture and the effects of early spring tillage on moisture in comparison with late spring tillage. For the first time root systems were photographically investigated. Studies were made of wind erosion on light soils and methods of prevention discovered. Field experiments on the percolation of irrigation water under varying conditions likewise contributed to knowledge of the effective distribution of water in crop production. Although at one time Dean Henry asked for King's resignation, he subsequently urged support for his work. In 1902, however, King left to accept a position in the United States Bureau of Soils. After leaving that post he prepared his classic, *Farmers of Forty Centuries* (1911), the standard account of methods of maintaining soil fertility in the Orient.[11] Open-minded, keen in powers of observation, and shrewd in his capacity to apply science to the practical problems of farming, King brought great prestige to the station.[12]

Before leaving Wisconsin, King, impressed by the new work in England on nitrogen fixation and by other chemical studies of soils, began significant experimental work on nitrates in plants, together with comparisons of the elemental composition of cropped and nearly virgin soils and the treatment of marsh soils to supply their lack of potassium. These pointed to the later comprehensive survey of Wisconsin soils which Alfred Vivian and A. R. Whitson conducted.[13]

The station horticulturist, Emmett S. Goff, like King, combined scientific investigations with practical applications. In his efforts to promote vegetable and fruit culture in as direct a manner as possible, he tested varieties, surveyed the economic aspects of fruitgrowing, tried out insecticides and sprayers, examined means of preserving orchards, and grew thousands of native plum seedlings in his search for a variety suitable to the Wisconsin climate. Investigations in the morphology of straw-

---

[11] King's writings included *The Soil* (1895), which was translated into Chinese and influenced a great part of the agricultural world, *Irrigation and Drainage* (1899), and *A Textbook of the Physics of Agriculture* (1899).

[12] *Reports of the Wisconsin Agricultural Experiment Station*, 1889–1902. L. S. Ivins and A. E. Winship, *Fifty Famous Farmers* (New York, 1924), 3–12; see also Glover. [13] See pp. 419–420.

berry plants laid a basis for the more successful culture of what came to be a valuable cash crop, while investigations of changes occurring during the curing of tobacco led to well-defined, useful results. Goff's repeated experiments over nearly two decades proved the greater vigor of tomato plants grown from fully matured seeds. The horticulturist also worked out a method of planting to achieve greater potato yields. New ways of making use of existing information were evidenced by his device for mechanically emulsifying kerosene and water to control sucking insects and by his tar-paper-disc device for combating maggots in cabbage. Goff's most important theoretical contribution was his observation of the formation and differentiation of the flower buds of fruit trees. These observations not only impressed botanists but were also welcomed by horticulturists, for they materially reduced the amount of guesswork in orchards. The studies of the horticultural department were ably carried on by Goff's successors after his untimely death in 1902.[14]

More spectacular, more commercially profitable, and in some ways more significant from the point of view of lasting results was the work in feeding and dairying in which Henry, Woll, Farrington, Russell, and Babcock collaborated. Stephen Moulton Babcock took his first degree at Tufts in 1866 after which he studied and taught at Cornell. In 1879 Göttingen conferred on him the doctorate in organic chemistry. As chemist at the New York State Agricultural Experiment Station at Geneva from 1882 to 1887 he observed phenomena which led him to question the dependability of prevailing methods of determining the nutritive value of foodstuffs. Jovial, hearty, fond of sports, preferring to whittle a piece of apparatus rather than to have it made in the machine shop, Babcock with his questioning mind and keen power of observation quickly made a place for himself at Wisconsin, to which he came from the New York Agricultural Experiment Station in 1887. He worked closely with Dean Henry, who, though trained as a botanist, had sensed the importance in a dairy state of feeding problems and had turned his attention to them. Indeed, Henry was among the

[14] *Reports of the Wisconsin Agricultural Experiment Station,* 1883–1901. L. H. Bailey, ed. *Cyclopedia of American Agriculture,* IV (1909), 576.

earliest agriculturalists to investigate the effect of proteins and minerals on the growth of farm stock. His studies, in which he was aided by a young chemist, Fritz W. Woll, included the effects of silage, dairy by-products, and other materials in feeding stock. In 1898 his *Feeds and Feeding* was published. Despite the shortcomings which subsequent new approaches were to reveal, this was a notable achievement. The youngest of the group was Harry L. Russell. After taking his first two degrees at Wisconsin, Russell worked in Europe with Koch and Pasteur, carried on investigations at the Zoological Station in Naples, and returned to Madison in 1893 to accept an assistant professorship in bacteriology. Before the decade was over his publications in agricultural bacteriology had won him nationwide recognition. These men turned their attention especially to the problems posed by the great development of the dairy interest throughout the state.

The most spectacular and widely publicized contribution was, of course, the development of an efficient milk-fat test. For a long time William D. Hoard and other enlightened dairymen had been gravely concerned over the ill effects of the prevailing practice of selling milk to creameries by weight alone. This opened the way to all sorts of inefficiency and fraud. Cheese factories and creameries were paying the same rate for milk high in butterfat as they did for an inferior product. This was naturally discouraging to producers who prided themselves on building up herds capable of yielding milk with a high butterfat content, and tended to encourage indifference among less enterprising and less scientifically-minded farmers. Worse, the prevailing practice of selling milk by weight alone was an invitation to dishonest dairymen to skim or water milk before taking it to the creamery. Honest producers, rightly indignant, were already refusing to take their product to creameries. In Dean Henry's words, the dairy industry was on the point of "going to pot."

In response to the need for an efficient milk-fat test Dean Henry had encouraged Frederick G. Short, one of the chemists at the station, to devise a method for determining the quality of milk. But the test which Short worked out in 1887 was, like other existing ones, inadequate. Dean Henry urged the new agricultural chemist, Stephen M. Babcock, to try his hand at devising something more practicable. Babcock was thoroughly aware of the need and had, while a member of the staff of the Geneva Agricultural Experiment Station, familiarized himself with existing laboratory milk tests. He also devised a mild viscometer which proved highly useful in dairy investigations. This instrument measured the viscosity of liquids by calculating the friction against a cylinder oscillating in them and enabled an investigator to detect the existence in food products of fats other than butterfat.[15] Sensitive as he was to the need, and well-equipped to undertake the problem by reason of his earlier interest, Babcock set aside laboratory investigations he regarded as more basic and intriguing and began the chore in January, 1890.

The procedure was to find an agent capable of liberating fat globules by dissolving the casein in a test tube and then to separate these by means of centrifugal force. In the beginning ether was used with promising results, but the ether test failed on the milk of an unusually high-grade Jersey, Sylvia. Jovial and lighthearted though he was, Babcock possessed the stubbornness of the true investigator. Not knowing, apparently, that Frederick G. Short had worked with sulphuric acid, he turned to it. Dean Henry, who had been familiar with all that Short did, was certain that Babcock was now on the wrong track. But Babcock discovered that his predecessor had used either too much or too little of the acid, and after making a vast number of tests, he hit on the precise formula. Babcock's contributions to the test which bears his name have been frequently weighed. The test bottle and the centrifuge were by no means new. He himself believed that his principal contribution was the reduction in the time of operation of the centrifuge. With typical modesty Babcock announced that his new test might offer more simplicity and economy in determining the fat content of milk. "Whether

---

[15] *Fifth Annual Report of the Board of Control of the New York Agricultural Experiment Station* (Geneva) 1886, pp. 297 ff.; Harry L. Russell, "The Man of Science, Stephen Moulton Babcock," (Wisconsin Alumni Research Foundation, Madison), 4.

this test will find a place among those already introduced, time alone can decide," he wrote. "In the hope that it may benefit some who are striving to improve their stock and enable creameries to avoid the evils of the present system, the test is given to the public." Actually, Babcock standardized the acid and the measurement of the milk sample, selected the proper characteristics for a simple test, and in so doing displayed the qualities of a great laboratory technician.[16]

The Babcock test caught on at once; it was overdue. Its simplicity, inexpensiveness, and rapidity of manipulation made it far superior to any other. Babcock refused to patent it although urged to do so in the interest of providing further funds for research if he would have none of the profits himself. In no time the Babcock test was known all over the country, and in New Zealand, Australia, and Europe as well. Stephen M. Babcock and the Wisconsin Agricultural Experiment Station had become famous.

The significance of the Babcock test is clear. For the first time the dairy industry possessed an adequate standard by which fair payment for milk could be determined. The manufacture of butter and cheese by factory methods was given a great boost. It was estimated that it saved not less than two tenths of one per cent of the fat, hitherto wasted, of all the milk taken to the Wisconsin creameries. This resulted from the fact that it drove the poor separators out of business and enabled creamery operators to determine the best possible methods for close skimming. The Department of Agriculture in 1900 estimated that it was saving Wisconsin alone not less than $800,000 a year, twice the annual current expenses of the whole University.[17] Nor did this take into account the economic advantages derived from the greatly improved herds which the milk-fat test encouraged. But Babcock's achievement cannot be measured in dollars and cents alone. It had a moral advantage—it was commonly said that the

[16] The test was described in Bulletin 24 of the Wisconsin Agricultural Experiment Station under the title *A New Method for the Estimation of Fat in Milk* (Madison, 1890). For a splendid discussion of the development of the test, see Glover.

[17] A. C. True and V. A. Clark, *The Agricultural Experiment Stations of the United States* (United States Department of Agriculture, Washington, 1900), 460.

test did more to make dairymen honest than the Bible itself.[18]

Many important details in the operation of the Babcock test were developed by painstaking co-workers, especially by Fritz W. Woll and Edward H. Farrington. They worked out the most efficient speed for the centrifuge. Charles S. Slichter assisted in devising tables based on 10,000 analyses which simplified the practical problem of payment for milks of varying richness and churnability. Additional formulae provided easy methods for determining solids other than butterfat in milk. These and other improvements and applications have been overshadowed by the spectacular nature of Babcock's original contribution.

Certainly in the popular mind the milk-fat test has obscured the more fundamental work which Babcock did on the nature of milk and its products. Again, much of this resulted from real and pressing problems in the dairy industry. Methods of extracting cream from milk, based on insufficient knowledge, were far from satisfactory. Back of many improvements in milking practices and in the construction and operation of separators lay patient laboratory and field investigations. The first work Babcock did at Wisconsin was to prove the existence of fibrinogen in milk. Noting a similarity of the grouping of fat globules to that which the fibrination of blood caused, he checked his observation with the blood fibrin test. The next step was the observation that creaming took place most freely when the coagulation caused by the formation of fibrin was slowed down so that the fat globules could rise freely. All this was followed by a far-reaching study of the methods of extracting cream from milk. In the course of his investigations Babcock discovered that the order of milking, stable conditions, and an expeditious procedure were important factors in high production.

The pasteurization of milk was not, of course, new, but satisfactory procedures had not been developed. The customary high heat destroyed the fibrin or other matter holding the fat globules together. Working with the station's bacteriologist, Harry L. Russell, Babcock attacked the problem. Investigations

[18] *Science,* 74:86 (July 24, 1931). See also de Kruif, *Hunger Fighters,* 278 ff., and Glover.

showed that lower heat satisfactorily reduced the number of bacteria without lowering the viscosity of the cream. As a result of these and other studies the first American apparatus was devised for the thorough pasteurization of milk and cream.

The combined attack of the chemists and the bacteriologists on the problem of cheese making led to results of great economic significance. In Russell, Babcock found a collaborator after his own heart. The prevailing methods of cheese making left much to be desired. In the first place chemical tests proved inadequate in locating the cause of the tainted milk which when used at the factories, as it inevitably was, resulted in floating curds and in "huffy cheese." In addition, the hot, dry curing rooms reacted unfavorably on the product, causing it to crack and to take on unpleasant flavors. The evil results were even more striking when the cheese passed from cold storage chambers back into heated stores. The cheese makers, speaking through Hoard, had long expressed the hope that the Experiment Station could provide a scientific basis for cheese curing.

It was clearly necessary to learn by laboratory methods a great deal about the bacteriological and chemical aspects of cheese making. Russell, Babcock, and their collaborators proceeded to do this. After ruling out bacteria as the cause of the breakdown of casein in cheese they sought another agent such as an enzyme. It was later shown that other investigators had, in using heat to destroy the bacteria, also destroyed the enzyme. Because they recognized this probability Babcock and Russell turned to chloroform and ether. Thus they isolated the enzyme which possessed a digestive action on proteid substances and which they named galactase. This discovery, which was reported in 1897, and the related observation of the coordinate influence of the rennet enzyme, pepsin, provided the answers for which the cheese makers had been asking and led to a revolution in the industry. For the discovery of galactase, together with empirical findings in the temperatures of curing rooms, enabled cheese to be produced satisfactorily in temperature as low as twenty-five to thirty degrees. The new cold-curing process permitted the marketing of a product, the quality of which did not vary with temperature changes in cold storage plants and in stores.[19] Meantime the investigators had also developed the Wisconsin curd test which enabled managers to reject hitherto undetectable tainted milk. At the turn of the century it was estimated that the curd test saved Wisconsin cheese makers from $100,000 to $200,000 annually.[20]

The uncertainties in making silage from corn yielded to an application of the methods used in getting to the bottom of the changes in cheese making. It was now possible to test the theory that the respiration of the cut tissues rather than bacterial ferment was responsible for the heating of the corn. The test demonstrated that bacteria were not solely the cause of the ensiling action. In consequence it was clear that improved silos were in order. Fortunately King was already providing the needed improvements in his new designs.

Important though all these contributions were, Russell's discovery of tuberculosis in the station dairy herd was the most sensational aspect of the activities of the bacteriologists. William Carlyle and John A. Craig had developed a sound empirical procedure for improving the herd which had come to be the pride not only of the station but of the whole dairy community. When Russell took up his duties in 1893 the dairy industry had just been aroused to the tuberculosis threat by the tests worked out by Leonard Pearson in Pennsylvania. Dairymen were panic-stricken as some of the choicest herds in the land were reported to be riddled by the disease. Hoard urged careful research and well-considered countermeasures. To Russell's surprise, the first two animals reacted when inoculated with the lymph he and Pearson had brought back from Robert Koch's laboratory. When slaughtered to check the test, both revealed tubercular lesions. The milk of the herd was marketed in Madison and when the great majority reacted positively Russell proposed their slaughter to demonstrate the reliability of the test.[21] When the herd was slaughtered the validity of the test was apparent. Experimental

[19] *14th, 15th, 16th, and 20th Annual Reports of the Wisconsin Agricultural Experiment Station,* 1897, 1898, 1899, 1903; see also Glover.

[20] True and Clark, *The Agricultural Experiment Stations of the United States,* 455-456.

[21] *11th Annual Report of the Wisconsin Agricultural Experiment Station,* 1894, p. 2.

science had triumphed over practical veterinary observations. The station at once undertook the task of meeting requests for testing herds. Short-course students, trained in giving the test, proved useful in its widespread application. At the same time Russell and his associates began laboratory studies of the transmission of tuberculosis through milk. It was found that no organisms were shed into the milk of the tubercular cows unless lesions had occurred in the udder. Experiments designed to determine whether diseased cows transmitted the disease to their offspring proved that, if the calves were at once separated from the mothers, infected cows might be safely used for breeding purposes. All this pointed the way to the establishment of the state laboratories in the interest of improving the herds of the state and safeguarding the public.

Russell, in association with Edwin G. Hastings and Ransom A. Moore, also laid the foundations for the study of soil bacteriology by initiating experiments with nitrogen-fixing bacteria. Effective research in this field began in 1906 with the appointment of Conrad Hoffman, who at once attacked the problem of the interrelations of chemical and bacterial elements in the soil. The tests devised by Emil Truog for determining the amount of acidity in soils had important applications. In studying the problem of liming in relation to the growth of legumes and their symbiotic bacteria, Edwin B. Fred and Edward J. Graul discovered that partial neutralization of the acidity of soils by the addition of lime was more effective than the complete change of the chemical condition.[22] The extension of these and other investigations and the application of findings can be traced in the successive reports of the station.

Let us now consider the work of the station in feeding problems. Trained as a botanist, Henry early turned his attention to livestock nutrition. As early as 1874 Wilbur Olin Atwater of the Maine State College had introduced into the United States the theories of the German school of agricultural chemists, notably those of Emil von Wolff. These theories required the analysis of dry matter and protein, carbohydrate and fat nutrients, and data from the analysis provided feeding standards. Henry Prentiss Armsby's *Manual of Cattle Feeding* (1880) developed these

[22] *Regents' Biennial Report*, 1915–16, pp. 113–114.

theories, and as a member of the staff from 1883 to 1887 Armsby, with Henry, organized tests of various feeds and filled in the tables of feeding standards. Both concluded that chemical analysis alone could not finally fix the value of feeding-stuffs of the same class and both believed that the German feeding standards should be submitted to empirical tests. Henry continued these over a long period, publishing his first results in 1892 and his classic manual, *Feeds and Feeding,* in 1898. It quickly became one of the most widely used texts and reference books in the English language.[23] Henry was among the earliest agriculturists to investigate the effects of proteins and minerals in silage, dairy by-products, and other materials commonly used in feeding stock.

Henry's interests in feeding problems converged with those of Babcock. The director of the Geneva Experiment Station had set Babcock to work at analyzing the intake and excrement of stock, and the young investigator was convinced that virtually nothing was really known about the nutritive aspects of food which stockfeeders had not themselves come to know in the course of their observations and experience. In other words, Babcock questioned the analytical procedure he had learned in Germany. Thus when he came to be on familiar terms with Dean Henry, he did not hesitate to twit him merrily for having relied exclusively on chemical analyses and tables in the preparation of his manual on feeding. Babcock's insatiable curiosity and shrewd skepticism convinced him that prevailing theories, which held that any feed was good if it contained the proper chemical constituents, needed to be checked carefully by controlled feeding experiments. Babcock's hunch that the energy content of foods was an insufficient criterion of their value was at last tested when he was finally given two cows from the station herd as subjects for one of the earliest recorded biological experiments. The cow fed on oats slumped while that given nothing but corn flourished. Since the oat-fed cow had been given all the feed it would consume, Babcock concluded that oats lacked some necessary substance for growth and life which corn possessed. This was the foundation of subsequent investigations, conducted

[23] In 1948 the twenty-first edition, under the authorship of Frank Morrison, was published.

largely by a group of young newcomers, which were to prove revolutionary. Although Babcock played an important role in the later work which, in truth, developed directly out of his initial experiment, the discussion of it may well be postponed since it falls within a new era in the research history of the station.[24]

✒

THE teaching program in the College of Agriculture developed within the already established framework of research on the one hand and extension on the other. This framework, as Glover has demonstrated in his history of the College of Agriculture, exerted a profound influence on the development of the agricultural program. Before any number of students arrived on the campus the Experiment Station and the farmers' institutes were already thriving and they continued to take a major portion of the time and energy of the staff. In addition, the problem of working out practical agricultural instruction had been recognized but in no sense solved when students began to appear in numbers.

The short course posed its own problems. Although its importance was recognized, the staff was at a loss at first to devise a practicable program for the handful of boys who came with no more than grammar school education at best and with virtual illiteracy or incompetency in the English language at worst. An early student recalled that professors casually skipped their classes, sometimes for weeks together, that they found nothing more practical at first for the boys to do than to work at brief stretches on a draining project.[25] Despite their early casual attitude, however, the faculty soon came to recognize that the key to a sound agricultural training lay in the short course, and over the years it has developed into a highly successful program. Laboratory instruction was finally incorporated, new courses were added, and graduates left full of enthusiasm for applying what they had learned, for cooperating with the station in its

[24] See Volume II, pp. 406 ff.
[25] *The Student Farmer*, 1:117–118 (April, 1907), cited by Glover.

research and extension program, and for sending other boys to take advantage of the offerings. In time experience with the short-course type of instruction influenced the long course itself. , The first impetus to any genuine growth in numbers in the short course came from the dairy course. This was established in 1889 partly in response to the report of an English inquirer which indicated that there existed nowhere in the United States any organized dairy instruction and partly as the result of the pressure of Hiram Smith.[26] A dairy house was constructed and a practical course designed to train creamery operators was offered under the direction of Babcock. Only two students appeared the first year. But the publicity attached to the invention of the milk-fat test brought seventy-two students the second year. The new dairy building was filled to capacity with the hundred students that were presently registered. Attendance varied between 100 and 169 until World War I, when a gradual decline began, thanks to the fact that Wisconsin creameries were at last able to train skilled operators and managers by apprenticeship. The course, which Professor Farrington took in hand in 1894, was based on the actual production of Cheddar cheese, fancy print butter, and pasteurized cream. Despite the high cost of equipment and instruction, the school was soon paying for itself. Its products were sold on the local market, a policy which occasioned considerable criticism on the grounds that the University was competing with private producers. When, in 1897, a legislative committee investigated this charge, and the more serious one involving the quality of the output, the criticisms quickly died, for the success of the enterprise from every point of view was obvious. Many of the men who had attended the course had already made distinguished records throughout the state.

The rapid development and growing popularity of the short course owed much to the success of the dairy course, which not only provided a practical model of instruction but which also broke down prejudice against the college among rank and file farmers. But the short course owed a great deal to other factors

---

[26] *18th Annual Report of the Wisconsin Dairymen's Association,* 1890, 18: 100–102.

too. It received an effective boost from the twenty scholarships which John Lendrum Mitchell of Milwaukee established in 1891. Most important of all, however, was the leadership provided by its director, Ransom A. Moore. Self-taught and possessing no degree, Moore threw himself into his work with an enthusiasm matched only by his sympathetic understanding and by his intelligence. In the early years of his directorship he rode around Dane County on his bicycle to enlist students. Possessing a remarkable gift for inspiring the respect and affection of farm boys, Moore succeeded in making their work interesting and significant. As the years passed he enlisted the cooperation of the boys in his program of breeding investigations. This not only contributed to the success of the program itself but also furthered the desire of those who had taken the short course to continue their education.[27]

Under the wise and helpful cooperation of Dean Henry, who became a champion of the kind of training provided by the short course, and under the leadership of Director Moore, the course was constantly improved without departing from its own essentially practical foundation. New subjects were added, including agricultural engineering, the judging of livestock, bacteriology, bookkeeping, shopwork, drafting, horticulture, feeding, agronomy, plant life, dairying, and veterinary science. To accommodate the expanding program a second year was added in 1896 and the annual term lengthened from twelve to fourteen weeks. In 1917 the term was extended to fifteen weeks, made up of three five-week sessions each complete in itself. Without militating against the boy whose school background was deficient the staff from time to time raised the academic standards in the course. Despite the development of more and better work in the County Agriculture Schools the short course continued to attract farm boys from all over the state. Many became important members of the legislature, more took active roles in farm organizations, and still more provided progressive leadership in their own communities. As befitted the first course of its kind in the country and one which readily met new problems and

[27] Moore's fascinating autobiography is printed in *Hoard's Dairyman*, vol. 72, October 25, 1927, to December 25, 1928.

pioneered in new areas, the short course exerted an incalculable influence not only in other states but in many foreign countries as well. Once the butt of ridicule, it had come to be universally recognized as a highly effective answer to the old and stubborn problem of an agricultural education for the rank and file rather than for the elite alone. That this development took place within an institution in which research projects enjoyed a priority was all the more significant.

The short course proved that if agricultural education was to attract farm boys it must be practically geared to their interests. But this lesson was only very slowly applied in the long course. Before the turn of the century the largest number of students enrolled in it at any one time was thirteen. Then, as Dean Henry noted, the long course began to grow in earnest.[28] This was the outcome, in part, of the expansion of experiment station staffs all over the country, for which college-trained men were required, of the introduction of agricultural instruction in secondary schools, and of the growing needs of the commercial establishments engaged in putting out feeds and fertilizers. But the quite sudden growth in enrollment in the long course also owed a good deal to the modifications in its curriculum.

When the college was founded the four-year program was still pretty much the compromise Professor Daniells had worked out in the seventies and eighties. Had it appealed to any considerable number of students it no doubt would have weaned boys away from the countryside, as virtually all farmers contended. It was a solidly scientific course, relieved by prescribed work in rhetoric or a foreign language and constitutional law. The student did not find his way into any agricultural courses until the second term of his junior year, when agriculture, forestry, veterinary science, agricultural chemistry, drawing, and economic entomology were open to him. The best that could be said for this program was that in the last year a student might take part in the special investigations of Henry and Babcock.

Two main reasons explain the hesitation to change this traditional sequence. In the first place, the faculty felt the necessity of holding up their heads in the University community. They

[28] *Regents' Biennial Report*, 1901–02, p. 15.

were fully aware that their colleagues in other divisions of the University suspected them of lowering standards in the interest of vocationalism. Indeed, in some respects the agricultural faculty bent over backward in exceeding reasonable standards for graduation. As Glover has suggested, Dean Henry, recollecting his own earlier desire to separate the college from the University, was overanxious about relations with the University. In attempting to reconcile the needs of scientist, educator, farmer, and human being in a single curriculum, Dean Henry was often painfully confused. This in part explains why the reorganization of the long course did not occur until his successor took over. In the second place, the lack of any important stimulus to break traditional practices likewise explained the slowness with which change came. The farm groups had pressed for a new type of short course, but they were indifferent to the long course; the students themselves were not critical of the existing pattern. For some time they did not even create an independent educational system of their own in extracurricular activities as arts and science students had once done when they felt the classical curriculum failed to give them the understanding of the modern world they wanted. Most of the students' societies were short-lived. Nevertheless, as time went on, there were indications that the students did try to achieve some measure of unity. Certainly the faculty was not indifferent to students' academic problems, as the successful development of an advising system in the latter part of Dean Henry's administration indicated.

The faculty was not resolutely set on maintaining the *status quo*. Certain changes, introduced in the early years of the century, brought to the forefront a basic problem that was to remain stubbornly present despite all compromises. Briefly, the problem involved on the one hand the maintenance of the older ideal of a well-balanced, general education in the agricultural sciences and, on the other, demands for an ever more specialized program as research extended the horizons of knowledge. The first notable change resulted from the institution of a new general science course in the College of Letters and Science. The student in the long course at the agricultural college, hereafter equipped in his first two years with the general sciences, was to be allowed to elect in his final two years a more specialized program in one of the established departments, such as agricultural chemistry, agricultural physics, animal husbandry, bacteriology, and horticulture, and to minor in some other. Babcock, however, was concerned lest the graduates of the long course be deficient in all but one or two of the agricultural fields and succeeded, in 1903, in introducing a further modification. This required the student in his last two years to be introduced to more than two fields of specialization. He was, in other words, not to finish the long course until he had familiarized himself with the application to agriculture of physics, chemistry, bacteriology, engineering, and, what was truly an innovation, economics.[29]

The first important break in what Glover has aptly called the rigid academic front was made in 1907. Both Henry, who was on the point of retiring, and Russell, who succeeded him, were agreed on the necessity and the desirability of viewing agricultural subjects as established academic disciplines properly within the reach of students in their first two years. The revolution, for it was that, may thus properly be discussed at this point, though it was to develop in the administration of Dean Russell. Entering freshmen at last were permitted to study agronomy and animal husbandry, in which their interest was already established and in which they could excel in greater measure than in the theoretical sciences taught in the College of Letters and Science. In the sophomore year courses in horticulture and in agricultural bacteriology and chemistry carried students still further into the professional program on which they had embarked.

It was at last clear that the fields of agricultural science were thoroughly established as academic disciplines. Thus initiated, students were ready in their last two years to take on specialized work without having to begin introductory work all over again. The change did not, to be sure, represent a full recognition of the lessons of the dairy course, for only a slight concession was made to the educational value of practical work under competent teachers. But it did point the way to the full recognition of the fact that vocational interests might provide a solid foundation on which to build specialized knowledge without sacrificing academic standards.

At the same time that the faculty accepted with enthusiasm the new curriculum of 1907, many—including Babcock, Otis, and Dean Russell—shared the fears which Dean Henry had felt lest the increased agricultural specialization militate against the broad education available at the University. This concern explains many of the curriculum changes in the years that followed. To quote Glover, "the ultimate evolution of the Long Course into a very flexible and satisfactory arrangement for the convenience of students of widely varying interests is accounted for in large part by this willingness of the faculty to search diligently for the appropriate regulations."[30] The problem was accentuated by the rapid multiplication of the departments and their courses—a process well under way in Henry's administration and speeded up in that of Russell. The founding of the departments of plant pathology, agricultural education, agricultural economics, genetics, poultry husbandry, economic entomology, and agricultural bacteriology resulted in a bewildering variety of choices despite the fact that some departments put their primary emphasis on graduate training in research. Although the faculty supplemented such changes and rules as it made with careful guidance of individuals, the majority of students were forced to make their own choices and to be responsible for achieving a balance between specialization, on the one hand, and general education in the arts and sciences and their application to agriculture, on the other. In view of the increasing demand for specialists in poultry and game management, market statistics, agricultural journalism, and education (including leadership in boys' and girls' clubs), to name only a few of the rising specialties, the problem often seemed as insoluble to students as it did to faculty. But all these changes reflected the same type of specialization which presented difficulties to all the other faculties including, as we have seen, that of the College of Letters and Science.

[30] Quoted from Wilbur H. Glover's manuscript, The History of the College of Agriculture.

The problem may be illustrated by reference to two fields, agricultural education and agricultural engineering. As the state imposed more and more requirements in the preparation of teachers of agriculture in the schools, as the programs in this field expanded and were adopted in almost all rural schools, and as the whole project received added stimulus from the federal funds provided by the Smith-Hughes Act, educational courses in the four-year program of necessity encroached on other offerings, and the agricultural education department came to attract the largest number of undergraduate majors. In part the problem thus posed was solved in 1907 when Henry, the dean emeritus, offered for the first time a teacher-training course in the summer session. Not until 1929 was an adequate solution achieved in agricultural education. In that year the college offered a nontechnical major for farmers, managers, and farm-equipment operators which could be combined with teacher-training and still be completed in four years. At the same time a solution was found for the parallel problem presented by the virtual impossibility of training a sound agriculturalist and a competent engineer in the same person in a four-year course. A new technical major was established which led to the degree of bachelor of science in agriculture in four years, the program being so constructed that only three additional semesters were needed to complete a full course in civil, mechanical, or electrical engineering.

The problem posed by the proliferations of subject matter and the ever-growing number of vocational specialities might be further illustrated by the development of agricultural economics. This course first became a required part of the four-year course in 1903, nine years after Professor William A. Scott of the School of Commerce had begun teaching it in the short course.[31]

While the long course was being revised in 1907 the faculty decided to meet the needs of a group desiring neither the full four-year program nor the short course. Never very large, this

---

[31] The development of agricultural economics and sociology as fields will be considered in connection with the history of research in the second and third decades of the twentieth century. See Volume II, pp. 420 ff.

group was offered the middle course. Most of those who chose it came from towns and cities and intended to go into teaching or farming. At least six months of practical farm experience was required before entering the second year. The program itself resembled the first two years of the long course, except that agricultural electives were substituted for the basic sciences in the second year. In 1912 the curriculum was modified in the direction of the practical pattern of the short course. Registration rose from the initial 35 in 1908 to a peak of 147 in 1914. It fell off during World War I and especially during the agricultural depression of the 1920's. This reflected a general trend: about the same percentage of the total University student body was of farm parentage in 1901, 1912, and 1925, but the proportion enrolling in the College of Agriculture fell from its peak of seven and a half per cent in 1912 to three per cent in 1925.[32]

A word must be said about the quality of teaching in the college. Although many no doubt continued to look upon teaching, whether in the long course or the short course, as an unfortunate interruption of research—a common attitude when students first came in any numbers—the college numbered among its great teachers men like A. S. Alexander, G. B. Mortimer, and E. B. Hart. Even those less gifted offered a great deal in associating long-course students with them in research projects and in publishing the results with them. Although some departments were virtually graduate research departments while others prided themselves on their teaching tradition, the college never formally tried to separate teaching altogether from research.

Thus despite the original emphasis on research and extension, the college slowly and somewhat haltingly developed a teaching program designed both for young farmers coming for a short winter term and for those seeking a full college program in preparation for specialized functions in agriculture. Both programs evolved in part by trial and error. Pragmatism governed the development of the short course to a greater degree than it did the long course, which was bound by academic traditions'

[32] J. A. James, "Results of a Study of Student Enrollment in Agriculture," *Proceedings of the Forty-Third Convention of the Association of Land Grant Colleges and Universities,* 1929, pp. 135–142.

and inhibitions. The problems were never entirely solved in working out a synthesis in the long course between the imperatives of basic scientific training, cultural education, practical experience, and specialized agricultural competence. But most of the problems were either close to solution or they disappeared as others arose to take their place. All in all, the educational success of the college was hardly less a testimony to leadership, devotion, and ability than was the outstanding success in research and extension.

AFTER 1908 the educational program of the college included the department of home economics. The transfer from the College of Letters and Science was the result of the failure of home economics to flourish on the Hill, the Nelson Act, which provided federal funds to home economics programs geared to agricultural education and problems, and the obvious bearing of home economics on rural as well as urban life. The home economics program, which had won an appropriation from the legislature in 1903 as a result of the activity of the women's clubs, continued to have this interest and support. Although it attempted to serve women in all aspects of homemaking and in all types of homes, the department succeeded in orienting itself in the pattern of education the College of Agriculture had evolved. In extension and in research, especially, but to some degree in academic studies and in social life, home economics was integrated with the college.

Throughout this period Abby L. Marlatt guided the immediate fortunes of the department. Professor Marlatt's greatest problem was to accommodate a constantly growing student population. At times home economics enrolled as many students as did the four-year agricultural course. Installed at first in the basement of Agricultural Hall, the department was forced to move, at the end of the semester, to the top floor of Lathrop Hall. The rapid increase in students compelled a further move. With the aid of the women's clubs, Professor Marlatt persuaded the legislature to grant an appropriation for a wing of the new

University Extension Division Building. Adequate for the time, the space was altogether insufficient by 1925, when the department included 300 full-time students in addition to a large number from the College of Letters and Science electing one course or more.

Professor Marlatt insisted on a broad type of training and on the maintenance of high standards. Her influence in these matters was felt not only at Wisconsin but throughout the nation. Her ideal of teaching included stimulating her students to think for themselves, to develop initiative, and to enliven and enrich what was done in the classroom by sustained research. Against the somewhat cavalier attitude of the administration of the college, Professor Marlatt aggressively defended her department and demanded recognition for her staff, whose class and laboratory work greatly exceeded that in any other part of the University. Her demands on her group, however, were matched only by her demands on herself.

The curriculum which Professor Marlatt set up included basic courses in chemistry, physics, physiology, and bacteriology; English and a foreign language; and the technical subjects of foods, textiles, architecture, and household management. As the staff expanded more specialized work was offered. Majors in applied bacteriology, hospital administration, home economics, journalism, and household art were added to the nonprofessional major designed for students preparing for a homemaking career and to the professional teacher-training program. At times the expansion of the curriculum occasioned the crossing of swords with Dean Russell. At times the administration of the program involved Professor Marlatt in tussles with the Dean of the College of Letters and Science. Whether she lost or won, however, she retained everyone's respect for her courage, her devotion and self-sacrifice, her tireless drive, and her insistence on high standards. In the students of the department and in the women of the state with whom she came in contact she had valuable support. Yet neither group possessed enough influence to insure the department what it needed. A practice cottage did become available in 1912 but really adequate facilities came only after World War I and as the result of a private gift. And it was not until 1930 that the department obtained a nursery school, long after most departments had come to take such an agency for granted.

The emphasis placed on teaching and on extension militated against research, though, as we shall see, some of the staff cooperated in the nutrition experiments at the Experiment Station. In extension work the department won an enviable reputation. Other departments, notably those at Iowa and Minnesota, won in some respects greater prestige, but none pushed ahead against greater odds or made better use of the resources at hand.

✑

THE pattern of activities which developed at the college during Dean Henry's administration (1891–1907) admirably exemplified the Van Hise ideal of a union of academic and practical interests. With Henry's retirement the pioneer era had passed. Dean Harry L. Russell, however, made the objectives of his predecessor his own. He carried them even further and in so doing developed methods which, whatever criticisms might be made of them, were bold, statesmanlike, and highly effective.

The problems which confronted Dean Russell differed in many ways from those which Henry had met, but they were not necessarily less difficult. The agricultural forces of the state were fairly well united during the larger part of Dean Henry's regime but this was no longer true in that of his successor. The Dairymen's Association continued to emphasize the ideal of greater production, a feeling Russell shared as Henry had done. But with the advance of the Progressive movement a considerable section of the farm population, led by the Society of Equity and supported by Charles McCarthy of the Legislative Reference Library, promoted the cooperative cause. This group was openly critical of the college and of Dean Henry. It bitterly denounced Russell's insistence that in view of the increasing population food production was paramount; that education was more important than government in the solution of farm problems; and that the farmers' hope lay in developing sound business methods rather than in cooperative production, buying, and marketing.

Deans of the College of Agriculture
Harry L. Russell and William A. Henry

Top: E. B. Hart and Stephen M. Babcock
Bottom: Henry C. Taylor and Benjamin H. Hibbard

Although the regents in general supported Russell, at least one of their members, Charles P. Cary, was outspokenly critical.

The cleavage in agricultural ranks made relations with the legislature difficult. Dean Russell's approach was "to contact the few key men who really ran things there." But to his critics this seemed to be mere conspiracy, and his forbearance failed to relieve all the tensions. Despite his efforts to avoid criticism for unbecoming lobbying, and despite his care not to appear at the legislature save in association with Van Hise lest he be charged with exerting undue influence in behalf of the college, he failed to enjoy the widespread confidence Dean Henry enjoyed.[33] The hostile critics of the University responsible for the investigation of 1915 succeeded in having the college's estimates cut. Although Governor Philipp prevented the threatened blows from falling, the efforts of the "business governor" to introduce budgetary controls made the task of finding funds for the rapidly expanding college an arduous one. Various limitations on the dean's freedom of action in financial matters were additional thorns.

These obstacles did not, however, seriously curtail the financial support of the institution. It is true that the building program, which moved smoothly ahead in the early years of the administration, slowed down after the Stock Pavilion (1909), the new Horticulture Hall (1912), the Agricultural Chemistry Building (1914), and the wing for the Soils Building were completed. However critical some farm organizations of left-wing sympathy were, most saw to it that their interests were translated into appropriations for the college. The gross expenditure of the college rose from $200,000 in 1906–07 to $1,500,000 in 1930–31, the last year of Dean Russell's administration.[34] There was little change in the sources of income: in both years state tax funds supplied approximately half, and federal grants and receipts of the college the other half. None could criticize the dean for any lack of sound practice in using funds for the attainment of their objective, as a careful balance was maintained among

[33] Records of the Board of Regents, H:525, February 8, 1913; Senator William A. Titus to Russell, March 31, 1923, cited by Glover.

[34] *University of Wisconsin Budget, 1930–1931*, p. 58; Russell to H. W. Hoyt, December 27, 1907, cited in Glover.

teaching, extension, and research. It was possible to concentrate efforts in the Experiment Station on research when the routine regulatory functions were transferred to the state department of agriculture, the state laboratory, and other agencies. This transfer of responsibility lifted the burdens which had piled up like a snowball ever since the commercial fertilizer regulatory act of 1895 set a precedent for asking the station to enforce the regulatory laws.

One of the major problems Dean Russell faced was the conservation of his staff's time without sacrificing the valuable associations with the farmers of the state. This he attacked in several ways. In the first ten years of his administration he built up an organization which enlarged the extension activities of the collegiate departments and absorbed the farmers' institute work. In so doing he maintained the integrity of the academic departments with their teaching disciplines and their research programs, insured a unity of effort, and prevented the waste involved in work carried on at cross-purposes. Russell also, in his determined effort to give scientific leaders more freedom for their work, multiplied departments to provide for new specialized research projects and new services. His report for 1909 listed as new departments: poultry husbandry, agricultural economics, agricultural education, plant pathology, and economic entomology. In succeeding years experimental breeding (genetics), agricultural journalism, and agricultural bacteriology were added.[35]

The decision to protect research investigators from the pressure of instruction and extension through the multiplication of departments raised new problems. As we have already seen the College of Letters and Science vigorously opposed mutiplication of departments in the College of Agriculture on the ground that all pure research should be conducted within its own departments, leaving the practical applications to other branches of the University. President Van Hise supported Dean Birge, reenforcing the case of the College of Letters and Science by the argument of efficiency. Despite the support which Regents Hoard and Swenson gave to Dean Russell, the Board at first agreed with Van Hise's contention. But Dean Russell insisted

[35] *26th Annual Report of the Wisconsin Agricultural Experiment Station,* 1909, pp. 10–12; *28th Annual Report,* 1911, p. 64.

that "it is quite as important for an Experiment Station to have under investigation problems related to pure as well as applied science, for no one can tell what practical application may be made from these more or less theoretical researches."[36] Thanks in part to Russell's insistence and strategy, and in part to the immediate success of Professor L. R. Jones, the new plant pathologist, in attacking threatening diseases in the truck gardens of the state, the College of Agriculture was permitted to set up a department of plant pathology in 1912. The controversy arising over the division of the bacteriology department, which Russell had managed for the entire University until he became dean, led to a compromise. Some of the lectures in the introductory courses were given in the general department and others in the department of agricultural bacteriology. Finally, in 1914 Professor William D. Frost and two instructors were transferred to agricultural bacteriology to expand the work of Professor Edwin G. Hastings. After considerable discussion, genetics—for a time called experimental breeding in deference to Hoard, who insisted that farmers would complain about the use of a technical term—was established as a department in the college. The movement to set up a separate department of economic entomology cut into the biological bailiwick of which Dean Birge was the recognized master, but the dean of Letters and Science at last deferred to the dean of Agriculture. In contrast the separation of agricultural economics was made by an amicable agreement.

Although Dean Russell's relations with his staff were not always free from friction, on the whole they were marked by stability and mutual confidence. Leon J. Cole, appointed professor of experimental breeding in 1910 as a result of Russell's diligent search, probably spoke for most of his colleagues when he testified that the dean was indeed strong-willed in matters concerning the budget, but that once he was convinced of the plans submitted to him, he did not waver in vigorous and sympathetic support of fundamental research.[37] Certainly he required free and willing service from the staff in return for the

[36] Harry L. Russell, "The Scope and Results of the Wisconsin College of Agriculture, 1903–1913" (mimeographed), 12, Papers of the Dean of the College of Agriculture.

[37] The American Society for Animal Production, *Records of Proceedings of 32nd Annual Meeting,* 1939, p. 465, cited in Glover.

professional courtesies and support the staff knew it could count on. At the same time he candidly made known his conviction that a fully empowered executive was best suited to decide on the practical details when a job was to be done. In opposing divided responsibility he was equally explicit. "I cannot see how homogeneity of department effort can be maintained on a basis which permits of three separate executives controlling these lines of work (instruction, investigation, extension)," he wrote, "unless the institution is on so large a basis as will permit of the time of the man being given wholly to each one of these three groups of activities."[38]

As an organizer, then, Dean Russell brought managerial efficiency to a rapidly growing institution. He spared no pains in developing and extending the program in instruction, in extension, and in research to cover all farm problems. His candor, efficiency, and dogged determination to protect the interests of the college, whether in the consolidation of wide-flung enterprises already launched or in the initiation of new ventures, proved a tower of strength.

DEAN Russell's reorganization of the college and the station involved fighting his program through the Board of Regents until the University found itself facing the accomplished fact of a College of Agriculture staffed, equipped, and functioning in the field of pure science. Yet contact with the actual problems of Wisconsin farmers, both in responding to local needs by initiating specific investigations and in making the results available, continued to give research the fullness which was Wisconsin's tradition and glory.

In establishing one new department after another in the interest of breaking fresh ground in research, Dean Russell was called on to iron out occasional conflicts resulting from the overlapping of programs and personnel. The overlapping itself did not trouble the dean, for he was convinced it was often beneficial. In part the problems which resulted were solved by a policy of ap-

[38] Russell to J. H. Skinner, February 23, 1914, cited in Glover.

pointments of members of the staff to two or even more departments. The relationship which thus developed was frequently highly fruitful. To cite a single example: such cooperation in attacking the problems of plant crops on farms brought forth a new discipline—plant pathology—which was a blend of botany, chemistry, bacteriology, physics, and genetics. The office of the dean, which included the director, and at last an assistant director, of the Experiment Station, coordinated research both in the planning and in later stages.

The support of research continued to be guided by established policies. In general the dean refused to sanction new projects unless an interested group of farmers had succeeded in providing legislative support. This had the advantage not only of safeguarding limited funds for the adequate support of a few carefully selected projects, but it also meant that farm groups desiring research aid had to organize effectively and were thus able to make more efficient use of scientific results once they were obtained. Dean Russell successfully resisted Governor Philipp's proposal to relegate the support of research to federal funds alone. Such a policy would indeed have been catastrophic, since the contribution of the state was almost three times that of the federal government.[39] The belittling attack on research, which the governor abetted if he did not inspire, was cogently refuted. It may be noted in passing that federal funds, which remained smaller than those of the state despite new legislation which augmented them from time to time, required the approval of given projects by the Department of Agriculture, a policy which Dean Russell, unlike some administrators elsewhere, believed to be more advantageous than disadvantageous. The advantages included both more careful research planning and the stimulus coming in many cases from the related investigations which the department was undertaking itself or sponsoring in other stations.

Grants from industrial concerns with a special relationship to agriculture proved an increasingly important source of financial support for research. In 1911 the Wisconsin Pea Packers' Asso-

[39] Emanuel L. Philipp to Dean James E. Russell [*sic*], April 9, 1915; Russell to Philipp, April 21, 1915, cited by Glover.

ciation gave the first such grant for a study of the diseases of canning peas. So successful were the results that cash grants in the form of annual research fellowships began to come from many other business enterprises. Among the concerns supporting specific projects were the Quaker Oats Company, which was interested in an investigation of the feed value of its by-products, and the Wisconsin Association of Manufacturers, which in 1926 initiated a five-year grant of $10,000 annually for a study of contagious abortion in cattle. One fertilizer company spent $20,000 to test the value of rock phosphate as stock feed only to discover its poisonous fluorine content. But the invention of a removal process brought a happy ending. From the start the station insisted on the control of the work, the choice of personnel, and the publication of results. It also insisted that a proposed project have general usefulness to farmers. In summarizing experience with this policy, Dean Russell noted that it had created little trouble; that in a number of cases applications were rejected on the score that it was impossible conscientiously to accept funds and to do the work from the standpoint of public interest; and that in more than one case companies had been forced to modify statements they made regarding the results of an investigation.[40]

Although the sale of produce had always provided a source of income of considerable importance, Babcock's decision not to patent his milk-fat test set a precedent for giving the results of scientific investigation to the public. The problem of scientific responsibility was far more important, however, in the case of Harry Steenbock's discovery of a way to recover vitamin A in its pure form. The University tardily and even reluctantly appropriated a small sum for the payment of some of the expenses involved in securing a patent. This step was taken too late, for the manufacturers of oleomargarine had begun to work on the problem early in 1924.[41] Professor Steenbock's next dis-

---

[40] *Experiment Station Record* (United States Department of Agriculture, February, 1932), 66:101–102; *Proceedings of the Forty-Third Annual Convention of the Association of Land Grant Colleges*, 1929, pp. 179–182.

[41] Harry Steenbock, The Relations of the Writer to the Wisconsin Foundation and the Events which led to its Organization, 1926, manuscript, Papers of the Dean of the College of Agriculture.

covery, the creation of vitamin D in foods by irradiation with ultraviolet light, raised even more far-reaching problems. The University again showed little or no interest. On the one hand, Steenbock knew that his application for a patent was open to the criticism that scientists might be tempted away from basic research in the hope of striking it rich. He knew, moreover, that a staff member in a state institution was looked on as a public servant. On the other hand, Steenbock resented the assumption that an investigator was in duty bound to hand over to the University the product of his researches. He also realized that the control of industrial firms subsidizing research was in no sense always easy, and that some universities had already forfeited control over scientific policy as a result. The patenting of his process would also protect the public against its unscrupulous use.

The hesitation of the regents to take action on being informed that offers had been made for patenting the process, that unauthorized use of irradiation had already begun, and that if granted, the patent would be assigned to the University, led Steenbock to propose the establishment of a trust to take over the patent. Dean Russell, Dean Slichter, and Harry L. Butler, a Madison attorney and alumnus of the University, together with Steenbock, drew up articles of incorporation and assembled an alumni group to constitute the Wisconsin Alumni Research Foundation. Authorized by the Board of Regents, the foundation was formally organized in November, 1925. Receipts from patents were to be divided between the inventor, who received 15 per cent, and the trust fund. Distribution to the University took the form of grants-in-aid of research, scholarships and fellowships, summer-research salary payments, lectures, and specific grants for designated investigation in the fields of natural science. In general the foundation did not pay research costs directly: Steenbock wisely insisted that the University itself, through its research committee, was to approve grants to particular projects. This prevented favoritism to any person or department and insured the independence of the research policy. It is sufficient to point out here that while the several colleges of the University were to profit from generous allocations for research purposes, the College of Agriculture in sharing such allocations augmented its research funds.

⟋𝒪

STEENBOCK's notable discovery of a process for the irradiation of food products to form vitamin D, which occasioned the new policy of patenting the results of research and utilizing the major portion of the proceeds for further investigation, was only one aspect of the highly significant work in nutrition experiments which, as we have seen, Babcock had initiated in the nineties. That early work, we may recall, indicated the need for the biological testing of feeds: the starving of cows on chemically balanced rations of oats and wheat pointed to the existence of some unknown factor necessary to growth and life in certain foods and the lack of it in others hitherto regarded as satisfactory from the point of view of chemical components. On Memorial Day, 1907, a group of younger colleagues, inspired by the early work of Babcock, initiated what were to become dramatic and highly significant nutrition experiments. The group included Edwin B. Hart, George C. Humphrey, Harry Steenbock, then a graduate student, and presently E. V. McCollum, who came from Yale where similar work was under way and who contributed, in addition to a metabolism approach, the idea of using rats in the feeding work. But many others contributed, and Babcock himself, who played the role of "the idea man," followed the investigations with great interest, making invaluable suggestions from time to time.

The story has been fascinatingly told by Paul de Kruif in his *Hunger Fighters* and, more fully and soberly, by Wilbur Glover in his history of the College of Agriculture. The mysterious elusive substance which was so necessary for life did not yield itself quickly to the varied attacks made in the Wisconsin laboratories or in those at Yale, London, and elsewhere. Farm experience occasionally provided startling confirmation for the strange but as yet only dimly glimpsed results. The missing element was at last brought to light by E. V. McCollum. It proved to be a complex of chemical substances to which the name vitamin was given. Even before McCollum made his discovery others, including Ejkman and F. G. Hopkins, had located such substances, and McCollum's findings were quickly followed by similar ones in the Yale laboratories of T. B. Osborne and L. B. Mendel. The McCollum discovery was fat-soluble vitamin A which controls growth and is found in butter, fat, and egg yolk. His first announcement of his discovery was in *Hoard's Dairyman* in 1914. Shortly afterward McCollum discovered water-soluble vitamin B, also found in egg yolk; he showed that this vitamin could also be extracted from a number of plants and, since it was destroyed when these plants were reduced to ashes, that it was an organic compound, not a simple element. These discoveries were turned to account almost at once in advertising the value of milk and in improving farm feeding processes. McCollum left in 1917 for Johns Hopkins University, where he discovered vitamin D.

But the secret of the relation of vitamins to protein was still unsolved, and mineral absorption was unknown. Discoveries, however, piled up excitingly one on the other. Steenbock found that white corn lacked the vitamin A which yellow corn possessed. Edwin B. Hart, in collaboration with James J. Halpin of the poultry husbandry department, discovered that leg weakness in chickens was the result of a vitamin D deficiency. Steenbock, working with Hart and Halpin, observed the value of sun rays in curing rickets—an observation others had noted—and in consequence made the next notable advance. To borrow de Kruif's words, he trapped the sun rays and further identified the nature of the new vitamin D. This vitamin was shown to be responsible for the absorption of calcium into bones. Thus at last, thanks to the work of many investigators, it was known that mineral and protein metabolism was related to the vitamins which persistent experimentation had revealed. Not only were many health problems now controlled by supplementing foods; methods had been discovered to seek the causes of many other farm perplexities. The subsequent work of Karl Paul Link in isolating dicumarol, the anticoagulant blood factor, proved to have important medical implications. Conrad A. Elvehjem's discovery of the antipellagra factor, nicotinic acid, which came later, was likewise full of significance for medicine. New experiments, launched in 1926, to determine the role of minerals in nutrition were to prove a boon to dairy farmers by enabling them to provide the phosphorus which the soil had not furnished the feed grown on it. And from these mineral experiments was to come Hart's discovery of the iron and copper treatment for anemia. By 1931, when Hart's twenty-five years of service as chairman of the department was celebrated, four hundred scientific articles and forty-four doctoral dissertations had resulted from the investigations in agricultural chemistry. It was truly an impressive record.

But the widely publicized significance of the nutrition experiments and their obvious implications for human well-being have tended to obscure other experimental work likewise of great scientific and practical importance. Much of this involved the cooperation of two or more departments, and some of it was closely related to programs sponsored by the Department of Agriculture and forwarded in many experiment stations. Indeed, the work in both pure and applied science came more and more to bear witness to the significant fact that achievements in research can be understood only in terms of a far-flung community of interests. Although the work at Wisconsin contributed to the growth of agriculture knowledge in almost every sphere, the most notable contributions were made in plant pathology, genetics, and bacteriology.

The work in plant pathology was really put on a solid basis when a special department, headed by Professor L. R. Jones of the University of Vermont, was organized in 1910. The breeding of a disease-resistant type of cabbage plant was followed by a significant set of experiments in soil temperature, in which John C. Walker and, subsequently, James G. Dickson participated. These experiments yielded the knowledge that soil temperature and genetic factors explained the ailments of even resistant varieties under unfavorable weather conditions. Indeed, the soil temperature experiments changed the whole way of thinking about plant diseases: it was clear that these were most fruitfully studied in terms of the interactions of plant and parasite under specific environmental conditions. As a result plant pathologists identified many diseases which the cooperating geneticists controlled by singling out the factor of resistance and by crossbreeding varieties to secure resistant types. The discovery of means of infecting the plants to be selected—artificial infection—yielded important new resistant strains of barley. Thus the dual strategy of combating plant disease by the selection of resistant plants and by controlling the soil environment through proper crop culture resulted from experiments involving heredity and environment. As a result Wisconsin growers of peas, beans, tomatoes, cabbages, and grains triumphed over adversities that had been as baffling as they were discouraging.[42] The work of Jones and the associated plant pathologists was in a sense quite as important as that of Babcock and his colleagues.

But this was not all. Walker initiated work in 1918 which, with the cooperation of Angell and Link, revealed that a specific chemical compound normally produced in the tissue of a plant may be the source of protection from diseases. Jones and G. W. Keitt developed a new strategy in their effort to combat diseases in plants and fruit trees which could not readily be changed by breeding for defense against disease. This involved studies of the genetics and the environmental relations of parasitic enemies for indications of vulnerability to counterattack. Although no weakness was detected in the apple scab fungus cycle, many important by-product discoveries were made. These include the fact that the active spores of the apple scab emerge in the spring from leaves of the previous season which lie on the ground during the winter and that the fungus has a sexual stage of reproduction. As a consequence many sources of trouble have been largely eradicated, and to a considerable degree control has been achieved over the apple scab, the cherry leaf spot, and crown gall and hairy root on nursery stock. Moreover in throwing light on the nature of excessive growths in the life cycle, these and related investigations may guide cancer research

[42] Lewis Ralph Jones, "Experimental Work on the Relation of Soil Temperature to Diseases in Plants," *Transactions of the Wisconsin Academy of Sciences, Arts, and Letters*, 1921, 20:433–457; James Geere Dickson, Wisconsin Soil Temperature Studies and their Application to Breeding for Disease Resistance, 1946, manuscript; John Charles Walker, Studies in Disease Resistance, 1946, manuscript; Edmond Joseph Delwiche, History of Pea Breeding and Cultural Work at Wisconsin, 1946, manuscript, all cited by Glover.

along fertile lines. Thus the concern for the prosperity of the farm population, which inspired the research of the plant pathologists, has not only brought relief to horticulturists but has furthered the understanding of many scientific problems.

The impact of specific farm problems in the initiation and conduct of research is also reflected in the work in animal breeding. The work at Wisconsin in this field was paralleled by the studies of Raymond Pearl at Maine and of investigators at Missouri and Minnesota; others, too, contributed to the infant science of genetics which was rediscovering and applying the Mendelian principles. In 1910, partly in response to the pressure of Hoard, the department of experimental breeding was established. Professor L. J. Cole inaugurated purely theoretical studies with the object of establishing broad scientific rules which might then serve for practical breeding purposes rather than undertaking empirical work to develop new types of plants and animals. In 1912 Cole undertook a study of inheritance in cattle through experiments in crossbreeding which yielded a mass of data not even yet fully analyzed. Other approaches, including the effect of poisons on the germ cells of animals, the development of artificial insemination and studies of the endocrine glands, and the control of sex were also sooner or later inaugurated with results varying from the negative and indeterminate to the positive and useful. The department of experimental breeding was much aided in its work by the animal husbandry and the poultry husbandry staffs. Masses of data were accumulated in the progeny records resulting from the breeding services which had been maintained and extended. Work in plant as well as in animal inheritance has led to important contributions in the field of genetics. E. W. Lindstrom directed this work until 1922, when he was succeeded by R. A. Brink. The investigation of the inheritance of chemical characteristics by plants brought immediate practical benefits and opened up new lines of inquiry. Improved varieties of soybeans, sweet clover, and corn were welcomed by practicing farmers, while the discovery of the critical functions of endosperm in seed formation advanced theory. In all this work the close relationship between the departments of plant pathology, horticulture, and agronomy proved invaluable.

The grain-breeding program begun by Ransom A. Moore, which rested on mass selection, and the definite breeding work of Benjamin D. Leith and Edmond J. Delwiche, the directors of the branch experiment stations in northern Wisconsin, resulted in new varieties of wheat which resisted the devastating stem rust. Improved varieties of peas, barley, and oats were also developed, and Wisconsin made significant contributions to the immensely practical hybridization of corn.[43]

Dean Russell's early work in bacteriology had led to notable results in the study of tuberculosis and cabbage rot as well as in other fields, but the appointment in 1906 of Professor Conrad Hoffman to the department of bacteriology opened a new and important line of work. Hoffman began the researches in soil bacteriology which developed into a world-famous project. The work of E. B. Fred, who joined the department in 1913, had a great part in this success. Within a year bacterial cultures were being supplied to legume growers, a service which developed into a large-scale enterprise until commercial manufacturers entered the field. The investigations in soil bacteriology led to the preparation of an encyclopedic work which was quickly recognized as the standard.

It is not easy to draw a clear-cut line between basic research and technical services to the farm population, but these on the whole may be said to have represented the application of scientific discoveries. The department of bacteriology, in addition to supplying legume growers with bacterial cultures, distributed cultures which greatly improved the quality of Swiss cheese. Tuberculin tests were also made available in quantity. In cooperation with the agricultural chemists the bacteriologists worked out methods for supplying much-needed alcohols during World War I. The scientists in the department of dairy husbandry designed tests which took much of the guesswork out of the making of ice cream, butter, and cheese. The soils department developed several tests for the chemical elements of soils and inaugurated the soils survey which made use not only of

[43] Wisconsin developed good northern varieties; see A. Richard Crabb, *The Hybrid-Corn Makers, Prophets of Plenty* (Rutgers, 1947), 199 ff.; manuscript, Outline of the History of the Department of Genetics, 1941, cited by Wilbur H. Glover.

chemical analysis but also of X-ray techniques. The value of the survey for land use and planning and for the adjustment of crops and soil was considerable. The department of horticulture initiated the certification of seed potatoes in 1913 while, as we have seen, the agronomy department devoted much time and energy to supervising the efforts of the Wisconsin Experiment Association. Farmers owed much also to the engineering department which designed many improvements in farm apparatus and which, in association with the soils department, emphasized erosion control, especially in the twenties. The department of veterinary science administered the laboratory production of hog cholera serum, refined tests for many diseases including the agglutination test, and pioneered in the use of johnin, a diagnostic agent. In its administration of the stallion enrollment law of 1905, the department of horse breeding, established by Professor A. S. Alexander, retired much unfit breeding stock.

Moreover, the list might be extended to a degree which would impress any reader as overwhelming. The department of economic entomology, set up in 1912, provided much aid in insect control campaigns in addition to maintaining a research program. This included the development of a new insecticide, sabadilla. The department of dairy industry carried forward the early studies of Babcock on the nature of milk and cream and provided innumerable services to the industry. In addition, although restricted by budgetary considerations, the department of home economics determined the course of vitamins in the cooking and canning of many foods.

Glover has pointed out that the amazing achievements of the Experiment Station were the more notable because frequently work was carried on without adequate facilities and personnel. Among the defects were the lack of histologists in the early years of the nutrition experiments and the absence of specially trained statisticians until 1935. Nor should the sacrifice and sustained labor of the staff be minimized.

Just as the scientific work of the station was conditioned by the pressure of actual problems in farm life, so the agricultural social sciences developed in a context of economic and cultural tensions and needs. The leaders of the dairy revolution assumed that farming should be a business with the same law of success as any other. This involved keeping accounts, choosing the most profitable line of production, and marketing in the most efficient way. *Hoard's Dairyman* long urged the importance of business methods and of carefully calculated net profits and looked for guidance to the lectures in farm management directed by Professor Daniel H. Otis in the animal husbandry department. In the social sphere the drift of farm population to the cities, including some of the most enterprising youth, gradually began to excite an interest in Wisconsin as it did elsewhere. Thoughtful observers were increasingly aware of the fact that social conditions such as neighborhood tradition and values often affected the economics of farming. In many experiment stations and in the Department of Agriculture itself the economic and social aspect of farming began to awaken interest in the first decade of the twentieth century—an interest which Henry, Russell, and others at Wisconsin shared. The Rural Life Conference which President Theodore Roosevelt summoned at the White House in 1908 gave focus to needs which were coming to be explicitly sensed. Thus the road was open to research in the whole field of the social and economic aspects of agriculture.

Although Wisconsin was not unique in this pioneering work it is fair to say that it took the lead.[44] In large measure this was the result of the driving interest of Henry C. Taylor, who may properly be regarded as the father of agricultural economics. Taylor as a member of the University department of political economy was encouraged by Richard T. Ely; but he believed more effective work could be done in the sympathetic environment of the agricultural college. Beginning in 1903 Taylor offered instruction in agricultural economics in the long course. In 1905 he published his textbook, *An Introduction to the Study of Agricultural Economics,* a remarkable achievement despite the fact that it did not include discussions of marketing, rural finance, agricultural labor, wages, costs of transportation, and taxation—subjects which were to become so important as the

[44] At Cornell, Professor George F. Warren undertook a detailed farm-management survey of Tompkins County which was completed in 1911. G. F. Warren and others, *An Agricultural Survey, Townships of Ithaca, Dryden, Danby, and Lansing, Tompkins County, New York* (Cornell University Agricultural Experi-

field developed. In spite of opposition from Professor Ely, Taylor transferred to the College of Agriculture in 1909.[45]

The Wisconsin combination of theory and practice was exemplified in the organization of the new department. Dean Russell insisted on associating Otis and his farm management program with Taylor. Otis devoted himself to instruction and extension work for the most part, although he did carry through a study of the management of twenty farms which provided compelling evidence of the advantages of farming with business methods. Taylor set himself to the problem of codifying the methods, materials, and objectives of agricultural economics. He urged the importance of careful economic analyses of the choice of crops, of the intensity of their cultivation, of independent ownership, and of market fluctuations. He had in fact already used experimental plots to determine costs of cultivation, the effects of market facilities, the advantages of various types of tenure, and the role of other economic factors in farming. Projects were worked out to throw light on all these and other matters, and the data thus accumulated were analyzed and interpreted.

Progress, however, was not unhindered. On the one hand many enlightened farm leaders were suspicious of what seemed to them the overly theoretical and academic aspects of the new program. This was true, at least at the start, of Hoard himself. On the other hand, the objective emphasis on fact-finding for which Taylor stood alienated the more radically minded farm leaders organized in the American Society of Equity. They were thoroughly committed to the program of cooperative marketing and were impatient with any approach which did not accept this as superior to any other. The powerful State Board of Public Affairs, the spearhead of the Progressive movement in the state, joined with the Society of Equity in criticizing Taylor for his effort to approach the whole problem of marketing in an objective way. Criticism by these groups abated somewhat when Taylor's careful study of the Plymouth cheese market pointed up the inadequacies of traditional pro-

ment Station, Bulletin 295). Elsewhere, too, the farm-management studies were gradually developing into the specialized field of agricultural economics.

[45] Taylor has told the outlines of this story in a manuscript account which is deposited in the Library of the College of Agriculture.

cedures. Taylor himself came to be sufficiently impressed by his findings and by the champions of cooperative marketing to propose that the college undertake the job of organizing cooperatives. The University, however, decided that such a venture went beyond the proper functions of investigation and education. The department did, nevertheless, furnish aid to the cooperative marketing movement without sacrificing any of its own objective canons. The work of Benjamin H. Hibbard in this field was especially noteworthy.[46] Meantime, the department was pushing forward other lines of investigation. In addition to the accounting studies in Otis' farm-management program, these included investigations in land use and policy. The publication in 1924 of Hibbard's *A History of Public Land Policies* brought these together in usable form. The work of George S. Wehrwein and others in the Institute of Land Economics, which Ely organized after the first World War, was notable both for its intensive scholarship and its broad grasp of basic problems.

Sensitive to the mounting interest in the social problems of rural life Taylor broadened the scope of the department the very year after it was organized by appointing Charles J. Galpin to a part-time position. As a teacher of agriculture in a rural New York school Galpin had become interested in the problem of social integration. This interest was sharpened by his experiences in helping a brother build and manage a Wisconsin milk-powder plant and in advising rural students in connection with his work in the Madison Baptist Church.[47] Taylor was keenly interested in Galpin's effort to describe objectively his observations in the rural New York community and encouraged him, in preparation for a teaching appointment in the department, to undertake a field survey of Walworth County. The results, published as a research bulletin under the title "The Social Anatomy of a Rural Community," indicated that despite recognizable relationships between farm families and schools, churches, and trading centers, these families were nevertheless without distinctive communities of their own. Subsequent field investigations explored the problem of farm tenancy, rural

[46] This dramatic conflict is interestingly discussed by Glover.

[47] Charles J. Galpin has told the story of his pioneer work in his charming autobiography, *My Drift into Rural Sociology* (Baton Rouge, 1938).

social organizations, and other matters long neglected both by scholars and by agricultural leaders. To supplement the field studies Galpin arranged annual rural-life conferences which provided significant data for his investigations. His book, *Rural Life*, is a classic in what ultimately came to be called rural sociology. Galpin trained investigators in his seminars, one of whom, John H. Kolb, made a significant study of primary groups in rural communities. When Taylor and Galpin left Wisconsin in 1922 to develop their work in the federal Department of Agriculture, they had built such solid foundations that there was no question of continuing their program. This was facilitated by the specific provision in the Parnell Act of 1925 which made federal funds available for research in the rural aspects of the social sciences. The outstanding work of the Wisconsin specialists in the economic and social problems of rural life won, in the years following 1925, international recognition.

Although at times members of the faculties and administrative officers in other departments of the University grumbled and even scoffed at the College of Agriculture and made no effort to conceal their feeling that it was supported overgenerously in relation to their own work, the relations between the college and Experiment Station and the rest of the University were on the whole friendly and cooperative. Few questioned the wisdom of the decision to develop this field within the University rather than in a separate institution. No one, of course, can say what the University would have been like in 1925 had agriculture been separated in the 1880's (as it came so near to being). It is possible that a separate institution, like the one at Ames, Iowa, would have developed into a highly distinguished and useful center of instruction, research, and dissemination. It is possible that more support would have been given to the other departments of the University. But it is inconceivable, had this pattern been developed, that Wisconisn could have achieved what it did in breaking down rigid barriers between related fields of knowledge and in bridging so remarkably the stubborn, traditional gulf between discovery and application.

12.

The Law School

THE legislative provision of 1891 for the construction of a law building on the Hill was a turning point in the history of the College of Law.[1] Moving up from the old quarters in the capitol, for the first time the college seemed to be an integral part of the University.

Yet this was not entirely the case, for the regents continued to insist that the College of Law be as nearly self-supporting as possible. Until the turn of the century law school finances were chiefly dependent on tuition fees—the fees being the only ones in the University which were more than incidental. Appropriations continued to be small in relation to those granted other branches of the institution. In 1901–02, for example, the amount expended per student on the College of Law was but 23 per cent of that spent in the College of Agriculture, 34 per cent of that in Letters and Science, and 42 per cent of that in Engineering. It was hard to see why the arguments advanced for the liberal support of other departments in the University did not equally apply to the College of Law.[2] In his report for the biennium ending in 1904 President Van Hise attributed the relatively slow growth of the College of Law, at least partly, to the high student fees necessitated by the policy of making

[1] In 1909 the name was changed from the College of Law to the Law School. *Laws of Wisconsin,* 1909, p. 48.

[2] Report of Dean Harry S. Richards, *Regents' Biennial Report,* 1903–04, pp. 123–234.

425

the college largely pay its own way.[3] "It is believed," he concluded, "that if the State fully appreciates that the College of Law is falling behind the other Colleges, relatively, because of lack of support, adequate funds will be furnished to make this College equal to any other of its kind in the Middle West."[4] In his report for the year 1907–08 Dean Harry S. Richards noted that the legislature had repealed the statutes permitting tuition fees to be charged in the College of Law and had established the same incidental fees and nonresident tuition fees as prevailed in the College of Letters and Science. This change marked the assumption by the state of complete responsibility for the support of the college and its final integration into the University.

Although the new building, which was occupied in 1893, was acclaimed as one of the finest of its kind, it was apparent almost at once that it had been built without taking into account future growth and expanding needs. Even when the regents moved out of the building in 1905 the problem of space remained acute. The failure to include any adequate provision for a growing library was at the heart of the problem. Partitions were removed to enlarge book space and reading-room facilities, but to little avail. The building itself, moreover, was not fireproof, which was an added danger to the library. By 1916 the problem had become so critical that the dean recommended abandoning the twenty-five-year old building and constructing a modern one better suited to the needs of the school. This seemed the best solution since the limit in the safe carrying capacity of the floors had been reached, and since the building was so constructed that an addition could not be made without introducing gross architectural inconsistencies.[5]

The startling discovery that the building was outmoded was in part the result of the growth of the library. In the early nineties the College of Law possessed only the most inadequate

---

[3] The raising of standards for admission and for graduation affected attendance, especially in short-term periods, and must be taken into account in any inspection of enrollment figures. The college numbered 126 in 1891–92, 266 in 1900–01, and 157 in 1907–08.

[4] Report of the president, *Regents' Biennial Report,* 1903–04, p. 32.

[5] *Regents' Biennial Report,* 1915–16, p. 158.

collection of textbooks and incomplete reports. Both the faculty and the Visitors urged the importance of building up the library. "A good library is indispensable to a good lawyer," the committee declared in 1893. "No law student can successfully prosecute the study of the law without the aid of a large, well-selected library."[6] Both Dean Edwin E. Bryant and his successor, Dean Richards, pointed out again and again that in legal study a library is the equivalent of a laboratory in the natural sciences. The adoption of the case method and also broadening the course of study during the second decade of the twentieth century to include comparative public law naturally required considerable expansion in purchases. While the state law library continued to be open to students until the fire in the capitol in 1904, the attorneys and judges of the supreme court were often inconvenienced by the presence of students using books which they themselves needed and which excessive use was wearing out. Thanks to an annual appropriation of $1,000 which the legislature granted in 1896 and to a special appropriation of $15,000 in 1905, the notable gaps in the series of state and federal reports were filled in. An adequate working library of reference texts and a sufficient number of *Wisconsin Reports* were purchased. Thus the library, which numbered 7,400 volumes in 1904, reported 18,000 volumes in 1910 and 30,000 titles ten years later. In 1905 a librarian was engaged and steps were taken to improvise more adequate reading rooms and stack space—efforts which proved only partly successful. Thus while the college took pride in the growth of its reference material, the problem of housing and servicing it remained unsolved until the addition of a library annex in the 1930's.

Until the early 1890's the law department depended largely on local practitioners and judges for instructors. President Adams was convinced that the history of American law schools in the seventies and eighties proved that success depended "far more upon energetic and systematic instruction on the part of young and vigorous professors than upon the learning of eminent judges

[6] *Ibid.*, 1893–94, p. 60.

and distinguished members of the bar called in to give the fruits of their success under circumstances that make their instruction of secondary importance." "At Harvard, at Columbia, at Cornell, and at Michigan, the four most successful law schools in the country today," he continued, "reliance is chiefly placed upon young and vigorous attorneys who are desirous of establishing a reputation primarily as teachers, and secondarily as writers."[7] The point President Adams made was the more significant by reason of the fact that while the work of some of the part-time instructors was of superior quality, that of others was impaired by age, infirmity, and professional obligations which resulted in frequent inability to keep appointments at the college.

The fact that Dean Bryant sympathized with President Adams on the matter of a full-time faculty, however, did not insure smooth sailing in the reorganization of 1900. The dean proposed to meet the salary for a new full-time instructor by reducing to two or three hours of instruction a week the programs of John M. Olin, Burr W. Jones, and Robert M. Bashford. Olin was greatly offended by the suggestion that he had missed an undue number of class appointments and that a two-hour class was too great a strain on his physical ability. He made it clear that the reduction in stipend was not the main thing —it was very small at most—but that he preferred to resign rather than to accept the new terms, among which he particularly disliked the proposal that the part-time staff be not expected to attend faculty meetings and that the full-time professors be made responsible for the college's internal affairs.[8] Bashford, like Olin, resented the proposal.[9] According to Associate Dean Gregory it was taken "very ill among the students, the lawyers, and in the town."[10] Edward P. Vilas believed that the loss of Olin would be "very serious." In a letter to President Adams, Gregory expressed the hope that Dean Bryant would advise a reconsideration and a continuance of the *status quo*. Bryant offered his own resignation. At this point Regent

[7] Reports to the Regents, D:29, June 19, 1894.
[8] *Ibid.*, D:591–592, April 17, 1900; Charles Kendall Adams to the regents, March 28, 1900, Records of the Board of Regents, E:304–305, April 17, 1900.
[9] John M. Olin to Edwin E. Bryant, May 30, 1900, Presidents' Papers.
[10] Charles Noble Gregory to Adams, June 1, 1900, Presidents' Papers.

Breese J. Stevens supported President Adams in maintaining that the plan was the right one and should be kept in all its essentials.[11] President Adams did, however, write diplomatically to Olin, expressing appreciation of his services; and Regent George H. Noyes similarly urged him to retain a connection with the school.

In a conversation between Olin and Bryant, the latter professed to be surprised that the part-time staff clung to the title of professor lest they lose dignity, and indicated that he would welcome them at faculty meetings dealing with standing recommendations and discipline. Dean Bryant, in informing Adams that the three men would continue their association with the school, indicated that in his opinion friction could be avoided. He added that all the men, and particularly Olin, had urged him to remain as dean.[12] President Adams refused to accept Bryant's resignation, and the dean reluctantly agreed "to abide in the ship till a better time to shift mates, and make it as easy for the 'admiral' of the educational fleet as I can."[13]

The outcome of the crisis only postponed the reshuffling of the faculty along the general lines that Bryant and Adams had envisioned. Bryant himself continued in the deanship until 1903. Although he favored the idea of a permanent teaching staff, in many ways Bryant represented the old order. He aimed to make, or rather to keep, the college as nearly self-supporting as possible—a policy his successor regarded as unfortunate since it put the college on a footing different from that of other branches of the University and militated against a sufficiently large budget to keep full-time outstanding professors.[14] Dean Bryant's conservatism was further reflected in his fear that a given candidate for an appointment might have "too many elements of the mugwump, insurgent, and rumpus-raiser on general principles to be a desirable addition to our University force."[15] However cautiously, Dean Bryant did lend his support to the movement for raising standards. He was untiring in his devotion to students and to the general interest of the college.

[11] Breese J. Stevens to Adams, June 12, 1900, Presidents' Papers.
[12] Bryant to Adams, June 18, 1900, Presidents' Papers.   [13] *Ibid.*
[14] *Ibid.*, June 9, 1900, Presidents' Papers.
[15] *Ibid.*, May 3, 1900, Presidents' Papers.

Although not primarily a legal scholar, he was the author of a number of favorably regarded treatises on pleading.

Dean Bryant found an able lieutenant in Charles Noble Gregory, who was appointed in 1893 to the newly created associate deanship. Gregory was the son of a prominent Madison attorney. Trained at the University, he had practiced in Madison and served on the board of education and the city council. An ardent advocate of reforms in local, state, and national government, Gregory played an important part in the enactment of Wisconsin's first corrupt practices act. As vice-president and member of the executive committee of the American Bar Association, he interested himself especially in legal education. It was he who introduced the case method of teaching, thus giving Wisconsin the distinction of pioneering in this type of instruction in the Middle West. He was also mainly responsible for expanding the course from two to three years. A champion of the study of international law, Gregory subsequently helped found the American Society of International Law, and many of his addresses in this field were published in professional journals. His departure in 1901 to accept the deanship of the law school at the State University of Iowa was a major loss, for his career at Iowa and later at George Washington University was a distinguished one.

In 1903 Harry Sanger Richards, trained at the Harvard Law School and at the time a professor at Iowa, was appointed to the deanship. Richards had edited case studies in private corporation law but his chief contributions lay in the field of legal education. His report on legal training in Great Britain was a workmanlike job, and his services on the committee on education of the American Bar Association and as president of the American Association of Law Schools were widely appreciated. During the first World War Richards accepted various government assignments, including one in the Bureau of Trade Intelligence.

Several factors explain why the college found it so hard to keep its teaching staff intact. The rapid expansion of the legal profession to meet the needs of corporate business increased the demand for able talent both in practice and in the multiplying law schools. At Wisconsin, as already noted, the College of Law for a considerable part of this period depended more largely on student fees than did any other part of the University. The administration, moreover, was slow to recognize the plea that professional school salaries must range higher than those in the arts if able men were to be retained as teachers. For all these reasons the turnover in personnel was amazingly rapid.

To cite a few examples: Walter Wheeler Cook, a brilliant scholar trained at Columbia, Leipzig, and Berlin, left Wisconsin after a four-year stay to accept a professorship at Chicago; H. Claude Horack remained only three years before taking a professorship at Iowa; Eldon R. James and Ernest G. Lorenzen went to Minnesota and to Yale, while William U. Moore migrated to Chicago before accepting a call to a Sterling professorship at Yale; and Henry W. Ballantine after a brief sojourn accepted the deanship of the law school at Illinois. Between 1902 and 1916, of the thirteen men to hold full-time positions on the law faculty, seven resigned to accept higher salaries in other institutions. As Dean Richards pointedly remarked, "the School cannot go ahead as it should if it is forced to be a training school for teachers in other schools."[16]

Fortunately the college enjoyed the part-time services of eminent practitioners. But in 1908 Bashford resigned after a sixteen-year association to accept a position on the state supreme court. Olin, a leading Madison attorney, whose teaching and stimulating personality had been an asset to the college for twenty years, retired in 1910. Five years later Burr W. Jones, shortly after he was appointed to the supreme court of Wisconsin, submitted his resignation, to the great regret of the faculty, students, and alumni, for he was a talented teacher and a respected writer in the field of evidence.

It was hard to keep together a faculty, although a few men did stay either long enough to make a real impression on the college or for the entirety of their active careers. Eugene Allen Gilmore, trained at the Harvard Law School, came to Wisconsin from private practice in Boston in 1902. He was joint editor of the *Documentary History of American Industrial Society*,

[16] *Regents' Biennial Report*, 1913–14, p. 151.

was active in the conservation movement, and was author of a treatise on partnership and of monographs on franchises, interstate commerce, riparian rights, and legal education. He represented Wisconsin in the National Conference of Commissioners on Uniform State Laws, served as president of the Association of American Law Schools (1919–20), and took an active part in the American Institute of Criminal Law and Criminology. Gilmore resigned in 1922 to become vice-governor and secretary of public instruction in the Philippine Islands and later became dean of the law school and president of the University of Iowa. Others whose careers at Wisconsin continued over long periods included Howard L. Smith, who studied abroad after receiving his degree at Wisconsin, practiced in Madison, and became a professor in 1900 and Jackson professor of law in 1914. His *Cases on Bills and Notes* (1910) was a testimony of his interest in this field. William H. Page, whose publication on wills, contracts, and codes had established his national reputation, joined the faculty in 1917. Oliver S. Rundell began his teaching at the school in 1910; John Dunne Wickhem, a prominent Milwaukee attorney, received his appointment in 1919 and remained until 1930 when he became a justice of the supreme court; and younger men, including Ray Andrews Brown and William G. Rice, began their work before 1925.

Productive scholarship was stimulated by the establishment in 1920 of the quarterly *Wisconsin Law Review*. The faculty, considering the difficulty in retaining professors, compared favorably with those of other Middle Western universities: it was competent rather than outstanding in productive scholarship. Though the staff was respected chiefly for contributions to legal education rather than to the traditional and developing fields in jurisprudence, some members did, through scholarly publications, give the Law School distinction in original work.

In conformity with the tendency of all the best law schools in the country the course of study was extended in 1895 from two to three years. At the same time the regents required that no student should be admitted to the College of Law who was unable to pass an examination for admission to one of the courses in the College of Letters and Science. According to

President Adams, these two actions "raised the school to a grade in point of admission and graduation equal to all but one of the best schools in the country."[17] As anticipated, however, the number of students in attendance fell off, partly because some sought two-year institutions and partly because many, on completion of the second year, were able to pass the state bar examinations and consequently were unwilling to return for a third year of instruction. The regents' committee on the College of Law thus raised the question whether it was not desirable for the legislature to require three years of study before admission to practice in the courts of the state. Despite the fact that several adjacent states had already enacted such legislation, nothing was done for the time, partly, no doubt, because of the retention by a Milwaukee law school of its two-year course.[18]

The effort of the bar throughout the country to raise the standards of the profession by requiring better preliminary education and longer periods of study was thoroughly appreciated by the Wisconsin law faculty, by the regents, and by the Visitors. Dean Richards emphasized over and over again the importance to the state of "developing and maintaining an enlightened bar ... particularly under the complex economic, social, and political systems that now prevail." "The material development of a State is futile if not impossible," he insisted, "unless the life and property of the citizen are protected by wise laws efficiently administered. Since the enactment of laws and their administration is largely in the hands of members of the Bar, the highest interests in the State and of the Bar, as well as the traditions and policy of the University, demand that the College of Law be maintained on a basis that will meet the needs of the time and furnish facilities of instruction at least equal to those provided in Universities of like rank."[19]

In response to such considerations the regents rescinded the provision in force since 1897 which enabled young men twenty-three years of age or more who were unable to satisfy the entrance requirements to enter without examination and to

<hr>

[17] *Ibid.*, 1895–96, p. 18.
[18] *Ibid.*, 1897–98, pp. 25–26.   [19] *Ibid.*, 1903–04, p. 117.

satisfy such requirements any time before receiving their law degree. The administration of the entrance requirements was also placed in the hands of the registrar of the University to promote more strict enforcement. On the recommendation of the Board of Visitors and the faculty, the regents in 1904 made a highly important decision: to exclude immature men and to make possible higher standards of instruction, admission was to be confined, beginning in 1905–06, to those who had completed the equivalent of the freshman year in the College of Letters and Science. It was further stipulated that, beginning in 1906–07, entering students must present credits equivalent to both the freshman and sophomore years in that college. Exceptions were made in the case of special students who demonstrated their capacity to do a high order of work; but they could not become candidates for the law degree. When the decision was made Dean Richards reported that 71 per cent of the students then in the school could comply with the two-year prelegal study rule. In accordance with the experience of other schools he anticipated a material falling off in attendance when the new requirements became effective. The entering class in 1905 was, to be sure, 19 per cent smaller than that of the preceding year, but attendance at the regular session in 1907–08 was only one less than in the preceding year, notwithstanding the rule requiring two years of college work. Very few special students were admitted, and standards were safeguarded still further by a provision to drop students failing to make a passing grade in a major part of their studies.[20]

The new departure was significant in more ways than one. The faculty unanimously felt that the changes resulted in a much more efficient body of students. The advanced stand taken by the University—Wisconsin was the first Middle Western institution to require two years of college work for entrance upon legal study—was widely influential. The large number of inquiries received from various schools concerning the new requirements and the general emulation of Wisconsin naturally gratified Dean Richards and the faculty. Yale, George Washington, Illinois, Minnesota, Texas, Washington, and Michigan

[20] *Ibid.*, 117–118; 1905–06, pp. 141–142; 1907–08, pp. 150–151.

had all announced the adoption of a two-year prelaw requirement. Dean Richards reported, "The advanced stand taken by
this university has served to accelerate the movement."[21]

At Wisconsin, as at many other institutions, it was possible
for a senior in the College of Letters and Science to elect part
of the first-year work in law and to count this towards the degrees in both arts and law. Dean Richards held that this was
pedagogically unsound since it forced students to carry at the
same time legal and nonlegal studies bearing no relation to
each other, and since it encouraged them to neglect either the
one or the other. Moreover, such a student was given full
second-year standing in the College of Law without having
completed the full course of the first year. He was compelled in
his second year to take certain basic courses with first-year law
school men and to follow more specialized ones with second-
year men. In addition the arrangement made it difficult to
comply with the requirements of the American Law School
Association without seriously interfering with the free choice
of studies in the College of Letters and Science.

Dean Richards recommended that Wisconsin adopt the practice of Columbia, California, Stanford, Chicago, Northwestern,
and other universities which permitted a student on completing
his junior year in arts to enter the College of Law and to count
the first year of professional work toward the degrees in both
arts and law. But the College of Letters and Science was against
such a concession, although Dean Richards kept hammering at
the problem. He pointed out that Harvard had responded to
the generally recognized need for making some concession to
students seeking both the arts and law degrees by permitting
them to obtain the first in three years, and that Chicago and
most other universities recognizing the combined course had
allowed the student completing his junior year to enter the
law school, carry all the work of the first year, and on its
successful completion obtain the A.B. degree. He himself
favored the latter plan, but the College of Letters and Science
continued to resist the proposal. In the spring of 1920, however,
the faculty of the Law School instructed Dean Richards to take

[21] *Ibid.*, 1907–08, pp. 151–153.

up with the dean of Letters and Science the question of so modifying the regulations governing the combined course as to permit students who had completed three years' work in the College of Letters and Science to secure the A.B. degree upon completing the required work of the first year in the Law School. The College of Letters and Science, following the example of an overwhelming number of universities, finally adopted this policy, but with a significant and important reservation: the specific requirements of the Letters and Science course, including the completion of the Letters and Science major, were not waived. In 1926 it was announced that candidates for degrees must have the equivalent of three full years of work in the College of Letters and Science, the requirement to become effective on January 1, 1929.

The Law School also suggested that University regulations governing the first two years in the College of Letters and Science be so modified as to permit students taking two years of prelegal work a larger choice in the field of history, political science, economics, and philosophy.[22] Since this concession was not forthcoming, the law faculty accepted in 1921 a report of a committee on prelegal courses. The report stipulated that the sixty hours of courses of college grade (two years) might be either the prescribed work for freshmen and sophomores in Letters and Science or a two-year prelegal course made up of a foreign language, English, science or mathematics, philosophy, history, and social studies.[23] The second alternative was of course open only to students entering the Law School from other universities. The solution was not entirely satisfactory to the law faculty; but later increases in freedom of election in the first two years in Letters and Science have substantially satisfied the wishes of the Law School.

Until the adoption early in the nineties of the case system of instruction which Harvard had launched twenty years earlier, the course of studies at Wisconsin followed the traditional pattern of law schools all over the country in relying

[22] Proceedings of the Law Faculty, 2:217–218, February 26, March 11, 1920. The proceedings are the minutes of the meetings of the law faculty and will be cited as such hereafter. *Regents' Biennial Report*, 1917–18, pp. 170–171.

[23] Minutes of the Meetings of the Law Faculty, 2:282–283, January 12, 1922.

on textbooks and lectures. In adopting the case system Wisconsin broke new ground for Middle Western law schools. This method of study required the students to deduce legal principles from the reports of cases submitted to them. It put the writing of the textbooks, so to speak, in their own hands. If properly chosen the cases showed the evolution of legal principles and their gradual modification and, in the words of the Visitors, tended "to produce graduates who practiced law as a fine art and not as a trade." But as the same committee noted, the new method required well-trained professors and necessitated a greater amount of independent work on the part of the students.[24] It did not at once win the general approval of students but it gradually became an accepted fact which even evoked considerable pride.

The change from a two-year to a three-year course and the requirement for two years of college training for admission both permitted and required modifications in the course of study. In the rearrangement the fundamental topics of the curriculum were grouped in the junior (first) year and the advanced courses in the middle and senior years. An increase in the number of courses offered, together with the more adequate preparation of the student body, enabled many to carry more subjects than those required for the degree. This reflected the growing tendency in professional education to provide for specialization by introducing or extending the elective principle. The first ten-week summer session in 1907 proved an immediate success, not only in helping candidates for the bar examination to brush up on certain fields but also in making it possible for regular students to shorten the time spent in residence.

The attorneys on the Board of Visitors and the Board of Regents urged additional emphasis on practical procedures. In response to such advice the courses in practice were extended in 1903 and supplemented by a practice court. Students received instruction in the drafting of legal papers, including pleadings. They were also required to prosecute and defend cases before a court conducted under the same rules as a circuit court. The

[24] *Regents' Biennial Report,* 1895-96, p. 57.

courses in practice were placed in charge of Robert M. Bashford, an experienced teacher, and Frank T. Boesel, a practitioner of long standing.[25] As a result, the time devoted to practice equaled, and in most cases exceeded, that given in similar courses in other law schools. The question of how far practice should be taught, however, raised many issues. A careful investigation of the practice offered in schools featuring such work indicated that they attracted students, enlarged their knowledge of substantive law, and enhanced their appreciation of its scope and meaning. Provision was made for additional instruction in framing common forms of contracts, liens, wills, abstracts, and the preparation of formal pleadings. At the same time Dean Richards reported that the moot trial, a traditional feature of the practice courses, was at best a shadow of a real action and that the actual results of some of the practice courses hardly warranted the time consumed and the expense involved.[26] Allowed to lapse for a time, the practice court was reinstated in 1911. No attempt was made to have a trial on the facts with a jury but the cause was brought to an issue, a verdict was prepared, judgments were entered, and appeals taken. Thus the student became "familiar with the ordinary steps in bringing an action and carrying it through to an issue, without attempting to simulate the actual details of a trial, which cannot be done in a moot court with any approach to the real conditions of a trial."[27] In addition to the work of the practice court, a number of clubs discussed legal questions, particularly in relation to the newer social and economic problems.

Despite these innovations, many felt that the course of study still failed to do justice to practical considerations. The faculty devoted an increasing amount of time to advising individual students in their work with the moot court and the clubs, which discussed and argued points of law. Special courses in brief-making and office practice were also introduced. Although the courses in code-pleading and code-practice and in the practice court offered "as complete a training in adjective law as can be done effectively in a law school," the faculty still felt that the

[25] Report of Dean Richards, *Regents' Biennial Report*, 1903–04. p. 119.
[26] *Ibid.*, 1909–10, p. 186.	[27] *Ibid.*, 1911–12, p. 142.

The Dean of the Medical School and the Dean of the Law School
Charles R. Bardeen and Harry S. Richards

Top: The Law Building, 1893. *Bottom:* The Medical Campus, 1923

law course as a whole failed to prepare students adequately for actual practice. However efficiently trained he might be, the graduate was sufficiently ignorant of many things pertaining to his profession to be an unsafe adviser. The remedy was sought in part in increasing the number of practical courses in brief-making and in office work. By 1916 the school was offering nineteen semester hours in such practical courses, fully as much in this field as in all the better schools.[28]

Yet the expansion of such practical courses raised problems too. Much of the routine practice work was of such a nature that it could be more readily and naturally acquired in the actual situations in law offices and courts. A majority of each year's graduating class did, to be sure, enter the offices of older lawyers before embarking on independent practice. But many did not. At the request of the faculty, therefore, the regents in 1914 required that all students entering after July 1, 1916, serve an apprenticeship of six months in a law office before receiving a degree. It was obvious, of course, that the success of the experiment rested in large part on the interest which the lawyer took in his apprentice.[29] In the main the system seemed to work fairly well. Increasing the requirements for a degree beyond those of other law schools, however, caused some dissatisfaction among the student body, which petitioned for its modification. Moreover, students studying law as a preliminary to a business career naturally objected to serving an apprenticeship as a condition of receiving the degree. Thus, on the recommendation of the faculty, the regents in 1920 modified the regulation by relieving from apprenticeship students who had secured eighty-two credits, who had been in residence three years and three months, and who had pursued certain designated practice courses. Substantially these requirements still remain in effect at Wisconsin.

The increasing number of students entering law schools to prepare for business or public careers suggested the importance of incorporating into the course of study instruction in administrative law. This was a field which few American law schools

[28] *Ibid.*, 1913–14, p. 149; 1915–16, pp. 155–156.
[29] *Ibid.*, 1915–16, 156–157.

covered in anything except the most elementary and unsatisfactory way, for, by and large, in contrast with most European schools of law, American institutions had grown up outside the universities and had only subsequently been incorporated into them. This explained in part why American law schools had emphasized a highly practical preparation for the profession rather than a comparative, philosophical, and historical approach to jurisprudence.

Despite the difficulties involved, Dean Richards was determined that Wisconsin should at least make a beginning in this latter approach. Before the end of the first decade of the twentieth century he had recommended the introduction of advanced courses in public administrative and comparative law, leading to a special degree. The political science department had already inaugurated some courses in public law and a cooperative arrangement might be worked out with it, Dean Richards believed, to the mutual advantage of both the department and the College of Law.[30] Lack of personnel in the Law School made it hard to go much beyond liaison work with the political scientists, but something, at least, was done. Courses were introduced in various phases of administrative law, including municipal corporations, taxation, and public offices. In 1911 the faculty voted to substitute for the traditional thesis new seminaries in public and private law, and attendance at these courses was henceforth required of third-year men. It was expected that the seminary training would give students a broader view of their profession, acquaint them with the interrelations of legal and social problems, and enable them to see the more cosmopolitan character which law in all countries tended to assume. Convinced of the necessity of examining common law anew in the light of both comparative law and of novel conditions of life, Dean Richards succeeded before World War I in introducing special work in Roman law and jurisprudence. The imperatives of new economic and social conditions within the country were, in his judgment, by no means the only practical reasons for approaching the study of law in terms of its historical evolution in changing social and

[30] *Ibid.*, 1907–08, pp. 155–156.

economic environments. Growing trade with Latin America also invited a larger knowledge of the legal systems and institutions of our southern neighbors.

Wisconsin was not the first school to enrich legal instruction by relating it more closely to the jurisprudence of other times and places as well as to modern social and economic conditions, but it was well in advance of many of the better schools in doing so. The development was important in more ways than one, for the interest in broadening the course of study in the direction of comparative and public law reflected the growing conviction that "law schools must not be content to be drill-masters for barristers, but must be the medium through which the lawyers of the new generation shall study other systems and by comparison seek to improve their own."[31] This implied, of course, the corollary that law thus broadly conceived was an essential part of a liberal education. The study of law as an aspect of civilization justified its recognition, in effect, not merely as a professional technique but as an important part of general university study.

The faculty believed that it was contributing to the public welfare and exemplifying the Wisconsin ideal of service to the commonwealth in training the majority of the practicing attorneys of the state, since by 1920 three-fourths of the members of the bar had taken their degree at the Law School. Moreover, the growing interest in preparing men for public careers in administrative law was an even more explicit response to the Van Hise philosophy.

In addition to such evidence of rapprochement with the Wisconsin Idea, the Law School found special ways of serving the public interest. We have already noted the important brief which Professor Gilmore prepared for the Wisconsin Conservation Commission. The most striking single effort to channel the talent of the faculty into a specific public project was the participation in the Wisconsin branch of the American Institute of Criminal Law and Criminology, which was launched in the autumn of 1909, members of the faculty taking an active part in the work of organization. Professors William U. Moore

[31] *Ibid.*, 1917–18, p. 170.

and Oliver S. Rundell served as secretary and as assistant secretary of the national organization, and other members of the faculty were active in committee work and in conferences. On November 27, 1909, a state conference on criminal law and criminology unanimously adopted a resolution requesting the regents to consider the advisability of establishing a professorship for the comparative and critical study of the results of remedial law.[32] The law faculty pointed out to Van Hise the great need of complete and accurate statistics concerning the actual results of the existing system of remedial law and called attention to the widespread criticism of the effectiveness of judicial processes and machinery.[33] After some delay the regents decided against appointing a special professor but did set aside an appropriation for the investigation of questions relating to the reform of criminal procedure. The faculty supervised the new work. To determine whether or not there had been undue delays in the institution, trial, and disposition of criminal cases, three counties were selected for special study. Rundell prepared a report of the investigation which was circulated as a bulletin of the University. A comparable investigation was carried out to determine the time element in civil cases.[34] All these activities aided considerably in bringing the Law School into more intimate relation with bench and bar and in forwarding criminal-law reform. Some of the recommendations of the Wisconsin branch of the American Institute of Criminal Law and Criminology were enacted into law by the 1911 legislature.

The first World War provided an occasion for demonstrating the readiness of the faculty to use its special knowledge in the public interest. Since virtually every student physically fit entered the armed forces, the faculty could readily be spared. Professor Howard L. Smith worked as a special agent of the War Trade Board in South America and Dean Richards acted as chief of the editorial division of the Bureau of War Trade Intelligence. Professor Rundell became a special legal investi-

---

[32] Papers of the Board of Regents, January 19, 1910.
[33] Minutes of the Meetings of the Law Faculty, February 25, March 2, 1910, pp. 230–231; Papers of the Board of Regents, March 2, 1910.
[34] *Regents' Biennial Report*, 1911–12, pp. 143–144.

gator of the War Trade Board, and Professor John D. Wickhem succeeded Dean Richards as chief of the editorial division.[35] The school also gave instruction in military law to the Student Army Training Corps unit on the campus.

The armistice brought back the students, and the readjustment involved no unusual difficulties. The expansion of the curriculum, already under way, continued. In 1923 labor law was introduced into the curriculum—a pioneering enterprise in the Middle West and particularly expressive of the Wisconsin approach in education. The experiment with the apprenticeship system and a renewed effort to advance legal education marked the postwar years. An era came to an end in 1929 with the death of Dean Richards. For over a quarter of a century the administrative head of a school which had come to be recognized as one of the leading centers for legal training in the country, Dean Richards consistently worked against sham sentiment, shoddy pretense, and flashy educational fads. "He aimed at something vastly higher than keeping an educational shop wherein were taught the latest tricks of an antisocial trade— wherein sharp practitioners learned to put a keen edge upon their weapons of reprisal and offence," declared the regents in their obituary resolution. Able, amiable, and devoted, Dean Richards certainly emphasized scholarship as opposed to salesmanship and showmanship. Yet his devotion to erudition did not beguile him into "parading mere dullness as depth or a subterfuge for seeking by being ponderous to delude the world into thinking him profound."[36] He indeed left the University and the state deeply indebted to him.

[35] *Ibid.*, 1919–20, pp. 110–111.
[36] Papers of the Board of Regents, April 24, 1929.

13.

The College of Engineering

THE halting beginnings of the College of Engineering have already been sketched. It has also been observed that this branch of the University, in its early years, suffered no more from the opposition and apathy of the University administration than did the agricultural college. It lacked, however, one important thing that the agricultural college and the Experiment Station possessed. The engineering college had no vociferous constituency to urge and badger the Board of Regents and the University authorities. Neither in this nor subsequent periods was this college able to find the means of forming an association with the manufacturing and industrial interests of the state comparable or even analogous to the association which the Experiment Station and the College of Agriculture formed with the agricultural groups. Nor was this because the engineering college refused to try. The failure resided, perhaps in large part, in the basic difference between agriculture and industry. From the nature of things, farming as an economic activity is competitive; industry tends, in our society, to be monopolistic. While the successful farmer is not without his special skills and knowledge, he works essentially the same type of soil as his neighbors; he is subject to the same sun, the same winds, the same floods, and the same droughts as his neighbors; his problems of transportation and marketing are similar. His success or failure is spelled in terms of his good luck and good judgment in dealing with a host of factors, both natural and man-made, which condition his occupation and bear equally upon him and his neighbors and competitors. In contrast, the manufacturer, although subject to forces beyond his control, also relied extensively on possession of the patented machine or the secret or patented process. The farmer might call upon the agricultural college to solve his problems, knowing that the information would help his competitors as well as himself, and yet be little disturbed by the knowledge. With manufacturers, however, it was different. Sole possession of patent rights was, and often still is, the key to industrial success. Manufacturers could not go nor did they want to go to the publicly supported engineering college for assistance in the invention of machines and processes which they could not patent and which might render their own machines or processes obsolete. Moreover, the diversity of industry, with its multitude of special problems, made it difficult to find a set of common problems such as the dairy farmers presented to the agricultural college. The diversity of industry, the prevalent corporate structure of the manufacturing enterprises, the importance of patents, combined with the need for engineering talent to solve industrial problems, served to bring into existence both the consulting engineer and the industrial engineer. The engineering college was expected to train them, but it should not compete with them in the practice of their professions. For these reasons the engineering college could be expected to train engineers for industry but not go very far beyond that point. In the development of public projects such as a water system and sewerage system the college was called upon for assistance. Thus these various factors gave the engineering college an orientation much different from that of the agricultural college.

Although the University was obligated under the terms of the Morrill grant to offer instruction in engineering and mechanic arts, for almost two decades after the passage of this act compliance was never more than nominal. Funds for the use of the department of engineering were modest at best, and facilities for instruction were almost nonexistent. In 1880 the University owned only one transit. Storm Bull, who had come

to the University as an instructor in engineering in 1879, re-
called twenty years later that until Chamberlin came to the
University, the engineering department was a stepchild. The
University never did more than permit the course to go on.[1]
This condition changed rapidly after Chamberlin's arrival.

Chamberlin's work in getting legislation to provide funds
for the expansion of engineering instruction and to provide a
legal basis for the organization of a college of engineering has
already been discussed in another connection. These two measures, the one providing for financial support of the college,
the other permitting reorganization, furnished the foundation
on which the college was to be built. Immediately after the
passage of the laws, the Board of Regents appointed a special
committee, consisting of President Chamberlin, William P.
Bartlett, and Frank Challoner, a graduate of the University
and a sturdy supporter of the engineering college, to prepare a
report on the curriculum of the college. Before the report was
submitted, Chamberlin went east to visit other engineering
colleges. Among those he visited in search of information and
suggestions were Michigan, Cornell, Harvard, Yale, Columbia,
Lehigh, Johns Hopkins, Rensselaer—oldest of the technical
schools in the United States—and Stevens Institute of Technology.[2]

Under the old organization, courses had been offered in civil
engineering, mechanical engineering, and in mining and metallurgical engineering. All were four-year courses. The primary
emphasis had been placed upon the acquisition of a knowledge
of the pure sciences on which these specialties rested. There
was very little work offered in the respective fields of applied
science.[3] The regents' special committee now recommended the
establishment of new courses and the reorganization of the old
ones. First of all the committee urged the establishment of a
course in railway engineering, the promise of which Chamberlin
had used to get legislative support from the railway lobby in
1889. It was proposed that this course consist of the civil engi-

[1] Storm Bull, "Technical Education at the University of Wisconsin," *The Wisconsin Engineer*, 3:1–17 (January, 1899).

[2] Reports to the Regents, C:20–25, June 18, 1889.

[3] *University Catalogue*, 1886–87, pp. 50–57.

neering courses related to railways and a number of special courses dealing with railway projects. The latter would include study of such matters as the survey of routes, earthwork computation, economics of railway location, specifications for railway construction and machinery, economics of railway construction, maintenance and management, structure and efficiency of locomotive engines, railway jurisprudence, hoisting and pumping machinery, bridge building, engineering architecture, "and such other subjects as may be found practicable and desirable in the development of the courses." The committee explained: "The design of the foregoing course is to prepare railway engineers in the ordinary sense of the term."[4] It also recommended that provision be made for one year of graduate work, the courses to consist of advanced instruction in the subjects of railway engineering.

The committee also proposed that the course in mechanical engineering be so modified as to train students in those subjects relating particularly to the mechanics of railroading. Lastly the committee proposed that a course be established in electrical engineering. This was to embrace instruction in magnetism, electricity, and electrodynamics, treated "mathematically and practically." The course should also include the study of various tests and measurements, methods of determining and standardizing electrical units, economics of electric distribution, transmission of power, electric motors and locomotives, lighting, dynamos, photometry, simple and multiple telephony, automatic signal systems, electrolysis, and electrometallurgy. The committee felt that students of electrical engineering should be grounded in both mechanical engineering and in theoretical physics. Provision should also be made for one year of graduate work. In view of the fact that the first electric lighting systems were not installed until 1882, the projected course in electrical engineering was much more of a pioneering venture than the course in railway engineering.

Lastly the committee considered the problem of whether the new college should employ regular professors to teach these courses or whether practicing engineers should be used as

[4] Reports to the Regents, C:21, June 18, 1889.

special lecturers. Acknowledging advantages in each system, the committee concluded: "Our judgment is that both methods may be employed to advantage, and that while the courses are developing themselves, special lecturers will afford the most readily adaptable method, and will besides give the widest and best advertisement to the course. Later on when a sufficient body of students shall have undertaken the courses, it seems altogether probable that regular systematic instruction will be required."[5] As it turned out, both methods were used effectively.

The report of the committee was adopted and the expansion of the college promptly began. It has already been observed that the College of Engineering was different from the College of Agriculture in its orientation. It must also be observed that in large measure the forces which shaped the College of Engineering were generated within the Board of Regents and the engineering faculty after it had been created. The engineering college would be concerned primarily with instruction of young engineers. Its research function would be only incidental. The College of Agriculture, on the other hand, perhaps in part because of its temporary failure to attract students, early became primarily concerned with research; its most important instructional activities were carried on by other means than conventional collegiate methods.[6]

Even before a full staff had been recruited, the college announced the enlarged program of instruction in engineering. Seven "systematic" courses were offered: civil, railway, mechanical, mining, metallurgical, and electrical engineering and railroad mechanics.[7] It became quickly apparent, however, that the program was too ambitious and that not all the courses would attract sufficient patronage to justify their continuance. In 1892 Leander M. Hoskins reported that no students had enrolled in the course in metallurgical engineering and recommended that it be dropped temporarily. The remaining courses

[5] *Ibid.,* 22.

[6] This difference has persisted to the present. In 1946–47, for example, some 64 per cent of the total University budget for organized research was allocated to the agricultural college and only 2½ per cent to the College of Engineering. Morton O. Withey, dean of the College of Engineering, "The Engineering College and Industry," an address delivered at Chilton, October 8, 1946.

[7] *University Catalogue,* 1889–90, p. 129.

were reorganized and revised "in the direction of specialization" and grouped under four sequences: two in civil engineering (consisting of railway engineering and structural engineering), mechanical and electrical engineering.[8] Two years later, the
two civil engineering courses were combined into one.[9] In 1897
the civil engineering course was divided again into two courses,
civil engineering and municipal and sanitary engineering.[10] In
1899 a fifth course was added, applied electrochemistry.[11] A
year later the offerings were extended again to include a premetallurgical course, and a new course in general engineering
was also created.[12] Thus by 1900 the college was again offering
seven systematic courses.

Although special lecturers were used for several years immediately after the reorganization, and the College of Engineering depended upon the College of Letters and Science for
instruction in mathematics, chemistry, physics, geology, and
allied disciplines, the engineering faculty itself was gradually
increased. When Chamberlin arrived at the University, Allan
D. Conover was professor of civil engineering and Storm Bull
held the chair of mechanical engineering, which had been
created as a separate professorship in 1885. Hoskins was an instructor. Charles I. King was superintendent of the department
of mechanic arts. In 1889 he was made professor of mechanical
practice. The same year Hoskins was promoted to the rank
of assistant professor of mechanics and soon thereafter to the
professorship of pure and applied mechanics. When Conover
resigned in 1890, he was succeeded by Charles D. Marx, of
Cornell, who resigned in 1891 to go to Stanford. The position
was then divided into a professorship of railway engineering,
to which Nelson O. Whitney—a practicing railway engineer—
was appointed, and a professorship of bridge and hydraulic

[8] Leander M. Hoskins to Thomas C. Chamberlin, Reports to the Regents, C:348,
June 13, 1892; *University Catalogue*, 1891–92, p. 138.
[9] *University Catalogue*, 1893–94, p. 108.   [10] *Ibid.*, 1896–97, p. 150.
[11] *Ibid.*, 1898–99, p. 178. As early as 1892, Professor John E. Davies had offered instruction in primary and secondary batteries. *Ibid.*, 1891–92, pp. 154–155.
Extended and later renamed "applied electrochemistry," this course was taken over
by Charles F. Burgess shortly after his graduation from the University in 1896. With
the support and encouragement of Professor Dugald C. Jackson, he expanded it
into a full engineering course leading to a degree.
[12] *Ibid.*, 1899–1900, p. 174.

engineering, to which Charles B. Wing, a recent graduate of the Cornell College of Engineering, was appointed. In 1891 Dugald C. Jackson, who had also trained at Cornell and who had served as a division engineer of the Edison company, became the new professor of electrical engineering. Albert W. Smith came at the same time as professor of machine design. David Starr Jordan carried Hoskins, Wing, and Smith off to Stanford in 1892 and thereby nearly disrupted the engineering college, but their places were taken by Edward R. Maurer, Frederick E. Turneaure, and Forrest R. Jones respectively. Arthur W. Richter became instructor in 1891. John G. D. Mack, Leonard S. Smith, and James R. Young joined the staff as instructors in 1893 and two years later Mack and Smith rose to the rank of assistant professor of machine design and topographical engineering respectively. Samuel Byrod Fortenbaugh became assistant professor of electrical engineering in 1894, but his distinguished career was to lie outside the engineering college. In 1895 Charles F. Burgess became instructor in electrical engineering.

Although this by no means completes the list of appointments during the period under study, it indicates the quality of the engineering college faculty. The men who came to constitute the expanding faculty were for the most part young men. The influence of Cornell upon the engineering college is suggested by the fact that a number of these men were trained there. Wing and Turneaure were graduates of Cornell, and Jackson and Mack had studied there after attending Pennsylvania State College and Rose Polytechnic Institute respectively. Whitney was a graduate of the University of Pennsylvania. But Wisconsin was also well represented. Conover and Hoskins were both graduates of the University, as were Maurer, Leonard S. Smith, Richter, Burgess, and others. Although Charles Kendall Adams had no marked sympathy for the College of Engineering, the youth, vigor, and capability of its faculty so impressed him that in 1894 he boasted to the Board of Regents: "In the matter of personnel, I believe that we have at Wisconsin the best engineering school in the Northwest. . . . We can put the college in such a condition as to convince the public that we have the best facilities for education in engineering that exist in the Northwest."[13]

Adams and others might well have been impressed, not only by the vigor of the faculty but by its productivity. Hoskins had published his first book, *Graphic Statics*, in 1892. Jackson brought out *Electricity and Magnetism and Construction of Dynamos* in 1893; *Electricity and Magnetism* in 1895; and *Alternating Currents and Alternating Currents Machinery* in 1896. Turneaure, in collaboration with John B. Johnson and Charles W. Bryan, had published *Theory and Practice of Modern Framed Structures* in 1893, and he was shortly to begin his investigations to determine the stress in bridges under moving-train loads. Moreover, the members of the college contributed to the technical journals, to the *Bulletin of the University of Wisconsin, Engineering Series,* and to the *Wisconsin Engineer,* established by the college in 1896. Although not conducting research on the scale that it was being done by the College of Agriculture, the faculty of the engineering college contributed to the rapidly growing literature of the profession.

The most important work of the college, however, was instruction. The rapidity with which this work increased is suggested by the fact that in 1890 only 89 students were registered in the college; in 1902–1903 the number of students enrolled in the engineering college had reached 585. The faculty had grown during the same period from four to over twenty.

For ten years after it had been reorganized, the College of Engineering was without a dean. The government of the college reposed in a Board of Engineers which consisted at first of all the members of the engineering faculty and subsequently of only the senior professors. This board served as a deliberative faculty body and also as the principal administrative body of the college. Either through the agency of a committee or an appointed agent, it handled problems ranging from the super-

[13] Charles Kendall Adams to the regents, Reports to the Regents, D:26, June 19, 1894.

vision of janitor service and student behavior to recommendations to the president and the Board of Regents for the creation
of new chairs and the appointment of new members of the
faculty.

Standards of admission to the college, fixed in part by the
Board of Engineers, followed in general the standards established
for admission to the College of Letters and Science. In 1894,
however, the Board of Engineers began to press for additional
mathematics as a prerequisite to admission to the college.[14] Sev-
èral years later, the board voted to accept the four-year courses
proposed by the board of education of Milwaukee for the high
school manual training program as adequate preparation for
admission to the engineering college provided "students taking
advantage of this course shall take History in the University."[15]
In general, however, the board exhibited little concern over
admission standards.

Early in 1895, the Board of Regents voted to increase all
student fees. While this increase applied to all colleges, it bore
most heavily upon the engineering students since the incidental
fee, which even residents of the state were required to pay, was
raised from $12 to $40 a year.[16] Before the announcement of
the increased fee was printed in the *University Catalogue*, the
Board of Engineers had appointed a committee to investigate
the problem. In view of the substantial increase in fees, the
committee reported, provision must be made at once for the
"worthy class of engineering students who pay their college
expenses by the proceeds of their individual work." In eastern
colleges of engineering, where large fees were charged, provision was made for these students by awarding scholarships.
This was true in both privately and publicly supported institutions and was generally considered to be good public
policy. Accordingly, the committee proposed that the engineering faculty recommend that the Board of Regents establish
forty-five scholarships, to be given for two-year periods, covering

[14] Records of the Board of Engineers, 1:55, June 11, 1894. The formal record
of the transactions of the Board of Engineers begins in 1890. The first two volumes are entitled Records of the Board of Engineers; thereafter, it is the
Record of the Engineering Faculty.

[15] *Ibid.*, 1:150, December 5, 1898.   [16] *University Catalogue*, 1894–95, p. 59.

the incidental fees. Half would be given to freshmen on a basis of competitive examinations, the other half to juniors on a basis of academic grades during their first two years. These scholarships would cost less than one-third of the increased amount expected to be collected from the higher fees, they would make it possible for worthy but impoverished young men to enroll in the college, and they would serve to elevate standards in the college.[17] The regents were unwilling to establish the scholarships, but the next year the incidental fee was reduced to $12 a year.[18]

Determination of the course of study and requirements for graduation was likewise largely the responsibility of the Board of Engineers, although the curriculum was subject, nominally at least, to review by the general faculty. The records do not reveal conflict either within the Board of Engineers or between it and the general faculty in the determination of the curriculum or the requirements for graduation. These matters seem largely to have been left to the representatives of the college. Indeed, in 1900, the general faculty declared that the engineering college might make minor changes in the curriculum without referring to the general faculty.[19] The record of the Board of Engineers shows that relatively little time was given to consideration of special elements in the curriculum. Shortly after the board had been constituted, the junior engineers presented a petition asking that they be relieved of the requirement of preparing and delivering a commencement oration. The board heard the petition and moved to comply with it.[20] In 1893 the board ruled that, except for juniors and seniors then enrolled, students proposing to graduate from one of the engineering courses must have a reading knowledge of French or German.[21] Subsequently, however, the board accepted Spanish, Italian, and Latin as substitutes for the French or German requirement. Indeed, on at least one occasion, Norse was presented and accepted—suggesting that the lan-

[17] Records of the Board of Engineers, 1:71, April 13, 1894.
[18] *University Catalogue,* 1895–96, p. 71.
[19] Minutes of the Meetings of the Faculty, 4:250, January 22, 1900.
[20] Records of the Board of Engineers, 1:7, September 28, 1891.
[21] *Ibid.,* 1:36, September 19, 1893.

guage requirement was regarded more as a "discipline" than as a tool for the young engineer. It was not until 1898 that the board determined that fifteen hours of work a week should constitute the minimum load and that no student should be permitted to enroll for more than eighteen hours without faculty permission.[22]

But if matters pertaining to the curriculum did not loom large in the deliberations of the Board of Engineers, maintenance of academic standards did. At its regular meetings, the board considered numerous cases of students who were delinquent in their grades. Those who were doing unsatisfactory work in all or most of their classes were notified that their connection with the college was to be terminated; those on the borderline were warned that unless their work improved, they would be required to withdraw. Also prominent at each meeting of the board were the petitions from students who had been dismissed for poor work asking to be reinstated. Not infrequently the student petitioner was conditionally readmitted to the college. Thus in 1893 the Board of Engineers permitted a delinquent student to re-enter the college but firmly decreed that he could return only with "the strict understanding that he does not take part in college athletics."[23] The high academic mortality rate in the engineering college, registered in the difference between the number who entered as freshmen in a given year and the number who graduated four years later, was caused only in part because students could not meet the expense of four years of professional training. The full program of solid work was a large element in this situation. Before the end of the century, provision was made to allow students to take five years to complete the four-year courses.

Although constantly concerned with the academic standings of the students in the college, the Board of Engineers took but little interest in other phases of student activities, partly because matters of discipline were handled by the general faculty, and partly no doubt because of the nature of the college. Occasionally the Board of Engineers took a brief, unenthusiastic

[22] *Ibid.*, 1:134, May 10, 1898.
[23] *Ibid.*, 1:26, January 6, 1893.

interest in student social gatherings.[24] Even more rarely was
the board concerned with problems of student conduct. When
it received the report charging that some engineering students
"were befouling the Reading Room with spitting," and others
were making loud and unseemly noises in the drafting room,
the board merely instructed the secretary "to write a notice for
posting, ordering Engineering students to stop spitting and to
avoid making disturbances in the Building."[25]

The College of Engineering prospered without a dean, but
President Adams was not wholly content with the arrangement.
The Colleges of Law, of Letters and Science, and of Agriculture all had deans. For the College of Engineering to be without
a dean constituted a hierarchical fault in the administrative
structure of the University and a source of vague embarrassment to the president. With three of the colleges neatly organized and directed by their respective chieftains, it was as
incongruous to have the fourth administered by a committee
of the faculty as it would be to have one company of a regiment commanded by a committee of master sergeants. In 1896
Adams first recommended to the Board of Regents that a dean
be appointed for the engineering college. Not only would
many administrative problems be solved by such an appointment but, Adams declared, "I think it must be admitted that
a College without a head is lacking somewhat in the active
and aggressive qualities which are necessary to impress the
extent and characteristics of the college upon the imaginations
of the people."[26] In short, the college would enjoy a better
reputation if it had a dean. But the Board refused to move. A
year later Adams repeated his recommendation. He conceded
that financial considerations might make it necessary to delay
the appointment, yet action was imperative.[27]

In June, 1897, the regents finally authorized the appointment of a dean, but Adams encountered difficulty in finding
a satisfactory man. A year later he reported that he had visited
Ann Arbor, Ithaca, Washington, Baltimore, and New York,

[24] *Ibid.*, 2:99, November 25, 1901.   [25] *Ibid.*, 1:28, March 13, 1893.
[26] Adams to the regents, Reports to the Regents, D:165, January 21, 1896.
[27] *Ibid.*, D:282, April 20, 1897.

but he had found no one for the position. He had offered the deanship to President Mendenhall of Worcester Polytechnic Institute of Massachusetts, but the offer had been refused. Since it seemed impossible to find the satisfactory dean immediately, Adams proposed a temporary reorganization of the engineering college into three departments. The senior professor in each department would be made head of the department and the Board of Regents would select a temporary dean from among the department heads. The temporary dean would then be responsible for allocating the funds of the college among the departments.[28] Apparently Adams had found the allocation of funds an extremely distasteful task which he was compelled to perform in cases of disagreement in the Board of Engineers.

But the temporary reorganization was not adopted. Within eight months Adams had found the man for the post. The man he recommended and the Board promptly appointed was John Butler Johnson, then professor of civil engineering at Washington University, St. Louis, where for a time Frederick E. Turneaure was his colleague. Johnson was born in Ohio in 1850. He had begun teaching in a country school at the age of seventeen and was in his middle twenties before he enrolled at the University of Michigan. He obtained a degree in civil engineering from that institution in 1878. After five years' service with the United States Lake Survey and the Mississippi River Commission, he accepted an appointment as professor at Washington University. His abundant industry and energy were attested by the fact that while at St. Louis he not only had done the teaching required of him, but also, as a consulting engineer, had designed water works for six municipalities and sewerage systems for three. He was active in a host of professional engineering organizations. He had launched the *Index of Current Engineering Literature,* the first two volumes of which were the product of his own labor. He had also found time to prepare several textbooks on engineering and had been instrumental in opening a lumber-testing laboratory at St. Louis.[29] Adams reported that Johnson was willing to come

[28] *Ibid.,* D:398–399, April 19, 1898.
[29] Adams to the regents, Reports to the Regents, D:469, January 17, 1899. *The Wisconsin Engineer,* 3:163–166 (May, 1899).

to the University for a salary of $3,500 and the use of a stenographer. The new dean proposed to make extensive changes in the college, but the changes would not be "so radical as to be regarded as revolutionary."[30]

Dean Johnson was energetic, ambitious, and active. At last Dean Henry of the agriculture college had a competitor almost as able, energetic, and ruthless as himself in seeking advantages for his college. Johnson's influence was felt almost at once not only in the engineering college but elsewhere in the University, particularly in the briefly revived interest in extension work and in the internal pressure quickly generated for the creation of a school of commerce in the College of Letters and Science. Johnson's own considered attitude toward engineering and engineering education was set forth briefly in an address before the students of the college in 1901.

Education in general, Johnson held, was a "means of gradual emancipation from the thralldom of incompetence." He divided all education into two kinds: that intended to give competence to serve and that intended to give competence to appreciate and enjoy. The learned professions, which included engineering, belonged to the first group. Engineering, he told the students, had little in common with society. The engineer dealt only with inanimate objects. "Neither do the ordinary social or political problems enter in any way into his sphere of operations."[31] The engineer need be little concerned with the social sciences and the humanities. His technical education must give him competence in using data, in observation, in translating theoretical knowledge into practice. But Dean Johnson was not opposed to cultural knowledge because it had no professional value to an engineer. On the contrary, he urged young engineers to greater cultural attainment for a happier life and more lucrative employment. He pictured engineers as engineers of men and capital as well as of materials. Hence, he urged engineering students to take courses in the new School of Commerce and to become acquainted with literature and history. The latter, he felt, would enrich life.[32] Johnson, of course, was keenly

---

[30] Reports to the Regents, D:469, January 17, 1899.
[31] John B. Johnson, "Two Kinds of Education for Engineers," *The Wisconsin Engineer*, 6:1, 3 (December, 1901). [32] *Ibid.*, 6:1–14.

aware of how basically the new technology, epitomized in the railroads and the factories, was altering the basic fabric of economic life, and he must have been aware of the close relation between the economic structure and social and political forms of society; yet he said nothing to suggest that he felt that engineers, as citizens and professional men, should be either concerned or interested in the social consequences of their actions. The engineer dealt only with the inanimate. In these attitudes Dean Johnson was, of course, in harmony with his contemporaries.

Johnson arrived in Madison in February, 1899.[33] He remained long enough to help get an appropriation for a new building for the college and then left for Europe. He returned to assume his duties in the autumn.

The new building had first been asked for in 1894. At that time the faculty complained that the college, then mostly housed in Science Hall, was already encroaching on the space of other departments; surveying instruments had to be kept in the janitor's supply room, and the library had to be used also as a drafting room and blowpipe laboratory. Moreover, more room was needed to permit the establishment of a department of architecture.[34] Instead of procuring a new building, the Board of Regents arranged for the enlargement of the engineering shops.[35] Two years later Adams was convinced of the need of a department of architecture, but the Board was unwilling, either then or later when Dean Johnson repeated the recommendation, to create such a department.[36] By 1898, however, Adams felt the time was propitious to seek a new building, and the request was laid before the Board to be presented to the legislature.[37] There were no other pressing demands that year for buildings, and the need of the engineers was great. The Board had appointed Johnson dean of the college shortly after the legislature met and he had come at once to Madison to

[33] The records of the Board of Engineers show that Johnson first attended a meeting of the faculty on February 23, 1899.

[34] Records of the Board of Engineers, 1:56–57, June 15, 1894.

[35] *Regents' Biennial Report*, 1893–94, p. 52.

[36] *Ibid.*, 1895–96, pp. 16–17.   [37] *Ibid.*, 1897–98, p. 32.

help push the building appropriation through the legislature. Unexpected assistance was received in February when Professors Robert W. Wood and Dugald C. Jackson succeeded in rendering an unusual service to the citizens of Madison and neighboring communities.

In February of 1899, with the ground bare of snow, a cold wave had moved across Wisconsin. Temperatures had dropped below zero and stayed there. Before the cold weather abated, service pipes leading from the water mains to residences had frozen. This minor calamity affected many communities in the vicinity of Madison. Ordinarily householders would have waited for the spring thaw to have running water available again. However, Professor Wood, of the physics department, soon to win the local nickname of "Wizard," and Dugald C. Jackson, professor of electrical engineering, contrived to thaw out the pipes by running an electric current through them from the mains, which had not frozen, to the residences. According to the awed but enthusiastic report of the experiment given by the *Wisconsin State Journal,* the device was first used at the homes of James D. Butler and ex-Senator William F. Vilas. It worked perfectly, heating the pipes sufficiently to thaw the ice in fifteen to thirty minutes.

The *Journal* could only compare it with the Babcock milk-fat test and declared, "One such boon emanating from the modest unassuming ranks of scholarship does more to still the carpings against higher education of uninformed and prejudiced critics than volleys of literature and speeches."[38] President Adams was not one to let the opportunity go unexploited. A circular was prepared for the president's signature describing how the trick was done, estimating the cost of the service, and providing sketches of how the electrical connections should be made. The circular was widely distributed. Even the *Engineering News,* published in New York, reported fully on this new, simple, and economical method of thawing out water pipes.[39]

No one would claim that this invention, which did help keep

[38] *Wisconsin State Journal,* February 22, 1899.
[39] *The Wisconsin Engineer,* 3:288–291 (May, 1899).

the plumbing in order, represented a great contribution, but it did have the effect of winning for the engineering college and the two professors much favorable publicity, for it had in it elements which appealed to Americans: it permitted a seemingly impossible job to be done quickly and simply. How much this incident contributed to the success of the request for a building appropriation it is impossible to say, but certainly it lost no support among the legislators. And funds were obtained for a new building.

Although the engineering college was primarily occupied with offering instruction to young engineers, it began relatively early to contribute to engineering literature. Besides the textbooks and other productions of the professors which found publication outside the University channels, papers were published in the *Wisconsin Engineer,* a college publication, and in the *University Bulletin.* The *Wisconsin Engineer* was launched in 1896. The Board of Regents agreed to appropriate the sum of fifty dollars to help start it.[40] The magazine, published quarterly for a number of years, was begun, in the words of the editor, so that Wisconsin engineering students would be represented among the technical journals of the country and thereby take a "more active part in the dissemination of engineering knowledge and experience." Moreover, the magazine was to serve "especially to make known the results of original investigation by students and others connected with the University and to publish communications of general interest from graduates who are engaged in the practice of their profession."[41] The first issue of the magazine ran to over one hundred pages, but later issues were thinner. Although it experienced many financial difficulties in the early years, it has continued regular publication. The contributions printed included many senior theses, either in whole or in part, along with technical papers by the professors. Occasionally historical pieces were printed. The senior theses dealt rather largely with reports of tests of machinery or materials or were formal papers presenting a solution of an engineering problem. It was the boast of

[40] Records of the Board of Regents, D:462, April 21, 1896.
[41] *The Wisconsin Engineer,* 1:3-4.

the editors that reports of tests of machinery often caused manufacturers to redesign machinery in terms of the college findings. The *University Bulletin, Engineering Series,* served as a vehicle for some of the more formal papers of the engineering faculty and as a means of distributing the addresses on engineering subjects by visiting specialists. Although the publications of the engineering college were in no way comparable to the research contributions found in the bulletins of the agricultural Experiment Station, they did furnish a means of publicizing the work of the college.

Some of the work done by the students and published in the *Wisconsin Engineer* represented the beginning of a life work. Charles W. Hart and Charles H. Parr, who graduated from the engineering course in 1896, collaborated on a thesis dealing with internal-combustion engines. The first such engine owned by the University was constructed on the basis of designs furnished by these two men. Built in the engineering shops by Paul F. Lueth and Halsten J. Thorkelson in 1897, it was an eight-horse-power engine, typical of the time, having neither carburetor nor electrical ignition system. During the late 1890's, in part because of the interest stimulated by Hart and Parr, experiments were conducted in the shops aimed at developing an electrical ignition system, a spark plug, and a carburetor. Two types of electrical ignition systems were experimented with, both subsequently perfected elsewhere; one involved the use of batteries and an induction coil, the other a magneto. In both cases the experimenters encountered difficulty in contriving a satisfactory timing mechanism.[42]

Hart and Parr, after trying to organize a plant for the manufacture of internal-combustion engines in Madison, found financial support and moved to Charles City, Iowa, where they developed a respectable business producing small farm engines. By the time of the first World War, Hart-Parr had become almost a household word on the farms of Iowa and surrounding states and their engines had served to give many a farm boy the experience which would enable him to deal confidently if not

[42] Interview, Carstensen with Russell W. Hargrave, March 5, 1947. Hargrave was a student assistant in the engineering shops at the time and subsequently a member of the engineering faculty.

always competently with his father's Tin Lizzie. Similarly the work of Charles F. Burgess in electrochemistry, as both student and teacher, was to launch him ultimately upon an active business career based upon his experimental work.

One other development in the college deserves at least brief notice, the attempt to develop a mechanics course comparable to the short course in the agricultural college. Chamberlin had proposed the organization of mechanics' institutes as early as 1889, and he had asked the legislature for the sum of $4,000 for this work. The legislature refused to give the money.[43] Similar plans were proposed from time to time, but until Dean Johnson arrived, no one within the college exhibited a marked interest in extension work.[44] In 1901, however, a summer school for apprentices and artisans was launched. The school was designed for carpenters, machinists, sheetmetal workers, and stationary, marine, and locomotive engineers.[45] Forty-five men enrolled in the six-weeks course, twenty-eight of whom the director, Professor Mack, called typical students; the remainder were students already members of the engineering college. The school had been well publicized, but the enrollment was not as large as the director anticipated. Professor Mack felt that this was to be explained first by the fact that the school was conducted at a rush time in industry when few men could be spared. Secondly, the expenses were too high for those who must pay tuition, laboratory fees, and board and room. If the school was to be continued, he urged, it should be transferred to the industrial cities of the state and should be conducted at a time when mechanics and others could attend.[46] The school for artisans never attained the popularity or support enjoyed by the agricultural short course, but it did represent an attempt on the part of the College of Engineering to serve the mechanics and artisans as the agricultural college served the farmers.

But whatever its failures in the direction of popular education, the engineering college was prosperous. Its graduates

[43] Chamberlin to George H. Paul and to Frank Challoner, February 8, 1889; Chamberlin to William P. Bartlett, February 27, 1889. See volume one, the chapter on extension, for discussion of mechanics' institutes.

[44] Cf. Records of the Board of Engineers, 1:128, February 7, 1898.

[45] *The Wisconsin Engineer*, 5:201–207 (May, 1901) contains the full announcement of the school.   [46] *Ibid.*, 6:28–39 (December, 1901).

were already widely scattered, many holding responsible positions. Its student patronage was increasing yearly. The new dean was vigorously promoting expansion and by 1900 was already looking forward with President Adams to having the strongest engineering school in that part of the country. "Inside of twelve years," Johnson informed Adams, "we can have here the greatest school of engineering west of New York, with nearly 1000 students, and with a faculty, buildings, and equipment equal to any in the world. . . . My only fear is that our numbers will increase more rapidly than we can care for them, and that the state may not wish to be burdened with the expense of so great an engineering department."[47] But neither Johnson nor Adams was to see that day. Johnson was killed in an accident early in the summer of 1902, only shortly before Adams died in California. Professor Turneaure was appointed in 1903 to succeed Johnson. He held this position until his retirement in 1937.

∅

IN 1900 Dean John Butler Johnson had predicted that the College of Engineering would have a student body of a thousand within twelve years. During the first seven years of the century it appeared that he had underestimated rather than overestimated the growth of the college. In the school year 1900–1901 the total enrollment in the college had reached 411; in 1907–1908 it reached 921. But the next year it began to drop. Ten years later only 552 students were enrolled. Shortly after World War I enrollment increased again to a high of 1,283 in 1921–1922, but by 1925–26 it had again fallen below a thousand.[48]

The rapid increase in enrollment was expected; the sharp drop, experienced also by other technical and engineering schools, was unforeseen. In September, 1908, Dean Turneaure pointed out that during the past ten years the enrollment of the colleges had increased at the average rate of seventy students a year. He cautioned that the growth might be checked

[47] Reports to the Regents, D:597, March 21, 1900.
[48] For a convenient summary of enrollment figures up to 1926 see *The Wisconsin Blue Book, 1927*, p. 369.

temporarily during periods of depression, "yet it is certain to continue at a comparatively high rate for many years to come, and I believe that we must look forward to an increase of from 50 to 75 students per year for many years. The field of employment for the engineering graduate is constantly widening, and if the instruction is wisely adapted to meet the needs of the country, there is certain to be a constantly increasing demand for the well-trained technical graduate."[49] Two years later the dean was less optimistic. The decrease in enrollment at Wisconsin had occurred partly because the introduction of advanced courses had encouraged students to take the first part of their college work in the College of Letters and Science or in other colleges, but there had also been a decrease in the demand for technically trained men, and the professional fields of commerce and agriculture had attracted students away from engineering.[50] Dean Turneaure also believed that the marked decrease in railroad construction had contributed to the decline.[51] Van Hise himself remarked in 1914 that "because of the astonishing expansion of business, industry and transportation, during the past twenty-five years, the colleges of engineering have had a phenomenal growth. In recent years, however, there has been rapidly introduced concentration in management, which has resulted, among other things, in relatively less demand for engineers." He foresaw no immediate rapid increase in the number of men required in engineering professions.[52] In 1916 Dean Turneaure reported that the decrease in attendance was accounted for almost entirely by the decrease in the number of civil engineering students. The number in mechanical engineering had grown, as had the enrollment in chemical engineering. He felt that the low point of attendance had been passed.[53] But the first World War decreased enrollment still further, so it was not until 1919 that enrollment again increased rapidly.

In 1900 work in the college was organized into seven system-

[49] *Regents' Biennial Report,* 1907–08, p. 140. In 1948, Dean Withey commented that the "present enrollment based on freshmen interested in engineering indicates that 50 per annum as an average rate of increase since 1900 is about right."
[50] *Ibid.,* 1909–10, p. 144.
[51] *Ibid.,* 1911–12, p. 134.
[52] *Ibid.,* 1913–14, p. 16.   [53] *Ibid.,* 1915–16, pp. 145–146.

atic courses: civil, sanitary, mechanical, electrical, and general engineering, applied electrochemistry, and premetallurgical engineering.[54] Six of these courses led to the degree of bachelor of science in engineering. The professional degrees of civil, mechanical, and electrical engineer were conferred on a basis of three years' professional work (later raised to five) and a thesis, or one year of advanced professional study and a thesis or the completion of a satisfactory project.

In 1904 Dean Turneaure urged that two new courses, one in chemical engineering, the other in mining engineering, be established.[55] A course in chemical engineering was promptly approved by the regents and Professor Charles F. Burgess placed in charge.[56] In June, 1907, the regents approved the establishment of the mining engineering course.[57] With the addition of these two courses, the engineering college offered a total of seven four-year courses leading to the degree of bachelor of science, and advanced work leading to five professional degrees —in civil, mechanical, electrical, chemical, and mining engineering.[58] In 1909 the engineering faculty voted to abolish the general engineering course, since the students once served by that course were now taken care of elsewhere, as well as the sanitary engineering course, since no one had ever graduated from it, and the studies offered under it would continue to be available elsewhere.[59] The course in applied electrochemistry was dropped from the catalogue in 1914.[60] This left five courses —civil, mechanical, electrical, chemical, and mining engineering—which led to the bachelor of science degree. Professional degrees in these fields were granted upon a basis of additional academic work and a thesis, or professional experience and a thesis. Graduate work, leading to the degrees of master of science and doctor of philosophy, was also offered in the College of Engineering.

Dean Johnson had urged that engineering training be com-

[54] *University Catalogue*, 1900–01, pp. 207–208.
[55] *Regents' Biennial Report*, 1903–04, pp. 108–110.
[56] *Ibid.*, 1905–06, p. 127.   [57] *Ibid.*, 1907–08, p. 142.
[58] *University Catalogue*, 1907–08, p. 293.
[59] Minutes of the Faculty of the College of Engineering, 1908–12, pp. 666–667, January 25, 1909.   [60] *University Catalogue*, 1913–14, p. 362.

bined with training in other fields. Various combinations were proposed. In 1904 Dean Turneaure reported that engineering and commerce seemed to meet the need of a number of students who did not want a wholly technical course.[61] In 1905 there was announced the establishment of five- and six-year courses leading to the degree of bachelor of science and professional degrees in engineering. These courses would enable a student also to carry additional studies in the other colleges. One course involved taking all essential studies in the course in commerce.[62] Some years later an agreement was made with the Law School whereby the Law School would accept the engineering work on the same basis as the work in the College of Letters and Science, thus making it possible for engineering graduates to secure a law degree two years after obtaining the bachelor of science degree in engineering.[63]

There was also some agitation to incorporate into the engineering courses certain studies of a nontechnical nature. In 1908 a five-year course was established in the engineering college.[64] President Van Hise welcomed this action and looked forward hopefully to the time when the engineering college, like the law college, could require two years' work in the liberal arts for admission.[65]

The attempts to lengthen the course and thus make room for liberal studies met with little success. The technical courses multiplied and engineering students were hard pressed to complete the prescribed courses within the allotted time. The faculty from time to time considered means of reducing the requirements of the several courses and modifying the methods of instruction. The University of Cincinnati, under the direction of Dean Herman Schneider, had in 1906 launched an

---

[61] *Regents' Biennial Report*, 1903–04, p. 106.

[62] *University Catalogue*, 1905–06, pp. 223–224.

[63] Statement by Dean Emeritus Frederick E. Turneaure, June, 1948.

[64] Minutes of the Faculty of the College of Engineering, 1905–08, p. 592, February 24, 1908; p. 600, April 27, 1908.

[65] *Regents' Biennial Report*, 1907–08, p. 14. Van Hise during the next couple of years carried on correspondence with M. E. Cooley, dean of the engineering department at Michigan, and J. G. Schurman, president of Cornell, urging that two years' work in liberal arts be required for admission to the College of Engineering. Van Hise to Cooley, November 6, 1909; Van Hise to Schurman, 1909–10 *passim*, all in the Presidents' Papers.

experiment in engineering education in which students divided their time between industrial shops and the classroom. The four-year course was lengthened to five years of eleven months each. One half of the time of the student was spent in industrial shops, the other half in the classroom. The plan won wide attention. By some it was construed as having been designed for the making of "skilled boiler makers." Charles R. Mann in his *Study of Engineering Education* found this cooperative method an effective form of engineering education.[66]

In November, 1908, Dean Turneaure proposed that this system be considered for adoption at Wisconsin, and a committee was appointed to investigate.[67] The committee reported that the Milwaukee manufacturers interviewed were favorable to the proposal. Students, however, expressed definite opposition on the ground that the system would break into their course work and that most of them took rather extensive shop courses during the summer either by attending the University or by working in shops during the period.[68] Accordingly the plan was dropped.

Meanwhile the summer school for artisans, begun in 1901, came to be used more and more by engineering undergraduates to accumulate experience and academic credits in shop work. In 1912 Dean Turneaure reported that the attendance of workers in the school for artisans had steadily declined but that a considerable demand existed for courses of college grade. In response to the demand the work of the summer school had been gradually modified until now almost all courses offered in summer school were of college grade.[69] In 1913 President Van Hise himself attended a meeting of the engineering faculty

[66] Charles R. Mann, *A Study of Engineering Education, Prepared for the Joint Committee on Engineering Education of the National Engineering Societies* (Carnegie Foundation for the Advancement of Teaching, Bulletin No. 11, New York, 1918), 78–83.

[67] Minutes of the Faculty of the College of Engineering, 1908–12, pp. 654–655, November 2, 1908.

[68] Dean Turneaure commented in June, 1948: "Mr. Schneider's scheme was successful, partly because the University of Cincinnati was located in a large city of many industries. The University of Wisconsin is not. Our study led to the conclusion that the scheme was not desirable here. Most of the students would prefer to finish in 4 years. The others would have to go to Milwaukee or some other manufacturing city to get their work training. This would force us to carry out a double program which we felt was impracticable."

[69] *Regents' Biennial Report*, 1911–12, p. 136.

to discuss the courses offered by the college. He asked the faculty to consider three questions: "Was the College of Engineering requiring the students to take too many separate subjects at the same time? Was the College of Engineering requiring more hours per week than could be well done by the average student? Was the College of Engineering requiring too many subjects of a specialized technical nature?"[70] The engineering college courses at this time required nineteen or twenty hours of work each semester and permitted virtually no elective studies. In response to Van Hise's inquiry, Professor Mack proposed that the foreign language for the engineering courses be dropped and that the senior thesis be made elective.[71] Subsequently the faculty formally went on record as agreeing that the required work in the first two years was too great and should be reduced.[72] The courses were then changed so as to reduce the amount of required work during the first two years and to increase the number of electives in the last two years. Although unwilling to abolish the language requirements, the faculty agreed that students who presented either three units of preparation in one language or four units of two languages might dispense with further language study.[73] Finally, in 1917, the faculty voted to drop the foreign language requirement entirely.[74] It provided, however, that students who entered the College of Engineering without foreign language preparation be required to secure eight additional credits for graduation in the field of foreign language, English, or history.[75] Professor Mack's proposal that the senior thesis be made elective was referred to the course committee,[76] but no action was taken immediately. In 1914 the subject came up again and was referred to a committee representing all departments of the college.[77] Although the committee failed to agree, a majority, upheld by the faculty, favored retaining the thesis requirement.[78] Five

---

[70] Minutes of the Faculty of the College of Engineering, 1912–15, p. 920, February 24, 1913.   [71] *Ibid.*, 921, February 24, 1913.
[72] *Ibid.*, 924, March 10, 1913.   [73] *Regents' Biennial Report*, 1913–14, p. 140.
[74] Minutes of the Faculty of the College of Engineering, 1915–20, p. 1132, April 2, 1917.
[75] *Regents' Biennial Report*, 1917–18, p. 160; *University Catalogue*, 1918–19, p. 299.
[76] Minutes of the Faculty of the College of Engineering, 1912–15, p. 925, March 19, 1913.   [77] *Ibid.*, 1030, November 23, 1914.
[78] *Ibid.*, 1056–1059, April 26, 1915; p. 1060, April 28, 1915.

years later the faculty voted to permit the course committee for each engineering curriculum to decide whether the
thesis should be required or elective for the course.[79] Under
this arrangement, the college announced the next year that
the senior thesis was required in the civil engineering course,
optional in electrical, mechanical, and mining; in chemical
engineering a course in special problems replaced the thesis.[80]

The various changes in course requirements were intended to
make possible a better use of the student's time. Closely allied
to this objective were a number of other attempts to develop
more effective means of presenting the subject matter of the
engineering courses. There had been many objections, at
Wisconsin and elsewhere, that the theoretical courses were unrelated to the technical courses. In 1918 one investigator reported: "There is almost unanimous agreement . . . that at
present the engineering curriculum, whatever its organization,
is congested beyond endurance. It is obviously absurd to require from the student more hours of intense mental exertion
than would be permitted him by law at the simplest manual
labor."[81]

Partly to meet such criticisms, Charles S. Slichter and his
associates, following an earlier experiment at Massachusetts Institute of Technology, developed a two-year course in mathematics in which the courses in algebra, trigonometry, and analytical geometry would be more logically presented. About both
of these attempts Charles R. Mann commented: "This emphasis on logical sequence has undoubtedly a fascination to certain
types of mind—teachers of mathematics, for example. Its effectiveness with the great majority of students may well be questioned."[82] But the course was successful. Dean Turneaure later
reported that it worked well and had been adopted by several
schools, although some instructors had found it hard to teach.[83]
In the teaching of English composition to engineering students, Professor Karl Young and his associates tried various

[79] *Ibid.*, 1915–20, p. 1305, May 24, 1920.
[80] *University Catalogue*, 1921–22, p. 314.
[81] Mann, *Engineering Education*, 25.
[82] *Ibid.*, 61.
[83] Statement by Dean Turneaure, June, 1948.

approaches to make the course more effective.[84] Perhaps the most successful experiment in integration was conducted by Professor Edward Bennett and his associates in bringing about a closer integration of the theoretical work in physics with the technical courses in electrical engineering. "The new plan," wrote Dean Turneaure in 1916, "provides for the giving of some of the technical instruction in electricity in the sophomore year, at the same time dividing the physics between the sophomore and junior years, the total amount of credits in the two departments being the same as at present. . . . There will be less duplication in instruction in the elements of electricity, the students will begin their work in the electrical laboratory somewhat earlier in their course, and by placing a substantial part of the physics instruction in the junior year the junior course can be made of a much more advanced character."[85] The course, although difficult to teach, was widely imitated in other schools.[86]

Although the amount of required work was reduced somewhat after 1913, the engineering courses continued to be exacting. In 1919 the faculty committee on the course of study said:

[84] Mann, *Engineering Education,* 64.
[85] *Regents' Biennial Report,* 1915–16, p. 146.
[86] Years later one of Professor Bennett's colleagues wrote: "The distinctive features of the treatment evolved by Professor Bennett and his co-workers assume their proper significance when contrasted with the practice prevailing in all schools at the time, and in many of the schools of today. Instead of following the usual sophomore physics treatment of electricity and magnetism often taught with little use of the calculus and using three different systems of units, the course in introductory electrodynamics made extensive use of the calculus and pioneered in the use of a unified system of units. The subject matter was developed in a systematic manner with logical transitions from the study of electrostatics to that of current electricity and magnetic theory.

"The laboratory experiments which accompanied the class work in electrodynamics were also unique. The equipment was especially designed so that the fundamental principles as expounded in the class room could be checked in orderly fashion, the initial experiments requiring only measurements of force, time and distance.

"The influence of the method and concepts developed in connection with this course spread to other schools and even to industry. Today there are several textbooks on the market which follow the general procedure of the text developed at Wisconsin and courses are being introduced in technical schools which follow closely the course in electrodynamics instituted here thirty years ago." J. W. Watson, Statement on the Department of Electrical Engineering, University Archives, prepared June, 1947.

Deans of the College of Engineering
John Butler Johnson and Frederick E. Turneaure

The Engineering Building, 1900

"It is expected that the students of average (fair) ability devote a total of 51 clock hours per week to meeting requirements of the engineering course." The committee recommended that the "attention of instructors should be directed to the possibility of increasing the effectiveness of instructional work by making a reduction in the number of topics or problems or reports, and using the time thus made available to require a more thorough analytical treatment."[87]

Van Hise had hoped that two years of liberal study would eventually be made preparatory to admission to the College of Engineering, but little progress was made in this direction. There was no general support for lengthening the courses to five or six years. The technical studies required were so numerous that virtually no liberal studies could be included in a four-year course. In 1912, for example, the civil engineering course, leading to the bachelor of science degree, required 155 semester hours of credit. Students were required to take from 18 to 21 hours a semester. Freshmen carried 19 hours both semesters. Except for 14 hours allotted in the freshman year to foreign languages and English composition, the entire course was devoted to scientific or technical training. A total of 17 hours of electives was permitted in the senior year although part of this credit was used for the senior thesis. The other engineering courses followed this pattern, although the electrical engineering course permitted the optional selection in the junior year of courses in political economy, economics, accounting, and commercial law.[88] Whatever may be said about the necessity of offering engineers more than technical training, the fact was that there simply was no time for any study that did not pertain directly to the business at hand. In 1922 Professor Edward Bennett reported that representatives of the land-grant colleges had considered the question of more general training of engineering students and the possible development of a five-year course. They also considered ways of providing for a number of nontechnical studies which would extend

[87] Minutes of the Faculty of the College of Engineering, 1915–20, p. 1268, October 24, 1919; p. 1276, November 24, 1919.
[88] *University Catalogue,* 1911–12, p. 349.

through the four-year course. The faculty voted that the course committee investigate the proposition.[89] In 1924 the electrical engineering department revised the course in electrical engineering to provide for a total of 28 hours of electives, fifteen of which were required to be selected from nonprofessional courses.[90] The number of electives was increased somewhat in the other courses. Yet at the end of the period under study the means had not been found of either requiring or encouraging engineering students to acquaint themselves with the historical and social processes that their work in laboratory, machine shop, factory, and mine was altering so fundamentally.

By 1925 the college possessed laboratory and other facilities that were extensive although not wholly adequate. Besides the engineering library, it possessed various laboratory facilities. The bridge engineering department had autographic extensometers and deflectometers, products of Dean Turneaure's experiments to determine bridge stresses under moving-train loads. The chemical engineering laboratories and the electrical laboratory were perhaps the least adequate. The college also had engineering shops, a hydraulic laboratory, a building for mining and metallurgical laboratories, a steam and gas-engineering laboratory, a general testing laboratory, a cement laboratory, and the use of facilities at the Forest Products Laboratory.

Although the college was primarily concerned with undergraduate instruction, Dean Johnson had encouraged engineering research just as he had looked forward to having the engineering college adapt its work to the extension service. In his first report as president, Van Hise had declared: "It is my earnest desire that investigative work be seriously begun in the College of Mechanics and Engineering.... There is an unrivalled opportunity at the present time for Colleges of Engineering to take up investigative work for the benefit of the people. While it is not possible in advance to give the money value which will accrue to the State from research in engi-

---

[89] Minutes of the Faculty of the College of Engineering, 1920–25, pp. 1456–1457, September 25, 1922.

[90] *University Catalogue*, 1924–25, p. 357; Watson, Statement on the Department of Electrical Engineering.

neering, no one who is familiar with the history of industrial development in the world, can doubt that research by the engineer is a source of enormous increase in the wealth of the nation." He felt that if the college were given funds to take up investigations, the state would have the money returned many times over. Already, he observed, the engineering departments of the Iowa State College and the University of Illinois received regular appropriations for research and investigation. Unless Wisconsin did likewise it might fall behind. "In the College of Engineering, as in the College of Agriculture, the best results, even if the narrow point of view of instruction alone be considered, can be obtained only at a college where investigations are being vigorously pursued."[91] The same year Dean Turneaure wrote: "There would seem to be no good reason why the engineering laboratories should not contribute their share of fruitful research in applied science, in the direction of improved methods of construction, new processes of manufacture, and other similar lines of work in the same way that the Agricultural College serves the agricultural interests of the State."[92] The regents responded slowly to the urging of the president and the dean. A small fund was provided for research and publication for the next two years and during the biennium 1906–1908 forty-five hundred dollars a year was made available.[93] Some funds were obtained from outside sources. Twenty-five hundred dollars a year was obtained by Professor Burgess for his investigations in chemical engineering and the American Engineering and Maintenance of Ways Association gave $5,500 for other research.[94] In 1908 Van Hise recommended increasing the research fund to $10,000 per year.[95] "No money," wrote Turneaure, "which has been spent in the college during the past two years has, in my judgment, gone further to improve the work of both instructors and students, and to enhance the standing of the college among engineers and educators, than the money which has been spent on research work."[96] But no increase was granted. In 1913 after repeated requests from the dean the research fund was increased

[91] *Regents' Biennial Report*, 1903–04, pp. 30–31.   [92] *Ibid.*, 106.
[93] *Ibid.*, 1907–08, p. 37.   [94] *Ibid.*
[95] *Ibid.*   [96] *Ibid.*, 148.

to $6,500. The Board of Regents also established the engineering experiment station as the agency within the college to administer the research program.[97] But a research program was not yet assured. The appropriation was later reduced to $2,200 a year. In 1916 and again in 1918 Dean Turneaure asked for a minimum of $10,000 a year for research, but to no avail. In 1918–1920 the engineering college had a research fund of about $3,000, an amount wholly inadequate for carrying on any sustained research work.[98]

That the College of Engineering did not establish a research program comparable to that of the College of Agriculture, particularly during those years when Van Hise encouraged and supported research in all colleges, is something of an anomaly. Yet this can be at least partly explained. First of all, the engineering college during these years did not form a close association with any politically potent groups within the state. It never found a means of making wide contacts with its potential constituency. This the agricultural college did by means of its bulletins, its short courses, farmers' institutes, and the county agricultural agents. In research, college instruction, and extension work, the College of Agriculture developed a program which won the support of the farmers and other economic groups whose prosperity was closely allied to that of the farmers. Mechanics' institutes had been attempted and had been given up. The summer school for artisans had been launched and, though it enjoyed some success, by 1910 it had practically ceased to be a school for artisans. Meanwhile, under the energetic leadership of Dean Reber, the University extension division had begun to offer various technical and vocational courses to the workers in the industrial shops of Milwaukee and elsewhere. Although some members of the engineering college faculty participated in the program, it was the extension division rather than the College of Engineering that received most of the

[97] *Ibid.*, 1913–14, pp. 143–144. This step had been taken by Illinois in 1903, by Iowa State College in 1904, by Pennsylvania State College in 1908, by Kansas State Agricultural College in 1910, and by Ohio State University in 1913. *Survey of Land-Grant Colleges and Universities*, U. S. Department of the Interior, Office of Education, Bulletin No. 9 (Washington, 1930), 1:816.

[98] *Regents' Biennial Report*, 1915–16, p. 151; 1919–20, p. 108.

public acclaim for the industrial work. Nothing had been developed to bring the Wisconsin manufacturers within the orbit of the engineering college. Dean Turneaure's proposal of a cooperative plan of education had been rejected. Such a cooperative venture, whatever its limitations, might have led to a closer cooperation between the engineering college and industrial activities in the state, but the experiment was not tried. In spite of the desire of the president and the dean of the college to develop a research program, it must be recognized first of all that the College of Engineering had no wide or articulate constituency within the state to support its repeated requests for research funds. In fact, the general unfriendliness of the legislature to industry probably provided positive resistance to college-sponsored research which would clearly benefit specific industries.

A second factor of some influence may be found in the fact that in the quest for research funds the College of Engineering had to compete with the other colleges. The College of Agriculture had a wide and vigorous constituency. Likewise the various departments in the College of Letters and Science contained many vigorous and energetic men, able and willing to bring to bear all the force at their command to win a share of the research funds available. The rapidly expanding University extension division was under the direction of Dean Reber, who was adept at obtaining funds.

Although members of the engineering faculty received little institutional support for research and writing, they produced a total of sixty-five technical papers which appeared before 1925 in the first nine volumes of the *Engineering Series* of the University *Bulletin,* in addition to the large number of papers presented to the various engineering societies. From the chemical engineering department alone, for example, came a total of 149 papers in the period from 1900 to 1928.[99] Experimental work was carried on in a number of lines. Dean Turneaure himself devised an instrument for measuring the stresses in railroad bridges under the impact of loaded trains. His successful de-

[99] Based on a statement prepared by Otto L. Kowalke, May 3, 1948. University Archives.

velopment of an extensometer and deflectometer won for him wide recognition in railway engineering circles. In the department of mechanics a series of notable studies was made on various aspects of construction materials.[100] Investigations of reinforced concrete and masonry were launched under Dean Johnson and continued under Dean Turneaure. The first major publication was *Tests on Reinforced Concrete Beams,* by Ernest A. Moritz.[101] A number of other studies were conducted subsequently on reinforced concrete and reinforced brick beams and columns. The first tests were followed by reports dealing with various other aspects of reinforced concrete and masonry. A series of durability studies was launched, the first report on which was published in 1910 by Morton O. Withey. The project was eventually organized so that the test could be carried to the year 2037 A.D. The first of the studies on the permeability of concrete was published in 1908 by Francis M. McCullough. These studies had been continued by Withey and his associates.

Professor Jesse B. Kommers, also of the mechanics department, published his first paper on the fatigue of metals in 1912. Besides numerous technical papers on the subject which appeared in this country and England, Professor Kommers, in collaboration with Professor H. F. Moore of the University of Illinois, published in 1927 a volume on *Fatigue of Metals,* the first book published in the United States on the subject.

The research work of the electrical engineering department, Professor Watson has declared, "has been extensive and varied but the chief emphasis has been in the field of circuit studies. Prior to 1925 this activity was carried on by several members of the staff who explored some of the little known phases relating to the characteristics of circuits and devices which have since become a part of modern communications systems." These studies have been published in a number of technical papers. Professor Edward Bennett was closely connected with Professor Earle M. Terry of the physics department in his pioneer work

[100] Many of the following statements are derived from a paper prepared by the late Professor Emeritus Edward R. Maurer, deposited in the University Archives, September, 1947.

[101] Ernest A. Moritz, *Tests on Reinforced Concrete Beams (Bulletin of the University of Wisconsin, Engineering Series,* Vol. 3, No. 4, Madison, 1906).

in radio. Bennett himself prepared a paper in the *Engineering Series* of the University *Bulletin*, "High Versus Low Antennae in Radio Telegraphy and Telephony," in 1916. After the death of Terry, technical supervision of the state station was assigned to members of the electrical engineering department.[102]

The department of chemical engineering sponsored research along a great many lines, but the most notable work was done in the fields of alloys, electroplating, gas testing, dry-cell batteries, and testing pyrometers.[103] In experiments with the production and testing of alloys of iron it was established that iron containing about one per cent of copper resisted corrosion to a notable degree. The discovery has materially influenced commercial practice. Moreover, theories proposed to explain the mechanism of corrosion of metals have enjoyed wide acceptance. Professor Oliver P. Watts in his experiments with electroplating found that nickel plated from a hot solution was ductile and would not peel like nickel plated from a cold solution. The Watts process has become practically universal in nickel-plating. The department was brought to experiment in gas calorimetry by the request of the Wisconsin Public Service Commission for a means of determining the heating value of gas. The methods and standards devised by the department were adopted by the Wisconsin Commission, by other state commissions, and by the American Gas Utilities Association. Tests and studies of dry-cell batteries, begun in 1907, served as the basis for the establishment of a leading battery manufactory. Tests on base-metal couples for pyrometers won wide attention and the recommendations were adopted by leading manufacturers.

In the department of mining and metallurgy Professor Richard S. McCaffery's studies of improvement in the Bessemer smelting process had attracted wide attention by 1920 and subsequent work along that line has resulted in important operating economy in blast-furnace steel making.[104] Early in the 1920's investigations were begun in the same department to develop

[102] Watson, Statement on the Department of Electrical Engineering.

[103] This paragraph is based upon Professor Kowalke's evaluation of the research of the work of the department.

[104] *Regents' Biennial Report*, 1919–20, p. 108; interview, Carstensen with Edwin R. Shorey, April 1, 1948.

better methods of reducing zinc and lead ore from the mines of southwest Wisconsin. Although the results were not published until 1931, the investigations had substantial effect in modifying milling practices in that region.[105]

This brief listing by no means completes even a bare outline of research and experimental work conducted by members of the faculty, but it suggests the main lines. Moreover, it should be noted that the engineering college was often called upon for technical service and information. The regents themselves as early as the middle 1880's had asked Professor Conover to prepare plans for the new science building and later to supervise the construction of the building. The University water works and later the central heating plant were designed and supervised by a member of the engineering faculty. Professor Storm Bull prepared plans for the new central heating plant and after his death in 1907, the responsibility for completing this project was given to Professor Halsten J. Thorkelson.

Members of the engineering faculty were also frequently called upon to provide various technical services for state boards and commissions. Dean Turneaure called attention in 1906 to the work of Professor William D. Taylor for the State Board of Assessment and Professor Leonard S. Smith's study of water-power resources.[106] In the next years such appointments increased. William D. Pence, professor of railway engineering, served the Tax and Railroad Commissions;[107] Professors John G. D. Mack and Charles F. Burgess were members of the joint engineering staff of the two commissions.[108] The department of mining and metallurgy, cooperating with the Geological and Natural History Survey, investigated Wisconsin clay deposits at the request of the state brickmakers' association.[109] In 1912, out of a total of forty-six men who served both on the University faculty and on a state board or commission, twelve were members of the engineering faculty.[110] In 1913 the electrical engineer-

[105] Edwin R. Shorey and La Verne W. Eastwood, *The Flotation of Southwestern Wisconsin Zinc Ores,* Engineering Experiment Station, Series No. 73, 1931.

[106] *Regents' Biennial Report,* 1905–06, pp. 134–135.

[107] *Ibid.,* 1909–10, p. 150.

[108] The *Wisconsin Engineer,* 16:142 (December, 1911).

[109] *Regents' Biennial Report,* 1911–12, p. 138.

[110] Charles McCarthy, *The Wisconsin Idea* (New York, 1912), 313–317.

ing department in cooperation with the Railroad Commission established a standards laboratory for testing electrical instruments for various public utilities of the state.[111] This agency is still in existence. In 1915, Professor Mack was appointed state engineer.

Thus throughout the first quarter of the century the engineering college was a substantial part of the University. Primarily devoted to the instruction of engineers, it also contributed basic and widely influential monographs in several fields of engineering and it served the state in many useful if not highly dramatic ways.

[111] *Regents' Biennial Report,* 1913–14, p. 143.

14.

The Medical School

ATTEMPTS to establish a medical school in Wisconsin, it will be recalled, started even before the territory attained statehood. On March 2, 1848, Governor Dodge approved a bill incorporating the Wisconsin Medical College. The act incorporating the University of Wisconsin on July 26, 1848, provided for four University departments, one of them a department of medicine. Similar creations on paper followed each other more or less regularly during the ensuing decades.[1] Yet not until 1893, forty-five years after the attainment of statehood, was a regular medical school opened in the state—the Wisconsin College of Physicians and Surgeons in Milwaukee, now the Marquette School of Medicine. And only in 1925, seventy-seven years after the act of incorporation, was the first full medical course established in the University of Wisconsin. The school which thus eventually reached maturity in 1925 grew out of very modest but solid beginnings, initiated and sustained with great courage and perseverance by men "who were more interested in an ideal than in gain."

This chapter is based on a manuscript by Dr. Erwin H. Ackerknecht, professor of the history of medicine, who in turn had at his disposal a 1937 manuscript of Dr. William H. O. Oatway and the departmental histories of Drs. Ovid O. Meyer, Paul F. Clark, Walter E. Sullivan, J. Murray Angevine, and Charles H. Bunting, the late Edgar J. Witzemann, and Miss Irene Blake for the departments of medicine, bacteriology, anatomy, pathology, biochemistry, and pharmacology, respectively.

[1] For details on this phase of Wisconsin medical history see William Snow Miller, "Medical Schools in Wisconsin: Past and Present," *Wisconsin Medical Journal,* 35:476–486 (June, 1936).

The first steps in medical instruction in the University can be traced back to the activity of a natural history instructor, Edward A. Birge, who later as dean and president played such a conspicuous role in the development of the University as a whole. Birge had come to Madison in 1875 as an instructor in the preparatory department. In 1881, after the preparatory department had been abolished, he began teaching the zoology courses that through emphasis on histology and embryology were destined to give future medical students a truly scientific background in biology. Together with existing botany, physics, and chemistry courses they provided the essentials for premedical instruction. Birge had prepared himself for such courses by studying in 1880–81 with Carl Ludwig, the renowned Leipzig physiologist, who had also been the teacher of such outstanding American scientists as Henry P. Bowditch and William H. Welch. These courses must be regarded as the germ cell of the present medical school.

In 1886 the State Medical Society, through a committee headed by Dr. John M. Dodson, urged the regents "to establish a preliminary course of medical study in the University (it being understood that this is not to be a medical department in any sense of the word)." The suggestion was favorably received by the new president, Thomas C. Chamberlin, who had to overcome certain hesitations of Birge's, and in the catalogue of 1887 a "special science course antecedent to medicine" was listed. The course lasted two years and comprised such subjects as zoology, vertebrate anatomy, histology, physiology, embryology, and bacteriology. The twenty-seven students who took this first course were given certificates and received advanced standing in other schools. The above-mentioned subjects were given by Birge alone until 1890, when he obtained an assistant. Students from Birge's classes had such an unusual preparation in histology and embryology that some of them (Joseph C. Bloodgood and Albert J. Ochsner) were used as teachers in these subjects in the very medical schools in which they were enrolled as students.

In 1892 the title of the course was changed to "premedical course." After Birge became dean of the College of Letters and

Science in 1891, most of the instruction was handled by William Snow Miller, Harry L. Russell, and their associates. Miller and Russell came to Wisconsin in 1892 and 1893 respectively.

William Snow Miller, who retired in 1924 but remained in close contact with the medical school until his death in 1939, thus participated in and influenced all the school's developmental stages. As a scientist he was one of the most distinguished to serve as a member of the staff. Dr. Miller was born in 1858 in Stirling, Massachusetts, and graduated in medicine from Yale in 1879. He was engaged in general practice in Southbury, Connecticut, from 1879 to 1887. Increasing deafness caused him to turn toward anatomical studies. He worked at the College of Physicians and Surgeons in New York City in 1887, at Clark University in 1888, and was pathologist at the City and Memorial Hospitals at Worcester from 1889 to 1892, lecturer in anatomy at Mount Holyoke in 1889, and instructor at Yale in 1891. At Wisconsin he became assistant professor of anatomy in 1895, associate professor in 1904, and professor in 1916. In 1918 he was lecturer in medicine at Johns Hopkins. Dr. Miller won international reputation for his studies of the microscopic structure of the lung in men and animals. His monograph on the lung (1937), summarizing the results of forty-seven years of study, was recently reprinted—an adequate testimony of its worth.

The seminar in the history of medicine that he founded in 1909 is still functioning. Because of the work of this seminar Fielding H. Garrison has called him a "pioneer in post-graduate training in the history of medicine" in this country. His valuable historical library is now part of the Medical School's library. The creation in 1946 of a regular chair of medical history at Wisconsin, the second in the country, is clearly a result of his labors.

Harry Luman Russell was born at Poynette in 1866 and graduated from the University of Wisconsin in 1888. In 1890 and 1891 he was in Europe studying bacteriology with Koch and Pasteur and working at the Naples Zoological Station. In 1892 he went to Johns Hopkins, where he was the first to take a doctorate under Dr. William H. Welch. In 1893 he took over the bacteriology courses in the premedical course at Wisconsin as an assistant professor. His interests and activities, however, shifted more and more to agricultural bacteriology, to the College of Agriculture, and to administrative tasks, and that part of his brilliant career is therefore more appropriately dealt with elsewhere. The same is true for William D. Frost, Edwin G. Hastings, and William S. Marshall, who began teaching with Russell in the premedical course in 1895, 1899, and 1893. Frost and Hastings transferred later to the College of Agriculture.

The next and decisive steps toward the creation of a medical school coincided with a change in administration. The new president, Charles R. Van Hise, took the initiative and in January, 1904, obtained from the regents the authorization to appoint a professor of anatomy as a first measure in this direction. The man chosen for this position was Charles Russell Bardeen, who already enjoyed an excellent scientific reputation and who held his post up to the time of his death in 1935. Bardeen's role at Wisconsin goes far beyond his scientific accomplishments. He was the first dean of the school, and no other single person deserves more credit for its development and accomplishments. To this end he had to abandon his own research work to a large extent. Bardeen's case is typical for a whole group of highly endowed men of whom Abraham Flexner once wrote that they "ought not be lightly sacrificed to executive routine to which, unfortunately, the American is a singularly easy victim." Bardeen himself stated a few years before his death in a letter to his friend, Dr. Yates of Milwaukee, "Wisely or unwisely, I have permitted my public interests to interfere with my scientific work to the serious detriment of the latter."

Bardeen was born in Kalamazoo, Michigan, in 1871, graduated from Harvard in 1893, and belonged to the first medical class at Johns Hopkins, graduating in 1897. He remained at Johns Hopkins till his departure for Wisconsin, serving as an assistant, associate, and associate professor in anatomy under Franklin Paine Mall. Before coming to Wisconsin he had already published papers on diphtheria antitoxin, brain pathology, muscle anatomy, a new freezing microtome, the physiology of the planaria musculata, the pathology of burns, and an outline of a course in normal histology. He was the first to show that the effect of X-rays was on the cell nucleus. He made permanent contributions also to descriptive embryology, experimental embryology, and anthropometry. His studies on the development of the skeleton and musculature are in every textbook of anatomy and embryology published since their completion.

In 1906 a first bulletin of "courses preparatory to the study of clinical medicine" appeared. In 1907 a bill establishing a College of Medicine was passed by the legislature.[2] The name was changed to School of Medicine in 1909. Bardeen became dean in 1907.

After the legislature had granted permission to establish the two-year course, Deans Birge and Bardeen worked out the details of organization for the new school. The plan as thus developed and approved by Van Hise was submitted to the regents in October and adopted. To a very large extent the school was organized from the scientific departments of the University which had been offering courses regularly included in a medical curriculum.[3] Instruction in the new college comprised the first two years of the ordinary medical school—the medical science or preclinical part of the curriculum. A condition for admission was successful completion of two years of college work, including premedical subjects. Students passing such a two-year preclinical course could go elsewhere for their clinical work and receive credit for the two years in medicine. This practice was actually followed until 1925. Already in his report of 1908 Dr. Bardeen was able to record a number of first-class medical schools that had offered to admit such students to advanced standing and to grant them full credit without special examination; and state boards of medical examiners had recognized the college. Wisconsin had been elected a member of the Association of American Medical Colleges and was represented on the A.M.A. committee on preliminary medical education. In 1910 Dr. Edward Evans, a member of the Board of Regents, wrote Van Hise: "In view of the tremendously unfavorable

[2] See Volume II, pp. 176 ff.
[3] Records of the Board of Regents, G:50–51, October 15, 1907.

criticism of Medical Schools and Medical Education in the United States by the Carnegie Foundation, which has just been published, I think it is a matter of congratulation that the University of Wisconsin in so far as she has taken up Medical Education receives words of very highest commendation from the same source."[4]

In 1907 the preclinical courses were actually started, twenty-six students, twenty-three men and three women, registering. This was made possible by the founding of a department of physiology in 1906. The first professor of physiology was Joseph Erlanger. In the same year Harold Cornelius Bradley was appointed assistant professor of physiology to teach physiological chemistry. Dr. Erlanger, born in San Francisco in 1874, took his medical degree at Johns Hopkins in 1899 and was associate professor of physiology there when called to Wisconsin. In 1910 he left for Washington University in St. Louis. In 1944 he was awarded the Nobel prize in medicine jointly with Herbert S. Gasser, who had been an instructor in physiology at Wisconsin from 1911 to 1913 and in pharmacology from 1915 to 1916.

Bradley, also a native of California, came from Yale where he had taken his doctorate in physiological chemistry in 1905. Physiological chemistry became an independent department in 1921 and was headed by Bradley until 1947. His winning personality made him an ideal choice for an active officer in scientific organizations or for larger campus responsibilities. To gain recognition for his relatively small department in the shadow of a much stronger and extremely successful biochemistry department in the College of Agriculture was no mean task.

With Russell's appointment as dean of the College of Agriculture in 1907, bacteriology was headed in this new era (till 1914) by Mazyck P. Ravenel. Ravenel also became director of the State Laboratory of Hygiene, founded by Russell and Cornelius H. Harper in 1903. In the twenty-three years since his graduation from the Medical School of South Carolina, Dr. Ravenel had done postgraduate work in Europe and had been connected with several scientific institutions in Charleston, Princeton, and Philadelphia. When he left in 1914 for Missouri, Dr. William D.

[4] Dr. Edward Evans to Charles R. Van Hise, June 14, 1910, Presidents' Papers,

Stovall was called from Tulane to become director of the State Laboratory of Hygiene and associate professor of hygiene. The State Laboratory of Hygiene was listed as part of the medical school for the first time in 1915. It is the central laboratory for the state Board of Health and supplies laboratory aid to health officers and physicians all over the state in the diagnosis and control of communicable diseases. After the opening of the Wisconsin General Hospital Dr. Stovall also became its clinical pathologist.

Medical bacteriology became, after Dr. Ravenel's departure, a subdepartment of the department of pathology and was headed by Dr. Paul Franklin Clark, who had previously been associated with the Rockefeller Institute for Medical Research and Johns Hopkins University. Of Dr. Clark's earlier research work, studies on immunity and experimental syphilis should be mentioned. Medical bacteriology became an independent department in 1935. Teaching in hygiene also was under Dr. Clark's supervision. One interesting feature of the early curricula of the new school up to 1914 was the offering of psychology courses given by Professor Jastrow to second-year medical students.

The second year of the preclinical courses, 1908, coincided with the opening of the departments of pathology and pharmacology-toxicology. The first professor of pathology and chairman of the department was Charles Henry Bunting, who took his B.S. at Wisconsin in 1896. He was a teacher of great distinction. His chief interest was in the diseases of the hematopoietic system, especially those of the lymphoid tissues. He acquired his medical degree at Johns Hopkins in 1901 and was professor of pathology at the University of Virginia before coming to Madison. He remained at the University until his retirement in 1945.

Arthur Solomon Loevenhart, the first chairman of the department of pharmacology-toxicology, had been an associate professor at Johns Hopkins. Some of his outstanding research work will be dealt with later. In the same year, 1908, Dr. Walter Joseph Meek, who was later to become assistant and associate dean and chairman of the department of physiology, joined the staff of the school.

The ability of Dr. Bardeen to choose the proper men is strikingly illustrated by the success achieved later by most of his appointees. That he drew so heavily on Johns Hopkins graduates, especially in the medical sciences, is to be understood from the unique role that that school played in American medical education at the beginning of the century, a role which attracted to it a student body of unusual quality.

The preliminary announcement of 1907, which was reprinted in all catalogues up to 1931, defined the aims of the college as follows: "1) To encourage a thorough preliminary medical education, and to offer facilities for a thorough preparation for clinical work; 2) To aid physicians and others in the state to keep up with the rapid advances in the application of science to medicine; 3) To promote the development of preventive medicine and hygiene; 4) To stimulate research in the sciences upon which modern medicine is based."[5] The steps for attaining the first goal have been sketched roughly above.

Realization of the second aim was envisaged in Dr. Bardeen's 1908 report through the application of the University's extension system to medicine. A tuberculosis exhibit was set up as the first example. The catalogue of 1915 gives detailed information on the subject. It lists a Bureau of Health Instruction headed by Dr. Hoyt E. Dearholt, a tuberculosis specialist of Milwaukee, and mentions traveling exhibits, bulletins on baby care and on rural hygiene, a weekly press bulletin, popular and special courses, and correspondence courses. By 1918 the work was divided between the Bureau of Health Instruction, headed by Dr. Dearholt, and the Bureau of Medical Instruction, headed by Dr. Rock Sleyster. In 1920 these activities seem to have reached a peak, the bureaus employing a number of the clinical staff members on half time. After 1921 extension work is not listed again until 1925. Then until 1936, when the name extension definitely disappeared, the catalogue listed an executive committee and an advisory council, the composition of which reflected the common interest of the University, the State Medical Society, and the state Board of Health in such projects. The school has not diminished its efforts in either popular

[5] *University Catalogue,* 1907–08, pp. 388–389.

health education or in medical postgraduate education, but forms have changed with changes in technology. In popular education, radio now plays a primary role, and the late Dr. Llewellyn R. Cole's addresses were distributed over twenty-three stations. Dr. Cole, professor of clinical medicine, from 1946 to 1948 also coordinated postgraduate courses and lectures which, with improved communication, could be centralized in Madison to a larger extent than before. The Medical Library extension service handles a great number of questions from laymen and doctors all over the state.

The school contributed considerably to the development of preventive medicine and public health in the state through its teaching and extension work and through specific divisions like the department of bacteriology, the State Laboratory of Hygiene, the Psychiatric Institute, the Student Health Service, and clinical services. Yet the specific goal of training public health officers, stated stubbornly in all programs from 1911 to 1937, did not materialize, as prospective candidates preferred special schools in the field which had been endowed elsewhere.

That stimulation of research was and has remained one of the main preoccupations of the school is evidenced in the work produced during these preclinical decades. We have already mentioned the work of Bardeen and Miller in anatomy. Another member of the department, Bennet Mills Allen (1903–13), later professor of zoology at the University of California, deserves to be remembered. Best known for his work in endocrinology, he did interesting embryological studies on the origin of sex cells while at Wisconsin. Walter E. Sullivan and Theodore H. Bast, who joined the department in 1920, have both found deserved recognition, the former for his work in primate anatomy, the latter for his intensive histological studies of the ear. In physiology Erlanger, Gasser, and Meek have been mentioned already. Dr. Erlanger's successor in 1910 was John A. E. Eyster, also a Johns Hopkins graduate. Dr. Eyster's work on cardiac physiology ranks among the most remarkable scientific achievements of the school.

In the pharmacology department Dr. Loevenhart and his associates developed a most amazing activity. Among the many problems Loevenhart dealt with, we can mention here only his studies on intracellular oxidation and on insomnia, the latter terminated by his untimely death in 1929. Best known of his studies was his work on the use of arsenical drugs in neurosyphilis, a project for which he was able to obtain extensive financial support as well as the cooperation of a neuropsychiatric group under Dr. William F. Lorenz and a bacteriological group under Dr. Paul F. Clark. These studies, which ran from 1919 to 1928, established among other things the effective use of tryparsamide. From 1923 to 1928 Chauncey D. Leake, on the campus as a graduate student from 1917 until he received his Ph.D. in 1923 and now vice-president of the University of Texas, taught in the pharmacology department. Dr. Leake showed also a strong interest in the history of medicine. The well-known Chinese pharmacologist, K. K. Chen, who took a B.S. at Wisconsin in 1920 and a Ph.D. in 1923, did part of his remarkable work on ephedrine in 1925–26 in the pharmacology department, where, unfortunately, no permanent position could be obtained for him.

Out of Dr. Loevenhart's work in forensic toxicology grew the appointment of a state toxicologist in 1923. The first incumbent was Dr. Clarence W. Muehlberger. Dr. Frank L. Kozelka has carried on this valuable work since 1933 in spite of the withdrawal of the state's financial support during the depression years, when the work was put on a private-fee basis.

Any report on the scientific activities of the school during the preclinical and later periods would be incomplete without mention of the late James S. Hipple, who as instrument maker and mechanician was connected with the school from 1912 until his retirement in 1947. Progress in experimentation depends to a large extent on apparatus, and Mr. Hipple showed rare talent in constructing mechanical devices for experimental as well as therapeutic purposes. In 1910 the library of Dr. Byron Robinson was received as a nucleus for a Medical School Library, another vital element for a school oriented toward systematic research.

From 1907 to 1917, when they were eventually united in Science Hall, the five departments of the school had been housed in a most unsatisfactory way in the attics and basements of at least three buildings, a fact which makes the accomplishments of the school during this period all the more admirable.

The preliminary announcement of 1907 said: "Lack of adequate clinical facilities prevents the establishment at Madison of the last half of the curriculum." The decisive step toward obtaining such clinical facilities was the foundation of the Student Health Service and the appointment of Dr. Joseph S. Evans in 1910 as its director as well as professor of clinical medicine in the medical school. As so often happens in medical history, the unfortunate consequences of an epidemic provided the stimulus for progress. After the outbreak of typhoid among students in 1908 which had resulted in several deaths, Doctors Erlanger and Bradley, who were both from California, the home of the first real student health program, convinced Dean Bardeen that the medical school should have a clinician and the University a student health program.

As a result Dr. Joseph Spragg Evans came to Madison in February, 1910. Thus Wisconsin became the second university in America to have a student health program, and the necessary courses in clinical diagnosis could be added to the second-year curriculum. Born in West Chester, Pennsylvania, in 1875, Evans received his medical degree at the University of Pennsylvania in 1899. After two years of postgraduate studies in bacteriology in Berlin, Vienna, and Paris, he returned to the Pennsylvania medical school in 1902 and was instructor in clinical medicine and associate in bacteriology until 1909. He was chairman of the department of medicine at Wisconsin from 1910 until his retirement in 1945. These official titles give only a very insufficient idea of his influence in the development of the school, which, without the impression that "the chief" made upon everybody he came in touch with, perhaps would never have been completed. In 1947 at the twentieth anniversary of the graduation of the first fourth-year class, Dr. William S. Middleton aptly called the school, to the building of which Dr. Evans had to a large extent sacrificed a promising research career, a product of "Bardeen's brain and Evans' heart."

Only a man of Evans' fiber could have weathered the vicious

attacks from all quarters made on the Student Health Service immediately after its initiation, attacks which, stimulated for obvious reasons by certain local doctors, recurred at intervals throughout the years.[6] The fact that the attitude of the Marquette Medical School in Milwaukee in all these crises was always friendly and cooperative deserves to be mentioned in this context. In spite of the early opposition the health service was quickly accepted by the students; and 837 patients were treated during the first semester (the total number of students at that time was 3,500) in the Cornelius house on State Street near Park. In 1910 Dr. Robert Van Valzah was brought from Pennsylvania for the clinical staff. Dr. Van Valzah, a keen clinician and bedside teacher, was clinical professor of medicine from 1918 until 1936 when ill health removed him from active practice.

In 1912 the Student Health Clinic was moved into the Olin house on Langdon Street, and in 1915 the house next door on the east, the Raymer house, was converted into an infirmary. In 1912 Dr. William Shainline Middleton, who had received his medical degree from the University of Pennsylvania in 1911, joined the staff of the Student Health Service. Advancing to professor of medicine in 1933 and dean, as successor of Dr. Bardeen, in 1935, Dr. Middleton has also had great influence on the development of the school and its clinical services.

The founding of the Wisconsin Psychiatric Institute in Mendota State Hospital in 1915 meant an important broadening of the clinical work of the school. Its first director, Dr. William F. Lorenz, became associate professor of neuropsychiatry in the same year. The institute, a laboratory of the State Board of Control, gives physicians free service in making Wassermann tests, examination of the spinal fluid, and blood-chemistry examinations. Dr. Lorenz was ably assisted by his nephew, Dr. William J. Blackwenn (appointed in 1922), and Dr. Hans H. Reese (appointed in 1924). The collaboration of this group in the neurosyphilis project has already been mentioned. In 1925 the laboratory was transferred by the legislature to the University campus. Also from 1915 dates the close cooperation with

[6] See pp. 520 ff.

the school of a local ophthalmologist, Dr. Frederick A. Davis, the author of interesting research papers, for instance on the inheritance of artificial eye defects in rabbits.

During the years 1916 and 1917 arrangements were made for the first medical school buildings: the student infirmary and Bradley Memorial Hospital. The $50,000 appropriated by the legislature for the building of an infirmary proved insufficient, but Carl Johnson and Thomas Brittingham, each donating $25,000, made the realization of the project possible. In 1916 Dr. and Mrs. Harold C. Bradley and Mr. and Mrs. Charles R. Crane donated $75,000 for the erection of a research hospital in memory of Mary Cornelia Bradley. The two hospitals were opened in 1919–20. During the great influenza epidemic of 1918, which claimed numerous victims on the campus, the University Club had to be transformed into an infirmary.

After 1920, owing to the enlarged clinical facilities, it was possible to associate with the school three noted Milwaukee men: the dermatologist, Otto H. Foerster; the orthopedic surgeon, Fred J. Gaenslen; and the plastic surgeon, George Van Ingen Brown. Dr. James C. Elsom, who had been with the University as professor of physical education since 1894, became physical therapist of the hospital in 1920, a position he retained until his retirement in 1937.

The usefulness and the necessity of the Student Health Service have become so obvious in the course of years that no further comments on this subject seem needed.

In 1919 the last round for the establishment of a full medical school in Madison started when the legislature eliminated the legal limitations against such a development that had been set up in 1915. It had become obvious that the school had to either expand or, in the long run, disappear. In a special report to the regents in December, 1919, Dean Bardeen declared that the medical school had reached "a critical stage." There were one hundred students in the sophomore class and one hundred and fifty freshmen. Already the point had been reached where it was difficult to place these students in good medical schools at the end of their first two years' preparation. He outlined three alternatives. The number of students admitted to the medical school could be restricted and no assurance given that a transfer could be arranged at the end of two years; the medical school might be given up entirely; or immediate steps could be taken to establish the complete four-year course. Dean Bardeen felt that the second alternative was preferable to the first, but that the third should prevail. The regents, the State Board of Education, and the legislature, he declared, had all looked forward to the completion of the four-year medical course at the University.[7]

Most schools that in the past had accommodated Wisconsin students for the last two years of the curriculum had, in the course of the reorganization that American medical schools underwent during this period, limited their student body to such an extent that they could no longer absorb any considerable number of outsiders. Yet in order to provide instruction in the last two years on a level with the preclinical instruction, a large teaching hospital was needed in Madison. While so far it had been possible to obtain new teaching facilities at relatively little expense, the building of a hospital required very considerable sums.

It was, therefore, fortunate that Governor Emanuel Philipp, who was a firm friend of the full-school plan, could point to the unexpended balance of the Service Recognition Fund as a source of funds for such a project. It was fortunate, too, that this project won the hearty support of the American Legion. A special session of the legislature in 1920 promptly allocated $1,300,000 out of this Service Recognition Fund for the building and furnishing of a hospital and a nurses' home as war memorials.[8] The last concrete was poured for the basement by December 20, 1920. Then, partly because of a change of administration, work stopped and the fate of the school was in suspense again. In July, 1922, work was resumed and in 1924 the hospital and the nurses' home were opened.

The first superintendent of the hospital was Dr. Robin C. Buerki who served until 1941. In the dedication ceremonies of the hospital in 1925, facilities for crippled children, the in-

[7] Papers of the Board of Regents, December 3, 1919.
[8] For details see Volume II, pp. 208 ff.

sane, and pregnant women in the state were particularly emphasized. The "State of Wisconsin General Hospital" was not primarily to serve a local community but rather such patients all over the state who otherwise could not afford the necessary specialized care and treatment offered by the hospital. Provision for their admission and transportation was made. Since its opening the hospital has always been filled to capacity. The immediate consequence of the opening of the hospital was the creation of a School of Nursing and the establishment of surgery and obstetrics departments and a number of specialized services that had not existed in the Student Health Service or the Bradley Memorial Hospital. From this time dates the connection with the hospital of Dr. Wellwood M. Nesbit as otolaryngologist and Dr. Ira R. Sisk as urologist. Dr. John E. Gonce, Jr., who had been with the school since 1919, headed the new pediatric division. The outpatient department has been directed since its beginning by Dr. Karver L. Puestow, whose special interest is gastroenterology.

On this solid clinical basis instruction in the third medical year could be started in 1925. This third-year class of twenty-six (twenty men and six women), who received the first medical degrees from the school in 1927, accommodated only a fraction of the preclinical classes. The classes in the clinical years were gradually increased in size during the following years to an average of sixty.

The medical school immediately inaugurated a new method in clinical teaching: the so-called preceptorial plan, a product of Dr. Bardeen's fertile mind that has found general attention. Dr. Bardeen realized that exclusive training in the artificial environment of the laboratory and hospital does not fully prepare the student for his future tasks as a practitioner in a world of economic realities and technical limitations. Therefore, to fill this educational gap, the oldest method of medical instruction, apprenticeship, has been resuscitated and integrated into the modern curriculum. Every fourth-year student spends one-fourth of his time (twelve weeks) with an outstanding practitioner as "preceptor" in one of ten different medical centers of the state. About one hundred physicians all over the state are involved in this plan. It so happens that the system has not only provided a unique educational experience for the student, but has also firmly cemented the relations between the school and the practitioners of the state.

In 1925 the legislature appropriated $840,000 from a surplus in the Soldiers' Rehabilitation Fund for the erection of another war memorial, the Service Memorial Institute, in the immediate neighborhood of the hospital. The building was occupied in 1928 and provided excellent housing for all nonclinical departments of the school except anatomy, which is still located in Science Hall. Thus after long sufferings, the school had grown within a decade from its uncertain beginnings into one of the best-equipped institutions of its kind in this country. Unlike most other medical schools in the United States, which started with clinical instruction and only later—and more or less grudgingly—accepted the medical sciences into their fold on an equal footing, this school has grown on a solid foundation in these sciences, a fact which is also reflected in its research record.

The events of the last twenty-three years of the medical school (or its first twenty-three years as a full-fledged medical school) are too recent to allow anything but a registration of facts which at present seem to be relevant.

In 1926 Dr. Erwin R. Schmidt became head of the department of surgery, which has grown up under his direction. In 1927 he brought Dr. Ralph M. Waters, an anesthetist of international reputation, into the department. Dr. Waters developed an extremely active and productive subdepartment of anesthesiology, remarkable for its successful and close cooperation with other departments. The appointment of Dr. Ernst A. Pohle as professor of radiology in the same year resulted in a strong development of the X-ray department in subsequent years. With the appointment of Dr. John W. Harris as professor of obstetrics and gynecology in 1928, this department was put on a full-time basis. In 1928 a subdivision of cardiology was created under Dr. Chester M. Kurtz. Cultivation of this branch of internal medicine has been greatly stimulated through the fundamental studies of the heart made by Doctors Eyster and Meek in the department of physiology. Since Dr. Loevenhart's premature death in 1929, pharmacological work has been carried on actively under the leadership of Dr. Arthur L. Tatum, who is known for his studies on different aspects of drug addiction and barbiturate poisoning.

In 1931 a real advance was made in the medical-surgical treatment of tuberculosis patients of the state when the roof of the hospital, the seventh floor, was converted into a beautiful air-conditioned special ward. In the same year the hospital and the student infirmary were connected through a new wing of the infirmary, and the Wisconsin Orthopedic Hospital for Children, designed for 125 patients, was opened on the hospital grounds.

Since the appointment in 1932 of Dr. Ovid O. Meyer, who has been chairman of the department of medicine since 1945, hematologic interests in the department have been particularly emphasized. In 1933 Dr. William A. Mowry, who had been on the staff of the school since 1923, opened the allergy service. Since 1936 Dr. Frederic E. Mohs has developed his successful work in "chemosurgery," the combination of chemical and surgical methods in the treatment of the superficial cancer. With the opening of the McArdle Memorial Laboratories in 1940, an active phase in cancer research was initiated. Medical technicians, occupational therapists, and physiotherapists have been trained in the school since 1937, 1944, and 1945, respectively.

The second World War, which again saw many of the staff members in service and greatly increased the teaching and practice load of those remaining, slowed down the continuous growth of the school for a short period. Since the end of the war the resident staff has been brought to twice its prewar size, new building projects are under consideration, research in the established fields has been intensified, and new developments in psychosomatic medicine, preventive medicine, physical medicine, the history of medicine, and dermatology have been undertaken.

15.

Student Life and Interests

R APID increase in student enrollment which had become
pronounced in the 1890's continued into the twentieth
century. By 1900 the student body exceeded two thousand; ten years later it had passed four thousand and, notwithstanding the slump which occurred during the first World War,
by 1920 it had reached seven thousand and within the next
decade, ten thousand. Depression and another war were to reduce this total but the end had not been reached. In this constant increase the College of Letters and Science continued,
with its numerous technical, quasi-professional, and professional
courses, to occupy the dominant position, while the colleges
of engineering, law, agriculture, and medicine drew propor-
tionately fewer students.

The constantly increasing student body naturally created a
mounting problem of housing. Except for the one women's
dormitory, the University had no residence halls at the time
Van Hise became president. Some students found rooms in the
dormitory, some in the houses of the Greek-letter societies, but
the great majority had to find places to live in the cavernous
rooming and boarding houses that continued to multiply
around the campus. Pleas for student dormitories from the
president, University officers, and students had little effect on
the legislature. An additional women's residence hall was
acquired before the first World War and, after that, a men's

dormitory. But as late as 1930, fewer than one-eighth of the students were occupying University dormitories.

University authorities had paid little attention to the rooming houses in which students lived. Housing regulations had been largely restricted to University-owned residence halls and to the Greek-letter societies. As far as the faculty was concerned, owners of rooming houses might rent to such students as they saw fit. As late as 1907 rooming houses, at the discretion of the owner, were occupied by both men and women. This situation was one which invited criticism. In 1905 a committee of the Visitors urged on by the University League complained that the University supplied rooming facilities for only one-seventh of the women; about the same number were accommodated in sorority houses and the rest lived in rooming houses in Madison. The committee found sixty-three boarding houses in which both men and women lived. "In some boarding houses young women have no place to receive callers save their bedrooms, no parlor privileges being provided for." The faculty was "awake to these conditions" and was preparing a list of approved houses in which the landladies had agreed to take only women. One difficulty in the way of a quick solution, the committee explained, was that "the University cannot guarantee to fill boarding houses, and the keepers cannot be expected to sacrifice profit to propriety."[1]

[1] Report of the Visitors, *Regents' Biennial Report*, 1905–06, pp. 185–186. The University League, made up largely of the wives of members of the faculty, was organized in 1901. Prominent among the objectives of the organization was the desire to help the young women at the University. It manifested great energy in helping to get a women's building, in making other provisions for women, and it was much concerned with the rooming-house situation in Madison. In May, 1901, after hearing a report by Miss Abby S. Mayhew on boarding and rooming houses, a committee with Miss Mayhew as chairman was formed to visit the houses and report conditions to the league. The committee reported the following September that but one boarding-house keeper had agreed to accept women only. During the next years the University League kept alive its interest in this matter although it became involved in many other activities. Having tried various voluntary means of obtaining segregated rooming houses, the league finally in February, 1905, adopted a petition which was sent to the faculty. "The University League respectfully petitions the Social Committee of the faculty to consider such regulations as would, in the judgment of the committee, better protect the young women students who room in houses in town.

"The league desire to call the attention of the committee to the fact that some women students do not have the use of a parlor in which to receive callers,

Possible faculty or regent intervention was forestalled in 1908 by the Women's Self-Government Association. The association, encouraged by the women's adviser, voted for rooming houses restricted exclusively to women students. A canvass of rooming-house owners was made and a list prepared of those who preferred to keep women and who further agreed to provide first-floor parlor privileges. These houses were recommended to women students.[2]

A year later, another step was taken to bring privately owned rooming houses within the purview of the University authorities. The Board of Regents appropriated money to provide for a "sanitary inspection" of student boarding and rooming houses. It was agreed that rooming and boarding houses should be inspected at least twice a year.[3] This decision was taken partly because of the University's growing sense of responsibility for student health. It seems also to have been based in part on the desire to give the student a little help in his unequal struggle against landlords, many of whom were unwilling to supply more than the minimum of heat, light, furniture, and free air to student tenants.

During the next few years, under the leadership of the dean of women and the chairman of the faculty committee on student life and interests, additional regulations were adopted to extend University supervision over rooming houses. In 1916 the Board of Regents formally voted to give the president the authority, upon the recommendation of the dean of women and

and also that in some cases where men and women room in the same house, the conditions are not all that might be desired." Secretary's Records, University League, pp. 86–87, used through the courtesy of Mrs. Robert Reynolds.

[2] *Regents' Biennial Report,* 1907–08, pp. 246–247; Report of the Adviser of Women, *ibid.,* 1909–10, p. 226. In her book, *The Dean of Women* (Boston, 1915), Lois Kimball Mathews discusses the various problems of deans of women. The author, then dean at Wisconsin, discussed rooming houses, undoubtedly with the Wisconsin situation in mind. She recalled the old days when parents moved to a university town with their children and took in a student roomer or two, or the young instructor and his wife eked out a meager salary by taking roomers: "The situation was very different from what it is now with a group of shrewd, experienced women depending for their living upon student patronage. The matter is regulated largely by the laws of supply and demand; any room rent is charged which the traffic will bear; and sometimes as little is given and as much is taken as can be managed without friction" (p. 72).

[3] Records of the Board of Regents, G:415, December 1, 1909.

the chairman of the committee on student life and interests, "to require a student to withdraw from any lodging place when in the opinion of the president and the officers named, the conditions justify this procedure."[4] On the other side, the University sought to safeguard the proprietor's interest by advising that all student roomers sign contracts for their rooms.[5]

Fraternities and sororities, which had become numerous and had begun to acquire chapter houses in the 1890's, continued to increase in numbers in the early years of this century. Some began to build their somewhat ostentatious houses. These associations represented different things to different University groups. To their own members, the fraternities offered a place to live, social prestige, a circle of friends, and often a focus of lasting interest; to other students, fraternity row was the gold coast of the University, the fraternity men were the sons of wealth, wasteful of time and money, dexterous in controlling University politics, aloof and unfriendly; to the faculty these associations often represented organizations which, because of the housing and boarding service offered, must be tolerated, regulated, and from time to time so controlled as to protect freshmen from their clutches; to many old alumni they were enduring points of interest in the vast stretches of the growing institution; to the regents, they were sometimes an annoyance, even an embarrassment; and to members of the legislature, they supplied an ever available target for attack because of their putative expensiveness, exclusiveness, lack of democracy, and immorality.

Through the years these organizations were the subject of a running argument, animated but of course inconclusive. Van Hise and many of the faculty felt that in an ideal world the University could very well get along without them, but that world had never emerged. Writing to the president of Smith College, Van Hise declared that if a college could provide halls under college supervision, he could "see no possible occasion for Greek-letter fraternities."[6] Thus it was the lack of University

---

[4] *Ibid.*, I:454, June 20, 1916.

[5] University Faculty Documents, No. 56, Records of the Secretary of the Faculty, October 1, 1917.

[6] Charles R. Van Hise to L. Clark Seelye, December 6, 1906, Presidents' Papers.

housing which conditioned all faculty and regent consideration of the fraternity problem. The legislature in 1907 threatened to abolish fraternities and in 1909 asked the regents to investigate the charges that the organizations were undemocratic.
This task the regents passed on to a faculty committee.[7] The
committee made a full investigation and brought in a report
which probably surprised no one. The committee found that
the fraternities were to an extent exclusive, but not extensively
antidemocratic, snobbish, or clannish. It reported that other
than well-to-do students were members. Indeed the committee found that about 27 per cent of the fraternity men were
partially self-supporting, 7 per cent entirely so. The management
of the chapter houses was not efficient, but it was improving. The
committee found that the fraternity members were definitely
deficient in scholarship and since the members came from better preparatory schools than the nonfraternity students, they
thought this condition was to be explained largely in terms of
the opportunities which existed for wasting time with congenial
companions. Overemphasis on social activities contributed to
this record. So far not much had been done by the faculty to
correct these evils. On the other hand, the fraternities offered
social advantages to their members. The moral standards of
the members differed little from those of other students. The
societies offered much needed housing for students. The only
adequate substitute for the fraternities, the committee felt,
would be an extensive University dormitory system. Until this
was provided, the committee declared, "No action looking
toward their abolition would seem justified." In the meantime,
the committee recommended, no freshmen should be permitted
to join, or live in the fraternity houses, and no student on probation ought to be initiated. The regents accepted the report
and used it as the basis of their report to the legislature the
next year.[8]

A committee of the regents tried to turn the report on fra-

[7] Records of the Board of Regents, G:415, December 1, 1909. The committee
was composed of Hugh A. Smith, Carl R. Fish, William U. Moore, Susan A.
Sterling, William L. Westermann, Cora S. Woodward, and Karl Young.
[8] Report of the Faculty Committee, Faculty File Book, July 1, 1910; Papers of
the Board of Regents, October 12, 1910.

ternities into an argument for legislative funds for the construction of student dormitories. But while members of the legislature might condemn the fraternity system on various grounds, a proposal looking forward to the eventual abolition of the societies but involving a substantial appropriation as a necessary part of the program found little support among the lawmakers.[9] Indeed, during the next years, fraternities and sororities continued to be attacked, but no one seriously proposed that they be abolished. They performed a necessary function. Dean Goodnight, in his formal report as chairman of the committee on student life and interests, defended fraternities on the grounds that they provided good room and board to their members at reasonable prices, and lamented that for the rest of the students boarding houses had practically disappeared. Outside of the fraternities and a limited number of boarding houses, he reported, "The men students depend upon restaurants, lunch wagons, and cafeterias. Since they can obtain service at these places at any hour and are at liberty to order as they please, a frequent result is irregular hours for eating, and in very many cases an ill-balanced ration. Young stomachs ordinarily recover quickly from such mistreatment, but where the abuse is of long duration, there is no doubt that much permanent injury is done. The clinic has many cases of malnutrition to treat."[10] "The fraternities," he wrote in 1918, "have always done at Wisconsin the work that should be done by dormitories and commons. Because they offered good lodgings and good table board —in this cafeteria era three substantial meals per day at regular hours are obtainable only in fraternity and sorority houses and women's dormitories—they had supported themselves without difficulty."[11] In 1920 he reported that with the establishment of good business management these organizations were able to provide board to their members for 88 cents a day and room for 61 cents. "This is certainly a cheaper rate than similar accommodations cost outside."[12]

In 1930, a regents' committee reported that of the eight

[9] Report of the Regents to the Legislature on the Fraternity System at the University, Papers of the Board of Regents, April 25, 1912.
[10] *Regents' Biennial Report*, 1915–16, p. 223.
[11] *Ibid.*, 1917–18, p. 238.   [12] *Ibid.*, 1919–20, p. 174.

Top: May Fête on the Upper Campus, 1915. *Bottom: The Sphinx* Board, 1914

The 1925 Prom, February 8, 1924

Top: The Lake Rush, 1908. *Bottom:* Class Rush, 1923

The First Sorority and the First Fraternity on the Campus
Early Photographs of Kappa Kappa Gamma and Phi Delta Theta

thousand students then enrolled in the University, less than seven hundred were accommodated in University-owned dormitories. The seventy-two fraternities and sororities, at the same time, provided housing for over fifteen hundred men and six hundred women.[13] The great majority of the students were still lodged in private rooming houses.

✐

WHEN Van Hise became president there was no system by which student opinion could be carried to the faculty in a responsible and orderly way. The women, to be sure, had their self-government association, but no similar organization existed for the men. To the extent that social and other student activities were controlled by the faculty, the control was through committees. The attitude and method of the faculty was explained by Dean Birge in 1907. "Our method of controlling the activities of student organizations outside of athletics is by means of committees. We have a Committee on Social Affairs and one on Musical and Dramatic Organizations. These are the only activities which we are at present endeavoring to regulate. I cannot say that our regulation is very efficient. The main attempt is to bring pressure to bear upon the students to secure the things which the faculty desires. Since students are continually asking for favors of one kind or another, a good deal can be accomplished this way, and I am not sure that a more vigorous method of control would bring about better results. It is difficult to say very much as to ways and means, since the problems are handled as they arise."[14] With this view Van Hise agreed. In a formal statement to the Board of Regents in December, 1907, Van Hise declared: "The most rapid progress is made in student affairs by the faculty standing with the front ranks of the best students, cultivating and improving their ideals, leading them and getting them to lead the mass of students in improving the conditions in the University. This has been my policy for the last four years, and I believe that there

[13] Papers of the Board of Regents, November 22, 1930.
[14] Edward A. Birge to Dean Evarts B. Greene, University of Illinois, December 18, 1907, Papers of the Dean of the College of Letters and Science.

has been marked improvement in the tone of the student body in various respects."[15]

In this spirit the president had created the student conference committee,[16] which by 1909 included representatives from each University class, from graduate students, and one each from the fraternities, literary societies, and other college organizations. "This committee," Van Hise wrote, "has no power whatever, except advisory. However, it is so influential that its recommendations are usually adopted by the classes and the various student organizations." Van Hise reported that such problems as hazing, student discipline, cheating, and regulation of social activities had thus been successfully handled by the students.[17]

This student participation in the regulation of various activities naturally suggested a further step. The conference committee proposed in the autumn of 1909 that a student court be established to deal with men students charged with violation of student rules and regulations.[18] The proposal formally recommended to the regents the establishment of such a court. The court was to consist of nine members, elected by the men students, and was to have power to investigate all infractions of University rules by men except those involving dishonesty in classroom work. The court, which did not operate during the summer session, was empowered to hold hearings and recommend action, including suspension, to the faculty discipline committee. A student might appeal the decision of the court to the faculty discipline committee or to the dean of his college.[19] The regents, upon the recommendation of Van Hise, approved the creation of this student court for the men.[20] The *Cardinal* applauded the action.[21] Van Hise's approval was unreserved. He declared that there had been no hazing in the fall of 1910 and that the faculty had upheld all the sentences pronounced by the student court. "The cases which have come before the student court have been handled with such firmness and wisdom

[15] Van Hise to the regents, December 17, 1907, Papers of the Board of Regents.
[16] *Daily Cardinal*, October 27, 1906.
[17] Van Hise to Homer C. Washburn, University of Oklahoma, January 13, 1909, Presidents' Papers.   [18] *Daily Cardinal*, November 9, 1909.
[19] Committee report adopted January 17, 1910, Faculty File Book.
[20] Records of the Board of Regents, G:424–425, 428, January 19, 1910.
[21] *Daily Cardinal*, January 19, 20, 1910.

that already this court has gained the respect and confidence of the student body."[22] In token of its confidence in the student court, the faculty recommended the next year that the regents repeal the old rule that any student convicted in a local court of a crime, misdemeanor, or disorderly conduct be automatically suspended from the University until readmitted by the faculty. This the regents did.[23] Thus such cases came, as in propriety they should, to the student court.

Meanwhile the success of the student court among the men served to encourage a similar development in the Women's Self-Government Association, and the president's student conference committee was formally recognized as the "legislative assembly of the University for all affairs concerning men."[24] Moreover, in 1910 all faculty committees dealing with student activities and interests, except for athletics, were consolidated into a single faculty committee on student affairs.[25]

Perhaps the most serious test of the student court and student self-government came in 1913 when the regents summarily dismissed a student for having brought out an unauthorized magazine containing "immoral and lascivious" material. The case was pending before the student court when the regents met and dismissed the student. The students protested and Van Hise championed their cause before the Board. To G. D. Jones, Van Hise declared that the regents ought not to override their own laws. Jones, on the other hand, felt that the regents were correct and justified in this instance. "We desire," he wrote Van Hise, "this rule and every other rule, for that matter, to show clearly that in all cases the regents reserve the right to deal summarily with any matter which arises in the university where in their judgment such action is for the interest of the university."[26] But the students regarded the act of the regents as rash

[22] Report of the president, *Regents' Biennial Report*, 1909–10, p. 7.

[23] Records of the Board of Regents, H:245, December 13, 1911.

[24] *Regents' Biennial Report*, 1911–12, p. 9; *Daily Cardinal*, January 18, 1912.

[25] The new committee met for the first time on October 12, 1910. Professors Dennis, Fish, and Roe each served a year as chairman of the committee. In 1914 Scott H. Goodnight became chairman and subsequently dean of men. See Minutes of the Committee on Student Life and Interests in the Office of the Dean of Men.

[26] Van Hise to G. D. Jones, March 17, 1913; and Jones to Van Hise, March 18, 1913, both in the Presidents' Papers.

and capricious. The conference committee presented its grievances to the regents charging that the regents had usurped powers granted to the student court. The regents justified their action on the basis that the case was exceptional and that prompt action had to be taken to protect the reputation of the University. Regent Hammond explained that the regents had even contemplated censure of the student court for not having taken prompt and decisive action, but instead had expelled the offending student and amended the constitution of the student court. He admitted that the regents might have been influenced by the fact that the offending student, when he appeared before them, had declared that he was under the jurisdiction of the student court, not the regents.

The student conference committee, after discussing the regents' explanation, agreed to abide by the regents' decision provided the Board would in the future give ample notice when it contemplated a change in the constitution of the student court.[27] Accordingly, Van Hise prepared a resolution in which the regents declared their "confidence in the principles of student self-government, and declare it to be their policy not to alter or abridge the power of the student conference or the student court, without an opportunity for representatives of the conference or court, to be heard upon the proposed change by the regent committee on by-laws and law, or some other committee of the regents designated for the purpose."[28] The regents also formally adopted an amendment to the constitution of the student court denying it jurisdiction in "such flagrant cases of action or behavior so contrary to the welfare of the university as to require immediate consideration."[29] Obviously, self-government was far from complete or secure. But it should be observed that the offending student was readmitted to the University by action of the regents some six months later.[30]

Self-government for the men was threatened by the regents in 1913, but the next year it was attacked by the students. There were many elements in the situation. The student conference committee, encouraged by the faculty committee on student

[27] Papers of the Board of Regents, April 16, 1913.
[28] Records of the Board of Regents, H:555, April 16, 1913.
[29] *Ibid.*, H:554–555. [30] *Ibid.*, I:44, October 8, 1913.

life, had adopted rules restricting social activities. The amount of money which could be spent in student elections had been strictly limited. The *Independent* thought this reform sufficiently important to warrant publishing an article on it.[31] Perhaps in consequence of these actions, control of the student conference committee passed from the fraternity to the non-fraternity groups. There followed a sustained attack upon the student conference committee and a referendum was held on whether the committee should be retained. By the narrow vote of 673 to 650, the male students of the University decided to retain this branch of student self-government.[32] Van Hise himself interpreted the attacks largely in terms of the resentment of the fraternity groups at having lost control and, what was closely related to this, the action of the conference committee in abolishing house parties.[33]

The faculty committee on student life meanwhile had recommended that one committee, with subcommittees on the separate extracurricular activities, be created. The chairman of this committee was to devote the major part of his time to the work of the committee. He would thus "in a measure perform the duties of the dean of men." The plan went into effect in 1914.[34] Two years later the office of dean of men was created and the chairman of the faculty committee, Associate Professor Scott H. Goodnight, was named to the position.

The student welfare committee of the faculty pressed various reforms upon the students through the student conference committee. Before the end of 1914 the chairman of the faculty committee proposed to the student conference committee a set of rules governing eligibility of students for participation in various student activities besides athletics.[35] These rules, adopted by the faculty the next May, provided that students must have been in residence at least one year and have earned 28 credits before becoming eligible to participate in "intercollegiate con-

[31] "Cleaning up College Politics," The *Independent*, 77:270 (February 23, 1914).
[32] *Daily Cardinal*, March 14, 1914.
[33] Van Hise to President George Edgar Vincent, University of Minnesota, March 23, 1914, Presidents' Papers.
[34] Report of the president, *Regents' Biennial Report*, 1913-14, p. 5.
[35] *Daily Cardinal*, December 11, 1914.

tests of any character . . . in any major musical or dramatic performance or trip, for representing the University in any public way, for membership in the Student Conference, the Student Court, the Women's Judiciary Committee, the Union Board, or the Athletic Board, for SGA office, Union committee chairmanship, or for any office or position of trust in the gift of any class, . . . a position upon the staff of any student publication, or for initiation to a fraternity or sorority." [36] Professor Goodnight also supported a series of regulations governing student social life, the fraternities, the auditing of accounts of student organizations, and a host of other matters. In 1915 he reported that "perhaps the most effective work that has been accomplished [by the committee] is the partial rectification of the wretched condition in class and publication finances." [37]

At the same time the student conference committee, which had come to have a membership of over fifty, was reorganized. A charter for the student senate, granting specific powers to the senate to regulate the nonacademic affairs of the male students, was prepared and approved by students, faculty, and regents. It went into effect in 1916. [38]

With the formal establishment of the student senate for the men of the University, more or less complete machinery for student government existed. The women had their association and their judiciary committee, the men their senate and student court. But student self-government did not flourish among the men, partly because of the disrupting effect of the war, partly for other reasons. The views of the dean of men were revealed in his first report to the president in 1916. The faculty committee of which he was chairman had, he reported, enforced the restriction of entertainment to Friday and Saturday nights. "It is impossible, of course," he wrote, "to prevent the individual student from wasting his time on these evenings, but we feel that by this policy the University clearly designates the midweek evenings as work evenings, and the student who fails to

---

[36] Faculty File Book, May 3, 1915.
[37] Report of the Committee on Student Life and Interests, Faculty File Book, June 7, 1915.
[38] *Daily Cardinal*, May 2, 3, 4, 19, and 30, 1916; Report of the president, *Regents' Biennial Report*, 1915–16, p. 12.

use them as such must accept the entire responsibility therefor."[39] The fraternities had been brought under control. "The present generation of fraternity men . . . has been subject to regulations from the beginning of its student days, and the fraternities now not only submit willingly to regulation, but also cooperate readily in an endeavor to raise the tone of fraternity life at Wisconsin."[40] He reported that auditing of accounts of student organizations had been instituted and announced that "In this manner a great reduction has been effected in the amount of petty graft formerly indulged in, and the finances of the classes and publications are handled in a more businesslike fashion."[41] Plans were being made to bring men's rooming houses under inspection by his office. "No small part of the time of the chairman is spent in adjusting personal differences which arise between lodgers and landladies, in aiding the latter in maintaining good order in their houses, and, in rare cases, in insisting upon the observance of reasonable sanitary regulations."[42] "We are quite aware," concluded the dean, "that there are many pathetic cases of poverty, of misguided energy, and occasional cases of wilful crime among our young men. To get in touch with these cases in time to be of assistance, to rectify, and at times to punish, is a phase of administrative work to which the chairman, in his new function of Dean of Men, expects to devote himself more in the future than during the biennial period just closed."[43] Indeed, with the appointment of a dean of men a new era had dawned.

Methodical, tireless, ubiquitous, self-reliant, Dean Goodnight extended the supervision of his office over student rooming houses, social life, and personal behavior of the students. His efforts to place the Greek-letter societies on a sound financial basis were perhaps in large measure responsible for saving these organizations from bankruptcy. His auditing of student organization accounts served to maintain solvency among them, which was a good thing to the extent that solvency was good, although some might possibly contend that solvency was not

[39] Report of the Committee on Student Life and Interests, *Regents' Biennial Report*, 1915–16, p. 218.
[40] *Ibid.*, 218, 219.
[42] *Ibid.*, 222.
[41] *Ibid.*, 221.
[43] *Ibid.*, 224.

the primary objective of student organizations. Conscientious to a fault, the dean kept his eye, directly and indirectly, on the Latin Quarter in search of rule breakers. He was quick to apprehend culprits wherever and whenever he found them, and was ever alert to investigate rumor and report of student violation of the rules. In the endless struggle between student and landlady, he placed his office on the side of the landladies who complied with University rules: "This office feels under a somewhat greater obligation towards the landladies of approved houses and they in turn feel freer to call upon the office for assistance in cases of misconduct on the part of lodgers."[44] Immediately after the war, he seemed to doubt his capacity to stem the mighty tide of dissipation and lawlessness. He confessed, "The passion for diversion, for extremes, for extravagances, for dissipation was more marked than at any time within the memory of members of the Committee." National prohibition also caused great trouble. "Although Madison was dry at the time neighboring village bars were doing an immense business and drinking was unusually prevalent among the men students. On the whole, it was a very trying year, interspersed with controversies of considerable magnitude between the Committee and the student body. . . . It was consoling to learn, however, that other institutions were having similar trouble."[45]

The dean of women, F. Louise Nardin, who had replaced Lois Kimball Mathews in 1918, was almost equally doleful in her first postwar report. But there had been some improvements under her urging. "Better fashions in dancing are appearing. And student sentiment gradually is arraying itself against poor scholarship, lax manners, and a blunted sense of honor. . . . Some students withdrew during the year," she reported, "because their behavior was considered destructive to the standards and the reputation of the University. The large elimination for delinquent scholarship removed from the community many others who were felt to be destructive influences. It is hoped that no succeeding year will bring to the University so many young women that are ethically unready."[46]

Perhaps student self-government was an impossibility dur-

---

[44] *Ibid.,* 1917–18, p. 239.
[45] *Ibid.,* 1919–20, pp. 172–173.   [46] *Ibid.,* 170.

ing and immediately after the first World War but the vigorous activity of Deans Goodnight and Nardin was not always calculated to strengthen it. In 1919 the *Cardinal* conducted a campaign to revive interest in the senate and student court.[47] In 1921 and 1922 a campaign was carried on to reorganize the student senate on a basis of representation by colleges instead of classes, but even so the senate, it was claimed, was in large measure restricted to legislating on minor matters.[48]

In the next few years interest did revive, but in 1925 the *Cardinal* declared that student government was ineffective, the student senate and the student court, weak and incapable.[49] A year later the members of the student court submitted their resignations to the regents explaining that the student court was "merely an agency to lull the University into the false belief that it has an effective student agent for its disciplinary problems," and recommended that the regents cancel the charter of the court.[50] The Board heard the petition and voted to accept the resignations, and it discontinued the court.[51] The members of the student court had stated that they believed that the men students did not want student self-government. It was to be revived later, but in 1926 men's self-government had become a casualty of the lack of interest on the part of the students.

✐

NEW student organizations continued to be formed and old ones to die and to be re-established with remarkable rapidity during this period. Some of the old ones, such as the literary societies, managed to survive with a suggestion of their former glory. Some of the student organizations were the product of faculty encouragement, some came about because of faculty-student interest, some were created and maintained by the students alone. There were dramatic and musical societies, of which Haresfoot was one of the popular and conspicuous, and there were athletic, political, artistic, religious, and a host of

[47] *Daily Cardinal,* January 6 and 7, 1919.
[48] *Ibid.,* November 6, 1921.
[49] *Ibid.,* April 25, 1925.
[50] Papers of the Board of Regents, June 19, 1926.
[51] Records of the Board of Regents, L:351, June 19, 1926.

other organizations. And as befitted the sons and daughters of a nation of joiners, the students of the University joined these organizations. The rise and fall in the financial status of the various organizations was recorded each year in that almost infallible index of organization prosperity, the *Badger*. When an organization was failing, it bought no space in the book. Some were of course entirely *sub rosa*. These existed outside University controls, neither seeking recognition nor courting publicity. In 1911 the faculty committee on student life and interests was informed that many "disreputable" organizations existed; the Humbser and Brewery Crowd were identified by name. It was reported that there were other clubs of "elusive nature" which stood for "excessive drinking," stealing of examination papers, et cetera.[52]

Van Hise believed that extracurricular activities were valuable and he urged that each student participate in one activity and one out-of-door sport.[53] This, of course, was not enough for many students. Faculty concern with overemphasis of "activities" had led to the restrictions on the number and kind of activities for which a student was eligible. But students' organizations continued to multiply. In 1921 the *Cardinal* reported that there were over one hundred and fifty clubs and societies on the campus with a total membership of over twenty thousand.[54] For a student body of little more than seven thousand this was indeed remarkable. Small wonder, too, that Dean Goodnight was proud of having managed to work out a calendar to keep the meetings of the organizations from too many conflicts in time and place.

While student publications did not multiply with the abandon of other student organizations, there was no lack of them. The *Cardinal* before the end of the century had become the only student daily newspaper. It continued to enjoy this monopoly except from June, 1912, until November, 1913, when it had a competitor in the form of the *Wisconsin Daily News*. In addition to the student newspapers, there were a number of other student publications reflecting the diversity of interests of

[52] Minutes of the Committee on Student Life and Interests, April 5, 1911.
[53] Report of the president, *Regents' Biennial Report*, 1913–14, p. 4.
[54] *Daily Cardinal*, September 30, 1921.

the student body. The *Wisconsin Alumni Magazine* had absorbed the remnants of the *Aegis* before the end of the century. In 1903 the *Wisconsin Literary Magazine* was launched by a group of faculty members and students.[55] This magazine, usually on the verge of insolvency, survived continuously until 1929. Sometimes threatened with bankruptcy, it was also threatened from time to time by faculty censorship. In 1924, for example, its editor, Kenneth Fearing, was compelled to resign under pressure of the deans and faculty advisers because the editorial policy of the magazine had been "irritatingly satirical and intolerably misanthropic, sour and biting."[56] Over the years it contained the literary outpourings of students and it published contributions by authors—not all students—who were more or less well known then or later. William Ellery Leonard, Esther Forbes, Marquis W. Childs, Vincent Starrett, Emily Hahn, Zona Gale, J. F. A. Pyre, Ring Lardner, Marjorie Kinnan Rawlings, Ernest L. Meyer, Louis P. Lochner, and Joseph E. Davies were among those whose pieces appeared in the magazine.

Sphinx, a humor magazine, was first published in 1899. Launched with the modest announcement that it would fill a place at Wisconsin similar to that filled at eastern colleges by the *Yale Record*, the *Harvard Lampoon*, and the *Princeton Tiger*, the *Sphinx* survived faculty censorship and other hazards until 1914 when the resignation of the business manager and the withdrawal of the editor from the University obliged it to suspend publication.[57] What was left of it combined with the *Wisconsin Literary Magazine* the next month.[58] Five years later, the *Octopus* appeared.

In addition to the newspapers and the literary and the humor magazines which enjoyed more or less permanence, a number of fugitive publications appeared for one issue or two and then disappeared forever, victims of faculty displeasure, printers' bills, or the exhaustion of the editors. The *Wisconsin Spectator* lasted almost a year, but the *Blackbird* got through just one issue before the Board of Regents expelled the editor. The *Pro-*

[55] *Ibid.*, November 10, 1903; *Wisconsin Literary Magazine*, December, 1903.
[56] *Daily Cardinal*, March 20, 1924.
[57] *Ibid.*, September 26, 1914.　　　　　　　[58] *Ibid.*, October 19, 1914.

letarian enjoyed an auspicious beginning when its first issue of twelve hundred copies was reported to have sold out in thirty minutes.[59] But its life was short.

In addition to the student publications of general interest, the engineering students launched and supported their own publication, the *Wisconsin Engineer,* which, with regent and college support, has managed to maintain an unbroken publication record since 1896. The College of Agriculture sponsored the *Student Farmer* in 1907 which later became the *Wisconsin Country Life Magazine.* In 1920 the *Wisconsin Law Review* was established.

The various student publications were for the most part stockholder organizations. In the *Cardinal,* Van Hise reported in 1907, the faculty held a majority of the stock, which gave them practical control, "but not as members of the faculty."[60] But there were further controls exercised by the faculty censor and by the regents in their annual allocation of funds to support these various publications. Censorship and financial support were occasionally definitely linked. Thus in 1905 the regent committee on student publications recommended that the Board refrain from granting its usual appropriation to the *Badger* "for the reason that the same was not fully submitted to the Professor of Rhetoric for examination and that undesirable matter appears therein which cannot fail to bring reproach upon the University."[61] There was hardly a student publication that at one time or another was not in trouble with the University censor for a violation of propriety or good taste. Even the *Daily Cardinal,* which tended more and more to become a practice ground for nascent journalists, was occasionally in trouble. Thus in 1909 the faculty censor wrote the business manager of the *Cardinal,* "I am now compelled to suggest, and on my authority to rule, that hereafter no cut shall appear presenting pictures of women in any garb other than the conventional apparel of polite society, and that no cuts shall appear

[59] *Ibid.,* March 13, 1924.
[60] Van Hise to Dean T. A. Clark, University of Illinois, February 21, 1907, Presidents' Papers.
[61] Papers of the Board of Regents, June 1, 1905.

in connection with theatrical advertising presenting girls in the ballet or chorus of comic operas and musical plays."[62]

The financial contribution of the regents to the student publications was substantial. In 1908, for example, the regents allocated $325 each to the *Literary Magazine,* the *Daily Cardinal,* and the *Wisconsin Alumni Magazine;* $162.50 each to the *Student Farmer* and the *Wisconsin Spectator;* $100 to the *Wisconsin Engineer,* and $75 to the *Sphinx.* In return each printed University advertising and sent copies of the paper to the regents, the normal schools, and the accredited high schools of the state.[63] Five years later the total appropriation of the regents for student publications amounted to $1,700.[64]

In 1913 Van Hise complained to the regents that the students were publishing too many papers and it was reported that Madison advertisers had objected that various petty extortions were practiced by members of the advertising departments of some of the student publications.[65] The regents accordingly appointed a committee to investigate all student publications. One of the immediate consequences of the president's complaint and the regents' investigation was that the *Wisconsin Daily News* merged with the *Cardinal* and the Cardinal Company itself was reorganized.[66]

The *Wisconsin Daily News* was organized in June, 1912. It claimed to represent the undergraduates. All shares of stock were sold to students and it proposed to be exclusively a student daily.[67] It was published during the summer session of 1912. In the autumn of 1912 Van Hise announced that the *Cardinal* was the only official paper in which the official faculty notices would be published. The *Daily News* immediately protested that the president was attempting to drive off its subscribers and discourage its advertisers. It accused the president of "partisan interference in student matters."[68] The *Daily News* insisted that it was ready "to give the students a better and fairer paper

[62] Thomas H. Dickinson to William J. Goldschmidt, copy to Van Hise, November 6, 1909, Presidents' Papers.

[63] Papers of the Board of Regents, October 21, 1908; Records of the Board of Regents, G:410, December 1, 1909.   [64] *Daily Cardinal,* October 9, 1913.

[65] *Ibid.*   [66] *Ibid.,* March 9, 1914.

[67] *Wisconsin Daily News,* June 18, 1912.   [68] *Ibid.,* September 23, 1912.

than they have ever received."[69] Van Hise was certain, however, that the paper was begun simply as a financial venture by Edwin P. Kohl who had been business manager of the *Cardinal* and had not been re-elected.[70] But during the eighteen months that the *Daily News* continued, it returned from time to time and with more or less vigor to the point that it was the only newspaper owned and controlled by students. It pointed out that the interests which controlled the *Cardinal* were not either "public or student. They are faculty and private."[71] In its capacity as student paper, the *Daily News* objected to faculty censorship and argued the case fully in its editorial columns.[72] But the energy which gave it birth and made it for a time possibly the bulkiest university newspaper in existence waned in time and after a year and a half it merged with the *Cardinal,* urged on by the regents and the faculty.

Besides interesting itself in the material which went into the student papers, the faculty concerned itself with the finances of the publications. Early in 1913 the committee on student interests proposed to the faculty a plan for the "control of student publications of the University."[73] The next year financial troubles of both the *Badger* and the *Cardinal* induced the committee on student interests to formulate, and the faculty to adopt, a set of regulations governing the financial management of all student publications. A written contract between the editorial management of the publication and the business manager was required. The contract was to state the remuneration to be received and to indicate respective areas of authority. The business manager was required to give bond and keep accurate records of all financial transactions. Advertisements could be printed only on written authorization of the advertiser, and advertisements had to be paid for in cash. Acceptance of merchandise or other forms of trade was forbidden. Copies of all contracts, agree-

[69] *Ibid.*
[70] Van Hise to Birge, July 2, 1912, Papers of the Dean of the College of Letters and Science.
[71] *Wisconsin Daily News,* September 27, 1912.
[72] *Ibid.,* February 14, 1913.
[73] Minutes of the Meetings of the Faculty, 7:111, 113, February 3, March 3, 1913.

ments, bonds, and account audits had to be filed with the committee on student life and interests.[74]

In 1915 the student life committee of the faculty proposed that a system of faculty "coaches" for student publications be established. It was proposed that the person employed be paid in part by the University and in part by the student publications. The *Cardinal* and the *Badger* together were to pay $400 annually for this service. While the students had accepted the faculty regulations on the financial side without much objection, the "coaching" system was promptly and energetically denounced. The *Cardinal* declared that the proposal was a threat to free expression of student opinion. It was bad enough to have a faculty "coach," but to require the *Cardinal* to help pay the salary of the person who would probably reduce or destroy student control of the paper was outrageous. The editor protested that the faculty committee had consulted no students on the matter, and the chairman of the committee, Professor Goodnight, had been unwilling to permit the committee to reconsider the proposition as requested by the *Cardinal* representatives.[75] The *Cardinal* board of control likewise objected to the plan. The board protested "most strongly against the institution of any such system." It offered "grave danger to student control. . . . It is impossible for the coaching system to be followed and have the staff retain its present responsibility and independence from one man dictation." The board further objected that the committee had violated the articles under which the *Cardinal* operated and had failed to consult either the editors of the paper or any students.[76]

The quick and apparently unanimous response of the students to this scheme had its effect. Two days later the *Cardinal* reported that the faculty committee action might be reconsidered, since many on the faculty had not realized the implications of the proposal.[77] Later the *Cardinal* reported that its advertisers joined the students in opposition to the coaching plan on the basis that the students would not be interested in a paper

[74] *Ibid.*, 186–187, June 1, 1914.
[75] *Daily Cardinal*, May 15, 1915.
[76] *Ibid.*
[77] *Ibid.*, May 17, 18, 1915.

controlled by the faculty.[78] The *Cardinal* then circulated student petitions to show that the student body supported its stand.[79] Just two weeks after the first public announcement was made of the faculty committee plan to impose a "coaching system" upon the student publications, the committee chairman, Professor Scott H. Goodnight, acknowledged that the proposal would not be presented to the faculty.[80] Censorship the students would apparently accept, since it was never very vigorous, but not yet were they willing to accept faculty "coaching" at their own expense in the conduct and control of their publications.

But if the students were able to forestall, temporarily at least, the extension of control of the faculty committee they had less success, in one respect, with the regents. The regents had early gone on record as disapproving liquor and tobacco advertising in student publications.[81] During the next years the successive editors and business managers of the *Cardinal* petitioned the regents to withdraw this rule so as to permit the paper to accept tobacco advertising. On occasion the students even reminded the regents that the College of Agriculture had conducted and was conducting experiments to increase the value of the Wisconsin tobacco crop. But, until after the resignation of President Birge, the regents steadfastly refused to modify their rule and permit cigarette advertising in the student publications.[82]

THERE had been periodic agitation among the students in the 1890's for some system of medical assistance, but University officials, in line with the general "salutary neglect" of students outside the academic sphere, showed only a perfunctory interest. There was a nurse at Chadbourne, but little other evidence of official solicitude for sick students. In 1905 the Edwin Booth and the Red Domino dramatic clubs announced their intention

[78] *Ibid.*, May 19, 1915.   [79] *Ibid.*, May 25, 1915.   [80] *Ibid.*, May 29, 1915.
[81] Records of the Board of Regents, F:538–539, April 16, 1907.
[82] *Ibid.*, J:62, October 10, 1917; J:73, December 5, 1917; J:408, December 3, 1919; Papers of the Board of Regents, December 2, 1914, January 21, 1925, and March 3, 1926.

of giving the proceeds from their annual play to endow a student ward at the Madison General Hospital. Student spokesmen declared that most universities already had some provision for paying hospital expenses for sick students.[83] A year later the University established a committee on University hygiene.[84]

In 1908 a mild epidemic of typhoid fever in the rooming house district led to an investigation by Professor Mazyck P. Ravenel and focused attention upon the necessity that the University assume some responsibility for student health. Coupled with this was the natural desire of the medical school, which until 1919 would be restricted to a two-year course, to have at least the shadow of a clinical department.[85] Early in 1909 the faculty hygiene committee reported that it had not only made investigations of University buildings and equipment, but had interested itself in student health also. It had campaigned to keep basketball players from spitting on the floor and had arranged to get the water in the gymnasium swimming tank changed once a week.[86]

In 1910 Van Hise reported that a "study of the question of student health led to the conclusion that it was necessary to have individual students looked after by the university authorities."[87] Accordingly, a proposition was brought to the regents under which a fee of $1 a semester would be levied on each student to provide funds for employment of a physician. The regents approved.[88] The appointment of Dr. Joseph S. Evans as professor of clinical medicine and medical adviser to all the students was announced in December.[89] Dr. Evans arrived at the University in February, 1910, to establish the student clinic and medical service, a field still largely uncharted in educa-

[83] *Daily Cardinal*, February 1, 1905.

[84] *Regents' Biennial Report*, 1909–10, p. 8.

[85] Mazyck P. Ravenel reported that he had checked milk, water, and ice supplies and had found no source of typhoid. He felt that it probably came from a carrier but had not been able to discover who it was. University of Wisconsin Press Bulletin, November 12, and 19, 1908.

[86] Papers of the Board of Regents, February 17, 1909.

[87] *Regents' Biennial Report*, 1909–10, p. 8.

[88] Records of the Board of Regents, G:395, October 20, 1909.

[89] *Daily Cardinal*, December 8, 1909. Evans himself opposed the establishment of student fees from the beginning and his wishes were respected. Interview, Curti and Cartensen with Dr. Joseph Evans, October 12, 1946.

tional institutions. Only at California had such an experiment already been launched.

Dr. Evans had been promised that he would have ample opportunity to continue research which he had started while he was in Philadelphia, but that prospect quickly went glimmering. Students at first regarded the new medical officer with suspicion, but not for long. During his first semester he treated almost a thousand students.[90] In the period from April 21 to May 20 there had been 1,356 visits to the clinic. It quickly became clear that one doctor could not hope to give the medical service which the students demanded, so a second doctor was asked for.[91] Dr. Evans also urged that provision be made for a student infirmary, and that more adequate housing and facilities be provided for the clinic itself.[92]

Dr. Robert Van Valzah was appointed to assist Evans. During the school year 1910–1911, the number of student patients increased from an average of 53 a day in October to 120 a day in January. In addition physical examinations were given to all entering freshmen in the fall of 1910; thereafter physical examinations were given to all entering students, whether freshmen or transfers.[93]

The first office was located at the Cornelius house on State Street next to the Administration Building. A student ward was provided in the Madison General Hospital and a small isolation hospital was secured on Warren Street. Next, the Olin house on Langdon Street was obtained and enlarged for the use of the clinic.[94] Quarters for a student infirmary were acquired in the house adjacent, and in 1917 the legislature appropriated funds for the construction of a student infirmary.[95] To these funds was added other money received by the regents as gifts, and the student infirmary and Bradley Memorial Hospital were constructed.[96]

But the course of the Student Health Service was far from

[90] *Regents' Biennial Report,* 1909–10, p. 134.
[91] Charles R. Bardeen to Van Hise, May 26, and June 10, 1910, both in the Presidents' Papers.
[92] *Regents' Biennial Report,* 1909–10, pp. 135–136.
[93] *Ibid.,* 1911–12, p. 150.   [94] *Ibid.,* 1913–14, pp. 58–59.
[95] *Ibid.,* 1917–18, p. 175.   [96] *Ibid.*

smooth. Just as the Madison landlords objected to University projects for student housing as an interference with their business and food vendors objected to University-run dining rooms and dairymen objected to the sales of dairy products by the College of Agriculture, so some doctors of Madison viewed the Student Health Service as an interference with their business. Despite the abandonment, at least technically, of the health fee, they complained that this was contract medicine. Although these objections bore most heavily upon the medical college and probably helped to delay the establishment of the last two years of the medical course for a number of years, they also influenced the student health program.

Objections were made even before the service was established. Thus Dr. John M. Dodson, dean of Rush Medical College, wrote to Dean Bardeen in December, 1909, opposing the "contract medicine" feature of the Student Health Service, and urging Bardeen not to allow its adoption—it was unfair to Madison physicians and to the medical profession. He declared that it was nothing more than a contract-medicine system "which, in self-interest ought to be opposed by every physician in private practice."[97] This Bardeen refused to concede and he was unwilling to agree that contract medicine was necessarily bad. Moreover, he was not convinced that Madison doctors had a monopoly on student practice. "I think," he wrote, "the regents can see as little reason why they should not hire a physician to look after the students at the students' expense as that they should not put up dormitories for students because it would interfere with the income of keepers of student rooming houses and boarding houses. They look upon the university as a state and not a city institution and do not feel that Madison physicians have a right to object on personal financial grounds to measures taken by the regents for the welfare of the student body."[98]

Dr. Charles Sheldon, secretary of the Wisconsin State Medical Society, attempted to arouse the State Medical Society against the plan, although Regent Edward Evans, then president of

[97] John M. Dodson to Bardeen, December 4, 1909, Presidents' Papers.
[98] Bardeen to Dodson, December 8, 1909, *Presidents' Papers.*

the State Medical Society, gave his own support and approval to the student clinic by saying that the service would not hurt Madison doctors, and that it was not socialized medicine. He asserted that when the University drew four thousand young people together in a community, it had a responsibility to help them maintain their health.[99] Dean Bardeen attempted to allay these criticisms. In a public statement in 1913 he took pains to emphasize that the expenses of the department of clinical medicine were met out of the general funds of the University, that students were not charged special fees.[100]

The clinical medicine department encountered another problem. The services of the doctors on its staff were sometimes sought by people who were not University students. So long as such people were legislators or public officials of some sort there were few objections. But private citizens sometimes came to the student clinic for treatment. This seemed to the doctors of Madison to be unfair competition. In 1914 Dean Bardeen wrote to Van Hise suggesting that charges be made for this work and other rules adopted. "It has been found that the main criticism now directed against this department [the student clinic] on the part of the physicians practicing in Madison is that so much work is done for people not students without charging." The dean reported that this work amounted to only about five per cent of the work done at the clinic building.[101]

Dean Bardeen accordingly proposed, and the regents adopted and published, rules to govern the services rendered by members of the clinic staff to persons not students of the University. For two hours each day three days a week, clinic doctors would treat nonstudent patients. To assure approval of the private physicians, a "referral" system was established providing: "Any patient thus applying for medical consultation should, whenever practicable, bring a letter from the family physician stating the purpose of the consultation and giving such data as may be of value in the case." Fees were to be paid in advance at the business office. Outside consultations by the members of the

[99] Evans to Charles Sheldon, undated, about March, 1910, Copy in the Presidents' Papers.
[100] *Daily Cardinal,* January 15, 1913.
[101] Bardeen to Van Hise, June 6, 1914, Presidents' Papers.

staff were permitted. Fees might be reduced or waived on the recommendation of the family physician.[102]

But these regulations did not wholly satisfy the private practitioners. The next year a determined effort was made to push a bill through the legislature which would limit the University clinic to "examination, diagnosis, or first aid, but not for continuous or extended treatment of illness or injuries. The furnishing of such services and facilities gratuitously or for hire, to others than students, is prohibited."[103] The bill, introduced by Senator J. Henry Bennett on February 18, came up for committee hearings on March 10. Dr. Albert J. Ochsner, described by the *Cardinal* as one of "Wisconsin's most illustrious alumni in the field of medicine," supported the bill because a medical clinic needed a city with a population of a quarter of a million to be effective for a medical course. He also opposed charity and contract medical service. Madison doctors also testified for the bill. A Madison attorney supported it for reasons of economy, and the local health officer supported it on the grounds that the state should not compete with its citizens. On the other hand, Dean Bardeen opposed it along with others, including Dr. Gilbert F. Seaman, a member of the Board of Regents, Professor Howard L. Smith of the Law School, President Van Hise, and the putative author of the bill, Senator Bennett. Probably most influential, however, was the testimony of Dean Germain of the Marquette Medical School and Father Moulinier, also of Marquette. Both deplored the "evident local interests" which had influenced the case.[104] The *Cardinal* announced: "We are sure that we voice the united opinion and sentiment of the student body when we say that this institution [the student clinic] is one of the most beneficent and valuable in the life of the University."[105]

In the face of this opposition the bill was modified. Senator Bennett himself introduced an amendment withdrawing the limitation placed on service which could be given students. The bill, thus amended, passed the Senate but was lost in the As-

[102] *Regents' Biennial Report*, 1913–14, p. 160.
[103] Senate Bill 222S, 1915.
[104] *Daily Cardinal*, March 11, 1915.
[105] *Ibid.*, March 12, 1915.

sembly.[106] A year later the student newspaper boasted that the author of the bill that had been intended to restrict the student clinic to students had himself come to the clinic. Seeking treatment for a chronic ailment, he had written to the Mayo brothers' clinic at Rochester, Minnesota. He had been referred to Dr. Evans for diagnosis. The story delighted all who had forgotten that Senator Bennett had virtually abandoned his bill when he discovered its portent.[107]

But the doctors of Madison and elsewhere were still not convinced of the propriety of the student clinic. Dr. Edward H. Ochsner and others wrote periodically to Van Hise registering an uncompromising disapproval of the system of student care at the University. Typically, these letters asserted that the system was unfair to the public, to the doctors, injurious to the patients, and inimical to medical progress.[108] And for all his skill in public relations, his capacity to deal with almost all politicians in virtually all University matters, Dr. Evans was never able to win completely the support of that group of his professional colleagues who viewed the Student Health Service as a step toward socialized medicine. But the construction of a student infirmary building in 1918–1919 attested that a large part of the victory had been won.

✍

OUTWARDLY there was little change in the kind of scrapes the students got themselves into, or in the excesses in which they indulged. Some problems of conduct and behavior were persistent and unyielding, perhaps none more than dishonesty in academic work. This problem had been more or less chronic since the Civil War and it continued to be a matter which faculty committees, student committees, the college faculties, and the University faculty considered from time to time. Honor systems, proctor systems, seating arrangements, grading penalties, and many other devices were proposed, experimented with,

---

[106] *Senate Journal*, 1915, p. 424; *Assembly Journal*, 1915, p. 1167.
[107] *Daily Cardinal*, June 30, 1916.
[108] Cf. Edward H. Ochsner to Van Hise, August 30, 1915.

fretted over, debated, and denounced. No solution was found and no system of student morality developed under which every student in the University did his own academic work. In 1926 a joint committee submitted a report on dishonesty in class-room work. Dishonesty in classroom work was more widespread, they said, than any faculty member or even the students sus-pected; it was found in small as well as in large classes, and many student leaders were involved. "Speaking generally," the committee declared, "there exists no student conscience in the matter; no vital sense of the wrongness or unfairness of dis-honesty in university work. This is true even of many who do not themselves engage in it. Anything like strict honesty would be regarded by most students as quixotic. The majority of fra-ternity men, for example, would not consider for membership anyone whom they suspected of cheating at tennis or poker, while they would have no objection to taking into their organi-zation one known to be dishonest in academic work. . . . The student body has travelled a long way toward making the prac-tice a-moral." The committee found, however, that there was less cheating in the Law School, which had adopted the proctor system, and the Medical School, which had the honor system, than in other parts of the University. Among other things the committee urged that the faculty look forward to the eventual introduction of the honor system throughout the University.[109]

At the point where student conduct touched Madison, and often the courts, there was little appreciable change from the nineties, except perhaps that it attracted more newspaper atten-tion. The rowdiness which got some students into barroom brawls and other escapades obtained, perhaps, in about the same proportion as uninhibited exuberance in the youthful popula-tion at large. The practice of hazing, which Chamberlin thought he had virtually abolished, reappeared under Adams, and mounted in violence despite periodic threats from the fac-ulty that it would have to go. It was abolished, theoretically, in

[109] Report of the special joint committee on dishonesty in classroom work, by Professors Eugene Byrne, Edwin B. Fred, Max C. Otto, and three students, Alice Brown, George Fiedler, and Richard Ratcliff. Papers of the Board of Regents, June 19, 1926.

1910, but it reappeared again and was banned once more a decade later, along with the freshman-sophomore class rush which occasionally threatened life and limb.

The tradition of requiring freshmen to wear green caps had become strong before the first World War and its enforcement characteristically required vigorous and forthright action by members of the sophomore class. Cap day, near the end of the school year, annually afforded an occasion for a large-scale conflict between freshmen and sophomores. During the war the green caps virtually disappeared and with them the freshman-sophomore rush. In 1919, however, an effort was made to revive the green cap and other traditions. "Freshmen," the *Cardinal* admonished on October 2, "wear your sea-green cap and live up to all the old Wisconsin traditions with the proper degree of respect." Eight days later, the freshmen apparently not having responded to this appeal, one hundred or so of the recalcitrant members were thrown into the lake in open defiance of the rule against hazing. Charges were brought against the offending sophomores and the student senate warned that the sophomores must throw no more freshmen into the lake, even though the freshmen violated the "traditions." Dean Bardeen of the Medical School had warned that the lake was too cold for ducking. Violators, it was announced, would be recommended to the faculty for expulsion. In the fall of 1920 the student senate again ruled that there was to be no hazing, but that violators of the "traditions" would be penalized. War veterans who had served overseas were to be excused from wearing green caps upon petition to the student senate.

However much the student senate protested to the contrary, it seemed that the traditions, particularly the wearing of the green caps and the attendant restrictions upon freshmen, could not be enforced without some discipline which entailed hazing. In the spring of 1921 the *Cardinal* announced that the student senate would meet daily to pass sentence on freshman violators of the traditions. Two months later cap night was the occasion of a freshman-sophomore encounter that approached riotous proportions. Eight men, it was reported, were hurt, two of them seriously. Dean Goodnight declared that he intended to use all his "power and influence" to obtain the abolition of cap night and the freshman-sophomore rush. The student senate responded by voting to abolish green caps, the class rush, and cap night, but immediately a large group of students petitioned to have the matter submitted to a referendum. This was agreed upon. In the autumn of 1922 a student referendum supported the proposal to require freshmen to wear green caps and to retain the class rush and cap night. But the "tradition" was in its last days. Before the end of the year Dean Sellery and others had taken a hand to try to make the green cap a badge of honor and the soon-to-be-sophomore men had agreed to give up hazing freshmen. This plan was not wholly successful, but as the academic year closed, the student court, at the suggestion of Robert B. Stewart, an influential senior, outlawed the green cap requirement. The action ended the history of that piece of headgear for freshmen at the University of Wisconsin, and with it the attendant hazing, class rush, and cap night.[110]

In their relations with the law enforcement officers of Madison the students managed to sustain an enduring feud. It had become pronounced in Chamberlin's time and little had been done to dissipate the notion that a Madison policeman was the natural enemy of the student. The police in general reciprocated the student sentiment, helping to lodge student miscreants in the city jail whenever possible. In this they were able to embarrass the students until 1911, since the rule obtained that any student convicted in court of a crime, misdemeanor, disorderly conduct, or other offense was to be suspended until readmitted to the University by faculty action.

The situation was more or less typical of every college and university town, although perhaps the antipathy was accentuated somewhat in Madison. In 1913 and 1914 the student-police feud reached a high point. The police seemed to be peculiarly inept and demonstrably unconcerned when the students wanted help. In the fall of 1914 there had been a series of incidents in

[110] Interview, Curti with George C. Sellery, December 16, 1948; memorandum by Dean Sellery, February 24, 1949; Robert B. Stewart to Sellery, February 21, 1949; *Daily Cardinal,* October 2, 10, 15, November 8, 1919; September 22, 23, 1920; April 10, June 5, 7, 10, September 22, 27, December 16, 1921; October 13, 1922.

which young bloods of Madison had set upon and beaten University students. Many reasons for this violence were given—that the University students dated the town girls, that they took over the dances, and that they made themselves obnoxious in other ways. In the autumn of 1914 a number of such incidents had been reported, but the Madison police did nothing. Then near one of the large hotels a Madison gang beat several students. It was alleged that a nearby policeman not only refused to assist the students, one of whom had only recently been released from the hospital after an operation, but actually encouraged the toughs. Student resentment, vaguely directed at the town gangs and the police, had been mounting. The time for action was now at hand. University students in automobiles drove through the Latin Quarter crying "Varsity Out," for a decade the rallying cry for student meetings. Over a thousand students —the *Madison Democrat* claimed two thousand—responded. The students formed a parade, marched through the streets of Madison and around the square. Groups of them set upon and beat any Madison citizens who looked as if they might at some time have been involved in the attacks on students. The police attempted to break up the student mob and managed to take several captive and get them into the jail. The action apparently released whatever restraints still existed. Students fought the police with enthusiasm and many boasted the next day about the night sticks, badges, and other mementos of battle taken from the foemen. Firemen were called and the water hoses turned on the students, who in turn responded by taking the hoses away from the firemen. They jubilantly carried one section of fire hose under a street light and chopped it to pieces.

The students had drawn up before the police station and jail, threatening to storm the building to free students held there. A cordon of police and deputies held the building and at one point, according to the newspaper report, when a rush impeded, the police fired their revolvers in the air. The act won a cheer from the besieging students. Energetic students brought up ammunition in the form of beer bottles and bricks with which to fire upon the police station. Some windows were smashed and other damage done before President Van Hise, who had been gotten out of bed to help quell the riot, arrived with the mayor of Madison. Van Hise spoke to the students telling them that they must not take the law into their own hands. He directed them to disperse, pledging that the students held in jail would have a fair trial. The students gave the president a cheer and withdrew. They then paraded triumphantly down State Street to the lower campus where they celebrated their victory over the police with a great bonfire.[111] A day later the newspapers congratulated everybody—police, students, and University authorities—that the expected repetition of the riot had not occurred.[112]

Incidents such as this continued to occur from time to time although seldom reaching the intensity of the riot of October 5. Football victories, the engineers' annual parade, and a number of class events often offered the occasion for an exuberant free-for-all fight or a friendly little intramural fight which might turn unexpectedly against the police authorities if they showed too much inclination to interfere. In May, 1920, a policeman shot and killed a student. Police had often enough pulled out guns during student riots, but this was the first time one had shot and killed. The police officer was placed in protective custody, and University officials spent a tense night fearing that an attempt would be made to storm the jail and perhaps lynch the policeman. To everybody's relief no such thing occurred.[113] Student resentment was intense. The faculty formally adopted a resolution which extended sympathy to the bereaved family, expressed "appreciation of the restraint and good order manifested by the students under the conditions which inevitably aroused strong resentment," regretted the deplorably inaccurate newspaper accounts which had been published, and recognized in "the tragic occurrence the danger of police authority unsupported by sound judgment and a competent understanding of student sympathy."[114] The officer was

[111] *Wisconsin State Journal*, and *Madison Democrat*, October 6, 1914.

[112] *Wisconsin State Journal*, October 7, 1914.

[113] Halsten J. Thorkelson, then business manager of the University, and several others stayed up most of the night, prepared to try to cut off such an attempt if it were made. Interview, Carstensen with Halsten J. Thorkelson, December 13, 1947.   [114] Minutes of the Faculty, 8:274–275, June 7, 1920.

brought to trial for manslaughter but because of the intense feeling in Madison a change of venue was obtained. The trial took place at Jefferson, and the police officer was acquitted, much to the distress of the students.[115]

Immediately after the first World War, excesses on the part of a few students attracted much attention in the press. This was, of course, the period of the flapper, of the discovery of Sex, of the coonskin coat, and of the hip flask. University students as well as many other young people aped the habits and behavior of their elders. Some drank, perhaps more than they could carry, and violated the rules of the University. National prohibition was an invitation to people everywhere to drink more or less clandestinely. President Birge refused to acknowledge that University students were doing more drinking than before and viewed the whole matter somewhat tolerantly. Dean Goodnight, who had long opposed drinking among students, was vigilant, however. When first local option and then national prohibition gave him additional support, he moved against discovered student drinkers with energy and regularity. He wrote to a regent in 1920: "It has always been our practice even before the prohibition amendment was adopted, to suspend students for a keg party if we got hold of them. I felt that this was an exceedingly serious affair—a deliberately pre-arranged drinking bout, the second of a series among seven freshmen. I therefore recommended that the whole seven be suspended." In justification for demanding suspension, he continued, "It was a deliberately pre-arranged drinking affair, and we felt that if students were going to smuggle booze and arrange parties of this sort in defiance of all laws and rules, they would have to take the consequences if they were caught. We do not believe that the University can afford to give notice by mild measures in a case of this kind, that we regard law violations as unimportant."[116] The dean

---

[115] The *Daily Cardinal* commented in an editorial that the students expected a conviction. "They hoped that the court would declare that no person, whether he wears an officer's badge or not, is entitled to wantonly take the life of a law-abiding citizen." *Daily Cardinal,* January 14, 1921. The student senate took notice of the action by announcing that the matter had ended. "There is no legal recourse from this decision. The case has been tried according to law, and we accept the decision." *Ibid.*

[116] Scott H. Goodnight to Walter J. Kohler, December 28, 1920. Presidents' Papers.

stood firmly for propriety and for strict adherence to University regulations. Not only did he stand willing to judge, but he himself went into the Latin Quarter to apprehend malefactors. "On the night of August first, Monday, I surprised a dancing party in the Alpha Sigma Phi fraternity," runs a typical letter. The dance was unchaperoned, it was not registered, and it was being held on a midweek evening—all violations of the University regulations. He recommended suspension.[117]

Scores of students who came to the University seemed to have had no respect for the proprieties of social behavior. They danced, they drank, and carried on in deliberate defiance of the regulations. And in 1922 despite the vigilance of the dean, a doctor of the University student clinic reported, according to a *Cardinal* editorial, that the University had something like a blue Monday. For the past five years, he reported, after each week end of social activity there was an increase in the number of excuses for sickness from University classes.[118]

Nor could the deans keep various wild accusations from being circulated about the conduct of the students—many of the charges old ones, dug up and reprinted in new dress. "We hear," wrote one crank, "of drunken debauches, girls removing their garments and dancing almost naked at a sorority house. We hear of wild parties at Middleton."[119] Even the *Cardinal* aired charges of drunkenness among students.[120] The women of the University, publicized in the nation's press as having taken to drink, held a mass meeting to vote their disapproval of drinking and to petition federal authorities to end prohibition violations in Madison.[121]

Stories of student dissipation in the 1920's seemed to be very attractive to the newspapers throughout the country, regardless of the reliability of the source: young people were going to the dogs fast and flaming youth was burning itself out. It made good newspaper copy. In 1925 when a Madison judge announced that terrible conditions existed in Madison, that a doctor had told

[117] Goodnight to Birge, August 2, 1921, Papers of the Dean of the College of Letters and Science.

[118] *Daily Cardinal,* January 7, 1922.

[119] H. W. M. to Professor Michael V. O'Shea, undated, about November, 1921, Presidents' Papers.

[120] *Daily Cardinal,* November 13, 1923.　　　　[121] *Ibid.,* November 16, 1923.

him that sixty per cent of the young men there were or had been venereal, he won national attention. He spoke about the Latin Quarter, about drinking and immorality. Although he seems to have been speaking about Madison in general, his mention of University students fixed attention on the University, and the story was printed with delight by the state newspapers and carried abroad on the wires of the news services. In some instances it was made to refer only to University students.[122] President Birge complained that such slanders were broadcast over the country, but that denials and statements of fact "do not offer any interesting news and the press agencies refuse to distribute them. The best we can do, therefore, is to 'endure it with a patient shrug.' "[123]

For all the dire newspaper predictions, the blown-up reports of student frivolity, irresponsibility, and all the rest, wise old Dean Charles Slichter had an answer. He knew, from his long experience, that the University was a training ground for distinguished careers and that each entering group of freshmen, despite the sometimes widely publicized escapades of some of its members, contained men and women who would help shape the future. "But actually," he wrote, "I did not teach freshmen. I taught attorneys, bankers, big businessmen, physicians, surgeons, judges, congressmen, governors, writers, editors, poets, inventors, great engineers, corporation presidents, railroad presidents, scientists, professors, deans, regents, and university presidents. For that is what those freshmen are now, and of course they were the same persons then."[124]

[122] The story, for example, had appeared on page one of the *Washington Post*, January 28, 1925. Wisconsin Representative Edward E. Browne wrote to Birge about it the next day. Browne to Birge, January 29, 1925. Birge in answering declared that since the judge was coming up for re-election soon, he was probably just trying to get some front-page publicity.

[123] Birge to Browne, February 4, 1925, Presidents' Papers.

[124] Charles S. Slichter, *Science in a Tavern* (Madison, 1938), 157–158.

16.

Athletics: The Newer Emphasis

S TUDENT interest in athletics had developed lustily in the 1890's; it approached fanaticism in the early 1900's. From the time the semester began in the fall until the last game had been played, football talk virtually usurped the University. The student newspaper was given over almost entirely to teaching yells and songs, announcing plans for mass meetings, and reciting the prowess of the team. What had been a welcome diversion became a distraction. Indeed, so intense was student feeling that loyalty to the football team was exacted from all students. At one boarding house a near tragedy resulted when an individualist not only refused to support the team but actually knocked it. Attempts on the part of the other students to impose conformity upon him caused a scuffle in which one student was shot in the foot.

Along with excessive student interest went other evils. The alumni of Wisconsin were encouraged to recruit good teams. In 1903 the *Wisconsin Alumni Magazine* declared: "Every loyal Wisconsin man must constitute himself a committee of one to spread the Wisconsin propaganda. We are not getting the men we should and this is a matter where the alumni are the ones to act. Every legitimate means should be used to turn the right sort of prospective students toward Madison. . . . We should draw from all the surrounding territory. There are Wisconsin alumni in every state in the union. They must wake up and begin the missionary work."[1] A month later the magazine sought to make a clear distinction between the "recruiting system" of other colleges under which athletes were offered cash, board, room, and other inducements, and the Wisconsin system under which "the superior educational, social, and athletic advantages" of the University were set forth most favorably.[2] Glosses of this type did not obscure the professionalism at Wisconsin any more than at other schools. In 1904 it was charged that various irregularities had marked the handling of athletic accounts. Although the accusation was denied, this constituted one more indictment of the game that threatened to take over the whole interest of the student body.[3]

However, athletics and intercollegiate football had many defenders. There were many who felt that it was enough that the game was popular with the students and others. Then, as now, it was often asserted that the fame of a university was spread by means of a winning football team and that participation in competitive sports built "character." Some people asserted that a football team, particularly a winning football team, had yet another justification: it afforded a relatively simple ceremonial symbol in which the students could find common cause. Thus, Professor Charles S. Slichter told a student mass meeting that their interest in athletics resulted from their demand for a means "to show that they are part of a great unit, the university. We appear at a football contest not as individuals, but as members of a great university."[4] A writer in the *Alumni Magazine* explained that, apart from "purely academic" work, athletics formed for the average student "the strongest and keenest interest of his college life. This may not be as it should be, and there is no question but what we are in a period of ultra-athleticism, if the expression be permitted. In a measure, this is natural, for athletics form practically the single element of community life in a state university like our own."[5]

Yet many felt that the abuses far outweighed the benefits of

---

[1] *Wisconsin Alumni Magazine* (Madison), 4:143 (January, 1903).
[2] *Ibid.*, 4:201 (February, 1903).
[3] *Daily Cardinal*, December 16, 1904.
[4] *Ibid.*, October 30, 1903.
[5] *Wisconsin Alumni Magazine*, 6:95 (December, 1904).

Wisconsin *vs.* Minnesota, a Scoreless Tie

Girls' Athletics in the Twenties

the game. In 1903 President Van Hise and members of the faculty began to move toward correction of some of the evils. In November, Van Hise proposed to President Harper of Chicago that steps be taken to cleanse and de-emphasize the game. He tentatively proposed that the football season end on the Saturday before Thanksgiving and that a rule be adopted requiring a year's residence at the University prior to participation in intercollegiate athletics.[6] The University faculty representative, Professor Charles Sumner Slichter, upon returning from the meeting of the conference of faculty representatives at Chicago late in November, 1903, reported to the students that the faculty representatives had considered a number of important athletic matters. Among the most important he listed the proselytizing of athletes by supporters of the various colleges. This evil had grown to such an extent that there was hardly a high school or college student of any athletic prominence in the West whose attendance was not solicited by the athletic managers or alumni of the larger institutions. It has been generally agreed at the conference that this practice was not confined to a few institutions but was as prevalent at one university as another. It was proposed that one year's residence be required before a student could participate in any intercollegiate athletics. Such a rule was proposed for adoption the next year.[7]

There was some evidence that the proposed reforms were taken seriously. At the opening of the 1904 football season the *Cardinal* boasted that the University was entering an era of "better standards." It was reported that men who had come to the University only to play football had "disappeared with the proverbial 'can tied to them' and we like to see them go."[8]

But the administration was not satisfied. At the end of the 1904 football season, President Van Hise launched a series of meetings with students, faculty, and alumni to bring about a reorganization of the Athletic Association, to make all students members of the association, and to change the composition of

<hr />

[6] Charles R. Van Hise to William Rainey Harper, November 23, 1903, Presidents' Papers.

[7] *Daily Cardinal*, December 2, 1903.

[8] *Ibid.*, September 30, 1904.

the athletic board. This was accomplished in March, 1905, and the new association, with Professor Thomas Sewall Adams as faculty supervisor, was launched.[9]

But the new association was unable to influence matters very much during the football season of 1905. The ten-game schedule, similar to that which had been played in former years, had been largely successful, but the faculty supervisor was far from satisfied that a mere change in the rules governing the Athletic Association of the University could have much beneficial effect. Accordingly, in December he proposed to the University faculty that a committee of seven "consider the condition of athletics in the University and make recommendations to the faculty."[10] This signaled a full attack upon the game by the faculty.

The action of the faculty, it should be noted, was only partly the result of local conditions. In part it was a response to the general attack which was made on football throughout the country in 1905. Following the 1905 season the *Chicago Tribune* had published a story describing the damage done during the season—eighteen college and high school students killed, one hundred and fifty-nine injured. A number of the colleges forthwith abolished football. President Theodore Roosevelt, an apostle of the strenuous life, called representatives of the three big eastern colleges to the White House to demand that the game be freed of brutality and foul play.[11]

The mood of the Wisconsin faculty at the time is suggested by an address given by Frederick Jackson Turner to the Madison Alumni Association in January, 1906. While acknowledging the value of college sports, he objected to the fierce rivalries which had been created, the tremendous interest in victory, the spirit which made nonsupport of the team an act of disloyalty, the too enthusiastic alumni support of athletics, and the exploitation of the game by the press. Human values were thus "put in wrong perspective and the fundamental purpose of

[9] *Ibid.,* November 28, December 3, 5, 8, 15, 16, 19, 1904; January 17, 18, March 2, 7, 9, 1905.

[10] Minutes of the Meetings of the Faculty, 6:8, December 4, 1905.

[11] John Allen Krout, *Annals of American Sport* (*The Pageant of America*, 15 vols., New Haven, 1924–1929), 15:246.

the University is lost sight of." Football, he charged, has "become a business, carried on far too often by professionals supported by levies on the public, bringing in vast gate receipts, demoralizing student ethics, and confusing the ideals of sport, manliness, and decency. Coaches and managers scour the country for material. Faculties are kept busy playing a game of hide and seek with the man who sells his athletic skill for personal gain, and who pretends to uphold the honor of the university." The public was, he declared, invading the walls of the University, "demoralizing student sentiment, exalting fictitious heroes, condoning brutality, setting up false ideas of the true honor of a university, and making it impossible for faculties and for the clean healthy masses of students to keep athletics honest and rightly related to a sane university life." He warned that "the brutality of the game must go, mercenary professionalism, immorality, deceit, and corruption of student sentiment must go, and, in their place, must come a game that students can play, a game kept subordinate to the intellectual life of the University, a game that leaves no slimy trail across the campus, no stain on the fair name of our alma mater." Football "will surely go, if students and alumni deceive themselves in the belief that the faculty will bear alone the burden of keeping the game free from taint and of restraining it within the bounds of moderation. They will cut it out, root and branch, if the forces of demoralization continue to vitiate the university atmosphere."[12]

The faculty committee appointed to "consider the condition of athletics in the University and make recommendations" was made up of Deans Birge and Turneaure and Professors Turner, Jackson, Munro, Slichter, and Trowbridge. The committee quickly agreed that any reform of athletics must extend to the other universities. Accordingly, the committee asked President Van Hise to propose to President Angell of Michigan that he call a conference of the Intercollegiate League of the Upper Mississippi Valley to discuss the athletic situation. This Angell

---

[12] Frederick Jackson Turner, Address before the Madison Alumni Association, January 31, 1906, Manuscript Division, State Historical Society of Wisconsin. The speech was reported in the *Madison Democrat*, February 1, 1906.

did.[13] The first meeting was held on January 19, 1906. Meanwhile the faculty committee proposed the selection and instruction of a University delegate to the conference. At faculty meetings on January 8 and 9, the matter was under discussion. Professor Turner was appointed faculty delegate and the faculty passed a resolution directing him to propose a public condemnation of the evils of football and a two-year suspension of intercollegiate contests, "to the end that rational, moral, and normal relations between athletics and intellectual activities may develop in each institution."[14]

The faculty action brought varying responses. W. J. Brier, president of the State Normal School of River Falls, Wisconsin, wrote Van Hise immediately saying that he hoped the report was true that the University had decided to abolish football.[15] The regents approved the faculty resolutions.[16] But the students circulated a petition to retain football. The petition pledged the student body to cooperate with the faculty in the elimination of graft and professionalism in collegiate athletics. Some fifteen hundred had signed. The petition was presented to President Van Hise on the day before Turner was to leave for the Chicago meeting.[17] Van Hise called a special meeting of the faculty to permit student representatives to appear and state their position. Thereafter the faculty discussed the matter and after "the consideration of various motions and amendments" adopted a resolution expressing the faculty appreciation of the offer of student cooperation and support for "purity in athletics," but refusing to modify its instructions to its delegate.[18]

[13] Report of the president, *Regents' Biennial Report*, 1905–06, p. 18.

[14] Minutes of the Faculty, 6:11–14, January 8 and 9, 1906; *Daily Cardinal*, January 19, 1906.

[15] "Professionalism has so saturated the game," he wrote, "that it has become a stench in the nostrils of the more sober and conservative people. The Coaches have dictated terms and rules, in their own interests, and there has been a strong following of the sporting element which has over-ridden the thoughtful and those who think there is still room for some profitable work and study in the Universities and Colleges. To my mind the football has lowered the morals and ideals of our higher institutions as much as would recognized prize fighting and horse racing." He hoped that the normal school regents would also prohibit the game. W. J. Brier to Van Hise, January 9, 1906, Papers of the Dean of the College of Letters and Science.

[16] Records of the Board of Regents, F:383, January 16, 1906.

[17] *Daily Cardinal*, January 17, 18, 19, 1906.

[18] Minutes of the Meetings of the Faculty, 6:16, January 18, 1906.

At Chicago the next day the conference had little difficulty in agreeing to abolish football "as now played" and quickly came to agreement on a number of proposals intended to reduce the number of contests and the expense of coaches and equipment, and to modify and strengthen the eligibility rules. The Wisconsin proposal to suspend all games for a period of two years was not pushed vigorously or widely supported.

The recommendations agreed upon were referred to the respective faculties. When the recommendations of the conference came before the Wisconsin faculty in early February, 1906, the anti-football element tried to pass a resolution suspending football at Wisconsin for two years. Failing that, they managed to attach to the faculty resolution approving the recommendations of the conference a declaration that "the faculty of the University of Wisconsin express their preference for the suspension of intercollegiate football for a period of two years by the agreement of the conference." President Angell was also asked to call a second conference.[19]

At the second meeting all the universities were in substantial agreement and the recommendations were adopted. In giving the substance of the important points of the reform measures, Van Hise wrote later in the year: "Among these are rules requiring a year of residence before participating in athletics; confining participation to three years; confining participation exclusively to students who have not taken any degree; excluding all students who have not been in continuous attendance between the first and second participations; taking financial control of athletics out of the students' hands; forbidding the employment of professional coaches by students, etc."[20] He might have added that the conference had gone so far as to fix the maximum student admission fee at fifty cents.[21] Although

[19] *Ibid.,* 6:17, February 6, 1906.
[20] Report of the president, *Regents' Biennial Report,* 1905–06, p. 18.
[21] The faculty voted to adopt the conference recommendations April 5, 1906. Minutes of the Faculty, 6:25. The regents adopted the recommendations on October 16, 1906, together with additions submitted by the faculty. *Daily Cardinal,* October 22, 1906. These became a part of the faculty rules printed in the fall in the *By-Laws and Laws of the Regents* (Madison, 1907), 122–126. The new regulations placed all athletics under the department of physical training and an athletic council, restricted competition to other college or university teams, placed paid coaches on the faculty, eliminated the training table, limited

willing to adopt the reforms proposed by the conference, a number of the faculty still felt that football must be suspended for two years; some wanted to abolish it altogether.[22]

But the students were determined that this was not to be done. They conducted a noisy campaign to retain the game. The *Cardinal* on March 27 announced that the faculty might still abolish football. That evening a group of over five hundred students called upon various members of the faculty at their homes to demonstrate their support of football and three professors were burned in effigy.[23] On the evening before the faculty meeting which was scheduled to consider the resolution abolishing football contests during the 1906 season, a great student mass meeting was held to adopt resolutions opposing such action.[24] A student committee presented petitions to the faculty at the meeting the next day. That meeting was another of those protracted, hotly contested affairs which extended from afternoon into the evening with only a brief adjournment for dinner. The great point at issue, apart from a minority attempt to win nothing short of abolishment, was whether the faculty would insist upon suspending football for the 1906 season. A compromise was finally reached under which the faculty agreed to permit intercollegiate football contests the next year provided that the big games scheduled with Michigan, Chicago, and Minnesota be canceled. Van Hise's active participation in reaching this compromise and Professor Turner's acquiescence apparently played a large part in carrying it through.[25]

Thus the faculty had retreated from the position that foot-

the football season to five games, provided that the season must end on the Saturday before Thanksgiving, and set forth rules of eligibility.

[22] Turner occupied a pivotal position in this discussion. Pyre ascribed to him the credit for having forestalled this action. In March, Turner received from Professor Smith of the Law School the following note: "Don't abandon us on this football proposition. With your help we can wipe it out once and for all. If we temporize now, when things are in their present shape, we shall be right back where we were in a few months, and the faculty will enjoy the contempt of everybody for having wanted to do right but not dared to. You see even Birge expects it to be wiped out. For Heaven's sake, don't let us disappoint him." Howard Smith to Turner, March 21, 1906. Turner Papers, State Historical Society of Wisconsin.

[23] *Daily Cardinal*, March 28, 1906.

[24] *Ibid.*, April 5, 1906.

[25] Minutes of the Faculty, 6:25, April 6, 1906; *Daily Cardinal*, April 6, 1906.

ball should be suspended entirely for two years and perhaps indefinitely to the position that the big games should be dropped for the 1906 season. Control of athletics had been taken from the students, however, and full development of an intramural program had been pledged. President Van Hise at the end of the year was not sure that the last steps had been taken. "It is believed," he wrote, "that the steps taken will be sufficient to reduce intercollegiate athletics to the subordinate place they should occupy in university life. If the steps taken are not sufficient, the temper of the faculty is such that additional steps will be taken to accomplish this end."[26]

No one seemed wholly satisfied with the results. Those on the faculty who had felt that intercollegiate competition in football was incompatible with amateur athletics regretted that football, the prime spectator sport and principal offender, had not been destroyed "root and branch." On the other side, a great number of students, alumni, and others, undeterred by or oblivious to the ethical considerations in the matter, felt that the faculty had already gone too far. It was all very well to talk about purity in athletics, but it was also important to win games. Moreover, with the adoption of rules which placed virtually complete control of athletics in the hands of the faculty, students felt they no longer had much responsibility in the matter. Turner warned that football would surely go if students and alumni expected that the faculty alone would bear the responsibility for keeping the game pure and in bounds. Yet shortly after the regents had given assent to the faculty rules, the *Cardinal* declared: "The faculty . . . has assumed the control of athletics in every sense of the word, and we need no longer worry about the degree and kind of participation which we are to enjoy."[27] Many students and others felt that reform had been carried far enough, so that now all efforts must be directed toward regaining the ground which had been lost. The same influences were obviously at work in the other universities of the Western Conference. Accordingly at the December, 1906, meeting of the faculty representatives, a

[26] Report of the president, *Regents' Biennial Report*, 1905–06, p. 19.
[27] *Daily Cardinal*, October 23, 1906.

six- or seven- instead of a five-game schedule was proposed.[28] The *Cardinal*, boasting that the evils of football had been eradicated, urged that the Wisconsin faculty accept this change.[29] The faculty, however, held firm but made one concession: it approved scheduling a "big" game with Minnesota in 1907.[30] Although petitioned each year, not until December, 1910, did the faculty agree to permit more than five games to be played.[31]

Control of finances continued to be bothersome. Financial control was assigned first to the newly constituted athletic board. Then a regents' committee sought to handle the matter. Later, finances were again returned to a faculty committee, and finally, in 1910, the University bursar was made treasurer of the athletic council by action of the regents.[32]

Meanwhile students and alumni continued to agitate for a full revival of football. In the student paper it was periodically argued that reform had been accomplished and the University should start winning football games; such arguments ignored the fact that although Wisconsin won no conference championship between 1901 and 1912, the football team each season won more games than it lost. Several regents interested themselves in the matter. During the 1907 season the *Cardinal* urged again and again that full student support be given the football team, so that the faculty would have evidence of widespread interest in the game.[33] It was even reported that the faculty proposed to abolish the game because of lack of student interest.[34] This brought a committee of Madison alumni to issue a public call for a meeting of students, alumni, and faculty at the gymnasium after the Minnesota game to discuss University athletics.[35] At the meeting contradictory resolutions were adopted approving full development of an athletic program at the Uni-

[28] *Ibid.*, December 3, 1906.   [29] *Ibid.*
[30] *Ibid.*, December 11, 1906, January 28, 1907.   [31] *Ibid.*, December 5, 1910.
[32] Records of the Board of Regents, G:521, April 20, 1910.
[33] *Daily Cardinal*, October 24, 1907.   [34] *Ibid.*, October 25, 1907.
[35] The call was issued through the *Wisconsin Alumni Magazine* and the newspapers. *Wisconsin Alumni Magazine*, 9:32–33 (October-November, 1907). The *Daily Cardinal* announced that the purpose of the meeting was to voice the common sentiment not only against the athletic situation at the University but against the paternal attitude which the faculty had taken toward all student activities. *Daily Cardinal*, November 18, 1907.

versity, urging adoption of a policy "calculated to develop at Wisconsin teams which can compete on an equality with other universities," and endorsing the policy of restricting participation to bona fide amateur students who conformed to the general scholastic standards.[36] There followed a conference with President Van Hise during which he assured the student conference committee that there was no motion before the faculty calling for the abolition of intercollegiate athletics, nor had any been offered.[37] The faculty, however, took formal notice of the alumni-student resolutions by protesting that their position had been misunderstood, that they did not contemplate abolition of intercollegiate athletics or the suspension of any branch thereof unless extraordinary conditions demanded it. The faculty went so far as to declare that they sympathized "with intercollegiate contests when not carried to obvious excess or tainted by corrupt practice."[38]

Although the faculty retained the five-game football schedule until 1910, the "de-emphasis" of athletics was short-lived. Unless intercollegiate competition were cut out, root and branch, such a thing was not possible within the context of social values existing at that time or in subsequent periods. Interest in winning teams was after all paramount to interest in sports, and

[36] *Ibid.*, November 25, 1907.
[37] *Ibid.*, November 27, 1907.
[38] *Ibid.*, December 3, 1907; Minutes of the Faculty, 6:88, December 2, 1907. Pyre, then on the faculty and one of the supporters of football, felt that the crisis of 1906–07 marked the end of an era in Wisconsin feeling and tradition. He felt the faculty had gone too far in insisting upon higher standards than the conference adopted. "No permanent good was accomplished by the procedure; but it caused students and alumni to believe themselves unsympathetically, and even unfairly, treated by the faculty, and to resent far more than they otherwise would have done the change to faculty control. They felt, not entirely without cause, that a party in the faculty ... stood ready for any opportunity to nick athletics in the heel.... The old glad confident Wisconsin spirit was depreciated by an alloy of sullenness and sneering criticism, on the part of too many students and alumni, which extended to other matters than athletics. This could not prevent the onward sweep of the university in numbers and power; but it introduced an element of discord at a time when this very growth demanded the application of every positive and vital force if the university was to preserve a spirit commensurate with its bulk." Pyre's defense of the game was both tolerant and generous, although it ignored the core of Turner's indictment. "It is a mistake to suppose that the extravagant enthusiasm lavished upon athletics by students and the alumni implies a proportionate over-estimate of their intrinsic importance. It is a mistake that arises from a puritanic failure to appreciate the significance of a ritual. That *esprit de corps* amongst the un-

winning teams increasingly demanded coaching, which became higher and higher priced, football players who must be recruited, and gate receipts rather in excess of what the students could provide at an admission fee of only fifty cents.

Even before the faculty had voted to permit the schedule to be lengthened to seven games, it gave evidence that the period of reformation was over. In June, 1909, the baseball team was invited to play a series of games with the teams of Keio and Waseda Universities of Tokyo. The faculty gave its unanimous consent, the student paper was delighted, and the versatile Charles McCarthy, legislative reference librarian and University publicist, helped to select the team and accompanied it as official representative of the University. He bore with him a letter from that great admirer of baseball, President William Howard Taft, to the American ambassador at Tokyo. The tour was a great success. In fact it was diplomatically impeccable, since the Wisconsin team won four games and lost four.[39]

The following years saw the re-establishment of football practices which the faculty had sought to abolish. The seven-game schedule was re-established in 1911 and extended to eight games in 1926. Pre-season or spring training, which had been eliminated, was reinstated. In the spring of 1912, the faculty refused to support the demands of the coach that men be excused from military drill for football practice. The coach resigned with a fanfare of excited student newspaper comment. The faculty action in this case, the *Cardinal* charged, was a bad blow for Wisconsin. "It was essentially un-Wisconsin."[40] The training

dergraduates and graduates of a school that we call 'college spirit' requires a rallying point or occasion for demonstration. Athletic contests and rivalries are convenient and pleasurable occasions for its manifestation. It matters little whether that spirit be associated with some intra-collegiate activity like the old games at Rugby, or, as has become traditional here, with intercollegiate rivalries. What matters is a tradition that fuses together all the forces of an institution in enthusiastic social consent. Such a spirit not only magnifies the power of an institution as a whole; it intensifies the generous impulses and stimulates the creative energy of the component individuals and hence must be counted one of the precious factors in the educational influence of the institution that possesses it." James F. A. Pyre, *Wisconsin* (New York, 1920), 328–330.

[39] *Daily Cardinal*, June 2, 8, 10, 1909; D. J. Flanagan, "Wisconsin vs. Japan in Baseball," The *Independent*, 67:1492–1496 (December 30, 1909); Edward A. Fitzpatrick, *McCarthy of Wisconsin* (New York, 1944), 244–245.

[40] *Daily Cardinal*, May 7, 8, 9, 12, 1912.

table, in something less than its original splendor, reappeared; and the stadium at Randall Field, like the stadiums of other universities, grew and with it the gate receipts. Student spectators, paying only fifty cents admission fee, were not profitable. In 1920 the *Cardinal* reported that the athletic department had given preference to outsiders in the purchase of football tickets.[41] It was planned by the opening of the 1921 season that the stadium would accommodate a crowd of twenty-five thousand spectators.[42] Thus the "simon-pure" athletics of 1907, of which the students had boasted, gave way to something certainly less pure. In 1911 the *Cardinal* reported a strong protest from Wisconsin athletes against having to sign a sworn statement of eligibility before participating.[43] The twin problems of eligibility and amateur status continued to be troublesome. The first was, of course, the simpler. Amateur status, however, posed many difficult, if not insoluble, problems after the initial compromise of permitting gate receipts to be collected at all was made. Other college and university faculties tried to find a workable and definable policy to govern intercollegiate athletic contests. As early as 1882, a "reluctant" Harvard faculty had been "precipitated . . . into a policy of oversight and regulation that for nigh fifty years afforded that learned body more grief than any learned subject."[44] Other faculties enjoyed no greater success than Harvard in attempting to control athletic contests.

After the difficulties of 1906–1907 the Wisconsin faculty seemed reluctant to move again. In 1912 the faculty of Northwestern University proposed a series of drastic modifications of conference rules: to limit the season to three games or less, to permit only student-coached teams to play, to reduce admission fees to twenty-five cents for all games, and to prohibit the employment of paid officials.[45] The Wisconsin faculty was unresponsive.

[41] *Ibid.*, December 3, 1920.
[42] *Ibid.*, March 13, 1921.   [43] *Ibid.*, December 12, 13, 1911.
[44] Samuel Eliot Morison, *Three Centuries of Harvard, 1636–1936* (Cambridge, 1937), 410.
[45] Thomas F. Holgate, Northwestern University, to the secretary of the University faculty, April 3, 1912, Faculty File Book.

Yet in 1914 the faculty did vote to discontinue intercollegiate rowing contests. This action, although protested by some alumni and student groups, was taken on the basis of an investigation by the department of clinical medicine which revealed that a large number of the members of the freshman crews suffered from the severe training. "The faculty of the medical school believe that the data presented by the clinical department showed conclusively that the severe training deemed necessary for preparing crews for intercollegiate contest puts so severe a strain on the heart that an undue proportion of men are seriously injured and that, therefore, a continuation of intercollegiate rowing is indefensible from the health standpoint."[46] Announcement of the faculty action was made in September, 1914.[47] The action, based on medical findings, was virtually unassailable for a time.[48]

An attack upon all intercollegiate athletics on the same basis apparently looked promising to some members of the faculty. In 1915 a request was made that an investigation be conducted to determine the effects of all competitive athletics and a report thereon made to the faculty.[49] The study was made; but the results, although revealing in many cases apparently undesirable cardiac effects, were not as conclusive as those which had been revealed by the investigation of rowing.[50] Moreover, not even the medical findings of 1914 prevented the reinstitution of rowing. In 1921 the faculty voted to permit intercollegiate competition in rowing under certain conditions presumed to offer sufficient safeguards to health.[51] That qualification itself, although largely unnoticed in this or for that matter any other competitive sport, indicated how irrelevant was the claim, by now virtually elevated into a myth, that there was a causal and favorable connection between participation in intercollegiate sports and physical well-being. The Roman in his day had not been concerned about the physical benefits received

[46] Papers of the Board of Regents, October 14, 1914.
[47] *Daily Cardinal,* September 29, 1914.
[48] Minutes of the Faculty, 7:245, April 12, 1915. Alumni protests were answered by reference to the medical findings.   [49] *Ibid.,* 7:241, March 1, 1915.
[50] Dr. Joseph S. Evans to Van Hise, October 20, 1915, Presidents' Papers.
[51] *Daily Cardinal,* March 2, 1921.

by the gladiator in participating in his rough sport. But the twentieth century American apparently must find, particularly in amateur sports, a virtuous principle to justify those great spectacles of conflict, force, and movement which appeal so deeply to so many.

✍

AN INCIDENTAL product of football enthusiasm has been the creation of that great ceremonial day of the athletic season, "Homecoming." Compounded equally of sentimentality and commercialism, it has become part of the fabric of American educational institutions today. As the day when the "old grads" return to their "alma mater," it has long since largely supplanted the class day of commencement week, the pageantry of which has yielded to mass production procedures brought about by the large number of degrees to be conferred. Moreover, the class reunions at commencement time are more or less restricted. "Homecoming" represented an attempt to heighten and intensify the alumni interest in football games with the other sentimental attachments to the institution.

During the 1890's and the first decade of the twentieth century, football supporters encouraged alumni to return to the alma mater on football Saturdays, and unorganized appeals were made to alumni to attend the pre-game mass meetings. The proposal for fixing a day and a game for all loyal alumni was not made, however, until 1911. It issued, appropriately enough, from the athletic department. Early in October, 1911, the *Cardinal* announced that an alumni homecoming on November 18, 1911, the day of the Minnesota game, had been proposed by C. C. Chambers in the first edition of the *Athletic Bulletin*. The picture of what it should be was presented by Chambers. "How great it would be if enough old Wisconsin men would come back to fill the entire bleachers. 'Red' Parker will undoubtedly be on hand to inspire the cheering. It is even possible that Senator La Follette might address a mass meeting before the game. A reunion and banquet for all old 'W' men would be a pleasant feature, and provision has already been made for seats for them near the side lines. The different organizations in the university could hold reunions and class headquarters could be established as at commencement time. The University Band could head a monster parade out to the Camp, and the undergraduate classes might vie with each other in introducing novel stunts in the cheering sections. There is sufficient dramatic talent in the university to provide a splendid entertainment the night preceding the game."[52]

The picture was apparently pleasing. Shortly afterwards it was announced that the athletic council had approved the plan and that an appropriation had been made to the athletic department to finance the affair.[53] Before the end of the month committees had been created to take charge of the burgeoning activities. Alumni responded. The plans included things that are still part of the event: three thousand homecoming buttons were procured to be sold at ten cents each to cover expenses; there was a mass meeting Friday night at which the coaches and prominent old grads spoke; and there was a bonfire.[54] Madison merchants even closed their stores on Saturday afternoon.[55] Once launched, nothing could keep it from being repeated, and nothing could change very much the basic pattern of the event.

[52] *Ibid.*, October 7, 1911.
[54] *Ibid.*, November 13, 17, 18, 20, 1911.
[53] *Ibid.*, October 12, 25, 1911.
[55] *Ibid.*

17.

The Wider Campus: Extension

I F CHAMBERLIN was the first president to project a broad
and generous University program in which service to the
state was both a justification and a goal, Van Hise was the
president who most vigorously pursued this course. In his inaugural address and time after time thereafter Van Hise dwelt
upon this theme. In his inaugural Van Hise stated that professors should serve as official advisers to the government and
should perform other services besides teaching, but "while
the professor performs important service outside the university
his greatest service is his own creative work and the production
of new scholars in the laboratory and seminary." Although he
was inclined to defend research in terms of its eventual "practical" value, he would exclude no type. "I . . . hold that the state
university, a university which is to serve the state, must see to
it that scholarship and research of all kinds, whether or not a
possible practical value can be pointed out, must be sustained."
He insisted that the chief function of the University was "to
add to the sum of human achievement," but he also felt that
"the University must give opportunity for training in all lines
of human endeavor."

Perhaps Van Hise never gave up that basic conviction that
to add to the sum of human achievement was the highest
obligation of the University, but he soon widened his conception of service to include a vigorous program of disseminating
the knowledge that had been created at the University or else-

where. He presented a characteristic statement of his view on this matter in an address before the National University Extension Association in 1915. Until the middle of the nineteenth century, he said, knowledge had accumulated rather slowly. After that time advancement of knowledge had been "greater than in a thousand and probably in five thousand years before. The result is that the accumulation of knowledge has far outrun the assimilation of the people." Thus it became a duty of the university to "carry to the people the knowledge which they can assimilate for their betterment along all lines."

Although Van Hise looked upon research aimed at adding to the store of knowledge as the basic obligation of the University and its fundamental service to the state, he and others began to speak of the threefold function of the University: research, resident instruction, and various activities intended to carry knowledge to the people. This last function, in many minds, was the principal "service" which the University performed. This slight misconception was perhaps warrantable, particularly during Van Hise's administration.[1]

Extramural service developed during this period along three more or less distinct lines, all very well publicized. One consisted of the service of members of the University staff on state boards, commissions, and regulatory bodies; the second consisted of the revival of University extension work; and the third involved a large expansion of the extension work of the College of Agriculture. The last two were of most consequence.

Although much was made of the service which members of the University performed for the state government, very little can be said about this service except that members of

[1] Charles R. Van Hise, "The University Extension Function in the Modern University," *Proceedings of the First National University Extension Conference, March 10–12, 1915*, pp. 8 ff. La Follette, for example, in his autobiography indicated that he thought the principal "service" performed by the University was outside the University. "In no state of the Union are the relationships between the university and the people of the state so intimate and so mutually helpful as in Wisconsin. We believe there that the purpose of the university is to serve the people, and every effort is made through correspondence courses, special courses, housekeepers' conferences, farmers' institutes, experimental stations and the like to bring every resident of the state under the broadening and inspiring influence of a faculty of trained men. At the same time the highest standards of education in the arts and the professions are maintained in the university itself." *La Follette's Autobiography* (Madison, 1913), 30.

the faculty did serve on various boards and commissions, with and without compensation, usually in the capacity of technical experts. This is not to say that the work was not important, or well done, or even significant, but merely that it is impossible to measure precisely what the result was.[2] Van Hise, in his inaugural address, had asked that the professors be given such work to do. He felt that faculty members had possession of much knowledge which might be useful in helping to solve various state problems. Nor did he ask in vain.

Robert M. La Follette, then governor, had already begun appointing professors to state positions. "I made it a further policy," La Follette recorded in his *Autobiography*, "in order to bring all the reserves of knowledge and inspiration of the university more fully to the service of the people, to appoint experts from the university wherever possible upon the important boards of the state—the civil service commission, the railroad commission and so on—a relationship which the university has always encouraged and by which the state has greatly profited."[3] In 1912 Charles McCarthy tabulated a list of forty-six people who were serving both the University and the state during 1910–11.[4] Howard J. McMurray compiled another list in 1940 which, though incomplete, indicated the extent of University and state interchange. This list contained the names of one hundred and ten people, in addition to the forty-six already listed by McCarthy, who had served both state and University in the period from 1905 to 1940.[5]

Although it is impossible to measure the influence of the University upon the state along these lines, some of these men for a time exercised a large influence.[6] John R. Commons, who was the author of the Industrial Commission Act, served as one

[2] Howard J. McMurray, after surveying the whole field of University influence on the state, was unwilling to venture a generalization. See Howard J. McMurray, Some Influences of the University of Wisconsin on the State Government of Wisconsin, manuscript doctoral dissertation, 1940, in the Library of the University of Wisconsin.

[3] *La Follette's Autobiography*, 31.

[4] Charles McCarthy, *The Wisconsin Idea* (New York, 1912), 313–317.

[5] McMurray, Influences of the University of Wisconsin, 54–60. McMurray found among other things that these men were predominantly specialists and technicians chosen to perform professional or technical tasks.

[6] McMurray discusses this problem on page 45.

of the commissioners; Thomas S. Adams, who helped draft the Wisconsin income-tax law, served on the Tax Commission; and Balthasar H. Meyer served on the Railroad Commission.[7] Whatever their influence, the very fact that University professors were serving in administrative and other posts of the state government itself presented a novel picture certain to be commented upon by visiting reporters sent to spy out La Follette's state. But the situation could not endure. In the first place the professors were associated with the Progressives, which made them largely politically unavailable after the defeat of McGovern in 1914.[8] On the other hand, many calls were made upon University professors simply because there was no one else available with the technical information or training needed at a given juncture. As the services of the state increased, however, and graduate and other schools responded to the needs of government service as they had earlier responded to the demands for trained engineers, men with expert knowledge became somewhat easier to find.

The use of academic experts in governmental affairs, while it declined in Wisconsin after the defeat of the Progressives in 1914, was still sufficiently novel to cause a stir when President Roosevelt brought his first "brain trust" together in 1933.

✐

It has been the custom, in certain quarters of the University community and elsewhere, to associate the beginning of University of Wisconsin extension work with the revival and expansion of certain phases of the work under the direction of Louis E. Reber. This, as we have already seen, is an error. Extension work actually began in 1885 and many of its solid achievements were already incorporated into the regular University program before Van Hise came to the presidency. Among the elements which remained a part of the University were the farmers' institutes, launched in 1885, the agricultural

---

[7] McMurray, Influences of the University of Wisconsin, 39–40.

[8] McMurray reports that he once asked John R. Commons whether he would have been as willing to serve the conservatives as he was to serve the progressives. Commons said, "Certainly, but only the progressives ever asked me." *Ibid.* p. 113.

short courses, and the summer school which was transformed into the summer session. General lecture courses, correspondence courses, and mechanics' institutes had been tried, but with little lasting success. The mechanics' institutes were dropped after a single season and correspondence courses after a couple of years. By 1903 there was slight interest in the lecture courses.

The movement to revive these and other phases of extension work, like so many of the movements which aimed to make the University more useful, was not initially an internal movement. Its beginning must perhaps be traced to Frank A. Hutchins, that self-effacing great teacher and imaginative founder of libraries in Wisconsin. He had a genius for creating quietly. He had come to Madison as a member of the staff of Superintendent of Public Instruction Oliver E. Wells, of Ely trial fame, and had been instrumental in the establishment of the Wisconsin Free Library Commission in 1895. This agency, consisting of a commission made up of the president of the University, the director of the Historical Society, the superintendent of public instruction, and several appointive members, was created to advise and counsel libraries. Its functions were quickly expanded under the secretaryship of Frank A. Hutchins. Notable among the achievements were the package library, assistance to small libraries, and, perhaps most important of all, the creation of the Legislative Reference Library.[9] This branch had been created by the legislature in 1901 and to it Hutchins brought Charles McCarthy. The function of the Legislative Reference Library as conceived by Hutchins and developed by McCarthy was first to supply legislators with all available information on problems of legislation. Out of this activity there developed the bill-drafting agency. Some of these activities were later described by McCarthy in *The Wisconsin Idea*. The Legislative Reference Library was quickly swamped with requests for information, first from legislators and later from people in various walks of life in the state. Its success was also registered by its imitation elsewhere.

It was from the men on the Free Library Commission that the demand came for a new University extension service, con-

---

[9] Cf. Conrad E. Patzer, *Public Education in Wisconsin* (Madison, 1924), 292.

ceived partly to satisfy the demands for information received by the library commission. These men, first Hutchins and McCarthy and later Henry E. Legler, who succeeded Hutchins as secretary in 1903, began to urge Van Hise, shortly after his election as president, to reinstitute extension work. There is no record of Van Hise's first responses to the proposal, but he apparently was not enthusiastic.[10]

In his first report to the Board of Regents, Van Hise had nothing to say about either extension work or service to the state. It is also significant that in his inaugural address, in which so many of the lines of effort of his administration were set forth, no mention was made of extension work, although he talked enthusiastically about service to the state. In 1905, however, Van Hise was converted to the possible value of reviving extension work. In an address before the Association of State Universities in November, 1905, he defended the short courses for farmers and housekeepers. "It seems to me that a state university should not be above meeting the needs of the people, however elementary the instruction necessary to accomplish this." These words, which he repeated in his report to the regents in 1906, echoed what Chamberlin had proclaimed fifteen years before. Van Hise told his fellow university presidents that Wisconsin was planning to enlarge "the scope of the regular University extension." Yet the plans were not yet specific. He spoke only in general terms about what extension was to accomplish.[11] This speech marks one of the first public espousals of extension work by Van Hise, an espousal that had come recently, since the president only a few months before had confessed, "I have given so little attention to correspondence work that I am unable to express an opinion upon the point you raise."[12]

In December, 1905, the executive committee of the regents approved an appropriation of $250 to revive the extension work

[10] Interview, Carstensen with Mrs. Burr W. Jones, July 17, 1947. Mrs. Jones, then Katherine MacDonald, was in a position to know of the discussions which went on. As assistant to the secretary of the commission, she attended the meetings often to keep minutes of the business transacted. Evidence of Van Hise's opposition, of course, did not show in the minutes.

[11] Address of Charles R. Van Hise to the Association of State Universities, Washington, November, 1905. Manuscript in the Presidents' Papers.

[12] Van Hise to Austin W. Stultz, New York, April 17, 1905, Presidents' Papers.

and in January appointed Edwin W. Pahlow, instructor of history, to be secretary of the department for the remainder of the year. "The development of this department of the university," the student newspaper declared, "is a part of President Van Hise's policy of extending the advantages of the university to as many people of the state as possible."[13] This action represented the beginning of revival. In March a general announcement was made that extension courses would again be offered on a wide scale.[14] The next month the regents, at Van Hise's request, approved an appropriation of $2,500 for the work.[15]

But nothing was going smoothly as yet. Pahlow left at the end of the academic year, and Henry E. Legler agreed to serve as secretary of the extension department without pay.[16] Legler continued in this capacity until almost the end of 1907, when Louis E. Reber arrived. In July, 1906, William H. Lighty, an acquaintance of Professor Ely, was employed to take charge of and organize the correspondence department. Lighty had been engaged in social settlement work in St. Louis.[17] Hutchins was appointed field organizer.

Van Hise, however, was not yet certain whether the agency should be small, employing two or three people, or large and vigorous. McCarthy, Legler, and Hutchins worked hard to convert Van Hise to a large program. In the summer of 1906 McCarthy, with the encouragement of Legler and Hutchins, conducted a survey of the private correspondence schools.[18]

[13] Regents' Executive Committee Minutes, F:104, December 4, 1905; F:134, January 29, 1906; *Daily Cardinal*, January 30, 1906.

[14] *Madison Democrat* and *Milwaukee Sentinel*, March 18, 1906.

[15] Records of the Board of Regents, F:404, April 17, 1906. Van Hise's later recollection of the re-establishment of University Extension is at odds with the official record. Cf. Report of the president, *Regents' Biennial Report*, 1907–08, p. 18.

[16] Minutes of the Wisconsin Free Library Commission, May, 1903–June, 1911, June 14, 1906, State Capitol. The minutes carefully specified that this was at the invitation of Van Hise.

[17] Regents' Executive Committee Minutes, F:304, August 6, 1906. William H. Lighty, *A Sketch of the Revivification of University Extension at the University of Wisconsin* (September, 1938), 10.

[18] There is some disagreement over who suggested this survey. Van Hise later claimed. that he called for the survey. McCarthy's biographer, E. A. Fitzpatrick, claims that McCarthy conceived and carried out the survey. Edward A. Fitzpatrick, *McCarthy of Wisconsin* (New York, 1944), 249–250. But whoever had the inspiration, it seems clear that the idea came from the library commission, not the University.

McCarthy's report on correspondence schools, consisting of nine typed pages, was forwarded to Van Hise by Legler early in August. McCarthy had found that some 35,000 people residing in Wisconsin were enrolled in private correspondence schools, and that approximately $800,000 was paid out annually for this instruction. He stated that the schools, when properly conducted, did much good; insisted that the University of Wisconsin had ample facilities to do better work than was being done; and recommended the vigorous development of University correspondence courses.[19] McCarthy also sent to the president a memorandum on a plan for extension.[20]

More telling perhaps was another phase of the campaign carried on in 1906. Legler and McCarthy solicited comments from leading Wisconsin citizens on the University extension work. Almost unanimously they supported the enlargement of this work. James H. Stout declared unequivocally that this move would make the University the "most democratic school in America." J. H. Puelicher of the Marshall & Ilsley Bank of Milwaukee gave the proposal his hearty support. John Barnes of the Railroad Commission declared that "such a school would bring the University in direct contact with very many who would be unable to attend it, and confer benefits of a practical kind upon them; would bring the school and the people closer together." James A. Sheridan of Sheridan and Wollaeger, Milwaukee, thought the extension would bring the University to the people and would quiet criticisms about the "aristocratic tendencies" of the University. Others interpreted the request for opinion as an invitation to speak their minds about the University. Thus the words in support of the proposed extension work were sometimes coupled with vigorous strictures of the University as it then existed.[21] McCarthy sent copies of all of these letters to Van Hise.

Meanwhile Lighty had come to Madison to organize the correspondence course work. He began immediately what Van Hise later called "wheedling out of the faculty members the

[19] Fitzpatrick, *McCarthy of Wisconsin*, 250.   [20] *Ibid.*, 287.
[21] Copies of these letters may be found in the Presidents' Papers, filed under extension, 1906–07.

commitments which should constitute the new university extension."[22] No decision had been made as to what these courses
were to be, or how they would fit in with the University program, if at all. Early in October upon Legler's urging, Van Hise
appointed a special committee, consisting of Dean Birge, Professors Elliott, Ely, Harper, Hubbard, Mack, and Turner, as
well as Legler, Lighty, and McCarthy, to investigate and report
on the nature of the correspondence work and the University
credits to be given for it.[23] The committee report, submitted to
Van Hise on October 16, 1906, supported the extension program,
observing that if the University did not respond to the demand,
other institutions would. Recognizing that some of the work
would not be of such a character as to merit academic credit,
the committee felt that much work of the University level
should be offered. Granting University credit would be beneficial since this would provide a steadying influence on the
students, even though few would go on to take degrees. Hence
it was proposed that some courses be outlined for which credit
would be given. Correspondence courses consisting of forty
lessons would yield five-fifths credits (five semester-hours) ; lecture courses of one hour a week through the academic year
would yield two-fifths credits toward a degree. No degree could
be earned by correspondence work alone, and only a limited
amount of credit from other correspondence course work could
be transferred to the University of Wisconsin. The committee
also recommended that the staffs of the normal schools be
drawn into the work wherever possible.[24]

The recommendations of the committee, the missionary work
of Legler, Hutchins, and McCarthy, the evidence of support
from prominent citizens in the state, and the energy displayed
by Lighty in organizing and publicizing the correspondence
courses all helped to dispel whatever lingering reservations Van
Hise may have had about the wisdom of launching a sustained
and vigorous University extension program. In October, 1906,

[22] Lighty, *A Sketch of the Revivification of University Extension*, 10.
[23] Henry E. Legler to Van Hise, October 2, 1906, and Van Hise to Legler,
October 8, 1906, Presidents' Papers, filed under extension.
[24] Report of the Committee on Credit for University Extension Work, October 16,
1906, Presidents' Papers, filed under extension.

Van Hise recommended and the regents approved a new budget of $7,500 for the extension work for the next year.[25] Moreover, in his report to the regents in 1906 Van Hise devoted some fifteen pages to a discussion of the University as an instrument of the state, four of which dealt with the steps already taken to revive extension and the large hopes entertained for this work. "It is the purpose of the reorganized extension department," he wrote, "not only to carry on extension lectures as heretofore, but to greatly extend work so as to assist all the groups of people that wish to undertake work of a serious character of whatever kind in any part of the state." He declared that "too much cannot be said as to the importance of University extension under which the University goes out to the people." The farmers' course was justified, he claimed, "if the fundamental conception be correct, that the University is to be managed in such a way as to be of greatest possible service to the state."[26] Clearly University Extension had now been brought within Van Hise's definition of service to the state.

The legislature of 1907 was asked to make a special appropriation for the work. Two bills were introduced for the purpose. One, which died in the Senate, provided an annual appropriation of $40,000 for extension work, $20,000 of which was to be used for agricultural extension.[27] The other, introduced by F. M. Jackson, amended the statutes to authorize the regents to carry on educational extension and correspondence teaching and provided an annual appropriation of $20,000 for the support of this work.[28] This bill moved slowly through the Assembly mill but was finally adopted by a unanimous vote.[29] In the Senate it was approved in two days, again by a unanimous vote,[30] and six days later it was signed by the governor.[31] The same legislature, although refusing to make an appropriation for agricultural extension, increased the amount available for farmers' institutes from $12,000 to $20,000 a year.

With additional funds available, plans to establish a large

[25] Records of the Board of Regents, F:491, October 16, 1906.
[26] Report of the president, *Regents' Biennial Report*, 1905–06, pp. 35, 37, 38.
[27] Senate Bill 137S, *Senate Journal*, 1907, pp. 130, 688, 711.
[28] Assembly Bill 404A, *Assembly Journal*, 1907, p. 146.
[29] *Ibid.*, 1075–1076.
[30] *Senate Journal*, 1907, p. 1014.   [31] *Laws of Wisconsin*, 1907, pp. 352, 1045.

organization could go forward. The first and most important step was the selection of a director of the department. Van Hise, then in the East, had begun to search for someone for this position, but it was Legler and McCarthy who pressed vigorously for a prompt appointment. Early in July, 1907, shortly after the governor approved the bill, each wrote to Van Hise urging that Frederick W. MacKenzie be given the position. Van Hise, after consultation with Dean Birge, was unenthusiastic. Legler dropped the matter; McCarthy, however, was incensed at Van Hise's declaration that he sought a scholar for the position, a man whom the faculty would accept as an equal. McCarthy responded: "You say you hope that 'the man who is called to the position of Secretary of Extension work shall be recognized by the Professors in the University as a man who is their equal in attainment.' I have not considered what the Professors might say about the thing so much as I have considered what the people of the state might want. . . . Frankly, I think, President Van Hise, that the professors in the University have, as a body, opposed this whole work and a man who would be acceptable to them would in my opinion be of no value to this movement." [32]

While this flurry had nothing to do with getting the job for the candidate proposed by Legler and McCarthy, it is apparent that it stirred Van Hise to greater action in search of a director.

---

[32] McCarthy continued, "I have scarcely met a professor in the University who has not been in some way opposed to this movement. I do not think we ought to consider the Professors in the University at all, especially in the light of the fact that the Governor of this state has assured me that the Professors in the University had been to him and had opposed the appropriation for this work. . . . I think it is a shame to have the spirit that we have had in the University in the past year toward this work and I want to say right here and put myself on record as saying it, if the same spirit is continued, I shall resign my little connection with the University and tell the people of the state what I think of the whole proposition. If this work cannot be done with the support of the faculty of the University of Wisconsin, it should be done without their support and I believe that if the University of Wisconsin cannot do it, that some other body ought to do it. . . . I am not afraid of the faculty, but I am disgusted and ashamed of it." McCarthy to Van Hise, July 29, 1907, Presidents' Papers. Van Hise rejoined with a defense of the faculty, acknowledging that some perhaps disapproved, but "as a whole the stronger men in the faculty have steadily supported the movement from the first conference which I held." He felt too that the professors had supported the development of correspondence courses. Van Hise to McCarthy, August 1, 1907, Presidents' Papers. McCarthy was not, however, willing to let Van Hise have the last word. "You say," he wrote, "that

Among the people to whom he now wrote was Louis E. Reber, dean of the college of engineering, Pennsylvania State College, and brother-in-law of Dugald C. Jackson of the Wisconsin engineering college, to explain the great plans at Wisconsin and to ask whether Reber knew anyone to suggest for the position. The extension work, Van Hise wrote, was likely to develop into "one of the most important branches of educational work. It seems to me that the amazing success of the private correspondence schools shows the unparalleled opportunity."[33] It was two weeks before Reber answered. Although he could think of no one who would meet the qualifications set forth by Van Hise, he felt the project was a worthy one of great promise.[34] Whether the first letter to Reber had been intended to feel him out on the subject, whether Van Hise was so pleased with Reber's response that he knew instantly that here was the man for the directorship, whether members of the Wisconsin engineering faculty had counseled the appointment of Reber, or whether the energetic McCarthy was forcing Van Hise to move, is not clear from the record. Van Hise had never met Reber. On the day before Reber answered, McCarthy had written to Van Hise again urging that a director be appointed. It was clear that if Van Hise did not have a man for the position, McCarthy and Legler would find one. That state of affairs Van Hise did not like. On the day that Van Hise received Reber's letter, he wrote asking him if he would consider the position.[35] The next day he wrote to McCarthy, but he was not wholly candid. He said he was considering two men for the position, Reber and Professor

you talked with the men on the faculty two years ago. Upon looking over my files I find that two years ago I proposed the outline of this plan to you and you then tried to get together some of the faculty, especially Mr. Tressler and others to meet me and so dead was the whole thing that you could not get anybody to even meet me to discuss the matter. From my correspondence in the files, I believe the whole matter was dead until a year ago in June. I believe firmly that the faculty do not want the thing now." McCarthy to Van Hise, August 6, 1907, Presidents' Papers. There is no record remaining of a faculty advisory committee meeting in 1905. Perhaps Van Hise was thinking of the special committee which reported in October, 1906, in support of the extension movement and favoring granting University credit for some of the work. The McCarthy Papers do not contain the correspondence which McCarthy referred to.

[33] Van Hise to Louis Ehrhart Reber, July 22, 1907, Presidents' Papers.
[34] Reber to Van Hise, August 7, 1907, Presidents' Papers.
[35] Van Hise to Reber, August 9, 1907, Presidents' Papers.

William T. Magruder, both seriously interested in technical education on a secondary level.[36] McCarthy promptly asked for information about these men. He himself began to investigate Magruder and was not wholly satisfied with what he learned. He confessed his doubts to Van Hise and expressed the fear of "an aristocracy in education." He felt that the man selected for the position must value the boy in the factory equally with the son of wealth. "I hope to see the day when the University of Wisconsin will do for the merchant and for the manufacturer what it has done for the farmer."[37] But Van Hise had made up his mind. He meant to have Reber for the position. Having had no response from Reber, Van Hise wrote again on the 14th, this time asking for an interview so that the proposition might be discussed.[38] The next day Reber agreed to an interview, which was arranged for August 22 in Boston. In setting the date for the conference Van Hise acknowledged that the position which Reber then held was one which offered many opportunities, but "the position of Director of Extension at Wisconsin," he declared, echoing words McCarthy had written a few days before, "would be developing a new line of education in state universities which I believe in the future is likely to become one of very great importance."[39]

The conference was a success in almost every way except that Reber asked for a salary of $4,500. The Board had authorized a maximum salary of only $4,000. Van Hise's attempts to have the executive committee increase the amount were unavailing. However, after more correspondence, Reber finally, late in September, accepted the position.[40] Before the end of the year he had come to Madison.

Louis Reber was born at Nittany, Pennsylvania, February 27,

[36] Van Hise to McCarthy, August 10, 1907, Presidents' Papers. Van Hise was in close touch with Magruder at this time. Presidents' Papers.

[37] McCarthy to Van Hise, August 14, 1907, Presidents' Papers.

[38] Van Hise to Reber, August 14, 1907, Presidents' Papers.

[39] Reber to Van Hise, August 15, 1907; Van Hise to Reber, August 17, 1907, both in the Presidents' Papers. Van Hise was vacationing in Massachusetts at the time.

[40] Van Hise to Magnus Swenson, August 23, 1907; Swenson to Van Hise, August 26; Van Hise to Reber, August 27; Reber to Van Hise, August 29, September 12; Van Hise to Reber, September 19; Reber to Van Hise, September 23, 1907, all in the Presidents' Papers.

1858. Entering Pennsylvania State College at twenty, he had graduated with honors four years later and promptly joined the faculty to teach mathematics. In 1883 he went to the Massachusetts Institute of Technology and a year later returned to Pennsylvania State to establish the department of mechanic arts. He became a full professor in 1887 and dean of the college in 1897. Ten years later, at the age of 49, he came to Wisconsin to assume control of the extension division, a position he held until his retirement in 1926. The initial steps toward the establishment of the extension division had been taken before he arrived. William H. Lighty had set up the correspondence courses, and Frank A. Hutchins was busily engaged in creating that remarkable organization, the department of debate and public discussion. Together they had already won wide and favorable publicity. An appropriation of $20,000 a year for the next two years had been obtained from the legislature. Van Hise was prepared to give the movement his full support, yet no one could say that the division had been created, or that its possibilities had been more than glimpsed. Indeed, in concept if not in organization, the University had proceeded little beyond the position taken by Chamberlin twenty years before. It was Reber who translated the somewhat vague aspiration of Van Hise for University service, the enthusiastic hopes of such men as McCarthy, Legler, Hutchins, and others, and the social uplift of Lighty into a powerful organization.[41]

In view of the large importance of this man who for almost

[41] After the extension division of the University of Wisconsin had become the model of university extension divisions, and visiting delegations came from other states and abroad to study the organization and methods, a number of people claimed or others claimed for them the credit for having created it. Van Hise certainly assumed that large credit belonged to him, as indeed it did. Without his support there would have been nothing. Edward A. Fitzpatrick in *McCarthy of Wisconsin* claims McCarthy was the originator (p. 259 *passim*). Former Superintendent of Public Instruction Charles P. Cary thought that he had initiated the movement. See his statement in *Louis Ehrhart Reber, Builder of University Extension* (Madison, 1944), 45. Birge gave Reber large credit for the success of the division (*ibid.*, 43). Reber himself declared in a letter to Hutchins, June 24, 1911, "I believe that I can say truly that the influence of your insight and knowledge of conditions coupled with the determination to help where help was needed, has contributed more toward the present development of University Extension than that of any other one factor." Works and Worth of Frank A. Hutchins, manuscript in the State Historical Society of Wisconsin.

twenty years directed University Extension at Wisconsin, whose
conception of its functions was widely influential, and whose
formal organization of the work, outlined in some detail in
1908, largely fixed the divisions and the pattern of extension
work from that time to the present,[42] his general conception of
the functions and organization of the division should be closely
examined. Reber was of course in agreement with Van Hise, who
often spoke about what extension should be and do. Again
and again in his speeches Van Hise had indicated his indebtedness to Lester F. Ward, whose *Applied Sociology* (1906) had
shown that "the greatest loss which we as a nation suffer is loss
of talent." Van Hise wanted, he told members of an extension
conference in 1915, "no mute inglorious Milton" in Wisconsin. "It should be the aim of University extension to make this
impossible; it should also be the aim of extension to assist the
ordinary individual as well as the man of talent. If society were
perfectly organized, each individual would have an opportunity
to develop to the fullest degree the endowments given him by
nature whether they be large or small. Doubtless this will never
be accomplished fully, but it should be the aim of extension
to assist every individual in this direction. This then is the
purpose of University Extension ... to carry light and opportunity to every human being in all parts of the nation; this
is the only adequate ideal of service for the University."[43] Van
Hise had already said these things often and he would repeat
them again and again.

On the same occasion Louis E. Reber declared: "Right or
wrong, you find here a type of University Extension that does
not disdain the simplest form of service. Literally carrying the
University to the homes of the people, it attempts to give them
what they need—be it the last word in expert advice; courses
of study carrying University credit; or easy lessons in cooking

[42] One student of the extension movement says that the pattern of University
extension work described by Van Hise in 1915, that is, the organization Reber
had created, "has not changed greatly in the succeeding twenty-five years, at
least not in its superficial characteristics," and the annual program of the National University Extension Association, formed at that time, still is disposed
around the major classifications outlined by Van Hise. James Creese, *The
Extension of University Teaching* (New York, 1941), 56.
[43] Van Hise, "The University Extension Function in the Modern University," 24.

and sewing. University Extension in Wisconsin endeavors to interpret the phraseology of the expert and offers the benefits of research to the household and the workshop, as well as to municipalities and state."[44]

Moreover, as Reber explained in his first formal report, the extension division was not content merely to make available the fruits of University knowledge. He declared: "As University extension is intended to disseminate all the benefits offered by the University to persons not resident at the institution, it is necessary that such an organization be developed throughout the state as will enable the extension division to reach the public in the most effective and helpful manner. It should be understood that it is the desire of the University to reach not only those who feel the need of assistance but also those who, not realizing a need, may upon learning the possibilities for self-improvement open to them through the several departments of extension be led to avail themselves of the opportunities thus offered."[45] Reber, in short, wanted to use the extension division as an agency by means of which all or any knowledge not only could but would be transmitted to those who sought it and to those who ought to have it. He was restrained by no rigid notions that certain activities were beneath the dignity of the University extension division. If the citizens of the state wanted to know about Plato or how to construct a sanitary sewage system, about astronomy or tuberculosis, he proposed to help them. Not even the inmates of the state prisons were safe. Various courses were ultimately organized for them.

This attitude, and the activities which flowed from it, did not escape criticism. Some felt that such education was not quite respectable institutionally. Some thought the University was lowering its standards and degrading itself in offering work which was frankly elementary and utilitarian. In his excellent history of the University, Professor James F. A. Pyre, who had

[44] Louis E. Reber, "The Scope of University Extension and Its Organization and Subdivision," *Proceedings of the First National University Extension Conference, March 10–12, 1915*, p. 25.

[45] Report of the University Extension Division, June 30, 1908, *Regents' Biennial Report*, 1907–08, p. 194.

served with the extension lecturers in the 1890's and again after 1906, passed over most of the extension work without comment. Occasional references to this division, however, suggest a certain watchfulness. Thus he observed at one point that "one's passion for service to his fellow man may run toward presenting him with some just impression of a value in art or morals or an elusive concept of gravitation, rather than toward providing him with cheaper electricity or subtilizing his philosophy of municipal sewage."[46]

Reber, Van Hise, and others were aware of such criticisms and tried to meet them. Even before the new extension division was launched Van Hise had made up his mind on the problem: the success of the short course in the College of Agriculture had done that for him. In his address before the Association of State Universities at Washington in November, 1905, Van Hise had talked about the short course and plans to increase this work. "It is sometimes thought that work of the kind mentioned is below the dignity of a university. This is a mis-conception." He pointed out that the names of the men and women who attended were not listed in the catalogue. "Thus our lists of students are in no way padded, and the standards of the University are not lowered. It seems to me that a state university should not be above meeting the needs of the people, however elementary the instruction necessary to accomplish this."[47] Ten years later, at Minneapolis, Van Hise discussed the matter more fully. His opinion had not changed. The idea of service, he declared, was that "the university shall carry to the people the knowledge which they can assimilate for their betterment along all lines. It may be suggested . . . that, while this idea of service cannot be gainsaid, it is not a function of the university but rather of some other instrumentality. If it is meant by this that it has not been the function of the traditional university, to this dissent cannot be made. But it seems to me that whether it is the function of the university should be decided by the simple criterion as to whether the university is the best fitted instrument to

[46] James F. A. Pyre, *Wisconsin* (New York, 1920), 348.
[47] Address of Charles R. Van Hise to the Association of State Universities, Washington, November, 1905. Manuscript in the Presidents' Papers.

do this work. If this is so, it should do it without reference to any person's conception as to the scope of the University."[48]

Reber likewise often dealt with the question of the propriety of the University's taking up this work. Like Van Hise he based his argument on the claim that a state university is a public service institution. In answer to the question whether the University should be engaged in this work, Reber asserted that "so long as there is no other agency prepared to do the work, the question admits of an affirmative answer only."[49] In 1924, President Birge, speaking before the National University Extension Conference, remarked that the extension work was criticized as not being of university grade. Like Reber and Van Hise and a host of others he answered the question partly by asking what university-grade work is. But more seriously he spoke along the lines Van Hise had marked out twenty years before and which Chamberlin had laid down in the late 1880's. "The university is the one agent of the state, which can and which does so embody the combined intellectual life of the community that it can apply that life on any level for the betterment of the community. The university can work wherever need appears. . . . The university is therefore the institution, and it is indeed the only institution whose campus can be coextensive with the state."[50]

If there was no apology in these justifications, it is clear that these men wanted their position to be understood. Although it was called University Extension, only a small part of the work was of accepted University standing. Indeed, it was, at its best, a people's university movement, intended to appeal to the people it was designed to serve. Nor was this an accidental de-

[48] Charles R. Van Hise, "The Idea of Service," address delivered at Minneapolis, 1915. Substantially the same address was presented at the First National University Extension Conference under the title "The University Extension Function in the Modern University," 7 ff.

[49] Louis E. Reber, "University Extension and the State University," *Science,* 34:825 (December 15, 1911). Chester Allen, now director of the extension field organization, recalled that Reber often declared: "Whenever any agency finds that it can take over educational activity started by the Extension Division and do it better, they are welcome to do it." Allen to Carstensen, December 1, 1947, University Archives.

[50] Edward A. Birge, Address Delivered at the Ninth National University Extension Association Conference, 1924, *Proceedings,* 164.

The Dean of University Extension
Louis E. Reber

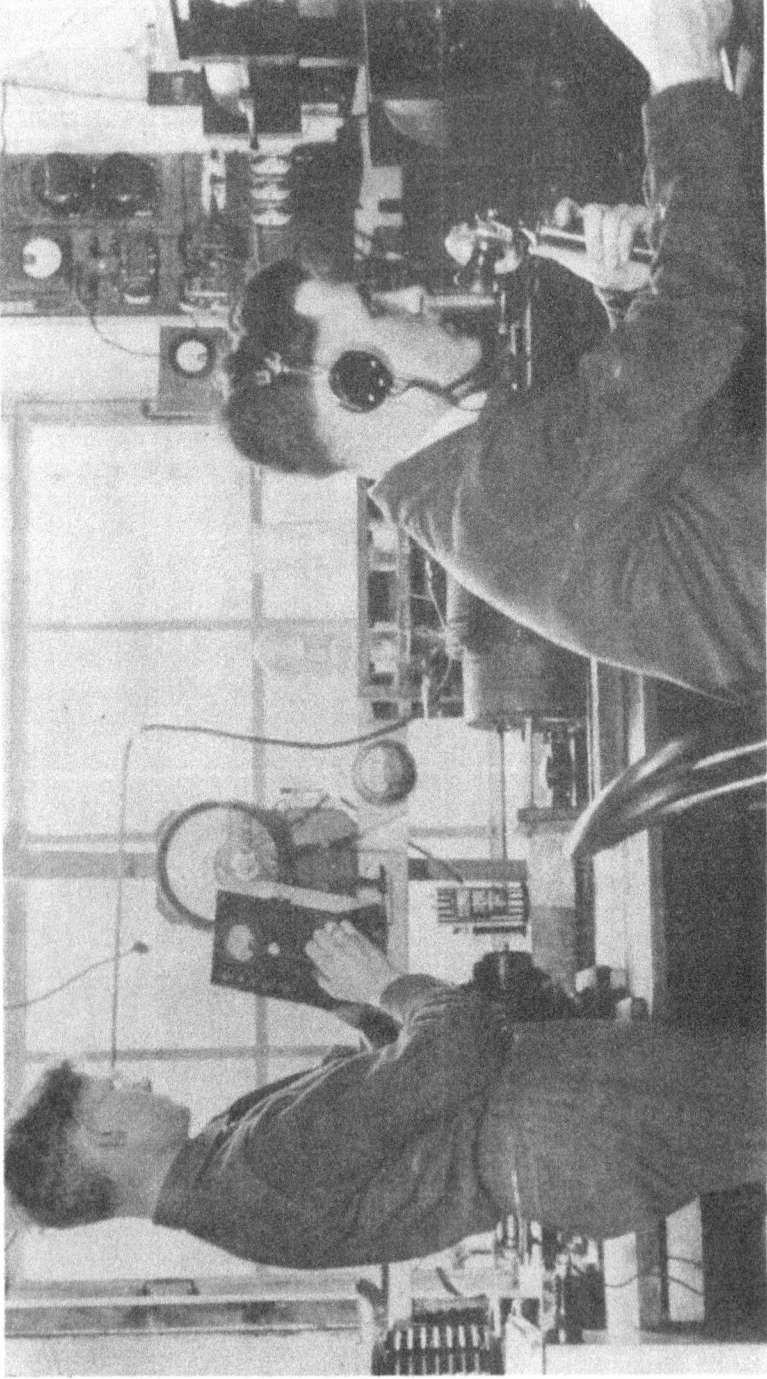

WHA in the Early Twenties

velopment. Reber, with Van Hise's full comprehension and support, conceived the function of the extension division to be largely outside the area of the conventional university scheme. Whatever might be said of it to the contrary, in terms of social uplift and of cultural benefits, its main purpose was to offer utilitarian courses at virtually any level.

Reber himself was dubious about using college teachers for the work. In his first report he indicated, somewhat obscurely, that university teachers would not be satisfactory. "Great as are the possibilities for good in this work, it is peculiarly true that the workers must be in thorough sympathy with it or disappointment will result. But with enthusiasm and fitness in its workers and the appreciation and support of the people of the state, no movement can prevent this division from adding to what President Eliot has called the greatest state university in the country, that element which will make it, in truth, 'The People's University'!"[51]

Although not unwilling to concede the resident departments a measure of control over courses offered for academic credit, Reber was a little suspicious of the resident instructors. "Correspondence study," he told one audience, "for purposes of university extension, must include courses of practically every grade. The teaching force must be selected with special reference to the peculiar relations between teacher and student. The resident instructor is frequently not well adapted to this work." Although willing to concede that "work for credit must be under the careful supervision of the residence departments," he felt that "departmental supervision is, in general, not necessary for the vocational courses, and is not as a rule desirable. There is danger that the influence of the old academic spirit may operate to make vocational correspondence study as applied to industrial workers ineffective and practically valueless."[52]

These then were the ideas that controlled the development

[51] Report of the University Extension Division, *Regents' Biennial Report,* 1907–08, p. 198.
[52] Louis E. Reber, "University Extension and the State University," *Science,* 34:825–833. A reprint of a paper read at the Minneapolis meeting of the American Association for the Advancement of Science.

of the new extension division. Consciously patterned after the proprietary correspondence schools, aimed at being all things to all men, evangelical in outlook, unreservedly committed to the assumption that one sure way to earthly salvation lay through education, the new extension division developed quickly, energetically, and conspicuously. The ideas which Reber and Van Hise expressed were not in themselves unusual. Others had had such ideas before. The remarkable thing was what was done within the framework of these ideas in terms of an organization conceived and created, a staff assembled, trained, and made effective.

In his first report, prepared in 1908, Dean Reber described the organization which had been created. "For convenience, expedition, and efficiency" the work had been divided into four departments: correspondence study, instruction by lectures, debating and public discussion, and general information and welfare.[53] The first two departments had been organized by Lighty and Hutchins before Reber arrived. Only the first of these divisions or departments was concerned with offering work for college credit. The department of correspondence study was created, according to Reber, to offer work of the widest possible variety. The range of study is suggested by the fact that the courses at the outset were divided into five general classifications: regular university work, special advanced work, high school and preparatory work, elementary school branches, and special vocational branches. Thirty-five departments of the University had prepared over two hundred courses. By September, 1908, the department claimed almost 1,200 registrations, over half of them in the special vocational branches, 330 in courses for university credit, and the rest scattered among the other three categories.[54] Thus whatever the impression created by the overenthusiastic reports which began to appear in the state and national press about the extension division, the fact should not be obscured that the bulk of the correspondence courses was utilitarian. Although the courses were conducted along

[53] Report of the University Extension Division, *Regents' Biennial Report*, 1907–08, p. 174. [54] *Ibid.*, 174–175.

lines followed by commercial correspondence schools, Reber introduced an important new feature. Because of the tendency of students to drop courses after completing only a few lessons the extension division provided for itinerant instructors who would meet classes of correspondence students at regular intervals to give assistance.[55] This device was especially used in the industrial education program launched in Milwaukee. These courses had the support of the manufacturers, a number of whom provided classrooms for such meetings and further encouraged their employees by giving them time off to attend the class meetings. In some cases manufacturers even paid the enrollment fees. Reber made a great point of justifying industrial education in terms of the money value of the courses.

To carry on the work of the correspondence department and the other work too, Reber demanded a special staff, first because the University staff, which contributed much in the beginning, had its own work to do, and second because he felt that the extension workers should possess special qualifications plus a "proper viewpoint."[56] In addition, Reber, who sought to establish a system of districts for the administration of extension, wanted some teachers stationed in each district. Besides the special staff, he wanted laboratories available at various centers.

Because of the special nature of the work he felt too that it would be necessary for most of the correspondence-study subjects to have special textbooks. These were to be written by men engaged in the profession and revised by teachers acquainted with pedagogical methods. It was Reber's intention that the work of textbook writing, when undertaken, would be done by people working on salary for the extension division.[57] The need for adequate courses in business administration, home economics, highway building, agriculture, and nature study was particularly emphasized.

These elements, in brief, constituted the first formally presented conception of the major department of the extension division. Subsequent years were to see the conception set forth in this first report realized along virtually all lines.

[55] *Ibid.*, 176.   [56] *Ibid.*, 183.   [57] *Ibid.*, 184.

The second department, that of debating and public discussion, was largely the creation of Frank A. Hutchins. The objective of this department was to arouse and stimulate among all classes of people an intelligent and active interest in important social and political questions. The department collected and maintained a lending library of books and periodicals on the living issues of the day.[58] The department of instruction by lectures was designed principally to supply speakers for various groups and lecture courses, both informational and entertaining.[59]

It was the object of the department of general information and welfare "to act as a medium between the great federal and state departments, national societies and state universities, on the one hand, and the people of the state on the other, in the dissemination of results of investigation and research."[60] The conception of this department was bold, for the function was, theoretically at least, nothing less than that of making the results of all research anywhere available to anyone who could use it. The work of the department was only partly passive. It would attempt to supply any information asked for, but also vital information about matters of public interest was assembled in bulletins for public distribution; and the department early arranged institutes intended, like the farmers' institutes, to bring to interested groups the latest and most reliable information about their vocation. The bakers' institute in Milwaukee was the first of such meetings.

In order to make the services of these four departments readily available throughout the state, Reber proposed the establishment of a field organization in which the state would be divided into eleven extension districts, each with a headquarters, a district representative, and such other field workers as might be called for. The conception and development of the field organization, with district representatives to serve as salesmen of the correspondence courses, counselors, publicists, and the rest, was of considerable importance to the effectiveness of the extension division. Although the division from the begin-

---

[58] *Ibid.,* 188–190.
[59] *Ibid.,* 186–187.   [60] *Ibid.,* 191.

ning sought and obtained wide newspaper publicity, and it circulated a vast number of pamphlets to inform people of the services available, it did not place full dependence upon the printed word. The district representatives and other field workers, talking agents of the division, were to see to it that "those who, not realizing a need, may upon learning of the possibility for self-improvement . . . be led to avail themselves of the opportunities."[61]

The quick success of the extension division in almost all its departments was registered in the rapid increase in the funds allotted to this work; the increase in the staff; the rapid and steady increase in the number of correspondence courses and extension classes taught and in the number of exhibits and information pamphlets prepared and sent out; the steady growth of the number of package libraries distributed; and the acquisition of buildings, first at Madison in 1915 and much later in Milwaukee in 1928. The legislative appropriation of funds for extension work began in 1907 when $20,000 a year was voted. The state appropriation was increased in 1909 to $50,000 annually, and the next year to $75,000. For the fiscal year 1914–15 the amount contributed by the legislature reached $225,000 but was then decreased thereafter to a little more than $160,000 in 1917–18.[62] During the next years the state appropriation increased again to over $200,000 and passed $245,000 for the year 1925–1926.[63] In the early 1920's the total amount collected in fees exceeded $20,000 annually. Thus, the whole amount devoted to extension work reached almost a half million dollars before Reber retired in 1926. The relatively large sums available for the work not only showed the willingness of the legislature to support this venture but probably explain the prominence of the University in this work, particularly before the first World War. In 1915 Van Hise pointed out that during the year 1913–14 Wisconsin devoted almost twice as much money

---

[61] *Ibid.*, 194.

[62] It should be noted that neither the increase in 1914 nor the decrease in 1917 was as large as the figure suggests. From 1913 to 1917 all fees were paid into the treasury and were expendable subject to legislative appropriation. After 1917 such fees went into a revolving fund and were available without legislative action. *Report of the Business Manager, 1917–18*, p. 14. [63] *Ibid.*, 1925–26, p. 12.

as any other institution in the country to University Extension of all kinds.[64]

These expenditures reflected continually expanding service, but Reber never succeeded in establishing the full field organization he planned. In 1908 he had called for the establishment of eleven districts with a representative in each district.[65] The first district, with headquarters at Milwaukee, was opened by July, 1908; the second, the Oshkosh district serving ten surrounding counties, was opened in June, 1909.[66] The third district with La Crosse as the headquarters was opened in August, 1911, and by the end of the 1910–12 biennium districts at Superior and Wausau had been authorized.[67] In 1913 the Eau Claire district was opened.[68] No more districts were organized, despite Reber's continued urging. Although disrupted during the first World War, the district organization continued substantially unchanged until Reber's retirement in 1926.

The correspondence department enjoyed a rapid growth. The total number of registrations for correspondence courses up to July 1, 1910, amounted to 4,246. In 1910 the Army and Navy Y.M.C.A. entered into an arrangement with the extension division permitting members of those armed services stationed abroad to enroll for courses.[69] In 1912 the total number of registrations passed 10,000.[70] By the end of the biennium in 1914 the number had increased to 15,000 and by July 1, 1916, to almost 25,000.[71] The number had passed 100,000 before Reber retired. New registrations, perhaps a more reliable indication

[64] Van Hise, "The University Extension Function in the Modern University," 22–23.

[65] Report of the University Extension Division, *Regents' Biennial Report,* 1907–08, p. 196.

[66] *Ibid.,* 1909–10, pp. 232–233.

[67] *Ibid.,* 1911–12, p. 154.

[68] *Ibid.,* 1913–14, p. 212.

[69] Papers of the Board of Regents, January 19, and April 20, 1910; William Howard Taft to Van Hise, March 4, 1910, Van Hise to Taft, March 7, October 13, 1910, all in the Presidents' Papers.

[70] *Regents' Biennial Report,* 1911–12, pp. 72–73.

[71] *Ibid.,* 1915–16, p. 187. The figures are somewhat misleading, both in the total number of registrations and in the annual increments, because of the system of carrying incomplete registrations over from one year to the next and counting the total registrations instead of total completions of courses; but the record still remains impressive.

of the growth of the department, increased annually until after the first World War. The new registrations recorded during the year 1914–15 numbered almost 4,000 and they exceeded 6,000 in 1916–17 and 10,000 in 1920–21. A decade later the number of new registrations during the year was over 17,000.[72] A partial explanation of the rapid expansion is to be found in the publicity which attended this work, the effectiveness of the field representatives in interesting individuals as well as industrial and other groups in the work, and the willingness of the department to prepare virtually any kind of correspondence course for which there was a demand. The demand was largely for utilitarian courses. In the period up to July 1, 1922, the number of registrations was 79,868. Of these 25,771 represented business courses and over 23,000, various engineering courses. Thus almost two thirds were in business and engineering. During the same time 6,542 people had registered for English, 1,000 or more for German, history, political science, and education, over 2,500 for Romance languages, 3,000 for economics, 5,700 for mathematics, and 2,700 for home economics.[73] Only 7 people had registered for courses in astronomy and 16 for bacteriology—the smallest registrations reported. During this period the courses were primarily taken for self-improvement rather than as work toward a university degree.

Another notable feature of the extension division consisted of preparing textbooks for the correspondence courses. Reber had pointed out in his first report that not only should the correspondence-study department have a faculty of its own but that it must have a staff to prepare textbooks.[74] This was worked out in the years that followed. Preparation of textbooks began during the next years. In 1913 a contract was made with the McGraw-Hill Book Company to publish business and engineering texts; and a year later Reber reported that three texts had already been published, that two more were

[72] Biennial Report of the Dean of the University Extension Division, 1930–32 (Bulletin of the University of Wisconsin, series number 1864, general series number 1648), 17.
[73] *Ibid.*, 1922 (series number 1268, general series number 1046), 7.
[74] Report of the University Extension Division, *Regents' Biennial Report,* 1907–08, p. 197.

in the hands of the printers, and that another four were nearly ready.[75] By 1914 twelve texts had been published, eleven by McGraw-Hill and one by Appleton. The texts were used not only by the University extension division; one or more, Reber claimed, were being used by at least thirty-six educational institutions. Fourteen university and college extension divisions had adopted the texts, and in addition numerous trade and technical schools were using some of the books.[76] Two years later a total of twenty-four texts were on the market, and some 87 colleges and universities as well as some 150 trade and technical schools were reported using one or more of them.[77] In 1922, ten years after the publication of correspondence course texts had been begun, the department reported thirty-one published and many more in preparation. Over a quarter of a million of these books had been sold, the royalties on which were paid to the extension division.[78] By 1917 the annual royalties amounted to over $2,000, and during the 1920–21 biennium they exceeded $13,000. By the fiscal year 1925–26, however, they had decreased to less than $6,000.[79] Over forty volumes were published in all, and royalties exceeded $100,000.[80]

The other extension departments enjoyed equally rapid growth—a growth often represented in the reports of the dean by dot maps showing the location of individuals and communities of Wisconsin served by the extension division. The department of debating and public discussion distributed almost two

[75] Biennial Report of the Dean of the University Extension Division, 1912 (Bulletin of the University of Wisconsin, series number 539, general series number 366), 73.

[76] Report of the University Extension Division, *Regents' Biennial Report,* 1913–14, pp. 171, 227–229.

[77] *Ibid.,* 1915–16, pp. 177–178.

[78] Biennial Report of the Dean of the University Extension Division, 1922 (Bulletin of the University of Wisconsin, series number 1268, general series number 1046), 11–12.

[79] *Report of the Business Manager,* 1917–18, p. 26; 1925–26, p. 21.

[80] *Louis Ehrhart Reber, Builder of University Extension,* 16. Hiring men to write texts was of course practiced by the private correspondence schools. Not much criticism of the practice by the extension division seems to have been made, although in 1920 Dean Slichter warned President Birge that the "La Follette bunch" was circulating stories about the exploitation of one instructor from the sale of whose texts the extension division collected royalties "equal or nearly equal to the instructor's salary." Slichter to Birge, March 15, 1920, Presidents' Papers. Later the regents arranged to share royalties with the authors.

thousand library packages in 1910–11, the number reaching five thousand five years later and almost ten thousand by 1919–20. It supplied innumerable calls for information from high school debating groups and others interested in public discussion.[81] Because it was self-consciously devoted to supplying factual material on living topics of the day, and could claim an active although impalpable contribution to adult education, this department of debating and public discussion was the darling of many of the reformers who saw it as a great agency of reform. The lecture department also showed great gains. It organized a summer Chautauqua and also lyceum courses.

The department of general information and welfare, which it will be recalled was conceived to be the division which would bring any useful knowledge to the people, performed a bewildering variety of functions. It produced a series of informational bulletins, the first to be published reflecting something of this catholic taste and sense of responsibility in their titles: *The Prevention and Cure of Tuberculosis* and *Frosts in Wisconsin.* It organized various institutes, the first of which was held at Milwaukee for bakers.[82] In 1909 a municipal reference bureau was established in this department to supply information to city officials and citizens, and a bureau of civic and social center development was established.[83] By 1910 the department had also assembled educational slides for circulation, prepared a milk exhibit, conducted a conference on criminal law, and established an institute of municipal and social service at Milwaukee.[84] During the next years the welfare institutes multiplied, and by 1914, besides the bureaus of municipal reference and of social and civic center development, bureaus of health and of community music had been established. The latter, directed by Peter W. Dykema, was one of the reasons for Governor Philipp's criticisms of the University a few years later.[85] Moreover the department, which two years before had merely collected and

---

[81] See Martin P. Anderson, A Study of Discussion in Selected Wisconsin Adult Organizations and Public Agencies, manuscript doctoral dissertation, 1947, in the Library of the University of Wisconsin.

[82] *Regents' Biennial Report,* 1907–08, p. 192.

[83] *Ibid.,* 1909–10, p. 243.

[84] *Ibid.,* 245–248.

[85] Interview, Curti and Carstensen with Dr. Joseph Evans, October 12, 1945.

distributed lantern slides, now contained a bureau of visual instruction which had begun the collection of motion-picture films. The University Press Bureau was assigned to the department in 1913.[86]

During the first World War, the department, like most of the others in extension, quickly turned to war work. The department of general information and welfare developed home service institutes and cooperated with the Red Cross in various training programs. The same years saw the development in the municipal reference bureau of a municipal and sanitary engineering service, the expansion of the bureau of community music to include drama, and the establishment of a bureau of postgraduate medical instruction in 1917 at the request of the State Medical Society.[87] After the war the extension division established a bureau of commercial and industrial relations, and in the reorganization which was carried through before the end of 1920, the department of general information and welfare became the department of group and community service. The department of lectures was incorporated into the new department.[88] After Reber retired in 1926 the department was renamed the department of public service. Most of the old bureaus remained in the new organization, which included bureaus of instruction, municipal information, recreation and community organization, community music, dramatic activities, economics and sociology, and business information.[89]

As long as Reber was dean, he claimed that the aims of the division were substantially the same as they had been since the beginning, but the changes in the department of general information and welfare suggest that many internal modifications had taken place. Moreover, a slight change of emphasis is discernible. The emphasis in the beginning was almost exclusively on utilitarian information. Although it could not be said that the extension division had abandoned this object, it was no longer concerned primarily with utilitarian activities. There were good reasons. As the extension division developed

[86] *Regents' Biennial Report,* 1913–14, pp. 196–200.
[87] *Ibid.,* 1917–18, pp. 203–216.
[88] *Ibid.,* 1919–20, pp. 130–146.   [89] *Ibid.,* 1927–28, p. 7.

it was natural that its activities would become more diverse. On the other hand, both the success and the stimulation of the extension division encouraged the creation of other agencies to take over some of the work begun by the division. With the adoption of the vocational education law of 1911, all cities of five thousand or more were required to establish vocational or continuation schools.[90] Likewise, industry soon began to institute training programs. With these agencies created, a part of the work of the extension division had been completed.

With a large segment of its first clientele provided for by the new educational agencies, the extension division developed more fully the courses offered for university credit. At the end of the period under study, provision was made for a permanent extension center in Milwaukee. That agency, while offering various adult and vocational courses, also developed many of the attributes of a junior college. In short, over the years, there was a perceptible movement in the class and course work from noncollegiate to collegiate work, and that movement has continued.

✐

MANY of the same forces which stimulated the revival of University Extension served also to stimulate the work of the College of Agriculture. It will be recalled that the farmers' institutes, established in 1885, were the first successful device developed by the college to reach large numbers of farmers. Under the first superintendent, William H. Morrison (1885–93), the pattern of the institutes was largely fixed; attention was placed principally on "practical" farm problems. The institute speakers included men from the College of Agriculture and successful local farmers. Little change was made in this system during the next thirty years. George A. McKerrow succeeded Morrison in 1893 and held the post until 1913. In 1891, partly to emphasize a relation with the University which to many people seemed tenuous, the office of the superintendent of the institutes was moved from the capitol to South Hall, then Agri-

[90] Patzer, *Public Education in Wisconsin,* 121, 207–210.

cultural Hall. About the only changes in the form of the institutes consisted in arranging local fairs in conjunction with the institutes, although making sure that the fair did not steal attention from the institute, and adding, in 1895, a cooking school to attract farmers' wives.

College officials thought that the institute workers were overzealous in keeping the discussion at the institutes turned toward practical matters. Dean Henry wanted more attention given to scientific discussion, but when, at the death of Morrison in 1893, he sought an institute leader who would be willing to develop the institutes along these lines, he encountered the opposition of the Dairymen's Association. These men wanted another practical farmer to lead the work. Russell likewise, when he became dean in 1907, sought to make changes but encountered opposition.[91]

The legislative appropriation for the work was increased from the original $5,000 a year granted in 1885 to $12,000 in 1887, and by twenty years later it had been increased to $20,000. The few attempts of politicians to decrease or abolish this annual grant failed.

The agricultural college extension work, however, was not wholly limited to the institutes. Experiment Station bulletins, which never reached great numbers of farmers, were published, and the various experiments were carried on at the request of interested groups. There was also the short course, instituted in 1885. After the turn of the century several new organizations were formed to extend the work of the college.

In 1901, under the leadership of Professor Ransom A. Moore, who had long directed the short course work, alumni and teachers of the College of Agriculture were organized into the Wisconsin Agricultural Experimental Association. Moore himself became secretary of the association and from that post exercised a controlling influence over the association for more than thirty years. The association began with the purpose of encouraging its members to conduct experiments with various types of seeds, in the control of plant diseases, and in testing

[91] Much material on the agriculture extension section was drawn from Wilbur H. Glover's manuscript, History of the College of Agriculture. Unless otherwise indicated all quoted material has been taken from Glover's manuscript.

new types of seeds and crops. Projects were also outlined on "livestock, soil, dairy records and horticulture." Although there was a small membership fee, in 1903 the legislature appropriated $1,000 for the work, primarily to cover the cost of printing the annual report. Two years later the amount was increased to $2,000, and in 1911 to $3,000. In 1928 it was increased to $5,000.

Although at first the membership was restricted to alumni of the agricultural college—mostly short-course boys—in 1908 the association established county units or orders open to others, and in 1921 membership in the organization was opened to all. In the meantime, ten years after the first county order had been established, fifty-five counties were organized.

The association was created in part to provide an agency which would afford the means of carrying on field tests and of providing accurate reports. Except for the seed work, however, it was relatively ineffective and became largely a means of disseminating information about new farm methods and practices. Its members, nevertheless, quickly became important seed producers and won a commanding position among the seed growers of the state. Under arrangements with the Experiment Station, members of the association obtained pedigreed seeds developed at the station and then enlarged and marketed the successful strains. "The association," wrote Wilbur H. Glover, "controlled the entire station output and offered it to its members at market prices of ordinary grains." This appears to have been a mutually satisfactory arrangement; the Experiment Station had an organization on which it could rely, and the members of the association, on the other hand, had a source of supply for their seed business. The association stimulated interest in and encouraged greater production of hay and grain, and within its membership grew up such specialized groups as the Alfalfa Order and the Hemp Order, devoted to the better propagation of alfalfa and hemp.

Besides the institutes and the experimental association, the college had established other lines of communication with farmers and farm groups. It encouraged dairy-testing associations, supported the hygiene laboratory, participated in the work of controlling bovine tuberculosis—a work in which Dean

Russell developed the dramatic tactic of slaughtering a "reactor" in the presence of farmers, opening the body, and showing evidence of the disease. Branch stations were established at Superior, Ashland, Iron River, and Ashland Junction between 1905 and 1912. And in 1904, a ten-day institute for experienced farmers was launched at Madison. One hundred and seventy-five farmers attended the first institute, and by 1910 the enrollment had passed one thousand and another institute had been organized for farmers' wives.

The revival of University Extension was a twofold stimulant to the College of Agriculture. On the one hand the University extension division sought and obtained wide and favorable publicity. Indeed, the publicity obtained by this division in 1907 almost overshadowed the rest of the University. In addition, the new director of the University extension division was something of an empire builder. He early showed signs of wanting to take over the extension work of the College of Agriculture. Within his first year at Madison he had brought the engineering and law colleges within his orbit. He intimated, in his first report, the necessity of making provision for agricultural education. How far Reber might have gone cannot, of course, be indicated, but it was clear that he stood ready to channel agricultural extension through his division if the opportunity offered. However, neither Dean Henry, who retired at the end of June, 1907, nor the new dean, Harry L. Russell, gave him that opportunity. An attempt to obtain $20,000 annually for agricultural extension failed in 1907.

In his first report as dean, Russell faced the question of extension service squarely. "The ever pressing problem in the development of our agricultural colleges is how to correlate the three main lines of agricultural effort, research, teaching at the college, and extension work throughout the state." The institution which had these three lines properly developed, he thought, would stand on the firmest basis. "No more important administrative question confronts us than the best possible arrangement whereby these three lines of work can be closely correlated."[92] Some colleges, Dean Russell declared, tried to meet the problem by providing separate staffs for research, instruc-

---

[92] *Regents' Biennial Report*, 1907–08, p. 123.

tion, and extension, a plan Russell opposed as tending "to destroy the solidarity of our agricultural work." Such division of function as had evolved, he said, was on a departmental rather than subcollege basis.[93] A year later, writing to the man who was to become the first secretary of the agricultural extension service, Russell declared: "My conception of the College of Agriculture in its full development is to have the institution rest on a three-legged foundation—research work of the Experiment Station, teaching work of the College here at Madison, and the extension work throughout the state. This position would be substantially the development of the extension side of the work, especially with reference to the extension teaching. The demonstration side of our teaching work will be, in the main, controlled by the respective departments, but even here much organization is needed to economize such work."[94]

The conception of "departmental solidarity" was the heart of Russell's plan of extension service. It had grown directly out of the experience of the college. Russell apparently was well satisfied with the decision, which had been reached only after careful and prolonged study. In 1916 he wrote G. D. Jones that the usual organization of extension "destroys departmental integrity to a marked degree. . . . Those colleges which have removed extension work from close contact with the departments . . . have in practically all cases introduced elements of friction."[95]

Russell did not want an administrative agency operating between the departments and the farmers or other groups to be served. The knowledge of the departmental experts was not going to be written down for the recipients except as the professors themselves should decide. In his determination that control of demonstration work remain within the departments, Russell differed fundamentally from Reber, who talked often about the "special" qualifications which were required for extension workers. Part of this difference could be found in the different objectives of the two extension services; but part of it reflected too a basic difference of attitude which no glosses could wholly conceal.

---

[93] *Ibid.*, 123–124.
[94] Harry L. Russell to K. L. Hatch, March 8, 1909. Quoted by Wilbur H. Glover. [95] Russell to G. D. Jones, April 8, 1916. Quoted by Glover.

Formal organization of the agricultural college extension services was made possible in 1909. The legislature, in response to the request of the dean, appropriated $30,000 annually for the work. Two years later the amount was increased to $40,000. Subsequently federal funds were also made available.

The first secretary, and later director, of the extension service was Kirk L. Hatch, who had called himself to the attention of Russell in 1907 or earlier by his work as principal of the Winnebago County Agricultural School at Winneconne. Hatch had approached Russell with a proposition that a farmers' short course, patterned after that at Madison, be held at the Winneconne school. He already had the promise of several professors from the College of Agriculture to help if Russell approved. Russell quickly fell in with the proposal. The farmers' course at Madison was already getting too big, and other states had been successful in holding courses at various centers away from their colleges. The short course was combined with the institute and was successfully carried off, with from 400 to 600 persons attending the various sessions. Because of Hatch's deep interest and the abundant evidence of his capability, Russell determined to make him head of the new service. One obstacle was that he had no college or university degree. At Russell's urging, he finished his work for a degree, his German requirement, incidentally, being completed by correspondence courses from the University extension division. In 1909 he was made assistant professor and secretary of the agricultural extension service. Four years later he was a full professor with the title of director of the extension service.

The agricultural college extension service, once formally established, expanded rapidly. As stated by Dean Russell, its object was to introduce the methods used by progressive farmers, or even better methods, into the "actual practice of the whole community." Research and propaganda work, he declared, could not be carried on successfully by the same staff, yet the most effective way of teaching the farmer how a thing should be done was to show him.[96] Thus the extension service was organized along two lines: demonstration work, which was done under

[96] Report of the Dean of the College of Agriculture, *Regents' Biennial Report*, 1909-10, p. 166.

the direction of the respective departments, and extension courses, which were given in cooperation with the county agricultural schools and elsewhere. Russell was able to list twelve departments in 1910 that were working directly with the farmers, and a number of other extension projects. By 1910 the ten-day farmers' course at the University had an enrollment of 1,125 representing 59 counties of the state. Moreover, some 400 women representing 32 counties also attended courses at the University. A number of similar one-week courses had been held in conjunction with the county agricultural schools. The college had also established a weekly press service intended to reach all the newspapers of the state and the agricultural journals as well.[97]

But the most effective link in the extension service had not yet been forged. This was the county agricultural representative or county agent. This position, already partly developed elsewhere,[98] may have been suggested too by the University extension organization. Reber, it will be recalled, had decided that the state must be divided into districts, with each district being placed under a representative of the University extension division. Reber planned to cover the state with eleven districts, only seven of which were organized before 1925, but Hatch and Russell proposed one representative in each county. The first county agricultural representative was appointed in Oneida County, February 12, 1912. Dean Russell declared, "A new and a most important kind of extension endeavor which has been inaugurated this past year is the establishment of a resident representative of the College in a county to give direct field instruction to adults in the summer, and courses of instruction to young people in winter. The representative gives a course in agriculture in the county training school for the training of

[97] *Ibid.*, 167–170.
[98] The county farm agent system had already become well established in the South by 1912 through the joint action of the Department of Agriculture and the General Education Board. The demonstration work of Seaman Knapp had attracted attention of the General Board. That agency in 1906 made an agreement with the Department of Agriculture under which Rockefeller funds were used to supplement United States Department of Agriculture funds in maintaining farm agents. The Department of Agriculture funds were available only in cotton-weevil-infected areas. Joseph C. Bailey, *Seaman A. Knapp* (New York, 1945), 215–243.

rural teachers, . . . organizes a boys' short course and a farmers' course in the winter, while the crop growing season is spent in the field carrying on practical test work and aiding the farmers in meeting their daily problems." By July the system was in operation in three counties. The University paid one half of the agent's salary; the county paid the rest and bore the other expenses.[99] Dean Russell looked forward to the rapid expansion of the system. He reported that already requests were on file from a dozen counties asking for such representatives.

Although the state superintendent of public instruction, perhaps only from habit, objected to a county agent's participating in the teacher-training program, the system of the county agricultural representatives was rapidly adopted. In 1913 the legislature passed a law specifically authorizing county boards of supervisors to establish and maintain such agents. The duties of the agents, as outlined in the law, were largely those described by Russell in his report of 1912, although the law provided that "it shall be his duty to keep in touch with all agencies in the state and elsewhere that will enable him to utilize the most improved knowledge in the furtherance of his work." The county must provide at least one thousand dollars a year toward the salary and provide for other expenses. The University was to contribute one thousand dollars a year. Appointments were to be made by the dean of the College of Agriculture upon the authorized request of the appropriate county official. The number of such representatives was limited to ten for the fiscal year of 1914 and to sixteen the next year; and the law appropriated funds sufficient to cover the University's portion of the expenses.[100]

In 1914 Congress passed the Smith-Lever Act under which the agricultural college received $10,000 for agricultural extension work, the sum to be increased through the years with matching funds from the state. With these and other funds one

[99] *Regents' Biennial Report,* 1911–12, pp. 111–112.
[100] *Laws of Wisconsin,* 1913, pp. 763–765. Giving the dean of the college authority to make appointments was undoubtedly in conflict with other laws giving sole power of appointment of University officers to the regents, but no difficulty seems to have resulted. Subsequently, however, appointment of county agents became a function of the regents, although the actual selection was made by the county boards and passed by the dean. Although various groups sought

more step was taken to round out the system—the development of extension specialists. The extension specialist was an expert in the work of one department, and his principal task was to keep the county representatives in touch with the work of his department.

The improvement of highways and the adoption of automobiles by the county agents as well as the greater effectiveness of demonstration and consulting work brought an end to the formal teaching activities of the county agents. Farm visits and field demonstrations became their primary tools.

Thus there had emerged, in the years from 1907 to 1915, an agricultural college extension service which, although often described as part of the University extension division, was in reality a separate agency. It differed fundamentally from University Extension. Agricultural extension was largely operated without collecting fees from those who received the benefit— much to the distress of Dean Reber—while the University Extension was more and more required to carry a larger part of its own cost. The agricultural college extension service was not involved in giving credit courses. It was simply an agency designed to provide the farmers with information about the best methods of farming. The lines of communication proceeded directly from the college to the farmer.

In the main the University extension service and the agricultural college extension service managed to work along somewhat parallel lines without conflict. Some difficulty was experienced early in 1912 over the control of the home economics extension work. The department was located in the agricultural college, but the University extension division had instituted correspondence and lecture courses in the subject. Russell objected, but no great crisis developed. Later the same year a rather more serious difficulty arose over lecturers and lecture fees. The agricultural extension service had adopted the policy of having the professors give extension lectures as part of their regular university duties. The extension division asked to have

to provide private funds for the county representative, this movement was opposed by Russell and Hatch in almost every case. The agents were made assistant professors in the college faculty to maintain departmental solidarity, although Russell was careful about using the title away from the University.

members of the agricultural faculty lecture for the standard fee of twenty dollars, but because the college was so pressed with its own calls for lecturers, the request was refused. However, John J. Pettijohn, then in charge of the lecture department, made independent arrangements with the professors of the agricultural college. Russell protested. Called upon to explain, Pettijohn retorted that the agricultural college had been uncooperative, and that he felt the agricultural extension lectures should be administered through his office. He protested that his office received many calls for agricultural lectures which could not be filled. Moreover, because the agricultural college made no charge for its lectures, he complained that it was "exceedingly difficult" for the extension division to promote its work on a fee basis. Russell then called for an administrative ruling or a decision by the regents on both points: should the men of the agricultural college be permitted to receive pay for lectures, something then against college policy, and under whose auspices should the lectures on agriculture be given?[101] Van Hise agreed to place the matter before the regents. This he did at the December meeting. The regents held that the extension division was not to use any of the agricultural staff for lecture programs.[102] Russell could chalk up a victory.

The next year however the situation was reversed. The regents turned the University Press Bureau over to the extension division in 1913.[103] Although Reber felt that all University publicity material should go out under its auspices, the agricultural college was sending its material out under a government frank. Van Hise in this case decided for Reber. In a letter addressed to both Russell and Reber he declared that all University publicity must go through the Press Bureau. The agricultural material, however, was to be prepared by the agricultural college editor and distinguished from the rest so that it could be later distributed by the agricultural college. "The working out of the above plan will require close cooperation of Mr. Holman

[101] Russell to Van Hise, October 1, 1912; J. J. Pettijohn to Reber, October 23, 1912; Russell to Van Hise, November 21, 1912; Van Hise to Russell, November 27, 1912, all in the Presidents' Papers.
[102] Van Hise to Reber and Russell, December 16, 1912, Presidents' Papers.
[103] Reber to Van Hise, October 4, 1913, Presidents' Papers.

and Mr. Hopkins . . . and this the University has the right to expect." [104]

When the extension division launched its community institutes there was more difficulty. Van Hise attempted to arrange a compromise by writing to Russell. "As you may know, it is my opinion that there should be a close cooperation between agriculture and extension. In some of the institutes it seems to me it is advantageous to include agricultural subjects. It may be that in the purely extension work of the College of Agriculture also it would be well to include social and other subjects which could be provided by the extension division." [105] But Russell was not satisfied. He felt that the community institutes of the University extension division often dealt incompetently with subjects which should be left in the hands of the agricultural college extension service. Accordingly he carried a protest to the Board of Regents. As a result the Board directed its committees on extension and on the agricultural college to meet and determine a policy. The committees reported a resolution on March 2, 1915, which was unanimously adopted by the Board. In the resolution the Board directed the University extension division to limit the subjects considered at the community institutes to "municipal activities" and the agricultural college to problems of "agriculture and rural life." The conflict over control of home economics was resolved temporarily by directing the two agencies to coordinate the work. The regents, the resolution concluded, "desire and expect" cordial cooperation between the departments. [106] While the Board decision did not end this conflict, it did serve to clarify the basis of disagreement.

✑

THE various extramural activities of the University—the governmental work of professors, the extension work of the agricultural college, and the University extension division—all contributed to the attainment of Van Hise's ideal of service to the

[104] Van Hise to Reber and Russell, November 11, 1913, Presidents' Papers.
[105] Van Hise to Russell, October 16, 1914, quoted by Glover.
[106] Papers of the Board of Regents, March 2, 1915.

state. Collectively and singly they were the most widely publi- · cized of the threefold functions of the University. The frank dedication of the University to service, and the lines which this service took, found wide support and enthusiastic—although not always well-informed—acclaim throughout the nation. Both in Wisconsin and in the nation at large the times were propitious. In 1900 the progressive wing of the Republican Party had come to power in Wisconsin under the leadership of Robert M. La Follette. In the years that followed Wisconsin enjoyed a reform movement while throughout the nation various groups and individuals sought to make government more responsive to the will of the people, to bring the growing industrial and financial associations under control of government, and to correct or at least ameliorate the conditions of the impoverished industrial workers in the slums which were a part of each industrial city.

For the reformers the first step consisted in spreading information among the people. For them, as for many others, knowledge and virtue were indivisible. Given knowledge the people would be virtuous and would want to do the right thing. The way to correct evils was to expose them. Thus the muckrakers insisted upon reporting the facts about conditions in the slums and factories; the workings of state and municipal political machines; the patent-medicine, meat-packing, and other industries; the operations of the financiers; and even the conduct of the United States Senate itself. Because the muckrakers and reformers were so deeply concerned with the exposure of wrong-doing and with the dissemination of knowledge, it is not to be wondered at that they came quickly to regard the University of Wisconsin as an institution which supported reform. La Follette himself sponsored that view.[107]

The doctrine of service preached by Van Hise was extolled, and the extension division became the darling of the reformers; its work became an object of interest throughout the nation. Thus in 1907 William Hard, in an article in the *Outlook* entitled "A University in Public Life," described how the University faculty served the state. But the University was not in politics: it simply furnished facts. "The University of Wisconsin

[107] *La Follette's Autobiography*, pp. 28–29.

has become a kind of 'consulting engineer' in the public life of the state of Wisconsin."[108] Other reporters, both with and without the encouragement of University officials, produced articles for magazines of national circulation. In 1908 Lincoln Steffens prepared an article which appeared in the *American Magazine*. The regents, forewarned, agreed to buy five hundred copies.[109] Although the article could not have pleased all of the regents with its slurring reference to the "Tory Regents," it was marked by unreserved enthusiasm for the work being done. "Sending a State to College" was largely concerned with agricultural and University extension work. Steffens observed that most of this work was utilitarian at present; but "Madison is using the conscious demand for 'utilitarian' instruction, to develop the unconscious demand that exists in the American people today for light."[110] He looked to the time when the University would "distribute scientific knowledge and the clear truth in plain terms to all the people for their self-cultivation and daily use."[111] Steffens, like many other reporters who came to Madison briefly, assumed that the Legislative Reference Library was a part of the University. This institution, he declared, was "the most remarkable example of state service by the University."[112] "In Wisconsin the University," he concluded, "is as close to the intelligent farmer as his pig-pen or his tool-house; the university laboratories are part of the alert manufacturer's plant; to the worker, the university is drawing nearer than the school around the corner and is as much his as his union is his or his favorite saloon. Creeping into the minds of the children with pure seed, into the debate of youth with pure facts, into the opinions of voters with impersonal, expert knowledge, the state university is coming to be a part of the citizen's own mind, just as the state is becoming a part of his will. And that's what this whole story means: the University of Wisconsin is a highly conscious lobe of the common community's mind of the state of the people of Wisconsin."[113]

Charles Johnston, writing in *Harper's Weekly* the next

---

[108] *The Outlook,* 86: 667 (July 21, 1907).
[109] Records of the Board of Regents, G:233, December 16, 1908.
[110] *American Magazine,* 67:361 (February, 1909).
[111] *Ibid.,* 362–363.   [112] *Ibid.,* 364.   [113] *Ibid.*

month under the arresting title "Tutoring Lawmakers: How the State University of Wisconsin Has Established a Working Alliance with the Legislature," repeated Steffens' mistake by describing the Legislative Reference Library as an agency of the University.[114]

A year later Edwin E. Slosson gave an enthusiastic report on the University.[115] It was impossible, he declared, to determine the size and location of the University of Wisconsin. "The most that one can say is that the headquarters of the institution is at the city of Madison and that the campus has an area of about 56,000 square miles."[116] He found the University influence almost universal and like Steffens found it to the good. "Under the influence of university men, Wisconsin has become the recognized leader in progressive and practical legislation, the New Zealand of the United States."[117] Like Steffens, too, he was impressed with the great declaration of academic freedom written by the Board at the time of the Ely trial and found that this declaration accounted "in large part" for the "prosperity and repute" of the school of economics.[118]

In the next years other articles, sometimes accurate in detail, emphasizing the work of the University and the extension division appeared in magazines of national circulation. Thus in 1912 an article appeared in *Review of Reviews* entitled "A University that goes to the People."[119] The next year the *Outlook* published an article by F. B. Morrison on "How a University Honors Farmers";[120] and the *World's Work* published Frank Parker Stockbridge's "A University that Runs a State";[121] and the *Independent* published an editorial on the "State Wide Forum in Wisconsin" explaining that the reason why so many new political ideas originated or were put into effect in Wisconsin was that the University had organized the whole state into a forum for the discussion of public affairs.[122] In these and many other articles, it was the work of the extension division,

[114] *Harper's Weekly*, 53:15 (March 27, 1909).
[115] Edwin E. Slosson, *Great American Universities* (New York, 1910), 210–244.
[116] *Ibid.*, 210.   [117] *Ibid.*, 215.   [118] *Ibid.*, 220–222.
[119] March Burchard Orvis, *The American Review of Reviews*, 45:457–465 (April, 1912).   [120] *The Outlook*, 103:146–147 (January 18, 1913).
[121] *World's Work*, 25:699–708 (April, 1913).
[122] The *Independent*, 76:245 (November 6, 1913).

or at least its stated objectives, that won most attention. In the work of the division, many thought they saw beyond courses in sanitary sewage, highway construction, and shop mathematics the promise of a new, completely informed America.

The state and national publicity given to these developments at Wisconsin naturally stimulated interest on the part of other institutions, whose representatives were welcomed at the University and whose visits were well advertised by the University Press Bulletin. Thus in 1908 when a party from Arkansas visited the University the visit was proudly reported by the Press Bulletin, as was a visit in 1911 of a representative from Queensland University. "The power of an idea is measured by its ability to beget itself," the Press Bulletin remarked. "The Wisconsin idea has the appearance of being prolific, for not only has nearly every State University in the United States followed Wisconsin's new extension policies, but now comes Australia under the influence of the Wisconsin spirit."[123] Other visiting delegations came and perhaps learned, and their visits were duly reported. None, however, won such attention as the Philadelphia Pilgrimage of 1913. The pilgrimage included the newly elected "reform" mayor, the city council, the superintendent of schools, college presidents, and a hundred or so educators, social workers, clubwomen, manufacturers, and businessmen. They matriculated as students in the extension division for four days.[124]

There is little doubt that Van Hise, Reber, and others encouraged this extensive and enthusiastic publicity, and that it helped in the legislature when funds were needed. The extension division with its field service and its relations with numerous groups, encouraged these groups to urge the legislature to appropriate funds. Thus in May, 1908, Van Hise, Reber, and Frederick W. MacKenzie gave addresses at the meeting of the Milwaukee Merchants and Manufacturers Association on the advantages of the extension program.[125] Less than a year later

---

[123] Copies of the University Press Bulletin are to be found in the Presidents' Papers.

[124] James S. Hiatt, "The Philadelphia Pilgrimage and the Wisconsin Idea." Reprinted from *The American School Board Journal* (July, 1913).

[125] The *Merchants and Manufacturers Association of Milwaukee Bulletin*, May, 1908.

the association reciprocated by sending out an appeal to all manufacturers of the state urging support of an appropriation of $150,000 by the legislature for extension work.[126]

These methods did not differ greatly from those used by University officials and the College of Agriculture in soliciting support, but some of the regents, notably G. D. Jones, opposed such activities, partly perhaps because of lack of sympathy for the division. In 1911 Jones wrote to Van Hise about the appropriations saying that he was "at sea in regard to the appropriations for University Extension."[127] Two months later he declared, "I find that even among our friends there is considerable criticism of what they consider the fictitious demand, apparently coming spontaneously, from various parts of the state, for an increase in the appropriation for general university extension work. Of course I sincerely believe this method of calling on parties from various parts of the state as though the demand were spontaneous and pressing is a mistake, and that we should more and more confine our attention to the regular University appropriation measures which are sanctioned by the Regents."[128]

The large claims made about the effectiveness of the extension department and some of the other public services of the University also caused resentment. The article by Stockbridge, for example, entitled "A University that Runs a State" suggested that virtually all that was good in Wisconsin came out of the University. Such articles, and articles like Steffens', picturing University students teaching businessmen how to run their businesses, drew acid comments not only from those who were out of sympathy with the progressive program and objectives, but from those who did not fancy being presented to the world as having to learn how to manage their affairs from University sophomores. Moreover, some came to doubt the value of the work of the extension division. Thus in 1914 T. J. Neacy, a prominent Milwaukee businessman, already widely known as "Injunction Tom," denounced the increasing appropriations for the extension division. The situation had reached the point,

---

[126] *Wisconsin Alumni Magazine*, 10:199–200 (February, 1909).
[127] G. D. Jones to Van Hise, January 27, 1911, Presidents' Papers.
[128] *Ibid.*, March 28, 1911, Presidents' Papers.

he declared, where anyone who criticized the administration of the University was accused of possessing ulterior motives. Neacy wrote, "On that score I can say that the dean of the extension division knows absolutely that no one for many years could be more loyal to the extension division or give more fully of his time and money to boost that department than I, and that I only quit in despair after a careful investigation of that institution in 1911 and 1912 had proved that it had nothing to show in return for the vast sums it had cost."[129]

There were other doubts, too. In 1915 G. D. Jones wrote to Van Hise to get assurances that Senator La Follette, who had appeared on earlier programs, would not be permitted to speak on the University extension Chautauqua programs again. Van Hise pointed out that the matter was under the jurisdiction of C. P. Cary, the regents' one-man committee on extension.[130] Cary meanwhile had informed Reber that the University facilities were to be used only by those officially connected with the University Chautauqua programs.[131] There were other objections. Lynn S. Pease protested against the "frivolity" of lyceum programs in letters to Reber and Van Hise.[132] Governor Philipp was critical too, largely because he felt that some of the people engaged in the work were not competent.[133]

Among the regents Jones was the most persistent critic. In 1915 he complained to Dean Birge about the method of appointments and promotions and the failure of the extension division to maintain standards as high as those that prevailed on the University faculty.[134] Birge tried to mollify Jones by pointing out that the extension work was definitely "an academic 'sideline.' " Any man who entered and stayed in was

[129] *Milwaukee Free Press*, June 22, 1914.
[130] Jones to Van Hise, March 13, 1915; and Van Hise to Jones, March 15, 1915, both in the Presidents' Papers.
[131] Cary to Reber, March 13, 1945, copy in the Presidents' Papers.
[132] Lynn S. Pease to Reber and Van Hise, 1913–14 *passim*, Presidents' Papers.
[133] Interview, Curti and Carstensen with Dr. Joseph Evans, October 12, 1945.
[134] Jones to Birge, August 27, 31, 1915; Birge to Jones, August 30, 1915, September 2, 1915. In his letter of August 31, Jones told Birge, "Promotions in all of the colleges are carefully worked out and the honor and credit of the university somewhat carefully safeguarded. This is not true in the university extension department. . . . I question whether we should have any man directly connected with the instructional side of this department of a rank higher than instructor. At our last meeting I think for the first time in my attendance at a

almost bound to forfeit academic promotion. Jones also complained to Dean Russell about incompetent extension workers: "I think there is a somewhat growing tendency of dissatisfaction as to the general working out of the University extension plan under Dean Reber's department, and I think this has come about largely from the employment of incompetent people by the extension department. The political science people naturally dislike to be charged with the responsibility for work of poorly equipped men, yet as it goes out under university auspices they know they are likely to be held responsible for it. The agricultural department similarly objects to the same thing as relating to it, and so on all the way around." He complained about Reber's liking for "the bombastic and braggadocio style of things."[135] A year later Jones wrote Van Hise that very little had been received "for much of the money we have spent on extension. It has been a new thing. It has been largely organized and operated on very thin material, wind and water have had too much to do with it in my opinion."[136]

But the opposition to the extension division was, as we have seen, less powerful than the support. Each successive year saw further expansion of that department. If the proponents of University Extension and the ideal of service to the state often claimed more than the record would support, the fact still remains that during the Van Hise administration the University of Wisconsin had found the means of vastly extending the area of its influence. It enjoyed the flattery of widespread imitation. If the influence of the University, particularly in the fields of social and political behavior, was neither as large nor as lasting as many enthusiasts claimed and predicted, the University under the banner of "service to the state" did occupy new areas, and it had indeed found concrete means of being of service to the state.

regents' meeting I lost my temper in dealing with this department. This is confidential."

[135] Jones to Russell, April 5, 1916. Quoted by Glover.
[136] Jones to Van Hise, May 7, 1917, Presidents' Papers.

Postscript

HE student, after he has completed his study of a
period or an institution, cannot isolate with complete
precision those elements which have been basic in the
process he has been studying. The factors and forces in operation in the creation of a university are often difficult to identify
and to evaluate with exactness. Nevertheless, after having carefully examined the founding and development of the University
of Wisconsin, and having tried to understand the factors and
the forces which contributed to giving this institution leadership among the state universities of the country, particularly
during the first two decades of the twentieth century, we have
been tempted to speculate upon the elements that gave Wisconsin the primacy that it enjoyed.

Four elements, certainly, were of large and perhaps pivotal
importance in shaping the institution: men, money, freedom,
and leadership. Take any of these away for the period from
1875 to 1915 and the story of Wisconsin would not have been
the story we have tried to tell. The first of these is, of course,
perfectly clear. Wisconsin, either by accident or design, attracted distinguished men to the University. More than that,
having attracted promising men, Wisconsin was during this
period able to hold them—an achievement which reflects enduring credit on regents and presidents alike. To attract these men,
Wisconsin by the middle 1890's was able to compete with such
institutions as Harvard, Chicago, and Stanford. To hold them

595

the University could and did offer freedom for research and
expression. E. E. Slosson, after visiting the University of Wisconsin in 1909, felt that the great declaration of academic freedom of 1894 and the adherence of the University to the spirit
as well as the letter of that declaration went a long way toward
explaining the greatness of the University. The sentiments
of this declaration beyond doubt contributed to the effectiveness of the Wisconsin Idea. Men officially encouraged in "fearless sifting and winnowing" could and did speak out; they
could and did contribute to better government, to improved
agriculture, and to more efficient industry.

The last factor, leadership, is the most elusive and the most
important. In our American state universities leadership must
come from or through the president. Although it is probably
true that no president by himself ever succeeded in making a
university great, it is doubtful whether any state university became great without a great president, and many an institution
has been reduced to second place or lower through the efforts
or mistakes of a president. The office is one in which decisions
of high importance are made or avoided; and the decisions of
the presidents, like the sins of the fathers, may be visited unto
the third and fourth generations.

Any review of the history of the University must notice that
preceding the great days of the Van Hise presidency there had
been three purposeful, forceful, and on the whole, successful
presidents. Bascom gave the institution standing and a sense
of high purpose; Chamberlin opened new and wider vistas of
learning; and Adams assiduously cultivated in the regents, the
legislature, and the state a larger understanding and deeper
appreciation of the University. At the very center of the great
faculty that served under Van Hise were men trained by
Bascom or appointed by Chamberlin and Adams. There is
no substitute for distinguished leadership and no question but
that an institution begins to falter when its leadership falters.

These elements, then, good men, sufficient funds, freedom
in research and teaching, and able leadership have been basic
in the emergence of Wisconsin as a leading state university.

Bibliographical Note

ALL the materials used in the preparation of these volumes have been cited in footnotes, but it has seemed advisable to append a brief description of the principal source materials. The University's records, on which a large part of the account rests, are abundant though as yet uncentralized. Many are still uncared for. Some, as indicated below, have been lost or destroyed; others are damaged.

The basic regents' records consist of a series of large volumes containing the official minutes of the meetings, a second series of volumes containing reports to the regents, a third containing the minutes of the executive committee, and a large miscellaneous collection containing papers of the Board of Regents. The official minutes have been kept from October, 1848, to the present. The volumes of reports to the regents contain those reports made to the Board by the president of the University, by members of the faculty, and by those regents' committees which the secretary of the Board considered of sufficient importance to copy into the permanent record. Some of these reports were subsequently printed in the annual or biennial reports of the regents. The collection designated Papers of the Board of Regents consists of all communications presented to the Board at its regular meetings; thus the Papers often but not always include documents which were later copied into the Reports volumes. These papers are unorganized up to 1868; thereafter the researcher will find one or more packets of papers for each regular meeting. Besides these manuscript materials, there are the published reports of the regents. From 1849 to 1921 the regents submitted reports to the governor for transmission to the legislature. From 1849 to 1883 the report was submitted annually; thereafter, until 1921, it was submitted biennially. Since 1921 no such report has been published, although the law still requires that the regents submit biennially an accounting of their stewardship. The report of the business manager, containing a statement of receipts and expenditures, has, perhaps, come to stand for the regents' report. In 1938 this was supplemented by a report from President Dykstra, an innovation which has been continued by President Fred.

Minutes of faculty meetings begin in 1850 and the record, with a few conspicuous gaps, has been maintained continuously. After 1886 the skeleton minutes are supplemented by a more or less continuous file of faculty documents made up principally of reports of faculty committees. Almost all the petitions, letters, and other communications received by the faculty have been lost or destroyed. In 1889 legal provision was made to establish the Colleges of Letters and Science, Agriculture, Engineering, and Law. The first full-time dean of the law school was appointed in 1889. Deans were appointed for the College of Letters and Science and the College of Agriculture in 1891, and for the College of Engineering in 1899. Little effort was made before the end of the century to distinguish between the records of the faculty of the College of Letters and Science and of the general University faculty. In the professional schools, however, separate faculty minutes begin in the 1890's. These records, although far from detailed, contain the major decisions of the respective faculties. The papers of the deans of the respective colleges are not complete; in no instance have they been carefully and completely preserved. The material available in the files of the agricultural college has been described in more extended form by Wilbur H. Glover in his manuscript, History of the College of Agriculture.

Departmental files have suffered in much the same way. Few departments have preserved their own records. The papers of the first University Extension Division (1891–1900) have been almost entirely lost, and most of the records of the extension division under Dean Reber (1907–26) are lost or destroyed.

The records of the president's office have also suffered from careless handling, wastepaper collection campaigns, and the other hazards to which neglected records are subject. The papers of the president's office before 1887 have been lost or destroyed. Fortunately the Henry Barnard papers have been preserved at New York University and were available to us. Scattered papers of presidents before Chamberlin were found in other collections, notably among the papers of the Board of Regents. Since 1887 the presidents' papers have been preserved although they are neither complete nor orderly. From 1887 until the end of the century copies of outgoing letters are preserved in press letter books and a fairly representative collection of incoming letters is preserved in files arranged in approximately alphabetical and chronological order. With the Van Hise administration, beginning in 1903, office procedure seems to have improved a little. The extant records are more abundant and are arranged in files roughly on a basis of school or fiscal years. Separate files containing legislative material were also established.

The University Catalogues constitute probably the most useful printed institutional record and rank in importance with the regents' reports, the regents' records, and the faculty minutes. The Catalogue for several years was printed as a supplement or appendix to the regents' reports. Not only does this record contain a host of details about the number of students, the required courses, the rules and regulations of the institution, but it has frequently provided a place in which the president could and did discuss educational philosophy.

The material on student life and activities includes the records of the student literary societies, the earliest of which began in 1850, the student newspapers, and the annual, first published in 1884. Several student diaries, referred to in the footnotes, and collections of student letters have also been useful.

Various official state documents also contain extensive materials relating to the University. The most important are the messages of the successive governors, the journals of the Assembly and the Senate, the session laws, and the periodic reports of the superintendents of public instruction. Newspaper files, particularly those of Madison and Milwaukee papers, have been valuable in supplementing both the official state publications and many of the University records.

The papers of former students of the University, faculty members, regents, and state officials, preserved in the manuscript room of the State Historical Society, are a valuable source of information. While specific reference has been made in the footnotes to each collection used, the most important of these deserve to be listed here. The papers of Governors Washburn, Davidson, McGovern, Philipp, and Blaine were useful, especially those of Governor Philipp. Unfortunately the La Follette papers, which might have yielded much information, were not open. Among other collections are the papers of John Catlin, Obadiah M. Conover, Horace A. Tenney, Jerome R. Brigham, Isaac N. Stewart, George H. Paul, Elisha W. Keyes, Samuel Fallows, John J. Orton, William F. Vilas, John M. Olin, William F. Allen, Richard T. Ely, Frederick Jackson Turner, Charles Kendall Adams, Edward Kremers, Charles McCarthy, Charles R. Van Hise, and Lyman C. Draper. Of these the Paul and Keyes collections were perhaps the most useful. George H. Paul was influential in Democratic politics. He was an informed, intelligent, and articulate member of the Board of Regents from 1874 to 1877 and from 1879 to his death in 1890. Elisha W. Keyes was prominent in Republican circles from the Civil War to the end of the century; from the 1870's on he was often referred to as "Boss" Keyes. He carried on a wide correspondence and his papers remained intact after his death. Keyes was a member of the Board of Regents from 1877 to 1889, but before, during, and after his service on the Board he kept himself informed about what was going on within the University.

Miscellaneous materials include the commencement annuals, which for a number of years contained all or nearly all of the addresses delivered during commencement week, the published addresses of the chancellor or president and members of the faculty, and the published reminiscences of men who had been associated with the University. Of special interest in this group are the following: John Bascom, *Things Learned by Living* (New York, 1913); *Life Story of Rasmus B. Anderson, written by himself with assistance of Albert O. Barton* (Madison, 1915); *Autobiography of Roujet D. Marshall,* edited by Gilson G. Glasier (2 vols., Madison, 1923, 1931); Burr W. Jones, *Reminiscences of Nine Decades* (Evansville, Wisconsin, 1937); John R. Commons, *Myself* (New York, 1934); Richard T. Ely, *Ground Under our Feet: an Autobiography* (New York, 1938); Edward Alsworth Ross, *Seventy Years of it: an Autobiography* (New York, 1936).

Mention should also be made of earlier histories of the University. Each of these to a certain extent may be considered a source since the author in each case was either a participant in or an observer of a part of the story he wrote: Stephen H. Carpenter, *An Historical Sketch of the University of Wisconsin from 1849 to 1876* (Madison, 1876); Consul Willshire Butterfield, *History of the University of Wisconsin* (Madison, 1879); William F. Allen and David Spencer, *Higher Education in Wisconsin* (Bureau of Education Circular of Information No. 1, 1889, Contribution to American Educational History No. 9, Washington, 1889); Reuben Gold Thwaites, *The University of Wisconsin, Its History and its Alumni* (Madison, 1900); James F. A. Pyre, *Wisconsin* (New York, 1920); and *The University of Wisconsin, Its History and its Presidents* (Madison, 1940–43) published in the *Wisconsin Alumnus,* contributed by various authors.

SOURCES OF INCOME OF . THE UNIVERSITY

1849-1949

SOURCES OF FINANCIAL SUPPOR⌐

Date	State Appropriation			Student Receipts[1]	Federal Government	Univ. & Agr Col. Income
	Operation	New Buildings	Total			

GROSS RECEIPTS

Date	Operation	New Buildings	Total	Student Receipts[1]	Federal Government	Univ. & Agr Col. Income
1850⁵		22,537.56	22,537.56	539.50		300.0⌐
1850–51⁶		2,462.44	2,462.44	629.67		
1852				1,063.21		650.0⌐
1853				923.48		3,255.2⌐
1854		12,735.33	12,735.33	643.58		6,800.0⌐
1855		2,264.67	2,264.67	946.60		12,404.1⌐
1856		1,675.00	1,675.00	1,675.25		9,923.9⌐
1857⁷			1,328.75			21,481.0⌐
1857–58		12,807.00	12,807.00	2,003.50		19,750.0⌐
1858–59		16,200.00	16,200.00	1,884.50		20,389.2⌐
1859–60		8,400.00	8,400.00	1,437.43		17,758.0⌐
1860–61		6,300.00	6,300.00	1,516.10		16,921.7⌐
1861–62						12,100.0⌐
1862–63						14,851.7⌐
1863–64						8,549.0⌐
1864–65						12,485.9⌐
1865–66				455.54		17,315.5⌐
1866–67				4,853.38		15,888.4⌐
1867–68	7,303.76		7,303.76	6,357.17		15,775.3⌐
1868–69	7,303.76		7,303.76	8,146.23		15,801.3⌐
1869–70	7,303.76	10,000.00	17,303.76	7,490.00		22,380.9⌐
1870–71	7,303.76	40,000.00	47,303.76	7,110.16		26,251.8⌐
1871–72	17,303.76		17,303.76	8,299.68		27,508.9⌐
1872–73	17,303.76		17,303.76	9,575.00		26,665.6⌐
1873–74	17,303.76		17,303.76	9,031.70		34,173.5⌐
1874–75	17,303.76	7,000.00	24,303.76	8,297.26		31,551.8⌐
1875–76	17,303.76	48,000.00	65,303.76	5,785.22		28,836.6⌐
1876–77	42,359.62	25,000.00	67,359.62	5,632.83		34,448.1⌐
1877–78	42,359.62		42,359.62	3,291.80		32,388.3⌐
1878–79	41,310.30		41,310.30	4,453.18		30,307.1⌐
1879–80	43,897.18		43,897.18	5,059.01		29,203.1⌐
1880–81	44,558.27		44,558.27	5,898.02		29,645.3⌐
1881–82	44,780.50	12,804.40	57,584.90	7,281.98		30,669.4⌐
1882–83	45,632.51		45,632.51	6,295.62		31,302.3⌐
1883–84	57,442.52	1,009.48	58,452.00	8,152.35		30,862.5⌐
1884–85	59,938.40	100,686.12	160,624.52	8,292.72		28,879.0⌐
1885–86	66,224.83	90,000.00	156,224.83	10,845.81		28,981.8⌐
1886–87	75,918.01	107,636.45	183,554.46	11,173.92		27,840.9⌐
1887–88	92,316.39	58,791.46	151,107.85	14,418.94	15,000.00	27,687.5⌐
1888–89	104,420.60	5,000.00	109,420.60	17,872.02	15,000.00	28,559.1⌐
1889–90	112,570.04		112,570.04	19,460.21	18,750.00	27,456.6⌐
1890–91	103,609.74		103,609.74	21,596.87	63,000.00	31,972.5⌐
1891–92	105,397.47	62,385.94	167,783.41	26,305.39	33,000.00	33,064.4⌐
1892–93	90,632.12	65,305.70	155,937.82	30,406.40	34,000.00	32,840.0⌐
1893–94	124,392.07	205,400.00	329,792.07	36,093.01	35,000.00	32,093.8⌐
1894–95	89,954.70	60,000.00	149,954.70	39,318.56	36,000.00	32,842.9⌐
1895–96	239,370.56	60,347.29	299,717.85	29,201.85	37,000.00	28,241.7⌐
1896–97	224,873.30	60,000.00	284,873.30	42,198.93	38,000.00	24,780.8⌐
1897–98	283,287.00		283,287.00	44,521.06	39,000.00	23,990.9⌐
1898–99	276,798.48		276,798.48	52,822.15	40,000.00	21,675.6⌐
1899–1900	289,798.48	135,000.00	424,798.48	63,302.62	40,000.00	23,826.4⌐

[1] Includes room rents to end of 1903–04.
[2] Including state patients.
[3] Residence halls, Union, intercollegiate athletics, and stores.
[4] Dairy and farm sales, theater, veterans' books and supplies, etc.

604

Exper. Farm Fund	Hospitals²	Gifts	Self-supporting Activities³	Miscellaneous⁴	Total Receipts	Date
			GROSS RECEIPTS			
				337.52	23,714.58	1850
				5,428.96	8,531.07	1850–51
				7,890.88	9,604.09	1852
				1,342.14	5,520.83	1853
				504.47	20,683.38	1854
				720.40	16,335.82	1855
				150.00	13,424.22	1856
				216.97	23,026.72	1857
				2,000.00	36,560.50	1857–58
					38,473.31	1858–59
				241.30	27,836.73	1859–60
				28.38	24,766.18	1860–61
				61.25	12,161.25	1861–62
					14,851.76	1862–63
				47.41	8,569.42	1863–64
				30.00	12,515.90	1864–65
29,358.72				31.32	47,160.91	1865–66
					20,741.85	1866–67
17,695.00				40.00	47,171.27	1867–68
3,593.05				80.00	33,924.41	1868–69
3,690.48				418.77	21,203.92	1869–70
				709.06	81,374.87	1870–71
				666.02	53,578.44	1871–72
				1,093.80	54,638.17	1872–73
				1,215.78	61,724.79	1873–74
			41.05	1,587.41	65,781.37	1874–75
			19.80	2,311.74	102,257.18	1875–76
			18.81	7,293.93	114,753.35	1876–77
			260.40	3,006.44	81,306.60	1877–78
			501.84	5,971.97	82,544.42	1878–79
			524.00	1,422.93	80,106.24	1879–80
			524.00	2,044.14	82,669.81	1880–81
			835.65	2,560.35	98,932.37	1881–82
			500.00	3,299.33	87,029.83	1882–83
			350.00	2,584.90	100,401.76	1883–84
			350.00	45,112.80	243,259.05	1884–85
			350.00	3,194.67	199,597.14	1885–86
			350.00	4,017.08	226,936.44	1886–87
			5,408.33	5,244.92	218,867.56	1887–88
			650.00	12,464.60	183,966.40	1888–89
			650.00	4,100.13	182,987.00	1889–90
			695.45	8,954.69	229,829.33	1890–91
			2,111.65	6,245.75	268,510.60	1891–92
			7,869.12	8,437.89	269,491.32	1892–93
			2,875.00	64,005.51	499,859.47	1893–94
			1,045.66	23,791.94	282,953.83	1894–95
			1,592.55	27,168.54	422,922.55	1895–96
			1,431.25	26,403.23	417,687.55	1896–97
			1,890.00	24,745.63	417,434.66	1897–98
			7,093.85	28,273.04	426,663.14	1898–99
			5,230.00	38,918.13	596,075.69	1899–1900

⁵ To November 20.
⁶ November 20, 1850, to December 31, 1851.
⁷ To September 30, 1857; from this date to September 30, 1901, the fiscal year extended from October first to ⸱tember thirtieth.

Date	State Appropriation			Student Receipts[1]	Federal Government	Univ. & Agr. Col. Income
	Operation	New Buildings	Total			
GROSS RECEIPTS						
1900–01	293,533.33		293,533.33	91,868.24	40,000.00	27,750.46
1901–02[2]	204,000.00	150,000.00	354,000.00	89,503.71	11,250.00	24,429.02
1902–03	409,000.00		409,000.00	104,308.65	40,000.00	26,000.11
1903–04	328,500.00	143,000.00	471,500.00	112,484.76	40,000.00	14,939.57
1904–05	510,500.00		510,500.00	115,650.35	40,000.00	39,098.85
1905–06	572,914.00	200,664.69	773,578.69	120,090.53	40,000.00	26,507.10
1906–07	622,085.00	200,000.00	822,085.00	138,559.33	52,000.00	26,304.10
1907–08	687,657.00	139,875.67	827,532.67	140,672.20	54,000.00	26,911.79
1908–09	750,360.70	397,628.03	1,147,988.73	169,603.05	61,000.00	29,896.95
1909–10	992,231.79	231,372.48	1,223,604.27	211,772.84	68,000.00	27,954.57
1910–11	1,061,052.25	166,848.00	1,227,900.25	250,009.57	75,000.00	31,854.29
1911–12	1,321,921.30	230,476.74	1,552,398.04	297,343.38	80,000.00	31,951.23
1912–13	1,099,666.99	379,801.57	1,479,468.56	301,172.09	80,000.00	31,874.54
1913–14	1,810,305.73	343,550.73	2,153,856.46	406,514.95	80,000.00	28,463.69
1914–15	1,666,722.51	69,205.02	1,735,927.53	452,090.15	90,000.00	34,997.91
1915–16	1,613,958.55	50,643.72	1,664,602.27	447,899.56	106,164.99	33,250.89
1916–17	1,614,100.92	198,932.63	1,813,033.55	489,587.41	119,635.81	36,443.86
1917–18	1,642,326.66	150,736.87	1,793,063.53	397,380.17	135,016.68	39,109.21
1918–19	1,821,801.22	94,126.34	1,915,927.56	427,872.23	147,962.39	42,217.28
1919–20	1,859,493.88	66,666.20	1,926,160.08	716,359.88	209,264.34	49,486.88
1920–21	2,214,170.69	327,374.05	2,541,544.74	889,736.34	231,936.13	37,294.13
1921–22	3,032,442.46	151,533.22	3,183,975.68	1,019,469.13	237,855.99	32,557.01
1922–23	2,890,161.12	348,396.55	3,238,557.67	1,025,554.55	249,393.59	32,324.90
1923–24	2,767,378.26	1,257,625.15	4,025,003.41	963,015.10	244,502.12	33,755.0
1924–25	3,334,203.30	210,326.41	3,544,529.71	948,615.42	238,283.82	36,648.4
1925–26	3,433,021.33	337,824.42	3,770,845.75	967,731.13	255,779.27	33,564.92
NET RECEIPTS						
1926–27	3,546,796.31	1,312,387.82	4,859,184.13	971,427.47	265,787.51	29,752.5
1927–28	4,068,394.75	463,150.93	4,531,545.68	1,041,576.76	275,779.27	39,270.8
1928–29	4,142,067.06	453,864.60	4,595,931.66	1,109,026.23	313,204.06	33,676.4
1929–30	4,085,785.08	210,460.72	4,296,245.80	1,332,092.21	336,815.18	34,597.0
1930–31	4,197,025.97	1,008,435.46	5,205,461.43	1,469,345.76	356,659.69	35,892.7
1931–32	4,142,689.95	472,062.44	4,614,752.39	1,365,248.84	349,742.15	23,062.5
1932–33	4,501,367.88	55,377.97	4,556,745.85	1,096,517.54	349,902.36	19,074.0
1933–34	3,751,062.20	2,205.70	3,753,267.90	1,127,107.94	350,197.03	22,160.3
1934–35	3,736,711.93	212.43	3,736,924.36	1,195,220.76	348,508.29	21,411.5
1935–36	3,893,819.47	7,714.42	3,901,533.89	1,333,587.37	603,907.04	20,886.7
1936–37	3,202,890.56		3,202,890.56	1,498,260.63	599,468.91	21,353.4
1937–38	3,842,515.08	20,700.32	3,863,215.40	1,599,413.69	675,013.07	20,974.6
1938–39	3,808,731.24	106,748.43	3,915,479.67	1,667,114.40	715,375.76	20,600.5
1939–40	3,740,165.98	125,348.21	3,865,514.19	1,773,651.84	741,732.01	18,925.7
1940–41	3,646,113.77	48,454.35	3,694,568.12	1,826,894.82	736,993.07	13,648.3
1941–42	4,037,290.77	200,000.00	4,237,290.77	1,768,209.95	741,598.58	12,499.4
1942–43	4,008,917.01		4,008,917.01	1,839,974.41	2,430,205.30	13,543.8
1943–44	4,379,843.24	461,200.00	4,841,043.24	1,548,412.26	3,403,073.59	10,897.5
1944–45	4,281,464.44		4,281,464.44	2,078,736.30	3,130,508.10	11,322.4
1945–46	6,026,556.08	8,000,000.00	14,026,556.08	2,184,080.13	1,682,265.87	13,714.8
1946–47	5,610,585.26		5,610,585.26	5,429,865.64	1,363,051.30	13,030.0
1947–48	7,903,757.74		7,903,757.74	7,000,251.90	1,096,669.72	11,999.0

[1] Includes room rents to end of 1903–04.
[2] Including state patients.
[3] Residence halls, Union, intercollegiate athletics, and stores.

Exper. Farm Fund	Hospitals[2]	Gifts	Self-supporting Activities[3]	Miscellaneous[4]	Total Receipts	Date
			GROSS RECEIPTS			
		8,363.15		40,825.83	502,341.01	1900–01
		3,022.54		39,237.70	521,442.97	1901–02
		5,626.91		55,942.49	640,878.16	1902–03
		7,585.35		65,156.15	711,665.83	1903–04
		17,598.30	6,853.95	67,462.94	797,164.39	1904–05
		1,050.00	7,672.62	72,450.78	1,041,349.72	1905–06
		580.00	9,666.44	76,066.13	1,125,261.00	1906–07
		2,200.00	9,873.99	104,378.82	1,165,569.47	1907–08
		400.00	33,902.54	110,410.82	1,553,202.09	1908–09
		15,881.87	40,254.62	152,775.47	1,740,243.64	1909–10
		13,872.55	65,409.30	153,078.83	1,817,124.79	1910–11
		9,475.52	73,660.85	144,227.41	2,189,056.43	1911–12
		10,745.17	79,539.76	165,676.27	2,148,476.39	1912–13
		12,721.14	177,067.46	234,630.84	3,093,254.54	1913–14
		13,710.44	196,847.07	234,545.36	2,758,118.46	1914–15
	2,441.50	16,739.64	206,256.85	287,974.60	2,765,330.30	1915–16
	3,076.00	21,799.98	220,118.99	310,203.88	3,013,899.48	1916–17
	4,736.00	24,863.43	193,125.73	314,159.19	2,901,453.94	1917–18
	1,457.75	117,028.60	355,818.84	524,020.99	3,532,305.64	1918–19
	6,693.14	80,228.15	321,783.34	397,263.98	3,707,239.79	1919–20
	50,375.78	37,561.03	374,218.23	519,448.79	4,682,115.17	1920–21
	61,652.04	203,407.03	379,158.36	562,144.68	5,680,219.92	1921–22
	63,032.19	157,547.99	413,109.78	726,088.16	5,905,608.83	1922–23
	68,480.34	145,105.95	423,181.86	772,466.04	6,675,509.88	1923–24
	221,719.57	138,365.99	506,377.06	682,681.59	6,317,221.62	1924–25
	441,275.84	164,576.79	493,786.04	823,781.03	6,951,340.77	1925–26
			NET RECEIPTS			
	553,062.57	144,828.58	844,733.46	740,951.87	8,409,728.10	1926–27
	624,248.15	123,535.99	884,111.99	467,834.87	7,987,903.51	1927–28
	636,957.16	147,194.85	1,208,731.53	409,049.45	8,453,771.41	1928–29
	695,070.48	178,688.58	1,247,775.19	459,575.26	8,580,859.79	1929–30
	736,237.57	208,533.08	1,241,547.69	415,621.80	9,669,299.77	1930–31
	873,613.34	179,839.01	1,151,024.23	324,867.82	8,882,150.33	1931–32
	144,813.45	183,475.61	809,256.95	224,822.32	7,384,608.14	1932–33
	165,297.48	280,346.31	824,751.29	243,681.24	6,766,809.58	1933–34
	200,056.79	352,764.56	950,596.63	312,290.69	7,117,773.59	1934–35
	231,846.49	317,561.81	985,619.82	322,871.09	7,717,814.25	1935–36
	1,085,497.69	502,910.48	1,104,245.73	372,254.31	8,386,881.72	1936–37
	1,105,760.75	362,590.42	1,448,317.86	381,468.74	9,456,754.62	1937–38
	1,096,366.42	853,819.56	1,535,973.32	384,932.31	10,189,661.97	1938–39
	1,230,951.55	1,370,508.27	1,593,338.14	433,213.20	11,027,834.92	1939–40
	1,250,267.42	697,376.16	1,797,262.03	479,488.83	10,496,498.78	1940–41
	1,201,845.10	676,886.33	1,737,580.16	648,373.02	11,024,283.39	1941–42
	1,248,135.31	425,398.66	1,564,718.13	711,866.27	12,242,758.94	1942–43
	1,281,450.61	414,842.55	1,365,478.97	851,577.33	13,716,776.05	1943–44
	1,469,800.46	492,035.84	1,623,186.66	995,593.85	14,082,648.07	1944–45
	1,506,410.06	600,652.71	2,693,641.93	1,388,470.06	24,095,791.64	1945–46
	1,899,537.46	1,148,096.69	4,853,233.03	2,567,841.37	22,885,240.76	1946–47
	1,938,566.19	1,151,152.19	6,584,621.18	2,992,930.13	28,679,948.14	1947–48

[4] Dairy and farm sales, theater, veterans' books and supplies, etc.
[5] To June 30; from this date the fiscal year has extended from July 1 to June 30.

607

AN ADDRESS BY CHARLES R. VAN HISE

May 23, 1913

An Address by Charles R. Van Hise

IT IS indeed most gratifying to us at the University of Wisconsin to be complimented by a visit of so large a group of distinguished people from Pennsylvania and other states in the east. What we have been doing here has been solely with the thought of advancing the welfare of the people of the state of Wisconsin. The idea that this work would bring us outside fame never entered our minds. We simply saw that there was work to be done, and we began to do that work. Nobody was more surprised than were we when it happened that the special things which have been undertaken at the University of Wisconsin began to attract outside notice. And when, a year ago or thereabouts, your Secretary wrote that some twenty or thirty people, as he then said, from Philadelphia, would like to visit the University of Wisconsin, I was much surprised that any group of people should think of taking a journey of a thousand miles for that purpose. When this year it appeared that the expedition was to consist of not twenty or thirty but more than one hundred, our surprise was turned into amazement. We could not understand why you should do such a thing, and we have not yet been able to understand it.

At the inauguration of A. Lawrence Lowell as President of Harvard, James Bryce was one of the speakers; and in his address he uttered the most pregnant sentence made at this celebration. He said, "a university should reflect the spirit of the times, without yielding to it."

It is the duty of a university to teach the truth as it sees it, and it is not only its duty to teach that truth, but it is its duty to advance knowledge. These are commonplaces for all universities of all countries; however, all that is involved in them is sometimes not fully appreciated. They mean that we must recognize that knowledge is nowhere fixed, that all things are fluid. The ideas which we hold today will not be held tomorrow in precisely the same form. The next generation will hold them in a very different form from that we now hold them in. This does not mean that the views which we now have may not be substantially sound, but it means that nowhere in the world have we attained perfection. No man knows everything about the simplest thing. The facts involved in the constitution of a grain of sand are far beyond our present knowledge—indeed are beyond the knowledge that any man ever shall have. All knowledge is incomplete. It is the duty of the University ever to move toward completion, with the certainty that it will never reach perfection anywhere, at any time, with regard to anything.

These principles recognized without question as applied to mathematics and other sciences, we must also apply to sociology, to morals, to politics, to religion, to all of the relations which obtain between man and man. It is the inflexible application of truth to these subjects which arouses opposition. It should not be the purpose of a university carelessly to question or recklessly to disturb current traditions, customs, or morals; but like every other human institution or human ideal, they are the legitimate field of sober inquiry. Nowhere is there fixity or completeness in regard to human relations any more than with regard to physical or chemical relations.

Following truth wherever it leads without regard to its bearing upon persons or nations is the spirit which the university must not yield. It is this spirit which makes the university a center of conflict. At a recent inauguration of a president of a great educational institution, he said his motto was to be Peace and Progress. Peace he may have, but not Progress. Peace and Progress are in irreconcilable conflict, and wherever there is progress there is no peace. This truth is no new discovery.

Heraclitus five centuries before Christ said, "Without conflict no life."

In the distant past, differences between men were settled by physical strife; man came into personal contact with man when there was difference of opinion. When the clan arose, it was demanded that the differences between men within the clan should be settled in another way than by physical conflict. When the clan developed into the nation this idea was extended to all the people of the larger group. We now have reached a situation in the world wherein physical conflict has been eliminated from the nation. The only physical conflict which remains on a large scale is international. Just as surely as strife between man and man in the clan, and between men in the different clans, when consolidated into a nation, has disappeared from the earth, just so physical strife between nation and nation will finally cease. While physical strife has ever been narrowed as civilization advanced, intellectual strife has continued to the present time. Indeed it has become more keen, and will continue throughout the future, for only through intellectual strife is there progress. The strife is now between ideals and ideas, not between man and man physically.

Since it is the function of the university to inspire, adjust, and advance civilization, it becomes the very *foci* of disturbance. There is between the university and the reactionary an irrepressible conflict. We may cry peace, but there will be no peace. Just so long as there are people who believe that the present situation is better than any future situation, who believe that the past is superior to the present, so long will these people criticize and oppose universities, wherever they are. The contest is unavoidable, and no one appreciates it more fully than those who have relations with a virile institution.

The spirit of authority, of despotism, represses and often aims to destroy universities. From time to time the Czar has found it necessary to close his higher educational institutions. Recently, when the great Tolstoy passed from this earth, the students decided to mark that momentous event by giving due recognition of his great service to the advancement of civilization; but the Czar forbade any notice whatever of Tolstoy's death. The result was student strikes. After a long contest the disturbance was ended by expelling some four thousand students; and about two hundred of the ablest men of the staff of the universities resigned or were removed. Many of the students, and some of the staff, were sent to Siberia. The Czar now has peace in his universities, but he has not progress; and just the moment the grip of authority is released from the throats of those institutions, that moment will the old situation be revived.

Just as the spirit of authority represses or destroys universities, so the spirit of freedom creates and inspires them. Charles Kendall Adams, formerly President of this University, was fond of telling how, after the disastrous Napoleonic Wars, came the great period of the founding of the German universities. These institutions have been powerful factors in changing that country from many detached, weak states,—some of them backward in their civilization,—into a great consolidated nation, having a foremost place among the nations of the world. All of you have read of the Siege of Leyden, during the attempt of Philip of Spain to over-ride the Netherlands, and how, after a terrific struggle which lasted for many months, the waters of the ocean were let in and relief came in ships that sailed over land. The Spaniards were terror-stricken, and Leyden was saved. In what way did the people of the Netherlands celebrate that event? They decided that the most appropriate recognition of the heroism of the defendants was the founding of a university, and the University of Leyden arose, which for more than five hundred years has shed light over that nation and throughout the world.

The search for truth, and the freedom in teaching truth, then, is the spirit which the university must not yield; but there is also to be considered the other side of Mr. Bryce's statement that the university should reflect the spirit of the times. The old classical college in this country had a curriculum which gave liberal training to men, and which prepared for certain learned professions, mainly three. Gradually, as the western state universities arose, and as the technical institutions were founded, it became recognized that science and applied science should be taught in the university alongside the traditional subjects and with equal privileges. By this procedure the "learned professions" were expanded so as to include not only law, medicine, and the ministry, but engineering and its various branches; and a little later there were included agriculture, domestic science, commerce, and other vocations. To make these various fields of knowledge learned professions is a reflection of the spirit of the times.

Often men think that some one subject, or group of subjects, is the chosen field of study, and should have a place of preference over other subjects. I am not so radical as to suppose that the old, well-organized subjects cannot be better taught in an institution than new and unorganized subjects; but I do hold that we should not insist *per se* that any subject have precedence to the extent of excluding any other subject from a university curriculum. Greek may be taught so that it is as narrowly technical as economic entomology, and economic entomology may be so taught that it is broadly liberalizing. It all depends upon the spirit and the method.

Consequently, we in these western universities have refused to circumscribe the field which may be the object of university study. Many subjects formerly excluded have been wisely introduced into our universities. The introduction of these new subjects has assisted in the advancement of knowledge and the uplifting of humanity.

Some years ago, also, we began to realize that our influence should be broadened. We were not the first to make this discovery. This was made many years ago at Oxford. In this country the University of Pennsylvania was the first institution, or one of the first, to introduce the method of extension into the United States. However, at Wisconsin, some eight or ten years ago, we took up this matter along somewhat different and broader lines than had previously been attempted. This story you have already heard, and I shall not repeat or amplify it. I only wish to indicate to you the underlying ideas which led us to the movement.

The first of these was the slowly dawning realization that

knowledge had far outrun the assimilation of the people. There have been greater advances in knowledge during the past sixty years than during two thousand years before that time. In a large measure this knowledge is not utilized by the people. We know enough about agriculture so that the agricultural production of the country could be doubled if the knowledge were applied. We know enough about disease so that if that knowledge were utilized, infectious and contagious diseases would be substantially destroyed in the United States,—and that within a score of years. We know enough about eugenics so that if that knowledge were applied, the defective classes would disappear within a generation. Similarly, in other fields, our knowledge has expanded far beyond its utilization.

It may be said that this new situation should be dealt with by introducing this new knowledge into the schools and thus training the children to apply it. But much of the advance has been accomplished during the past fifteen or twenty years, since men who are still in active life left the schools—men who have from twenty-five to fifty years to live. If the teaching of new knowledge were confined to the rising generation, the same situation would obtain fifteen or twenty years hence. Therefore, if we expect new knowledge to be applied at any time to the then existing stage of advancement, it must be carried out to the people. Adults must continue their education throughout life.

This has been one of the underlying purposes of the broad extension movement in Wisconsin. When this view was first broached to an eminent eastern educator, he said to me, "What about your university ideals?" I replied that we do not put the names of those doing extension work in our catalog; we do not say we have ten thousand, or fifty thousand, or two hundred thousand students if we chance to come into contact with that number of people. The admission requirements of the university and the qualifications for the academic degrees remain the same. We do not see how it demeans us to do work for the advancement of the people simply because it has not been traditional for a university to undertake such work. We laid down the fundamental principle that the State University of Wisconsin is willing to undertake any line of educational work for which

it is the best fitted instrument, without regard to the precon-
ceived notions of anybody, anywhere, concerning the scope of
a university. One other idea is fundamental in our extension
work, and that is to find a way for the boy or girl of parts whatever the conditions of birth. You well know that all of the in-
tellect of Philadelphia is not born in the aristocratic circle. You
well know that where your factories are, in the congested
quarters, there is just as likely to be a boy or girl of parts born
as in the homes of the wealthy. The late Mr. Lester F. Ward, in
his book on applied sociology, has proved this in a book of some
two hundred pages; but it is no more than the poet Gray saw
a hundred and fifty years ago—that in the country churchyard
may lie a "mute, inglorious Milton."

We, in the State of Wisconsin, wish to create a situation in
which mute, inglorious Miltons shall become an impossibility.
The greatest waste of this nation is its waste of talent. If we
could only fully utilize our talent, there would be no limit to our
progress; no one could forecast its speed.

Wealth is not equally distributed among us. Some are more
fortunate in this respect than others. It has been proposed by
many that we divide wealth equally and start anew. However,
that proposal has not met the approval of the larger number of
the people. What we own seems to me a relatively immaterial
thing. The richest man is not always the happiest. Democracy
does not depend upon the horizontal distribution of wealth;
it does, however, depend upon opportunity. And if the time
shall arise in this country, in this twentieth century, when the
boy or girl of parts shall be unable to find a way, then we shall
have lost democracy. It is, then, the second great fundamental
aim of the university extension movement to forever retain in
this commonwealth the essentials of democracy; and to do this,
the opportunities of our boys and girls of parts to obtain an
education broad and complete, fitted to the demands of the
present time, must be provided.

This rainbow we had in the sky. We went seeking for a man
to bring the rainbow to earth; and our search carried us to
Pennsylvania. There in State College was found a man to whom
this rainbow was painted. When the colors glowed most radi-

antly, the man was asked to come to Wisconsin to make the rainbow a reality. Dean Louis E. Reber is the man; and he has accomplished this seemingly impossible task.

Very slowly in this country was elementary education democratized. Indeed, in many other countries this is not true to the present time. Even in England the public school does not mean what it does in this country, and free education of the common people is very imperfect. For a long time in the United States it was supposed that public funds should not go further than to support elementary education; but gradually the idea dawned in the middle west that secondary education was also the lot of all the people. The high school arose, and has extended from the Mississippi Valley both east and west to the Atlantic and the Pacific.

When this was achieved it was believed that the very acme of public expense had been reached for education; that we could not possibly ask the state to support higher education. But the people of the West and South were not content; although those who opposed higher state education went so far as to say of the men holding the opposite point of view that they were desirous of getting their hands into the public treasury for the benefit of a few, that the plan was undemocratic, was indeed an assault upon property, and should not be permitted. But notwithstanding this position, the middle western and southern states began quietly to develop university education as a public function. The principle of public support for higher education is now fully recognized for all the country except a few eastern states. It is accepted doctrine that the right of the boy to secure the highest education in the land shall not depend upon the amount of money which he may possess, but upon his inherent capacity, moral and intellectual. It is the aim of the state university to democratize higher education, to open all the facilities of knowledge to all the people of the commonwealth. If this be attained, it will be a new thing in the world.

One of the distinctive features of the University of Wisconsin has been its relation to government. It is often supposed, and especially have I found the opinion in the East, that Wisconsin is a radical state, in favor of all sorts of strange and irrational things. However, if one considers the characteristics of the Wisconsin advances of government during recent years, it will be appreciated that the state is really conservative. The Wisconsin movement did not begin by putting upon the whole people the solution of various intricate problems; it began by the development of government by experts; indeed this is the distinctive feature of the Wisconsin system. The Tax Commission was first established. A larger achievement was the creation of the Public Utilities' Commission, and I see here the man, Senator W. H. Hatton, who had a more important part in the preparation of the law than any other man. The purpose of this law was the control of the public utilities so that they should recognize their public obligations as well as their private duties. There were appointed on the Public Utilities' Commission by Senator, then Governor, R. M. La Follette, three experts, one a statistician, one a lawyer, and the third a professor of transportation in the University of Wisconsin.

Another commission has been established in this state to cover the relation of employers and employees. This is the Industrial Commission. There was taken from the University a professor as one of the members of the Industrial Commission, John R. Commons. He has spent two years upon the work of that Commission. Its work has become organized, and Professor Commons has decided that the state pays him so much that he cannot remain there, as he has not been able to discover a way to spend the five thousand dollars per annum that is paid him; therefore, he is returning to the University for thirty-five hundred dollars per annum. He has contributed his constructive ideas to the state work, and is coming back to us, to work in his chosen field of political economy for the advancement of knowledge and the creation of scholars.

Another commission is now proposed by Governor Francis E. McGovern—that relating to markets. It is the idea to have this commission do for industry what the Public Utilities' Commission has done for the railroads, telegraphs, and telephones, and what the Industrial Commission has done for labor. If the proposed law be enacted, another expert commission will have been established in this state by the Legislature now in session.

We hope that the State of Wisconsin may have the honor of first passing a law for a comprehensive State Market Commission; and thus round out the four commissions needed to regulate and control property in Wisconsin in the interest of the people; for we must recognize that in this twentieth century no one owns property as an absolute right. Every man is a trustee to the nation and to succeeding generations for the property committed to his care. This we perfectly understand in regard to the great captains of industry, who hold vast resources; but not always do we appreciate that the doctrine applies equally to the man who has little. It is now as it was in biblical times, each shall be held responsible for the talents entrusted to him; and the man who owns forty acres of land is just as responsible to the state and to the people of succeeding generations for his trusteeship as is the man who is at the head of a great corporation. We, in this state, do not hold to the idea of responsibility limited to a special class; we hold to the idea of the responsibility for all.

Some states have begun their forward movement by the adoption of the initiative, referendum, and recall. Only after ten years or more of the development of government by experts, only after ten years of carrying out knowledge to the people on the broadest scale, have we in this state begun to think of the initiative, the referendum, and the recall. While realizing that these great measures are coming, and that the people are destined in the future to take a larger and larger part in the immediate direction and control of their own affairs, our conservative instincts are against putting extremely complex problems of government upon the people without preparation. for their solution. This seems to us beginning at the wrong end. The movement to carry government back to the people, if undertaken without preparation, will, I fear, lead to unfortunate results. We in Wisconsin are trying, through the methods discussed, to get ready for the initiative, referendum, and a modified recall. If we develop government by experts, if the

University ever remains ready to carry knowledge to the people, if we develop a system of education so broad that every one may find a way, we shall hope that there will be advance and not retrogression through the introduction of these last new devices of representative government.

Since the University has been interested in the advance of government in this state, it has been said by some of our friends (the statement that they are our friends is always carried prefixed) that the University is in politics. If by this it is meant that the University has ever been organized in the past or in the present, in whole or in part, in the interest of any individual or faction or party, the statement is absolutely false. If, however, it is meant that the University is attempting to lead in the advancement of the people; if it is meant that problems which relate to water powers, to forests, to marketing, to the public utilities, to labor, are legitimate fields of university inquiry and teaching, then the university is in politics, and will remain there so long as it is a virile institution worthy of the support of the people of this state.

Because we at the University have been trying to get the state ready for the initiative, referendum, and recall, one of our friends in a recent article in The World's Work described the University of Wisconsin as a university that rules a state. Now, I have no doubt that the author thought he was complimenting us and doing us a favor; but everywhere the weapon has been seized by those opposed to the type of university here advocated. The University does not rule the state; the University has never attempted to rule the state. The University professors carefully refrain from offering advice or assistance except as they are called upon to do so. As a matter of fact the committees of the Legislature and individual members do ask the professors for expert advice and opinion with regard to many matters; they are giving such assistance as they can. When the enactment of laws regarding weeds, drainage, water powers, or many of the technical questions now before the Legislature come up, and the members find that the knowledge which they desire may be obtained through some of the professors of the University, the members sensibly ask the assistance of such professors in formulating measures. We at the University are ready to lend a hand wherever we may, but never now nor in the past have we attempted to control, to rule, or to impose our authority or our ideas. This would be contrary to the spirit of freedom in the University.

Because of the principle already developed that the universities are chief centers of progress and therefore of disturbance, they have been described as the nurseries of revolution, of social democracy, of anarchy. But on the contrary, universities because of their leadership are the safety-valves of the nation. It is only when the just aspirations of the people have been repressed; it is only when the call to remedy injustice has been unheard, that revolution and anarchy have come. If my time were not already exhausted I could cite many illustrations, but this is not necessary in a company of this kind, all of whom are familar with the history of this and of other nations. But if you will let your mind revert to the French Revolution, if you will recall the revolution in England, if you will let your memory run back to our own Civil War, in fact, if you will think of a great crisis of any nation, you will find almost without exception that for any instance the underlying cause is that great wrongs have remained unredressed; and this has led to revolution, and sometimes to anarchy.

In this twentieth century, when for the first time we discover that our natural resources are limited in quantity, when a man cannot have for the asking a farm, or a forest, or a mine, we find ourselves confronted with a new situation. A man in the pioneer days on the prairies might shoot a rifle in any direction, and no one might hinder him; but now that the men of the nation have multiplied and are nearer together, we have been obliged to make laws regulating the use of firearms.

These new conditions of the new century confront our nation with a new crisis. We must pass from the period of individualism which was the characteristic of the nineteenth century, to the period of social responsibility which will be the characteristic of the twentieth century. This will be as great a readjustment of ideals as has ever been demanded by seer or prophet of any people at any time. This is the reason why the wise, constructive leadership of men of thought is so necessary at this time. Therefore the universities, while confessedly the very centers of unrest, the sources of disturbance, contain the possible leaders who may point the way to the inevitable readjustment without disaster.

In asking that a state maintain a free university, we are asking much of a democracy. We are asking that the people shall be willing to believe that truth should prevail wherever it leads,— that truth will prevail and that without regard to their own ideas, without regard to their preconceptions. When the time comes that state university appropriations are subject to a referendum, the question will be clearly before the people, whether or not they can rise to this plane. We shall then know, and not until then shall we certainly know, whether a democracy can maintain a university on as high a plane as a monarchy. For my part, I believe that it may. If a democracy cannot maintain a university which will not yield to the spirit of the times, it will be the most serious charge that has ever been made against a democracy. I recognize that the danger is no doubtful one; I recognize that this test will be the great crucial one in the progress of the state universities of this country. It is a very different thing to convince a majority of a legislature once in two years of the wisdom of the work of a university, and to convince the majority of the people of a commonwealth; and yet, unquestionably, the latter problem in the near future will confront many of the state universities. It has already come in Oregon.

It is too much to hope that in no state shall we ever have any back-set. It is too much to believe that every state university will continue its forward movement without check. Your coming to Wisconsin, more than five score of you from the East, will, I believe, be of assistance to us in maintaining a university on the highest plane, for, strangely enough, the things which brought you from Pennsylvania, New York, New Jersey, Maryland and Massachusetts to Wisconsin are the very things which have been attacked by one group of people in this state.

Thus, if perchance we at the University of Wisconsin have been able or shall be able to assist you in the advance of your commonwealths, you also, reciprocally, have done equally well, have helped us to maintain the ideals for which we are striving.

I thank you for your support, for your assistance. Your visit to us will be a powerful factor in preventing the State of Wisconsin from halting in the advancement of true democracy in the advancement of education of all grades, for all the people of the entire commonwealth.—*An address to the Philadelphia City Club's Expedition, at the Golf Club, Madison, May 23, 1913.*

INDEX

Index

mal dept., 364, 445. *See also* Chadbourne Hall
Ferber, Edna, II, 8
Ferguson, Ben, I, 140n
Fernow, Bernhard Eduard, I, 637; II, 20
Fetter, Frank A., II, 339
Feuling, John B., I, 336, 339, 419
Field, Jennie, I, 374
Field House, II, 222
Finances, early conditions of, I, 68, 130–31, 133, 135ff, 139, 142–44; first state support, 120, 296; plan for expenditures, 1851, I, 131; prosperity of Univ., 135–36, 589, 591–92; effect of free tuition on, 367; control of funds, 527ff; expenditures in 1890's, 582–83; expenditures by major units, I, 583n; legislative concern in, 597; II, 97–100; Van Hise and, II, 91–95; Birge and, 128; accounting system reorganized, 160; investigation of, 169–74. *See also* Income; University Fund
Finch, Vernor C., II, 354
Fischer, Richard, II, 349
Fish, Carl Russell, history faculty member, I, 639, 642; II, 337; reputation as teacher, 311, 337; and first World War, II, 112, 119, 338
Fiske, George C., II, 320, 321
Fiske, H. S., I, 725
Fitzpatrick, Edward A., II, 272–73
Flexner, Abraham, report on Allen, II, 271–72; quoted, 483
Flowers, D. M., and hazing episode, I, 551–53
Foerster, Otto H., II, 492
Fogo, William M., I, 597
Foley, James L., I, 190, 195
Follen, Charles, I, 31
Fond du Lac, proposed for site of territorial capital, I, 39
Football, early history of, I, 388, 572, 695–97, 700–1, 702–3, 710; and eastern colleges, 695–97; evils of deplored, 695–96; II, 535–39; student enthusiasm for, I, 698ff; II, 533, 538, 540–45; gate receipts, I, 698; II, 545; proposals to abolish, II, 540–41, 542–43
Forbes, Esther, II, 513
Forest Products Laboratory, II, 183, 358, 472
Fortenbaugh, Samuel Byrod, II, 450
Foster, William Z., II, 143

Four Lakes, named site of territorial university, I, 39–40
Fourth Lake, I, 40, 66. *See also* Lake Mendota
France, University of, I, 16
Francke, August Hermann, I, 30
Frank, Glenn, appointed president, II, 158, 222, 225; on Univ. during first World War and after, 222–23; on freedom of research, 229; and Experimental College, 320
Frank, Michael, I, 481
Frankenburger, David Bower, prof. of rhetoric and oratory, I, 344, 650; on selective studies, 400
Franklin, Benjamin, secular ideal of learning, quoted, I, 8, 12n; on practical education, 25; on German universities, 30
Franklin, Walter S., I, 450
Fraternities, growth of, I, 392, 503, 665; II, 500; criticism of, I, 392, 665–67; II, 165n, 174, 183, 190, 500–2; faculty regulation of, II, 500–2, 509; and student conference committee, 507
Fratt, Nicholas D., I, 601
Fred, Edwin Broun, and researches on soils, II, 359, 393, 419
Free Library Commission, II, 7
Freeman, John Charles, criticized by regents, I, 331–32; as lecturer, 344, 451–52, 650; on separate agricultural college, 470; and extension lectures, 724, 729; mentioned, 566; II, 13, 235
Free Press (Milwaukee), II, 8, 21, 196
French, study of, I, 73, 84, 100, 114, 646; dept. of, 335, 339–40
French House, founded, II, 322
French *philosophes*, I, 13, 16
Frieze, Henry, I, 32
Frost, William D., II, 358, 409, 483
Fuchs, John P., first prof. of modern languages, I, 83, 114, 177; views on women students, 117–18; on faculty appointments, 157; scholarship, 182–83

GABRIEL, Ralph, I, 694
Gaenslen, Fred J., II, 492
Gale, Zona, activities as writer, I, 688; II, 8, 513; as regent, 158, 228, 290
Galpin, Charles J., II, 423–24
Gamper, John, II, 219–20
Gardiner Lyceum, I, 28

Composed, printed, and bound for the
UNIVERSITY OF WISCONSIN PRESS